Music Therapy Methods in Neurorehabilitation: A Clinician's Guide

Music Therapy Methods in Neurorehabilitation: A Clinician's Guide

Editor: Christina Hampton

AMERICAN
MEDICAL PUBLISHERS
www.americanmedicalpublishers.com

AMERICAN
MEDICAL PUBLISHERS
www.americanmedicalpublishers.com

Cataloging-in-Publication Data

Music therapy methods in neurorehabilitation : a clinician's guide / edited by Christina Hampton.
p. cm.
Includes bibliographical references and index.
ISBN 979-8-88740-284-0
1. Brain damage--Patients--Rehabilitation. 2. Music therapy. 3. Central nervous system--Diseases--Patients--Rehabilitation. 4. Brain damage--Alternative treatment. 5. Central nervous system--Diseases--Alternative treatment. 6. Neurology.
I. Hampton, Christina.
RC387.5 .M87 2023
617.481 044--dc23

American Medical Publishers,
41 Flatbush Avenue,
1st Floor, New York,
NY 11217, USA

ISBN 979-8-88740-284-0 (Hardback)

Contents

Preface VII

Chapter 1 **The Role of Rhythm in Speech and Language Rehabilitation: The SEP Hypothesis** 1
Shinya Fujii and Catherine Y. Wan

Chapter 2 **Brain Responses to Musical Feature Changes in Adolescent Cochlear Implant Users** 16
Bjørn Petersen, Ethan Weed, Pascale Sandmann, Elvira Brattico, Mads Hansen, Stine Derdau Sørensen and Peter Vuust

Chapter 3 **Music Lessons Improve Auditory Perceptual and Cognitive Performance in Deaf Children** 30
Françoise Rochette, Aline Moussard and Emmanuel Bigand

Chapter 4 **Residual Neural Processing of Musical Sound Features in Adult Cochlear Implant Users** 39
Lydia Timm, Peter Vuust, Elvira Brattico, Deepashri Agrawal, Stefan Debener, Andreas Büchner, Reinhard Dengler and Matthias Wittfoth

Chapter 5 **Rhythm Perception and Production Predict Reading Abilities in Developmental Dyslexia** 50
Elena Flaugnacco, Luisa Lopez, Chiara Terribili, Stefania Zoia, Sonia Buda, Sara Tilli, Lorenzo Monasta, Marcella Montico, Alessandra Sila, Luca Ronfani and Daniele Schön

Chapter 6 **The Musician Effect: Does it Persist Under Degraded Pitch Conditions of Cochlear Implant Simulations?** 64
Christina D. Fuller, John J. Galvin III, Bert Maat, Rolien H. Free and Deniz Başkent

Chapter 7 **Neurobiological, Cognitive and Emotional Mechanisms in Melodic Intonation Therapy** 80
Dawn L. Merrett, Isabelle Peretz and Sarah J. Wilson

Chapter 8 **Moving to Music: Effects of Heard and Imagined Musical Cues on Movement-Related Brain Activity** 91
Rebecca S. Schaefer, Alexa M. Morcom, Neil Roberts and Katie Overy

Chapter 9 **Individual Differences in Beat Perception Affect Gait Responses to Low- and High-Groove Music** 102
Li-Ann Leow, Taylor Parrott and Jessica A. Grahn

Chapter 10 **Musically Cued Gait-Training Improves Both Perceptual and Motor Timing in Parkinson's Disease** 114
Charles-Etienne Benoit, Simone Dalla Bella, Nicolas Farrugia, Hellmuth Obrig, Stefan Mainka and Sonja A. Kotz

Chapter 11 **Reducing Chronic Visuo-Spatial Neglect Following Right Hemisphere Stroke Through Instrument Playing** 125
Rebeka Bodak, Paresh Malhotra, Nicolò F. Bernardi, Gianna Cocchini and Lauren Stewart

Chapter 12 **The Combination of Rhythm and Pitch can Account for the Beneficial Effect of Melodic Intonation Therapy on Connected Speech Improvements in Broca's Aphasia** 133
Anna Zumbansen, Isabelle Peretz and Sylvie Hébert

Chapter 13 **Music-Supported Motor Training After Stroke Reveals No Superiority of Synchronization in Group Therapy** 144
Floris T. Van Vugt, Juliane Ritter, Jens D. Rollnik and Eckart Altenmüller

Chapter 14 **Music Mnemonics Aid Verbal Memory and Induce Learning - Related Brain Plasticity in Multiple Sclerosis** 153
Michael H. Thaut, David A. Peterson, Gerald C. McIntosh and Volker Hoemberg

Chapter 15 **Less Effort, Better Results: How does Music Act on Prefrontal Cortex in Older Adults During Verbal Encoding? An fNIRS Study** 163
Laura Ferreri, Emmanuel Bigand, Stephane Perrey, Makii Muthalib, Patrick Bard and Aurélia Bugaiska

Chapter 16 **New Learning of Music After Bilateral Medial Temporal Lobe Damage: Evidence from an Amnesic Patient** 174
Jussi Valtonen, Emma Gregory, Barbara Landau and Michael McCloskey

Chapter 17 **Structural Changes Induced by Daily Music Listening in the Recovering Brain After Middle Cerebral Artery Stroke: A Voxel-Based Morphometry Study** 187
Teppo Särkämö, Pablo Ripollés, Henna Vepsäläinen, Taina Autti, Heli M. Silvennoinen, Eero Salli, Sari Laitinen, Anita Forsblom, Seppo Soinila and Antoni Rodríguez-Fornells

Chapter 18 **Music as a Mnemonic to Learn Gesture Sequences in Normal Aging and Alzheimer's Disease** 203
Aline Moussard, Emmanuel Bigand, Sylvie Belleville and Isabelle Peretz

Chapter 19 **Intact Brain Processing of Musical Emotions in Autism Spectrum Disorder, but More Cognitive Load and Arousal in Happy vs. Sad Music** 212
Line Gebauer, Joshua Skewes, Gitte Westphael, Pamela Heaton and Peter Vuust

Permissions

List of Contributors

Index

Preface

The world is advancing at a fast pace like never before. Therefore, the need is to keep up with the latest developments. This book was an idea that came to fruition when the specialists in the area realized the need to coordinate together and document essential themes in the subject. That's when I was requested to be the editor. Editing this book has been an honour as it brings together diverse authors researching on different streams of the field. The book collates essential materials contributed by veterans in the area which can be utilized by students and researchers alike.

Neurorehabilitation or neurological rehabilitation is a complex medical program that is designed for assisting people with diseases, injury or disorders of the nervous system. The aim of neurorehabilitation is to help people recover from nervous system damage and minimize and compensate for any functional change that may occur due to it. It has been observed that neurorehabilitation can help improve neurological functions, reduce symptoms and improve the overall well-being of the patients. Neurological Music Therapy (NMT) is one of the techniques used in neurorehabilitation programs. It is a therapeutic technique that aims to improve people's mental health and overall well-being by utilizing music's innate ability to uplift the mood. Making music, writing songs, singing, dancing, listening to music, and discussing music are examples of this goal-oriented intervention. This type of treatment may be beneficial for people suffering from depression and anxiety, and improve the quality of life for those suffering from physical ailments. Music has the ability to change physiological characteristics in the body such as blood pressure, heart rate, and respiration. This book explores all the essential aspects of using music therapy methods for neurorehabilitation. With state-of-the-art inputs by acclaimed experts of this field, this book targets students and professionals. It will also provide interesting topics for research which interested readers can take up.

Each chapter is a sole-standing publication that reflects each author´s interpretation. Thus, the book displays a multi-facetted picture of our current understanding of application, resources and aspects of the field. I would like to thank the contributors of this book and my family for their endless support.

Editor

1

The role of rhythm in speech and language rehabilitation: the SEP hypothesis

Shinya Fujii[1]* and Catherine Y. Wan[2]

[1] Heart and Stroke Foundation Canadian Partnership for Stroke Recovery, Sunnybrook Research Institute, Toronto, ON, Canada
[2] Department of Radiology, Boston Children's Hospital, Harvard Medical School, Boston, MA, USA

Correspondence:
Shinya Fujii, Heart and Stroke Foundation Canadian Partnership for Stroke Recovery, Sunnybrook Research Institute, 2075 Bayview Avenue, Toronto, ON M4N 3M5, Canada
e-mail: sfujii@sri.utoronto.ca

For thousands of years, human beings have engaged in rhythmic activities such as drumming, dancing, and singing. Rhythm can be a powerful medium to stimulate communication and social interactions, due to the strong sensorimotor coupling. For example, the mere presence of an underlying beat or pulse can result in spontaneous motor responses such as hand clapping, foot stepping, and rhythmic vocalizations. Examining the relationship between rhythm and speech is fundamental not only to our understanding of the origins of human communication but also in the treatment of neurological disorders. In this paper, we explore whether rhythm has therapeutic potential for promoting recovery from speech and language dysfunctions. Although clinical studies are limited to date, existing experimental evidence demonstrates rich rhythmic organization in both music and language, as well as overlapping brain networks that are crucial in the design of rehabilitation approaches. Here, we propose the "SEP" hypothesis, which postulates that (1) "sound envelope processing" and (2) "synchronization and entrainment to pulse" may help stimulate brain networks that underlie human communication. Ultimately, we hope that the SEP hypothesis will provide a useful framework for facilitating rhythm-based research in various patient populations.

Keywords: rhythm, speech, language, rehabilitation, the SEP hypothesis

INTRODUCTION

Human beings have universally engaged in rhythmic musical activities such as drumming, dancing, singing, and playing musical instruments since ancient times (e.g., Mithen, 2005; Fitch, 2006; Conard et al., 2009). The presence of rhythmic sounds in the environment can result in spontaneous motor responses such as tapping, clapping, stepping, dancing, and singing (e.g., Kirschner and Tomasello, 2009; Sevdalis and Keller, 2010; Fujii et al., 2014). Rhythm serves as a potent catalyst to elicit positive affect (e.g., Zentner and Eerola, 2010), co-operation (e.g., Reddish et al., 2013), and social bonding (e.g., Freeman, 2000). In recent years, researchers have begun to explore the therapeutic potential of rhythm in speech and language rehabilitation. In this paper, we discuss the importance of rhythm as a medium of human communication and social interaction. Specifically, we discuss the important role of rhythm in speech perception and production, and summarize the relevant neuroscience literature. In addition, we present the "SEP" hypothesis, which postulates that (1) sound envelope processing and (2) synchronization and entrainment to a pulse, may help stimulate brain networks that underlie human communication. Finally, we provide examples of speech and language disorders [Parkinson's disease, stuttering, aphasia, and autism] that can potentially benefit from rhythm-based therapy.

RHYTHM AS A MEDIUM OF COMMUNICATION

Rhythm, or the temporal organization of perceived or produced events, mediates communication and social interaction. For example, normal rhythm or rate of syllable production during speech is typically three to eight syllables per second (3–8 Hz) across many languages (Malecot et al., 1972; Crystal and House, 1982; Greenberg et al., 2003; Chandrasekaran et al., 2009). This rate range corresponds to natural movement frequencies of articulators including tongue, palate, cheek, jaw, and lips coupled with voicing (Peelle and Davis, 2012). If the rate is faster than 8 Hz, however, speech intelligibility is significantly reduced (e.g., Ahissar et al., 2001), suggesting that our brain may be "tuned" to the natural rhythm of vocal production.

Primate studies have shown a similar rhythmic tuning to communicative gestures such as lip-smacking (Fitch, 2013; Ghazanfar et al., 2013; Ghazanfar and Takahashi, 2014). Lip-smacking is often directed at another animal during face-to-face interactions, and is characterized by regular cycles of vertical jaw movement, often involving a parting of the lips (e.g., Ghazanfar et al., 2012). For example, Ghazanfar et al. (2013) used three types of video clips as visual stimuli in which monkey avatars were lip-smacking at frequencies of 3, 6, and 10 Hz. Interestingly, the preferential viewing times were significantly longer for the smacking rate of 6 Hz, which corresponds to the natural syllable production rate, compared with those of 3 and 10 Hz. Moreover, the monkeys in the study responded to the avatars in the video with their own rhythmic lip-smacking expressions, as if they were communicating with real monkeys. Based on these observations, Ghazanfar et al. (2013) suggested that monkey lip-smacking and human speech rhythms share a similar sensorimotor mechanism, and that human speech might have evolved from the rhythmic gestures or motor actions normally produced by our primate ancestors.

The idea that rhythmic motor actions mediate communication is supported by another primate study, which showed that rhythmic non-vocal sounds created by drumming actions served as communicative signals (Remedios et al., 2009). The mean rate of drumming actions by the macaque monkeys were around five beats per second (Remedios et al., 2009), which also corresponded to the natural syllable production rate during speech. Further investigation with functional magnetic resonance imaging (fMRI) showed that neural responses when animals listened to rhythmic drumming sounds overlapped with those when they listened to vocalizations (Remedios et al., 2009).

Human studies have also shown the importance of gestures and rhythmic motor actions for communication and social interaction. For example, lip movements affect the way in which people perceive speech syllables (McGurk and MacDonald, 1976). In congenitally blind individuals, verbal communication is often accompanied by hand gestures, although they have never seen hand gestures, and the listener cannot see the speaker's movements (Iverson and Goldin-Meadow, 1998). Developmental studies have shown that newborn infants imitate adult facial and manual gestures (e.g., Meltzoff and Moore, 1977) and synchronize body movements with the articulated structure of adult speech (e.g., Condon and Sander, 1974). Furthermore, 3- to 4-month-old infants show altered vocalizations and synchronized limb movements in response to rhythmic dance music (Fujii et al., 2014), while 5- to 24-month-old infants engage in more rhythmic limb movements and smile more during music listening (Zentner and Eerola, 2010). Older preschool children spontaneously play the drum in synchrony when a human adult partner plays the drum (Kirschner and Tomasello, 2009). Thus, rhythmic sounds and motor actions are fundamental for communication and social interaction throughout development.

THE ROLE OF RHYTHM IN SPEECH

Rhythm is essential to the understanding of speech. In order to comprehend spoken language, listeners are required to perceive temporal organization of phonemes, syllables, words, and phrases from an ongoing speech stream (Kotz and Schwartze, 2010; Patel, 2011; Peelle and Davis, 2012). An important source of acoustic information that conveys rhythm in speech is the *sound envelope*, which is defined as the acoustic power summed across all frequencies for a given frequency range (Kotz and Schwartze, 2010; Patel, 2011; Peelle and Davis, 2012). As illustrated in **Figure 1**, the phrase "Happy birthday to you" can be broken down into six syllables (i.e., "Ha/ppy/birth/day/to/you"), and these boundaries correspond to the pattern of the sound envelope (denoted by vertical dashed lines). Thus, burst patterns of the sound envelope represent rhythm or temporal organization in vocalization.

A number of studies have demonstrated the importance of rhythm or sound envelope in speech comprehension (e.g.,

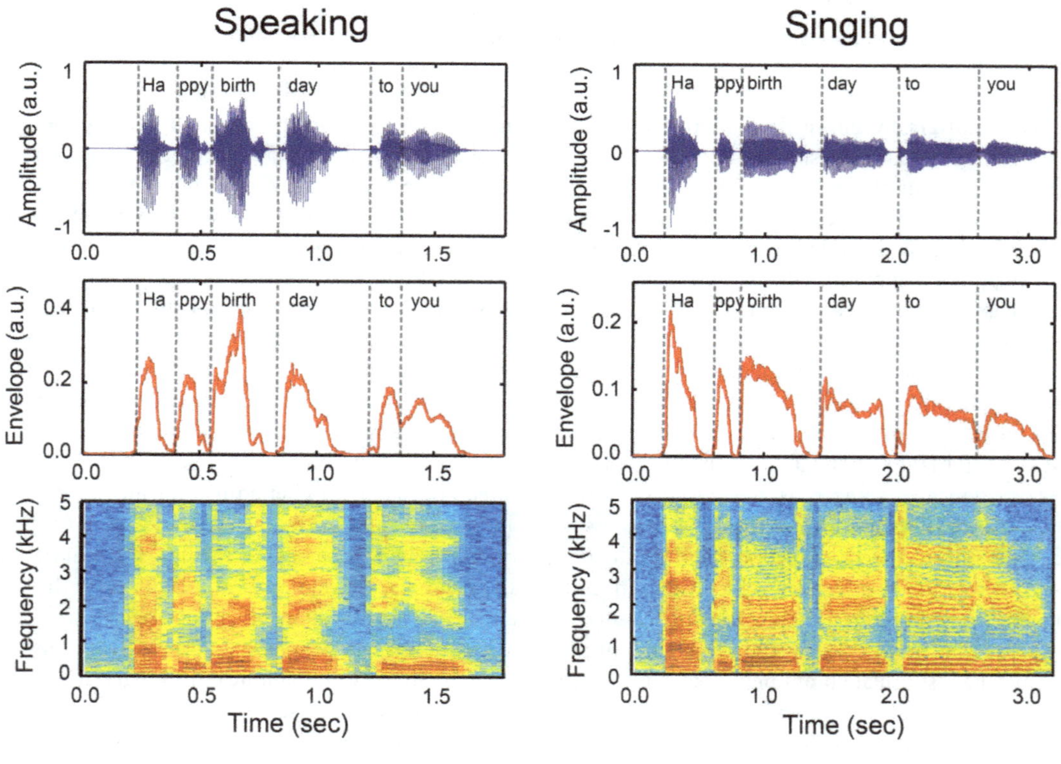

FIGURE 1 | An example of sound wave (upper panels), amplitude envelope (middle panels), and power spectrum (bottom panels) when a person speaks (left) and sings (right) "Happy birthday to you" that can be divided into six syllables (i.e., Ha/ppy/birth/day/to/you, see vertical dashed lines). Sound envelope is an important acoustic information that conveys temporal organization of phonemes and syllables or rhythm in vocalization. Note that rhythm in singing (right) has a more salient pulse- or beat-based timing compared with rhythm in speech (left).

Drullman et al., 1994a,b; Nazzi et al., 1998; Ahissar et al., 2001; Smith et al., 2002; Elliott and Theunissen, 2009; Bertoncini et al., 2011). For example, Shannon et al. (1995) tested the importance of rhythm in speech by minimizing the fine spectral information while preserving the sound envelope. Near perfect speech recognition performance was observed when individuals were presented with these speech stimuli. Consistent with this finding, smearing of the rhythm or sound envelope in speech sounds significantly reduced sentence intelligibility (e.g., Drullman et al., 1994a,b; Elliott and Theunissen, 2009). The reliance on rhythm or sound envelope to discriminate speech sounds has also been reported in infants (Nazzi et al., 1998; Bertoncini et al., 2011). Smith et al. (2002) further investigated the different roles of envelope and fine spectral structure in human auditory perception. They created sound stimuli called "auditory chimeras," which consisted of the envelope of one sound and the fine spectral structure of another (Smith et al., 2002). Interestingly, when the two features (i.e., envelope and fine spectral structure) were in conflict, the pitch and location of sounds were determined by the fine spectral structure, while the words identified were based on the envelope (Smith et al., 2002). Thus, along with fine spectral information, sound envelope or rhythm is essential for speech intelligibility.

NEURAL CORRELATES OF RHYTHMIC SPEECH PERCEPTION

A question arises then, regarding how rhythm or sound envelope is processed in the brain. fMRI studies have shown that the processing of sound envelope or low-frequency temporal feature in the acoustic signal is associated with activities in the inferior colliculus of the brainstem, the medial geniculate body of the thalamus, the Heschl's gyrus (HG), the superior temporal gyrus (STG), and the superior temporal sulcus (STS) (Giraud et al., 2000; Boemio et al., 2005). The "asymmetric sampling in time (AST)" hypothesis postulates that low-frequency temporal features in the acoustic signals are lateralized to the right hemisphere, whereas high-frequency fine spectral features of the acoustic signals are lateralized to the left hemisphere (Poeppel, 2003; McGettigan and Scott, 2012). Consistent with this hypothesis, electroencephalography (EEG) studies have also shown that sound envelope processing is right lateralized (Abrams et al., 2008, 2009). Similarly, phase pattern of theta band (4–8 Hz) responses recorded from the temporal cortex using magnetoencephalography (MEG), especially in the right hemisphere, is correlated with the degree of speech intelligibility (Luo and Poeppel, 2007). Thus, the neural mechanisms underlying rhythm or sound envelope processing are likely to involve the brainstem, the thalamus, and the auditory regions in the temporal cortex, which may be lateralized to right hemisphere (see pink arrows and "R" in **Figure 2B**).

In parallel with the brainstem-thalamo-cortical (temporal auditory regions) pathway, there is another possible pathway for rhythm perception in speech, which involves the brainstem, the cerebellum, the thalamus, the supplementary motor area (SMA), the basal ganglia (BG), and the prefrontal cortex (light blue arrows in **Figure 2B**) [see Kotz and Schwartze (2010)]. Here, early auditory input is transmitted to the cerebellum via the cochlear nuclei of the brainstem (Huang et al., 1982; Wang et al., 1991; Xi et al., 1994; Kotz and Schwartze, 2010). The cerebellum is responsible for the encoding of event-based temporal structure, and relays information to the SMA via the thalamus, which further transmits information to the prefrontal cortex (Kotz and Schwartze, 2010). The SMA and the prefrontal cortex transmit temporal information to the BG, which transmits information back to the cortex via the thalamus forming the BG-thalamo-cortical loop (Kotz et al., 2009; Kotz and Schwartze, 2010, 2011). This closed-loop circuit is assumed to have functions to continuously evaluate temporal relations, extract temporal regularity, and engage in sequencing of temporal events and analysis of hierarchical structure (Kotz et al., 2009; Kotz and Schwartze, 2010, 2011; Schwartze et al., 2011). For example, when we listen to the six syllables of "ha/ppy/birth/day/to/you," they are grouped into four words "happy/birthday/to/you" and perceived as one phrase (**Figure 1**). Thus, rhythm perception in speech can be regarded as finding the hierarchical structure of temporal events (Kotz et al., 2009; Kotz and Schwartze, 2010; Przybylski et al., 2013). The prefrontal cortex integrates information from the temporal cortex with that being processed in the BG-thalamo-SMA loop circuit to optimize speech comprehension (Kotz and Schwartze, 2010). Taken together, the sound envelope or rhythm is processed in the cortical and subcortical auditory-motor systems.

NEURAL CORRELATES OF RHYTHMIC SPEECH PRODUCTION

In the previous section, we described the neural correlates of sound envelope or rhythm processing in speech perception. We now consider the neural correlates of rhythmic speech production. The directions into velocities of articulators (DIVA) model provide a useful framework to consider the neural mechanisms (see Guenther et al., 2006; Bohland et al., 2010; Tourville and Guenther, 2011). According to the DIVA model, rhythmic speech production is achieved by sequential control of the velocities of articulators including the upper and lower lips, the jaw, the tongue, and the larynx. In this model, the bilateral ventral primary motor cortex (vM1), which corresponds to the cortical homunculus of speech articulators (Penfield and Rasmussen, 1950; Penfield and Roberts, 1959), is responsible for outputting motor commands to the muscles of articulators [see also Kalaska et al. (1989), Ludlow (2005), Brown et al. (2008), and Olthoff et al. (2008)]. The vM1 receives inputs from the SMA connected with the BG and the thalamus (green arrows in **Figure 2C**) [see also Jurgens (1984) and Luppino et al. (1993)]. This is supported by fMRI studies that showed bilateral activities in the BG, thalamus, and SMA during speech production (e.g., Bohland and Guenther, 2006; Tourville et al., 2008). The BG-thalamo-SMA circuit is hypothesized to play a role in sequencing and self-initiation of speech, or rhythmic speech production in the DIVA model. This is based on clinical studies that showed speech production problems including involuntary vocalizations, echolalia, lack of prosody, stuttering-like output, variable rate, and difficulties with complex speech sequences following the impairment of the BG-thalamo-SMA circuit (e.g., Jonas, 1981; Ziegler et al., 1997; Ho et al., 1998; Pickett et al., 1998; Vargha-Khadem et al., 1998; Pai, 1999; Watkins et al., 2002).

In the DIVA model, the bilateral vM1 also receives inputs from left ventral premotor cortex (vPMC) and adjacent posterior inferior frontal gyrus (pIFG) (see red arrow and "L" in **Figure 2C**). These areas (i.e., left vPMC and pIFG) are hypothesized to

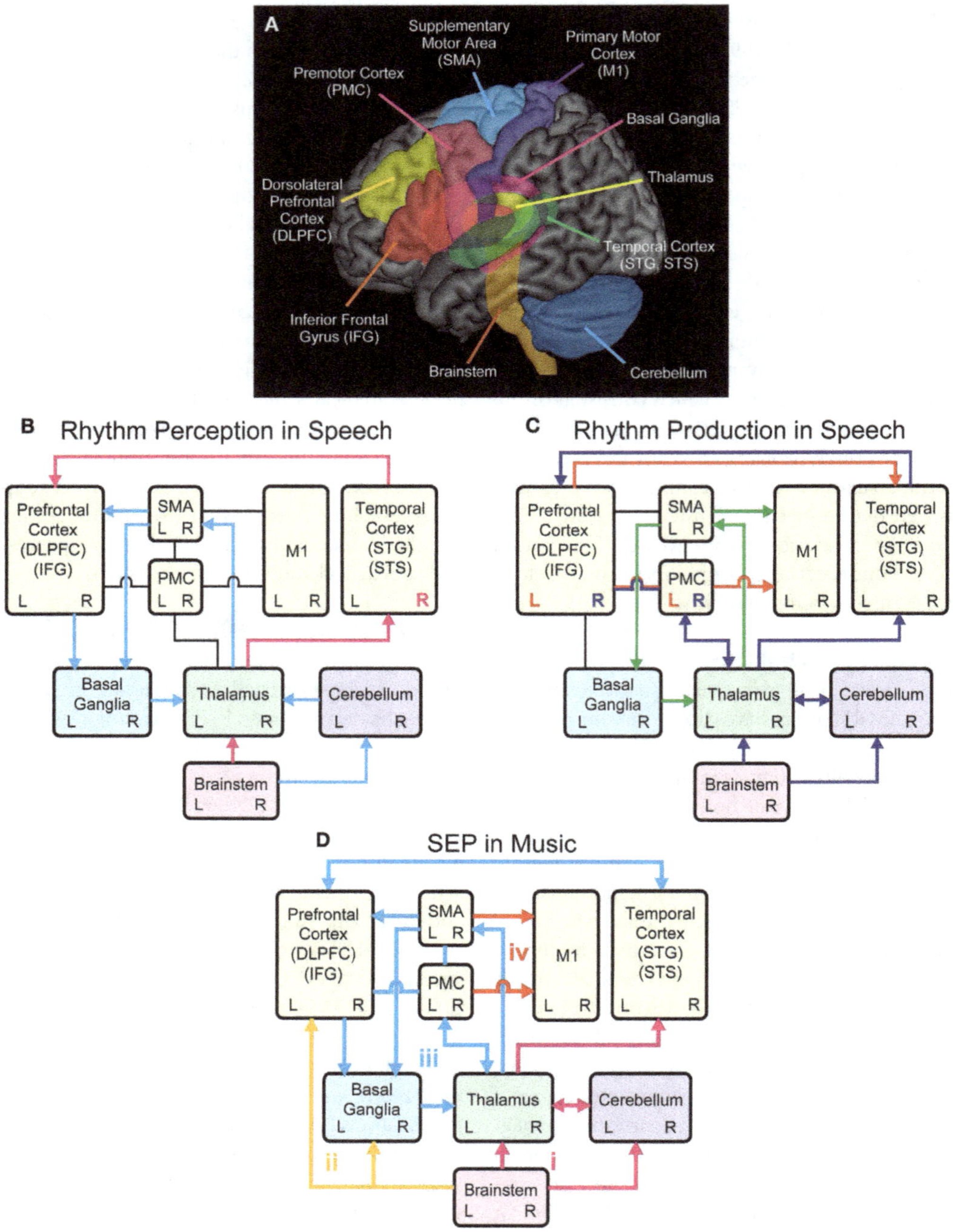

FIGURE 2 | Schematic models of shared brain network for rhythm perception and production in speech and music. (A) Possible shared brain regions for rhythm processing in music and speech. **(B)** A model for rhythm perception in speech. The temporal cortex receives auditory inputs from the brainstem via the thalamus, which further transmits information to the prefrontal cortex (pink arrows). Processing of sound envelope or low-frequency temporal feature in the acoustic signals may be lateralized to the right hemisphere in the temporal cortex (see pink R). The cerebellum also receives the auditory inputs from the brainstem and relays information to the SMA via the thalamus, and further transmits information to the prefrontal cortex to process temporal events. The SMA and the prefrontal cortex transmit information to the basal ganglia (BG), which transmits information back to the cortex via the thalamus forming the BG-thalamo-cortical loop (light blue arrows). **(C)** A model for rhythm production in speech. The M1 receives inputs from the SMA, which forms the SMA-BG-thalamo loop, for rhythmic speech production (green arrows). The M1 also receives inputs from the left PMC and IFG, which transform speech sounds into motor commands (see red arrow and L). The left PMC and IFG also transmit information to the temporal cortex, which is associated with sensory predictions. The temporal cortex monitors the sensory predictions and the auditory feedback received from the brainstem via the thalamus. The feedback errors from the temporal cortex are sent to right PMC and IFG, which is interconnected with the thalamus and the cerebellum (see blue arrows and R). **(D)** A model for Sound Envelope Processing (SEP) and Synchronization and Entrainment to a Pulse (SEP) in music. Rhythm-based therapy may help stimulate brain networks involving (i) the auditory-afferent circuit consisting of brainstem, thalamus, cerebellum, and temporal cortex (pink arrows) for precise encoding of sound envelope and temporal events; (ii) the subcortical-prefrontal circuit for emotional and reward-related processing (yellow arrows); (iii) the BG-thalamo-cortical circuit for processing beat-based timing (light blue arrows); and (iv) the cortical-motor efferent circuit for motor output (red arrows).

form the "speech sound map," which transform speech sounds (e.g., phonemes and syllables) into motor commands (Guenther et al., 2006; Bohland et al., 2010; Tourville and Guenther, 2011). In other words, the speech sound map is "mental syllabary" or repository of learned speech motor program [see also Levelt and Wheeldon (1994) and Levelt et al. (1999)]. The speech sound map has anatomical correspondence with Broca's area (e.g., Dronkers et al., 2007) and has functional correspondence with the "mirror-neuron system" (Rizzolatti et al., 1996; Kohler et al., 2002). Language function is generally regarded as left lateralized because impairments of these brain regions (i.e., left vPMC and pIFG) lead to significant deficit of speech production (e.g., Dronkers, 1996; Kent and Tjaden, 1997; Hillis et al., 2004; Duffy, 2005).

The speech sound map (i.e., left vPMC and pIFG) is hypothesized to project not only to the vM1 to form the motor commands but also to the bilateral auditory areas in the temporal cortex (Guenther et al., 2006; Tourville and Guenther, 2011) (see red arrow in **Figure 2C**). The auditory areas include two locations along the posterior superior temporal gyrus (pSTG): the lateral one near the STS, and the medial one at the junction of the temporal and parietal lobes deep in the sylvian fissure (Guenther et al., 2006; Tourville and Guenther, 2011). These auditory areas are activated not only during speech perception but also during speech production (e.g., Buchsbaum et al., 2001; Hickok and Poeppel, 2004). The projections from the speech sound map to these auditory areas are responsible for predicting the sound being produced, which is compared with the actual auditory feedback being processed in the HG and the adjacent anterior planum temporale (PT) (Guenther et al., 2006; Tourville and Guenther, 2011). If the auditory feedback does not fall within the predicted range, the error signals are sent back to the right vPMC and pIFG according to the DIVA model (Guenther et al., 2006; Tourville and Guenther, 2011) (see blue arrows and "R" in **Figure 2C**). The right vPMC and pIFG are interconnected with the cerebellum via the thalamus, forming the "feedback control map," which transforms the sensory error signals into corrective motor commands (Tourville and Guenther, 2011). This is based on fMRI studies that showed increased hemodynamic responses in the right PMC, pIFG, and the cerebellum during speech production under perturbed auditory feedback conditions (Tourville et al., 2008). Taken together, it is assumed that the BG-thalamo-cortical (vM1 and SMA) circuit is essential for rhythmic speech production, and the other areas (vPMC, pIFG, temporal cortex, and cerebellum) also play important roles for sensorimotor transformation and integration processes.

THEORETICAL RATIONALE UNDERLYING THE ROLE OF RHYTHM FOR SPEECH AND LANGUAGE REHABILITATION: THE "OPERA" AND "SEP" HYPOTHESES

The aim of this section is to provide a rationale underlying the role of rhythm for speech and language rehabilitation considering the above mentioned neural correlates of rhythm perception and production in speech. Here, we present the "SEP" hypothesis, which is a rhythm-specific extension of the "OPERA" hypothesis (Patel, 2011, 2012, 2014), to explain how and why musical rhythm can benefit speech and language rehabilitation.

The OPERA hypothesis is a conceptual framework that postulates how general musical activities can facilitate speech and language processing (Patel, 2011, 2012, 2014). The OPERA hypothesis assumes that five conditions are needed to drive the benefit of musical activities for speech and language processing: (1) overlap: there is anatomical overlap in the brain networks during the processing music and speech, (2) precision: music places higher demands on these shared networks than does speech, in terms of the precision of processing, (3) emotion: musical activities that engage this network elicit strong positive emotion, (4) repetition: musical activities that engage this network are frequently repeated, and (5) attention: musical activities that engage this network are associated with focused attention. In other words, condition (1) describes shared neural underpinnings for both music and speech activities while (2)–(5) are distinctions of musical activities that may drive the neural plasticity enhancing the abilities of speech and language processing.

While the OPERA hypothesis provides a useful conceptual framework for general musical processing, it has a number of limitations that preclude its application to rhythm-based therapy. First, the OPERA hypothesis describes the possible overlap in brain networks during music and speech processing, but the explanation is restricted to perception (i.e., afferent process from cochlea to auditory cortex level). Within the context of rhythm, however, it is important to clarify the overlapping brain networks during sensorimotor coupling and production (i.e., cortical auditory-motor interaction and efferent process from the motor cortex to the spinal cord). Second, the OPERA hypothesis covers many aspects of general musical processing that include pitch and timbre. Here, we specifically discuss how rhythm itself meets with the five conditions of the OPERA hypothesis (i.e., overlap, precision, emotion, repetition, and attention). Third, under the OPERA hypothesis, it is not clear whether rhythm *per se* would have therapeutic potential in patient populations.

In order to address the above limitations, we propose the "SEP" hypothesis, which postulates two additional components to describe how and why rhythm in particular can be beneficial for speech and language rehabilitation: (1) sound envelope processing and (2) synchronization and entrainment to a pulse. The first key component of the SEP hypothesis, sound envelope processing, is adapted from the OPERA hypothesis (Patel, 2011, 2012, 2014), which postulates the major sources of overlap in the brain networks during rhythm perception in music and speech [see also Peretz and Coltheart (2003), Corriveau and Goswami (2009), Kotz and Schwartze (2010), and Goswami (2011)]. The second key component in the SEP hypothesis, synchronization and entrainment to a pulse, postulates the major sources of overlap in the brain networks not only for rhythm perception but also for rhythm production and sensorimotor coupling in music and speech (Guenther et al., 2006; Kotz et al., 2009; Bohland et al., 2010; Kotz and Schwartze, 2010, 2011; Tourville and Guenther, 2011).

In the SEP hypothesis, we assume that the overlap in brain networks for rhythm processing between speech and music involve the brainstem, cerebellum, thalamus, BG, M1, SMA, PMC, prefrontal cortex (DLPFC and IFG), and temporal cortex (STG and STS). As illustrated in **Figure 2D**, we propose four key circuits in the shared brain network to explain the potential benefit of rhythm-based therapy: (a) the auditory afferent circuit consisted of brainstem, thalamus, cerebellum, and temporal cortex (pink arrows) for precise encoding of sound envelope and temporal events; (b) the subcortical–prefrontal circuit for emotional and reward-related processing (yellow arrows); (c) the BG-thalamo-cortical circuit for processing beat-based timing (light blue arrows); and (d) the cortical motor efferent circuit for motor output (red arrows).

AUDITORY AFFERENT CIRCUIT

According to the OPERA hypothesis, musical activities place high demands on precise encoding of acoustic features including the sound envelope (Patel, 2011, 2012, 2014). This notion is supported by neuroimaging studies that showed more precise encoding of sounds in the brainstem of musicians compared with non-musicians (e.g., Musacchia et al., 2007, 2008; Parbery-Clark et al., 2011, 2012; Strait and Kraus, 2014; Strait et al., 2014). Interestingly, individuals with more musical training exhibit better encoding of speech sounds in the brainstem, larger cortical responses, and better speech sound perception (Strait and Kraus, 2014; Strait et al., 2014). Although the role of the cerebellum for speech and music perception is not mentioned in the OPERA hypothesis, we also include the cerebellum as a part of the auditory afferent circuit because it receives input from the cochlear nuclei (Huang et al., 1982; Wang et al., 1991; Xi et al., 1994; Kotz and Schwartze, 2010) and plays an important role in encoding the absolute duration of time intervals in successive acoustic events (Kotz and Schwartze, 2010; Teki et al., 2011a,b). For example, a recent neuroimaging study showed that perception of changes in musical rhythm (so-called "groove") with drum sounds is associated with activity in the cerebellum and the STG (Danielsen et al., 2014). In addition, musicians showed enhanced activity in the cerebellum compared to non-musicians during temporal perception (Lu et al., 2014) and have larger volumes of cerebellum than non-musicians (Hutchinson et al., 2003). Taken together, we postulate that musical rhythm perception or sound envelope processing in music places high demand on the auditory afferent circuit consisted of the brainstem, thalamus, cerebellum, and temporal cortex (pink arrows in **Figure 2D**). This corresponds to the second condition of the OPERA hypothesis ("precision").

SUBCORTICAL–PREFRONTAL CIRCUIT

Rhythm perception or sound envelope processing in music may engage neural activities in the subcortical–prefrontal circuit relevant for emotional processing. A primate study has shown that rhythmic drumming sounds serve as communicative signals and engage the emotional network in the subcortical areas including the amygdala and the putamen (Remedios et al., 2009). Human neuroimaging studies have shown that listening to music elicit pleasant emotion by engaging the reward system in the subcortical and cortical areas including the midbrain (e.g., ventral tegmental area, periaqueductal gray, and pedunculopontine nucleus), the nucleus accumbens, the striatum, the amygdala, the orbitofrontal cortex, and the ventral medial prefrontal cortex (Blood and Zatorre, 2001; Menon and Levitin, 2005; Salimpoor et al., 2011, 2013; Koelsch, 2014). Recent behavioral studies have also shown that listening to musical rhythm elicits positive affect and a desire to move (Zentner and Eerola, 2010; Witek et al., 2014). Similarly, perception of poetry in the presence of rhyme and regular meter lead to enhanced positive emotions, suggesting that perceiving rhythmic vocalizations may result in positive emotions (Obermeier et al., 2013). Thus, we assume that musical rhythm engages the subcortical–prefrontal circuit for emotional and reward-related processing to elicit positive affect, leading to repetition of actions to reinforce the pleasure actions (yellow arrows in **Figure 2D**). This meets the conditions of (3) emotion and (4) repetition in the OPERA hypothesis.

BG-THALAMO-CORTICAL CIRCUIT

Synchronization and entrainment to a pulse in music may place high demands on information process in the BG-thalamo-cortical circuit. This notion is based on the fact that musical rhythm is more periodic while speech rhythm is quasi-periodic (Peelle and Davis, 2012). Compared with speech rhythm, musical rhythm has a more salient pulse- or beat-based timing. For example, for the phrase "happy birthday to you," the onsets of syllable in the sound envelope are more equally time spaced in singing compared to speaking (**Figure 1**). Neuroimaging studies suggest that perception of beat-based timing (i.e., perception of time intervals with respect to a regular pulse) involve brain networks in the BG, the SMA, the PMC, and the DLPFC (Teki et al., 2011a,b). In fact, beat perception and synchronization increase activities in the BG, SMA, PMC, DLPFC, and STG, and enhance connectivity between the BG with the SMA, PMC, and STG (Chen et al., 2006, 2008a,b; Grahn and Brett, 2007; Grahn and Rowe, 2009; Hove et al., 2013; Kung et al., 2013). Animal studies also suggest the importance of brain networks involving the BG and cortical auditory-motor areas for beat perception and synchronization capabilities (Patel et al., 2009; Schachner et al., 2009; Hasegawa et al., 2011). In addition, tapping to a beat is associated with increased cortical responses in the DLPFC and the inferior parietal lobule (Chen et al., 2008b), which are assumed to be responsible for auditory and temporal attention (Zatorre et al., 1999; Lewis and Miall, 2003; Singh-Curry and Husain, 2009). This attention-related brain network has been shown to be more engaged in precise synchronization performance with the musical beat (Chen et al., 2008b). Taken together, synchronization and entrainment to a pulse in music engages enhanced BG-thalamo-cortical activity (light blue arrows in **Figure 2D**), and this fulfills the fourth and fifth conditions of the OPERA hypothesis ("repetition" and "attention").

CORTICAL MOTOR EFFERENT CIRCUIT

Synchronization and entrainment to a pulse in music can modulate the neural pathway for cortical motor output (red arrows in **Figure 2D**). Not only vocalizations but also other body movements can be synchronized and entrained to the pulse of music, such as tapping, clapping, stepping, dancing, and singing. In terms of the motor-output process in the brain, involvements of both the dorsal and ventral portions of the M1, PMC, and PFC are likely. Neuroimaging studies have shown that cortical hand motor areas are involved not only in hand motor control but also in language processing (e.g., Meister et al., 2003, 2009a,b), suggesting the importance of cortical hand motor areas for human communication. In addition, a recent transcranial magnetic stimulation (TMS) study has shown that listening to groove music modulates cortico-spinal excitability (Stupacher et al., 2013), suggesting that musical rhythm perception itself may also stimulate the motor-output pathway from the M1 to spinal cord. In sum, there are four circuits of interest in the SEP hypothesis, which may help to stimulate the brain networks underlying human communication.

EXAMPLES OF SPEECH AND LANGUAGE DISORDERS THAT CAN BENEFIT FROM RHYTHM-BASED THERAPY: APPLICATION OF THE "SEP" HYPOTHESIS FOR REHABILITATION

The SEP hypothesis postulates that rhythm-based therapy elicits functional and structural reorganization in the neural networks for human communication in various patient populations via sound envelope processing and synchronization and entrainment to a pulse. In this section, we present examples of speech and language disorders and consider the role of rhythm in speech and language rehabilitation under the framework of the SEP hypothesis. We note, however, that the number of rhythm-based techniques currently available is very limited.

PARKINSON'S DISEASE

Parkinson's disease is a neurodegenerative disorder characterized by progressive deterioration of motor function due to a loss of dopaminergic neurons in the substantia nigra (DeLong, 1990; Wichmann and DeLong, 1998; Blandini et al., 2000). In addition to the more commonly known symptoms such as muscular rigidity, tremor, and postural instability, abnormalities of voice and speech (beyond those associated with aging) are highly prevalent. Indeed, it has been estimated that over 80% of patients with PD develop voice and speech problems at some point (Ramig et al., 2008). Examples of deficits reported by clinicians include mono-pitch, monoloudness, hypokinetic articulation, and altered speech rate and rhythm (Darley et al., 1969). Analysis of the speech rate of patients with PD showed impaired rhythm and timing organization, such as an accelerated rate of articulation during speaking, as well as a reduction in the total number of pauses (Skodda and Schlegel, 2008; Skodda et al., 2010). When combined with the debilitating motor limb deficits, the loss of speech intelligibility and communication skills can significantly impair the quality of life of patients with PD (Streifler and Hofman, 1984).

To date, only a handful of studies have examined the speech deficits in Parkinson's disease using neuroimaging technique (e.g., Liotti et al., 2003; Pinto et al., 2004; Rektorova et al., 2007, 2012). These studies must be interpreted with caution because the results vary depending on treatment status of patients with PD. For example, patients with PD with no medication and no deep brain stimulation showed significant dysarthria accompanying with a lack of activity in the orfacial motor cortex (M1) and cerebellum while increased activities in the PMC, SMA, and DLPFC compared with the healthy controls (Pinto et al., 2004). These abnormal cortical activities disappeared and the dysarthria symptoms improved after the deep brain stimulation of subthalamic nucleus (STN) in these patients (Pinto et al., 2004). The other fMRI studies investigated mild to moderate patients with PD with levodopa medication (Rektorova et al., 2007, 2012). Compared to healthy controls, patients with PD with the levodopa medication had increased activity in the orofacial sensorimotor cortex (Rektorova et al., 2007) and enhanced functional connectivity in the networks seeded from the periaqueductal gray matter of the midbrain (a core subcortical structure involved in human vocalization) (Rektorova et al., 2012). However, speech productions in these patients with PD with levodopa medication was comparable with that in the controls except for speech loudness, suggesting that the increased brain activity and connectivity might reflect the effects of pharmacological treatment or successful compensatory mechanisms (Rektorova et al., 2007, 2012).

Besides the deep brain stimulation and pharmacological treatments, Lee Silverman Voice Treatment (LSVT) technique has received research attention as a rehabilitation method (Ramig et al., 2001, 2004, 2007; Liotti et al., 2003; Sapir et al., 2011; Sackley et al., 2014). LSVT is designed to improve vocal function in patients with PD by enhancing loudness, intonation range, and articulatory functions. LSVT emphasizes use of loud phonation and high intensity vocal exercises to improve respiratory, laryngeal, and articulatory during speech. Compared with placebo therapy, LSVT has resulted in improvements in speech production parameters such as increases in sound pressure level (i.e., loudness) and semitone standard deviation of fundamental frequency (i.e., prosody), and these improvements were sustained even 12 months after cessation of treatment (e.g., Ramig et al., 2001). The neural correlates of LSVT have been studied by administrating levodopa medication for 4 weeks to mild and moderate patients with PD (Liotti et al., 2003). The results showed that the improvement of speech loudness following the LVST accompanied by neural activities in the striatum, insula, and DLPFC (Liotti et al., 2003).

Under the SEP hypothesis, patients with PD can benefit from synchronization and entrainment to a pulse in music to stimulate the subcortical–prefrontal network and the BG-thalamo-cortical network. As illustrated in **Figure 3**, the BG-thalamo-cortical network functions normally in healthy individuals (top left panel), whereas the network becomes abnormal in PD because of the degeneration of the dopamine-producing neurons in the substantia nigra pars compacta (SNc) (top right panel). The projections from the SNc to the striatum regulates the cortico-strital projections, and if the dopamigeneric neurons in the SNc are depleted, it leads to reduced inhibition in the "direct" pathway to the BG output nuclei (i.e., GPi: internal segment of globus pallidus and SNr: substantia nigra pars reticulata), which carries dopamine "D1" receptors. The degeneration of dopamigeneric neurons in the SNc also leads to increased inhibition in the "indirect" pathway to the BG output nuclei (GPi/SNr) via external segment of globus pallidus (GPe) and STN carrying dopamine "D2" receptors. Net action of the degeneration of dopanigeneric neurons in the SNc leads to the hyper-activation of the BG output nuclei (GPi/SNr) inhibiting activities of thalamocortical projection neurons, which in turn negatively affects motor output [for more detail, see DeLong (1990), Wichmann and DeLong (1996), Blandini et al. (2000), Galvan and Wichmann (2008), and Smith et al. (2012)].

In this model, we assume that pleasurable musical rhythm induces increased endogenous dopamine release in the striatum (bottom left panel in **Figure 3**). This is based on a previous study, which showed an increase in dopamine release and hemodynamic response in the striatum during listening pleasurable music

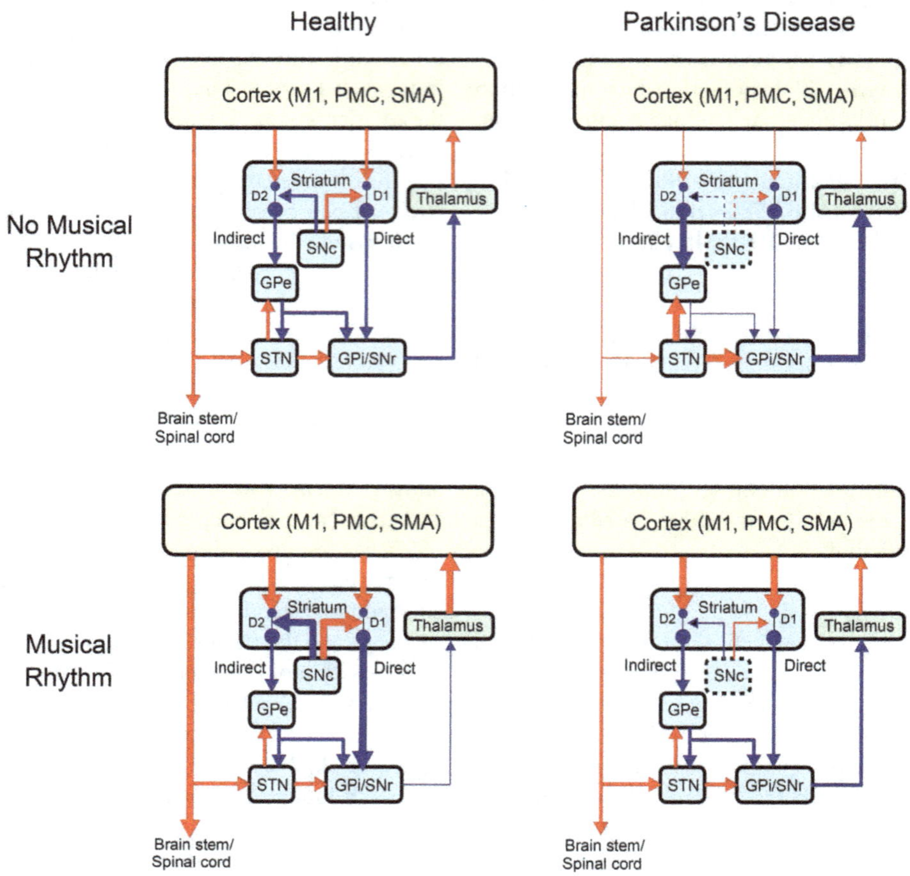

FIGURE 3 | A schematic model of changes in the basal ganglia-thalamo-cortical motor network with Parkinson's disease and/or musical rhythm [modified from Galvan and Wichmann (2008)]. The left and right panels show the network without and with Parkinson's disease, while the upper and lower panels show the network without and with musical rhythm, respectively. Blue arrows indicate inhibitory projections, while red arrows indicate excitatory projections. Changes in the thickness of the arrows indicate increase (thicker arrow) or decrease (thinner arrow) of the projections relative to the normal situation. The dashed lines around the SNc (substantia nigra pars compacta) indicate degeneration of dopaminergic neurons caused by Parkinson's disease. GPe, external segment of globus pallidus; GPi, internal segment of globus pallidus; SNr, substantia nigra pars reticulata; STN, subthalamic nucleus; M1, primary motor cortex; PMC, premotor cortex; and SMA, supplementary motor area. Striatum has "direct" and "indirect" pathways to the basal ganglia (BG) output nuclei (GPi/SNr). Light blue, green, and yellow colors denote BG, thalamus, and cortex, respectively. D1 and D2 indicate subtypes of dopamine receptor. Parkinson's disease induces hyper-activation of BG output nuclei (GPi/SNr) inhibiting activities of the thalamocortical projection neurons, which in turn decreases motor output, while musical rhythm induces hypo-activation BG output nuclei and thereby facilitates thalamo-cortical motor output.

(Salimpoor et al., 2011). In our model, the increased dopamine release leads to increased inhibition in the BG output neuclei (GPi/SNr) and thereby facilitates thalamo-cortical motor output and a desire to move. This idea is also supported by the other studies that showed modulation in the cortico-spinal excitability (Stupacher et al., 2013) and increased activity and connectivity in the brain network including the striatum, PMC, and SMA during perceiving and synchronizing with the musical beats (Chen et al., 2006, 2008a,b; Grahn and Brett, 2007; Grahn and Rowe, 2009; Kung et al., 2013). We also postulate that pleasurable musical rhythm may increase dopamine release even in patients with PD considering that some of the GNc neurons (approximately 30–50%) remain intact even at the time of death (e.g., Davie, 2008). Indeed, a number of studies have shown improvements of motor function in patients with PD during rhythmic auditory stimulation (RAS) (e.g., Thaut et al., 1996; McIntosh et al., 1997; de Bruin et al., 2010; Nombela et al., 2013), suggesting that musical rhythm may facilitate thalamo-cortical motor output in patients with PD (bottom right panel in **Figure 3**).

If our model is correct, then musical rhythm may reduce reliance on levodopa medication and/or deep brain stimulation. However, there remain a few untested assumptions. For example, patients with PD show impaired emotional recognition in music (e.g., van Tricht et al., 2010), suggesting that the ventral portion of the striatum is also affected in patients with PD. Therefore, dopamine release in the striatum may not be increased by music in patients with PD as seen in healthy individuals. Positron emission tomography (PET) can be used to test this hypothesis (Laruelle, 2000; Salimpoor et al., 2011), and whether this may be affected by intervention. A recent study has shown improved perceptual and motor timing in patients with PD after a 4-week music training program with rhythmic auditory cueing (Benoit et al.,

2014), suggesting a possible benefit of RAS on the treatment of PD. However, the participants of that study consisted only of mild to moderate patients with PD (Benoit et al., 2014). Future studies will need to clarify whether the RAS is also beneficial for severe patients with PD, and how the therapeutic effect is different. It may also be important to test whether RAS (simple metronome stimulation as well as rhythmic musical stimulation) improves speech function in patients with PD, given gait functions have been a topic of research interest (e.g., Thaut et al., 1996; McIntosh et al., 1997; de Bruin et al., 2010; Nombela et al., 2013). Additional neuroimaging studies are required to examine the brain networks underlying speech and hand/foot motor processes in patients with PD.

STUTTERING

Stuttering is a developmental condition that affects fluency of speech. It begins during the first few years of life, and affects approximately 5% of preschool-aged children (Bloodstein, 1995). Symptoms include repetition of words or parts of words, as well as prolongations of speech sounds, resulting in disruptions in the normal flow of speech.

As illustrated in **Figure 2C**, during normal speech production, the left IFG and PMC projects to the M1 for vocal-motor output and the right IFG and PMC are monitoring sensory feedback together with the temporal cortex and the cerebellum (blue arrows). However, individuals who stutter show abnormalities in the left IFG and PMC and compensatory hyperactivity in the right IFG and the cerebellum (Fox et al., 1996; Brown et al., 2005; Kell et al., 2009), suggesting that stuttering is associated with poor feed-forward motor command and excessive reliance on auditory feedback control (Max et al., 2004; Civier et al., 2010, 2013). In addition, stuttering is associated with reduced activity and connectivity in the brain network including the BG and the SMA (e.g., Toyomura et al., 2011; Chang and Zhu, 2013), suggesting that stuttering may be due to dysfunction in the BG-thalamo-cortical circuit to produce timing cues for the initiation of the next motor segment in speech (Alm, 2004).

To date, examples of fluency shaping methods for stuttering include altered auditory feedback (e.g., Hargrave et al., 1994; Ryan and Van Kirk Ryan, 1995; Stuart et al., 1996; Armson and Kiefte, 2008), prolonged speech that uses slow and exaggerated speech production (e.g., O'Brian et al., 2010), training of oral-motor co-ordination (e.g., Riley and Ingham, 2000), and the Lidcombe technique, a response-contingent program that involves parents to shape the child's utterances (e.g., Lattermann et al., 2008). The altered auditory feedback methods are considered to be effective to change the excessive reliance on auditory feedback control, while the other speech production trainings would help to reform feed-forward speech commands. Yet, a therapy that focuses specifically on stimulating the BG-thalamo-cortical circuit to enhance rhythmic speech production would also be warranted (Alm, 2004).

The SEP hypothesis assumes that individuals who stutter may benefit from rhythm-based therapy using synchronization and entrainment to a pulse for stimulating the BG-thalamo-cortical circuit. Behavioral studies support this notion by showing that the presence of rhythmic auditory signals such as metronome beats, when synchronized with speech production, induces strong fluency-enhancing effects in individuals who stutter (e.g., Brady, 1969, 1971). A recent fMRI study also supports this notion by showing that BG activities of stuttering speakers increased to the level of normal speech controls when speaking with the metronome beats (Toyomura et al., 2011).

Nevertheless, given that stuttering is a relapse-prone disorder (Craig, 2002), long-term management strategies are likely to be useful when dealing with this disorder over a lifetime. Accordingly, future studies need to test how long the metronome-induced fluency sustains after removing the rhythmic sounds. It has been suggested that the BG-thalamo-SMA circuit is dominant for self-initiation of speech, while the PMC-thalamo-cerebellar circuit is dominant for externally cued speech (Alm, 2004). Therefore, one of the challenges for future studies is to transition from the externally cued (PMC-centered) speech to self-initiated (SMA-centered) speech in the treatments using metronome-guided cues. To engage the BG-thalamo-SMA circuit, it may be useful to use non-isochronous metronome stimuli to promote the patients to find a pulse and initiate rhythmic speech by themselves. In addition, future studies need to test whether structural and functional reorganization occur in the BG-thalamo-cortical circuit after the intervention using the rhythmic auditory cues. Concurrently, more basic studies are needed to clarify whether the neural underpinnings of stuttering overlap with those of rhythm processing in music. Investigations of the abilities of musical rhythm processing in individuals who stutter using an amusia battery (e.g., Peretz et al., 2003; Fujii and Schlaug, 2013) may help further our understanding of possible overlapping brain networks. In addition, there is a need to test whether synchronization to a pulse in music have the similar fluency-enhancing effect for stuttering speakers compared with the synchronization to a metronome.

APHASIA

Aphasia is a common and devastating consequence of stroke or other brain injuries that results in language-related dysfunction. When speech production is impaired, the patients are broadly classified into the category of "non-fluent aphasia." In such cases, a lesion in the left posterior frontal region (Broca's area) is often observed. Many patients with large left hemisphere lesions have poor prognosis, despite having received years of intensive speech therapy (Lazar et al., 2010). However, emerging evidence suggests that some techniques have the potential to improve the verbal communication skills of these patients, as well as to reorganize the underlying neural processes related to language. For example, inspired by the clinical observation that patients with non-fluent aphasia can sing words even though they are unable to speak (Gerstmann, 1964; Yamadori et al., 1977), melodic intonation therapy (MIT) has received much research attention over the past few years. The main components of this speech therapy technique are (1) melodic intonation, (2) the use of formulaic phrases and sentences, and (3) slow and periodic verbalization with left-hand tapping (Schlaug et al., 2008, 2010). Within a therapy session, the therapist instructs the patient to intone (or "sing") simple phrases while slowly tapping their left hand with each syllable.

Emerging evidence involving open-label studies has revealed some positive treatment effects (Wilson et al., 2006; Schlaug et al., 2008; Wan et al., 2014). However, the question of "why" MIT works remains the subject of intense debate. The contribution of singing is supported by the neuroimaging findings of right hemisphere lateralization of singing processing when compared to speaking (e.g., Ozdemir et al., 2006), as well as by studies showing reorganization of right hemisphere structure and function following therapy (e.g., Schlaug et al., 2008). However, it is important to note that the latter studies often included patients with very large lesions that sometimes cover most of the left hemisphere, thus precluding analysis of language-related areas within that hemisphere. In addition, although melodic intonation is usually emphasized as a major difference of singing compared with speaking, the difference between singing rhythm and speaking rhythm has been overlooked (see **Figure 1** as an example).

Recent studies have highlighted the potential role of rhythm in aphasia treatment. For example, aphasia recovery, as denoted by correct syllable production, was examined by comparing singing therapy, rhythmic therapy, and standard speech therapy (Stahl et al., 2011, 2013). The results showed that, when compared to singing therapy, the rhythmic therapy was similarly effective (Stahl et al., 2011, 2013). Moreover, patients with lesions that cover the BG were found to be highly dependent on the external rhythmic cues (Stahl et al., 2011). Taken together, this study highlights the role of rhythm in aphasia recovery.

The SEP hypothesis postulates that the rhythmic components (e.g., singing rhythm, left-hand tapping) of MIT can help to facilitate sound envelope processing and synchronization and entrainment to a pulse. That is, the predictability of formulaic phrases and sentences requires precise encoding of pulse or periodic timing of vocalizations, while left-hand tapping can facilitate synchronization and entrainment to the pulse. Thus, under the SEP framework, MIT may be interpreted as an effective way to engage (a) the auditory afferent circuit to encourage precise encoding of sounds, (b) the subcortical–prefrontal circuit to motivate patients, (c) the BG-thalamo-cortical circuit to facilitate beat-based timing process, and (d) the efferent cortical motor circuit to promote the motor output (**Figure 2D**).

A rationale for MIT is the potential to engage and unmask language-capable regions in the unaffected right hemisphere such as the structural reorganization of arcuate fasciculus, a fiber bundle connecting the posterior superior temporal region and the posterior inferior frontal region (Schlaug et al., 2008, 2010; Wan et al., 2014). The SEP hypothesis assumes that sound envelope processing may be lateralized to the temporal cortex in the right hemisphere (**Figure 2B**). If MIT engages high demands on the right temporal cortex to encode sound envelope precisely, it may also increase the connectivity from the right temporal cortex to the right inferior frontal gyrus (IFG). Importantly, rhythmic therapy in aphasia patients with left basal ganglia lesion resulted in improved production of common formulaic phrases that are known to be supported by right BG-thalamo-cortical network (Stahl et al., 2013), suggesting that rhythm therapy for aphasia might also induce alterations in the right BG-thalamo-cortical network. The left-hand tapping in MIT might be also interpreted as a way to recruit enlarged involvement of contralateral right motor areas (i.e., dorsal and ventral portions of the right M1, PMC, and PFC) and thereby facilitate motor output of the unaffected hemisphere.

AUTISM

One of the core features of autism spectrum disorder (ASD) is impairment in language and communication. For children with ASD, the ability to speak early is associated with improved quality of life. Research has reported the presence of motor and oral-motor impairments in ASD children who have expressive language deficits (Belmonte et al., 2013; McCleery et al., 2013).

To date, very few interventions have specifically targeted the oral-motor aspects in ASD. One is the prompts for restructuring oral muscular phonetic targets (PROMPT) model, which is a play-based technique that involves vocal modeling and physical manipulations of the children's oral-motor system to facilitate the production of a speech target (Chumpelik, 1984). A pilot study reported speech improvements in five non-verbal children with ASD after receiving PROMPT intervention (Rogers et al., 2006). Another therapy technique that incorporates a motor component is auditory-motor mapping training (AMMT), which is an active multisensory therapy designed to facilitate speech output in completely non-verbal children with autism (Wan et al., 2010). This technique aims to promote speech production directly by training the association between speech sounds and articulatory actions using slow and melodic intonating vocalizations with bimanual motor activities (Wan et al., 2010). While some of the components of AMMT overlap with those of MIT in phasia, a unique aspect of AMMT is the use of a set of tuned drums and bimanual motor actions to facilitate sound-motor mapping. An initial proof-of-concept study indicated the therapeutic potential of AMMT in facilitating speech development in autism (Wan et al., 2011).

Similar to MIT in aphasia, we assume that AMMT can be categorized into non-rhythmic and rhythmic components. The former relates to intoned vocalizations, and the latter relates to spoken syllables being linked with the bimanual motor actions on the tuned drums. Under the SEP framework, the rhythmic component in AMMT can be useful in a number of ways. First, perception of rhythmic drumming and vocal sounds may stimulate the auditory afferent circuit for the precise encoding of sound envelope or temporal events. Indeed, it has been shown that ASD is associated with developmental abnormalities in the brainstem and cerebellum *in utero*, which can lead to abnormal timing and sensory perception in ASD (Trevarthen and Delafield-Butt, 2013). Second, synchronization and entrainment of rhythmic vocalizations and bimanual motor actions may be effective to stimulate the speech motor and language networks in ASD. In the DIVA model, the left vPMC and pIFG are involved in both speech production and sensorimotor mapping and have functional correspondence to the mirror-neuron system (Rizzolatti et al., 1996; Kohler et al., 2002; Guenther et al., 2006; Tourville and Guenther, 2011). A number of neuroimaging studies have suggested that ASD is associated with abnormalities in the IFG and posterior superior temporal sulcus (pSTG) (Herbert et al., 2002; De Fosse et al., 2004; Kleinhans et al., 2008; Mengotti et al., 2011; McCleery et al., 2013). Moreover, another neuroimaging study suggests that motor dysfunction in ASD is associated with abnormality in BG-thalamo-SMA circuit (Enticott et al., 2009). Thus, synchronization and entrainment of rhythmic vocalizations and bimanual motor actions in AMMT may help ameliorate speech production and sensorimotor mapping deficits in ASD by engaging the BG-thalamo-cortical (SMA, PMC, IFG, and STG) circuit.

CONCLUSION

In this paper, we consider the role of rhythm in speech and language rehabilitation. The emerging research field of music and neuroscience led us to propose the SEP hypothesis, which postulates that (1) sound envelope processing and (2) synchronization and entrainment to a pulse, may help to stimulate brain networks for human communication. Within the SEP framework, we present four possible circuits that may help to stimulate the brain networks underlying human communication: (i) the auditory afferent circuit consisted of brainstem, thalamus, cerebellum, and temporal cortex for precise encoding of sound envelope and temporal events; (ii) the subcortical–prefrontal circuit for emotional and reward-related processing; (iii) the BG-thalamo-cortical circuit for processing beat-based timing; and (iv) the cortical motor efferent circuit for motor output. We hope that future studies combining neuroimaging techniques and randomized control designs with the SEP framework will help to evaluate the efficacy of the rhythm-based therapies.

ACKNOWLEDGMENTS

Shinya Fujii was supported by a fellowship from the Japan Society for the Promotion of Science (JSPS). Catherine Y. Wan was supported by a fellowship from the Nancy Lurie Marks Family Foundation.

REFERENCES

Abrams, D. A., Nicol, T., Zecker, S., and Kraus, N. (2008). Right-hemisphere auditory cortex is dominant for coding syllable patterns in speech. *J. Neurosci.* 28, 3958–3965. doi:10.1523/JNEUROSCI.0187-08.2008

Abrams, D. A., Nicol, T., Zecker, S., and Kraus, N. (2009). Abnormal cortical processing of the syllable rate of speech in poor readers. *J. Neurosci.* 29, 7686–7693. doi:10.1523/JNEUROSCI.5242-08.2009

Ahissar, E., Nagarajan, S., Ahissar, M., Protopapas, A., Mahncke, H., and Merzenich, M. M. (2001). Speech comprehension is correlated with temporal response patterns recorded from auditory cortex. *Proc. Natl. Acad. Sci. U.S.A.* 98, 13367–13372. doi:10.1073/pnas.201400998

Alm, P. A. (2004). Stuttering and the basal ganglia circuits: a critical review of possible relations. *J. Commun. Disord.* 37, 325–369. doi:10.1016/j.jcomdis.2004.03.001

Armson, J., and Kiefte, M. (2008). The effect of SpeechEasy on stuttering frequency, speech rate, and speech naturalness. *J. Fluency Disord.* 33, 120–134. doi:10.1016/j.jfludis.2008.04.002

Belmonte, M. K., Saxena-Chandhok, T., Cherian, R., Muneer, R., George, L., and Karanth, P. (2013). Oral motor deficits in speech-impaired children with autism. *Front. Integr. Neurosci.* 7:47. doi:10.3389/fnint.2013.00047

Benoit, C. E., Dalla Bella, S., Farrugia, N., Obrig, H., Mainka, S., and Kotz, S. A. (2014). Musically cued gait-training improves both perceptual and motor timing in Parkinson's disease. *Front. Hum. Neurosci.* 8:494. doi:10.3389/fnhum.2014.00494

Bertoncini, J., Nazzi, T., Cabrera, L., and Lorenzi, C. (2011). Six-month-old infants discriminate voicing on the basis of temporal envelope cues (L). *J. Acoust. Soc. Am.* 129, 2761–2764. doi:10.1121/1.3571424

Blandini, F., Nappi, G., Tassorelli, C., and Martignoni, E. (2000). Functional changes of the basal ganglia circuitry in Parkinson's disease. *Prog. Neurobiol.* 62, 63–88. doi:10.1016/S0301-0082(99)00067-2

Blood, A. J., and Zatorre, R. J. (2001). Intensely pleasurable responses to music correlate with activity in brain regions implicated in reward and emotion. *Proc. Natl. Acad. Sci. U.S.A.* 98, 11818–11823. doi:10.1073/pnas.191355898

Bloodstein, O. (1995). *A Handbook of Stuttering.* San Diego, CA: Singular Publishing Group, Inc.

Boemio, A., Fromm, S., Braun, A., and Poeppel, D. (2005). Hierarchical and asymmetric temporal sensitivity in human auditory cortices. *Nat. Neurosci.* 8, 389–395. doi:10.1038/nn1409

Bohland, J. W., Bullock, D., and Guenther, F. H. (2010). Neural representations and mechanisms for the performance of simple speech sequences. *J. Cogn. Neurosci.* 22, 1504–1529. doi:10.1162/jocn.2009.21306

Bohland, J. W., and Guenther, F. H. (2006). An fMRI investigation of syllable sequence production. *Neuroimage* 32, 821–841. doi:10.1016/j.neuroimage.2006.04.173

Brady, J. P. (1969). Studies on the metronome effect on stuttering. *Behav. Res. Ther.* 7, 197–204. doi:10.1016/0005-7967(69)90033-3

Brady, J. P. (1971). Metronome-conditioned speech retraining for stuttering. *Behav. Ther.* 2, 129–150. doi:10.1016/S0005-7894(71)80001-1

Brown, S., Ingham, R. J., Ingham, J. C., Laird, A. R., and Fox, P. T. (2005). Stuttered and fluent speech production: an ALE meta-analysis of functional neuroimaging studies. *Hum. Brain Mapp.* 25, 105–117. doi:10.1002/hbm.20140

Brown, S., Ngan, E., and Liotti, M. (2008). A larynx area in the human motor cortex. *Cereb. Cortex* 18, 837–845. doi:10.1093/cercor/bhm131

Buchsbaum, B. R., Hickok, G., and Humphries, C. (2001). Role of left posterior superior temporal gyrus in phonological processing for speech perception and production. *Cogn. Sci.* 25, 663–678. doi:10.1207/s15516709cog2505_2

Chandrasekaran, C., Trubanova, A., Stillittano, S., Caplier, A., and Ghazanfar, A. A. (2009). The natural statistics of audiovisual speech. *PLoS Comput. Biol.* 5:e1000436. doi:10.1371/journal.pcbi.1000436

Chang, S. E., and Zhu, D. C. (2013). Neural network connectivity differences in children who stutter. *Brain* 136, 3709–3726. doi:10.1093/brain/awt275

Chen, J. L., Penhune, V. B., and Zatorre, R. J. (2008a). Listening to musical rhythms recruits motor regions of the brain. *Cereb. Cortex* 18, 2844–2854. doi:10.1093/cercor/bhn042

Chen, J. L., Penhune, V. B., and Zatorre, R. J. (2008b). Moving on time: brain network for auditory-motor synchronization is modulated by rhythm complexity and musical training. *J. Cogn. Neurosci.* 20, 226–239. doi:10.1162/jocn.2008.20018

Chen, J. L., Zatorre, R. J., and Penhune, V. B. (2006). Interactions between auditory and dorsal premotor cortex during synchronization to musical rhythms. *Neuroimage* 32, 1771–1781. doi:10.1016/j.neuroimage.2006.04.207

Chumpelik, D. (1984). The PROMPT system of therapy: theoretical framework and applications for developmental apraxia of speech. *Semin. Speech Lang.* 5, 139–155. doi:10.1055/s-0028-1085172

Civier, O., Bullock, D., Max, L., and Guenther, F. H. (2013). Computational modeling of stuttering caused by impairments in a basal ganglia thalamo-cortical circuit involved in syllable selection and initiation. *Brain Lang.* 126, 263–278. doi:10.1016/j.bandl.2013.05.016

Civier, O., Tasko, S. M., and Guenther, F. H. (2010). Overreliance on auditory feedback may lead to sound/syllable repetitions: simulations of stuttering and fluency-inducing conditions with a neural model of speech production. *J. Fluency Disord.* 35, 246–279. doi:10.1016/j.jfludis.2010.05.002

Conard, N. J., Malina, M., and Munzel, S. C. (2009). New flutes document the earliest musical tradition in southwestern Germany. *Nature* 460, 737–740. doi:10.1038/nature08169

Condon, W. S., and Sander, L. W. (1974). Neonate movement is synchronized with adult speech: interactional participation and language acquisition. *Science* 183, 99–101. doi:10.1126/science.183.4120.99

Corriveau, K. H., and Goswami, U. (2009). Rhythmic motor entrainment in children with speech and language impairments: tapping to the beat. *Cortex* 45, 119–130. doi:10.1016/j.cortex.2007.09.008

Craig, A. R. (2002). Fluency outcomes following treatment for those who stutter. *Percept. Mot. Skills* 94, 772–774. doi:10.2466/PMS.94.2.772-774

Crystal, T. H., and House, A. S. (1982). Segmental durations in connected speech signals: preliminary results. *J. Acoust. Soc. Am.* 72, 705–716. doi:10.1121/1.388251

Danielsen, A., Otnaess, M. K., Jensen, J., Williams, S. C., and Ostberg, B. C. (2014). Investigating repetition and change in musical rhythm by functional MRI. *Neuroscience* 275, 469–476. doi:10.1016/j.neuroscience.2014.06.029

Darley, F. L., Aronson, A. E., and Brown, J. R. (1969). Clusters of deviant speech dimensions in the dysarthrias. *J. Speech Hear. Res.* 12, 462–496. doi:10.1044/jshr.1203.462

Davie, C. A. (2008). A review of Parkinson's disease. *Br. Med. Bull.* 86, 109–127. doi:10.1093/bmb/ldn013

de Bruin, N., Doan, J. B., Turnbull, G., Suchowersky, O., Bonfield, S., Hu, B., et al. (2010). Walking with music is a safe and viable tool for gait training in Parkinson's disease: the effect of a 13-week feasibility study on single and dual task walking. *Parkinsons Dis.* 2010, 483530. doi:10.4061/2010/483530

De Fosse, L., Hodge, S. M., Makris, N., Kennedy, D. N., Caviness, V. S. Jr., McGrath, L., et al. (2004). Language-association cortex asymmetry in autism and specific language impairment. *Ann. Neurol.* 56, 757–766. doi:10.1002/ana.20275

DeLong, M. R. (1990). Primate models of movement disorders of basal ganglia origin. *Trends Neurosci.* 13, 281–285. doi:10.1016/0166-2236(90)90110-V

Dronkers, N. F. (1996). A new brain region for coordinating speech articulation. *Nature* 384, 159–161. doi:10.1038/384159a0

Dronkers, N. F., Plaisant, O., Iba-Zizen, M. T., and Cabanis, E. A. (2007). Paul Broca's historic cases: high resolution MR imaging of the brains of Leborgne and Lelong. *Brain* 130, 1432–1441. doi:10.1093/brain/awm042

Drullman, R., Festen, J. M., and Plomp, R. (1994a). Effect of reducing slow temporal modulations on speech reception. *J. Acoust. Soc. Am.* 95, 2670–2680. doi:10.1121/1.408467

Drullman, R., Festen, J. M., and Plomp, R. (1994b). Effect of temporal envelope smearing on speech reception. *J. Acoust. Soc. Am.* 95, 1053–1064. doi:10.1121/1.408467

Duffy, J. R. (2005). *Motor Speech Disorders: Substrates, Differential Diagnosis, and Management.* St. Louis, MO: Elsevier Mosby.

Elliott, T. M., and Theunissen, F. E. (2009). The modulation transfer function for speech intelligibility. *PLoS Comput. Biol.* 5:e1000302. doi:10.1371/journal.pcbi.1000302

Enticott, P. G., Bradshaw, J. L., Iansek, R., Tonge, B. J., and Rinehart, N. J. (2009). Electrophysiological signs of supplementary-motor-area deficits in high-functioning autism but not Asperger syndrome: an examination of internally cued movement-related potentials. *Dev. Med. Child Neurol.* 51, 787–791. doi:10.1111/j.1469-8749.2009.03270.x

Fitch, W. T. (2006). The biology and evolution of music: a comparative perspective. *Cognition* 100, 173–215. doi:10.1016/j.cognition.2005.11.009

Fitch, W. T. (2013). Speech science: tuned to the rhythm. *Nature* 494, 434–435. doi:10.1038/494434a

Fox, P. T., Ingham, R. J., Ingham, J. C., Hirsch, T. B., Downs, J. H., Martin, C., et al. (1996). A PET study of the neural systems of stuttering. *Nature* 382, 158–161. doi:10.1038/382158a0

Freeman, W. J. (2000). "A neurobiological role of music in social bonding," in *The Origins of Music,* eds N. Wallin, B. Merkur, and S. Brown (Cambridge MA: MIT Press), 411–424.

Fujii, S., and Schlaug, G. (2013). The Harvard beat assessment test (H-BAT): a battery for assessing beat perception and production and their dissociation. *Front. Hum. Neurosci.* 7:771. doi:10.3389/fnhum.2013.00771

Fujii, S., Watanabe, H., Oohashi, H., Hirashima, M., Nozaki, D., and Taga, G. (2014). Precursors of dancing and singing to music in three- to four-months-old infants. *PLoS ONE* 9:e97680. doi:10.1371/journal.pone.0097680

Galvan, A., and Wichmann, T. (2008). Pathophysiology of parkinsonism. *Clin. Neurophysiol.* 119, 1459–1474. doi:10.1016/j.clinph.2008.03.017

Gerstmann, H. L. (1964). A case of aphasia. *J. Speech Hear. Disord.* 29, 89–91. doi:10.1044/jshd.2901.89

Ghazanfar, A. A., Morrill, R. J., and Kayser, C. (2013). Monkeys are perceptually tuned to facial expressions that exhibit a theta-like speech rhythm. *Proc. Natl. Acad. Sci. U.S.A.* 110, 1959–1963. doi:10.1073/pnas.1214956110

Ghazanfar, A. A., and Takahashi, D. Y. (2014). Facial expressions and the evolution of the speech rhythm. *J. Cogn. Neurosci.* 26, 1196–1207. doi:10.1162/jocn_a_00575

Ghazanfar, A. A., Takahashi, D. Y., Mathur, N., and Fitch, W. T. (2012). Cineradiography of monkey lip-smacking reveals putative precursors of speech dynamics. *Curr. Biol.* 22, 1176–1182. doi:10.1016/j.cub.2012.04.055

Giraud, A. L., Lorenzi, C., Ashburner, J., Wable, J., Johnsrude, I., Frackowiak, R., et al. (2000). Representation of the temporal envelope of sounds in the human brain. *J. Neurophysiol.* 84, 1588–1598.

Goswami, U. (2011). A temporal sampling framework for developmental dyslexia. *Trends Cogn. Sci.* 15, 3–10. doi:10.1016/j.tics.2010.10.001

Grahn, J. A., and Brett, M. (2007). Rhythm and beat perception in motor areas of the brain. *J. Cogn. Neurosci.* 19, 893–906. doi:10.1162/jocn.2007.19.5.893

Grahn, J. A., and Rowe, J. B. (2009). Feeling the beat: premotor and striatal interactions in musicians and nonmusicians during beat perception. *J. Neurosci.* 29, 7540–7548. doi:10.1523/JNEUROSCI.2018-08.2009

Greenberg, S., Carvey, H., Hitchcock, L., and Chang, S. (2003). Temporal properties of spontaneous speech: a syllable-centric perspective. *J. Phon.* 31, 46485. doi:10.1016/j.wocn.2003.09.005

Guenther, F. H., Ghosh, S. S., and Tourville, J. A. (2006). Neural modeling and imaging of the cortical interactions underlying syllable production. *Brain Lang.* 96, 280–301. doi:10.1016/j.bandl.2005.06.001

Hargrave, S., Kalinowski, J., Stuart, A., Armson, J., and Jones, K. (1994). Effect of frequency-altered feedback on stuttering frequency at normal and fast speech rates. *J. Speech Hear. Res.* 37, 1313–1319. doi:10.1044/jshr.3706.1313

Hasegawa, A., Okanoya, K., Hasegawa, T., and Seki, Y. (2011). Rhythmic synchronization tapping to an audio-visual metronome in budgerigars. *Sci. Rep.* 1, 120. doi:10.1038/srep00120

Herbert, M. R., Harris, G. J., Adrien, K. T., Ziegler, D. A., Makris, N., Kennedy, D. N., et al. (2002). Abnormal asymmetry in language association cortex in autism. *Ann. Neurol.* 52, 588–596. doi:10.1002/ana.10349

Hickok, G., and Poeppel, D. (2004). Dorsal and ventral streams: a framework for understanding aspects of the functional anatomy of language. *Cognition* 92, 67–99. doi:10.1016/j.cognition.2003.10.011

Hillis, A. E., Work, M., Barker, P. B., Jacobs, M. A., Breese, E. L., and Maurer, K. (2004). Re-examining the brain regions crucial for orchestrating speech articulation. *Brain* 127, 1479–1487. doi:10.1093/brain/awh172

Ho, A. K., Bradshaw, J. L., Cunnington, R., Phillips, J. G., and Iansek, R. (1998). Sequence heterogeneity in parkinsonian speech. *Brain Lang.* 64, 122–145. doi:10.1006/brln.1998.1959

Hove, M. J., Fairhurst, M. T., Kotz, S. A., and Keller, P. E. (2013). Synchronizing with auditory and visual rhythms: an fMRI assessment of modality differences and modality appropriateness. *Neuroimage* 67, 313–321. doi:10.1016/j.neuroimage.2012.11.032

Huang, C. M., Liu, G., and Huang, R. (1982). Projections from the cochlear nucleus to the cerebellum. *Brain Res.* 244, 1–8. doi:10.1016/0006-8993(82)90897-6

Hutchinson, S., Lee, L. H., Gaab, N., and Schlaug, G. (2003). Cerebellar volume of musicians. *Cereb. Cortex* 13, 943–949. doi:10.1093/cercor/13.9.943

Iverson, J. M., and Goldin-Meadow, S. (1998). Why people gesture when they speak. *Nature* 396, 228. doi:10.1038/24300

Jonas, S. (1981). The supplementary motor region and speech emission. *J. Commun. Disord.* 14, 349–373. doi:10.1016/0021-9924(81)90019-8

Jurgens, U. (1984). The efferent and afferent connections of the supplementary motor area. *Brain Res.* 300, 63–81. doi:10.1016/0006-8993(84)91341-6

Kalaska, J. F., Cohen, D. A., Hyde, M. L., and Prud'homme, M. (1989). A comparison of movement direction-related versus load direction-related activity in primate motor cortex, using a two-dimensional reaching task. *J. Neurosci.* 9, 2080–2102.

Kell, C. A., Neumann, K., Von Kriegstein, K., Posenenske, C., Von Gudenberg, A. W., Euler, H., et al. (2009). How the brain repairs stuttering. *Brain* 132, 2747–2760. doi:10.1093/brain/awp185

Kent, R. D., and Tjaden, K. (1997). "Brain functions underlying speech," in *Handbook of Phonetic Sciences,* eds W. J. Hardcastle and J. Laver (Oxford: Blackwell), 220–255.

Kirschner, S., and Tomasello, M. (2009). Joint drumming: social context facilitates synchronization in preschool children. *J. Exp. Child Psychol.* 102, 299–314. doi:10.1016/j.jecp.2008.07.005

Kleinhans, N. M., Muller, R. A., Cohen, D. N., and Courchesne, E. (2008). Atypical functional lateralization of language in autism spectrum disorders. *Brain Res.* 1221, 115–125. doi:10.1016/j.brainres.2008.04.080

Koelsch, S. (2014). Brain correlates of music-evoked emotions. *Nat. Rev. Neurosci.* 15, 170–180. doi:10.1038/nrn3666

Kohler, E., Keysers, C., Umilta, M. A., Fogassi, L., Gallese, V., and Rizzolatti, G. (2002). Hearing sounds, understanding actions: action representation in mirror neurons. *Science* 297, 846–848. doi:10.1126/science.1070311

Kotz, S. A., and Schwartze, M. (2010). Cortical speech processing unplugged: a timely subcortico-cortical framework. *Trends Cogn. Sci.* 14, 392–399. doi:10.1016/j.tics.2010.06.005

Kotz, S. A., and Schwartze, M. (2011). Differential input of the supplementary motor area to a dedicated temporal processing network: functional and clinical implications. *Front. Integr. Neurosci.* 5:86. doi:10.3389/fnint.2011.00086

Kotz, S. A., Schwartze, M., and Schmidt-Kassow, M. (2009). Non-motor basal ganglia functions: a review and proposal for a model of sensory predictability in auditory language perception. *Cortex* 45, 982–990. doi:10.1016/j.cortex.2009.02.010

Kung, S. J., Chen, J. L., Zatorre, R. J., and Penhune, V. B. (2013). Interacting cortical and basal ganglia networks underlying finding and tapping to the musical beat. *J. Cogn. Neurosci.* 25, 401–420. doi:10.1162/jocn_a_00325

Laruelle, M. (2000). Imaging synaptic neurotransmission with in vivo binding competition techniques: a critical review. *J. Cereb. Blood Flow Metab.* 20, 423–451. doi:10.1097/00004647-200003000-00001

Lattermann, C., Euler, H. A., and Neumann, K. (2008). A randomized control trial to investigate the impact of the Lidcombe program on early stuttering in German-speaking preschoolers. *J. Fluency Disord.* 33, 52–65. doi:10.1016/j.jfludis.2007.12.002

Lazar, R. M., Minzer, B., Antoniello, D., Festa, J. R., Krakauer, J. W., and Marshall, R. S. (2010). Improvement in aphasia scores after stroke is well predicted by initial severity. *Stroke* 41, 1485–1488. doi:10.1161/STROKEAHA.109.577338

Levelt, W. J., Roelofs, A., and Meyer, A. S. (1999). A theory of lexical access in speech production. *Behav. Brain Sci.* 22, 1–38; discussion 38–75. doi:10.1017/S0140525X99001776

Levelt, W. J., and Wheeldon, L. (1994). Do speakers have access to a mental syllabary? *Cognition* 50, 239–269. doi:10.1016/0010-0277(94)90030-2

Lewis, P. A., and Miall, R. C. (2003). Distinct systems for automatic and cognitively controlled time measurement: evidence from neuroimaging. *Curr. Opin. Neurobiol.* 13, 250–255. doi:10.1016/S0959-4388(03)00036-9

Liotti, M., Ramig, L. O., Vogel, D., New, P., Cook, C. I., Ingham, R. J., et al. (2003). Hypophonia in Parkinson's disease: neural correlates of voice treatment revealed by PET. *Neurology* 60, 432–440. doi:10.1212/WNL.60.3.432

Lu, Y., Paraskevopoulos, E., Herholz, S. C., Kuchenbuch, A., and Pantev, C. (2014). Temporal processing of audiovisual stimuli is enhanced in musicians: evidence from magnetoencephalography (MEG). *PLoS ONE* 9:e90686. doi:10.1371/journal.pone.0090686

Ludlow, C. L. (2005). Central nervous system control of the laryngeal muscles in humans. *Respir. Physiol. Neurobiol.* 147, 205–222. doi:10.1016/j.resp.2005.04.015

Luo, H., and Poeppel, D. (2007). Phase patterns of neuronal responses reliably discriminate speech in human auditory cortex. *Neuron* 54, 1001–1010. doi:10.1016/j.neuron.2007.06.004

Luppino, G., Matelli, M., Camarda, R., and Rizzolatti, G. (1993). Corticocortical connections of area F3 (SMA-proper) and area F6 (pre-SMA) in the macaque monkey. *J. Comp. Neurol.* 338, 114–140. doi:10.1002/cne.903380109

Malecot, A., Johnston, R., and Kizziar, P. A. (1972). Syllabic rate and utterance length in French. *Phonetica* 26, 235–251. doi:10.1159/000259414

Max, L., Guenther, F. H., Gracco, V. L., Ghosh, S. S., and Wallace, M. E. (2004). Unstable or insufficiently activated internal models and feedback-biased motor control as sources of dysfluency: a theoretical model of stuttering. *Contemp. Issues Commun. Sci. Disord.* 31, 105–122.

McCleery, J. P., Elliott, N. A., Sampanis, D. S., and Stefanidou, C. A. (2013). Motor development and motor resonance difficulties in autism: relevance to early intervention for language and communication skills. *Front. Integr. Neurosci.* 7:30. doi:10.3389/fnint.2013.00030

McGettigan, C., and Scott, S. K. (2012). Cortical asymmetries in speech perception: what's wrong, what's right and what's left? *Trends Cogn. Sci.* 16, 269–276. doi:10.1016/j.tics.2012.04.006

McGurk, H., and MacDonald, J. (1976). Hearing lips and seeing voices. *Nature* 264, 746–748. doi:10.1038/264746a0

McIntosh, G. C., Brown, S. H., Rice, R. R., and Thaut, M. H. (1997). Rhythmic auditory-motor facilitation of gait patterns in patients with Parkinson's disease. *J. Neurol. Neurosurg. Psychiatr.* 62, 22–26. doi:10.1136/jnnp.62.1.22

Meister, I. G., Boroojerdi, B., Foltys, H., Sparing, R., Huber, W., and Topper, R. (2003). Motor cortex hand area and speech: implications for the development of language. *Neuropsychologia* 41, 401–406. doi:10.1016/S0028-3932(02)00179-3

Meister, I. G., Buelte, D., Staedtgen, M., Boroojerdi, B., and Sparing, R. (2009a). The dorsal premotor cortex orchestrates concurrent speech and fingertapping movements. *Eur. J. Neurosci.* 29, 2074–2082. doi:10.1111/j.1460-9568.2009.06729.x

Meister, I. G., Weier, K., Staedtgen, M., Buelte, D., Thirugnanasambandam, N., and Sparing, R. (2009b). Covert word reading induces a late response in the hand motor system of the language dominant hemisphere. *Neuroscience* 161, 67–72. doi:10.1016/j.neuroscience.2009.03.031

Meltzoff, A. N., and Moore, M. K. (1977). Imitation of facial and manual gestures by human neonates. *Science* 198, 75–78. doi:10.1126/science.198.4312.75

Mengotti, P., D'Agostini, S., Terlevic, R., De Colle, C., Biasizzo, E., Londero, D., et al. (2011). Altered white matter integrity and development in children with autism: a combined voxel-based morphometry and diffusion imaging study. *Brain Res. Bull.* 84, 189–195. doi:10.1016/j.brainresbull.2010.12.002

Menon, V., and Levitin, D. J. (2005). The rewards of music listening: response and physiological connectivity of the mesolimbic system. *Neuroimage* 28, 175–184. doi:10.1016/j.neuroimage.2005.05.053

Mithen, S. (2005). *The Singing Neanderthals: The Origins of Music, Language, Mind, and Body.* London: Weidenfeld & Nicolson.

Musacchia, G., Sams, M., Skoe, E., and Kraus, N. (2007). Musicians have enhanced subcortical auditory and audiovisual processing of speech and music. *Proc. Natl. Acad. Sci. U.S.A.* 104, 15894–15898. doi:10.1073/pnas.0701498104

Musacchia, G., Strait, D., and Kraus, N. (2008). Relationships between behavior, brainstem and cortical encoding of seen and heard speech in musicians and non-musicians. *Hear. Res.* 241, 34–42. doi:10.1016/j.heares.2008.04.013

Nazzi, T., Bertoncini, J., and Mehler, J. (1998). Language discrimination by newborns: toward an understanding of the role of rhythm. *J. Exp. Psychol. Hum. Percept. Perform.* 24, 756–766. doi:10.1037/0096-1523.24.3.756

Nombela, C., Hughes, L. E., Owen, A. M., and Grahn, J. A. (2013). Into the groove: can rhythm influence Parkinson's disease? *Neurosci. Biobehav. Rev.* 37, 2564–2570. doi:10.1016/j.neubiorev.2013.08.003

Obermeier, C., Menninghaus, W., Von Koppenfels, M., Raettig, T., Schmidt-Kassow, M., Otterbein, S., et al. (2013). Aesthetic and emotional effects of meter and rhyme in poetry. *Front. Psychol.* 4:10. doi:10.3389/fpsyg.2013.00010

O'Brian, S., Packman, A., and Onslow, M. (2010). "The camperdown program," in *Treatment of Stuttering: Established and Emerging Interventions*, eds B. Guitar and R. McCauley (Philadelphia, PA: Wolters Kluwer/Lippincott Williams & Wilkins), 256–276.

Olthoff, A., Baudewig, J., Kruse, E., and Dechent, P. (2008). Cortical sensorimotor control in vocalization: a functional magnetic resonance imaging study. *Laryngoscope* 118, 2091–2096. doi:10.1097/MLG.0b013e31817fd40f

Ozdemir, E., Norton, A., and Schlaug, G. (2006). Shared and distinct neural correlates of singing and speaking. *Neuroimage* 33, 628–635. doi:10.1016/j.neuroimage.2006.07.013

Pai, M. C. (1999). Supplementary motor area aphasia: a case report. *Clin. Neurol. Neurosurg.* 101, 29–32. doi:10.1016/S0303-8467(98)00068-7

Parbery-Clark, A., Strait, D. L., and Kraus, N. (2011). Context-dependent encoding in the auditory brainstem subserves enhanced speech-in-noise perception in musicians. *Neuropsychologia* 49, 3338–3345. doi:10.1016/j.neuropsychologia.2011.08.007

Parbery-Clark, A., Tierney, A., Strait, D. L., and Kraus, N. (2012). Musicians have fine-tuned neural distinction of speech syllables. *Neuroscience* 219, 111–119. doi:10.1016/j.neuroscience.2012.05.042

Patel, A. D. (2011). Why would musical training benefit the neural encoding of speech? The OPERA hypothesis. *Front. Psychol.* 2:142. doi:10.3389/fpsyg.2011.00142

Patel, A. D. (2012). The OPERA hypothesis: assumptions and clarifications. *Ann. N. Y. Acad. Sci.* 1252, 124–128. doi:10.1111/j.1749-6632.2011.06426.x

Patel, A. D. (2014). Can nonlinguistic musical training change the way the brain processes speech? The expanded OPERA hypothesis. *Hear. Res.* 308, 98–108. doi:10.1016/j.heares.2013.08.011

Patel, A. D., Iversen, J. R., Bregman, M. R., and Schulz, I. (2009). Experimental evidence for synchronization to a musical beat in a nonhuman animal. *Curr. Biol.* 19, 827–830. doi:10.1016/j.cub.2009.03.038

Peelle, J. E., and Davis, M. H. (2012). Neural oscillations carry speech rhythm through to comprehension. *Front. Psychol.* 3:320. doi:10.3389/fpsyg.2012.00320

Penfield, W., and Rasmussen, T. (1950). *The Cerebral Cortex of Man: A Clinical Study of Localization of Function.* New York, NY: Macmillan.

Penfield, W., and Roberts, L. (1959). *Speech and Brain Mechanisms.* Princeton, NJ: Princeton University Press.

Peretz, I., Champod, A. S., and Hyde, K. (2003). Varieties of musical disorders. The montreal battery of evaluation of amusia. *Ann. N. Y. Acad. Sci.* 999, 58–75. doi:10.1196/annals.1284.006

Peretz, I., and Coltheart, M. (2003). Modularity of music processing. *Nat. Neurosci.* 6, 688–691. doi:10.1038/nn1083

Pickett, E. R., Kuniholm, E., Protopapas, A., Friedman, J., and Lieberman, P. (1998). Selective speech motor, syntax and cognitive deficits associated with bilateral damage to the putamen and the head of the caudate nucleus: a case study. *Neuropsychologia* 36, 173–188. doi:10.1016/S0028-3932(97)00065-1

Pinto, S., Thobois, S., Costes, N., Le Bars, D., Benabid, A. L., Broussolle, E., et al. (2004). Subthalamic nucleus stimulation and dysarthria in Parkinson's disease: a PET study. *Brain* 127, 602–615. doi:10.1093/brain/awh074

Poeppel, D. (2003). The analysis of speech in different temporal integration windows: cerebral lateralization as "symmetric sampling in time". *Speech Commun.* 41, 245–255. doi:10.1016/S0167-6393(02)00107-3

Przybylski, L., Bedoin, N., Krifi-Papoz, S., Herbillon, V., Roch, D., Leculier, L., et al. (2013). Rhythmic auditory stimulation influences syntactic processing in children with developmental language disorders. *Neuropsychology* 27, 121–131. doi:10.1037/a0031277

Ramig, L. O., Fox, C., and Sapir, S. (2004). Parkinson's disease: speech and voice disorders and their treatment with the Lee Silverman voice treatment. *Semin. Speech Lang.* 25, 169–180. doi:10.1055/s-2004-825653

Ramig, L. O., Fox, C., and Sapir, S. (2007). Speech disorders in Parkinson's disease and the effects of pharmacological, surgical and speech treatment with emphasis on Lee Silverman voice treatment (LSVT(R)). *Handb. Clin. Neurol.* 83, 385–399. doi:10.1016/S0072-9752(07)83017-X

Ramig, L. O., Fox, C., and Sapir, S. (2008). Speech treatment for Parkinson's disease. *Expert Rev. Neurother.* 8, 297–309. doi:10.1586/14737175.8.2.297

Ramig, L. O., Sapir, S., Countryman, S., Pawlas, A. A., O'Brien, C., Hoehn, M., et al. (2001). Intensive voice treatment (LSVT) for patients with Parkinson's disease: a 2 year follow up. *J. Neurol. Neurosurg. Psychiatr.* 71, 493–498. doi:10.1136/jnnp.71.4.493

Reddish, P., Fischer, R., and Bulbulia, J. (2013). Let's dance together: synchrony, shared intentionality and cooperation. *PLoS ONE* 8:e71182. doi:10.1371/journal.pone.0071182

Rektorova, I., Barrett, J., Mikl, M., Rektor, I., and Paus, T. (2007). Functional abnormalities in the primary orofacial sensorimotor cortex during speech in Parkinson's disease. *Mov. Disord.* 22, 2043–2051. doi:10.1002/mds.21548

Rektorova, I., Mikl, M., Barrett, J., Marecek, R., Rektor, I., and Paus, T. (2012). Functional neuroanatomy of vocalization in patients with Parkinson's disease. *J. Neurol. Sci.* 313, 7–12. doi:10.1016/j.jns.2011.10.020

Remedios, R., Logothetis, N. K., and Kayser, C. (2009). Monkey drumming reveals common networks for perceiving vocal and nonvocal communication sounds. *Proc. Natl. Acad. Sci. U.S.A.* 106, 18010–18015. doi:10.1073/pnas.0909756106

Riley, G. D., and Ingham, J. C. (2000). Acoustic duration changes associated with two types of treatment for children who stutter. *J. Speech Lang. Hear. Res.* 43, 965–978. doi:10.1044/jslhr.4304.965

Rizzolatti, G., Fadiga, L., Gallese, V., and Fogassi, L. (1996). Premotor cortex and the recognition of motor actions. *Brain Res. Cogn. Brain Res.* 3, 131–141. doi:10.1016/0926-6410(95)00038-0

Rogers, S. J., Hayden, D., Hepburn, S., Charlifue-Smith, R., Hall, T., and Hayes, A. (2006). Teaching young nonverbal children with autism useful speech: a pilot study of the Denver model and PROMPT interventions. *J. Autism Dev. Disord.* 36, 1007–1024. doi:10.1007/s10803-006-0142-x

Ryan, B. P., and Van Kirk Ryan, B. (1995). Programmed stuttering treatment for children: comparison of two establishment programs through transfer, maintenance, and follow-up. *J. Speech Hear. Res.* 38, 61–75. doi:10.1044/jshr.3801.61

Sackley, C. M., Smith, C. H., Rick, C., Brady, M. C., Ives, N., Patel, R., et al. (2014). Lee Silverman voice treatment versus standard NHS speech and language therapy versus control in Parkinson's disease (PD COMM pilot): study protocol for a randomized controlled trial. *Trials* 15, 213. doi:10.1186/1745-6215-15-213

Salimpoor, V. N., Benovoy, M., Larcher, K., Dagher, A., and Zatorre, R. J. (2011). Anatomically distinct dopamine release during anticipation and experience of peak emotion to music. *Nat. Neurosci.* 14, 257–262. doi:10.1038/nn.2726

Salimpoor, V. N., Van Den Bosch, I., Kovacevic, N., McIntosh, A. R., Dagher, A., and Zatorre, R. J. (2013). Interactions between the nucleus accumbens and auditory cortices predict music reward value. *Science* 340, 216–219. doi:10.1126/science.1231059

Sapir, S., Ramig, L. O., and Fox, C. M. (2011). Intensive voice treatment in Parkinson's disease: Lee Silverman voice treatment. *Expert Rev. Neurother.* 11, 815–830. doi:10.1586/ern.11.43

Schachner, A., Brady, T. F., Pepperberg, I. M., and Hauser, M. D. (2009). Spontaneous motor entrainment to music in multiple vocal mimicking species. *Curr. Biol.* 19, 831–836. doi:10.1016/j.cub.2009.03.061

Schlaug, G., Marchina, S., and Norton, A. (2008). From singing to speaking: why singing may lead to recovery of expressive language function in patients with Broca's aphasia. *Music Percept.* 25, 315–323. doi:10.1525/mp.2008.25.4.315

Schlaug, G., Norton, A., Marchina, S., Zipse, L., and Wan, C. Y. (2010). From singing to speaking: facilitating recovery from nonfluent aphasia. *Future Neurol.* 5, 657–665. doi:10.2217/fnl.10.44

Schwartze, M., Keller, P. E., Patel, A. D., and Kotz, S. A. (2011). The impact of basal ganglia lesions on sensorimotor synchronization, spontaneous motor tempo, and the detection of tempo changes. *Behav. Brain Res.* 216, 685–691. doi:10.1016/j.bbr.2010.09.015

Sevdalis, V., and Keller, P. E. (2010). Cues for self-recognition in point-light displays of actions performed in synchrony with music. *Conscious. Cogn.* 19, 617–626. doi:10.1016/j.concog.2010.03.017

Shannon, R. V., Zeng, F. G., Kamath, V., Wygonski, J., and Ekelid, M. (1995). Speech recognition with primarily temporal cues. *Science* 270, 303–304. doi:10.1126/science.270.5234.303

Singh-Curry, V., and Husain, M. (2009). The functional role of the inferior parietal lobe in the dorsal and ventral stream dichotomy. *Neuropsychologia* 47, 1434–1448. doi:10.1016/j.neuropsychologia.2008.11.033

Skodda, S., Flasskamp, A., and Schlegel, U. (2010). Instability of syllable repetition as a model for impaired motor processing: is Parkinson's disease a "rhythm disorder"? *J. Neural Transm.* 117, 605–612. doi:10.1007/s00702-010-0390-y

Skodda, S., and Schlegel, U. (2008). Speech rate and rhythm in Parkinson's disease. *Mov. Disord.* 23, 985–992. doi:10.1002/mds.21996

Smith, Y., Wichmann, T., Factor, S. A., and DeLong, M. R. (2012). Parkinson's disease therapeutics: new developments and challenges since the introduction of levodopa. *Neuropsychopharmacology* 37, 213–246. doi:10.1038/npp.2011.212

Smith, Z. M., Delgutte, B., and Oxenham, A. J. (2002). Chimaeric sounds reveal dichotomies in auditory perception. *Nature* 416, 87–90. doi:10.1038/416087a

Stahl, B., Henseler, I., Turner, R., Geyer, S., and Kotz, S. A. (2013). How to engage the right brain hemisphere in aphasics without even singing: evidence for two paths of speech recovery. *Front. Hum. Neurosci.* 7:35. doi:10.3389/fnhum.2013.00035

Stahl, B., Kotz, S. A., Henseler, I., Turner, R., and Geyer, S. (2011). Rhythm in disguise: why singing may not hold the key to recovery from aphasia. *Brain* 134, 3083–3093. doi:10.1093/brain/awr240

Strait, D. L., and Kraus, N. (2014). Biological impact of auditory expertise across the life span: musicians as a model of auditory learning. *Hear. Res.* 308, 109–121. doi:10.1016/j.heares.2013.08.004

Strait, D. L., O'Connell, S., Parbery-Clark, A., and Kraus, N. (2014). Musicians' enhanced neural differentiation of speech sounds arises early in life: developmental evidence from ages 3 to 30. *Cereb. Cortex* 24, 2512–2521. doi:10.1093/cercor/bht103

Streifler, M., and Hofman, S. (1984). "Disorders of verbal expression in parkinsonism," in *Advances in Neurology*, eds R. Hassler and J. Christ (New York: Raven Press), 385–393.

Stuart, A., Kalinowski, J., Armson, J., Stenstrom, R., and Jones, K. (1996). Fluency effect of frequency alterations of plus/minus one-half and one-quarter octave shifts in auditory feedback of people who stutter. *J. Speech Hear. Res.* 39, 396–401. doi:10.1044/jshr.3902.396

Stupacher, J., Hove, M. J., Novembre, G., Schutz-Bosbach, S., and Keller, P. E. (2013). Musical groove modulates motor cortex excitability: a TMS investigation. *Brain Cogn.* 82, 127–136. doi:10.1016/j.bandc.2013.03.003

Teki, S., Grube, M., and Griffiths, T. D. (2011a). A unified model of time perception accounts for duration-based and beat-based timing mechanisms. *Front. Integr. Neurosci.* 5:90. doi:10.3389/fnint.2011.00090

Teki, S., Grube, M., Kumar, S., and Griffiths, T. D. (2011b). Distinct neural substrates of duration-based and beat-based auditory timing. *J. Neurosci.* 31, 3805–3812. doi:10.1523/JNEUROSCI.5561-10.2011

Thaut, M. H., McIntosh, G. C., Rice, R. R., Miller, R. A., Rathbun, J., and Brault, J. M. (1996). Rhythmic auditory stimulation in gait training for Parkinson's disease patients. *Mov. Disord.* 11, 193–200. doi:10.1002/mds.870110213

Tourville, J. A., and Guenther, F. H. (2011). The DIVA model: a neural theory of speech acquisition and production. *Lang. Cogn. Process.* 26, 952–981. doi:10.1080/01690960903498424

Tourville, J. A., Reilly, K. J., and Guenther, F. H. (2008). Neural mechanisms underlying auditory feedback control of speech. *Neuroimage* 39, 1429–1443. doi:10.1016/j.neuroimage.2007.09.054

Toyomura, A., Fujii, T., and Kuriki, S. (2011). Effect of external auditory pacing on the neural activity of stuttering speakers. *Neuroimage* 57, 1507–1516. doi:10.1016/j.neuroimage.2011.05.039

Trevarthen, C., and Delafield-Butt, J. T. (2013). Autism as a developmental disorder in intentional movement and affective engagement. *Front. Integr. Neurosci.* 7:49. doi:10.3389/fnint.2013.00049

van Tricht, M. J., Smeding, H. M., Speelman, J. D., and Schmand, B. A. (2010). Impaired emotion recognition in music in Parkinson's disease. *Brain Cogn.* 74, 58–65. doi:10.1016/j.bandc.2010.06.005

Vargha-Khadem, F., Watkins, K. E., Price, C. J., Ashburner, J., Alcock, K. J., Connelly, A., et al. (1998). Neural basis of an inherited speech and language disorder. *Proc. Natl. Acad. Sci. U.S.A.* 95, 12695–12700. doi:10.1073/pnas.95.21.12695

Wan, C. Y., Bazen, L., Baars, R., Libenson, A., Zipse, L., Zuk, J., et al. (2011). Auditory-motor mapping training as an intervention to facilitate speech output in non-verbal children with autism: a proof of concept study. *PLoS ONE* 6:e25505. doi:10.1371/journal.pone.0025505

Wan, C. Y., Demaine, K., Zipse, L., Norton, A., and Schlaug, G. (2010). From music making to speaking: engaging the mirror neuron system in autism. *Brain Res. Bull.* 82, 161–168. doi:10.1016/j.brainresbull.2010.04.010

Wan, C. Y., Zheng, X., Marchina, S., Norton, A., and Schlaug, G. (2014). Intensive therapy induces contralateral white matter changes in chronic stroke patients with Broca's aphasia. *Brain Lang.* 136C, 1–7. doi:10.1016/j.bandl.2014.03.011

Wang, X. F., Woody, C. D., Chizhevsky, V., Gruen, E., and Landeira-Fernandez, J. (1991). The dentate nucleus is a short-latency relay of a primary auditory transmission pathway. *Neuroreport* 2, 361–364. doi:10.1097/00001756-199107000-00001

Watkins, K. E., Vargha-Khadem, F., Ashburner, J., Passingham, R. E., Connelly, A., Friston, K. J., et al. (2002). MRI analysis of an inherited speech and language disorder: structural brain abnormalities. *Brain* 125, 465–478. doi:10.1093/brain/awf057

Wichmann, T., and DeLong, M. R. (1996). Functional and pathophysiological models of the basal ganglia. *Curr. Opin. Neurobiol.* 6, 751–758. doi:10.1016/S0959-4388(96)80024-9

Wichmann, T., and DeLong, M. R. (1998). Models of basal ganglia function and pathophysiology of movement disorders. *Neurosurg. Clin. N. Am.* 9, 223–236.

Wilson, S. J., Parsons, K., and Reutens, D. C. (2006). Preserved singing in aphasia: a case study of the efficacy of melodic intonation therapy. *Music Percept.* 24, 23–36. doi:10.1525/mp.2006.24.1.23

Witek, M. A., Clarke, E. F., Wallentin, M., Kringelbach, M. L., and Vuust, P. (2014). Syncopation, body-movement and pleasure in groove music. *PLoS ONE* 9:e94446. doi:10.1371/journal.pone.0094446

Xi, M. C., Woody, C. D., and Gruen, E. (1994). Identification of short latency auditory responsive neurons in the cat dentate nucleus. *Neuroreport* 5, 1567–1570. doi:10.1097/00001756-199408150-00006

Yamadori, A., Osumi, Y., Masuhara, S., and Okubo, M. (1977). Preservation of singing in Broca's aphasia. *J. Neurol. Neurosurg. Psychiatr.* 40, 221–224. doi:10.1136/jnnp.40.3.221

Zatorre, R. J., Mondor, T. A., and Evans, A. C. (1999). Auditory attention to space and frequency activates similar cerebral systems. *Neuroimage* 10, 544–554. doi:10.1006/nimg.1999.0491

Zentner, M., and Eerola, T. (2010). Rhythmic engagement with music in infancy. *Proc. Natl. Acad. Sci. U.S.A.* 107, 5768–5773. doi:10.1073/pnas.1000121107

Ziegler, W., Kilian, B., and Deger, K. (1997). The role of the left mesial frontal cortex in fluent speech: evidence from a case of left supplementary motor area hemorrhage. *Neuropsychologia* 35, 1197–1208. doi:10.1016/S0028-3932(97)00040-7

2

Brain responses to musical feature changes in adolescent cochlear implant users

Bjørn Petersen[1,2]*, Ethan Weed[1,3], Pascale Sandmann[4], Elvira Brattico[5,6], Mads Hansen[1,7], Stine Derdau Sørensen[3] and Peter Vuust[1,2]

[1] *Center for Functionally Integrative Neuroscience, Aarhus University Hospital, Aarhus, Denmark*
[2] *Royal Academy of Music, Aarhus, Denmark*
[3] *Department of Aesthetics and Communication – Linguistics, Aarhus University, Aarhus, Denmark*
[4] *Central Auditory Diagnostics Lab, Department of Neurology, Cluster of Excellence "Hearing4all", Hannover Medical School, Hannover, Germany*
[5] *Brain and Mind Laboratory, Department of Biomedical Engineering and Computational Science, Aalto University, Aalto, Finland*
[6] *Cognitive Brain Research Unit, Institute of Behavioral Sciences, University of Helsinki, Helsinki, Finland*
[7] *Department of Psychology and Behavioural Sciences, Aarhus University, Aarhus, Denmark*

Correspondence:
Bjørn Petersen, Center for Functionally Integrative Neuroscience (CFIN), Nørrebrogade 44, Building 10G, 5th Floor, Aarhus C 8000, Denmark
e-mail: bjorn@pet.auh.dk

Cochlear implants (CIs) are primarily designed to assist deaf individuals in perception of speech, although possibilities for music fruition have also been documented. Previous studies have indicated the existence of neural correlates of residual music skills in postlingually deaf adults and children. However, little is known about the behavioral and neural correlates of music perception in the new generation of prelingually deaf adolescents who grew up with CIs. With electroencephalography (EEG), we recorded the mismatch negativity (MMN) of the auditory event-related potential to changes in musical features in adolescent CI users and in normal-hearing (NH) age mates. EEG recordings and behavioral testing were carried out before (T1) and after (T2) a 2-week music training program for the CI users and in two sessions equally separated in time for NH controls. We found significant MMNs in adolescent CI users for deviations in timbre, intensity, and rhythm, indicating residual neural prerequisites for musical feature processing. By contrast, only one of the two pitch deviants elicited an MMN in CI users. This pitch discrimination deficit was supported by behavioral measures, in which CI users scored significantly below the NH level. Overall, MMN amplitudes were significantly smaller in CI users than in NH controls, suggesting poorer music discrimination ability. Despite compliance from the CI participants, we found no effect of the music training, likely resulting from the brevity of the program. This is the first study showing significant brain responses to musical feature changes in prelingually deaf adolescent CI users and their associations with behavioral measures, implying neural predispositions for at least some aspects of music processing. Future studies should test any beneficial effects of a longer lasting music intervention in adolescent CI users.

Keywords: cochlear implants, adolescents, music perception, mismatch negativity, music training, rehabilitation, auditory cortex

INTRODUCTION

The cochlear implant (CI) is a neural prosthesis that provides profoundly deaf individuals with the opportunity to gain or regain the sense of hearing. The implant transforms acoustic signals into electric impulses, which are delivered to an electrode array implanted within the cochlea. The electrodes stimulate intact auditory nerve fibers at different places in the cochlea, thus mimicking the tonotopic organization of the healthy cochlea (Loizou, 1999; McDermott, 2004). The clinical impact of the device is extraordinary, allowing postlingually deafened adults to restore speech comprehension and children to acquire language. Adults with prelingual hearing loss may achieve some auditory alerting functions, but rarely speech comprehension (e.g., Petersen et al., 2013a).

The majority of postlingually deafened adult CI users achieve good speech perception in quiet but their perception of music remains poor. Several studies show that due to low spectral resolution and compromised temporal fine-structure information, discrimination of pitch, melody, timbre, and emotional prosody is significantly poorer in CI users than in normal-hearing (NH) listeners (Leal et al., 2003; Kong et al., 2004; Gfeller et al., 2005, 2007; Olszewski et al., 2005; Cooper et al., 2008; Timm et al., 2012; Agrawal, 2013). Nevertheless, there are examples of CI users who seem to enjoy music after repeated listening (Gfeller and Lansing, 1991; Gfeller et al., 2005) and some studies show significantly improved music discrimination after computer-assisted training (Gfeller et al., 2000a, 2002b; Galvin et al., 2007) and after long-term one-to-one musical ear training (Petersen et al., 2012). These findings suggest that CI users typically do not extract all of the (degraded) information available from the CI signal (Moore and Shannon, 2009) and that targeted auditory training maximizes the benefits of the implant (Fu and Galvin, 2008). Beyond the potential beneficial effects on music enjoyment and social functioning, improved music perception may have positive implications for the quality of life in CI users (Gfeller et al., 2000b; Drennan and Rubinstein, 2008; Lassaletta et al., 2008; Wright and Uchanski, 2012; Petersen et al., 2013b). Furthermore, musical training might transfer to non-musical domains and may have beneficial effects on speech perception in noisy surroundings (Qin and Oxenham, 2003; Parbery-Clark et al., 2009; Won et al., 2010) and on the ability to recognize gender and identity of the speaker (Vongphoe and Zeng, 2005).

In this context, the new generation of prelingually deaf children, who have grown up with the assistance of CIs and who have now become teenagers, is of particular interest. While postlingually deafened CI users rely on auditory development formed by previous hearing experience in processing auditory information from the CI, most current adolescent CI users are congenitally deaf and have only heard sound through their implant. In addition, most young CI users were not diagnosed until they were 2–3 years old and subsequently received their CI after the first 3–5 years of life, that is, beyond the sensitive period for cochlear implantation (Sharma et al., 2002b; Kral and Sharma, 2012).

Initially, cochlear implantation was offered primarily to adults, whereas children were included in CI-programs at a later stage (in Denmark since 1993) and only in moderate numbers. Thus, information about this new population of CI users, their educational placement, and linguistic development has so far been sparse. A recent Danish survey indicate that a majority of young CI users communicate by auditory methods (36%) or auditory methods supported by lip-reading (47%), whereas as few as 5% depend on sign language. Background noise, small talk, slang language, joking, irony, and phone conversation with strangers, however, are reported to represent very challenging daily communicative situations (Rosenmeier and Møller Hansen, 2013). While the findings are an encouraging indication of the overall success of pediatric cochlear implantation (Bosco, 2012), these difficulties highlight the need for continuing specialist teaching throughout adolescence (Archbold et al., 2008; Geers et al., 2008; Harris and Terlektsi, 2011). Adolescence is an age when self-identify is forming and social relations, including music listening and preferences, are particularly important in the life of a teenager (North et al., 2000). Considering that well-functioning communicational skills are crucial for adolescent CI users' well-being, self-esteem, social functioning, and educational prospects (Hansen, 2012), it is pivotal to understand the neural substrates of their speech and music processing to further develop their hearing and speech skills. Nevertheless, while a few behavioral studies have been conducted on adolescent CI users who were prelingually deaf (Geers et al., 2008; Gfeller et al., 2012), no information is currently at hand concerning the neural correlates of musical sound perception and musical training in adolescent CI users.

Auditory processing in CI users can be studied by recording auditory event-related potentials (ERP) using electroencephalography (EEG) (Sharma et al., 2002a; Pantev et al., 2006; Debener, 2008; Sandmann et al., 2009, 2014). One component of the auditory ERP is the mismatch negativity (MMN), which is related to change in different sound features such as pitch, timbre, harmony, intensity, and rhythm (Näätänen et al., 2001, 2007). In contrast to subjective behavioral measures, the MMN represents a reliable and objective marker for CI users' ability to accurately discriminate auditory stimuli (Sandmann et al., 2010; Torppa et al., 2012) typically elicited pre-attentively, in the absence of participants' attention toward the stimuli. MMN latency and amplitude reflect the magnitude of perceptual difference between deviant and standard stimulus and are associated with auditory behavioral measures (Näätänen et al., 2007).

A few MMN studies have investigated auditory brain processing of music in children and adult CI users. For instance, Koelsch (2004) reported timbre-evoked MMN responses with reduced amplitudes in postlingually deaf CI users compared to NH control participants. In a study with postlingually deaf adult CI recipients, Sandmann et al. (2010) reported smaller MMN amplitudes for frequency and intensity deviations in CI users compared to NH controls, and found no robust MMNs to duration deviants in neither of the two groups. In a study with early-implanted CI children (mean age 6 years, 10 months), Torppa et al. (2012) reported comparable magnitudes and latencies of MMN responses to three and seven semitone pitch changes in CI and NH children, and significant MMNs to timbre only for a change from piano to cymbal in both groups. Interestingly, Torppa et al. (2014) in a recent longitudinal study found enhanced development of P3a (attention toward salient sounds) to pitch, timbre, and rhythm changes in CI children who sang regularly, not observed in CI children who did not sing.

Using a newly developed musical multi-feature paradigm, Timm et al. (2014) found distinct MMN responses to pitch, timbre, and intensity, but not to rhythm in postlingually deafened adults with CI. In the present study, we wished to study for the first time the neural prerequisites for music perception, and particularly for musical feature change discrimination, in prelingually deaf adolescent CI users by applying the same paradigm as in Timm et al. (2014). We hypothesized that if any MMN would be found to musical feature changes it would testify the existence of neural predispositions for musical feature processing even in prelingually deaf CI users who were not exposed to any musical (or speech) sounds during the critical period of development. Additionally, we wanted to test whether these adolescent CI users would have any beneficial effect even from a short but intensive music training program. For this purpose, the CI users were measured before and after a musical intervention lasting 2 weeks (20 h), consisting of singing, rhythm, and ear training as well as computer-assisted musical quizzes. We predicted that adolescent CI users would show MMNs, which would differ from those of NH peers, particularly with smaller MMN amplitudes and longer latencies to changes in the acoustic properties of musical sounds, reflecting their impaired musical skills as in behavioral tests. Moreover, we expected to observe a relation between the behavioral effects of music training and the MMN amplitude and latency.

MATERIALS AND METHODS

PARTICIPANTS

The participants were all recruited from Frijsenborg Efterskole (post-school) in the city of Hammel, Denmark. Frijsenborg Efterskole has specialized in teaching hearing-aid (HA) and CI users and employs teachers who are specialized in teaching hearing-impaired pupils and provides modern aids that promote teaching and communication, such as multi-frequency FM equipment. The hearing-impaired pupils make up 25% of the students. The remaining part of the pupils is typical NH age mates.

The participants were recruited through a procedure in which they received oral as well as written information about the project. Since all participants, except one, were below the age of 18 years, their parents received written information also and were required to give informed consent on behalf of their children. The participants received no monetary compensation for their time. The study was conducted in accordance with the Helsinki declaration and approved by the Research Ethics Committee of the Central Denmark Region and is part of a broader study.

All of the school's 12 adolescent CI users signed up for the study, but, due to illness, one had to withdraw from the project. The remaining 11 CI users (6 girls, 5 boys, $M_{age} = 17.0$ years, age range: 15.6–18.8 years), committed themselves to 2 weeks of music training and two sessions of EEG recording and behavioral tests – one before and one after the training period. In the following, T1 and T2 refer to EEG recordings and behavioral tests administered before and after the 2-weeks intervention period, respectively.

The CI participants had a severe-profound/profound congenital or prelingual hearing loss and had received their CI at different points of time in childhood or adolescence (M_{age} at implant = 7.5 years; range: 2.2–14.9 years) between 1997 and 2011, with the majority of participants implanted between 2001 and 2003. The mean implant experience was 9.5 years (range: 1.8–15.2). Nine CI users had bilateral implants, in all cases received sequentially (M_{age} at implant 2 = 12.0 years; range: 10.5–16.6 years; mean experience w. CI 2 = 5.2; range: 0.1–6.2) and two CI participants had unilateral implants combined with a contra-lateral HA. All of the participants used the Nucleus Freedom device from Cochlear Corporation. All CI participants had NH, monolingual Danish-speaking parents. The clinical and demographic data of the 11 CI participants are shown in **Table 1**.

The NH reference group consisted of 10 participants (2 girls, 8 boys; $M_{age} = 16.2$ years, age range: 15.3–17.0 years), who committed themselves to two sessions of EEG recording and tests with a 14-day-interval. The NH reference group followed their normal school schedule during the project and received no musical training. By testing the NH participants twice, we acquired measurements that could be used for direct comparisons with the CI group before and after training.

Musical background

To account for past and recent musical training and experience, the participants filled out a questionnaire concerning their musical background. All NH participants had attended music classes in primary school, as had all CI participants except one. Four CI participants had sung in a choir, which was only the case for two in the NH group. Two in each group stated that they had played in a band at some point. Four CI users had received musical instrument lessons, which was also the case for five NH participants, typically guitar, bass, or drums and in all cases for a short period of time. Based on this information, we judged the musical background in the two groups to be comparable.

THE MUSIC TRAINING PROGRAM

The music training program aimed at strengthening the participants' perception of the fundamental resources in music: pitch, rhythm, and timbre in a combination of active music-making sessions and computer-based listening exercises. The active training part totaled 20 h, scheduled over 6 days, and distributed over 2 weeks. The activities were formed by three elements: rhythm training, singing, and ear training and were led by two masters' students from Royal Academy of Music, Aarhus and the first author,

Table 1 | Clinical and demographic data of the 11 participants in the CI group.

Participant (gender)	Age at project start (years)	Etiology of deafness	Side of first implant	Contra-lateral use of HA	CI 1 experience (years)	CI 2 experience (years)	Use of sign-language[e]	Use of lip-reading[e]	Ability to speak on the phone
CI GROUP									
CI 1 (F)	17.8	[a]Cong. non-spec.	L		10.1	5.9	4	5	X
CI 2 (F)	15.5	[b]Pendred	R	X	4.1		1	2	X
CI 3 (F)	16.5	Unknown	L		11.1	5.6	5	5	X
CI 4 (M)	16.6	[c]CMV	L	X	3.0		1	2	X
CI 5 (M)	18.8	Cong. non-spec.	R		9.9	5.7	4	2	
CI 6 (M)	17.3	Cong. non-spec.	R		11.4	6.1	3	4	X
CI 7 (F)	16.2	Pendred	R		11.8	5.0	3	3	
CI 8 (M)	16.6	Meningitis	L		13.4	6.0	3	2	X
CI 9 (F)	17.4	[d]Her. non-spec.	R		15.7	6.2	4	3	X
CI 10 (M)	16.7	CMV	L		1.8	0.1	3	5	X
CI 11 (F)	17.6	Cong. non-spec.	L		12.0	6.1	5	5	X
Mean	17.0				9.5	5.2	3.3	3.5	
Range	(15.6–18.8)				(1.8–15.2)	(0.1–6.2)			

[a] *Non-specified congenital hearing loss.*

[b] *Pendred Syndrome.*

[c] *Cytomegalovirus.*

[d] *Non-specified hereditary hearing loss.*

[e] *Indicated on a scale where 5 is "everyday" and 1 is "never."*

who has previous experience with music training of adult and pediatric CI users (Petersen et al., 2011, 2012). Training took place in the school's two music classrooms, which were acoustically well suited and well equipped.

Rhythm training

The intention of the rhythm training sessions was to establish a fundamental sense of meter, period, and subdivision in a motivating and physically engaging manner. The sessions involved recurrent exercises including coordination of foot stomping, clapping, and "rapping". All exercises were in 4/4-time in tempos between 80 and 110 BPM. The exercises were performed in a circle, standing up.

Singing

The purpose of the singing training was to establish a sense of basic musical attributes such as high/low, up/down, far/close, and melodic direction. The singing training involved technical instructions about breath control/belly support and exercises, such as glissando (up/down), and imitation of short phrases with focus on long/short, strong/weak, and open/closed vowel sounds in different vocal registers.

Ear training

The ear training part aimed at improving the participants' general music perception skills, particularly timbre, pitch, and melody in a standard classroom setting. The group was introduced to different instruments in live demonstrations. For perception of pitch and melody, the participants were required to identify the direction of two notes (up, down) or three notes (up-down, down-up) or recognize familiar melodies presented on piano or other instruments.

Musical quizzes

To support the ear training sessions, several computer applications, presented as musical quizzes, were developed and made available through download from a website. The quizzes were adapted and expanded versions of applications described in Petersen et al. (2012), aiming to train discrimination of melodic contour, timbre, melody, and rhythm. All quizzes were designed with a familiarization part followed by a number of trials, which required the user to match presented sounds with corresponding icons on the screen. The participants were asked to train everyday for 10–20 min during the 2-weeks training period.

EEG RECORDING

Stimuli and procedure

Electroencephalography was recorded with a musical multi-feature MMN paradigm (Vuust et al., 2011), in a version previously adapted for a study with adult CI users (Timm et al., 2014). The musical multi-feature paradigm presents musical standards, pseudorandomly violated by different deviants in the context of musical four-tone patterns. The four-tone patterns consist of major triads arranged in an "Alberti bass" configuration, an accompaniment commonly used in the Western musical culture.

In the adapted configuration, deviant patterns were similar to standards, except that the third tone of the pattern was exchanged with one of six deviants: (1) pitch deviant (Pitch1$_{D1}$), which was created by raising the standard note by two semitones, (2) pitch deviant (Pitch2$_{D2}$), which was created by raising the standard by four semitones, (3) timbre deviant (Gui$_{D3}$), which was created by replacing the standard piano timbre with the sound of an electric guitar, (4) timbre deviant (Sax$_{D4}$), which was created by replacing the standard piano timbre with the sound of a saxophone, (5) intensity deviant (Int$_{D5}$), which was created by reducing the original intensity by 12 dB, and (6) rhythm deviant (Rhy$_{D6}$), which was created by anticipating the third note by 60 ms. In contrast to the more subtle deviants encompassed in the original multi-feature paradigm aimed at musicians and non-musicians (Vuust et al., 2011), the deviants in the present study were enhanced, thus taking the crude sound representation of the CI into consideration. Each tone was in stereo, 44,100 in sample frequency, and 200 ms in duration, having an inter-stimulus-interval (ISI) of 5 ms. For the Rhy$_{D6}$ deviant, the note prior to the third note was shortened to 140 ms and the ISI between third and fourth note extended to 65 ms. The position of the fourth note was preserved, thus leaving the metric pulse uninterrupted. To make the stimuli more musically interesting, we changed the key every sixth measure, allowing for the six different types of deviants to appear in four different keys. The order of the four possible keys (F, G, A, and C) was pseudo-randomized, so that each key appeared six times in the duration of the paradigm. The keys were kept in the middle register of the piano with the bass note between F3 and C4. The stimuli were presented in Presentation software (Neurobehavioral Systems). The paradigm presented a total of 4608 stimuli, making the duration of whole experiment approximately 18 min, including two 1-min-pauses (**Figure 1**). For more details about the paradigm, see Timm et al. (2014).

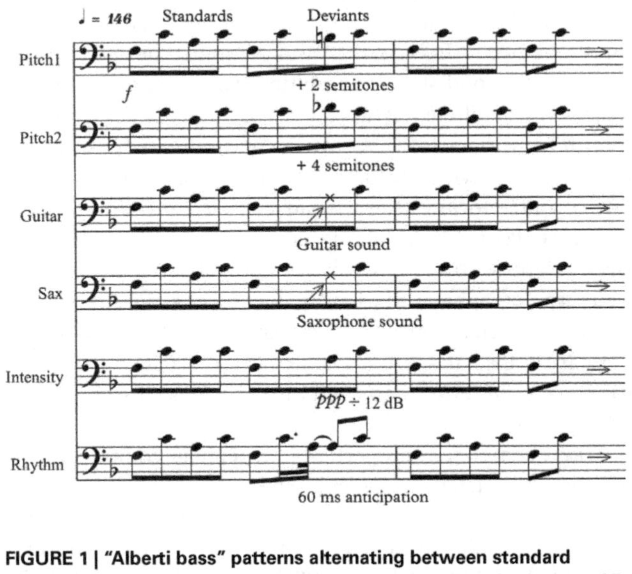

FIGURE 1 | "Alberti bass" patterns alternating between standard sequence played with piano sounds and a deviant, here in the key of F. Deviants were introduced randomly and patterns were pseudorandomly transposed to the keys of G, A, or C with an interval of six bars. Each tone was 200 ms in duration, with an ISI of 5 ms, yielding a tempo of approximately 146 beats/min. Comparisons were made between the third note of the standard sequence and the third note of the deviant sequence.

EEG data recording and analysis

Recording of EEG took place in an acoustically dampened room at Frijsenborg Efterskole. Participants were seated in front of two active loudspeakers (Genelec 8020B; Genelec Oy, Iisalmi, Finland) placed to their left and right side with a 45° angle, approximately 0.5 m distance from the participants' ear. Participants were instructed to ignore the auditory stimuli and watch an animated subtitled movie presented without sound.

The stimuli were presented at 65 dB SPL. CI users used their everyday processor settings during the EEG session. To assure the most comfortable level, participants were exposed to the stimuli briefly before the EEG recording, thus getting an opportunity to adjust their processor settings. To assure comparable conditions for CI participants, bilateral CI users were asked to use only their preferred implant and bimodally aided participants were asked to remove their hearing aid.

Electroencephalography was recorded from 30 Ag/AgCl electrodes placed according to the International 10–20 system and using a BrainAmp amplifier system (Brainproducts, Gilching, Germany). Two additional electrodes were placed below the left and right eye to record the electrooculogram. For CI users, some channels could not be used because of the location of the CI device. Data were recorded with a sampling rate of 500 Hz using the position FCz as reference, and were analog filtered between 0.02 and 250 Hz. Electrode impedances were maintained below 5 kΩ prior to data acquisition.

Electroencephalography data were analyzed with custom scripts and EEGLAB 12.0.2.4b (Delorme, 2004) running in the MATLAB environment (Mathworks, Natick, MA, USA). The preprocessing was done using a two-step procedure, optimized for artifact correction with independent component analysis (ICA) (e.g., Debener et al., 2010). In the first step, the raw data were offline filtered (1–40 Hz) and epoched into continuous 2 s intervals. Intervals containing unique, non-stereotyped artifacts were rejected (threshold: 3 SD). Infomax ICA was computed on the remaining data. In the second step, the resulting ICA weights were applied to the raw data filtered between 0.5 and 30 Hz. Note that the different filter settings for ICA training and ERP analysis was done according to previous recommendations (Debener et al., 2010) and accounted for the otherwise adverse effect of slow amplitude drifts (<1 Hz) on ICA data decomposition. Independent components representing eye-blinks, horizontal eye movement, and electrocardiographic artifacts were identified semi-automatically and were corrected from all datasets using CORRMAP (Viola et al., 2009). Next, the data were segmented from -100 ms to 400 ms relative to stimulus onset, and components representing CI artifacts and other non-cerebral activity were identified by visual inspection of various component properties. Independent components representing CI artifacts were identified by the centroid on the side of the implanted device, and by the time course of component activity (for details on the reduction of CI artifacts by means of ICA, see Gilley, 2006; Debener, 2008; Sandmann et al., 2009). The total number of rejected ICA components was (means and SEM): 8 ± 0.7 for the CI users before training, 9 ± 0.7 for the CI users after training, 10 ± 0.7 for the NH listeners in the first session, and 9 ± 0.9 for the NH listeners in the second session. The data were then pruned of unique, non-stereotyped artifacts (threshold: 3 standard deviations), and unused channels were interpolated (mean: 2 electrodes; SEM: 0.4; range: 1–3 electrodes) using the EEGLAB function eeg_interp.m, before re-referencing the data to a common average reference. Finally, ERPs were obtained by time-domain averaging, and the pre-stimulus interval from −100 to 0 ms was used for baseline correction.

MMN quantification

Difference waveforms were computed for each participant by subtracting the response to the standard stimulus from each of the six deviant stimuli. MMN's were identified with the following procedure. First, a grand-average difference wave was constructed for each deviant by combining the difference waves from the two recording sessions. This was done separately for the NH and the CI group. Next, a 40 ms time window was defined, centered on the most negative point at 75–205 ms in the grand-average difference waves. Finally, the MMN was measured as the peak amplitude within the 40 ms window at the Fz electrode site for each participant, deviant type, and recording session. To avoid erroneously high or low values, three data points on either side of the peak were included in the peak measurement (14 ms duration in total). MMN latency was measured as the peak amplitude between 75 and 205 ms at Fz electrode for each participant, deviant type, and recording session.

BEHAVIORAL MEASUREMENTS

Musical multi feature discrimination task

All participants completed a music discrimination test before and after the intervention period. The purpose was to obtain a behavioral measurement of auditory discrimination accuracy of the six musical deviants also used in the MMN paradigm. The test was designed as a three-alternative forced-choice task (3-AFC), in which the participants were presented with a similar four-tone piano pattern as used in the EEG experiment, restricted, though, to the key of C major. The pattern was presented thrice in a row, twice in the standard, and once in the deviant condition. The deviant patterns were presented equally often and were repeated 6 times in random order, occurring as either the first, the second, or the third pattern, adding to a total of 36 trials. Participants were instructed to click pictorial representations of the pattern, indicating at which position the deviating pattern had occurred. The scores were converted to percent correct hit rates for the six deviant conditions.

Dantale II test. To measure speech comprehension, we used the Danish speech material Dantale II (Wagener et al., 2003). In the applied configuration, this sentence test adapts to the respondent's performance by increasing or decreasing the volume of the speech, holding the background noise at a constant level. The result of the test is given as the speech reception threshold (SRT) in this case the signal-to-noise ratio for 50% word intelligibility. The participants completed three lists, one training list and two trial lists, thus testing perception of 100 words in total. All participants listened through headphones, as did the test administrator. Bilateral CI users were allowed to use both CIs, whereas bimodally aided users were required to switch off their HA but keep it plugged. This measure was taken to secure that conditions were as comparable as possible and to exclude any assistance from potential residual hearing. CI users as well as NH participants completed the test at both recording sessions (T1 and T2). The rationale for testing NH participants twice was first to identify any effects of time and, second, to identify learning effects, which have been reported previously (Pedersen and Juhl, 2013).

STATISTICAL METHODS

MMN responses

In a first step, we tested for significant MMN amplitudes by performing two-tailed one-sample t-tests on each of the deviant difference waves using the ttest.m function in Matlab (Mathworks, Natick, MA, USA). Following this, similar to previous MMN studies on CI users (Sandmann et al., 2010; Timm et al., 2014), we tested for main effects of group, time, and deviant type, and possible interactions between these effects by performing mixed-effects ANOVAs separately on MMN amplitudes and latencies with the between-subjects factor Group (NH and CI) and the within-subjects factors Time (T1 and T2) and deviant type (1–6). *Post hoc* tests were performed using Bonferroni-corrected t-tests.

Behavioral tests

The analysis of the behavioral data from the musical multi-feature discrimination test was performed in a separate mixed-effects ANOVA with the between-subjects factor of Group (NH and CI) and the within-subjects factors of time (T1 and T2) and deviant type (1–6).

To identify significant training effects and group differences as measured by the Dantale II test, we analyzed the SRT values using independent (between groups) and paired (within groups) t-tests.

Correlation analyses between EEG results, behavioral results, and clinical data were done using Spearman's product–moment test. For all tests, the level for significance was set at 0.05, and the significant results are reported. All tests were performed in SPSS (IBM SPSS Statistics for Windows, Version 21.0. Armonk, NY, USA: IBM Corp.).

RESULTS

MMN AMPLITUDES

For the CI users, the musical multi-feature paradigm elicited significant MMNs for deviants Gui_{D3}, Sax_{D4}, Int_{D5}, and Rhy_{D6} at both T1 and T2. For the two pitch deviants, the CI users exhibited a significant MMN only for Pitch1_{D1} and only at T1. For the NH listeners, our analyses showed significant MMNs for all six deviants at both times of testing, except for the T1 Int_{D5} (**Figures 2A–C; Tables 2** and **3**).

Our mixed-effects analysis of the MMN amplitudes showed a significant main effect of Group, $F(1, 19) = 8.43$; $p = 0.009$, driven by overall smaller MMN mean amplitudes in the CI users compared to the NH participants (mean value for combined MMNs across all deviants: CI users: T1: $-0.54\,\mu$V, SD: 0.49, T2 $-0.47\,\mu$V SD: 0.58; NH controls: T1 $-0.66\,\mu$V, SD: 0.61, T2 $-0.94\,\mu$V, SD: 0.58).). Furthermore, we found a significant main effect of deviant type [$F(5, 95) = 15.77$; $p < 0.001$], predominantly deriving from significantly larger amplitudes elicited by the Sax_{D4} compared to the other five deviants. There was also a significant interaction between Group and Time [$F(1, 19) = 7.3$; $p = 0.014$] driven by a significantly larger overall MMN negativity in the NH group at T2 compared to the CI group ($p = 0.002$; NH: $-0.94\,\mu$V; CI: $-0.47\,\mu$V). The *post hoc* comparison of the two groups at T1 was not significant. The Group by Deviant Type interaction was non-significant. Also, the three-way interaction Group × Time × Deviant Type was non-significant. Explorative t-tests showed a significant difference between the MMN amplitudes of the two groups for Pitch1_{D1} [$t(1, 19) = -2.53$; $p = 0.02$], Gui_{D3} [$t(1, 19) = -2.32$; $p < 0.037$], and Rhy_{D6} [$t(1.19) = -2{,}38$; $p < 0.028$], in each case driven by larger mean amplitudes in the NH participants compared to CI users.

MMN LATENCIES

The mixed-effects analysis on MMN latencies showed a significant main effect of Group, $F(1, 19) = 83.55$; $p < 0.001$, driven by overall shorter MMN mean latencies in CI users than in the NH participants (mean value for combined MMN latencies: CI users: 127.15, SD: 31.75, NH listeners: 141.97, SD: 31.40). Furthermore, we found a significant main effect of Time [$F(1, 19) = 5.05$; $p = 0.037$], driven by overall longer MMN latencies in both groups at T2 compared to T1 (mean latency difference: 2.43 ms). Finally, we found a significant main effect of Deviant Type, $F(5, 95) = 258.66$, $p < 0.001$ and an interaction between Deviant Type and Group, $F(5,95) = 122.6$, $p < 0.001$. The three-way interaction Group × Time × Deviant Type was non-significant.

Post hoc t-tests for mean latencies across T1 and T2 with respect to Deviant Type showed that for CI users Gui_{D3} and Rhy_{D6} deviants were significantly longer compared with MMN latencies in the NH participants [Gui_{D3}, $t(1, 19) = -5.9$; $p < 0.001$; Rhy_{D6}, $t(1, 19) = -8.4$, $p < 0.001$]. In contrast, for deviants Pitch1_{D1}, Pitch2_{D2}, and Int_{D5}, we found significantly shorter latencies in the CI users compared to the NH group at T1and T2 [Pitch1_{D1}, $t(1, 19) = 12.58$; $p < 0.001$; Pitch2_{D2}, $t(1, 19) = 9.74$; $p < 0.001$; Int_{D5}, $t(1, 19) = 20.71$, $p < 0.001$] (**Figures 2A–C; Tables 2** and **3**).

BEHAVIORAL MUSICAL MULTI FEATURE DISCRIMINATION TEST

Our mixed-effects analysis showed a significant main effect of Group, $F(1, 19) = 13.04$; $p = 0.002$, driven by an overall 19.72% point lower score in CI users compared with NH participants. Furthermore, the analysis showed an interaction between Deviant Type and Group, $F(5, 19) = 13.79$, $p = 0.001$. According to *post hoc* t-tests, this interaction was driven by significantly lower overall hit rates by the CI users for discrimination of Pitch1_{D1} [$T(5, 19) = 5.27$, $p = < 0.001$], Pitch2_{D2} [$T(5, 19) = 4.13$, $p = 0.001$], Gui_{D3} [$T(5, 19) = 2.41$, $p = < 0.037$], and Int_{D5} [$T(5, 19) = 2.63$, $p = 0.023$] compared to NH controls. The groups did not differ for the Sax_{D4} or Rhy_{D6} deviants (**Figure 3**). We found no effect of Time.

DANTALE II TEST

The CI users produced mean speech recognition threshold values of 1.0 at T1 and of 0.04 at T2, indicating a (non-significant) improvement in their ability to recognize speech in background noise. The CI users' mean SRT values were significantly higher than those of the NH participants at both T1 and T2 ($p < 0.001$) and displayed also a high variability ranging from -3.9 to 10.9 dB SNR.

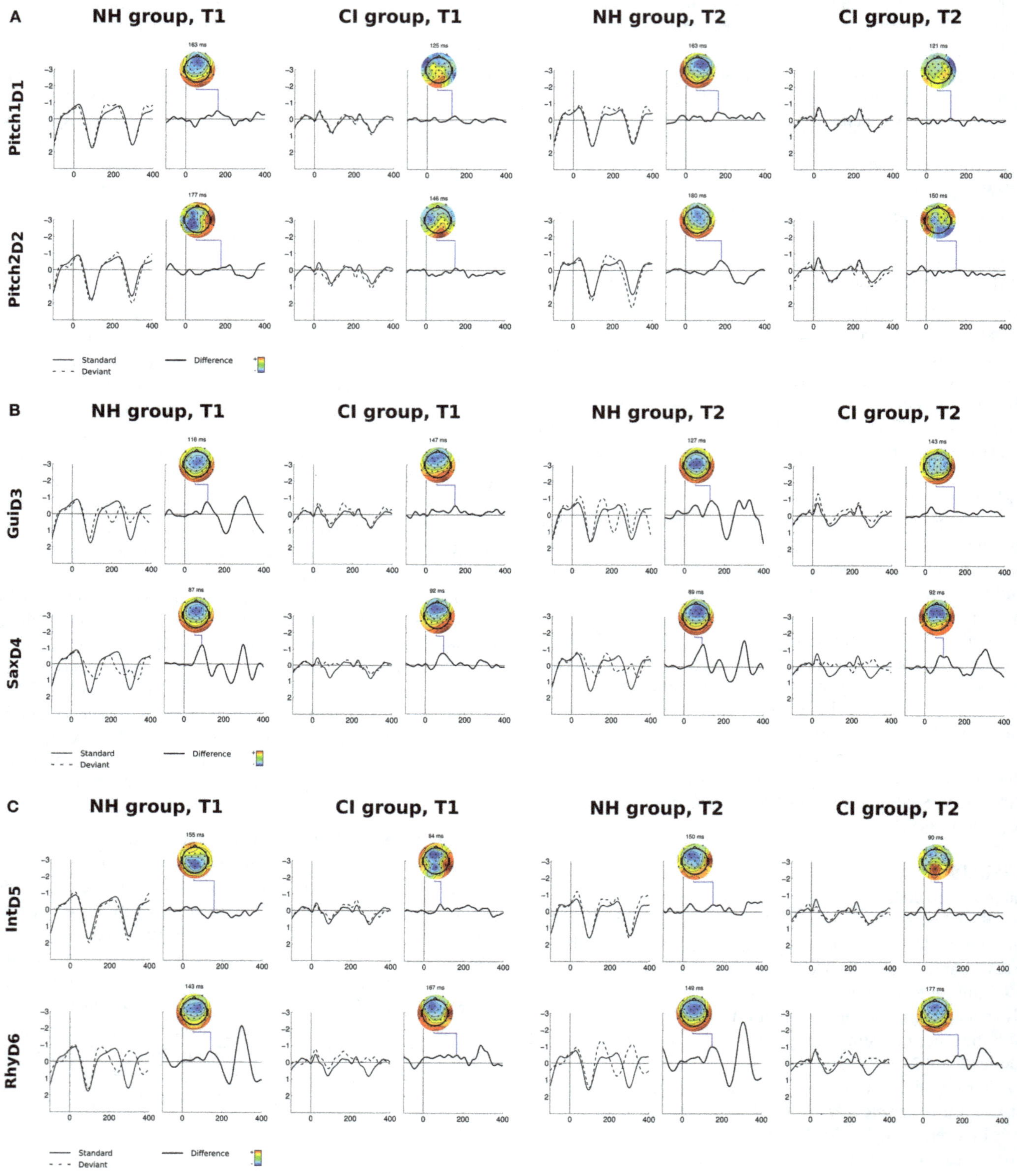

FIGURE 2 | (A–C) Grand-average ERPs and EEG voltage isopotential maps for six types of deviants (vertical) in the two experimental groups at T1 (left) and T2 (right). For each deviant, left panels show responses to the standard (solid line) and to the deviant (dotted line). Right panels show difference waves. Isopotential maps illustrate the difference between the responses to deviants and standards averaged in an interval of ±3 ms around maximal peak amplitudes. X-axis values are in milliseconds; Y-axis values are in microvolts.

Table 2 | Amplitudes and latencies of the MMN in response to different musical features in CI users at T1 and T2.

CI users		T1 results				T2 results			
Deviant	**Interval (ms)**	**Peak amplitude (μV)**	***t***	**SD**	**Latency (ms) (SD)**	**Peak amplitude (μV)**	***t***	**SD**	**Latency (ms) (SD)**
$Pitch1_{D1}$	103–143	−0.45	−3.49**	0.43	125 (11.8)	−0.27	−1.54	0.58	121 (9.7)
$Pitch2_{D2}$	128–168	−0.19	−1.18	0.55	146 (10.2)	−0.22	−1.72	0.42	150 (11.7)
Gui_{D3}	125–165	−0.63	−6.41**	0.33	147 (8.8)	−0.45	−3.80**	0.39	143 (11.8)
Sax_{D4}	72–112	−0.88	−6.06**	0.51	92 (11.0)	−0.88	−6.55**	0.44	92 (12.7)
Int_{D5}	67–107	−0.42	−3.10*	0.45	84 (8.0)	−0.36	−2.34*	0.51	90 (11.6)
Rhy_{D6}	152–192	−0.57	−5.24**	0.36	167 (10.2)	−0.63	−4.62**	0.45	177 (7.2)

*(*p = 0.01; **p < 0.001).*

Table 3 | Amplitudes and latencies of the MMN in response to different musical features in normal-hearing controls at T1 and T2.

NH participants		T1 results				T2 results			
Deviant	**Interval (ms)**	**Peak amplitude (μV)**	***t***	**SD**	**Latency (ms) (SD)**	**Peak amplitude (μV)**	***t***	**SD**	**Latency (ms) (SD)**
$Pitch1_{D1}$	143–183	−0.68	−5.48**	0.39	163 (11.6)	−0.57	−6.73**	0.27	163 (8.3)
$Pitch2_{D2}$	158–198	−0.39	−3.45**	0.36	177 (12.6)	−0.76	−5.05**	0.47	180 (10.2)
Gui_{D3}	101–141	−0.86	−4.61**	0.59	116 (10.4)	−1.13	−5.32**	0.67	127 (11.4)
Sax_{D4}	68–108	−1.30	−6.94**	0.59	87 (7.2)	−1.41	−5.62**	0.79	89 (7.8)
Int_{D5}	132–172	−0.34	−1.98	0.54	155 (9.6)	−0.42	−5.94**	0.22	150 (12.1)
Rhy_{D6}	126–166	−0.72	−5.24**	0.43	143 (11.1)	−1.11	−15.56**	0.22	149 (9.4)

**p = 0.01; **p < 0.001.*

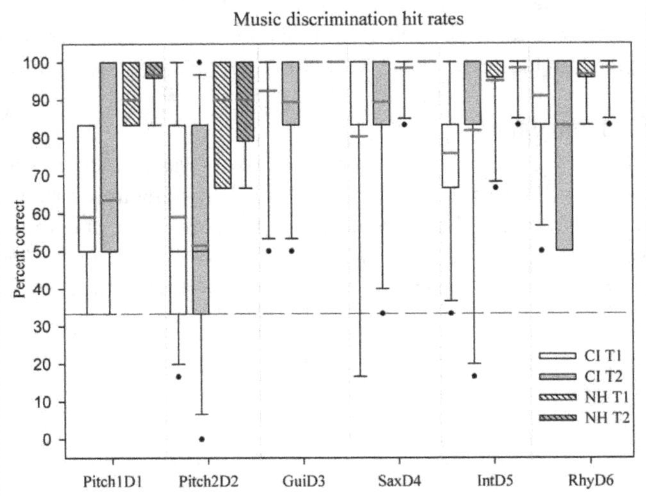

FIGURE 3 | Box plot showing mean hit rates of the two groups for the six deviants at T1 and T2. Whiskers (error bars) above and below the box indicate the 90th and 10th percentiles. Solid black line represents the median, gray line represents the mean. Dots represent outlying points. Dashed line represents chance level.

The mean SRT for NH participants was −6.9 at T1 and −7.7 at T2, which represented a significant improvement [$t(1, 9) = 3.31$, $p = 0.009$] (**Figure 4**).

CORRELATIONS

Correlation analyses were performed for CI users between MMN amplitudes and latencies and behavioral music discrimination scores and Dantale II T2 results and demographic data. Because our ANOVAs showed no main effect of Time, we computed values that were averaged across T1 and T2 for MMN amplitudes and behavioral music discrimination data.

For the MMN data, a significant positive association was found between mean amplitudes for the Gui_{D3} ($r = 0.798$) and Rhy_{D6} ($r = 0.605$) and age, indicating that younger CI users had larger MMN responses than older CI users for these two deviants. Furthermore, we found a significant negative association between hearing age (implant experience) and mean latency for the Rhy_{D6} ($r = -0.838$), indicating that CI users with higher hearing age had MMN responses with shorter latency for this deviant (**Figure 5**). A similar non-significant association was found for the Sax_{D4} deviant ($r = -0.592$, $p = 0.055$).

Hit rates for behavioral discrimination of the six different musical deviants showed a general positive association with each other. Significant correlations were found between discrimination of IntD5 and $Pitch1_{D1}$ ($r = 0.699$), Gui_{D3} ($r = 0.642$), Sax_{D4} ($r = 0.907$), and Rhy_{D6} ($r = 0.789$) and between Rhy_{D6} and $Pitch2_{D2}$ ($r = 0.665$) and Sax_{D4} ($r = 0.807$). Further associations were found between behavioral discrimination scores and Dantale II SRTs, in all cases, however, driven by an extraordinarily high SRT by a single outlier.

DISCUSSION

The current study measured behavioral and electrophysiological correlates of music perception in prelingually deaf adolescents before and after a 2-week music training program. A group of age-matched NH listeners served as controls. Overall, the results revealed smaller MMN amplitudes and shorter MMN latencies in CI users than in NH listeners. More specifically, the adolescent CI users showed robust MMN responses for deviations in timbre, intensity, and rhythm. For pitch deviants, we found no consistent MMNs in CI users, which was also reflected in the CI users' poor hit rates for behavioral pitch discrimination. The findings suggest that even though these adolescents received their implants beyond the optimal age for cochlear implantation (Kral and Sharma, 2012) and have formed their perception of sound solely through the implant, their auditory pathways have been sufficiently developed to allow some discrimination of details in music, predominantly within timbre, timing, and intensity. The study complements previous MMN studies with adult and pediatric CI users (Sandmann et al., 2010; Zhang, 2011; Torppa et al., 2012, 2014), showing potential ability also in prelingually deaf, late-implanted adolescent CI users to process features of music, even when embedded in a complex auditory context.

Consistent with our hypothesis, we found significantly diminished overall amplitudes in the CI users compared to NH controls. The difference, however, reflected differential responses depending on deviant type, with smaller MMN amplitudes elicited by the Pitch1$_{D1}$, Gui$_{D3}$, and Rhy$_{D6}$ deviants and comparable amplitudes elicited by the Sax$_{D4}$ and Int$_{D5}$ deviants. In line with this, we found significantly poorer overall behavioral discrimination scores, which confirm that MMN responses for changes in various kinds of stimuli are reflected in discrimination accuracy (Näätänen et al., 2007). Contrary to our hypothesis, we found significantly shorter overall MMN latencies in the CI users compared to NH peers. Again the difference was linked to deviant type; Gui$_{D3}$ and Rhy$_{D6}$ deviants showed significantly longer latencies, whereas the Int$_{D5}$ and the two pitch deviants were elicited significantly earlier than those of the NH reference. Latencies for pitch, however, should be judged with caution, given the fact that the pitch MMNs were non-significant for Pitch1$_{D1}$ at T2 and for Pitch2$_{D2}$ at both time points.

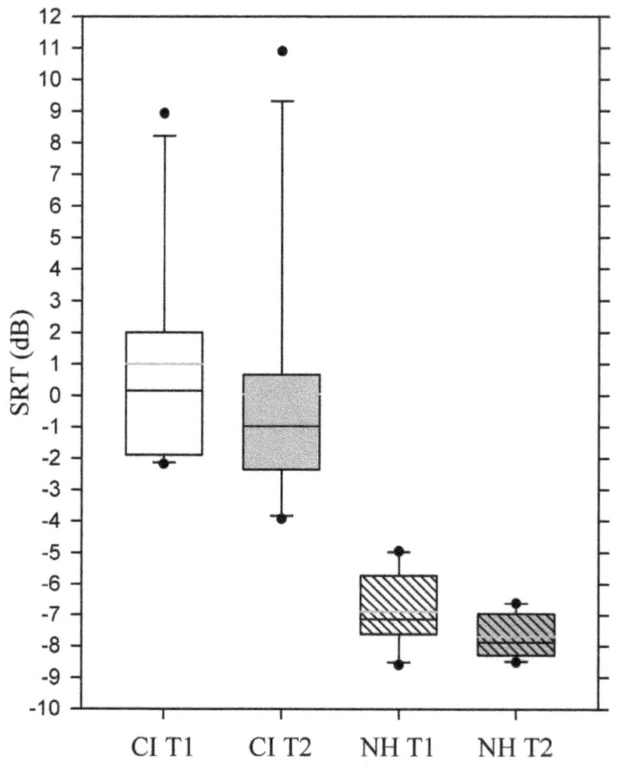

FIGURE 4 | Box plot showing mean speech recognition thresholds for the two experimental groups at T1 and T2. Whiskers (error bars) above and below the box indicate the 90th and 10th percentiles. Solid black line represents the median, gray line represents the mean. Dots represent outlying points. Note that a more negative value corresponds to a better performance.

MUSIC TRAINING

For most of the young CI users, this project was their first experience with structured and targeted music making and certainly challenging. Indeed, they generally responded with great enthusiasm to the different exercises and tasks and also displayed a marked progress in their musical competences. Nevertheless, in contrast

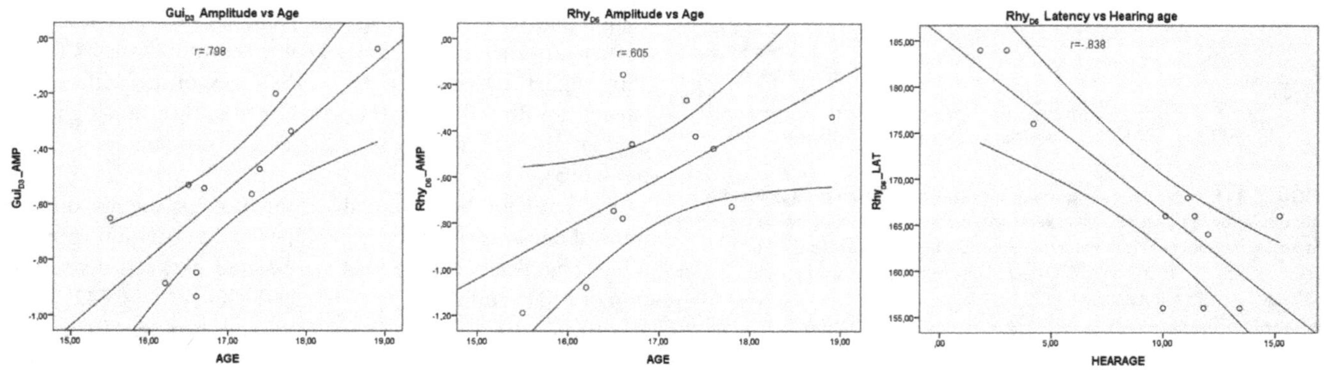

FIGURE 5 | Scatter plots illustrating the correlation between the mean MMN amplitude to the Gui$_{D3}$ and age (left panel), mean amplitude to the Rhy$_{D6}$ deviant and age (middle panel), and mean MMN latency for the Rhy$_{D6}$ deviant and hearing age (=implant experience) in the adolescent CI users.

to our hypothesis, we were unable to observe any progress in the young CI users' discrimination skills at either a neuronal or behavioral level. This lack of progress could be due to the brevity of the program. Moreover, the broad-spectrum and music-making nature of the training may have been insufficiently focused to reliably strengthen the specific auditory skills in demand for the tests in such a short period of time. It is important to emphasize, however, that because of interference with the participants' school activities, an extended training period was not an option and that the music-making approach was deliberately chosen to ensure maximum appeal to the participants. Evenly important, according to self-report, the CI participants spent much less time training with the musical quizzes than requested. Despite instant feedback and progressive design, the quizzes offered little excitement in comparison with current computer games and may simply have appeared less appealing. Future studies should investigate the possible advantages of applications, preferably for smart phones or tablet computers, which offer auditory training of music discrimination skills in an adaptive, socially interactive, and game-like design (Lee and Hammer, 2011).

Contrary to our predictions, we found an overall progress in MMN amplitude in the NH group, who received no music training. We could speculate that NH subjects show training effects simply by being a second time exposed to the same sound stimulation (Paukkunen, 2011). Instead, CI users, even if they had a musical training, did not show any advantage at T2, probably as a consequence of their deficits in musical sound processing. To be visible, the exposure to sounds in CI users should most likely be very long and intensive, whereas in normal subjects some transient neural effects are observable even already after 20 min of discrimination training (Jäncke et al., 2001; Brattico et al., 2003; Lappe et al., 2011).

RHYTHM

Previous behavioral studies with postlingually deaf CI users have documented that discrimination of complex rhythm is difficult (Leal et al., 2003; Kong et al., 2004; Drennan and Rubinstein, 2008). In that respect, we were encouraged to find that the adolescent CI users were able to produce significant MMN responses to a change in rhythm as fast as 60 ms and produce discrimination scores that were not significantly different from the NH reference. This is an indication of the ability of these young CI users to extract fast temporal information despite prelingual deafness and late implantation, as well as the accuracy with which timing features are transmitted in current CI technology. Ability to discriminate rhythm may assist young CI users in general when listening to music, especially for genres that tend to have strong rhythmic elements paired with lyrics (Gfeller et al., 2012). Moreover, poor perception of rhythm has been associated with poor perception of syllable stress and dyslexia (Overy, 2003; Overy et al., 2003; Huss, 2011), and it is possible that training of rhythm, on a long-term, could form a beneficial part in auditory–oral therapy for young CI users (Looi and She, 2010; Petersen et al., 2012).

Our results are in contrast with Timm et al. (2014) who found no robust MMN response to the rhythm deviant in their adult CI users. The authors speculated that one of the sources to this absence of MMN could possibly be that the relatively small deviation of 60 ms was too difficult to extract, especially when embedded in a complex auditory scene. There may be several sources to the discrepancy between the two studies. First, the CI users in the present study were significantly younger (mean age 17 vs. 43.5 years), which may influence neural processing of auditory stimuli. Second, the adolescent CI users all used the most updated implant device in contrast to the adult CI users' selection of brands and models, which might result in some differences in timing accuracy. A minor difference in the way the rhythm deviant was presented in the two studies may also have contributed to the different results. In the present study, the position of the fourth note was preserved, thus leaving the metric pulse uninterrupted. In the Timm et al. (2014) study, the position of the fourth note was altered in accordance with the early third note, thereby shifting the metric pulse. Thus, the rhythm deviant in the present study deviates in three ways. First, it cuts the preceding note short, which could be perceived as a deviation of duration. Second, the third note comes early, violating the rhythmic flow and, third, the fourth note comes late, caused by the longer gap between notes 3 and 4. By inspecting the difference wave plots for the rhythm deviant (**Figure 2C**), it appears that this multifaceted deviation evokes not only a significant MMN in the 143–173 ms window after stimulus onset but also a consistent and even stronger negative peak around 325 ms. This effect is identical and consistent across groups and time points and we speculate that it reflects a second MMN in response to the late fourth note.

TIMBRE

Both the guitar and the saxophone deviants elicited significant brain responses in our two experimental groups. This is in contrast to findings by Torppa et al. (2012) who in a study with CI and NH children found significant MMNs only to a large change from piano to cymbal but not to changes from piano to violin or to cembalo. They did, however, find indications of a general improvement with age in the children's ability to detect changes between instruments, which could partly explain this discrepancy. Our findings are in line with Timm et al. (2014) who found similar strong MMN responses to timbre changes in postlingually deaf adult CI users. Interestingly, in both studies the saxophone deviant showed the largest effect compared to the remaining deviants and amplitude and latency that were not significantly different from those of NH listeners. It should be emphasized, however, that the latency of the MMN for this particular deviant was quite different in the two studies, elicited around 92 ms in the present and around 165 ms in the Timm et al. (2014) study. Since both the stimuli and the experimental settings were identical, we speculate that differences in age may be the primary source of this difference in timing.

As opposed to the saxophone deviant, CI users' MMN responses to the guitar deviant showed significantly smaller amplitudes and significantly longer latencies than those of NH controls, indicating reduced discrimination accuracy. The neurophysiological findings were reflected in behavioral performance in which the CI users produced discrimination scores, which were comparable to the NH level for the saxophone but not for the guitar deviant. This suggests that the sound of a saxophone, which is characterized by a slow attack and a soft tone, represents a larger deviation from the piano tone than the sharp distinct sound of the guitar. Moreover, in an MMN study, which is based on the theory of predictive coding (Baldeweg, 2006), an unexpected occurrence of a saxophone sound in a stream of piano notes represents not only a change of timbre but also a change in timing and intensity, which could also partly explain the observed difference.

So are adolescent CI users as good or almost as good as NH peers in discrimination of timbre? No, probably not. Discrimination of timbre involves perception of several acoustic parameters, particularly the temporal envelope (rise time, duration, and decay) and harmonic spectrum of a sound, and is usually poor in CI users (Gfeller et al., 2002a; McDermott and Looi, 2004; Drennan and Rubinstein, 2008; Spitzer et al., 2008; Timm et al., 2012). The fact that the adolescent CI users were able to detect changes in timbre does not necessarily mean that they would be able to recognize a musical instrument. It does, however, indicate that they possess some basic prerequisites for developing this skill and that the implant transmits sufficient spectral information to allow detection of changes in timbre (Koelsch, 2004). Previous studies have showed enhanced abilities to discriminate timbre after computer-assisted training (Fujita and Ito, 1999; Leal et al., 2003; Pressnitzer et al., 2005; Driscoll et al., 2009) and long-term individual training (Petersen et al., 2012). Improved perception of timbre may add positively to the esthetic enjoyment of music listening and may also be beneficial in other aspects of listening such as recognition of gender or speaker in auditory-only acoustic communication, which are notoriously challenging with CIs (Vongphoe and Zeng, 2005).

PITCH

Except for the Pitch1_{D1} deviant at T1, the CI group did not exhibit significant MMN responses to changes in pitch of neither two nor four semitones and produced pitch discrimination scores, which were significantly below the NH level. This pitch discrimination deficit may indicate that the neuronal connections of the auditory pathways were not established in the appropriate time window of opportunity, leaving the potential for developing pitch processing abilities very limited (Sharma et al., 2005; Sharma, 2006). Despite ability to produce significant MMNs for pitch deviants, the adult CI users in the study by Timm et al. (2014) showed significantly diminished amplitudes, longer latencies, and lower hit rates for the two and four semitones pitch deviants compared to NH controls. This indicates that, at least for small pitch change detection, the advantages of postlingually deafened CI users, who rely on auditory skills developed prior to their hearing loss, over prelingually deaf adolescent CI users, whose auditory development is based exclusively on implant experience, may be rather small.

Interestingly, Torppa et al. (2012) in a recent study found magnitude and timing of MMN responses to three and seven semitone changes of pitch in early-implanted CI children that were comparable to those of NH controls. The authors suggested that harmonic components of the presented piano tones may be sufficiently separated in frequency to allow accessibility of spectral cues to a change in pitch to the CI children. While the children in the Torppa et al.' study had a mean age at switch-on of 21.5 months (range 14–37 m), the adolescents in the present study were implanted significantly later (mean age at switch-on: 7.4 years). We speculate that the delayed stimulation of the auditory system is the primary cause of the poor pitch processing observed in the adolescent CI users. Furthermore, the previous study used a multi-feature MMN paradigm, which presented repeated piano tones in contrast to the present study, which presented deviants in a complex musical context and randomly changing keys.

We observed a significant MMN for the Pitch_{D1} at T1 but not at T2, implying a reverse effect of the training. However, considering the intensive focus on pitch and melody included in both the singing and ear training activities, we hardly believe that is the case. More likely, the inconsistent pitch MMNs reflect the suboptimal recording conditions and possible variability across sessions in participant behavior, which may have prevented the weak pitch responses from passing the statistical thresholds. Alternatively, pitch MMNs were elicited but could not be identified due to overlap by other potentials. Finally, the rather short SOA used here prevented identifying a latency longer than 200 ms. Considering that the NH children showed MMN latencies to pitch deviants close to 200 ms, it may well be that we simply missed it.

INTENSITY

Electrical hearing produces a much narrower dynamic range than acoustic hearing (Galvin et al., 2007; Veekmans et al., 2009). We were therefore surprised to find MMN responses to the Int_{D5} deviant, which were not significantly different in amplitude from those of the NH listeners. It should be emphasized, however, that the NH responses were surprisingly weak for these deviant and non-significant at T2, indicating a generally small effect of this deviation. Furthermore, although significantly poorer than the NH reference, the CI users' hit rates for discrimination of intensity were well above chance. This indicates that despite the limited dynamics of the implant, the 12 dB decrement in intensity is transmitted reliably even in prelingually deaf adolescent CI users. The results are partly consistent with a previous MMN level-study with adult CI users, in which Sandmann et al. (2010) found significant MMN responses to a 12 dB intensity decrement but not to two smaller 4 and 8 dB intensity decrements. Future studies should investigate discrimination of changes of intensity in adolescent CI users in more detail.

While our two experimental groups produced similar but small MMN amplitudes in response to the Int_{D5} deviant, the latencies differed significantly. The MMNs of the CI users peaked around 84 ms while those of the NH listeners peaked around 150 ms. This difference may reflect different processing of this particular deviant. However, as with the MMN responses for pitch, we cannot exclude the possibility that the latency values for intensity in the CI group may reflect activity that is different from the activity reflected in the later peaks among NH participants.

SPEECH PERCEPTION IN NOISE

The marked improvement in the CI users' SRT s suggested a transfer effect from the music training. The similar and significant progress in the non-trained NH group, however, indicates that these improvements are the results of a test learning effect, as seen in previous studies (Pedersen and Juhl, 2013). The Dantale

II test requires the ability to identify words in spoken sentences in background noise and subsequently match these with a matrix of optional words on a computer screen, a complex task that relies on both reading skills and working memory and may benefit from previous exposure. These requirements may also explain the huge variability observed in the CI group reflecting possible differences in the participants' linguistic and cognitive development (Burkholder and Pisoni, 2003). Naturally, the variance may also reflect other factors such as history of hearing loss and CI functionality. None such predictive factors, however, were identified in our correlational analyses.

MUSICAL MULTI-FEATURE PARADIGM

Our results indicate that the fast, musical, multi-feature paradigm presenting deviants embedded in a complex musical pattern can elicit distinct MMNs not only in postlingually deaf adults but even in prelingually deaf adolescent CI users. Since MMNs are elicited pre-attentively with no behavioral task, this paradigm may be used for objective evaluation of CI users' auditory skills in general and ability to discriminate musical sounds in particular. Because it is fast with a recording time of only 20 min and highly flexible with regard to both the nature and the deviation magnitude of the properties which it investigates, this paradigm could be a useful tool for assessing auditory rehabilitation following cochlear implantation. In a clinical context, MMN responses could be of relevance as an objective marker for measuring auditory discrimination abilities in CI patients, especially pediatric CI users, whose assessment of auditory discrimination and implant outcome is challenging. The paradigm does, however, run at a fast pace and a future revision should evaluate the effects of a reduced tempo, allowing analysis of effects in the 200–400 ms, particularly the P3a (Torppa et al., 2012).

THE IMPACT OF HEARING AGE

The adolescent CI users in our study represented a huge range of age at implantation as well as communication background. Nevertheless, apart from the indication of an association between higher hearing age and shorter latencies for rhythm and saxophone, we found none of these factors predictive of either neurophysiological or behavioral performance. Especially with regard to the behavioral tests, this suggests that skills associated with cognition, concentration, attention, and memory may have a stronger impact than implant experience and prior use of sign language. As an interesting single case, CI 5, who is profoundly deaf, raised as a sign language user and who received his implant at the age of 9 years was able to score in the high average level of his group in both speech and music tests.

LIMITATIONS

Recording and analyzing EEG with CI users represent a number of challenges. Due to the position of the implant, some electrodes cannot be used, resulting in a number of interpolated channels. Furthermore, due to the electric signal from the implant, it is necessary to use elaborate preprocessing procedures to reduce the CI artifact (Sandmann et al., 2009; Viola et al., 2011), allowing interpretation of the resulting evoked potentials of interest. Finally, in this particular study, recordings were done in the field, thus potentially degrading the signal-to-noise ratio as compared to recordings made in the shielded settings of the laboratory. In sum, these challenges may have resulted in data, which were less consistent than desired. Furthermore, measuring ERPs in a group of healthy individuals and a special group such as CI users implies an intrinsic difficulty of picking up the same peak for both groups. We cannot preclude that the applied peak-identification method, which identified MMN peaks algorithmically and separately in the two groups, erroneously may have led us to peaks from the two groups that in fact belonged to different ERP components.

The adolescent CI users in this study belong to the first generation of children who were offered CIs. Since, at the time, neo-natal hearing screening was not a standard procedure and some concerns about the safety of the surgery existed, they were in general both diagnosed and implanted later in childhood than is typical today. Therefore, they may not be fully representative of the future generations of early-implanted adolescents. We will, however, argue that the study and its findings are relevant, particularly considering the considerable number of teenagers worldwide making up this generation.

SUMMARY AND CONCLUSION

Our findings provide novel insight on neural processing of musical sounds in a new generation of deaf adolescents, who have grown up with the assistance of CIs. The results showed that despite prelingual deafness and late implantation, adolescent CI users possess prerequisites for some discrimination of musical sounds, as indicated by their significant MMN responses particularly to changes in timbre, rhythm, and intensity. Compared to a NH reference, however, the CI users' general discrimination abilities were characterized by significantly weaker brain responses and poorer behavioral performance. This was particularly true for their discrimination of small changes in pitch, which showed a severe deficit, reflected in inconsistent brain responses, and poor behavioral performance. Evidently, perception of music – especially melody – is degraded in these adolescent CI users, as also signified by the challenges observed in relation to singing. This, however, does not necessarily reduce music appreciation. Unlike postlingually deaf adult CI users, prelingually deaf CI users make no comparisons with previous music listening experience and may be quite satisfied with the representation provided by the implant, perceiving possibly particularly the rhythmic content of music (Gfeller et al., 2012). The lack of findings with an ear training program lasting only 2 weeks in CI users shows their refractoriness to auditory interventions. Thus, we encourage future research on the effects of longitudinal music training, preferably involving a combination of music making and training applications offering an adaptive and game-like interface. As observed here, the great compliance and enthusiasm of the participants indicate that such measures could be relatively easily implemented.

ACKNOWLEDGMENTS

The authors wish to acknowledge all of the participants and their parents for their unrestricted commitment to the study as well as the staff at Frijsenborg Efterskole for invaluable help and support in organizing and scheduling tests and training. Furthermore, they wish to thank Susanne Mai, Minna Sandahl, and

Anne Marie Ravn from the Department of Audiology, Aarhus University Hospital and Jesper Dahl at Gentofte Hospital for provision of clinical data and Professor Therese Ovesen at the ENT department of Aarhus University Hospital for her help and support. Finally, they thank Nynne Horn, Andreas Højlund Nielsen, and Martin Dietz for assistance and counseling on EEG recording and analysis. EEG facilities were generously provided by Center of Functionally Integrative Neuroscience, Aarhus University Hospital. This work was supported by a grant from the Danish Ministry of Culture's Research Foundation (Bjørn Petersen) and by the Cluster of Excellence "Hearing4all" (Pascale Sandmann).

REFERENCES

Agrawal, D. (2013). Electrophysiological responses to emotional prosody perception in cochlear implant users. *NeuroImage Clin.* 2, 229–238. doi:10.1016/j.nicl.2013.01.001

Archbold, S., Sach, T., O'Neill, C., Lutman, M., and Gregory, S. (2008). Outcomes from cochlear implantation for child and family: parental perspectives. *Deaf. Educ. Int.* 10, 120–142. doi:10.1097/MAO.0b013e3182522906

Baldeweg, T. (2006). Repetition effects to sounds: evidence for predictive coding in the auditory system. *Trends Cogn. Sci.* 2006, 93–94. doi:10.1016/j.tics.2006.01.010

Bosco, E. (2012). Long term results in late implanted adolescent and adult CI recipients. *Eur. Arch. Otorhinolaryngol.* 270, 2611–2620. doi:10.1007/s00405-012-2264-4

Brattico, E., Tervaniemi, M., and Picton, T. W. (2003). Effects of brief discrimination-training on the auditory N1 wave. *Neuroreport* 14, 2489–2492. doi:10.1097/00001756-200312190-00039

Burkholder, R. A., and Pisoni, D. B. (2003). Speech timing and working memory in profoundly deaf children after cochlear implantation. *J. Exp. Child Psychol.* 85, 63–88. doi:10.1016/S0022-0965(03)00033-X

Cooper, W. B., Tobey, E., and Loizou, P. C. (2008). Music perception by cochlear implant and normal hearing listeners as measured by the Montreal battery for evaluation of Amusia. *Ear Hear.* 29, 618–626. doi:10.1097/AUD.0b013e318174e787

Debener, S. (2008). Source localization of auditory evoked potentials after cochlear implantation. *Psychophysiology* 45, 20–24. doi:10.1111/j.1469-8986.2007.00610.x

Debener, S., Thorne, J. D., Schneider, T. R., and Viola, F. (2010). "Using ICA for the analysis 50 of multichannel EEG data," in *Simultaneous EEG and fMRI: Recording, Analysis, and Application,* Vol. 1, eds M. Ullsperger and S. Debener (New York, NY: Oxford University Press), 121–134.

Delorme, A. (2004). EEGLAB: an open source toolbox for analysis of single-trial EEG dynamics including independent component analysis. *J. Neurosci. Methods* 134, 9–21. doi:10.1016/j.jneumeth.2003.10.009

Drennan, W. R., and Rubinstein, J. T. (2008). Music perception in cochlear implant users and its relationship with psychophysical capabilities. *J. Rehabil. Res. Dev.* 45, 779–789. doi:10.1682/JRRD.2007.08.0118

Driscoll, V. D., Oleson, J., Jiang, D., and Gfeller, K. (2009). Effects of training on recognition of musical instruments presented through cochlear implant simulations. *J. Am. Acad. Audiol.* 20, 71–82. doi:10.3766/jaaa.20.1.7

Fu, Q. J., and Galvin, J. J. III (2008). Maximizing cochlear implant patients' performance with advanced speech training procedures. *Hear. Res.* 242, 198–208. doi:10.1016/j.heares.2007.11.010

Fujita, S., and Ito, J. (1999). Ability of nucleus cochlear implantees to recognize music. *Ann. Otol. Rhinol. Laryngol.* 108, 634–640. doi:10.1177/000348949910800702

Galvin, J. J., Fu, Q. J., and Nogaki, G. (2007). Melodic contour identification by cochlear implant listeners. *Ear Hear.* 1169, 518–533. doi:10.1097/01.aud.0000261689.35445.20

Geers, A., Tobey, E., Moog, J., and Brenner, C. (2008). Long-term outcomes of cochlear implantation in the preschool years: from elementary grades to high school. *Int. J. Audiol.* 47, S21–S30. doi:10.1080/14992020802339167

Gfeller, K., Driscoll, V., Smith, R. S., and Scheperle, C. (2012). The music experiences and attitudes of a first cohort of prelingually-deaf adolescents and young adults CI recipients. *Semin. Hear.* 33, 346–360. doi:10.1055/s-0032-1329224

Gfeller, K., and Lansing, C. R. (1991). Melodic, rhythmic, and timbral perception of adult cochlear implant users. *J. Speech Hear. Res.* 34, 916–920. doi:10.1044/jshr.3404.916

Gfeller, K., Mehr, S. A., Woodworth, G., and Knutson, J. (2002a). Effects of frequency, instrumental family, and cochlear implant type on timbre recognition and appraisal. *Ann. Otol. Rhinol. Laryngol.* 111, 349. doi:10.1177/000348940211100412

Gfeller, K., Witt, S., Adamek, M., Mehr, M., Rogers, J., Stordahl, J., et al. (2002b). Effects of training on timbre recognition and appraisal by postlingually deafened cochlear implant recipients. *J. Am. Acad. Audiol.* 13, 132–145.

Gfeller, K., Olszewski, C., Rychener, M., Sena, K., Knutson, J. F., Witt, S., et al. (2005). Recognition of "real-world" musical excerpts by cochlear implant recipients and normal-hearing adults. *Ear Hear.* 26, 237–250. doi:10.1097/00003446-200506000-00001

Gfeller, K., Turner, C., Oleson, J., Zhang, X., Gantz, B., Froman, R., et al. (2007). Accuracy of cochlear implant recipients on pitch perception, melody recognition, and speech reception in noise. *Ear Hear.* 28, 412–423. doi:10.1097/AUD.0b013e3180479318

Gfeller, K., Witt, S., Stordahl, J., Mehr, M., and Woodworth, G. (2000a). The effects of training on melody recognition and appraisal by adult cochlear implants recipients. *J. Acad. Rehabil. Audiol.* 33, 115–138.

Gfeller, K., Christ, A., Knutson, J. F., Witt, S., Murray, K. T., and Tyler, R. S. (2000b). Musical backgrounds, listening habits, and aesthetic enjoyment of adult cochlear implant recipients. *J Am. Acad. Audiol* 11, 390–406.

Gilley, P. M. (2006). Minimization of cochlear implant stimulus artifact in cortical auditory evoked potentials. *Neurophysiol. Clin.* 117, 1772–1782. doi:10.1016/j.clinph.2006.04.018

Hansen, N.-H. M. (2012). *Langtidsstudie af unge hørehæmmede efter Frijsenborg Efterskole.* CEFU, Center for Ungdomsforskning: Danmarks Pædagogiske Universitetsskole. Aarhus: Aarhus University. [In Danish].

Harris, M., and Terlektsi, E. (2011). Reading and spelling abilities of deaf adolescents with cochlear implants and hearing aids. *J. Deaf Stud. Deaf Educ.* 16, 24–34. doi:10.1093/deafed/enq031

Huss, M. (2011). Music, rhythm, rise time perception and developmental dyslexia: perception of musical meter predicts reading and phonology. *Cortex* 47, 674–689. doi:10.1016/j.cortex.2010.07.010

Jäncke, L., Gaab, N., Wüstenberg, T., Scheich, H., and Heinze, H. J. (2001). Short-term functional plasticity in the human auditory cortex: an fMRI study. *Brain Res. Cogn. Brain Res.* 12, 479–485. doi:10.1016/S0926-6410(01)00092-1

Koelsch, S. (2004). Music perception in cochlear implant users: an event-related potential study. *Neurophysiol. Clin.* 115, 966–972. doi:10.1016/j.clinph.2003.11.032

Kong, Y. Y., Cruz, R., Jones, J. A., and Zeng, F. G. (2004). Music perception with temporal cues in acoustic and electric hearing. *Ear Hear.* 25, 173–185. doi:10.1097/01.AUD.0000120365.97792.2F

Kral, A., and Sharma, A. (2012). Developmental neuroplasticity after cochlear implantation. *Trends Neurosci.* 35, 111–122. doi:10.1016/j.tins.2011.09.004

Lappe, C., Trainor, L. J., Herholz, S. C., and Pantev, C. (2011). Cortical plasticity induced by short-term multimodal musical rhythm training. *PLoS ONE* 6:e21493. doi:10.1371/journal.pone.0021493

Lassaletta, L., Castro, A., Bastarrica, M., Perez-Mora, R., Herran, B., Sanz, L., et al. (2008). Changes in listening habits and quality of musical sound after cochlear implantation. *Otolaryngol. Head Neck Surg.* 138, 363–367. doi:10.1016/j.otohns.2007.11.028

Leal, M. C., Shin, Y. J., Laborde, M. L., Calmels, M. N., Verges, S., Lugardon, S., et al. (2003). Music perception in adult cochlear implant recipients. *Acta Otolaryngol.* 123, 826–835. doi:10.1080/00016480310000386

Lee, J., and Hammer, J. (2011). Gamification in education: what, how, why bother? *Acad. Exch. Q.* 15. Available at: http://www.gamifyingeducation.org/files/Lee-Hammer-AEQ-2011.pdf

Loizou, P. C. (1999). Introduction to cochlear implants. *IEEE Eng. Med. Biol. Mag.* 18, 32–42. doi:10.1109/51.740962

Looi, V., and She, J. (2010). Music perception of cochlear implant users: a questionnaire, and its implications for a music training program. *Int. J. Audiol.* 49, 116–128. doi:10.3109/14992020903405987

McDermott, H. J. (2004). Music perception with cochlear implants: a review. *Trends Amplif.* 8, 49–82. doi:10.1177/108471380400800203

McDermott, H. J., and Looi, V. (2004). Perception of complex signals, including musical sounds, with cochlear implants. *Int. Congr. Ser.* 1273, 201–204. doi:10.1016/j.ics.2004.08.034

Moore, D. R., and Shannon, R. V. (2009). Beyond cochlear implants: awakening the deafened brain. *Nat. Neurosci.* 12, 686–691. doi:10.1038/nn.2326

Näätänen, R., Paavilainen, P., Rinne, T., and Alho, K. (2007). The mismatch negativity (MMN) in basic research of central auditory processing: a review. *Neurophysiol. Clin.* 118, 2544–2590. doi:10.1016/j.clinph.2007.04.026

Näätänen, R., Tervaniemi, M., Sussman, E., Paavilainen, P., and Winkler, I. (2001). Primitive intelligence" in the auditory cortex. *Trends Neurosci.* 24, 283–288. doi:10.1016/S0166-2236(00)01790-2

North, A. C., Hargreaves, D. J., and O'Neill, S. A. (2000). The importance of music to adolescents. *Br. J. Educ. Psychol.* 70, 255–272. doi:10.1348/000709900158083

Olszewski, C., Gfeller, K., Froman, R., Stordahl, J., and Tomblin, B. (2005). Familiar melody recognition by children and adults using cochlear implants and normal hearing children. *Cochlear. Implants. Int.* 6, 123–140. doi:10.1002/cii.5

Overy, K. (2003). Dyslexia and music. From timing deficits to musical intervention. *Ann. N. Y. Acad. Sci.* 999, 497–505. doi:10.1196/annals.1284.060

Overy, K., Nicolson, R. I., Fawcett, A. J., and Clarke, E. F. (2003). Dyslexia and music: measuring musical timing skills. *Dyslexia* 9, 18–36. doi:10.1002/dys.233

Pantev, C., Dinnesen, A., Ross, B., Wollbrink, A., and Knief, A. (2006). Dynamics of auditory plasticity after cochlear implantation: a longitudinal study. *Cereb. Cortex* 16, 31–36. doi:10.1093/cercor/bhi081

Parbery-Clark, A., Skoe, E., and Kraus, N. (2009). Musical experience limits the degradative effects of background noise on the neural processing of sound. *J. Neurosci.* 29, 14100–14107. doi:10.1523/JNEUROSCI.3256-09.2009

Paukkunen, A. K. (2011). The effect of measurement error on the test-retest reliability of repeated mismatch negativity measurements. *Neurophysiol. Clin.* 122, 2195–2202. doi:10.1016/j.clinph.2011.04.004

Pedersen, E. R., and Juhl, P. M. L. (2013). User-operated speech in noise test: Implementation and comparison with a traditional test. *Int. J. Audiol.* 53, 336–344. doi:10.3109/14992027.2013.860486

Petersen, B., Gjedde, A., Wallentin, M., and Vuust, P. (2013a). Cortical plasticity after cochlear implantation. *Neural Plast.* 2013:318521. doi:10.1155/2013/318521

Petersen, B., Hansen, M., Derdau, S., Ovesen, T., and Vuust, P. (2013b). *Aspects of Music With Cochlear Implants – Music Listening Habits and Appreciation in Danish Cochlear Implant Users.* Ballerup: The Danavox Jubilee Foundation. Presented at ISAAR, 2013.

Petersen, B., Hansen, R. H., Beyer, K., Mortensen, M. V., and Vuust, P. (2011). Music for little digital ears – music training with preschool children using cochlear implants. *Int. J. Pediatr. Otorhinolaryngol.* 75, 66. doi:10.1016/S0165-5876(11)70339-1

Petersen, B., Mortensen, M. V., Hansen, M., and Vuust, P. (2012). Singing in the key of life: a study on effects of musical ear training after cochlear implantation. *Psychomusicology* 22, 134–151. doi:10.1111/j.1749-6632.2009.04796.x

Pressnitzer, D., Bestel, J., and Fraysse, B. (2005). Music to electric ears: pitch and timbre perception by cochlear implant patients. *Ann. N. Y. Acad. Sci.* 1060, 343–345. doi:10.1196/annals.1360.050

Qin, M. K., and Oxenham, A. J. (2003). Effects of simulated cochlear-implant processing on speech reception in fluctuating maskers. *J. Acoust. Soc. Am.* 114, 446–454. doi:10.1121/1.1579009

Rosenmeier, S. L., and Møller Hansen, N.-H. (2013). *CI-unges trivsel og uddannelse.* Survey Report. Copenhagen: Rädgivende Sociologer Aps. [In Danish].

Sandmann, P., Eichele, T., Buechler, M., Debener, S., Jancke, L., Dillier, N., et al. (2009). Evaluation of evoked potentials to dyadic tones after cochlear implantation. *Brain* 132, 1967–1979. doi:10.1093/brain/awp034

Sandmann, P., Kegel, A., Eichele, T., Dillier, N., Lai, W., Bendixen, A., et al. (2010). Neurophysiological evidence of impaired musical sound perception in cochlear-implant users. *Neurophysiol. Clin.* 121, 2070–2082. doi:10.1016/j.clinph.2010.04.032

Sandmann, P., Plotz, K., Hauthal, N., De Vos, M., Schönfeld, R., and Debener, S. (2014). Rapid bilateral improvement in auditory cortex activity in postlingually deafened adults following cochlear implantation. *Clin. Neurophysiol.* doi:10.1016/j.clinph.2014.06.029

Sharma, A. (2006). Central auditory development in children with cochlear implants: clinical implications. *Adv. Otorhinolaryngol.* 64, 66–88.

Sharma, A., Dorman, M. F., and Kral, A. (2005). The influence of a sensitive period on central auditory development in children with unilateral and bilateral cochlear implants. *Hear. Res.* 203, 134–143. doi:10.1016/j.heares.2004.12.010

Sharma, A., Dorman, M. F., and Spahr, A. J. (2002a). Rapid development of cortical auditory evoked potentials after early cochlear implantation. *Neuroreport* 13, 1365–1368. doi:10.1097/00001756-200207190-00030

Sharma, A., Dorman, M. F., and Spahr, A. J. (2002b). A sensitive period for the development of the central auditory system in children with cochlear implants: implications for age of implantation. *Ear Hear.* 23, 532–539. doi:10.1097/00003446-200212000-00004

Spitzer, J. B., Mancuso, D., and Cheng, M. Y. (2008). Development of a clinical test of musical perception: appreciation of music in cochlear implantees (AMICI). *J. Am. Acad. Audiol.* 19, 56–81. doi:10.3766/jaaa.19.1.6

Timm, L., Agrawal, D., Viola, C., Sandmann, P., Debener, S., Buchner, A., et al. (2012). Temporal feature perception in cochlear implant users. *PLoS ONE* 7:e45375. doi:10.1371/journal.pone.0045375

Timm, L., Vuust, P., Brattico, E., Agrawal, D., Debener, S., Büchner, A., et al. (2014). Residual neural processing of musical sound features in adult cochlear implant users. *Front. Hum. Neurosci.* 8:181. doi:10.3389/fnhum.2014.00181

Torppa, R., Huotilainen, M., Leminen, M., Lipsanen, J., and Tervaniemi, M. (2014). Interplay between singing and cortical processing of music: a longitudinal study in children with cochlear implants. *Front. Psychol.* 5:1389. doi:10.3389/fpsyg.2014.01389

Torppa, R., Salo, E., Makkonen, T., Loimo, H., Pykäläinen, J., Lipsanen, J., et al. (2012). Cortical processing of musical sounds in children with cochlear implants. *Neurophysiol. Clin.* 123, 1966–1979. doi:10.1016/j.clinph.2012.03.008

Veekmans, K., Ressel, L., Mueller, J., Vischer, M., and Brockmeier, S. J. (2009). Comparison of music perception in bilateral and unilateral cochlear implant users and normal-hearing subjects. *Audiol. Neurotol.* 14, 315–326. doi:10.1159/000212111

Viola, F. C., Thorne, J., Edmonds, B., Schneider, T., Eichele, T., and Debener, S. (2009). Semi-automatic identification of independent components representing EEG artifact. *Clin. Neurophysiol.* 120, 868–877. doi:10.1016/j.clinph.2009.01.015

Viola, F. C., Thorne, J. D., Bleeck, S., Eyles, J., and Debener, S. (2011). Uncovering auditory evoked potentials from cochlear implant users with independent component analysis. *Psychophysiology* 48, 1470–1480. doi:10.1111/j.1469-8986.2011.01224.x

Vongphoe, M., and Zeng, F. G. (2005). Speaker recognition with temporal cues in acoustic and electric hearing. *J Acoust. Soc. Am.* 118, 1055–1061. doi:10.1121/1.1944507

Vuust, P., Brattico, E., Glerean, E., Seppanen, M., Pakarinen, S., Tervaniemi, M., et al. (2011). New fast mismatch negativity paradigm for determining the neural prerequisites for musical ability. *Cortex* 47, 1091–1098. doi:10.1016/j.cortex.2011.04.026

Wagener, K. F., Josvassen, J. L. F. A. U., Ardenkjaer, R., and Ardenkjaer, R. (2003). Design, optimization and evaluation of a Danish sentence test in noise. *Int. J. Audiol.* 42, 10–17. doi:10.3109/14992020309056080

Won, J. H., Drennan, W. R., Kang, R. S., and Rubinstein, J. T. (2010). Psychoacoustic abilities associated with music perception in cochlear implant users. *Ear Hear.* 31, 796–805. doi:10.1097/AUD.0b013e3181e8b7bd

Wright, R., and Uchanski, R. M. (2012). Music perception and appraisal: cochlear implant users and simulated cochlear implant listening. *J. Am. Acad. Audiol.* 23, 350–365. doi:10.3766/jaaa.23.5.6

Zhang, F. (2011). Mismatch negativity and adaptation measures of the late auditory evoked potential in cochlear implant users. *Hear. Res.* 275, 17–29. doi:10.1016/j.heares.2010.11.007

3

Music lessons improve auditory perceptual and cognitive performance in deaf children

Françoise Rochette[1]*, Aline Moussard[2] and Emmanuel Bigand[1]

[1] *Laboratoire d'Etude de l'Apprentissage et du Développement (LEAD – CNRS 5022), Université de Bourgogne, Dijon, France*
[2] *Rotman Research Institute, Baycrest, University of Toronto, Toronto, ON, Canada*

***Correspondence:**
Françoise Rochette, Laboratoire d'Etude de l'Apprentissage et du Développement (LEAD – CNRS 5022), Université de Bourgogne, Pôle AAFE, Esplanade Erasme. BP 26513, Dijon Cedex 21065, France
e-mail: francoise.rochette@u-bourgogne.fr

Despite advanced technologies in auditory rehabilitation of profound deafness, deaf children often exhibit delayed cognitive and linguistic development and auditory training remains a crucial element of their education. In the present cross-sectional study, we assess whether music would be a relevant tool for deaf children rehabilitation. In normal-hearing children, music lessons have been shown to improve cognitive and linguistic-related abilities, such as phonetic discrimination and reading. We compared auditory perception, auditory cognition, and phonetic discrimination between 14 profoundly deaf children who completed weekly music lessons for a period of 1.5–4 years and 14 deaf children who did not receive musical instruction. Children were assessed on perceptual and cognitive auditory tasks using environmental sounds: discrimination, identification, auditory scene analysis, auditory working memory. Transfer to the linguistic domain was tested with a phonetic discrimination task. Musically trained children showed better performance in auditory scene analysis, auditory working memory and phonetic discrimination tasks, and multiple regressions showed that success on these tasks was at least partly driven by music lessons. We propose that musical education contributes to development of general processes such as auditory attention and perception, which, in turn, facilitate auditory-related cognitive and linguistic processes.

Keywords: congenitally deaf children, music training, auditory working memory, phonetic discrimination, auditory perception

INTRODUCTION

One of every 800 children in France is born with congenital deafness (Chen et al., 2007). The technological development of devices for the restoration of the auditory function is progressing. Hearing aids optimize residual auditory capacities, especially at low and medium frequencies, though they remain relatively ineffective for the perception of higher frequencies. Cochlear implants are sensory aids that convert auditory information into electrical impulses transmitted to the auditory nerve through multiple stimulating electrodes (currently between 16 and 22) located throughout the cochlea. Despite low spectral resolution, reduced temporal fine-grained structure, and reduced dynamic range due to the number of electrodes (Zeng et al., 2008 for a review), those receiving pediatric cochlear implants develop higher speech and language outcomes than non-implanted peers. Hereafter in this text, the term "deaf children" will refer to both hearing aid and cochlear implant pediatric users suffering from pre-lingually profound deafness (i.e., without auditory knowledge prior to the use of their devices).

Sensory deprivation has long-lasting repercussions on brain development and behavioral outcomes (Pisoni et al., 2008; Kral, 2013). In deaf children, the duration of deafness (i.e., from birth to auditory rehabilitation) is negatively correlated with neural development (Kral, 2013), as well as perceptual, linguistic, and cognitive abilities (Geers et al., 2007; Pisoni et al., 2008; Peterson et al., 2010; Havy et al., 2013). As the development and organization of cortical auditory pathways critically depends on sensory experience (Kral et al., 2000; Sharma et al., 2002; Kral and Eggermont, 2007), the restoration of auditory function with technical devices is alone insufficient for the children to "hear" properly. Deaf children must learn to interpret auditory signals to build meaningful sound representations and listening strategies. This learning often has to be supported by auditory training therapies (Wu et al., 2007). In a previous study (Rochette and Bigand, 2009), we trained a small sample of severe to profoundly deaf children through interactive auditory games targeting four main auditory-related processes such as discrimination and identification of sounds, auditory scene analysis, and auditory working memory. After 20 half-hour weekly training sessions, these children showed a significant improvement in each of the trained tasks, as well as transfer of benefits to linguistic sound perception (phonetic discrimination), which had not been trained.

Music may constitute a powerful stimulus to train perceptive and auditory-related skills in deaf children. Musical activity involves a broad brain network and engages various perceptual and cognitive processes. Music practice produces neuroanatomical and neurofunctional modifications in expert musicians, but also after short periods of practice in adults and children (see

Wan and Schlaug, 2010 for a review). Trainor et al. (2003) tested 4–5 years-old normal-hearing children in an EEG paradigm after 1 year of musical training with the Suzuki method to assess changes in activation patterns in response to auditory stimuli (event related potentials, ERPs). After training, children showed faster development of the auditory brain responses (enhanced early ERP components P1, N1, and P2) compared to non-musically trained matched children (see also Hyde et al., 2009 for a similar study using fMRI). Interestingly, music practice also enhances functions that are seemingly unrelated to the musical activity (e.g., Moreno, 2009). In normal-hearing children, positive effects of musical training have been observed in non-musical abilities including visuo-spatial skills (Bilhartz et al., 1999), IQ (Schellenberg, 2004; Moreno et al., 2011), phonetic discrimination (Anvari et al., 2002; Degé and Schwarzer, 2011; Chobert et al., 2012), reading abilities (Anvari et al., 2002; Moreno et al., 2009), and verbal memory (Nutley et al., 2014). In particular, the link between music and language abilities and their overlapping processes is of great interest. Music and language have common characteristics: both systems are composed of discrete elements (phonemes and notes), organized into temporal and hierarchical structures (words and chords), rely on auditory processing of complex acoustical elements and convey rich meanings (Patel, 2008). Studies have shown large overlap in brain regions involved in the processing of music and language at the cortical (Tillmann et al., 2006; Koelsch et al., 2009) and subcortical (Strait and Kraus, 2014) levels. These commonalities, in both processes and brain networks, may underlie transfer effects from one domain to another in the normal population. Thus, training with one type of material (e.g., music) should improve their efficiency to process other types of stimuli (e.g., language; see Besson et al., 2011; Kühnis et al., 2013).

To date, only a few studies have examined the effects of musical training in hearing impaired populations. After training adults for 6 months, Petersen et al. (2012) showed improvement in perception of musical acoustic features, such as timbre, melodic contour, and rhythm, as well as in perception of emotional prosody. In children, Chen et al. (2010) compared pitch interval recognition in 27 children with cochlear implants (mean age = 6.7 years). Thirteen of these children were musically trained. The perception of musical sounds was significantly better in musically trained children and correlated with the duration of musical training. This suggests that training induced experience-dependent changes in the auditory pathway. Moreover, if musical training improves general auditory perception, then it is likely that the perception of non-music sounds, such as linguistic stimuli, would also improve. Only two published studies have investigated the effect of music training on transfer to the linguistic domain in children (Yucel et al., 2009; Torppa et al., 2014). In the first (Yucel et al., 2009), 18 cochlear-implanted children were enrolled in a training program based on auditory–verbal learning. In addition to this program, nine children received musical stimulation at home from their parents. Children were tested at 1, 3, 6, 9, 12, and 24 months on phonetic discrimination, word identification, comprehension of simple auditory instructions, and sentence repetition. The music group showed greater improvement at 3 months for a task requiring the comprehension of auditory instructions, suggesting a limited effect of music training on children's auditory perception and cognition. However, several methodological issues may have attenuated possible gains from musical training, including potential differences in the group demographics, ceiling effects in the tasks, and limitations due to parent-administered training. Moreover, the musical training was limited to pitch or rhythm discrimination in one- or two-note items. In the second such study (Torppa et al., 2014), musically trained deaf children showed improved perception of prosodic cues in words, as well as improved working memory (digit span). However, the type of music training (instrumental practice, singing, or dance) and its duration/frequency was heterogeneous and the sample of musically trained children was small ($N = 8$). Taken together, these data suggest that there is a clear need for additional studies to examine the effects of musical training on deaf children, particularly studies that address transfer to non-music abilities.

The goal of the present study was to assess whether music lessons, given in a small group setting and led by a professional music teacher, affect deaf children's abilities in auditory perception, auditory cognition, and linguistic domains. In a cross-sectional design, we compared 14 profoundly deaf children who completed weekly music lessons for a period of 1.5–4 years and 14 deaf children who did not receive music lessons. Auditory perception (discrimination and identification tasks) was tested with environmental sounds, as well as linguistic sounds (phonetic discrimination task). Higher level of auditory processing (auditory scene analysis) and auditory working memory were also assessed using environmental sounds. As music is a rich acoustic stimulus and because of shared general mechanisms for auditory perception across domains, we hypothesized that music training would improve auditory-related performance in non-music domains, specifically an improvement in perceptual tasks using environmental and linguistic sounds, as well as in auditory scene analysis. As a result of better perception and because music training involves many cognitive processes including auditory attention and working memory, we also expected enhanced performance in higher level of auditory-related cognitive abilities such as auditory working memory.

MATERIALS AND METHODS

PARTICIPANTS

Twenty-eight profoundly deaf children were recruited through the CEOP institute (Centre Experimental Orthophonique et Pédagogique de Paris, a specialized institute, which offers adapted schooling and therapies for children with severe and profound hearing impairment). Fourteen children (mean age = 8.6 years, SD = 1), enrolled full-time at the institute, followed weekly 1-h music lessons for 2.6 years on average (i.e., since their admission to the institute; SD = 0.80). The other 14 participants (mean age = 7.9 years, SD = 1.4) did not receive musical instruction. They were enrolled in the institute at 50% and followed a classic schooling program (mainstream) during the other 50%. All 28 children generally received significant auditory stimulation from their parents and from the school as they were orally educated (i.e., teaching based on auditory strategies). Children were classified as profoundly deaf (highest degree of deafness), with an unaided bilateral hearing loss of >91 dB. They were either using hearing

Table 1 | Demographic data of participants (HA, hearing aid; CI, cochlear implant).

Participants	Sex	Age in months (years)	Age at correction in months	Duration of use of the device in months	Threshold 2000 Hz <50 dB	Threshold 4000 Hz <50 dB	Threshold 8000 Hz <50 dB	Type of device	Brand and processor of CI
MUSIC GROUP									
S1	M	114 (9.5)	60	54	Yes	No	No	HA	
S2	F	113 (9.4)	59	54	Yes	No	No	HA	
S3	F	119 (9.9)	18	101	Yes	Yes	Yes	CI + HA	Nucleus CP 810
S4	M	111 (9.3)	10	101	Yes	Yes	No	HA	
S5	M	104 (8.7)	39	65	Yes	No	No	HA	
S6	F	112 (9.3)	18	94	No	No	No	HA	
S7	M	97 (8.1)	10	87	Yes	Yes	Yes	CI + HA	Nucleus freedom
S8	F	84 (7)	18	66	Yes	Yes	Yes	CI + HA	Nucleus CP 810
S9	F	99 (8.3)	24	75	Yes	Yes	Yes	CI + HA	Nucleus CP 810
S10	M	108 (9)	4	104	Yes	No	No	HA	
S11	F	95 (7.9)	14	81	Yes	Yes	Yes	CI + HA	Bionics harmony
S12	F	87 (7.3)	16	71	Yes	Yes	Yes	CI + HA	Nucleus freedom
S13	F	84 (7)	7	77	Yes	No	No	HA	
S14	M	112 (9.3)	24	88	Yes	No	No	HA	
Mean		102.8 (8.6)	22.93	79.86					
SD		11.8 (1.0)	17.72	16.77					
CONTROL GROUP									
S15	M	88 (7.3)	28	60	Yes	Yes	No	HA	
S16	M	112 (9.3)	18	94	Yes	Yes	Yes	CI + HA	Nucleus freedom
S17	F	83 (6.9)	22	61	Yes	Yes	No	HA	
S18	F	75 (6.3)	41	4	Yes	Yes	Yes	CI + HA	Medel Sonata
S19	F	95 (7.9)	17	78	Yes	Yes	No	HA	
S20	M	94 (7.8)	11	83	Yes	Yes	No	HA	
S21	M	78 (6.5)	18	60	Yes	Yes	Yes	CI + HA	Nucleus CP 810
S22	F	91 (7.6)	26	65	Yes	No	No	HA	
S23	M	79 (6.6)	7	72	Yes	Yes	No	HA	
S24	F	123 (10.3)	6	117	Yes	Yes	Yes	CI + HA	Nucleus CP 810
S25	M	77 (6.4)	16	61	Yes	Yes	Yes	CI + HA	Nucleus freedom
S26	M	90 (7.5)	20	70	Yes	Yes	Yes	CI + HA	Nucleus CP 810
S27	F	116 (9.7)	19	97	Yes	Yes	No	HA	
S28	F	124 (10.3)	18	106	Yes	Yes	Yes	CI + HA	Nucleus CP 810
Mean		94.6 (7.9)	19.07	73.43					
SD		17.2 (1.4)	8.84	27.21					

Duration of use of the device for HA + CI corresponds to the duration of utilization of CI.

aids alone or hearing aids in conjunction with cochlear implants[1]. Given the difficulty of recruiting a large and homogeneous sample of deaf children, we chose to mix children with these different types of auditory device, making sure that the type of device was equally represented in both groups.

T-test for independent samples did not revealed significant differences between groups for age [$t(26) = 1.46$, $p = 0.16$], age at correction [$t(26) = 0.73$, $p = 0.47$], duration of utilization of the device [$t(26) = 0.75$, $p = 0.46$], and type of correction [hearing aids versus cochlear implants, $t(26) = -0.36$, $p = 0.71$]. Perfect matching between experimental and control groups is extremely difficult when working with profoundly deaf children. Although the experimental group was slightly (but not significantly) older than the control group, we prioritized matching children in terms of age of hearing correction and duration of utilization of the device (i.e., length of auditory experience), and we limited our population to orally educated children only, these factors being strongly associated with the outcome of auditory abilities and language development in deaf children.

As perception of vowels relies on the perceptive analysis of formants frequencies from 2000 Hz, pure-tone detection at 50 dB (with hearing devices) was assessed for 2000, 4000, and 8000 Hz. **Table 1** presents the participant details (sex, chronological age,

[1] French criteria for pediatric cochlear implantation in pre-lingually deaf children are: profound or total deafness (loss of >91 dB), perceptive thresholds at 2000 and 4000 Hz >60 dB after 3–6 months of regular bearing of devices, no pathologies of middle and external ears, no morphological disease of the cochlea (as measured by a complete radiological assessment), and no neurological disease (as measured by magnetic resonance imaging).

age at correction, duration of hearing device usage, perceptual thresholds, and the type of hearing device).

The music lessons consisted of the standard music courses delivered by the CEOP institute. They were performed by a music teacher and completed in small groups of five or six children. The training consisted of five progressive levels of difficulty, which increased after about 4 months of training at a given level. The first level focused on the binding between motor activities and auditory perception. Children used their voice and interacted with real instruments (drums, flutes, maracas, whistles, bells, keyboard, cymbales, and ocarinas) to discover what and how different sounds could be produced. The goal of this level was to explore the many sounds that could emanate from the voice or the various musical instruments by interacting with them in any way the children could imagine. This served to train invariant recognition of the instrument sounds. The second level consisted of the children engaging in sensorimotor activities. The children were encouraged to move their bodies along with the sounds they heard. They could, for example, sway to the rhythm of the music, shift from one foot to the other, rock on their chair. They were instructed to synchronize their movements to the rhythm of the music. Alternatively, a child performed a rhythmical movement with an instrument and their classmate had to adapt their musical activity to this movement. The third level consisted of exercises involving memory processes. For example, a child, hidden behind a folding screen, played a sequence of three or four notes with different instruments. The other children had to reproduce the same sequence by choosing the right instruments amongst several options. The fourth level consisted of analyzing the emotional value of musical pieces and the children's feelings toward those pieces of music. The fifth level consisted of the children playing simple self-written pieces of music together. For example, a child chose a drum and decided to play it on the third and fourth beat of the measure while another child chose a bell and decided to play it on the second and fourth beat. The teacher sets the basic rhythm by playing each of the four beats of the measure on a drum for a period of time. The children played the music for two or three measures and repeated this play in a loop. When a child made a mistake, the others were invited to identify the problem.

PROCEDURE

The auditory performance of children was assessed with the "Sound in Hands" apparatus (see **Figure 1**; Rochette and Bigand, 2009), which is comprised of two speakers (70 cm apart and each 70 cm from the participant), a response platform, and a computer for sound generation. Sound level was adjusted to be comfortable for the children.

The Sound in Hands apparatus uses interactive games with a variety of environmental sounds to test four main operations involved in auditory perception and cognition (McAdams and Bigand, 1993): discrimination, identification, auditory scene analysis, and auditory working memory. All the tasks were carried out in a single session for a total duration of 30 min on average. Before each of the four tasks, children were invited to interact with the response platform used for the task, to familiarize themselves with its functioning (e.g., which sounds could be produced and how). The five tasks are further described below.

FIGURE 1 | Illustration of the "Sound in Hands" platform dressed for the identification task.

Identification and discrimination tasks evaluated the quality of the analysis of micro- and macro-temporal properties of relevant features of the signal. The discrimination task was done with the "magic hexagon" pierced by 12 holes (**Figure 1**). The children heard a continuous sound stream (i.e., the sound of a bulldozer). Five out of the 12 holes were magnetized. The introduction of a magnetic pawn (the "magic pawn") in the magnetized holes modified the continuous auditory stream (to the sound of a maneuvering truck) whereas the introduction of the magic pawn in the not magnetized holes did not modify the auditory stream. A pile of blue and white pawns was at the child's disposal. If a modification was perceived, the child had to fill the hole with a blue pawn. Conversely, if no modification was perceived, the child had to fill the hole with a white one. One point was given for each correct answer (maximum score = 12 points).

The identification task was executed with the keyboard. Each key produced an environmental sound, which was represented by a picture on the key (**Figure 1**). The child was presented with sounds in a randomized order and had to reproduce each sound (e.g., plane, frog, thrush, moped, nightingale, cicada) by pushing the corresponding key on the keyboard. Two points were given for a correct answer on the first attempt, and one point for a correct answer on the second attempt (maximum score = 12 points).

The auditory scene analysis task examined the blending and segregation of an auditory signal (Bregman, 1990). The auditory scene analysis task was conducted with a pegboard in which the 24 holes are filled with white magnetic pawns. Two auditory streams were simultaneously produced (cat and horse). Removing a pawn could shut down one of the two streams. When a change was detected, the child had to fill the hole with a yellow pawn. If the signal was not modified, the child filled the hole with a red pawn. One point was given for each correct answer (maximum score = 24 points).

In the auditory working memory task, the experimenter generated a sequence of two sounds that the child had to reproduce by ear in the same order, using the keyboard. Pictures on the keys indicated the sound that each key produced (steps in the water, crow, tit, rain, sheep, and goat). To avoid a contamination of the memory task by a process of identification of the sounds, children were authorized to proceed by trial and error to find which keys corresponded to the sounds before they provided the correct sequence to the experimenter. When the child succeeded for two trials in a row, an element was added to the sequence, up to a maximum of five elements. Two points were given for a correct reproduction of the sequence. Only one point was given if the child needed a second presentation of the sequence (maximum score = 16 points).

In the phonological discrimination task, children were presented with pairs of mono- or bi-syllabic nonsense words and they were asked to judge whether the two items of each pair were identical or different. The task was composed of three subtests. The first subtest was composed of pairs of mono-syllabic non-words, where the two non-words could vary in vowel composition (oral versus nasal, as in /o/ versus /Õ/; or "weak" vowels, as /i/ versus /y/) in the discordant pairs. The second subtest held vowels constant within pairs and assessed the discrimination of word-initial voiced (e.g., /b/) versus voiceless (e.g., /p/) consonants, again in mono-syllabic non-words. In the third subtest, discordant pairs were formed by placing voiced or voiceless consonants in the middle or at the end of bi-syllabic words. One point was given for each correct answer (maximum score = 36 points).

During the tasks, children were not given any feedback about their accuracy. The scores obtained in each task were converted into percentage of correct answers. To evaluate the effects of music lessons on our different measures, scores were analyzed with a Group (2) by Tasks (5) Repeated Measures ANOVA. For the tasks in which a training effect was found, multiple regressions were used to evaluate the effect of covariates such as the duration of music lessons, chronological age, the duration of deafness, the length of device use (length of auditory experience), perceptual threshold, and the type of device they use (cochlear implant versus hearing aids).

RESULTS

The results are presented in **Figure 2**. A main effect of Group [$F(1, 26) = 14.55$, $p < 0.001$, partial eta-squared $\eta^2 = 0.36$] and an interaction between Group and Tasks [$F(4, 104) = 43.12$, $p < 0.001$] were found. Musically trained children obtained significantly higher scores in the auditory scene analysis task [$F(1, 26) = 6.92$, $p < 0.05$, $\eta^2 = 0.21$], in the phonetic discrimination task [$F(1, 26) = 6.74$, $p < 0.05$, $\eta^2 = 0.21$], and in the auditory working memory task [$F(1, 26) = 19.79$, $p < 0.001$, $\eta^2 = 0.43$]. Groups did not significantly differ in discrimination and identification tasks, despite a tendency for higher scores in the music group.

In order to evaluate the respective contribution of various factors, which may impact the children's task performance, multiple regressions were run for the tasks in which an effect of music training was found (i.e., auditory scene analysis, auditory working memory, and phonetic discrimination). The following factors, supposed to potentially influence task performance, were included in our regression model: music lessons (presence/absence), duration of music lessons (in months), chronological age (in months),

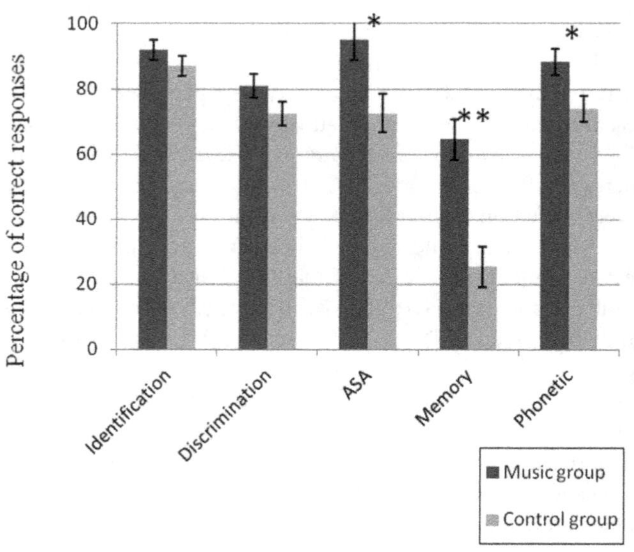

FIGURE 2 | Scores of auditory performance for the music and the control groups. Stars represent significant differences between groups: $*p < 0.05$, $**p < 0.01$. Errors bars represent one standard error.

duration of deafness (in months), length of device use (i.e., length of auditory experience; in months), perceptual threshold (yes/no), and type of device they use (cochlear implant/hearing aids). **Table 2** presents the significant factors contributing to task performance. For auditory scene analysis, the results of the regression indicated that these factors explained 67% of the variance of the children's scores. It was found that the presence of music lessons, the duration of music lessons, the age at correction (in favor of early corrected children), and the duration of use of the device (in favor of greater length of auditory experience) significantly predicted performance for auditory scene analysis. For the auditory working memory task, results of the regression showed that 60% of the variance was explained by our model. Performance for auditory working memory was significantly predicted by the presence of music lessons and the perceptual threshold at 4000 Hz (in favor of children that were able to hear 4000 Hz sounds at 50 dB). The percentage of variance explained for phonetic discrimination was only 27%, with the presence of music lessons as the only variable predicting scores.

Further correlations were performed to investigate the link between tasks using linguistic and non-linguistic sounds. Scores for phonetic discrimination were correlated with three of the tasks using environmental sounds: identification [$r(26) = 0.42$, $p < 0.05$], auditory scene analysis [$r(26) = 0.47$, $p < 0.05$], and auditory working memory [$r(26) = 0.51$, $p < 0.01$].

DISCUSSION

Despite advanced technology for the rehabilitation of hearing impairments, auditory training therapies remain crucial for children to learn to interpret auditory signals, create meaningful sound representation, and develop listening strategies. The goal of the present cross-sectional study was to assess the efficacy of music lessons to improve auditory perception and auditory cognition

Table 2 | Results from the multiple regressions including R^2, F, β, and t statistics.

Task	Music lessons (Yes/no)	Duration of music lessons (in months)	Age at correction (in months)	Duration of use of device (in months)	Threshold 4000 Hz (<50 dB)	Full Model
Auditory scene analysis	$t(22) = 3.37$, $\beta = 1.20^{**}$	$t(22) = 2.69$, $\beta = -1.07^{*}$	$t(22) = 2.88$, $\beta = 0.60^{**}$	$t(22) = 5.11$, $\beta = 0.98^{***}$		$R^2 = 0.67$, $F(5, 22) = 8.81^{***}$
Auditory working memory	$t(23) = 5.16$, $\beta = 0.83^{***}$				$t(23) = 2.39$, $\beta = 0.47^{*}$	$R^2 = 0.60$, $F(4, 23) = 8.57^{***}$
Phonological discrimination	$t(24) = 2.63$, $\beta = 0.52^{*}$					$R^2 = 0.27$, $F(3, 24) = 2.96$, $p = 0.053$

$^{*}p < 0.05$, $^{**}p < 0.01$, $^{***}p < 0.001$.

in deaf children. Four main processes of auditory cognition (discrimination, identification, auditory scene analysis, and auditory working memory) were evaluated using environmental sounds. Transfer to linguistic sounds was assessed using a phonetic discrimination task. Results showed that musically trained children performed significantly better than their non-musician counterparts for auditory scene analysis, auditory working memory, and phonetic discrimination. Moreover, multiple regressions revealed that music lessons was one of the main factors explaining children's performance for the auditory scene analysis and the auditory working memory tasks (though other variables contributed to the performance in these tasks, such as age at correction, duration of use of device, and perceptual thresholds). Interestingly, for the phonetic discrimination task, only music lessons accounted for group differences, strongly suggesting the impact of musical training on transfer to the linguistic domain.

Although we observed a trend for better performance in musically trained children, identification and discrimination tasks using environmental sounds did not differ between groups. This could be due, in part, to the fact that low-level of auditory perception is already intensively trained in deaf children through their regular therapies. For example, early stages of typical speech therapy require children to examine sounds parameters such as changes in frequency, tempo, duration, or timbre in stimuli that often include environmental sounds. This might explain the ceiling effect we observed in the identification task and might have hidden potential differences between groups in our two perceptive tasks using environmental sounds. However, when examining auditory perceptual abilities using linguistic sounds (phonological discrimination), we observed better performance for musically trained children compared to controls. This suggests that music training contributes to develop abilities at a perceptual level and allows children to create more efficient auditory representations of sounds. Moreover, even when including other factors that may contribute to performance on the linguistic task, only musical training significantly influenced performance. Rhythm exercises from the music curriculum may have contributed to this effect. Rhythm has been shown to be a crucial gateway for phonological representations (Leong et al., 2011; Rauscher and Hinton, 2011) and strong associations between poor perception of musical meter, reading, and phonological representations were found in dyslexic children (Huss et al., 2011). In a recent study using the child version of the Montreal Battery of Evaluation of Amusia (MBEA; Peretz et al., 2003), Hopyan et al. (2012) found that pediatric cochlear implant users performed significantly below the matched normal-hearing children in the rhythm subtest. The rhythm component of the music lessons may have contributed to the development of the deaf children's sensitivity to the rhythmic structure in speech which, in turn, may have allowed for the development of higher quality of phonological representations (Kotz and Schwartze, 2010).

Better performance in the musically trained children in the auditory scene analysis task suggests that higher levels of auditory perception such as stream segregation and the representation of auditory scenes are enhanced by music training. These results may be due to the acoustic richness of musical training sessions and the graded nature of the training (i.e., increased task difficulty at each stage). For example, in the exercises in which children created musical pieces, children developed their ability to analyze auditory streams composed of at least two sources. This may have contributed to enhanced listening strategies. The current finding is consistent with previous studies showing that abilities related to auditory scene analysis, such as speech in noise perception, which is impaired in deaf children (Kral and Sharma, 2012), can be enhanced with auditory training therapies (Strait and Kraus, 2014). Interestingly, in the normal-hearing adults, Skoe and Kraus (2012) showed that a limited period of music practice in childhood (3 years on average) influences how the brain further encodes and processes sounds later in life. Thus, in deaf children, it is possible that listening strategies taught at a young age would have a lifelong impact, if the children keep using these strategies beyond the context of musical lessons.

There are two potential interpretations for the results from the auditory working memory performance, in which musically trained children show better performance than controls. First, enhanced auditory representation and listening strategies, as evident by better performance in phonological discrimination and auditory scene analysis by the musically trained children, may have facilitated encoding and storage in working memory. Some studies highlighted a causal link between poor encoding of sounds and difficulties in working memory in deaf children (Pisoni and Cleary, 2003; Pisoni et al., 2011; Nittrouer et al., 2013). This is consistent with the observation of enhanced auditory (but not necessarily visual) working memory in normal-hearing children and adults after musical practice, compared to matched non-musician, (in children: Moreno et al., 2011; Strait et al., 2012; in adults: Berti et al., 2006; Hansen et al., 2013; Parbery-Clark et al., 2009). Alternatively, the music exercises relied on working memory for an important part and this might have enhanced general working memory ability, beyond auditory-specific working memory (see George and Coch, 2011 for enhanced visuo-spatial memory in normal hearing adult musicians). This would be consistent with studies showing that music training improves various high level cognitive processes in normal-hearing children (e.g., Schellenberg, 2004). Future studies could test whether or not musical training could generally improve working memory processes of deaf children in a non-auditory context.

Surprisingly, we did not found any effect of type of device or amodal versus bimodal aid (as CI users also wore HA in the contralateral ear). Due to limited spectral resolution and reduced temporal fine-grained structure in cochlear implants (Kong et al., 2005; Zeng et al., 2008), encoding pitch information remains a challenge (McDermott, 2004; Looi et al., 2008) and a hearing aid in the non-implanted ear could have positively influenced music processing and thus the gain from music training (Kong et al., 2005). Further studies will explore interactions between music training and type of device to determine which profiles of children would benefit most from the training.

The main limitation of the study is the cross-sectional nature of the study design, which does not allow to draw causal conclusions regarding musical training as the present results could be due, at least in part, to pre-existing differences between groups or confounding factors (e.g., perceptive threshold levels, chronological age). Although our multiple regression analysis suggested music factor as an influential factor even after accounting for other possible confounds, it is possible that other factors not examined presently could underlie the group differences reported here. In addition, schooling programs would differ between the two groups for 50% of their time, which could also have influenced the children's performance. Longitudinal studies using a randomized controlled trial design and blind testers are necessary to further replicate these findings. Further study would also need to investigate effects of training at the neural level. Using a deviant detection task (tone, duration, intensity, and timbre) in pediatric cochlear implant users that were not musically trained, Torppa et al. (2012) observed smaller amplitudes for the P1, MMN, and P3a components as well as longer latency of the MMN than in matched normal hearing children. Further studies will investigate if music training could improve these neural indices in deaf children.

As a final note, it is important to mention that a great advantage of music is to be an enjoyable stimulus. Contrary to the post-lingually cochlear-implanted adults who report little appreciation in listening to music due to the spectral limitation of the device and the comparison with their prior musical knowledge (McDermott, 2004; Looi et al., 2008), deaf children show interest and pleasure in listening to music (Nakata et al., 2005). They appreciate activities involving music such as listening to music, dancing, singing, or instrumental practice (Gfeller et al., 1999). As in normal-hearing children, music has the power to modify their mood (Hopyan-Misakyan et al., 2009). Moreover, motivation and enjoyment have been shown to improve learning effects and to boost brain plasticity (Sutoo and Akiyama, 2004). Thus, while clinical rehabilitation with children remains a challenge due to lack of engaging training program and difficulty to keep children's attention and motivation, music could represent a highly effective rehabilitation tool (Bruner, 1960; Kim, 2013).

To conclude, this study provides evidence that music may constitute a relevant tool for deaf children rehabilitation. Music lessons promote improved auditory perception and the development of finer sound representations and listening strategies. Moreover, improvements in these processes appear to have downstream effects on higher-order auditory cognition (i.e., auditory working memory). Interestingly, these results provide support for cross-domain transfer into the linguistic domain. Therefore, musical training may be an interesting and useful vehicle for enhancing the basic linguistic processes that are necessary for improving higher-order linguistic processes (i.e., vocabulary and reading abilities).

ACKNOWLEDGMENTS

We wish to thank the CEOP Institute for children recruitment and above all, the children and their parents for their implication in the study. We thank Dr. Melissa Pangelinan and Dr. Patrick Bermudez for their insightful comments on the manuscript.

REFERENCES

Anvari, S. H., Trainor, L. J., Woodside, J., and Levy, B. A. (2002). Relations among musical skills, phonological processing, and early reading ability in preschool children. *J. Exp. Child Psychol.* 83, 111–130. doi:10.1016/S0022-0965(02)00124-8

Berti, S., Münzer, S., Schröger, E., and Pechmann, T. (2006). Different interference effects in musicians and a control group. *Exp. Psychol.* 53, 111–116. doi:10.1027/1618-3169.53.2.111

Besson, M., Chobert, J., and Marie, C. (2011). Transfer of training between music and speech: common processing, attention and memory. *Front. Psychol.* 2:94. doi:10.3389/fpsyg.2011.00094

Bilhartz, T. D., Bruhn, R. A., and Olson, J. E. (1999). The effect of early music training on child cognitive development. *J. Appl. Dev. Psychol.* 20, 615–636. doi:10.1016/S0193-3973(99)00033-7

Bregman, A. S. (1990). *Auditory Scene Analysis: The Perceptual Organization of Sound.* Cambridge, MA: MIT Press.

Bruner, J. (ed.) (1960). *The Process of Education.* Cambridge, MA: Harvard University Press.

Chen, J. K.-C., Chuang, A. Y. C., McMahon, C., Hsieh, T.-H., and Li, L. P.-H. (2010). Music training improves pitch perception in prelingually deafened children with cochlear implants. *Pediatrics* 125, 793–800. doi:10.1542/peds.2008-3620

Chen, S. H., Liu, H., Xu, Y., and Larson, C. R. (2007). Voice F0 responses to pitch-shifted voice feedback during English speech. *J. Acoust. Soc. Am.* 121, 1157–1163. doi:10.1121/1.2404624

Chobert, J., François, C., Velay, J.-L., and Besson, M. (2012). Twelve months of active musical training in 8- to 10-year-old children enhances the preattentive processing of syllabic duration and voice onset time. *Cereb. Cortex* 24, 956–967. doi:10.1093/cercor/bhs377

Degé, F., and Schwarzer, G. (2011). The effect of a music program on phonological awareness in preschoolers. *Front. Psychol.* 2:124. doi:10.3389/fpsyg.2011.00124

Geers, A. E., Nicholas, J. G., and Moog, J. S. (2007). Estimating the influence of cochlear implantation on language development in children. *Audiol. Med.* 5, 262–273. doi:10.1080/16513860701659404

George, E. M., and Coch, D. (2011). Music training and working memory: an ERP study. *Neuropsychologia* 49, 1083–1094. doi:10.1016/j.neuropsychologia.2011.02.001

Gfeller, K., Witt, S., Spencer, L., Stordhal, J., and Tomblin, B. (1999). Musical involvement and enjoyment of children who use cochlear implants. *Volta Rev.* 100, 213–233.

Hansen, M., Wallentin, M., and Vuust, P. (2013). Working memory and musical competence of musicians and non-musicians. *Psychol. Music* 41, 779–793. doi:10.1177/0305735612452186

Havy, M., Nazzi, T., and Bertoncini, J. (2013). Phonetic processing during the acquisition of new words in 3-to-6 year-old-French-speaking deaf children with cochlear implants. *J. Commun. Disord.* 46, 181–192. doi:10.1016/j.jcomdis.2012.12.002

Hopyan, T., Peretz, I., Chan, L. P., Papsin, B. C., and Gordon, K. A. (2012). Children using cochlear implants capitalize on acoustical hearing for music perception. *Front. Psychol.* 3:425. doi:10.3389/fpsyg.2012.00425

Hopyan-Misakyan, T. M., Gordon, K. A., Dennis, M., and Papsin, B. C. (2009). Recognition of affective speech prosody and facial affect in deaf children with unilateral right cochlear implants. *Child Neuropsychol.* 15, 136–146. doi:10.1080/09297040802403682

Huss, M., Verney, J. P., Fosker, T., Mead, N., and Goswami, U. (2011). Music, rhythm, rise time perception and developmental dyslexia: perception of musical meter predicts reading and phonology. *Cortex* 47, 674–689. doi:10.1016/j.cortex.2010.07.010

Hyde, K. L., Lerch, J., Norton, A., Forgeard, M., Winner, E., Evans, A. C., et al. (2009). Musical training shapes structural brain development. *J. Neurosci.* 29, 3019–3025. doi:10.1523/JNEUROSCI.5118-08.2009

Kim, S.-I. (2013). Neuroscientific model of motivational process. *Front. Psychol.* 4:98. doi:10.3389/fpsyg.2013.00098

Koelsch, S., Schulze, K., Sammler, D., Fritz, T., Müller, K., and Gruber, O. (2009). Functional architecture of verbal and tonal working memory: an FMRI study. *Hum. Brain Mapp.* 30, 859–873. doi:10.1002/hbm.20550

Kong, Y. Y., Stickney, G. S., and Zeng, F. G. (2005). Speech and melody recognition in binaurally combined acoustic and electric hearing. *J. Acoust. Soc. Am.* 117, 1351–1361. doi:10.1121/1.1857526

Kotz, S. A., and Schwartze, M. (2010). Cortical speech processing unplugged: a timely subcortico-cortical framework. *Trends Cogn. Sci.* 14, 392–399. doi:10.1016/j.tics.2010.06.005

Kral, A. (2013). Auditory critical periods: a review from system's perspective. *Neuroscience* 247, 117–133. doi:10.1016/j.neuroscience.2013.05.021

Kral, A., and Eggermont, J. J. (2007). What's to lose and what's to learn: development under auditory deprivation, cochlear implants and limits of cortical plasticity. *Brain Res. Rev.* 56, 259–269. doi:10.1016/j.brainresrev.2007.07.021

Kral, A., Hartmann, R., Tillein, J., and Heide, S. (2000). Congenital auditory deprivation reduces synaptic activity within the auditory cortex in a layer-specific manner. *Cereb. Cortex* 10, 714–726. doi:10.1093/cercor/10.7.714

Kral, A., and Sharma, A. (2012). Developmental neuroplasticity after cochlear implantation. *Trends Neurosci.* 35, 111–122. doi:10.1016/j.tins.2011.09.004

Kühnis, J., Elmer, S., Meyer, M., and Jäncke, L. (2013). The encoding of vowels and temporal speech cues in the auditory cortex of professional musicians: an EEG study. *Neuropsychologia* 51, 1608–1618. doi:10.1016/j.neuropsychologia.2013.04.007

Leong, V., Hämäläinen, J., Soltész, F., and Goswami, U. (2011). Rise time perception and detection of syllable stress in adults with developmental dyslexia. *J. Mem. Lang.* 64, 59–73. doi:10.1016/j.jml.2010.09.003

Looi, V., McDermott, H., and McKay, C. (2008). Music perception of cochlear implant users compared with that of hearing aids users. *Ear Hear.* 29, 421–434. doi:10.1097/AUD.0b013e31816a0d0b

McAdams, S., and Bigand, E. (1993). *Thinking in Sound: The Cognitive Psychology of Human Audition.* Oxford: Oxford University Press.

McDermott, H. J. (2004). Music perception with cochlear implants: a review. *Trends Amplif.* 8, 49–82. doi:10.1177/108471380400800203

Moreno, S. (2009). Can music influence language and cognition? *Contemp. Music Rev.* 28, 329–345. doi:10.1080/07494460903404410

Moreno, S., Bialystok, E., Barac, R., Schellenberg, E. G., Cepeda, N., and Chau, T. (2011). Short-term music training enhances verbal intelligence and executive function. *Psychol. Sci.* 22, 1425–1433. doi:10.1177/0956797611416999

Moreno, S., Marques, C., Santos, A., Santos, M., Castro, S. L., and Besson, M. (2009). Musical training influences linguistic abilities in 8-year-old children: more evidence for brain plasticity. *Cereb. Cortex* 19, 712–723. doi:10.1093/cercor/bhn120

Nakata, T., Trehub, S., Kanda, Y., Shibasaki, A., and Schellenberg, E. G. (2005). Music recognition by Japanese children with cochlear implants. *J. Physiol. Anthropol. Appl. Human Sci.* 24, 29–32. doi:10.2114/jpa.24.29

Nittrouer, S., Caldwell-Tarr, A., and Lowenstein, J. H. (2013). Working memory in children with cochlear implants: problems are in storage, not processing. *Int. J. Pediatr. Otorhinolaryngol.* 77, 1886–1898. doi:10.1016/j.ijporl.2013.09.001

Nutley, S. B., Darki, F., and Klingberg, T. (2014). Music practice is associated with development of working memory during childhood and adolescence. *Front. Hum. Neurosci.* 7:926. doi:10.3389/fnhum.2013.00926

Parbery-Clark, A., Skoe, E., Lam, C., and Kraus, N. (2009). Musician enhancement for speech-in-noise. *Ear Hear.* 30, 653–661. doi:10.1097/AUD.0b013e3181b412e9

Patel, A. D. (2008). *Music, Language and the Brain.* New York, NY: Oxford University Press.

Peretz, I., Champod, A.-S., and Hyde, K. L. (2003). Varieties of musical disorders the montreal battery of evaluation of amusia. *Ann. N. Y. Acad. Sci.* 999, 58–75. doi:10.1196/annals.1284.006

Petersen, B., Mortensen, M. V., Hansen, M., and Vuust, P. (2012). Singing in the key of life – a pilot study on effects of musical ear training after cochlear implantation. *Psychomusicology* 22, 134–151. doi:10.1111/j.1749-6632.2009.04796.x

Peterson, N. R., Pisoni, D. B., and Miyamotoa, R. T. (2010). Cochlear implants and spoken language processing abilities: review and assessment of the literature. *Restor. Neurol. Neurosci.* 28, 237–250. doi:10.3233/RNN-2010-0535

Pisoni, D. B., and Cleary, M. (2003). Measures of working memory span and verbal rehearsal speed in deaf children after cochlear implantation. *Ear Hear.* 24(1 Suppl.), 106S–120S. doi:10.1097/01.AUD.0000051692.05140.8E

Pisoni, D. B., Conway, C. M., Kronenberger, W. G., Horn, D. L., Karpicke, J., and Henning, S. C. (2008). "Efficacy and effectiveness of cochlear implants in deaf children," in *Deaf Cognition: Foundations and Outcomes*, eds M. Marschark and P. Hauser (New York, NY: Oxford University Press), 52–101.

Pisoni, D. B., Kronenberger, W. G., Roman, A. S., and Geers, A. E. (2011). Measures of digit span and verbal rehearsal speed in deaf children after more than 10 years of cochlear implantation. *Ear Hear.* 32(1 Suppl.), 60S–74S. doi:10.1097/AUD.0b013e3181ffd58e

Rauscher, F. H., and Hinton, S. C. (2011). Music instruction and its diverse extra-musical benefits. *Music Percept.* 29, 215–226. doi:10.1525/mp.2011.29.2.215

Rochette, F., and Bigand, E. (2009). Long-term effects of auditory training in severely or profoundly deaf children. *Ann. N. Y. Acad. Sci.* 1169, 195–198. doi:10.1111/j.1749-6632.2009.04793.x

Schellenberg, E. G. (2004). Music lessons enhance IQ. *Psychol. Sci.* 15, 511–514. doi:10.1111/j.0956-7976.2004.00711.x

Sharma, A., Dorman, M. F., and Spahr, A. J. (2002). A sensitive period for the development of the central auditory system in children with cochlear implants; implications for age of implantation. *Ear Hear.* 23, 532–539. doi:10.1097/00003446-200212000-00004

Skoe, E., and Kraus, N. (2012). A little goes a long way: how the adult brain is shaped by musical training in childhood. *J. Neurosci.* 32, 11507–11510. doi:10.1523/JNEUROSCI.1949-12.2012

Strait, D., and Kraus, N. (2014). Biological impact of auditory expertise across the life span: musicians as a model of auditory learning. *Hear. Res.* 308, 109–121. doi:10.1016/j.heares.2013.08.004

Strait, D. L., Parbery-Clark, A., Hittner, E., and Kraus, N. (2012). Musical training during early childhood enhances the neural encoding of speech in noise. *Brain Lang.* 123, 191–201. doi:10.1016/j.bandl.2012.09.001

Sutoo, D., and Akiyama, K. (2004). Music improves dopaminergic neurotransmission: demonstration based on the effect of music on blood pressure regulation. *Brain Res.* 1016, 255–262. doi:10.1016/j.brainres.2004.05.018

Tillmann, B., Koelsch, S., Escoffier, N., Bigand, E., Lalitte, P., and Friederici, A. D. (2006). Cognitive priming in sung and instrumental music: activation of inferior frontal cortex. *Neuroimage* 31, 1771–1782. doi:10.1016/j.neuroimage.2006.02.028

Torppa, R., Faulkner, A., Huotilainen, M., Järvikivi, J., Lipsanen, J., Laasonen, M., et al. (2014). The perception of prosody and associated auditory cues in early-implanted children: the role of auditory working memory and musical activities. *Int. J. Audiol.* 53, 182–191. doi:10.3109/14992027.2013.872302

Torppa, R., Salo, E., Makkonen, T., Loimo, H., Pykäläinen, J., Lipsanen, J., et al. (2012). Cortical processing of musical sounds in children with cochlear implants. *Neurophysiol. Clin.* 123, 1966–1979. doi:10.1016/j.clinph.2012.03.008

Trainor, L. J., Shahin, A. J., and Roberts, L. E. (2003). Effects of musical training on auditory cortex in children. *Ann. N. Y. Acad. Sci.* 999, 506–513. doi:10.1196/annals.1284.061

Wan, C. Y., and Schlaug, G. (2010). Music making as a tool for promoting brain plasticity across the life span. *Neuroscientist* 16, 566–577. doi:10.1177/1073858410377805

Wu, J. L., Yang, H. M., Lin, Y. H., and Fu, Q. J. (2007). Effects of computer-assisted speech training on Mandarin-speaking hearing-impaired children. *Audiol. Neurootol.* 12, 307–312. doi:10.1159/000103211

Yucel, E., Sennaroglu, G., and Belgin, E. (2009). The family oriented musical training for children with cochlear implants: speech and musical perception results of two year follow-up. *Int. J. Pediatr. Otorhinolaryngol.* 73, 1043–1052. doi:10.1016/j.ijporl.2009.04.009

Zeng, F. G., Rebscher, S., Harrison, W. V., Sun, X., and Feng, H. (2008). Cochlear implants: system design, integration and evaluation. *IEEE Rev. Biomed. Eng.* 1, 115–142. doi:10.1109/RBME.2008.2008250

4

Residual neural processing of musical sound features in adult cochlear implant users

Lydia Timm[1]*, Peter Vuust[2,3], Elvira Brattico[4,5], Deepashri Agrawal[1], Stefan Debener[6,7], Andreas Büchner[7,8], Reinhard Dengler[1,7] and Matthias Wittfoth[9]

[1] Department of Neurology, Hannover Medical School, Hannover, Germany
[2] Center of Functionally Integrative Neuroscience, Aarhus University, Aarhus, Denmark
[3] Royal Academy of Music, Aarhus, Denmark
[4] Brain and Mind Laboratory, Department of Biomedical Engineering and Biomedical Science, Aalto University School of Science, Aalto, Finland
[5] Cognitive Brain Research Unit, Institute of Behavioral Sciences, University of Helsinki, Helsinki, Finland
[6] Neuropsychology Laboratory, Department of Psychology, Carl von Ossietzky University of Oldenburg, Oldenburg, Germany
[7] Cluster of Excellence Hearing4All, Oldenburg/Hannover, Germany
[8] Department of Otolaryngology, Hannover Medical School, Hannover, Germany.
[9] Department of Clinical Psychology and Sexual Medicine, Hannover Medical School, Hannover, Germany

Correspondence:
Lydia Timm, Department of Neurology, Hannover Medical School, Hannover 30625, Germany
e-mail: lt@brainproducts.com

Auditory processing in general and music perception in particular are hampered in adult cochlear implant (CI) users. To examine the residual music perception skills and their underlying neural correlates in CI users implanted in adolescence or adulthood, we conducted an electrophysiological and behavioral study comparing adult CI users with normal-hearing age-matched controls (NH controls). We used a newly developed musical multi-feature paradigm, which makes it possible to test automatic auditory discrimination of six different types of sound feature changes inserted within a musical enriched setting lasting only 20 min. The presentation of stimuli did not require the participants' attention, allowing the study of the early automatic stage of feature processing in the auditory cortex. For the CI users, we obtained mismatch negativity (MMN) brain responses to five feature changes but not to changes of rhythm, whereas we obtained MMNs for all the feature changes in the NH controls. Furthermore, the MMNs to deviants of pitch of CI users were reduced in amplitude and later than those of NH controls for changes of pitch and guitar timber. No other group differences in MMN parameters were found to changes in intensity and saxophone timber. Furthermore, the MMNs in CI users reflected the behavioral scores from a respective discrimination task and were correlated with patients' age and speech intelligibility. Our results suggest that even though CI users are not performing at the same level as NH controls in neural discrimination of pitch-based features, they do possess potential neural abilities for music processing. However, CI users showed a disrupted ability to automatically discriminate rhythmic changes compared with controls. The current behavioral and MMN findings highlight the residual neural skills for music processing even in CI users who have been implanted in adolescence or adulthood.

Highlights:

- Automatic brain responses to musical feature changes reflect the limitations of central auditory processing in adult Cochlear Implant users.
- The brains of adult CI users automatically process sound features changes even when inserted in a musical context.
- CI users show disrupted automatic discriminatory abilities for rhythm in the brain.
- Our fast paradigm demonstrate residual musical abilities in the brains of adult CI users giving hope for their future rehabilitation.

Keywords: cochlear implant, auditory evoked potentials, mismatch negativity, music multi-feature paradigm, music perception

INTRODUCTION

A cochlear implant (CI) is a device, which can restore hearing in patients with severe and profound sensori-neural hearing loss. The outer and middle ear is bypassed with a microphone and a speech processor, which converts the acoustical signals into electric pulses. These pulses are brought into the cochlear nerve via the transmitter coil and thus stimulate directly the hearing nerve fibers. Despite the limitations of their implant, most CI users are able to derive information for speech intelligibility, depending on the age when the device has been implanted. Usually younger implantees (implantation age <4 years) reach better levels of speech understanding than older implantees as long as the critical time window for speech acquisition is considered (Kral and O'Donoghue, 2010). However, for post-lingually deafened CI users the levels of speech understanding are depending on factors such as: duration of implant use, amount of training, and rehabilitation as well as psychological factors like: personal acceptance of the implant and environmental reactions (Gfeller et al., 2008; Driscoll et al., 2009). Since the CI was mainly created as a prosthesis to enhance speech perception, music perception remains comparably poor (Koelsch et al., 2004; Gfeller et al., 2006; Cooper et al., 2008; Limb and Rubinstein, 2012). These differences arise mainly because of the missing spectral fine structure information, which is not well processed by the current CIs (McDermott, 2004). Behavioral measures of CI users' auditory capabilities compared to NH controls, however, imply a number of confounding factors such as fluctuations in attention, differences in familiarity with and motivation in relation to performing auditory tasks, and so on. In the electrophysiology lab, the mismatch negativity (MMN) brain response is instead elicited while the subject is performing a task unrelated to the sounds, allowing the study of automatic auditory skills in the brain (Alho et al., 1998; Brattico et al., 2006; Näätänen et al., 2012). Even though the number of published experiments so far is very small, the MMN has emerged as a reliable marker for CI users' ability to accurately discriminate stimuli without the trade-off of subjective behavioral responses (Kraus et al., 1993; Lonka et al., 2004; Kelly et al., 2005; Sandmann et al., 2010; Zhang et al., 2011; Torppa et al., 2012).

The MMN is a component of the auditory event-related potential (ERP) recorded with electroencephalography (EEG) in response to sound features (such as pitch, timber, and intensity), or abstract rules (such as musical scale relations) deviating from those of a predictable auditory environment (Näätänen, 1992; Näätänen et al., 2001, 2011a). The MMN is sensitive to discrimination learning (Näätänen et al., 1993) and hereby to auditory and musical competence (Vuust et al., 2005; Vuust and Roepstorff, 2008; Brattico et al., 2009; Tervaniemi, 2009), being it elicited even by small changes in stimulus features at a level near just-noticeable difference thresholds (Näätänen et al., 2007) and provides an objective measure of central auditory processing functions. Traditionally, the MMN is obtained by using the oddball paradigm, which includes a repetitive sound and an infrequent change in one feature of the sound, such as its frequency or duration or timber. With a stimulus trial lasting, for instance, about one second, the oddball paradigm would require about 15 min of sound repetitions to reach an acceptable signal-to-noise ratio necessary to obtain averaged brain responses to a single sound feature change. Hence, to obtain MMN responses to several feature changes, several hours of recordings would be needed. Obviously, that is not affordable with a clinical population (and difficult even with healthy subjects); consequently, most MMN and, more broadly, ERP papers using traditional oddball paradigms provide brain responses to a single feature change (e.g., Näätänen et al., 2012). That, however, is unsatisfactory because the neuroauditory profile of the subjects is not accurate when only one feature is studied. For instance, the evolving of schizophrenia seems to be reflected in the MMN to frequency chances whereas the genetic aspects of the disease may be more closely associated with the deficient MMN to duration changes [for a review, see Näätänen and Kahkonen (2009)]. Indeed, the first version of the multi-feature paradigm, introduced by Näätänen et al. (2004) was later applied by Sandmann et al. (2010) to demonstrate that MMNs to changes in a repeated sound occurring 50% of the times may be elicited even in CI users. In addition, Torppa et al. (2012) have demonstrated how a new multi-feature change detection paradigm can be used in order to demonstrate cortical processing of musical sound in young CI users. They have found significant (although in some cases reduced) neural responses to several feature changes in children using CIs, which did differ from those of the NH control group only in response to changes in musical instrument, sound duration, and gap but not for other sound features, demonstrating the potentials of music intervention in CI children. The possibility to measure MMNs to several sound feature changes in a laboratory session lasting less than 20 min opens thus new opportunities for basic research with young children and for opening new interventional avenues.

Recently, Vuust et al. (2011) have introduced a new fast musical multi-feature paradigm that tests sound feature deviations in a complex auditory setting resembling music. This paradigm can be used as a tool of objective assessment of music-expertise neural skills in normal-hearing listeners (Vuust et al., 2011, 2012a,b). In the musical multi-feature paradigm, deviant sound features (such as pitch, timber, intensity, and rhythm) are embedded in the "Alberti bass," where three different pitches alternate in a four-note pattern changing over the 12 keys. The stimuli therefore provide a more musical context than the original multi-feature paradigm in which one sound feature alternated with a deviant one (cf. Torppa et al., 2012). Indeed, the musical multi-feature paradigm has evidenced differences between different kinds of musicians, which were closely related to the style-specific aspects of the music practiced (Vuust et al., 2012a).

Based on the correlation between musical expertise and the amplitude of the MMN obtained in a normal-hearing population including musicians (Vuust et al., 2012a), we hypothesized that adult CI users would show distinct MMNs for musical features with different magnitudes of deviations depending on the feature and the characteristics of their corrected hearing. Compared to NH controls, we anticipated longer latencies in the CI users as well as smaller MMN amplitudes, indexing their impaired music processing. However, without previous studies measuring brain processing of several features in a musical context in adult CI users, we could hypothesize a difference between musical feature processing in CI users, without any more specific expectation on which direction this difference would be evidenced.

MATERIALS AND METHODS

PARTICIPANTS

Twelve adult right-handed CI users (age range in years: 21–56, mean: 43.5, SD: 9.97) and 12 age- and sex-matched, right-handed participants with normal-hearing ability (age range in years: 21–57, mean: 43.3, SD: 11.09) were included. Prior to the experiment, all CI users had been using their implant for at least 12 months.

Table 1 | Patient demographics.

Subject	Age	Sex	Implant type	Duration of profound deafness (years)	Age at implantation (years)	Etiology	Freiburger monosyllabic in quiet (%)	Implanted ear
P1	34	F	AB Clarion CII	1.59	26	Sudden	90	Right
P2	55	M	AB HiRes 90 K	6.76	53	Progressive	65	Right
P3	56	F	AB HiRes 90 K	10.3	52	Genetic	90	Right
P4	44	F	Nucleus RE 24	17	39	Measles	85	Right
P5	43	M	AB HiRes 90 K	0.34	42	Progressive	90	Left
P6	40	M	Medel SONATA	<0.2	35	Hypoxia	65	Right
P7	50	M	Nucleus RE 24	<0.2	47	Otosclerosis	45	Right
P8	46	F	Nucleus RE 24	3.17	40	Genetic	90	Right
P9	35	F	Nucleus RE 24	5.67	29	Progressive	90	Right
P10	21	F	Nucleus RE 24	7	13	Genetic	65	Left
P11	48	F	Nucleus RE 24	17.75	43	Mumps	90	right
P12	51	M	Medel SONATA	1.25	46	Sudden	80	Left

All CI users were implanted during adulthood except one participant who received the implant at age 13. Moreover, all CI users were post-lingually deafened with the duration of profound deafness not exceeding 18 years (years of profound deafness: 5.93, SD: 6.24) (please see **Table 1** for detailed patient demographics). Additionally, their hearing abilities exceeded 20% as assessed by the Freiburger monosyllabic words test in quiet environment, a standard German speech intelligibility test in which participants repeat monosyllabic words presented at a level of 65 dB. All experimental procedures were approved by the local ethics committee and the study protocol conformed to the Declaration of Helsinki. Participants gave written informed consent before data collection and received monetary compensation for their time.

STIMULI

The auditory stimuli in the present experiment were similar to the musical multi-feature paradigm developed by Vuust et al. (2011), with only small adaptations due to the characteristics of the CI patient group. Unlike the oddball paradigm, the multi-feature paradigm allows us to record auditory evoked potential (AEP) responses to many auditory feature deviations in a relatively short time and with a comparably good signal-to-noise ratio. Instead of a usual stimulus probability (80% standards; 20% deviants), our current musical multi-feature paradigm allows each "standard" to be followed by a "deviant" resulting in an equal probability of standards and deviants.

The musical multi-feature paradigm is an extension of the "optimal paradigm" (Näätänen et al., 2004) but with a richer musical context and higher complexity obtained by presenting standards and deviants within an "Alberti bass" configuration. This configuration is commonly used in the Western musical culture in both classical and improvisational music genres. For the present study, we presented this musical 4-tone pattern, with a key change between F-major, G-major, A-major, or C-major on every sixth measure. The original paradigm by Vuust et al. (2011) was adapted to the CI patient group by limiting the amount of key changes, in order to meet the average frequency range of the CI user devices. The keys were kept in the middle register of a piano with the bass note between *F*3 and *E*4, while their order was pseudo-randomized; each key was repeated six times during the experiment. In addition, whenever a key change occurred, the standard pattern was repeated six times in order to facilitate the difference between standard and deviant pattern in the presence of a key change. Those standard patterns occurring after key change were omitted from the average.

Sound stimuli were generated using the sample sounds of an acoustic piano (Wizoo) from the software sampler "Halion" in Cubase (Steinberg Media Technologies GmbH). Deviant patterns were similar to the standards, except that the third tone of the pattern was modified with Pro Tools (Pro Tools 7.4, Avid) as illustrated in **Figure 1**.

The first pitch deviant ($\text{Pitch1}_{\text{D1}}$) was created by exchanging the third tone of the Alberti pattern with a sound, which was two semitones higher. The second pitch deviant ($\text{Pitch2}_{\text{D2}}$) was created in the same manner using a substitute four semitones higher. Note that $\text{Pitch2}_{\text{D2}}$ produces both a pitch and contour violation, whereas $\text{Pitch1}_{\text{D1}}$ only produces a pitch violation. The two timber deviants were created by exchanging the third note for either a guitar (Gui_{D3}) or a saxophone (Sax_{D4}) sound (both timber deviants were normalized in loudness according to the standard pattern). The intensity deviant (Int_{D5}) was generated by reducing the original loudness of the third tone by 12 dB, whereas the rhythm deviant (Rhy_{D6}) was created by anticipating the third note by 60 ms. Each single note was presented in stereo (44,100 Hz sample frequency), and with a duration of 200 ms and with a 5 ms inter-stimulus-interval form the previous tone (except the rhythm deviants). The deviants occurred always in the same fixed order as depicted in **Figure 1**. The stimuli were presented with Presentation software (Neurobehavioral Systems). The total duration of the experiment was 20 min.

PROCEDURE

EEG experiment

Upon arriving to the lab, participants signed the consent form and were subsequently prepared for EEG recordings. The EEG was recorded from 30 scalp channels using active electrodes (Acticap, Brain Products, Munich, Germany) placed according to the

Stimulus (Alberti Bass)

Keys randomized: A major F-major C-major G-major

S:	Standard	
D1:	Pitch1$_{D1}$	2 semitones higher
D2:	Pitch2$_{D2}$:	4 semitones higher
D3:	Gui$_{D3}$:	Guitar
D4:	Sax$_{D4}$:	Saxophone
D5	Int$_{D5}$:	12 dB reduction
D6	Rhy$_{D6}$:	60 ms earlier

FIGURE 1 | Stimuli. The main stimulus: "Alberti bass" patterns alternating between standard sequence and a deviant sequence played with a piano sound. Patterns were periodically transposed to four different keys with an interval of six bars. Each tone was 200 ms in duration, with an inter-stimulus-interval of 5 ms, yielding a tempo of approximately 140 beats/min. Comparisons were made between the third note of the standard sequence and the third note of the deviant sequence.

10–20 system (Klem et al., 1999) with a BrainAmp (Brain Products, Munich, Germany). For the CI users, three to six channels mainly from the temporal (T12/T8) to the occipital electrodes (P08) had to be unattached due to interferences with the implant transmission coil (channels range: 3–6, mean: 3, SD: 1). Two electrodes were attached to record the EOG (below and at the outer canthus of the right eye). The reference electrode was attached to the nose-tip and was used as the common reference. Sampling rate was 250 Hz, the data were analog filtered (0.1–80 Hz), and electrode impedances were kept below 10 kΩ. During the EEG recordings, participants were comfortably seated in a shielded chamber and passively listened to the auditory sequences via loudspeakers positioned on their left and right side with an angle of 45°. Loudness was kept at a sound pressure level of 60 dB. All participants watched a silenced documentary throughout the whole experimental procedure.

Behavioral experiment

After the EEG recordings, all participants performed a discrimination task to measure a behavioral index of their auditory discrimination accuracy. In this three alternative choice task, participants were presented with the same four-tone pattern as used in the previous EEG experiment. The pattern was presented three times in a row (3 × 4-pattern), twice in the standard condition and once with in a deviant condition. The deviating pattern could occur either on the first, the second, or the last position in the presentation of the 3 × 4-pattern. All deviant conditions were presented equally often and were repeated 10 times in random order. Participants were instructed to press a corresponding key (1, 2, 3) indicating at which position the deviating pattern had occurred. Hit rates of CI users and NH controls were analyzed and averaged across the six deviant conditions.

DATA ANALYSIS

Electroencephalography data were analyzed in the MATLAB (Mathworks, Nattick, MA, USA) environment using EEGLAB 9.0.5.6b (Delorme and Makeig, 2004). Data were filtered offline using a FIR filter with the lower edge of the frequency pass band at 1 Hz and a higher edge of the frequency pass band at 30 Hz. The recordings were screened for infrequent or un-stereotyped artifacts using an inbuilt probability function (pop_jointprob) with a threshold of three standard deviations (Debener et al., 2008). After performing an Infomax independent component analysis (ICA), ocular and cardiac artifacts were identified using the CORRMAP plug-in (Viola et al., 2009) and removed from the data. Artifacts caused by electrical interference of the CI were identified with respect to their independent components (ICs) (Debener et al., 2008; Viola et al., 2011, 2012). Evaluation of whether an IC was artifact driven was determined by (i) visual inspection of IC scalp projection (e.g., centroid of activity on the implanted side), (ii) whether on and offset of the AEP component were in phase with stimulus on and offset, or (iii) whether the activity power spectrum of the IC showed a periodic-like spectral distribution in the frequency domains up to 20 Hz (Torppa et al., 2012). Consequentially, ICs found to reflect an artifact induced by the implant were removed from the data.

For the CI users, the missing channels were spherically interpolated with respect to the neighboring channels to enable voltage topographic maps. Following ICA-based artifact attenuation, data were segmented in 100 ms pre-stimulus and 400 ms post-stimulus epochs. After baseline correction (−100 to 0 ms), single subject averages of the six types of deviant stimuli as well for the standard stimuli were conducted. Single-subject MMN latencies and amplitudes were measured by subtracting the AEP waveform of the deviant from the standard waveform resulting in

Table 2 | Amplitudes and latencies of the MMN in response to different musical features for both groups.

Deviant	Interval (ms)	CI users				NH controls				
		Amplitude mean (μV)	t	SD	latency (ms) (SD)	Interval (ms)	Amplitude mean (μV)	t	SD	latency (ms) (SD)
$Pitch1_{D1}$	180–220	−0.61	−2.81*	0.75	202 (15.3)	136–176	−1.80	−7.45**	0.83	148 (14.4)
$Pitch2_{D2}$	180–220	−0.71	−3.11*	0.79	206 (19.7)	136–176	−2.48	−7.48**	1.15	148 (12.3)
$Guit_{D3}$	140–180	−1.38	−5.07**	0.94	165 (14.1)	120–160	−2.72	−7.76**	1.23	134 (14.0)
Sax_{D4}	140–180	−1.10	−5.22**	0.73	169 (14.7)	140–180	−1.71	−4.53**	1.31	165 (13.0)
Int_{D5}	138–178	−1.49	−4.77**	1.08	150 (17.3)	138–178	−1.39	−4.22**	1.14	162 (16.4)
Rhy_{D6}	128–168	−0.24	−1.41	0.74	143 (11.1)	128–168	−1.91	−6.50**	1.01	140 (14.1)

$*p=0.01$; $**p<0.001$.

six difference-waves. For the MMN quantification, group- and deviant-specific time windows of 40 ms were chosen from the respective grand-average MMN peak amplitude. MMN amplitude voltages for all electrodes were then calculated as the mean amplitude within these 40 ms time windows (see **Table 2** for time windows). In line with previous studies (Näätänen et al., 2007; Duncan et al., 2009) reporting that the largest negative MMN peak is typically obtained at Fz, MMN significance analysis against the zero baseline was carried out on electrode Fz. Since the mastoids were not accessible in all CI users, we chose P08 to evaluate possible polarity reversals of the MMN response (Sandmann et al., 2010).

STATISTICS

Two-tailed t-tests were carried out for all six deviant categories in both groups to ascertain that MMN amplitudes differed significantly from zero. A repeated measure ANOVA with within-subject factor deviation (five levels: $Pitch1_{D1}$, $Pitch2_{D2}$, Gui_{D3}, Sax_{D4}, Int_{D5}) and Group as between-group factor was computed for MMN latencies. For further statistical analysis, the effects of feature deviation on the MMN amplitudes and scalp distributions in terms of frontal and central electrodes as well as group-specific differences were calculated on a subset of electrodes (*F*3, Fz, *F*4, C3, Cz, C4). A repeated measures ANOVA was performed on the MMN mean amplitudes and latencies. Within-subject factors were Deviation (five levels: $Pitch1_{D1}$, $Pitch2_{D2}$, Gui_{D3}, Sax_{D4}, Int_{D5}), Frontality (two levels: F-line, C-line), and Laterality (left, middle, or right), while Group was a between-subject factor. Effects of electrode factors alone are not reported as meaningless with respect of the hypothesis tested concerning group differences (they only reflect the scalp topography of the MMN). A Greenhouse-Geisser correction was applied when necessary, and will be indicated in the following section with epsilon values; degrees of freedom will be presented uncorrected. *Post hoc* t-tests were used to reveal group-specific differences.

RESULTS

MMN AMPLITUDES

In NH controls, the fast multi-feature paradigm elicited significant MMNs in all the six feature deviants whereas in CI users significant MMNs were found for all but the Rhy_{D6} (see **Table 2**). For the MMN amplitudes, we found a significant main effect of Group ($F_{1,22}=8.57$; $p=0.008$), deriving from overall diminished MMN in CI users compared to NH controls (mean value for combined MMNs as measured on Fz: CI users: −0.92 μV, SD: 0.88; NH controls: −2.00 μV, SD: 1.11). We also obtained significant within-subject effects of Deviation ($F_{4,88}=4.57$; $p<0.001$) (see **Table 2**). Furthermore, we found a significant interaction Deviation × Group ($F_{4,88}=3.86$; $p=0.008$). *Post hoc* t-tests for amplitude at *Fz* with respect to deviation showed the largest differences between the two groups for the $Pitch1_{D1}$ ($t=3.64$; $p=0.001$) and $Pitch2_{D2}$ ($t=4.39$; $p<0.001$) deviations. A significant difference was also found for the Gui_{D3} with smaller amplitudes in the CI users than in NH controls ($t=3.03$; $p=0.006$). We found no significant differences for the MMN amplitudes to saxophone and intensity between CI users and NH controls (Sax_{D4}: $t=1.4$, $p=0.17$; Int_{D5}: $t=0.20$, $p=0.83$). MMN amplitude for $Rhythm_{D6}$ differed significantly between CI users and NH controls ($t=4.57$, $p<0.001$) (please see **Figure 2** for MMNs to musical multi-feature deviations).

As illustrated in **Figure 3**, and indicated with *post hoc* paired t-tests the topography maps show that the MMNs of CI users were differently lateralized than those of the NH controls. This was testified also by the significant interactions between the between-subject factor and the two electrode factors: Laterality × Group ($F_{2,44}=5.20$; $p=0.02$), Frontality × Laterality × Group ($F_{2,44}=10.74$; $p=0.001$), and Frontality × Deviation × Group ($F_{4,88}=5.48$; $p=0.004$). Further investigating these interactions, planned t-tests showed that significant MMN lateralization was obtained for feature deviations $Pitch1_{D1}$ (comparing $F3<F4$: $t=3.32$, $p=0.007$) and Gui_{D3} ($F3<F4$: $t=2.33$, $p=0.040$), whereas no significant differences for *F*-line vs. *C*-line were observed for the different feature deviations (all $p>0.6$) in CI users. In the NH controls, both pitch deviants showed a more frontal ($Pitch1_{D1}$ $F4>C4$: $t=2.49$, $p=0.030$; $Pitch2_{D2}$ $F4>C4$: $t=4.94$, $p<0.001$) and rightwards lateralization ($Pitch1_{D1}$ $F4>F3$: $t=7.83$, $p<0.001$; $Pitch2_{D2}$ $F4>F3$: $t=3.51$, $p=0.005$). The MMN to feature deviation Gui_{D3} showed strongest amplitude on the C-line, with no significant lateralization effect (all $p>0.061$).

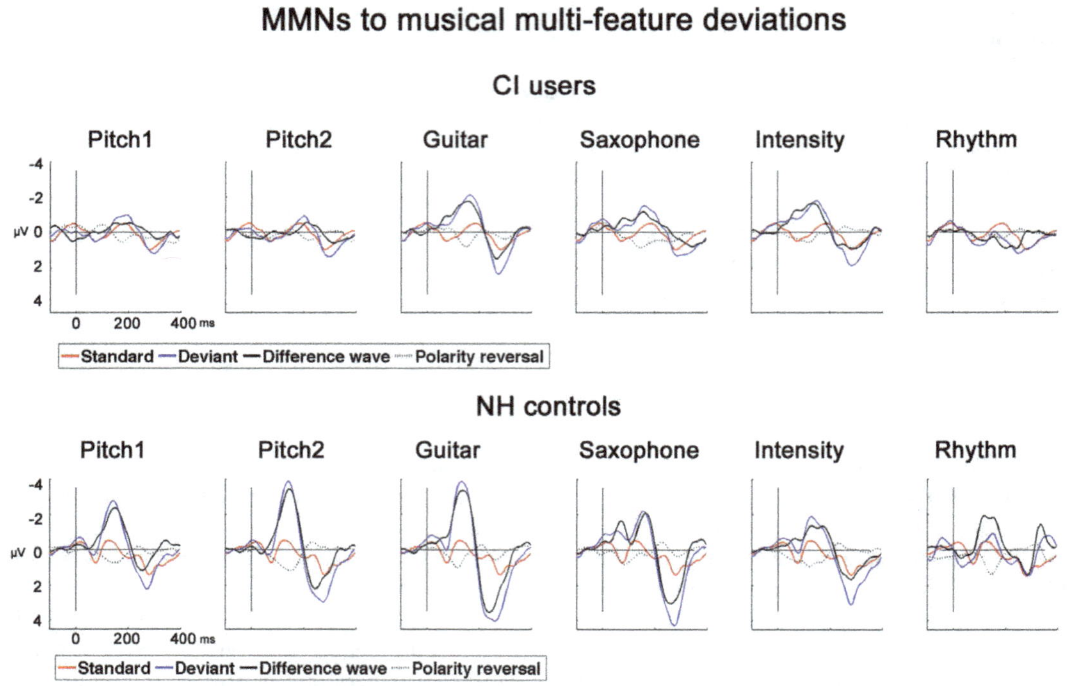

FIGURE 2 | MMNs to musical multi-feature deviations in CI users and NH controls. Grand-average AEPs for CI users and NH controls for six types of deviations recorded at Fz. Standard (red), deviant (blue), difference wave (black), polarity reversal was obtained at P08 (dotted line).

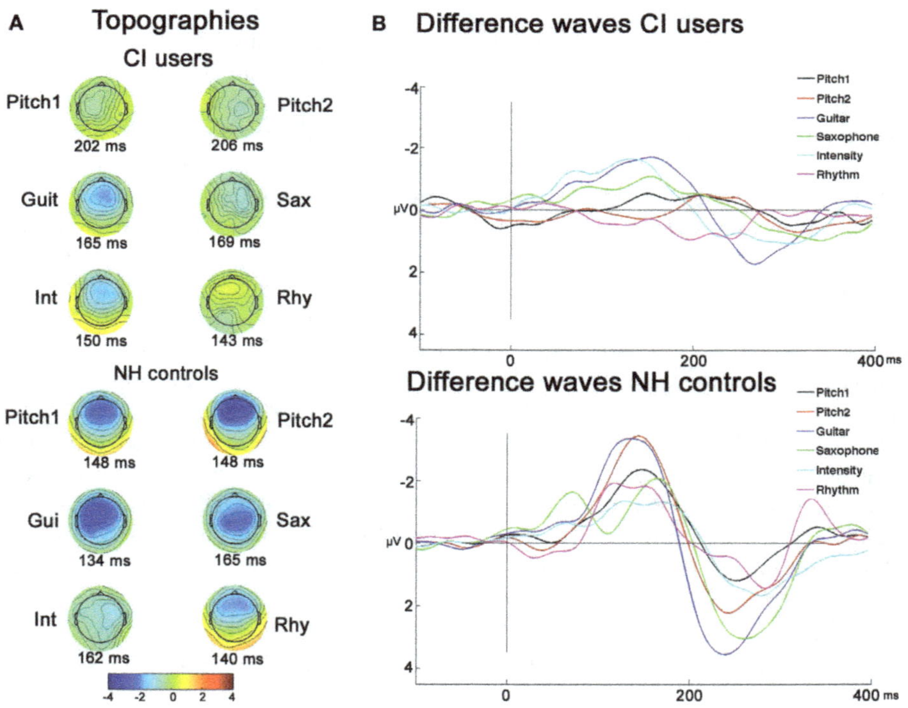

FIGURE 3 | Topographies and grand-average difference-waves of CI users and NH controls. (A) EEG voltage isopotential maps of the difference between the responses to deviants and standards averaged in an interval of ±20 ms around maximal peak amplitudes. **(B)** Grand-average difference-waves of CI users and NH controls.

Table 3 | Hit rates of CI users and NH controls.

	CI user hit rate		NH controls hit rate	
	(%)	SD	(%)	SD
Pitch1$_{D1}$	65	2.42	87	0.90
Pitch2$_{D2}$	74	3.07	98	0.40
Gui$_{D3}$	85	1.12	97	0.64
Sax$_{D4}$	92	1.20	96	1.20
Int$_{D5}$	68	3.20	92	1.42
Rhy$_{D6}$	77	2.40	76	2.01

MMN LATENCIES

The MMN latencies were modulated by the six feature deviations in both groups as tested with repeated measures ANOVA in a general linear Model and showed significant within-subject effect for Deviation ($F_{4,88} = 13.75$, $p < 0.001$) as well as an interaction Deviation × Group ($F_{4,88} = 22.16$, $p < 0.001$). Furthermore a significant main effect of Group was found for the MMN latencies ($F_{1,22} = 125.42$, $p < 0.001$). The two MMNs with the longest latency in the CI users were elicited by the two pitch deviants and differed significantly from the two pitch MMN latencies of the NH controls (Pitch1$_{D1}$: $t = 8.74$; $p < 0.001$; Pitch2$_{D2}$: $t = 8.50$; $p < 0.001$). The shortest MMN latency for the NH group was obtained for the Gui$_{D3}$: this latency differed significantly from the one observed in CI users ($t = 5.32$; $p < 0.001$). Comparable to the results of the MMN amplitudes, we found no group-specific differences for the Sax$_{D4}$ MMN latency ($t = 0.645$, $p = 0.52$) or the Int$_{D5}$ MMN latency ($t = 1.78$, $p = 0.88$). The Rhy$_{D6}$ MMN, was found for the NH controls only (see **Table 2** for detailed latency and amplitudes measures).

BEHAVIORAL EXPERIMENT

All subjects showed a high accuracy with above-chance hit rates. We found lower hit rates for CI users compared to NHs in most feature deviation categories, including Pitch1$_{D1}$ ($t = -2.69$, $p = 0.013$), Pitch2$_{D2}$ ($t = 2.46$, $p = 0.022$), Gui$_{D3}$ ($t = 2.86$, $p = 0.009$), and the deviation Int$_{D5}$ ($t = 2.45$, $p = 0.22$), whereas the groups did not differ for the Sax$_{D4}$ ($t = 0.684$, $p = 0.50$), or Rhy$_{D6}$ ($t = 0.01$, $p = 1.0$) deviations (see **Table 3** for Hit rates).

CORRELATIONS BETWEEN MMN AND BEHAVIORAL OR DEMOGRAPHIC MEASURES

Additional correlations for the CI users group only, including MMN amplitudes at Fz, patient demographics, and hit rates showed significant positive correlations for the Freiburger speech score and hit rates for Pitch2$_{D2}$ ($r = 0.597$, $p = 0.04$), Gui$_{D3}$($r = 0.704$, $p = 0.011$), and Rhy$_{D6}$($r = 0.801$, $p = 0.002$) (please see **Figure 4**). The same hit rates were also significantly negatively correlated (e.g., the higher the hit rate the larger the MMN amplitude) with the MMN amplitude for feature deviation Pitch1$_{D1}$ (Pitch2$_{D2}$: $r = -0.588$, $p = 0.044$), Gui$_{D3}$ ($r = -0.586$, $p = 0.045$), and Rhy$_{D6}$ ($r = -0.747$, $p = 0.005$).

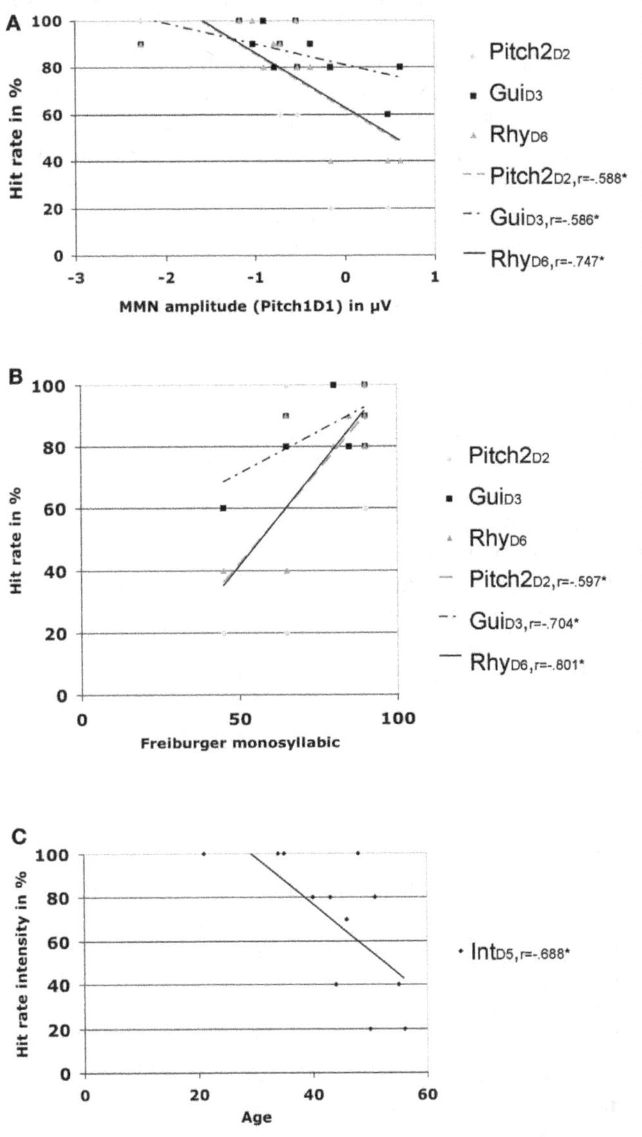

FIGURE 4 | Hit rates and correlations. (A) Correlations of different hit rates with MMN amplitude for deviation Pitch1 in CI users. **(B)** Correlations of different hit rates with the Freiburger monosyllabic speech scores in CI users. **(C)** Correlations of hit rates for intensity with age in CI users.

Age was negatively correlated with the hit rate for Int$_{D5}$ ($r = -0.688$, $p = 0.013$) and the MMN latency for feature deviation Pitch1$_{D1}$ ($r = -0.619$, $p = 0.032$) with older CI users showing prolonged latencies for the pitch MNN (see **Figure 2**).

DISCUSSION

Electroencephalography studies with CI users yield challenges regarding recording, analysis and comparison with NH controls. Due to the implant itself fewer electrodes may be used, which results in a higher amount of topographical interpolated channels. In addition, the implant interferences with the EEG signal require a careful inspection and understanding of the origins of the CI artifact in order to be able to visualize and interpret the resulting evoked potentials of interest. Nevertheless, our results show evidence for CI users' processing of prominent sound features embedded in a complex sound context. CI users in our study had five robust MMNs out of six for sound features formerly described as difficult for these subjects to perceive. We observed significant differences between CI users and NH controls for the MMN amplitude and latencies depending on the feature deviation, especially for the two pitch deviations. The timber deviant to saxophone as well as the intensity deviant elicited similar MMNs in both groups. CI users did not elicit a significant MMN for the rhythm feature even in a complex musical context, which might be explained by the relatively small magnitude of the rhythm deviation within a complex auditory context. In sum, we here extend the findings of earlier MMN studies (Ponton and Don, 1995; Sandmann et al., 2010; Zhang et al., 2011; Torppa et al., 2012), showing that CI users may be able to process musical features such as pitch and intensity even in a complex music-like context. Furthermore, the differences in the MMN scalp distributions and latencies between the different deviant types observed in the present suggest that partially separate neural populations process and store distinct auditory sensory memory traces for different sound features, such as pitch, timber, and intensity (Caclin et al., 2006; Näätänen et al., 2011b). Hemispheric asymmetries between CI users and NH controls for AEPs have been shown earlier by studies indicating a topographical (e.g., more ipsilateral) displacement due to the implantation (Sandmann et al., 2009; Gordon et al., 2010).

PITCH

The findings of the Pitch1$_{\mathrm{D1}}$ in CI users indicate the capability of CI users to perceive differences as small as two semitones. However, less neural efficiency for pitch processing was observed with CI users as evidenced by their diminished MMN amplitudes and lower hit rates to both pitch deviants compared to controls. Especially under consideration of the correlation with the Freiburger speech scores, the pitch results indicate a dependency between the perception of small pitch differences and good speech perception. This extends the results of Torppa et al. (2012), who found that small pitch deviations might be sufficiently salient thus eliciting a MMN. While in their study young CI users were implanted early in life in our study adult CI users were implanted significantly later in life. In Torppa et al.'s study, children early implanted with a CI showed adequately and equally good processing of pitch when compared to NH control children for deviations of three to four semitones of repeated piano tones without any musical context or minimal acoustic variation. In our study, we elicited MMN in adult CI users who were mainly implanted late in life in response to a pitch deviation as little as two semitones, inserted in a music-like context. The findings indicate that the automatic neural processing of pitch [as indexed by the MMN (Näätänen et al., 2011a) is not limited to the often-referred five to seven semitones, when tested behaviorally (Gfeller et al., 2002; Donnelly et al., 2009)]. We found a robust MMN in CI users for the second pitch deviation with four semitones. The threshold of 2–4 semitones elicits a MMN in CI users is considerably good. Recently Lonka et al. (2013) presented similar findings on how the MMN in adult CI users to quasi four semitones (3200 Hz deviants to 4000 Hz standards) is robust and enhanced over the measurement time of 2.5 years.

Behavioral studies, which indicated pitch thresholds of at least five to seven semitones in CI users, often involve judgments of the direction of pitch differences (Gfeller et al., 2002; Drennan and Rubinstein, 2008). Our findings, on the contrary, reflect that neural automatic detection of a pitch change within a complex pitch pattern, takes place even with smaller deviations. Similar findings were reported by Peretz et al. (2009), who obtained a significant MMN to small pitch changes inserted in a complex melody context in patients with congenital amusia, despite no conscious awareness of those changes. The musical richness of context in our study and the previous one on congenital amusics might provide additional cues enabling sound-processing impaired subjects to at least neurally process feature changes. Since the MMN is an index of pre-attentive processing, however, this neural detection may not be sufficient for participants to make clear behavioral discriminations. This explanation is also supported by Leal et al. (2003) who described the differences between pitch discrimination and pitch identification abilities in adult CI users and the impaired prerequisite for the latter to detect the direction of the pitch change. These findings are, nevertheless, potentially important because they hint at the possibility of rehabilitation even in adult CI users who were implanted later in life, thanks to the presence of residual auditory discrimination capabilities in the brain.

TIMBER

Both timber feature deviations (e.g., guitar and saxophone) elicited MMNs in CI users and NH controls. This corroborates earlier findings by Koelsch et al. (2004) showing significant MMNs for timbers differing from the standard piano sound in adult CI users. However, these timber deviants were implemented in a less musical setting than the one used in the current study, thus allowing less generalization of the findings to everyday life situations involving perception of complex auditory scenes.

Behavioral timber discrimination accuracy has been shown to be reflected by the MMN response to timber changes (Näätänen et al., 2007). The timber of an instrument is mainly defined by its temporal and spectral envelope. The gross temporal envelope and the sound onset are comparably good perceived by CI users, whereas the spectral envelope and especially the fine structure are partly missing (Drennan and Rubinstein, 2008; Heng et al., 2011). This might explain the comparable morphologies between the CI users and NH controls in the difference-waves for the two timber deviations, as well as the reduced MMN specifically to the guitar deviant. The guitar as a plugged string instrument has a sharper attack time, and therefore a steeper envelope compared to the slower, by air-excited saxophone. Again, one needs to differentiate between the acoustic change mechanism underlying the two MMNs in our experiment and the general timber identification abilities in adult and experienced CI users. These behavioral identification abilities are hampered depending on the target instrument of the identification task, musical training and a high inter-individual variability (Galvin et al., 2009). This hampered neural and behavioral timber abilities in CI users may be also driven by the fact that the required spectro-temporal fine structure, necessary to differentiate between timbers, is not fully provided by the current CI decoding strategies (Timm et al., 2012). The general consequence of such limitations in the CI device is a perceptual difficulty with complex sound environments (Moore, 2003).

INTENSITY

Although hit rates for intensity differed significantly between groups, we found no group differences in MMN amplitudes or latencies. Instead, the intensity deviation showed the most comparable MMN morphologies between groups, along with the timber deviations. This is not surprising since intensity is usually well implemented in CI users. It is, however, plausible that CI users would be more uncertain about what they hear in general, and therefore behaviorally perform worse than NH despite the apparent similarity between the neural responses between the groups on this sound feature. This assumption is further supported by our findings of the negative correlation between the intensity hit rate and the CI users' age. However, the amplitude range of the MMN in our adult CI users group was remarkably large compared to earlier studies (Sandmann et al., 2010; Torppa et al., 2012) and fosters the reliability of the current musical multi-feature paradigm.

RHYTHM

In music, changes in sound duration are necessary in order to be able to detect changes in rhythm and tempo. Interestingly, the rhythm deviant did not elicit a significant MMN in the CI users. Behavioral studies have shown that the rhythm perception is working well for adult CI users (Limb, 2006; Drennan and Rubinstein, 2008). However, the complexity and lack of attention toward the auditory stimuli in our experiment may have driven the lack of MMN to rhythm feature deviations, as already indicated by the low behavioral hit rate for this feature. This may give rise to the question, whether the behavioral rhythm tests, currently used with CI users within their rehabilitation training, give reliable results about their musical rhythm perception. It may rather be that simple clapping or single note rhythms are more easily perceivable with a CI, whereas rhythm nuances embedded in a complex auditory scene are more difficult to extract. This argument is corroborated by the relative minimal rhythm deviation of 60 ms used in our study, since various studies have indicated that adult CI users with a longer duration of profound deafness have difficulties in more complex rhythm discriminations with small rhythmic changes (Leal et al., 2003; Kong et al., 2004). Future studies should focus on the ability of adult CI users to understand and appreciate musical expression based on rhythmic and temporal variations.

SUMMARY

Our findings extend the insight on the neural abilities for musical feature processing in adult CI users who were implanted after childhood. Particularly, we showed that by using a music-like stimulation paradigm, CI users' brains are able to extract more information from sound than previously reported, as indexed by the distinct MMNs to several musical features. This indicates the existence of residual feature encoding abilities in adult CI users. The musical multi-feature paradigm with which we tested these perceptual abilities is advantageously short and musically enriched compared to previous music-related MMN studies. Within 20 min, we were able to test for six types of deviations embedded in an ecologic musical setting. Our findings imply that it might be necessary to work with realistic stimulus changes in order to capture residual auditory processing skills. In turn, the neural processing of deviations in rhythm was seemingly more difficult in the present paradigm, thus explaining the previously reported differences in our study between behavioral data and AEPs as shown here in relation to the rhythm deviant.

The multi-feature paradigm implemented here may be adopted for clinical routine as it may give objective data of the capability of current implants in an everyday-like listening condition. However, to meet this goal future research in AEP method needs to reach sensitivity at the single subject level to enhance reliability of individual multi-attribute profiles of sound discrimination abilities. Further experiments should include a more parametric approach toward the single deviant categories leading to a more pronounced MMN and specific information about a magnitude of the deviance effect (Horvath et al., 2008; Näätänen, 2009). Additionally, differences between uni- and bi-lateral CI users could be tested giving more information concerning the lateralization of the MMN. This paradigm might also be suitable for auditory brainstem responses. Therefore, experiments including patients with an auditory brainstem implant are warranted, since there is evidence that the novelty detection reflected by the MMN might be driven by much earlier processes of deviant detection encoding mechanisms (Slabu et al., 2012).

ACKNOWLEDGMENTS

This work and its first author were supported by the Georg Christoph Lichtenberg Stipendium of Lower Saxony, Germany. The first author would like to thank all participants and the staff at the German Hearing Centre Hannover. We wish also to thank the Academy of Finland (project number 133673) and University of Helsinki (project number 490083) for financial support.

REFERENCES

Alho, K., Winkler, I., Escera, C., Huotilainen, M., Virtanen, J., Jaaskelainen, I. P., et al. (1998). Processing of novel sounds and frequency changes in the human auditory cortex: magnetoencephalographic recordings. *Psychophysiology* 35, 211–224. doi:10.1111/1469-8986.3520211

Brattico, E., Pallesen, K. J., Varyagina, O., Bailey, C., Anourova, I., Jarvenpaa, M., et al. (2009). Neural discrimination of nonprototypical chords in music experts and laymen: an MEG study. *J. Cogn. Neurosci.* 21, 2230–2244. doi:10.1162/jocn.2008.21144

Brattico, E., Tervaniemi, M., Näätänen, R., and Peretz, I. (2006). Musical scale properties are automatically processed in the human auditory cortex. *Brain Res.* 1117, 162–174. doi:10.1016/j.brainres.2006.08.023

Caclin, A., Brattico, E., Tervaniemi, M., Näätänen, R., Morlet, D., Giard, M. H., et al. (2006). Separate neural processing of timbre dimensions in auditory sensory memory. *J. Cogn. Neurosci.* 18, 1959–1972. doi:10.1162/jocn.2006.18.12.1959

Cooper, W. B., Tobey, E., and Loizou, P. C. (2008). Music perception by cochlear implant and normal hearing listeners as measured by the montreal battery for evaluation of amusia. *Ear Hear.* 29, 618–626. doi:10.1097/AUD.0b013e318174e787

Debener, S., Hine, J., Bleeck, S., and Eyles, J. (2008). Source localization of auditory evoked potentials after cochlear implantation. *Psychophysiology* 45, 20–24. doi:10.1111/j.1469-8986.2007.00610.x

Delorme, A., and Makeig, S. (2004). EEGLAB: an open source toolbox for analysis of single-trial EEG dynamics including independent component analysis. *J. Neurosci. Methods* 134, 9–21. doi:10.1016/j.jneumeth.2003.10.009

Donnelly, P. J., Guo, B. Z., and Limb, C. J. (2009). Perceptual fusion of polyphonic pitch in cochlear implant users. *J. Acoust. Soc. Am.* 126, EL128–EL133. doi:10.1121/1.3239464

Drennan, W. R., and Rubinstein, J. T. (2008). Music perception in cochlear implant users and its relationship with psychophysical capabilities. *J. Rehabil. Res. Dev.* 45, 779–789. doi:10.1682/JRRD.2007.08.0118

Driscoll, V. D., Oleson, J., Jiang, D., and Gfeller, K. (2009). Effects of training on recognition of musical instruments presented through cochlear implant simulations. *J. Am. Acad. Audiol.* 20, 71–82. doi:10.3766/jaaa.20.1.7

Duncan, C. C., Barry, R. J., Connolly, J. F., Fischer, C., Michie, P. T., Näätänen, R., et al. (2009). Event-related potentials in clinical research: guidelines for eliciting, recording, and quantifying mismatch negativity, P300, and N400. *Clin. Neurophysiol.* 120, 1883–1908. doi:10.1016/j.clinph.2009.07.045

Galvin, J. J. III, Fu, Q., and Oba, S. I. (2009). Effect of a competing instrument on melodic contour identification by cochlear implant users. *J. Acoust. Soc. Am.* 125, 98–103. doi:10.1121/1.3062148

Gfeller, K., Oleson, J., Knutson, J. F., Breheny, P., Driscoll, V., and Olszewski, C. (2008). Multivariate predictors of music perception and appraisal by adult cochlear implant users. *J. Am. Acad. Audiol.* 19, 120–134. doi:10.3766/jaaa.19.2.3

Gfeller, K., Turner, C., Mehr, M., Woodworth, G., Fearn, R., Knutson, J. F., et al. (2002). Recognition of familiar melodies by adult cochlear implant recipients and normal-hearing adults. *Cochlear Implants Int.* 3, 29–53. doi:10.1002/cii.50

Gfeller, K. E., Olszewski, C., Turner, C., Gantz, B., and Oleson, J. (2006). Music perception with cochlear implants and residual hearing. *Audiol. Neurootol.* 11(Suppl. 1), 12–15. doi:10.1159/000095608

Gordon, K. A., Wong, D. D., and Papsin, B. C. (2010). Cortical function in children receiving bilateral cochlear implants simultaneously or after a period of interimplant delay. *Otol. Neurotol.* 31, 1293–1299. doi:10.1097/MAO.0b013e3181e8f965

Heng, J., Cantarero, G., Elhilali, M., and Limb, C. J. (2011). Impaired perception of temporal fine structure and musical timbre in cochlear implant users. *Hear. Res.* 280, 192–200. doi:10.1016/j.heares.2011.05.017

Horvath, J., Czigler, I., Jacobsen, T., Maess, B., Schroger, E., and Winkler, I. (2008). MMN or no MMN: no magnitude of deviance effect on the MMN amplitude. *Psychophysiology* 45, 60–69. doi:10.1111/j.1469-8986.2007.00599.x

Kelly, A. S., Purdy, S. C., and Thorne, P. R. (2005). Electrophysiological and speech perception measures of auditory processing in experienced adult cochlear implant users. *Clin. Neurophysiol.* 116, 1235–1246. doi:10.1016/j.clinph.2005.02.011

Klem, G. H., Luders, H. O., Jasper, H. H., and Elger, C. (1999). The ten-twenty electrode system of the international federation. The international federation of clinical neurophysiology. *Electroencephalogr. Clin. Neurophysiol. Suppl.* 52, 3–6.

Koelsch, S., Wittfoth, M., Wolf, A., Muller, J., and Hahne, A. (2004). Music perception in cochlear implant users: an event-related potential study. *Clin. Neurophysiol.* 115, 966–972. doi:10.1016/j.clinph.2003.11.032

Kong, Y. Y., Cruz, R., Jones, J. A., and Zeng, F. G. (2004). Music perception with temporal cues in acoustic and electric hearing. *Ear Hear.* 25, 173–185. doi:10.1097/01.AUD.0000120365.97792.2F

Kral, A., and O'Donoghue, G. M. (2010). Profound deafness in childhood. *N. Engl. J. Med.* 363, 1438–1450. doi:10.1056/NEJMra0911225

Kraus, N., Micco, A. G., Koch, D. B., Mcgee, T., Carrell, T., Sharma, A., et al. (1993). The mismatch negativity cortical evoked potential elicited by speech in cochlear-implant users. *Hear. Res.* 65, 118–124. doi:10.1016/0378-5955(93)90206-G

Leal, M. C., Shin, Y. J., Laborde, M. L., Calmels, M. N., Verges, S., Lugardon, S., et al. (2003). Music perception in adult cochlear implant recipients. *Acta Otolaryngol.* 123, 826–835. doi:10.1080/00016480310000386

Limb, C. J. (2006). Cochlear implant-mediated perception of music. *Curr. Opin. Otolaryngol. Head Neck Surg.* 14, 337–340. doi:10.1097/01.moo.0000244192.59184.bd

Limb, C. J., and Rubinstein, J. T. (2012). Current research on music perception in cochlear implant users. *Otolaryngol. Clin. North Am.* 45, 129–140. doi:10.1016/j.otc.2011.08.021

Lonka, E., Kujala, T., Lehtokoski, A., Johansson, R., Rimmanen, S., Alho, K., et al. (2004). Mismatch negativity brain response as an index of speech perception recovery in cochlear-implant recipients. *Audiol. Neurootol.* 9, 160–162. doi:10.1159/000077265

Lonka, E., Relander-Syrjanen, K., Johansson, R., Näätänen, R., Alho, K., and Kujala, T. (2013). The mismatch negativity (MMN) brain response to sound frequency changes in adult cochlear implant recipients: a follow-up study. *Acta Otolaryngol.* 133, 853–857. doi:10.3109/00016489.2013.780293

McDermott, H. J. (2004). Music perception with cochlear implants: a review. *Trends Amplif.* 8, 49–82. doi:10.1177/108471380400800203

Moore, B. C. (2003). Coding of sounds in the auditory system and its relevance to signal processing and coding in cochlear implants. *Otol. Neurotol.* 24, 243–254. doi:10.1097/00129492-200303000-00019

Näätänen, R. (1992). "Attention and brain function," in *Attention and Brain Function.* London: Lawrence Erlbaum Ass, 102–211. Available at: http://www.questia.com/read/14362952/attention-and-brain-function

Näätänen, R. (2009). Somatosensory mismatch negativity: a new clinical tool for developmental neurological research? *Dev. Med. Child Neurol.* 51, 930–931. doi:10.1111/j.1469-8749.2009.03386.x

Näätänen, R., and Kahkonen, S. (2009). Central auditory dysfunction in schizophrenia as revealed by the mismatch negativity (MMN) and its magnetic equivalent MMNm: a review. *Int. J. Neuropsychopharmacol.* 12, 125–135. doi:10.1017/S1461145708009322

Näätänen, R., Kujala, T., Escera, C., Baldeweg, T., Kreegipuu, K., Carlson, S., et al. (2011a). The mismatch negativity (MMN) – a unique window to disturbed central auditory processing in ageing and different clinical conditions. *Clin. Neurophysiol.* 123, 424–458. doi:10.1016/j.clinph.2011.09.020

Näätänen, R., Kujala, T., and Winkler, I. (2011b). Auditory processing that leads to conscious perception: a unique window to central auditory processing opened by the mismatch negativity and related responses. *Psychophysiology* 48, 4–22. doi:10.1111/j.1469-8986.2010.01114.x

Näätänen, R., Kujala, T., Escera, C., Baldeweg, T., Kreegipuu, K., Carlson, S., et al. (2012). The mismatch negativity (MMN) – a unique window to disturbed central auditory processing in ageing and different clinical conditions. *Clin. Neurophysiol.* 123, 424–458. doi:10.1016/j.clinph.2011.09.020

Näätänen, R., Paavilainen, P., Rinne, T., and Alho, K. (2007). The mismatch negativity (MMN) in basic research of central auditory processing: a review. *Clin. Neurophysiol.* 118, 2544–2590. doi:10.1016/j.clinph.2007.04.026

Näätänen, R., Pakarinen, S., Rinne, T., and Takegata, R. (2004). The mismatch negativity (MMN): towards the optimal paradigm. *Clin. Neurophysiol.* 115, 140–144. doi:10.1016/j.clinph.2003.04.001

Näätänen, R., Schröger, E., Karakas, S., Tervaniemi, M., and Paavilainen, P. (1993). Development of a memory trace for a complex sound in the human brain. *Neuroreport* 4, 503–506. doi:10.1097/00001756-199305000-00010

Näätänen, R., Tervaniemi, M., Sussman, E., Paavilainen, P., and Winkler, I. (2001). "Primitive intelligence" in the auditory cortex. *Trends Neurosci.* 24, 283–288. doi:10.1016/S0166-2236(00)01790-2

Peretz, I., Brattico, E., Jarvenpaa, M., and Tervaniemi, M. (2009). The amusic brain: in tune, out of key, and unaware. *Brain* 132, 1277–1286. doi:10.1093/brain/awp055

Ponton, C. W., and Don, M. (1995). The mismatch negativity in cochlear implant users. *Ear. Hear.* 16, 131–46.

Sandmann, P., Eichele, T., Buechler, M., Debener, S., Jancke, L., Dillier, N., et al. (2009). Evaluation of evoked potentials to dyadic tones after cochlear implantation. *Brain* 132, 1967–1979. doi:10.1093/brain/awp034

Sandmann, P., Kegel, A., Eichele, T., Dillier, N., Lai, W., Bendixen, A., et al. (2010). Neurophysiological evidence of impaired musical sound perception in cochlear-implant users. *Clin. Neurophysiol.* 121, 2070–2082. doi:10.1016/j.clinph.2010.04.032

Slabu, L., Grimm, S., and Escera, C. (2012). Novelty detection in the human auditory brainstem. *J. Neurosci.* 32, 1447–1452. doi:10.1523/JNEUROSCI.2557-11.2012

Tervaniemi, M. (2009). Musicians – same or different? *Ann. N. Y. Acad. Sci.* 1169, 151–156. doi:10.1111/j.1749-6632.2009.04591.x

Timm, L., Agrawal, D., Viola, F. C., Sandmann P., Debener, S., Büchner, A., et al. (2012). Temporal feature perception in cochlear implant users. *PLoS ONE* 7:e45375. doi:10.1371/journal.pone.0045375

Torppa, R., Salo, E., Makkonen, T., Loimo, H., Pykalainen, J., Lipsanen, J., et al. (2012). Cortical processing of musical sounds in children with cochlear implants. *Clin. Neurophysiol.* 123, 1966–1979. doi:10.1016/j.clinph.2012.03.008

Viola, F. C., De Vos, M., Hine, J., Sandmann, P., Bleeck, S., Eyles, J., et al. (2012). Semi-automatic attenuation of cochlear implant artifacts for the evaluation of late auditory evoked potentials. *Hear. Res.* 284, 6–15. doi:10.1016/j.heares.2011.12.010

Viola, F. C., Thorne, J., Edmonds, B., Schneider, T., Eichele, T., and Debener, S. (2009). Semi-automatic identification of independent components representing EEG artifact. *Clin. Neurophysiol.* 120, 868–877. doi:10.1016/j.clinph.2009.01.015

Viola, F. C., Thorne, J. D., Bleeck, S., Eyles, J., and Debener, S. (2011). Uncovering auditory evoked potentials from cochlear implant users with independent component analysis. *Psychophysiology* 48, 1470–1480. doi:10.1111/j.1469-8986.2011.01224.x

Vuust, P., Brattico, E., Glerean, E., Seppanen, M., Pakarinen, S., Tervaniemi, M., et al. (2011). New fast mismatch negativity paradigm for determining the neural prerequisites for musical ability. *Cortex* 47, 1091–1098. doi:10.1016/j.cortex.2011.04.026

Vuust, P., Brattico, E., Seppanen, M., Näätänen, R., and Tervaniemi, M. (2012a). The sound of music: differentiating musicians using a fast, musical multi-feature mismatch negativity paradigm. *Neuropsychologia* 50, 1432–1443. doi:10.1016/j.neuropsychologia.2012.02.028

Vuust, P., Brattico, E., Seppänen, M., Näätänen, R., and Tervaniemi, M. (2012b). Practiced musical style shapes auditory skills. *Ann. N. Y. Acad. Sci.* 1252, 139–146. doi:10.1111/j.1749-6632.2011.06409.x

Vuust, P., Pallesen, K. J., Bailey, C., Van Zuijen, T. L., Gjedde, A., Roepstorff, A., et al. (2005). To musicians, the message is in the meter pre-attentive neuronal responses to incongruent rhythm are left-lateralized in musicians. *Neuroimage* 24, 560–564. doi:10.1016/j.neuroimage.2004.08.039

Vuust, P., and Roepstorff, A. (2008). Listen up! polyrhythms in brain and music. *Cogn. Semiot.* 3, 131–159. doi:10.1515/cogsem.2008.3.fall2008.134

Zhang, F., Hammer, T., Banks, H. L., Benson, C., Xiang, J., and Fu, Q. J. (2011). Mismatch negativity and adaptation measures of the late auditory evoked potential in cochlear implant users. *Hear. Res.* 275, 17–29. doi:10.1016/j.heares.2010.11.007

5

Rhythm perception and production predict reading abilities in developmental dyslexia

Elena Flaugnacco[1,2], Luisa Lopez[3], Chiara Terribili[3], Stefania Zoia[1], Sonia Buda[3], Sara Tilli[3], Lorenzo Monasta[4], Marcella Montico[4], Alessandra Sila[2], Luca Ronfani[4] and Daniele Schön[5,6]*

[1] *Child Neurology and Psychiatry Ward, Institute for Maternal and Child Health - IRCCS Burlo Garofolo Pediatric Institute, Trieste, Italy*
[2] *Center for the Child Health – Onlus, Trieste, Italy*
[3] *Developmental Neuropsychiatry Ward, Villaggio Eugenio Litta, Rome, Italy*
[4] *Epidemiology and Biostatistics Unit, Institute for Maternal and Child Health - IRCCS Burlo Garofolo Pediatric Institute, Trieste, Italy*
[5] *Institut de Neurosciences des Systémes, Aix-Marseille Université, Marseille, France*
[6] *INSERM, U1106, Marseille, France*

Correspondence:
Daniele Schön, Faculté de Médecine la Timone, UMR 1106 - Institut de Neurosciences des Systèmes, Aix-Marseille Université, Aile rouge - 5éme étage, 27 bd Jean Moulin 13005, Marseille, France
e-mail: daniele.schon@univ-amu.fr

Rhythm organizes events in time and plays a major role in music, but also in the phonology and prosody of a language. Interestingly, children with developmental dyslexia—a learning disability that affects reading acquisition despite normal intelligence and adequate education—have a poor rhythmic perception. It has been suggested that an accurate perception of rhythmical/metrical structure, that requires accurate perception of rise time, may be critical for phonological development and subsequent literacy. This hypothesis is mostly based on results showing a high degree of correlation between phonological awareness and metrical skills, using a very specific metrical task. We present new findings from the analysis of a sample of 48 children with a diagnosis of dyslexia, without comorbidities. These children were assessed with neuropsychological tests, as well as specifically-devised psychoacoustic and musical tasks mostly testing temporal abilities. Associations were tested by multivariate analyses including data mining strategies, correlations and most importantly logistic regressions to understand to what extent the different auditory and musical skills can be a robust predictor of reading and phonological skills. Results show a strong link between several temporal skills and phonological and reading abilities. These findings are discussed in the framework of the neuroscience literature comparing music and language processing, with a particular interest in the links between rhythm processing in music and language.

Keywords: dyslexia, phonological awareness, temporal processing, rhythm, music

INTRODUCTION

Music is a complex activity that taps onto several sensory-motor, cognitive and emotional mechanisms. Over the last two decades many studies have tested the hypothesis that music training (implying formal training and/or regular practice) can impact non-musical abilities. Most of these studies have addressed this issue by comparing a population of musicians, either professional or amateur, and a population of non-musicians, namely participants with little or no music training. Overall, these studies have shown a clear effect of music-dependent brain plasticity affecting brain activity both at the functional and structural level in adults (Herholz and Zatorre, 2012) and children with as little as one year of musical practice (Hyde et al., 2009).

Music shares many basic processes with other human activities, and this is particularly evident when comparing music and speech (Besson and Schön, 2011). Both rely on sound processing and require a precise—though often categorical—representation of several sound features, such as timbre, pitch, duration, and their interactions. As an example, these representations allow discrimination between *legato* and *staccato* violin sounds as well as [ba] and [pa] phonemes.

While a common belief is that music is mostly challenging with respect to pitch, music making puts a high challenge on all these sound features, and most importantly on complex spectral features, because sound quality (and not just being in tune) is what a musician has to work on from the very start. This may explain why music training enhances processing of sound features that play a major role in speech processing as well (Kraus and Chandrasekaran, 2010). Adult musicians have a more faithful representation of speech sound features in the brainstem, both in terms of pitch and formants (Wong et al., 2007). These representations are also more robust to noisy conditions (Parbery-Clark et al., 2012). This subcortical music-induced plasticity may depend upon the numerous corticofugal (descending) projections from the cortex to the brainstem auditory relays.

One of the most important properties of music being its structuring sounds in time and in a tonal space, it is not surprising that music-dependent brain plasticity goes well beyond subcortical and primary auditory and sensorimotor cortex, thus affecting more integrated functions. For instance, there is evidence that music training facilitates language learning. Children taking music classes are better at segmenting a new artificial language on the sole basis of its statistical properties (François et al., 2012), an ability that seems to rely heavily on the dorsal pathway (Rodriguez-Fornells et al., 2009). Other studies show an overall enhancement of verbal intelligence in children taking music classes (Moreno et al., 2011), possibly tapping onto several integrated brain functions.

A number of studies have also reported an association between music and reading skills. For example, pitch perception was positively correlated with phonemic awareness and reading abilities in children (Anvari et al., 2002) and the variability in tapping to a beat correlated with performance on reading and attention tests (Tiernay and Kraus, 2013a). A meta-analysis of 25 cross-sectional studies found a significant association between music training and reading skills (Butzlaff, 2000). Importantly, music seems to be able, to a certain extent, to drive an improvement in reading skills in normal readers (Moreno et al., 2009).

The fact of showing, on one side that music and language share several sensory and cognitive processes, and on the other side that music training enhances several language abilities, has brought several researchers to hypothesize that music training may be effective in rehabilitation of several motor and cognitive disorders in different clinical populations (Tallal and Gaab, 2006; Besson et al., 2007; Särkämö et al., 2008; Schön et al., 2008; Altenmüller et al., 2009; Kraus and Chandrasekaran, 2010; Goswami, 2011; Patel, 2011; Amengual et al., 2013).

Our study focuses on the relation between musical abilities and reading skills in children with developmental dyslexia. Developmental dyslexia is a disorder characterized by a specific and long lasting difficulty in reading acquisition, limited to written text decoding with no sensory or neurological deficits (Snowling and Hulme, 2012).

Reading results are slow and inaccurate, despite adequate intelligence, socio-cultural background and instruction. Difficulties arise typically from a phonological core deficit with an indirect impact on reading comprehension, requiring lexical, morpho-syntactic, memory and prediction abilities that are not directly affected by this disorder (Lyon et al., 2003).

In Italy, prevalence of developmental dyslexia ranges from 1.5 to 5% (Cornoldi and Tressoldi, 2007). A recent epidemiological study involved a sample of more than 1500 children attending the fourth grade of primary school in Friuli Venezia Giulia, a region in the north of Italy, and found prevalence slightly higher than 3%, thus lower than that reported in opaque language speaking countries such as United Kingdom or France (Barbiero et al., 2012).

While the neurobiological and genetic basis of developmental dyslexia is now widely accepted in the scientific community, it is not clear whether there is a specific neuropsychological function that, once impaired, determines such heterogeneous landscape of difficulties in reading acquisition. Indeed, if the reading disorder is best described in terms of phonological deficits and to a certain extent visual deficits, there are other deficits of working memory, sequencing, mental calculation, motor coordination or music processing that are often associated with the main reading disorder (Ramus, 2004; Snowling and Hulme, 2012).

These observations have brought to the emergence of multiple hypotheses relative to the functional deficit of developmental dyslexia that may be accounted for by a multifocal brain abnormality approach (Pernet et al., 2009). Nonetheless, several authors agree in defining the phonological deficit as the core deficit of developmental dyslexia, primarily due to a dysfunction of the auditory system yielding a poor temporal processing. Interestingly, several studies have shown that children with developmental dyslexia also show an impairment of music temporal processing; compared to normally developing children they are impaired in tapping along a song (Overy et al., 2003), show greater variability when asked to tap along a metronome (Thomson and Goswami, 2008) and are quite poor in segmentation and grouping tasks, both in speech and music (Petkov et al., 2005). Furthermore, Wolff (2002) found that children with dyslexia tended to overanticipate the cued stimulus by as much as 100 ms, unlike their control matched peers, and showed difficulties reproducing patterned rhythms of tones.

What still remains to be understood is the precise temporal scale(s) that may be impaired, thus causing a phonological deficit. For instance, Tallal (1980, 2004) has suggested a rapid temporal processing deficit which would prevent the discrimination of different phonemes, in particular contrastive consonants such as [t]-[d] that acoustically differ in terms of rapid transient formants. While several studies supported a notion of causal link between impaired perception of rapid spectrotemporal cues and impaired literacy (Reed, 1989; De Martino et al., 2001; Tallal, 2004), recent research has suggested a rather limited role for rapid auditory processing in developmental dyslexia (Heath and Hogben, 2004a,b).

An alternative hypothesis seems to rely on a longer time scale, that of amplitude envelope, and more precisely that of "rise time" which in the case of speech can be very important to distinguish different voice onset times (VOT) allowing to categorize /ch/ of chip vs. /sh/ of ship or /b/ of bull vs. /p/ of pool (Rosen, 1992). There is, indeed, growing literature attesting the presence of impaired amplitude envelope perception in developmental dyslexia, across languages with different phonological structures and languages with different writing systems (for a review see Goswami et al., 2011b, 2013). More precisely, a specific deficit in accurately processing sound rise time (the time taken for sounds to reach their maximum amplitude) has been postulated (Goswami et al., 2010). Rise times are critical in speech signal, as they reflect the patterns of amplitude modulation that facilitate syllabic segmentation. Thus, a poor perception of amplitude envelope structure may lead to poor phonological development (Goswami, 2011). By contrast to rapid spectrotemporal modulations, more linked to acoustic processing, slower spectrotemporal modulations and the amplitude envelope are linked to syllabic and prosodic structure, in particular to speech rhythm and intonational patterning (Greenberg, 2006).

Impaired auditory perception of slow ($<10\,\text{Hz}$) temporal modulations in speech is thus likely to cause poor perception of speech rhythm and syllable stress (Goswami, 2011; Leong et al., 2011). Indeed, children with developmental dyslexia have a deficit in both rhythm and meter perception, also when using musical stimuli (Huss et al., 2011).

Following the idea of a neural oscillatory phase-locking to speech modulation patterns (e.g., Ghitza, 2011; Giraud and Poeppel, 2012), the perceptual difficulties commonly observed in developmental dyslexia could be underpinned by impaired phase alignment between speech and neural activity as well as poor firing coupling between different neuronal oscillatory rates (Abrams et al., 2009; Lehongre et al., 2011; Leong and Goswami, 2014).

In this work we present data collected on an Italian highly selected sample of children with developmental dyslexia. In the light of what has been documented in the literature, we investigate the relation between musical temporal, phonological, and decoding (reading) skills. The starting point is the hypothesis of a temporal sampling deficit as possible cause of the poor phonological representation and reading ability. We present a multivariate approach first describing correlations between reading and temporal processing outcomes. Then, we analyse, within the limits of a cross sectional approach, the (predictive) links between several "temporal processing" measures and reading abilities. Finally, we interpret our findings within the theoretical framework described above and give our contribution to the development of a targeted and rehabilitative hypothesis of developmental dyslexia via music training.

METHODS

PARTICIPANTS

Out of 225 children aged 8–11 years with a diagnosis of developmental dyslexia, referred to the health units and rehabilitation centers (IRCCS Burlo Garofolo and ASS1 local health units in Trieste and Villaggio Eugenio Litta in Grottaferrata, Rome), we included 48 children based on the following criteria.

Inclusion criteria

Italian native language; reading performance (accuracy and/or speed) failed on at least two of three school grade standardized Italian tests, as stated in the Original National Guidelines (PARCC DSA, 2011): text, words, pseudowords (speed scores: z-score <-1.8 standard deviations from the mean, accuracy: <5th percentile); hearing, vision and neurological examination within normal range; normal or corrected-to-normal visual acuity; General IQ >85 at the Wechsler Intelligence Scale for Children III.

Exclusion criteria

Comorbidity with Attentional Deficit Disorders with Hyperactivity (ADHD), Specific Language Impairment (SLI), Oppositional Defiant Disorder (ODD), severe emotional-relational impairments, previous formal musical or painting education for more than one year, on-going treatment.

The assessment was carried out by neuropsychologists and neurologists. Children participated only upon formal signed informed consent from their parents.

After the enrolment, the 48 children underwent the following neuropsychological assessment, which includes standardized test and phonological and musical tasks (22 children in Trieste and 26 in Grottaferrata), with mean age of 9 years and 8 months. Two children did not complete the testing.

NEUROPSYCHOLOGICAL ASSESSMENT

Parents completed a detailed anamnestic questionnaire providing information about their child's health, relevant family history, and socioeconomic background.

STANDARDIZED ABILITY TESTS

General cognitive abilities

General cognitive abilities and working memory were assessed using the Wechsler Intelligence Scale for Children III (Orsini and Picone, 2006).

Auditory attention

Auditory Attention was measured using a subtest from the BIA Battery (Marzocchi, 2010) wherein children have to count the number of occurrences of a given sound.

Phonological awareness

Phonological awareness was assessed using the pseudowords repetition test from the Promea Battery (Vicari, 2007).

Reading abilities

The ability to read a text aloud was measured using an Italian standardized test for reading abilities (*MT Reading test*, Cornoldi and Colpo, 2011). Because different texts were used depending upon the school grade, statistics were based on the standardized clinical cut-off.

The ability to read single words and pseudowords aloud was measured on a standardized list of 102 Italian words and 48 Italian pseudowords (*DDE-2*, Sartori et al., 2007). Again, statistics were based on the standardized clinical cut-off (percentiles).

PHONOLOGICAL AWARENESS TASKS

Phonemic blending

The phonemic blending test included 38 words (nouns) of increasing difficulty, selected from VARLESS Italian data base (Burani et al., 2011). Difficulty was estimated on the basis of the number of syllables, frequency in oral speech and written language, accent regularity, and orthographic complexity. Children had to blend sounds into words (e.g., hear [d]-[o]-[g] and produce [dog]). Every child performance was recorded with the Open Source sound editor and recorder Audacity 1.3 (beta). Dependent variables: number of correct items and time to perform the test.

Phonemic segmentation

The phonemic segmentation task also included 38 words, with the same selection criteria described above for the phonemic blending task. Children had to segment every word into its basic sounds (e.g., hear [frog] and produce [f]-[r]-[o]-[g]). Every child performance was recorded with Audacity 1.3 (beta). Dependent variables: number of correct items and time to perform the test.

PSYCHOACOUSTIC TASKS

MLP Amplitude envelop onset (rise time)

In this experiment children listened to a sequence of three identical pure tones (800 ms each) with headphones. The onset of one of the tones was varied adaptively (longer ramping) to find the subject's threshold using a Maximum Likelihood Procedure

(MLP, Grassi and Soranzo, 2009). Children had to detect the longest ring tone (first, second or third?) by choosing one of three telephone pictures.

MLP Temporal anisochrony

In this experiment children listened to a sequence of five identical complex tones (100ms each) with headphones and had to report whether or not a cartoon rabbit was able to perform regular jumps. The gap between tones 3–4 and 4–5 was varied adaptively to find the subject's threshold using a Maximum Likelihood Procedure (MLP, Grassi and Soranzo, 2009).

MUSICAL TASKS

Tapping

Children had to tap along a 90 pulse/minute metronome for 40 s. Each sound lasted 50 ms, was built using a sinusoidal sound ($f = 1200$), and ramped with a 1 ms ramp at the onset and offset. Children listened to the metronome using an open headphone at approximately 75 dB and performed the task holding a pencil in their dominant hand and tapping it on a wooden box containing a microphone. They were instructed to tap as regularly as possible and did a short training before the recording to verify that they understood the task. Stimulation and acquisition were run using Audacity 1.3. Tap onsets were calculated using a custom Matlab program and a semi-automatic (supervised) procedure. Analyses were run on the coefficient of variation (i.e., the mean of the inter-tapping intervals divided by the standard deviation).

Rhythm reproduction

Children had to listen and reproduce 10 different rhythms (3–8 tones each; durations spanned from triplets of eight notes to half notes). Each sound of the sequence lasted 65 ms and was built using a MIDI woodblock sound. The sequences were taken and adapted from Fries and Swihart study (1990). Children listened to the sequence using an open headphone at approximately 75 dB and immediately reproduced it holding a pencil in their dominant hand and tapping it on a wooden box containing a microphone. They were instructed to tap as accurately as possible and did a short training before the recording to verify that they understood the task. Stimulation and acquisition were run using Audacity 1.3.

Every item performance was scored by two independent judges from 1 to 9 depending on its similarity to the template stimulus (9 = identical). The final mark for each child was the average of the twenty scores (inter judge correlation was 0.89).

Perception of musical meter

The musical meter task tested and published by Huss et al. (2011) was adapted for this study. Only trials that had metrical structure critical for children with developmental dyslexia were selected. Therefore the task included 18 trials of different metrical arrangements of a series of notes with an underlying pulse rate of 500 ms (120 bpm), each series being delivered twice within one trial. Half of the trials delivered an identical series of notes twice ("same" trials), and half delivered two slightly different series of notes ("different" trials). In the "different" trials, the change in metrical structure was caused by adding 100 ms to the accented notes. The task was to make a same-different judgment. Same and different trials were delivered in pseudo-random order.

Each sequence comprised a simple rhythm (2–5 notes) repeated 3 times, to keep short-term memory demands low. Trial length was approximately equated across variations in the number of notes by varying the length of individual notes. Ten trials (5 same, 5 different) were in 4/4 time and 8 trials (4 same, 4 different) were in 3/4 time, with accent conveyed by increasing the intensity of the relevant note in the sequence by 5 dB.

STATISTICAL ANALYSIS

Statistical analysis was performed with SPSS 13.0 and Intercooled Stata 9.0.

Spearman correlation analysis (based on ranks) was performed to test the strength of a relationship between variables. The 95% confidence interval for Rho was calculated with Fisher method.

The interdependence among the measured variables, namely the joint measured variations in response to possible latent (unobserved) variables, was calculated by using a factor analysis with Varimax rotation (maximizing the variances of the squared correlations between variables and factors).

Logistic regression analyses were carried out in order to evaluate which measures were associated with the six dependent variables of the reading tests. All associations were adjusted for sex, school level, city of recruitment and IQ were always controlled (see **Tables 7, 8**). Reading outcomes were dichotomized into highly pathological and pathological to increase robustness of the test.

RESULTS

Figures 1–3 illustrate the outcomes of reading, phonological awareness and temporal processing tests.

CORRELATIONS

Correlations between all the temporal processing tasks and measures of phonology and literacy are provided in **Tables 1, 2**. An overview of significant values in **Table 1** (**$p < 0.001$ and *$p < 0.05$) shows that each reading outcome measure, with the exception of the MT text reading test, correlated significantly with rhythm reproduction and tapping tasks. The difference observed for the MT test may be due to the fact that it includes different school-level adapted texts, which in turn increases variability. Nevertheless, the outcome of this test correlates with amplitude envelope onset (rise time). Perception of the musical meter task shows a weak correlation with word reading time measure but a strong correlation with auditory attention test ($r = 0.434$, $p < 0.01$). The auditory attention test also correlates with WISC III digit span test ($r = 0.378$, $p < 0.01$) and rhythm reproduction ($r = 0.292$, $p < 0.05$), but not with phonological awareness or other reading outcomes.

As observed in **Table 2**, rhythm reproduction and tapping measures correlate with phonological tests, in particular with phonemic blending task and pseudoword repetition tests.

Overall, **Tables 1, 2** suggest that there is a strong relationship between reading outcomes, phonological awareness, and

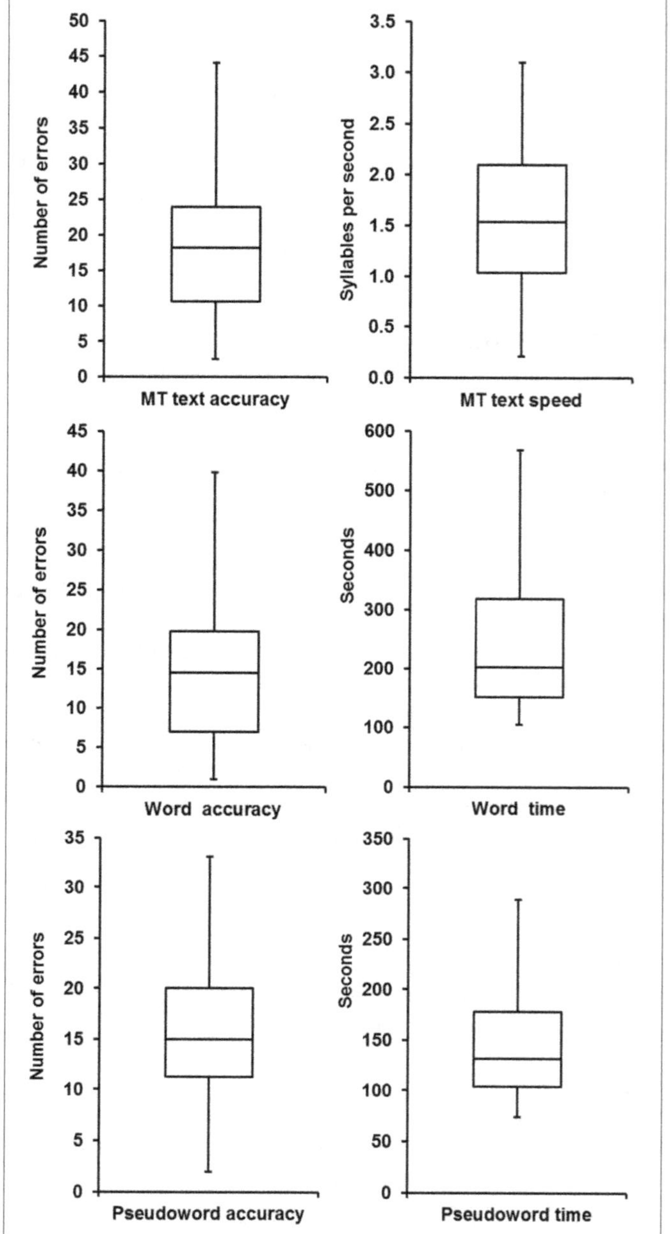

FIGURE 1 | Box plots of the reading outcomes. The bottom and top of the box show the first and third quartiles, the band inside the box the median. The edges of the whiskers represent the values closest to the median between the minimum absolute value and Q1 − 1.5IQR for the lower whisker, and the maximum absolute value and Q3 + 1.5IQR for the upper whisker, where Q1 and Q3 are the first and third quartiles respectively, and IQR is the interquartile range.

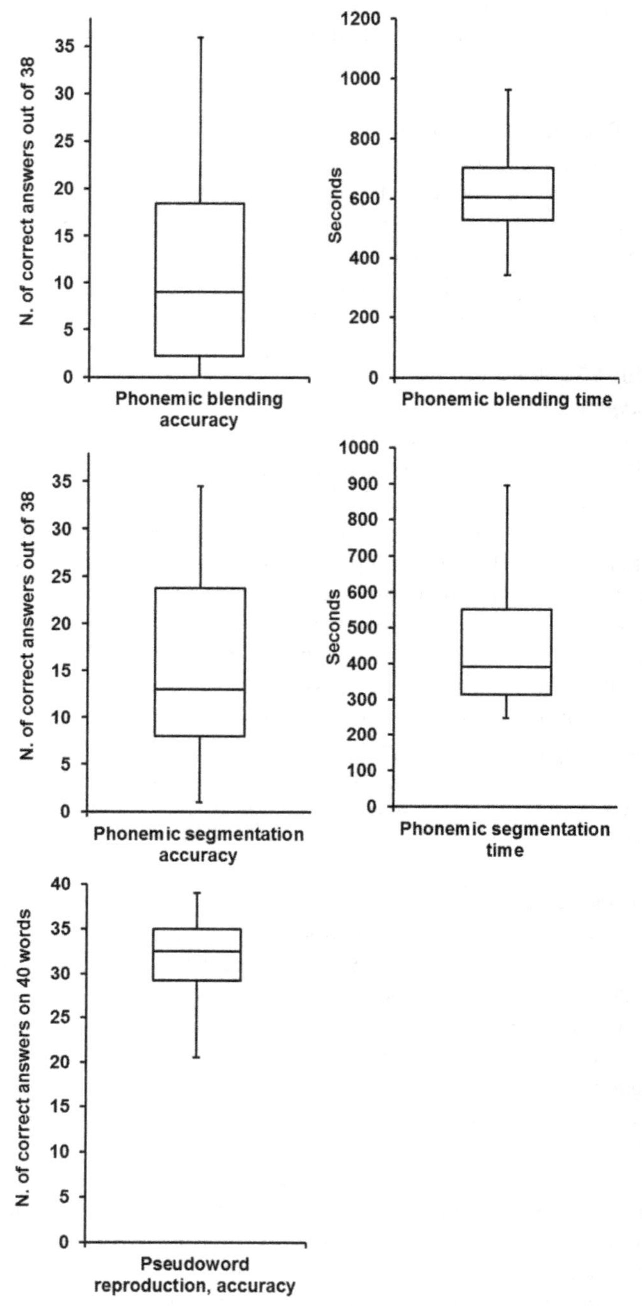

FIGURE 2 | Box plots of the phonological awareness measures.

rhythm reproduction and tapping measures (**Figure 4**). The interdependence among these variables was tested with a factor analyses.

Table 3 shows the correlation between the different temporal tasks. Overall and as expected there is a rather strong correlation between tasks, exception made for the task measuring the rise time threshold which only shows a weak to moderate correlation with the meter perception task.

FACTOR ANALYSIS

The factor analysis included accuracy and speed measures in the tests measuring reading abilities, phonological awareness, temporal processing, auditory attention, and digit span. Preliminary testing showed that our model was satisfactorily adequate. Indeed the Kaiser-Meyer-Olkin (KMO) index measuring the sampling adequacy gave a value of 0.764 (recommended is >0.6). Also the Bartlett's test of sphericity rejecting the null hypothesis of an identity matrix was significant ($p < 0.001$, recommended is <0.05). Finally, following two different methods to estimate the

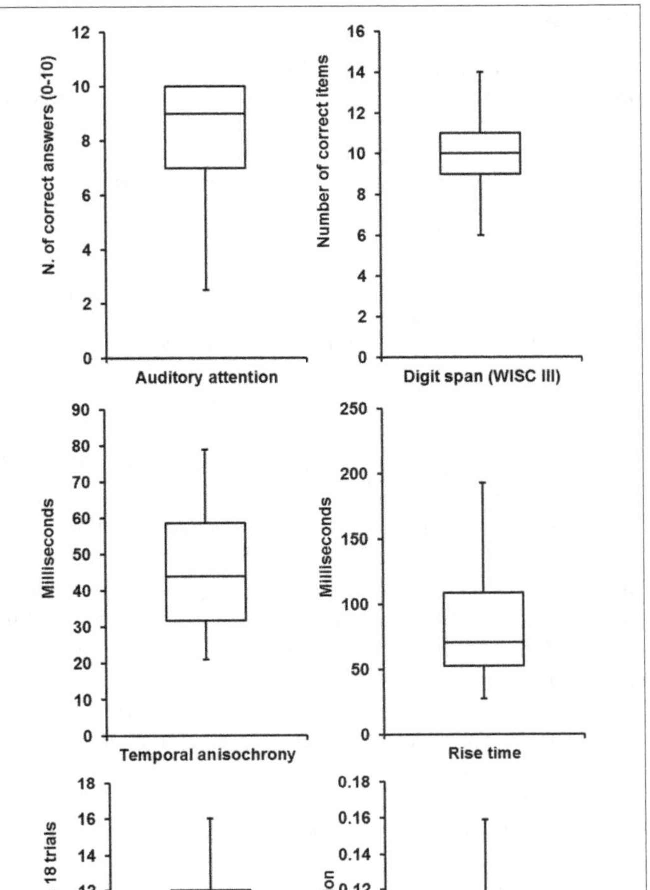

FIGURE 3 | Box plots of the temporal processing measures.

number of factors (software package F A C T O R, Unrestricted Factor Analysis 9.2 by Urbano Lorenzo-Seva and Pere J. Ferrando) and the eigenvalue criterion $\geq$1, three factors were extracted explaining a variance of 61.389% (**Table 4**).

Table 1 | Spearman correlations between reading measures and phonology and temporal processing tasks.

	Tapping	Rhythm reprod.	Meter percep.	Rise time	Temporal anisoch.	Pseudo-word reproduct. accuracy	Phonemic segment. accuracy	Phonemic blending accuracy
MT text accuracy	0.006 (−0.288/0.299)	−0.280 (−0.528/0.011)	−0.154 (−0.425/0.143)	0.301 (0.012/0.544)	−0.135 (−0.409/0.162)	−0.165 (−0.434/0.132)	−0.342 (−0.575/−0.057)	−0.131 (−0.406/0.166)
MT text speed	−0.346 (−0.578/−0.062)	0.387 (0.109/0.609)	0.269 (−0.023/0.519)	−0.274 (−0.523/0.018)	−0.161 (−0.431/0.135)	0.240 (−0.054/0.495)	0.065 (−0.229/0.349)	0.305 (0.0159/0.547)
Word accuracy	**0.360** (0.074/0.591)	**−0.445** (−0.651/−0.178)	−0.245 (−0.499/0.049)	0.204 (−0.091/0.467)	0.278 (−0.013/0.526)	−0.224 (−0.483/0.071)	−0.168 (−0.437/0.128)	**−0.380** (−0.603/−0.101)
Word time	**0.452** (0.182/0.658)	**−0.438** (−0.646/−0.170)	−0.317 (−0.556/−0.029)	0.239 (−0.055/0.495)	0.189 (−0.108/0.454)	−0.238 (−0.495/0.056)	−0.025 (−0.313/0.267)	**−0.396** (−0.615/−0.119)
Pseudoword accuracy	0.191 (−0.108/0.459)	**−0.357** (−0.586/−0.074)	−0.162 (−0.432/0.134)	0.303 (0.014/0.545)	0.000 (−0.290/0.291)	−0.285 (−0.531/0.006)	−0.189 (−0.454/0.107)	−0.170 (−0.439/0.126)
Pseudoword time	0.292 (−0.001/0.539)	−0.229 (−0.487/0.065)	−0.284 (−0.530/0.007)	0.069 (−0.226/0.352)	0.159 (−0.138/0.429)	−0.123 (−0.399/0.174)	−0.020 (−0.308/0.272)	0.312 (-0.553/−0.024)

In parenthesis the 95% confidence interval. Critical values (double-tailed) levels of significance for our sample size are 0.294 and 0.347 for p values of 0.05 and 0.01 respectively (not corrected for multiple comparisons) and 0.472 for p = 0.05 Bonferroni corrected for multiple comparisons. Values with a non-corrected p value < 0.01 (reasonably controlling for false positive) are reported in bold.

Table 2 | Spearman correlations between temporal processing tasks and phonology tasks.

	Tapping	Rhythm reproduction	Meter perception	Rise time	Temporal anisochrony
Pseudoword reproduction, accuracy	**−0.380** (−0.606/−0.097)	**0.380** (0.100/0.603)	0.131 (−0.165/0.406)	−0.209 (−0.470/0.087)	−0.246 (−0.500/0.048)
Phonemic segmentation accuracy	−0.252 (−0.508/0.045)	0.340 (0.055/0.574)	0.200 (−0.095/0.464)	−0.090 (−0.371/0.205)	−0.015 (−0.304/0.277)
Phonemic blending accuracy	**−0.527** (−0.710/−0.276)	**0.442** (0.173/0.649)	0.259 (−0.034/0.511)	−0.015 (−0.304/0.277)	−0.101 (−0.380/0.195)

Critical p values are the same as in ***Table 1*** *exception made for the Bonferroni corrected p value, here 0.428. Values with a non-corrected p value < 0.01 (reasonably controlling for false positive) are reported in bold.*

The first factor shows high factor loadings (i.e., correlation coefficients between variables and factors) for speed and accuracy scores in all reading tests and surprisingly in rise time threshold. Thus, this first factor can be interpreted as describing reading abilities.

The second factor shows high factor loadings for the temporal anisochrony threshold and auditory attention test while slightly lower factor loadings for tapping coefficient of variation, accuracy in rhythm reproduction task, musical meter perception task, pseudoword repetition test and the verbal short term memory test of WISC III. It can thus be interpreted as a factor describing broad auditory temporal processing.

The third factor shows high factor loadings for accuracy in the phonemic blending and phonemic segmentation tests and slightly lower loading for the pseudoword repetition and rhythm reproduction tasks. It can thus be interpreted as a factor describing broad phonological processing.

LOGISTIC REGRESSION

In the logistic regression analyses (**Tables 5–8**), the reading outcome measures were considered as the dependent variables.

Analyses of the MT text reading test point to the meter perception task as a good predictor of reading accuracy ($or = 0.641$, $p = 0.02$). Reading speed was only associated with the controlled variables IQ and school-level.

Analyses of the word reading test point to the mother school level as a good predictor of reading accuracy ($or = 6.371$, $p = 0.006$) and to the meter perception task as a good predictor of reading speed ($or = 0.270$, $p = 0.032$).

Analyses of the pseudoword reading test point to the rhythm reproduction test as a good predictor of reading accuracy ($or = 0.429$, $p = 0.026$). Reading speed was not significantly associated to any variables entered in the model.

DISCUSSION

This study explored whether and to what extent different levels of temporal processing are associated to reading and phonological abilities.

We found that rhythm reproduction were strongly associated with most reading outcome measures and phonological awareness. Furthermore, tapping tasks correlated with some aspects of language and rise time correlated with text reading, in accordance with previously published studies (Goswami et al., 2002; Thomson and Goswami, 2008).

Intriguingly, the factor analysis identified three significant factors: the first grouping reading tests and rise time thresholds; the second spanning broad auditory temporal processing, including pseudoword repetition and verbal short term memory; the third describing phonological processing but also including rhythm reproduction.

Last but not least, the logistic regression analyses indicated the meter perception task as a good predictor of text reading accuracy and word reading speed, while rhythm reproduction was the best predictor of pseudoword reading accuracy. Finally, maternal formal education level was also a good predictor of word reading accuracy.

We will first discuss the results of these complementary analyses, bridging temporal processing skills on one side and phonological awareness and literacy on the other. We will then present some considerations on the different temporal scales that are addressed by our tasks and by other tasks and models described in the literature. Finally, we will consider the use of music training as a possible rehabilitation of developmental dyslexia and give some tentative recommendations.

BRIDGING TEMPORAL PROCESSING AND READING SKILLS

Correlations between the temporal processing tasks, phonology measures, and literacy confirm previously published data in the literature (Anvari et al., 2002; Overy et al., 2003; Huss et al., 2011). The temporal task showing the highest correlation is the rhythm reproduction task, followed by the tapping task. These tasks are the two most complex temporal tasks because they both require listening and motor coordination. The rhythm reproduction task also requires working memory and grouping events in meaningful chunks, even though the sequences were not long. By contrast the tapping task is a sensorimotor synchronization task which does not require working memory or chunking because the stimulus was a simple metronome.

The perceptual metrical tasks also require grouping events in chunks on the basis of a metrical hierarchy (e.g., strong-weak-weak). The independent variable was the duration of the strong beat which was sometimes lengthened by 100 ms. This is somewhat related to the two psychoacoustic tests measuring rise time and temporal anisochrony thresholds because lengthening the strong beat produces both a change in the

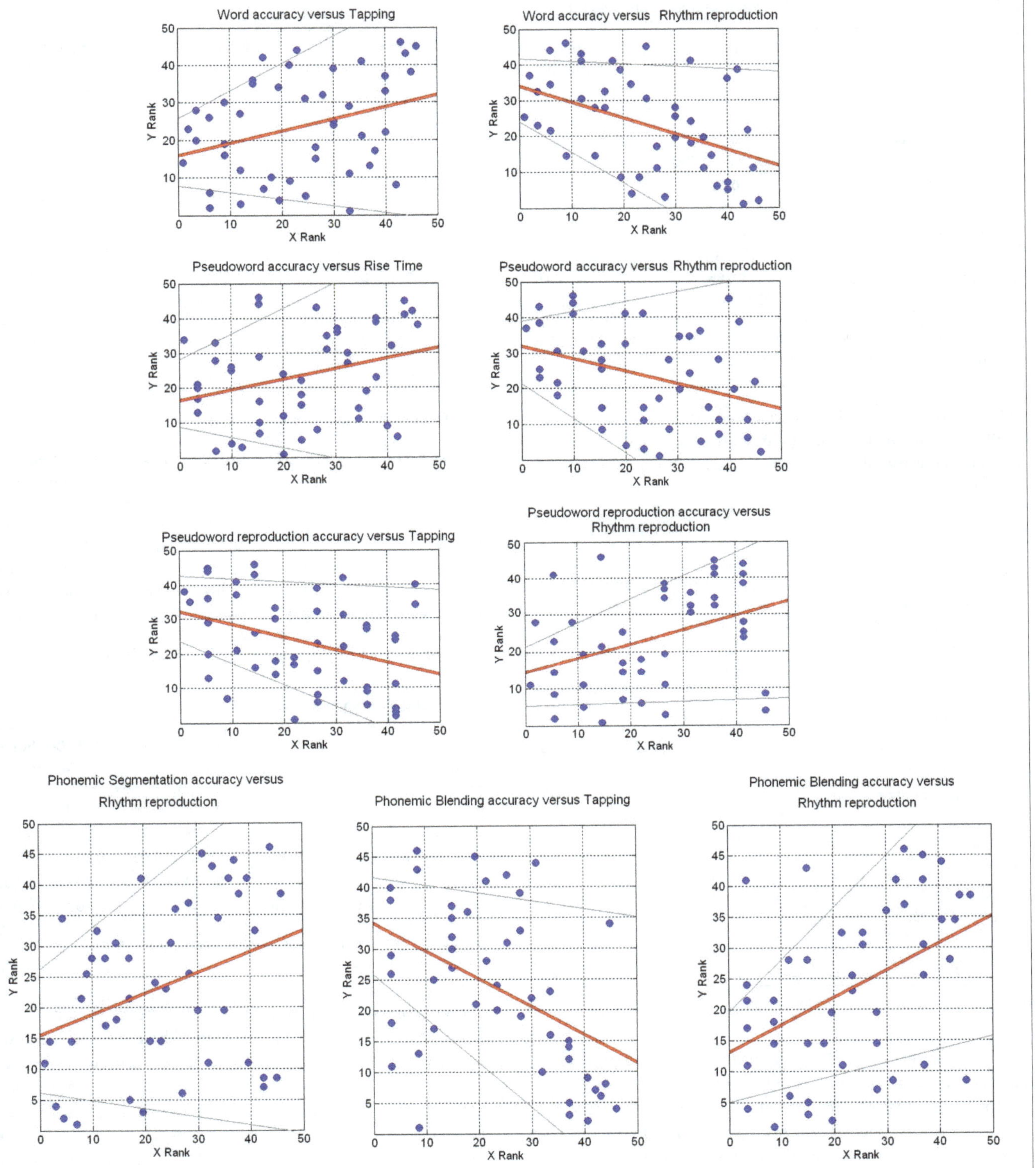

FIGURE 4 | Scatter plots of ranked variables to illustrate high *r* values between temporal tasks and reading and phonological tasks. Red lines indicate the linear regression. Gray lines indicate 98.5 confidence interval.

temporal envelope of the note—like in the rise time task—and a change in the temporal relation with the preceding and following notes—like in the temporal anisochrony task. Interestingly, the temporal anisochrony task did not correlate with any phonological or literacy measures. By contrast, both the metrical and rise time tasks correlated with some literacy measures (word and text reading) pointing to a greater role of temporal envelope compared to temporal isochrony.

Table 3 | Spearman correlations between temporal processing tasks.

	Tapping	Rhythm reproduction	Meter Perception	MLP Rise time	MLP Temporal anisochrony
Tapping					
Rhythm reproduction	**−0.618** (−0.771/−0.396)				
Meter Perception	**−0.425** (−0.639/−0.151)	0.319 (0.028/0.560)			
MLP Rise time	0.203 (−0.096/0.468)	−0.186 (−0.455/0.113)	−0.294 (−0.540/−0.000)		
MLP Temporal anisochrony	**0.385** (0.103/0.610)	**−0.379** (−0.605/−0.097)	**−0.354** (−0.586/−0.067)	−0.084 (−0.369/0.214)	

*Critical p values are the same as in **Table 1** exception made for the Bonferroni corrected p value, here 0.411. Values with a non-corrected p value < 0.01 (reasonably controlling for false positive) are reported in bold.*

Table 4 | Varimax with Kaiser Normalization rotated factor loadings for all tests of reading, phonological awareness, temporal processing, attention and verbal short term memory, using the option "Blank" (<l0.40l).

	Component		
	1 (6.112)	**2 (1.644)**	**3 (1.453)**
MT text reading speed	−0.816		
Word reading accuracy	0.803		
Word reading time	0.874		
Pseudoword reading accuracy	0.813		
Pseudoword reading time	0.826		
Phonemic segmentation			0.842
Phonemic blending			0.818
Pseudoword repetition	−0.443		0.527
Auditory attention		0.671	
Digit span		0.486	
Metrical task		0.548	
Tapping		−0.586	
Rhythm reproduction		0.551	0.511
Rise time	0.540		
Temporal anisochrony		−0.802	

The initial eigenvalues for each factor are reported in parenthesis.

Table 5 | Logistic regressions.

MT Text Accuracy	Odds ratio	Std. Err.	*P* > |z|	95% Confidence interval	
City	0.343	0.268	0.170	0.074	1.584
School level	1.085	0.295	0.763	0.637	1.849
IQ	0.939	0.036	0.096	0.872	1.011
Sex	0.238	0.200	0.088	0.046	1.238
Metrical task	0.641	0.124	**0.022**	0.439	0.938

Values with a non-corrected p value < 0.01 are reported in bold.

Table 6 | Logistic regressions.

Pseudoword reading accuracy	Odds ratio	Std. Err.	*P* > |z|	95% Confidence interval	
City	1.386	1.137	0.690	0.278	6.920
School level	1.081	0.329	0.797	0.595	1.964
IQ	0.937	0.0368	0.099	0.868	1.012
Sex	0.871	0.708	0.865	0.177	4.283
Rhythm Reproduction	0.429	0.163	**0.026**	0.203	0.903

Values with a non-corrected p value < 0.01 are reported in bold.

Results of the factor analysis confirm and extend results of the correlation matrix. Interestingly, all temporal tasks except the rise time task appear in the same factor, which also includes the auditory attention and verbal working memory (digit span) tasks. This raises the issue of the relation between attention and working memory on one side, and temporal skills on the other side. More precisely, in the case of the metrical and rhythmic reproduction tasks (but it is also the case in the text reading task), children need a global representation of the stimuli, while a serial and local representation of stimulus parts necessarily produces a poor performance. This global representation possibly needs an attentional window spanning approximately 2 s. This is also the case of the psychoacoustic task because the change to be detected was embedded in a five-note sequence for the temporal anisochrony. In the case of tapping, the temporal window is shorter when considering the interval between successive taps, but this shorter window possibly engenders a larger temporal windows, due to the emergence of a metrical structure, yielding a more global percept of several taps. In other words, when tapping along a metronome, the child will group taps together in series of two, three of four (the latter being the most likely here), with the first tap of each group being perceived as the most relevant. The third factor of the analysis shows the rhythmic task together with the phonological awareness tasks. Thus, while an attentional and memory component may indeed play a role, there seems to be a cognitive process in the rhythm reproduction task that is independent of selective attention and verbal working memory processes and that is strongly related to phonological

Table 7 | Logistic regressions.

Word reading accuracy	Odds ratio	Std. Err.	*P* > |z|	95% Confidence Interval	
City	0.626	0.519	0.572	0.124	3.173
School level	0.658	0.189	0.146	0.375	1.156
IQ	0.968	0.039	0.418	0.895	1.047
Sex	2.050	1.773	0.407	0.376	11.170
Mother School Level	6.371	4.277	**0.006**	1.709	23.748

Values with a non-corrected p value < 0.01 are reported in bold.

Table 8 | Logistic regressions.

Word reading time	Odds ratio	Std. Err.	*P* > |z|	95% Confidence interval	
City	24.179	47.008	0.101	0.535	1092.288
School level	5.789	5.443	0.062	0.917	36.550
IQ	0.830	0.079	0.052	0.688	1.002
Sex	3.764	6.777	0.462	0.110	128.281
Metrical Task	0.2698	0.165	**0.032**	0.081	0.893

Values with a non-corrected p value < 0.01 are reported in bold.

processing. While the tapping does not appear in the third factor, this is due to the thresholding criterion we used (eigenvalue ≤ 0.4), but the tight relationship between the rhythmic task and tapping is visible in the high correlation values between these two variables.

Another interesting result of the factor analysis is the presence of the rise time task together with all reading measures. In speech, amplitude modulations in the temporal envelope (rise time) are one of the critical acoustic features underlying syllable rate and speech rhythm, and allow to distinguish between stressed and unstressed syllables (Leong et al., 2011). Indeed, amplitude modulations in the signal give a cue to the moment of occurrence of a sound that is used to build the rhythmic structure of speech (Leong and Goswami, 2014). Temporal envelope may also provide distinctive phonetic cues such as voice onset time and manner of articulation, that are necessary to discriminate otherwise similar phonemes (e.g., tie/die, bad/pad, Goswami et al., 2011a). Thus, temporal envelope is a key determinant in both perception of speech prosody and development of phonological awareness that are fundamental skills to achieve a "normal" developmental trajectory of reading (Goswami et al., 2011a). A growing body of literature attests to the presence of impaired perception of temporal envelope in developmental dyslexia, in adults and children and across languages with different phonological structures and writing systems (Goswami et al., 2011b). Interestingly, this result confirms the correlation analyses showing that this measure of rise time threshold is the only one that does not clearly correlate with the other temporal measures, exception made for a weak correlation with the meter perception task. In other words this task seems to measure a temporal scale which is not present in the other temporal tasks and which could be relevant for phonetic and prosodic processing, indispensable to all reading measures.

Correlation and factor analyses do not take into account certain sources of covariance such as age, sex, IQ and so on. However, the sources of correlation due to these variables can be controlled in regression analyses such as the logistic regression use here. In the logistic regression the dependent variables (e.g., text reading accuracy) are categorized into two categories corresponding to a severe or moderate level of dyslexia. Thus, after controlling for the effects of variables city, school-level, QI and sex, the model tests whether there is still one or more (continuous) independent variables that constitute a significant predictor of the reading outcome category. Interestingly the two measures that best predict reading outcomes are not the phonological awareness, attention or working memory tasks but the two tasks that present a greater temporal complexity, the rhythm reproduction and the metrical perceptual task. Both tasks measure a rather global level of temporal processing, including amplitude modulation, grouping events into chunks and applying a metrical hierarchy.

Although it was not the main aim of the present work, an interesting result is that mother school level was a good predictor of word reading abilities. This is probably linked to the fact that word recognition is influenced by the lexical/vocabulary development of the child (Sénéchal et al., 2006) and that maternal education is a stronger predictor of intellectual attainment than paternal education (Bradley and Corwyn, 2002). Recent research has shown the positive effect of reading during the first year of life (early literacy) on verbal competence and future academic skills (Sénéchal and LeFevre, 2002), pointing to other powerful compensatory strategies.

DIFFERENT TEMPORAL SCALES

One aim of the present work was to compare how different temporal skills relate to phonological and reading abilities. In doing this we had to choose a limited number of tasks, each testing a different aspect of temporal processing. We will try here to discuss how there different levels relate to each other, and how they may possibly be linked to reading disabilities in developmental dyslexia.

The smallest temporal scale is at the millisecond level. Hornickel and Kraus (2013) found that poor readers have more variable neural responses to speech; there seems to be a higher level of inconsistency in the poor reader brain's response to sound from one trial to another. Interestingly, weaker response consistency is absent with simple sounds (e.g., clicks) and present in both the formant transition (consonant) and in the more stationary part of the signal (vowel). Nonetheless, decreased consistency is maximal in the formant transition which is the most complex part of the signal. Even though the actual jitter is difficult to estimate, the lower brainstem response consistency can be accounted for by variability of the order of the millisecond or even less. While this temporal scale can be best studied by using neuroimaging techniques such as brainstem responses or cortical EEG, one should also consider that the fine-structure of speech sound (above 600 Hz) contains the formant patterns that are for instance the only acoustic cues to place of articulation ("dait" vs. "bait," Rosen, 1992).

In her rapid auditory processing theory, Tallal (1980) proposed that the phonological deficit in developmental dyslexia could be due to impaired processing of brief, rapidly presented sounds. She proposed that children with language learning impairment (LLI) are specifically impaired in their ability to discriminate between speech sounds that are characterized by brief and rapidly successive acoustic changes. This is the case of some formant transitions characterizing the phonetic distinctive features of some consonant contrasts such as /ba/ and /da/, that can only be differentiated by the acoustic cues present within the initial 40 ms (Tallal, 2004). Tallal suggests a window of 40 ms as the critical time window of the rapid spectrotemporal acoustic changes in formant transitions that would be necessary to track temporal order across ongoing speech. Thus, the key temporal scale would be of the order of tens of milliseconds. Because recent studies have suggested a limited role for rapid auditory processing in developmental dyslexia (Heath and Hogben, 2004a,b; Thomson et al., 2013) and due to time constraints in the testing session, this time scale level was not tested in the present study, although the tapping task may draw upon temporal processing on a rapid time scale (Tiernay and Kraus, 2013b). Nonetheless, in line with the other temporal tasks that do not require speech processing and have some link with music, one possible test would be to ask children to discriminate between different musical instruments carefully manipulating the distinctive spectrotemporal features.

We have already discussed of the temporal sampling deficit framework suggested by Goswami (2011) claiming that amplitude modulations in the envelope are one of the critical acoustic properties underlying syllable rate and speech rhythm. These fluctuations range between 2 and 50 Hz, are characterized by loudness, length, attack and decay and can convey different types of linguistic information: segmental cues to manner of articulation, voicing and vowel identity. The dynamic envelope cues (changes in amplitude) can also be important suprasegmental prosodic cues to mark stresses, facilitate syllabification and normalize speech rate variations in segmental and prosodic contrasts (Rosen, 1992). In other words, whereas rapid spectro-temporal cues are thought to be linked particularly to formant transitions (Tallal, 2004), slower spectro-temporal modulations are rather linked to syllabic and prosodic structure, thus to stress patterns and speech rhythm. Already during infancy, stress patterns are important to segment, namely extract words and syllables from the speech stream, and have thus a phonological relevance (Mattys and Jusczyk, 2001), which may explain why a deficit in temporal sampling of slow amplitude modulations may deviate a normal language developmental trajectory. In the present study the measure that is more closely related to this time scale is the onset rise time threshold because it manipulates the dynamic features of amplitude envelope. However, the durational (length) and intensity (loudness) features of amplitude envelope play an important role in the metrical tasks wherein meter was marked by greater loudness of the strong beat and different trials were marked by an increased length of a strong beat note (100 ms).

Both the meter perception and rhythm reproduction tasks also require building a longer temporal structure wherein the different inter-stimuli intervals are categorized in terms of relative durations (typically simple fractions: 1/2, 1/3, 1/4 or their reciprocal) and grouped together in larger units. The temporal scale here is longer, below 2 Hz, because these larger units may contain several notes. This would correspond in speech to word segmentation (several syllables) and prosodic phrasal boundaries (several words). Moreover, these grouping phenomena give rise to the emergence of the metrical structure, the alternation of strong and weak beats which typically corresponds to the a musical bar and falls again in a rather slow temporal window (below 2 Hz). An interesting theoretical account of the perception of musical meter is given in terms of continuous attentional modulations that would be coupled via entrainment to the metrical structure of the musical stimulus (Large and Jones, 1999). In this sense, meter should not be seen as a static and quantized hierarchy of slowly alternating strong and weak beats, but as a more dynamic process that evolves in time.

The last temporal scale that we would like to address is of a somewhat different quality and not specific to the auditory domain. It concerns the ability to predict events in time. This is a more general cognitive mechanism, sometimes referred to as Bayesian inference. For instance, making a good guess by prior probabilities (i.e., our experience of the world as we know it) about which words are most likely to be heard or seen. This is especially true when the environment is "noisy" and the choice of the signal representation is ambiguous, which is the case in natural speech but also in reading (due to time pressure and competition between similar words) and even more so in children with developmental dyslexia (Norris, 2006). The use of our prior experience of the world allows predicting what event may happen and possibly when it will happen. This prior knowledge allows for a better perception of degraded speech (Sohoglu et al., 2012) as well as reading a degraded text or a text full of errors (e.g., "Aoccdrnig to a rscheearch at CmabrigdeUinervtisy"). Thus, there is intrinsic to this prediction mechanism a temporal dimension which is in this case less precisely defined, because it depends upon the context and the object to be predicted (e.g., a letter, a syllable, a word). Nonetheless, both music and speech heavily repose on this type of inference, and working on this avenue may be interesting for future research.

To conclude this section, one should keep in mind that all the different time scales that we presented above are strongly interrelated, and that the serial presentation from short to long time scale does not mean that the levels are serial or independent from each other or that embedding of one level into another only takes place in one direction.

MUSIC REHABILITATION OF DEVELOPMENTAL DYSLEXIA

The issue raised here between the lines is whether and how music can help children with developmental dyslexia to restore a normal developmental trajectory of reading abilities. While there is not yet a clear cut answer to these questions, our data, together with other previously published results strongly suggest that music should have a positive effect on reading abilities. The reasons of this benefit are probably multiple and are still debated and will thus require further research in the years to come.

From a perspective on music and rehabilitation, it is interesting to consider the OPERA hypothesis proposed by Patel (2011), stating that music brings to adaptive brain plasticity of the same neural network involved in language processing. More precisely, this hypothesis claims that music training can drive adaptive plasticity in speech processing networks if certain conditions are respected. Firstly, a sensory or cognitive process used by both speech and music is mediated by overlapping brain networks. Secondly, music places higher demands on that process than speech. Thirdly, music engages that process with emotion, repetition, and attention (Patel, 2013).

From a more precise perspective on music and rehabilitation of developmental dyslexia, several authors have hypothesized a rehabilitation centered on rhythm, capable of developing several temporal skills that may in turn transfer to reading skills (Overy et al., 2003; Tallal and Gaab, 2006; Goswami, 2011). Nonetheless, it is not an easy issue to understand what specific aspects of temporal processing should be targeted by a possible music intervention.

Some authors suggest to work at a global level on rhythm and meter, both in perception and production (Goswami, 2011). Other researchers point to spectrotemporal processing as the best candidate to improve phonetic discrimination/categorization (Tallal and Gaab, 2006) or on both local and global dimensions, suggesting perceptual and creative games center on the musical pedagogy of Zoltan Kodaly (Overy et al., 2003).

Putting together our results with the general framework of music and language rehabilitation suggested by Patel and the more specific frameworks suggested for developmental dyslexia we will give some tentative but scientifically grounded recommendations when considering a music intervention with this population.

Our first recommendation (R1) is to use a group setting rather than an individual setting. This will possibly boost the playful and positive emotional aspects of the training and will possibly maximize rhythmic entrainment. Indeed, Kirschner and Tomasello (2009) showed that if the musical activity is realized in a social/imitative context, the synchronization ability of young children (2–3 years old) improves more compared to a context without a human partner (i.e., a computer game).

Our second recommendation (R2) is to use a fully active setting with music making and active musical games wherein music, body movements, emotions, and intentionality influence each other in a complex dynamical process (Maes et al., 2014). This will also maximize the demands on the audio-motor loop as well as on anticipatory and predictive processing, that is prediction, preparation, anticipation of events to come. In other words, music making in a social context (R1&R2) will set a high demand on Bayesian inferential efficiency, allowing for a faster prediction of future events (Bubic et al., 2010).

Our third recommendation (R3) is to focus on rhythm rather than on pitch accuracy as it is often the case in classical music pedagogy. This can be easily associated to movement and dance and, despite the idea that music has to be perfectly in tune, there are a plethora of musical games or even styles that are not too demanding on pitch accuracy, such as beat boxing, body tapping, rap and so on. This type of rhythmic activity seems to us to be the most appropriate in the rehabilitation of developmental dyslexia. On one side it will improve global temporal skills (meters and rhythm processing, sequencing, temporal prediction). On the other side, the lack or limitation of pitch and tonality will force the music teacher to make a larger use of the spectral dimension, by using different timbres produced with the mouth, body or different percussive instruments which may in turn facilitate fast temporal processing of speech sounds.

Our last recommendation (R4) is to keep variety high. While repetition is intrinsic to musical structure, the music teacher, by contrast to the computer game, can propose an almost infinite number of befittingly variations of a given game/exercise/song, that will possibly emerge in the musical interaction between the teacher and the children or the children themselves. This high variety is important in our view, to capture children attention but also to maximize the chances of a generalization process and thus a transfer to language and reading.

CONCLUSIONS

In this study we investigated the link between different levels of temporal processing and reading skills in developmental dyslexia. We confirmed and extended previous findings describing a strong relation between timing and reading abilities. However, due to time constraints of the testing session we could not assess all temporal processing levels (for instance the fine structure level, important for phonetic discrimination). Moreover while the three statistical analyses point into a similar direction, results are only partially concordant, possibly due to the intrinsic heterogeneity of a population of dyslexic children.

Despite these limitations, our results show a strong association between reading skills and meter perception and rhythm processing. These two measures of temporal processing do not only involve timing mechanisms, but also other competences that are notoriously poor in children with developmental dyslexia, such as auditory attention (Facoetti et al., 2010) and working memory (Swanson et al., 1996). Future work should try to better tease apart the role of attention and memory in temporal processes and their link to reading skills.

The next step should be to develop interventions based on musical training for children with developmental dyslexia, and to test their efficacy through randomized controlled trials, although sufficient numerosity to allow adequate statistical power to detect treatment effects may be difficult to achieve due to the high cost and risk of drop out. A multicenter study may overcome these obstacles. To conclude, the literature review literature and our findings suggest that music training, focused on rhythm, could be beneficial for children with dyslexia, or maybe even for children identified earlier as at risk based on low phonological abilities.

ACKNOWLEDGMENTS

This work was funded by the Mariani Foundation, grant no. R-11-85. We wish to thank Giorgio Tamburlini for helpful comments on this manuscript and all the families and children for their patience.

REFERENCES

Abrams, D. A., Nicol, T., Zecker, S., and Kraus, N. (2009). Abnormal cortical processing of the syllable rate of speech in poor readers. *J. Neurosci.* 29, 7686–7693. doi: 10.1523/JNEUROSCI.5242-08.2009

Altenmüller, E., Marco-Pallares, J., Münte, T. F., and Schneider, S. (2009). Neural reorganization underlies improvement of stroke-induced motor dysfunctions by music-supported therapy. *Ann. N. Y. Acad. Sci.* 1169, 395–405. doi: 10.1111/j.1749-6632.2009.04580.x

Amengual, J. L., Rojo, N., Veciana de Las Heras, M., Marco-Pallarés, J., Grau-Sánchez, J., Schneider, S., et al. (2013). Sensorimotor plasticity after music-supported therapy in chronic stroke patients revealed by transcranial magnetic stimulation. *PLoS ONE* 8:e61883. doi: 10.1371/journal.pone.0061883

Anvari, S. H., Trainor, L. J., Woodside, J., and Levy, B. A. (2002). Relations among musical skills, phonological processing, and early reading ability in preschool children. *J. Exp. Child Psychol.* 83, 111–130. doi: 10.1016/S0022-0965(02)00124-8

Barbiero, C., Lonciari, I., Montico, M., Monasta, L., Penge, R., and Vio, C. (2012). The submerged dyslexia iceberg: how many school children are not diagnosed? Results from an Italian study. *PLoS ONE* 7:e48082. doi: 10.1371/journal.pone.0048082

Besson, M., and Schön, D. (2011). "What remains of modularity?" in *Language and Music as Cognitive Systems,* eds P. Rebuschat, M. Rohrmeier, J. Hawkins, and I. Cross (Oxford: Oxford University Press), 283–291. doi: 10.1093/acprof:oso/9780199553426.003.0029

Besson, M., Schön, D., Moreno, S., Santos, A., and Magne, C. (2007). Influence of musical expertise and musical training on pitch processing in music and language. *Restor. Neurol. Neurosci.* 25, 399–410.

Bradley, R. H., and Corwyn, R. F. (2002). Socioeconomic status and child development. *Annu. Rev. Psychol.* 53, 371–399. doi: 10.1146/annurev.psych.53.100901.135233

Bubic, A., von Cramon, D. Y., and Schubotz, R. I. (2010). Prediction, cognition and the brain. *Front Hum Neurosci.* 4:25. doi: 10.3389/fnhum.2010.00025

Burani, C., Barca, L., and Arduino, L. S. (2011). *Lexical and Sublexical Variables for 626 Italian Simple Nouns.* Data Base. Available online at: http://www.istc.ip.rm.cnr.it/material/database

Butzlaff, R. (2000). Can music be used to teach reading? *J. Aesthet. Educ.* 34, 167–178. doi: 10.2307/3333642

Cornoldi, C., and Colpo, G. (2011). *MT Reading Test.* Florence: Organizzazioni Speciali.

Cornoldi, C., and Tressoldi, P. (2007). "Definizione, criteri e classificazione," in *Difficoltà e Disturbi Dell'apprendimento,* ed C. Cornoldi (Bologna: Il Mulino), 9–52.

De Martino, S., Espesser, R., Rey, V., and Habib, M. (2001). The temporal processing deficit hypothesis in dyslexia: new experimental evidence. *Brain Cogn.* 46, 104–108. doi: 10.1016/S0278-2626(01)80044-0

Facoetti, A., Trussardi, A. N., Ruffino, M., Lorusso, M. L., Cattaneo, C., Galli, L., et al. (2010). Multisensory spatial attention deficits are predictive of phonological decoding skills in developmental dyslexia, *J. Cogn. Neurosci.* 22, 1011–1025. doi: 10.1162/jocn.2009.21232

François, C., Tillmann, B., and Schön, D. (2012). Cognitive and methodological consideration on the effects of musical expertise on speech segmentation. *Ann. N.Y. Acad. Sci.* 1252, 108–115. doi: 10.1111/j.1749-6632.2011.06395.x

Fries, W., and Swihart, A. A. (1990). Disturbance of rhythm sense following right hemisphere damage. *Neuropsychologia* 28, 1317–1323. doi: 10.1016/0028-3932(90)90047-R

Ghitza, O. (2011). Linking speech perception and neurophysiology: speech decoding guided by cascaded oscillators locked to the input rhythm. *Front. Psychol.* 2:130. doi: 10.3389/fpsyg.2011.00130

Giraud, A. L., and Poeppel, D. (2012). Cortical oscillations and speech processing: emerging computational principles and operations. *Nat. Neurosci.* 15, 511–517. doi: 10.1038/nn.3063

Goswami, U. (2011). A temporal sampling framework for developmental dyslexia. *Trends Cogn. Sci.* 15, 3–10. doi: 10.1016/j.tics.2010.10.001

Goswami, U., Fosker, T., Huss, M., Mead, N., and Szûceta D. (2011a). Rise time and formant transition duration in the discrimination of speech sounds: the Ba–Wa distinction in developmental dyslexia. *Dev. Sci.* 14, 34–43. doi: 10.1111/j.1467-7687.2010.00955.x

Goswami, U., Gerson, D., and Astruc, L. (2010). Amplitude envelope perception, phonology and prosodic sensitivity in children with developmental dyslexia. *Read. Writ.* 23, 995–1019. doi: 10.1007/s11145-009-9186-6

Goswami, U., Huss, M., Mead, N., Fosker, T., and Verney, J. P. (2013). Perception of patterns of musical beat distribution in phonological developmental dyslexia: significant longitudinal relations with word reading and reading comprehension. *Cortex* 49, 1363–1376. doi: 10.1016/j.cortex.2012.05.005

Goswami, U., Thompson, J., Richardson, U., Stainthorp, R., Hughes, D., Rosen, S., et al. (2002). Amplitude envelope onsets and developmental dyslexia: a new hypothesis. *Proc. Natl. Acad. Sci. U.S.A.* 99, 10911–10916. doi: 10.1073/pnas.122368599

Goswami, U., Wang, H. L., Cruz A., Fosker T., Mead N., and Huss M. (2011b). Language-universal sensory deficits in developmental dyslexia: English, Spanish, and Chinese. *J. Cogn. Neurosci.* 23, 325–337. doi: 10.1162/jocn.2010.21453

Grassi, M., and Soranzo, A. (2009). MLP: a MATLAB toolbox for rapid and reliable auditory threshold estimations. *Behav. Res. Meth.* 41, 20–28. doi: 10.3758/BRM.41.1.20

Greenberg, S. (2006). "A multi-band framework for understanding spoken language" in *Understanding Speech: An Auditory Perspective,* eds S. Greenberg and W. Ainsworth (Mahweh, NJ: LEA), 411–434.

Heath, S. M. and Hogben, G. H. (2004a). Cost-effective prediction of reading difficulties. *J. Speech Lang. Hear. Res.* 47, 751–765. doi: 10.1044/1092-4388(2004/057)

Heath, S. M., and Hogben, J. H. (2004b). The reliability and validity of tasks measuring perception of rapid sequences in children with dyslexia. *J. Child Psychol. Psychiatry* 45, 1275–1287. doi: 10.1111/j.1469-7610.2004.00313.x

Herholz, S. C., and Zatorre, R. J. (2012). Musical training as a framework for brain plasticity: behavior, function, and structure. *Neuron* 76, 486–502. doi: 10.1016/j.neuron.2012.10.011

Hornickel, J., and Kraus, N. (2013). Unstable representation of sound: a biological marker of dyslexia. *J. Neurosci.* 33, 3500–3504. doi: 10.1523/JNEUROSCI.4205-12.2013

Huss, M., Verney, J. P., Fosker, T., Mead, N., and Goswami, U. (2011). Music, rhythm, rise time perception and developmental dyslexia: perception of musical meter predicts reading and phonology. *Cortex* 47, 674–689. doi: 10.1016/j.cortex.2010.07.010

Hyde, K. L., Lerch, J., Norton, A., Forgeard, M., Winner, E., Evans, A. C., et al. (2009). Musical training shapes structural brain development. *J. Neurosci.* 29, 3019–3025. doi: 10.1523/JNEUROSCI.5118-08.2009

Kirschner, S., and Tomasello, M. (2009). Joint drumming: social context facilitates synchronization in preschool children. *J. Exp. Child Psychol.* 102, 299–314. doi: 10.1016/j.jecp.2008.07.005

Kraus, N., and Chandrasekaran, B. (2010). Music training for the development of auditory skills. *Nat. Rev. Neurosci.* 11, 599–605. doi: 10.1038/nrn2882

Large, E. W., and Jones, M. R. (1999). The dynamics of attending: how we track time-varying events. *Psychol. Rev.* 106, 119–159. doi: 10.1037/0033-295X.106.1.119

Lehongre, K., Ramus, F., Villiermet, N., Schwartz, D., and Giraud, A. L. (2011). Altered low-gamma sampling in auditory cortex. Accounts for the three main facets of dyslexia. *Neuron* 72, 1080–1090. doi: 10.1016/j.neuron.2011.11.002

Leong, V., and Goswami, U. (2014). Impaired extraction of speech rhythm from temporal modulation patterns in speech in developmental dyslexia. *Front. Hum. Neurosci.* 8:96. doi: 10.3389/fnhum.2014.00096

Leong, V., Hamalainen, J., Soltesz, F., and Goswami, U. (2011). Rise time perception and detection of syllable stress in adults with developmental dyslexia. *J. Mem. Lang.* 64, 59–73. doi: 10.1016/j.jml.2010.09.003

Lyon, R., Shaywitz, S. E., and Shaywitz, B. A. (2003). Defining dyslexia, comorbidity, teachers' knowledge of language and reading. *Ann. Dyslexia* 53, 1–14. doi: 10.1007/s11881-003-0001-9

Maes, P. J., Leman, M., Palmer, C., and Wanderley, M. M. (2014). Action-based effects on music perception. *Front. Psychol.* 4:1008. doi: 10.3389/fpsyg.2013.01008

Marzocchi, G. M. (2010). *BIA Italian Battery for Children with Attention Deficit and Hyperactivity Disorder.* Trento: Erickson.

Mattys, S. L., and Jusczyk, P. W. (2001). Phonotactic cues for segmentation of fluent speech by infants. *Cognition* 78, 91–121. doi: 10.1016/S0010-0277(00)00109-8

Moreno, S., Bialystok, E., Barac, R., Schellenberg, E. G., Cepeda, N. J., and Chau, T. (2011). Short-term music training enhances verbal intelligence and executive function. *Psychol. Sci.* 22, 1425–1433. doi: 10.1177/0956797611416999

Moreno, S., Marques, C., Santos, A., Santos, M., Castro, S. L., and Besson, M. (2009). Musical training influences linguistic abilities in 8-year-old children: more evidence for brain plasticity. *Cereb. Cortex* 19, 712–723. doi: 10.1093/cercor/bhn120

Norris, D. (2006). The Bayesian reader: explaining word recognition as an optimal Bayesian decision process. *Psychol. Rev.* 113, 327–357. doi: 10.1037/0033-295X.113.2.327

Orsini, A., and Picone, L. (2006). *Italian standardization of Wechsler Intelligence Scale for Children III*. Florence: Organizzazioni Speciali.

Overy, K., Nicolson, R. I., Fawcett, A. J., and Clarke, E. F. (2003). Dyslexia and music: measuring musical timing skills. *Dyslexia* 9, 18–36. doi: 10.1002/dys.233

Parbery-Clark, A., Anderson, S., Hittner, E., and Kraus N. (2012). Musical experience offsets age-related delays in neural timing. *Neurobiol. Aging* 33, 1483.e1–1483.e4. doi: 10.1016/j.neurobiolaging.2011.12.015

PARCC DSA. (2011). *Raccomandazioni Cliniche sui DSA. Risposte a Quesiti*. Available online at: www.lineeguidadislessia.it

Patel, A. D. (2011). Why would musical training benefit the neural encoding of speech? The OPERA hypothesis. *Front. Psychol.* 2:142. doi: 10.3389/fpsyg.2011.00142

Patel, A. D. (2013). Can nonlinguistic musical training change the way the brain processes speech? The expanded OPERA hypothesis. *Hear. Res.* doi: 10.1016/j.heares.2013.08.011

Pernet, C., Andersson, J., Paulesu, E., and Demonet, J. F. (2009). When all hypotheses are right: a multifocal account of dyslexia. *Hum. Brain Mapp.* 30, 2278–2292. doi: 10.1002/hbm.20670

Petkov, C. I., O'Connora, K. N., and Benmoshea, G. (2005). Auditory perceptual grouping and attention in dyslexia. *Cogn. Brain Res.* 24, 343–354. doi: 10.1016/j.cogbrainres.2005.02.021

Ramus, F. (2004). Neurobiology of dyslexia: a reinterpretation of the data. *Trends Neurosci.* 27, 720–726. doi: 10.1016/j.tins.2004.10.004

Reed, M. (1989). Speech perception and the discrimination of brief auditory cues in reading disabled children. *J. Exp. Child Psychol.* 48, 270–292. doi: 10.1016/0022-0965(89)90006-4

Rodriguez-Fornells, A., Cunillera, T., Mestress-Misse, A., and De Diego Balaguer, R. (2009). Neurophysiological mechanisms involved in language learning in adults. *Philos. Trans. R. Soc. Lond. B Biol. Sci.* 364, 3711–3735. doi: 10.1098/rstb.2009.0130

Rosen, S. (1992). Temporal information in speech: acoustic, auditory and linguistic aspects. *Philos. Trans. R. Soc. Lond. B Biol. Sci.* 336, 367–373. doi: 10.1098/rstb.1992.0070

Särkämö, T., Tervaniemi, M., Laitinen, S., Forsblom, A., Soinila, S., Mikkonen, M., et al. (2008). Music listening enhances cognitive recovery and mood after middle cerebral artery stroke. *Brain* 131, 866–876. doi: 10.1093/brain/awn013

Sartori, G., Job, R., and Tressoldi, P. E. (2007). *DDE-2 Battery for Reading and Writing Disorders*. Florence: Organizzazioni Speciali

Schön, D., Boyer, M., Moreno, S., Besson, M., Peretz, I., and Kolinsky, R. (2008). Songs as an aid for language acquisition. *Cognition* 106, 975–983. doi: 10.1016/j.cognition.2007.03.005

Sénéchal, M., and LeFevre, J. A. (2002). Parental involvement in the development of children's reading skill: a five-year longitudinal study. *Child Dev.* 73, 445–460. doi: 10.1111/1467-8624.00417

Sénéchal, M., Ouellette, G., and Rodney, D. (2006). "The misunderstood giant: on the predictive role of early vocabulary to future reading," in *Handbook of Early Literacy Research*. Vol. 2, eds D. Dickinson and S. B. Neuman (New York, NY: Guilford), 173–182.

Snowling, M. J., and Hulme, C. (2012). Annual research review: the nature and classification of reading disorders - a commentary on proposals for DSM-5. *J. Child Psychol. Psychiatry* 53, 593–607. doi: 10.1111/j.1469-7610.2011.02495.x

Sohoglu, E., Peelle, J. E., Carlyon, R. P., and Davis, M. H. (2012). Predictive top-down integration of prior knowledge during speech perception. *J. Neurosci.* 32, 8443–8453. doi: 10.1523/JNEUROSCI.5069-11.2012

Swanson, H. L., Ashbaker, M. H., and Lee, C. (1996). Learning disabled readers working memory as a function of processing demands. *J. Exp. Child Psychol.* 61, 242–275. doi: 10.1006/jecp.1996.0016

Tallal, P. (1980). Auditory temporal perception, phonics and reading disabilities in children. *Brain Lang.* 9, 182–198. doi: 10.1016/0093-934X(80)90139-X

Tallal, P. (2004). Improving language and literacy is a matter of time. *Nat. Rev. Neurosci.* 5, 721–728. doi: 10.1038/nrn1499

Tallal, P., and Gaab, N. (2006). Dynamic auditory processing, musical experience and language development. *Trends Neurosci.* 29, 382–390. doi: 10.1016/j.tins.2006.06.003

Thomson, J., Leong, V., and Goswami, U. (2013). Auditory processing interventions and developmental dyslexia: a comparison of phonemic and rhythmic approaches. *Read. Writ.* 26, 139–161. doi: 10.1007/s11145-012-9359-6

Thomson, J. M., and Goswami, U. (2008). Rhythmic processing in children with developmental dyslexia: auditory and motor rhythms link to reading and spelling. *J. Physiol.* 102, 120–129. doi: 10.1016/j.jphysparis.2008.03.007

Tiernay, A., and Kraus, N. (2013b). The ability to move to a beat is linked to the consistency of neural responses to sound. *J. Neurosci.* 33, 14981–14988. doi: 10.1523/JNEUROSCI.0612-13.2013

Tiernay, A. T., and Kraus, N. (2013a). The ability to tap to a beat relates to cognitive, linguistic, and perceptual skills. *Brain Lang.* 124, 225–231. doi: 10.1016/j.bandl.2012.12.014

Vicari, S. (2007). *PROMEA Memory and Learning Tests for Developmental Age*. Florence: Organizzazioni Speciali.

Wolff, P. H. (2002). Timing precision and rhythm in developmental dyslexia. *Read. Writ.* 15, 179–206. doi: 10.1023/A:1013880723925

Wong, P. C., Skoe, E., Russo, N. M., Dees, T., and Kraus, N. (2007). Musical experience shapes human brainstem encoding of linguistic pitch patterns. *Nat. Neurosci.* 10, 420–422. doi: 10.1038/nn1872

6

The musician effect: does it persist under degraded pitch conditions of cochlear implant simulations?

Christina D. Fuller*[1,2]*, John J. Galvin III*[1,2,3,4]*, Bert Maat*[1,2]*, Rolien H. Free*[1,2] *and Deniz Başkent*[1,2]**

[1] *Department of Otorhinolaryngology/Head and Neck Surgery, University Medical Center Groningen, University of Groningen, Groningen, Netherlands*
[2] *Research School of Behavioral and Cognitive Neurosciences, Graduate School of Medical Sciences, University of Groningen, Groningen, Netherlands*
[3] *Division of Communication and Auditory Neuroscience, House Research Institute, Los Angeles, CA, USA*
[4] *Department of Head and Neck Surgery, David Geffen School of Medicine, UCLA, Los Angeles, CA, USA*

Correspondence:
Deniz Başkent, Department of Otorhinolaryngology/Head and Neck Surgery, University Medical Center Groningen, University of Groningen, PO Box 30.001, Hanzeplein 1, Groningen, 9700 RB, Netherlands
e-mail: d.baskent@umcg.nl

Cochlear implants (CIs) are auditory prostheses that restore hearing via electrical stimulation of the auditory nerve. Compared to normal acoustic hearing, sounds transmitted through the CI are spectro-temporally degraded, causing difficulties in challenging listening tasks such as speech intelligibility in noise and perception of music. In normal hearing (NH), musicians have been shown to better perform than non-musicians in auditory processing and perception, especially for challenging listening tasks. This "musician effect" was attributed to better processing of pitch cues, as well as better overall auditory cognitive functioning in musicians. Does the musician effect persist when pitch cues are degraded, as it would be in signals transmitted through a CI? To answer this question, NH musicians and non-musicians were tested while listening to unprocessed signals or to signals processed by an acoustic CI simulation. The task increasingly depended on pitch perception: (1) speech intelligibility (words and sentences) in quiet or in noise, (2) vocal emotion identification, and (3) melodic contour identification (MCI). For speech perception, there was no musician effect with the unprocessed stimuli, and a small musician effect only for word identification in one noise condition, in the CI simulation. For emotion identification, there was a small musician effect for both. For MCI, there was a large musician effect for both. Overall, the effect was stronger as the importance of pitch in the listening task increased. This suggests that the musician effect may be more rooted in pitch perception, rather than in a global advantage in cognitive processing (in which musicians would have performed better in all tasks). The results further suggest that musical training before (and possibly after) implantation might offer some advantage in pitch processing that could partially benefit speech perception, and more strongly emotion and music perception.

Keywords: musician effect, music training, cochlear implant, speech perception, emotion identification, music perception, pitch processing

INTRODUCTION

In normal hearing (NH), musicians show advantages in auditory processing and perception, especially for challenging listening tasks. Musicians exhibit enhanced decoding of affective human vocal sound (Wong et al., 2007; Musacchia et al., 2008; Strait et al., 2009; Besson et al., 2011), better perception of voice cues, and better perception of pitch cues in both speech (prosody) and music (Schon et al., 2004; Thompson et al., 2004; Chartrand and Belin, 2006). But perhaps more importantly, some transfer of musical training to better speech understanding in noise has also been observed, although evidence for such transfer has been mixed (Parbery-Clark et al., 2009; Kraus and Chandrasekaran, 2010; Ruggles et al., 2014). This "musician effect" might be due to better processing of voice pitch cues that can help to segregate speech from noise (Micheyl et al., 2006; Besson et al., 2007; Oxenham, 2008; Deguchi et al., 2012), suggesting that there may be differences between musicians and non-musicians in terms of sound processing at lower levels of the auditory system. Alternatively, the musician effect may be due to better functioning of higher-level processes, such as better use of auditory working memory and attention (Bialystok and DePape, 2009; Besson et al., 2011; Moreno et al., 2011; Barrett et al., 2013).

Previously, the musician effect has been studied in NH listeners under conditions in which the spectro-temporal fine structure cues important for complex pitch perception are fully available. It is not yet known if this effect would persist when the acoustic signal is degraded and when the pitch cues are less available, whether due to signal processing and transmission in hearing devices or by hearing impairment. Such is the case with the cochlear implant (CI), the auditory prosthesis for deaf individuals who cannot benefit from traditional hearing aids. Instead of amplifying acoustic sounds, CIs directly stimulate auditory neurons via electrodes placed inside the cochlea. While the CI users can understand speech transmitted through the device to some degree, this speech signal is greatly reduced in spectral resolution and spectro-temporal fine structure. Further, other factors related to electrode-neuron interface may additionally limit CI performance, such as nerve survival patterns (e.g., Başkent and Shannon, 2006; Bierer, 2010) or potential mismatch in the frequency-place mapping of electric stimulation, especially due to differing electrode array positions inside the cochlea (e.g., Başkent and Shannon, 2007; Holden et al., 2013). As a result, there is large variation in speech perception abilities of CI users post-implantation (Blamey et al., 2013). Furthermore, difficulty understanding speech in noise or in the presence of competing talkers is common among CI users (Friesen et al., 2001; Stickney et al., 2004). The spectro-temporal degradations also severely limit CI users' pitch perception, which is important for recognizing vocal emotion and voice gender, but also for segregating speech from background noise (Fu et al., 2004; Luo et al., 2007; Oxenham, 2008; Fuller et al., under revision). Problems in pitch processing directly and negatively affect musical pitch and timbre perception, and in turn music perception and appreciation (Gfeller et al., 2002a; McDermott, 2004; Galvin et al., 2007; Heng et al., 2011; Limb and Roy, 2014).

Due to aforementioned benefits of the musician effect on speech and music perception, one can argue that music training before or after implantation can also provide some advantages to CI users. In support of this idea, music experience before and after implantation has been shown to benefit CI users' music perception (Gfeller et al., 2000). Further, explicit music training has been observed to significantly improve melodic contour identification (MCI) (Galvin et al., 2007, 2012), and timbre identification and appraisal (Gfeller et al., 2002a; for a review on music appreciation and training in CI users, see Looi et al., 2012). On a potential connection of music training to speech, however, while some CI studies have shown that better music perception was associated with better speech perception (Gfeller et al., 2007; Won et al., 2010), this connection was not always confirmed by other studies. Fuller et al. (2012) showed that previous musical experience with acoustic hearing did not significantly affect CI users' speech performance after implantation. In that study, as is typical for this patient population, few CI participants were trained musicians before implantation, and many reduced their involvement with music after implantation. It is possible that explicit training after implantation may help postlingually deafened CI users to better associate the degraded pitch patterns via electric hearing to pitch patterns developed during previous acoustic hearing. Alternatively, the spectral degradation with CIs may be so severe that previous music experience provides only limited benefit. Thus, it remains unclear whether the musician effect can persist under conditions of spectro-temporal degradation as experienced by CI users.

Acoustic CI simulations have been widely used to systematically explore signal processing parameters and conditions that may affect real CI users' performance. In a typical CI simulation (e.g., Shannon et al., 1995), the input signal is first divided into a number of frequency analysis bands, then the temporal envelope is extracted from each band and used to modulate a carrier signal (typically band-limited noise or sine-wave), and finally the modulated carrier bands are summed. Parameter manipulations can include the number of spectral channels (to simulate different amounts of spectral resolution), the frequency shift between the analysis and the carrier bands (to simulate different electrode insertions), the envelope filter cut-off frequency (to simulate limits on temporal processing), and the analysis/carrier band filter slopes (to simulate different degrees of channel interaction). CI simulations have also been used to elucidate differences and similarities between acoustic and electric hearing under similar signal processing conditions. Friesen et al. (2001) showed that while NH sentence recognition in noise steadily improved as the number of spectral channels in the acoustic CI simulation increased, real CI performance failed to significantly improve beyond 6–8 channels. Luo et al. (2007) found that temporal envelope cues contributed more strongly to NH listeners' vocal emotion recognition with an acoustic CI simulation than in the real CI case. Kong et al. (2004) showed that NH listeners' familiar melody recognition (without rhythm cues) steadily improved as the number of channels were increased in the CI simulation, while real CI performance remained at chance levels despite having 8–22 channels available in the clinical speech processors.

In the present study, CI simulations were used to differentiate the performance between NH musicians and non-musicians, to identify the effect of long-term musical training, when pitch cues must be extracted from a signal that is spectro-temporally degraded given the limited number of channels. The purpose was two-fold; one, to explore to what degree the musician effect would persist under pitch conditions weakened due to spectro-temporal degradations, and two, to explore if the musician effect could potentially be relevant to CI users, for example, by training them with music pre- or post-implantation to increase hearing performance. To achieve this purpose, we systematically investigated the musician effect in a relatively large group of NH participants in three experiments comprised of various speech and music perception tasks, each of which relied on pitch cues to differing degrees. Varying the importance of the pitch cues across the listening tasks might provide insight into mechanisms associated with the musician effect. Speech intelligibility in quiet and in noise was tested using words and sentences. Voice pitch cues would be expected to contribute little to speech understanding in quiet, and possibly more to speech understanding in noise. Vocal emotion identification was tested with and without normalization of amplitude and duration cues that co-vary with fundamental frequency (F0) contours (Luo et al., 2007; Hubbard and Assmann, 2013). Voice pitch cues would be expected to contribute strongly to vocal emotion identification, especially when amplitude and duration cues are less available. MCI was tested with and without a competing masker, in which the pitch and the timbre of the masker and target contours were varied. Pitch cues would be expected to contribute most strongly to MCI, compared to the other listening tasks. All participants were tested in all tasks while listening to unprocessed stimuli or stimuli processed by an 8-channel acoustic CI simulation, using a typical simulation method based on literature. We had three hypotheses: (1) As a direct result of their musical training, musicians would exhibit better music perception. (2) Based on previous studies that showed a transfer from music training to speech perception, we hypothesized that musicians would better understand speech in noise. (3) Based on previous studies that showed a stronger pitch perception in musicians, we hypothesized that musicians would better identify vocal emotion in speech. We further hypothesized that due to better use of pitch cues and better listening skills, musicians would outperform non-musicians also with the CI simulations. However, if musicians outperformed non-musicians in all tasks, this would indicate overall better functioning of high-level auditory perceptual mechanisms. Alternatively, if the musician effect were stronger for listening tasks that relied more strongly on pitch cues, this would indicate that music training mainly improved lower-level auditory perception.

EXPERIMENT 1: SPEECH INTELLIGIBILITY

RATIONALE

In Experiment 1, we conducted two tests to explore the musician effect on speech intelligibility: (1) word identification in quiet and in noise at various signal-to-noise ratios (SNRs), and (2) sentence identification in various types of noise. In the test of word identification, there was no semantic context, but the words were meaningful; in the test of sentence identification, there was strong semantic context. Musician effect had been previously observed for speech recognition in noise, but with speech materials with intact spectro-temporal fine-structure cues (Parbery-Clark et al., 2009; Kraus and Chandrasekaran, 2010). To explore the effect of spectral degradation on speech intelligibility along with the musician effect, NH musicians and non-musicians were tested while listening to unprocessed speech or to an acoustic CI simulation.

MATERIALS AND METHODS

Participants

Twenty-five musicians and non-musicians, matched in age and gender, participated in the study (**Table 1**). Based on previous studies (Micheyl et al., 2006; Parbery-Clark et al., 2009), the inclusion criteria for "musician" were defined as: (1) having begun musical training before or at the age of 7 years, (2) having 10 years or more musical training (i.e., playing an instrument), and (3) having received musical training within the last 3 years on a regular basis. The inclusion criteria for "non-musician" were defined as: (1) not meeting the musician criteria, and (2) not having received musical training within the 7 years before the study. **Table 1** shows significant differences between the two participant groups in the number of years of musical training and the starting age of training, confirming a good partition of participants in terms of their music training. There were two small irregularities in participant selection. One non-musician participant started music training at the age of 6 due to mandatory musical training at preliminary school. Another non-musician participant did have 10 years of irregular musical training, but did not have any musical training in the 7 years before the study. Participants were recruited from University of Groningen and from music schools in the area. Further inclusion criteria for all subjects were having NH (pure tone thresholds better than 20 dB HL at the audiometric test frequencies between 250 and 4000 Hz, and 25 dB HL or better at 8 kHz) and being a native Dutch speaker. Exclusion criteria were neurological disorders, especially dyslexia, psychiatric disorders, or untreated past hearing-related problems.

The Medical Ethical Committee of the University Medical Center Groningen (UMCG) approved the study. Detailed information about the study was given and written informed consent was obtained before participation in the study. A financial reimbursement was provided in line with the guidelines of subject reimbursement of Otorhinolaryngology Department of UMCG.

Stimuli

Word identification. Stimuli included meaningful, monosyllabic Dutch words in CVC format [e.g., bus ("bus," in English), vaak ("often"), nieuw ("new"), etc.], taken from the NVA test (Bosman and Smoorenburg, 1995). The corpus contains digital recordings of 12 lists, each of which contains 12 words spoken by a female talker. Steady speech-shaped noise (provided with the database) that matched the long-term spectrum of the recordings was used for tests conducted with background noise.

Sentence identification. Stimuli included meaningful and syntactically correct Dutch sentences with rich semantic context (Plomp and Mimpen, 1979). The corpus contains digital recordings of 10 lists, each of which contains 13 sentences spoken by a female talker. Each sentence contains 4–8 words. Sentence identification was measured in three types of noise: (1) Steady speech-shaped noise (provided with the database) that matched the long-term spectrum of the recordings, (2) fluctuating noise, the steady speech-shaped noise additionally modulated by the mean temporal envelope of the sentence recordings, and (3) 6-talker speech babble (taken from ICRA noise signals CD, ver.0.3; Dreschler et al., 2001).

Participants were trained with the CI simulation using a different corpus of sentence materials (Versfeld et al., 2000). The training sentences were also meaningful and syntactically correct Dutch sentences with rich semantic context. However, the training sentences were somewhat more difficult compared to the test sentences. The training corpus contains digital recordings of 39 lists, each of which contains 13 sentences spoken by a female talker. Each sentence contains 4–9 words.

Table 1 | Demographics of the participants.

	Musicians	Non-musicians	Comparison of the two groups (*t-test*)
Mean age (range)	22.9 years (18–27)	22.4 years (19–28)	$t_{(48)} = -0.78$; $p = 0.440$
Gender	7 males; 18 females	7 males; 18 females	N.A.
Mean years of musical training (range)	14.6 years (10–20)	1.6 years (0–10)	$t_{(48)} = -15.96$; $p < 0.001$
Mean age of the start of musical training (range)	5.8 years (3–7)	9.1 years (6–13)	$t_{(33)} = 3.26$; $p < 0.001$

CI simulation

An acoustic CI simulation was used to replicate some of the spectral and temporal degradations inherent to CI sound transmission (e.g., Shannon et al., 1995). An 8-channel sinewave vocoder based on the Continuous Interleaved Sampling (CIS) strategy was implemented using Angelsound™ and iStar software (Emily Shannon Fu Foundation, http://angelsound.tigerspeech.com/; http://www.tigerspeech.com/istar). In the simulation, the acoustic input was first band-limited to 200–7000 Hz, which approximates the input frequency range used by many commercial CI devices, and then bandpass-filtered into eight frequency analysis bands (4th order Butterworth filters with band cutoff frequencies according to Greenwood, 1990, frequency-place formula). Eight channels were used in the CI simulation because previous studies have shown that CI users can only access 6–8 spectral channels (e.g., Friesen et al., 2001). For each channel, the temporal envelope was extracted using half-wave rectification and lowpass filtering (4th order Butterworth filter with cutoff frequency = 160 Hz and envelope filter slope = 24 dB/octave). These envelopes were used to modulate a sinusoidal carrier with a frequency that was equal to the center frequency of the analysis filter. The modulated carriers were summed to produce the final stimulus and the overall intensity was adjusted to be the same as the original signal. **Figure 1** shows spectrograms for four example Dutch words presented in quiet, for unprocessed speech (left panel) and with the CI simulation (right panel). Similarly, **Figure 2** shows spectrograms for an example Dutch sentence presented in quiet, for unprocessed speech (left panel) and with the CI simulation (right panel).

Experimental setup

All tests were conducted in an anechoic chamber. Participants were seated in front of a touchscreen (A1 AOD 1908, GPEG International, Woolwich, UK), facing a loudspeaker (Tannoy precision 8D; Tannoy Ltd., North Lanarkshire, UK) at a distance of 1 meter. Stimuli were presented using iStar custom software via a Windows computer with an Asus Virtuoso Audio Device soundcard (ASUSTeK Computer Inc, Fremont, USA). After conversion to an analog signal via a DA10 digital-to-analog converter (Lavry Engineering Inc., Washington, USA) the speech stimulus was played at 65 dBA in free field. The root mean square (RMS) intensity of all stimuli was normalized to the same value. The levels were calibrated with a manikin (KEMAR, GRAS) and a sound-pressure level meter (Type 2610, Brüel Kjær and Sound & Vibration Analyser, Svan 979 from Svantek). Participants' verbal responses on the speech tests were recorded using a DR-100 digital voice recorder (Tascam, California, USA), and were used to double-check responses as needed.

PROCEDURE

The order of the training and testing sessions was the same for all participants. In each experiment, participants received a short training specific to that experiment. The testing was conducted sequentially in this order: word identification, emotion identification, sentence identification, and MCI. The speech intelligibility data (word and sentence identification) are presented in this section (Experiment 1), the emotion identification data in Experiment 2, and the MCI data in Experiment 3.

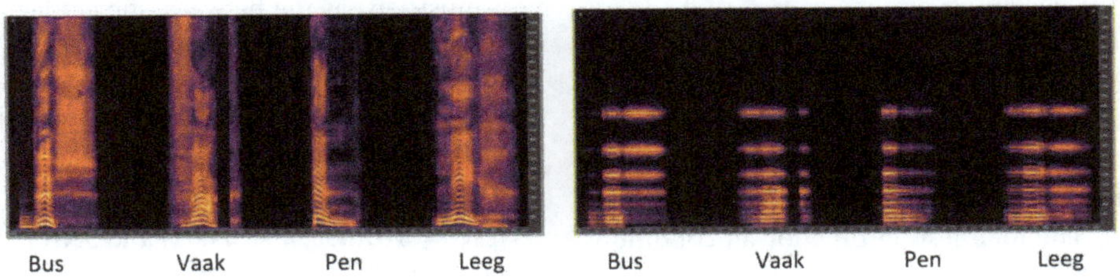

FIGURE 1 | Spectrograms for Dutch monosyllabic words "Bus," "Vaak," "Pen," and "Leeg" ("Bus," "Often," "Pen," and "Empty" in English), shown for unprocessed speech (left panel) or with the CI simulation (right panel).

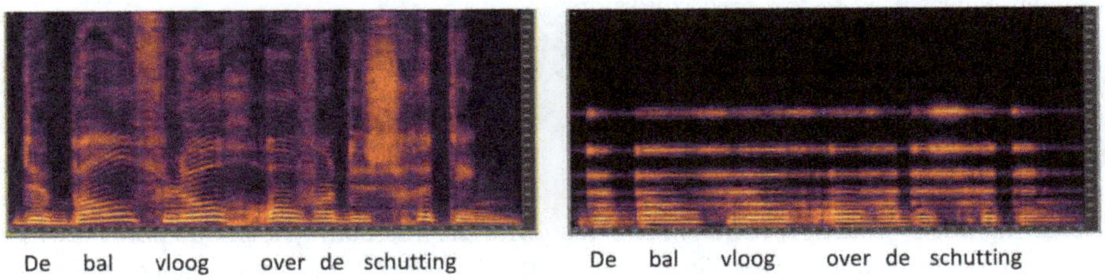

FIGURE 2 | Spectrograms for Dutch sentence "De bal vloog over de schutting" ("The ball flew over the fence" in English), shown for unprocessed speech (left panel) or with the CI simulation (right panel).

Training

Participants were trained with the CI simulation and in quiet condition only. Two sentence lists were randomly chosen from the 39 training lists for each participant. The first list was used for passive training, and the second list was used for active training. During passive training, each sentence was played through the loudspeaker and the text was shown simultaneously on the screen. Participants were asked only to listen and to read. After each sentence was presented, the participant pressed "*continue*" on the touchscreen to proceed to the next sentence. After completing the passive training, the touchscreen was turned off. During active training, a training sentence from the second list was played, this time without visual text being displayed. Participants were asked to repeat what they heard as accurately as possible, and to guess if they were unsure of the words. A native Dutch speaker observer, situated in an adjacent room and listening to subjects' responses over headphones, scored the responses using the testing software. Participants were required to score better than 85% correct during active training before beginning formal testing; all participants met this criterion with only one round of active training.

Word identification

Word identification was measured with unprocessed speech and the CI simulation in quiet and in steady, speech-shaped noise at 3 SNRs (+10, +5, and 0 dB). One list of 12 words was used to test each condition (eight lists in total). Word lists were randomly chosen from the 12 lists in the test corpus, and no list was repeated for a participant. The order of the conditions was set to progress from relatively easy to relatively difficult: (1) Unprocessed in quiet, (2) CI simulation in quiet, (3) Unprocessed +10 dB SNR, (4) CI simulation +10 dB SNR, (5) Unprocessed +5 dB SNR, (6) CI simulation +5 dB SNR, (7) Unprocessed 0 dB SNR, and (8) CI simulation 0 dB SNR. During testing, a word was randomly selected from within the list and presented via the loudspeaker. The participant was asked to repeat the word as accurately as possible. The observer listened to the responses and scored each correctly repeated phoneme using testing software that calculated the percentage of phonemes correctly recognized. No trial by trial feedback was provided. The total testing time for all conditions was 12–18 min.

Sentence identification

Sentence identification was measured with unprocessed speech and the CI simulation in three types of noise: (1) speech-shaped steady noise, (2) speech-shaped fluctuating noise, and (3) 6-talker babble. One list of 13 sentences was used to test each condition (6 lists in total). Sentence lists were randomly chosen from the 10 lists in the test corpus, and no list was repeated for a participant. Similar to word identification testing, the test order for sentence identification was fixed: (1) Unprocessed in steady noise, (2) CI simulation in steady noise, (3) Unprocessed in fluctuating noise, (4) CI simulation in fluctuating noise, (5) Unprocessed in babble noise, and (6) CI simulation in babble noise. For sentence identification in noise, the speech reception threshold (SRT), defined as the SNR needed to produce 50% correct sentence identification, was measured using an adaptive, one-up/one-down procedure (Plomp and Mimpen, 1979), in which the SNR was adjusted from trial to trial according to the accuracy of the response. During testing, speech and noise were presented at the target SNR over the loudspeaker and the participant was asked to repeat the sentence as accurately as possible. If the participant repeated all words in the sentence correctly, the SNR was reduced by 2 dB; if the participant did not repeat all words in the sentence correctly, the SNR was increased by 2 dB. The reversals in SNR between trials 4–13 was averaged and reported as the SRT for the test condition. To better target the SRT within the limited number of sentences in the test list, the initial SNR was different for each noise type and listening condition, based on preliminary testing. For steady noise, the initial SNRs were −4 and +2 dB for unprocessed speech and the CI simulation, respectively. For fluctuating noise, the initial SNRs were −8 and +6 dB for unprocessed speech and the CI simulation, respectively. For babble, the initial SNRs were −4 and +6 dB for unprocessed speech and the CI simulation, respectively. Note that the first sentence was repeated and the SNR increased until the participant repeated the entire sentence correctly. The total testing time for all conditions was 15–20 min.

RESULTS

Word identification

Figure 3 shows boxplots for word identification performance by musicians (white boxes) and non-musicians (red boxes) listening to unprocessed stimuli (left panel) or the CI simulation (right panel), as a function of noise condition. Performance generally worsened as the noise level increased, for both listening conditions, and performance with the CI simulation was generally poorer than that with unprocessed stimuli. In the CI simulation, musicians generally performed better than non-musicians. A split-plot repeated measures analysis of variance (RM ANOVA) was performed on the data, with group (musician, non-musician) as the between-subject factor, and listening condition (unprocessed, CI simulation) and SNR (quiet, +10, +5, and 0 dB) as within-subject factors. The complete analysis (with Greenhouser-Geisser corrections due to sphericity violations) is presented in **Table 2**. There were significant main effects for subject group [$F_{(1,\,48)} = 7.76$; $p = 0.008$], listening condition [$F_{(1,\,48)} = 1098.55$; $p < 0.001$] and SNR [$F_{(2.63,\,126.36)} = 409.85$; $p < 0.001$]. There was a significant interaction between listening condition and SNR [$F_{(2.81,\,134.67)} = 148.54$; $p < 0.001$]. Despite the overall main group effect, *post-hoc t-tests* showed a significant difference between musicians and non-musicians only at the +5 dB SNR with CI simulation [$t = -2.94$; $df = 48$; $p = 0.005$], namely, at one condition out of eight tested.

Sentence identification

Figure 4 shows boxplots for SRTs by musicians (white boxes) and non-musicians (red boxes) listening to unprocessed stimuli (left panel) or the CI simulation (right panel), as a function of noise type. With unprocessed speech, performance was generally best with the fluctuating noise and poorest with the steady noise. With the CI simulation, performance was generally best with steady noise and poorest with babble. Performance with unprocessed speech was much better than with the CI simulation. Differences between musicians and non-musicians were generally small. A split-plot RM ANOVA was performed on the data, with group

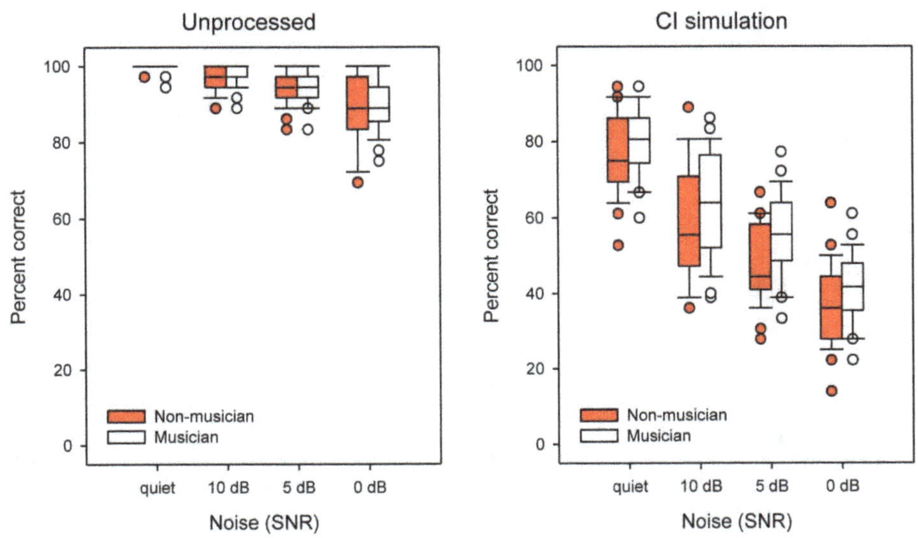

FIGURE 3 | Boxplots of word identification scores for musicians and non-musicians shown as a function of SNR. The left and right panels show data with unprocessed stimuli or with the CI simulation, respectively. The error bars show the 10 and 90th percentiles and the circles show outliers.

Table 2 | Experiment 1: Results of a split-plot RM ANOVA (with Greenhouse-Geisser correction) for word identification.

		Observed power
BETWEEN-SUBJECT FACTOR		
Group	$F_{(1, 48)} = 7.76$; $p = 0.008$*	0.78
WITHIN-SUBJECT FACTORS		
Listening condition	$F_{(1, 48)} = 1098.55$; $p < 0.001$*	1.00
SNR	$F_{(2.63, 126.36)} = 409.85$; $p < 0.001$*	1.00
SNR × listening condition	$F_{(2.81, 134.67)} = 148.54$; $p < 0.001$*	1.00
SNR × group	$F_{(2.63, 126.36)} = 2.02$; $p = 0.449$	0.20
Listening condition × group	$F_{(1, 48)} = 1.02$; $p = 0.051$	0.50
Listening condition × SNR × group	$F_{(2.81, 134.67)} = 0.95$; $p = 0.416$	0.25

*Significant ($p < 0.05$).

as the between-subject factor, and listening condition and noise type (steady, fluctuating, babble) as within-subject factors. The complete analysis is presented in **Table 3**. There were significant main effects for listening condition [$F_{(1, 48)} = 3771.1; p < 0.001$] and noise type [$F_{(1.56, 74.97)} = 95.01$; $p < 0.001$], but not for group [$F_{(1, 48)} = 2.85$; $p = 0.098$]; note that the observed power was relatively weak for the group comparison (0.38). There was a significant interaction between listening condition and noise type [$F_{(1.80, 86.54)} = 273.90$; $p < 0.001$]. *Post-hoc* tests did not show any significant differences between groups with the different noise types.

EXPERIMENT 2: IDENTIFICATION OF EMOTION IN SPEECH

RATIONALE

In Experiment 2, a vocal emotion identification task was used to test whether there was a musician effect for a speech-related test that heavily relied on perception of pitch cues in speech. To avoid any influence of semantic content on performance, a nonsense word was used to produce the target emotions. Although pitch cues strongly contribute to emotion identification, other cues such as duration and amplitude co-vary with pitch and can also be used for this purpose (Luo et al., 2007; Hubbard and Assmann, 2013). Accordingly, vocal emotion identification was tested for speech stimuli in two versions; once with pitch, duration and amplitude cues preserved across stimuli, and once with duration and amplitude cues normalized across stimuli, leaving in mainly the pitch cues. When duration and amplitude cues are minimal, vocal emotion identification is more difficult, especially under conditions of CI signal processing in which pitch cues are also weakened (Luo et al., 2007). Testing with normalized stimuli would thus allow performance to be compared between musicians and non-musicians when mainly pitch cues are available, with other acoustic cues minimized.

As in Experiment 1, musicians and non-musicians were tested while listening to unprocessed stimuli or to a CI simulation. Participants, CI simulation, and general experimental setup were identical to Experiment 1. The differences in design are explained below.

STIMULI

Stimuli included digital recordings made by Goudbeek and Broersma (2010). The original corpus contains a nonsense word [nutohɔmsɛpikɑŋ] produced by eight professional Dutch actors according to eight target emotions. The actors, who were all trained or were in training at a drama school, were instructed to imagine emotions in a scenario or by reliving personal episodes in which the target emotion occurred. Based on a pilot study with three participants, the four actors (two female, two male), and the four emotions representing all corners of the emotion matrix were chosen for formal testing (Goudbeek and Broersma, 2010). Target

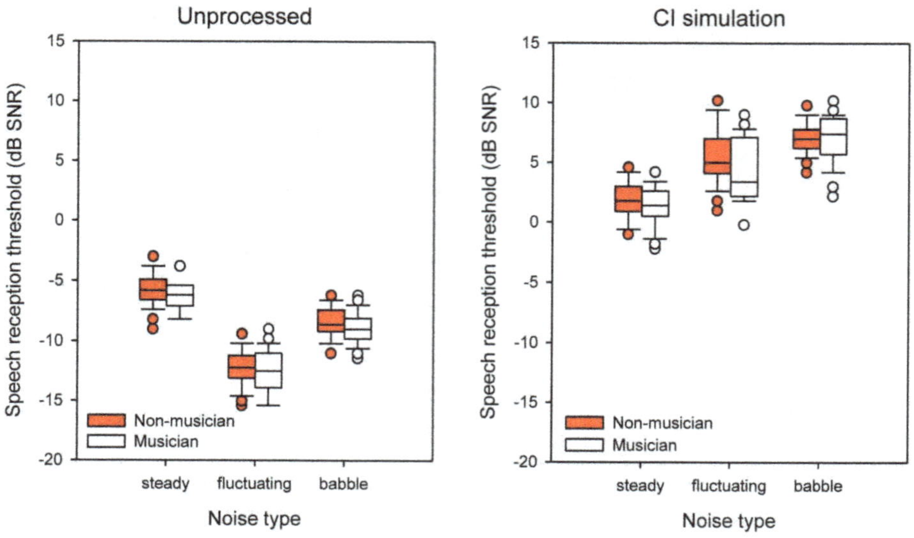

FIGURE 4 | Boxplots of SRTs for musicians and non-musicians shown as function of different noise types for different noise conditions. The left and right panels show data with unprocessed stimuli or with the CI simulation, respectively. The error bars show the 10 and 90th percentiles and the circles show outliers.

Table 3 | Experiment 1: Results of a split-plot ANOVA (with Greenhouse-Geisser correction) for sentence identification.

		Observed power
BETWEEN-SUBJECT FACTOR		
Group	$F_{(1, 48)} = 2.85; p = 0.098$	0.38
WITHIN-SUBJECT FACTORS		
Listening condition	$F_{(1, 48)} = 3771.1; p < 0.001$*	1.00
Noise type	$F_{(1.56, 74.97)} = 95.01; p < 0.001$*	1.00
Noise type × listening condition	$F_{(1.80, 86.54)} = 273.90; p < 0.001$*	1.00
Noise type × group	$F_{(1.56, 74.97)} = 0.46; p = 0.587$	0.11
Listening condition × group	$F_{(1, 48)} = 0.17; p = 0.682$	0.07
Listening condition × noise type × group	$F_{(1.80, 86.54)} = 1.05; p = 0.350$	0.22

**Significant (p < 0.05).*

emotions included: (1) Anger (high arousal, negative valence), (2) Sadness (low arousal, negative valence), (3) Joy (high arousal, positive valence), and (4) Relief (low arousal, positive valence). This resulted in a total of 32 tokens (4 speakers × 4 emotions × 2 utterances).

For the intact stimuli, duration ranged 1.06–2.76 s and amplitude ranged 45–80 dBA. For the normalized stimuli, duration was normalized to 1.77 s using a script in PRAAT (version 5.3.16; Boersma and Weenink, 2012) without changing the fundamental frequency, and amplitude normalized to 65 dBA using Matlab (i.e., the mean duration and amplitude of the intact stimuli). **Figure 5** shows spectrograms for the four target emotions with all cues intact (top panels) or with normalized duration and amplitude cues (bottom panels); the left panels show unprocessed speech and the right panels show speech processed with the CI simulation.

PROCEDURE

For all participants, conditions were tested in a fixed order: (1) Original (with all cues intact), unprocessed stimuli, (2) Original, CI simulation, (3) Normalized (in duration and amplitude), unprocessed, and (4) Normalized, CI simulation. Stimuli were presented using Angelsound software™. Before formal testing, participants were familiarized with the test procedure while listening to unprocessed stimuli, namely, the target emotions (intact stimuli only) produced by four actors not used for formal testing. During training, a target emotion was randomly selected from the stimulus set and presented over the loudspeaker. Subjects were asked to indicate the emotion of the stimulus by touching one of four response boxes on the touchscreen labeled "anger," "sadness," "joy," and "relief." Visual feedback was provided on the screen, and in case of an incorrect answer, the correct response and incorrect response were replayed. The actual data collection was identical to training, except that no audio-visual feedback was provided and only the selected test stimuli were used. The software calculated the percent correct and generated confusion matrices. The total testing time for all conditions was 8–16 min.

RESULTS

Figure 6 shows boxplots for emotion identification by musicians (white boxes) and non-musicians (red boxes) listening to unprocessed stimuli (left panels) or the CI simulation (right panels); the top panels show performance with pitch, duration, and amplitude cues preserved and the bottom panels show performance with normalized duration and amplitude cues. Note that in some cases, median and 25th/75th percentiles could not be displayed because performance was similarly good amongst participants; as such, only error bars and outliers are displayed. In general, "relief"

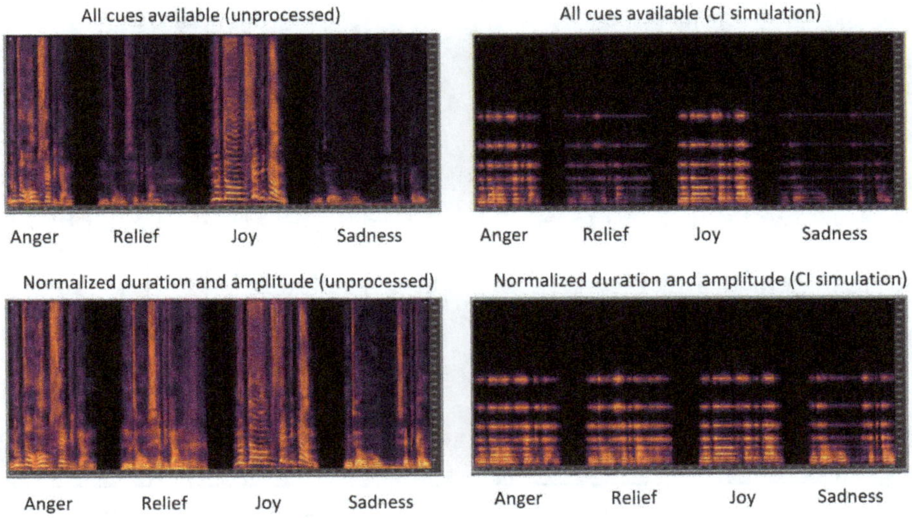

FIGURE 5 | Spectrograms for Dutch nonsense words produced according to four target emotions. The left panels show unprocessed speech and the right panels show speech processed with the CI simulation. The top panels show speech with duration, amplitude, and pitch cues intact. The bottom panels show speech with normalized duration and amplitude cues, but with preserved pitch cues.

was the least reliably recognized emotion. Performance generally worsened when duration and amplitude cues were normalized. There was a small advantage for musicians in all test conditions. A split-plot RM ANOVA was performed on the data, with group as the between-subject factor, and listening condition and cue availability (all cues, normalized duration and amplitude) as within-subject factors. The complete analysis is presented in **Table 4**. There were significant main effects for group [$F_{(1, 48)} = 4.66; p = 0.036$], listening condition [$F_{(1, 48)} = 323.85; p < 0.001$] and cue availability [$F_{(1, 48)} = 18.59; p < 0.001$].

EXPERIMENT 3: MELODIC CONTOUR IDENTIFICATION

RATIONALE

In Experiment 3, a MCI (Galvin et al., 2007) task was used to test musicians' and non-musicians' perception of musical pitch and ability to use timbre and pitch cues to segregate competing melodies. Participants were asked to identify a target melodic contour from among a closed-set of responses that represented various changes in pitch direction. MCI was measured for the target alone, and in the presence of a competing contour. The timbre of the target contour and the pitch of the competing contour were varied to allow for different degrees of difficulty in segregating the competing contours. As in Experiments 1 and 2, participants were tested while listening to unprocessed stimuli or the CI simulation. The degradations imposed by CI simulation were expected to have a profound effect on MCI performance, given that melodic pitch was the only cue of interest and would not be well represented in the CI simulation. As this experiment was a more direct measure of music perception, musicians were expected to perform better than non-musicians.

Participants, CI simulation, and general experimental setup were identical to Experiments 1 and 2. Details of the experimental stimuli and procedures are described below.

STIMULI

Stimuli for the MCI test consisted of nine 5-note melodic contours (see **Figure 7**) that represented different changes in pitch direction: "Rising," "Flat," "Falling," "Flat-Rising," "Falling-Rising," "Rising-Flat," "Falling-Flat," "Rising-Falling," "Flat-Falling." The lowest note in a given contour was A3 (220 Hz). The spacing between successive notes in the contour was 1, 2, or 3 semitones. Presumably, the 1 semitone spacing would be more difficult than the 3 semitone spacing, as the contours would be represented by a smaller cochlear extent. The duration of each note was 250 ms, and the silent interval between notes was 50 ms. The target contour was played by either a piano or an organ sample, as in Galvin et al. (2008). MCI was measured for the target alone or in the presence of a competing contour, as in Galvin et al. (2009). The competing contour ("masker") was always the "Flat" contour, played by piano sample. The pitch of the masker was varied to overlap the pitch of the target, or not. The overlapping pitch was A3 (220 Hz); the non-overlapping pitch was A5 (880 Hz). Thus, there were six conditions: (1) piano target alone (no masker), (2) piano target with the A3 piano masker, (3) piano target with the A5 piano masker, (4) organ target alone (no masker) (5) organ target with the A3 piano masker, and (6) organ target with the A5 piano masker. It was expected that MCI performance would be best with no masker, better with the organ than the piano, and better with the A5 than the A3 masker. As such, performance with the organ target with the A5 piano masker (i.e., maximum pitch and timbre difference) would be expected to be better than that with the piano target with the A3 piano masker (minimum pitch and timbre difference). The masker onset and offset was identical to the target contour; thus the notes of the masker and the target occurred simultaneously. **Figure 8** shows spectrograms for the Rising target contour played either by the piano (top panels) or the organ (bottom panels). In each panel, the target contour is shown, from left to right, with

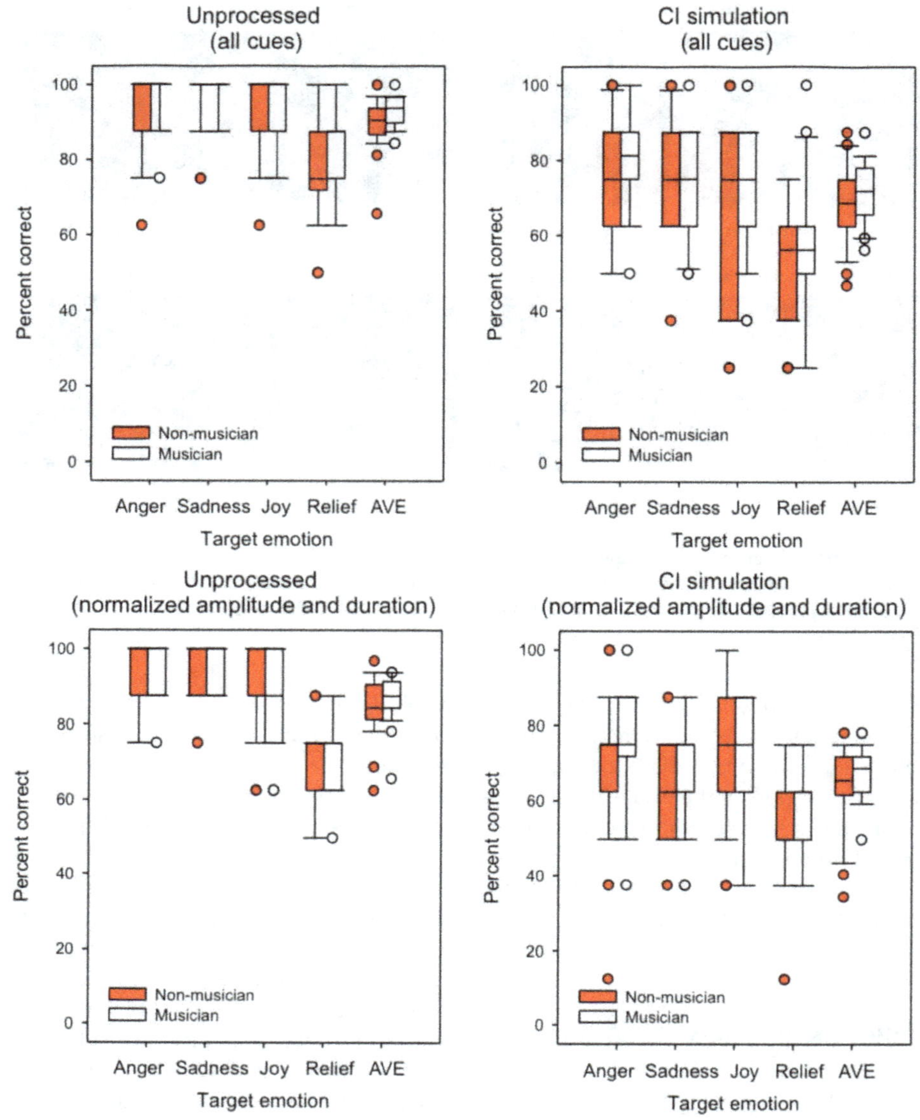

FIGURE 6 | Boxplots for identification of each emotion and overall emotion identification for musicians and non-musicians. The left and right panels show data with unprocessed stimuli or with the CI simulation, respectively. The top panels show performance with pitch, duration, and amplitude cues preserved and the bottom panels show performance with normalized duration and amplitude cues. The error bars show the 10 and 90th percentiles and the circles show outliers.

no masker, with the overlapping A3 piano masker, and with the non-overlapping A5 piano masker.

PROCEDURE

MCI testing procedures were similar to previous studies (Galvin et al., 2007, 2008, 2009). Before formal testing, participants were trained in the MCI procedure. The piano and organ samples were used for training; only the target contours were presented. During training for both piano and organ (both normal and CI simulated stimuli), a contour was randomly selected and presented via the loudspeaker. The participant was instructed to pick the contour that best matched the stimulus from among nine response choices shown on the screen; the response boxes were labeled with both a text descriptor (e.g., "Rising," Falling," Flat," etc.) and an illustration of the contour. After responding, visual feedback was provided and in the case of an incorrect response, audio feedback was provided in which the correct response and the participant's (incorrect) response were played in sequence.

Testing methods were the same as for the training, except that no feedback was provided. For all participants, the test order was fixed: (1) piano target (no masker), unprocessed, (2) piano target (no masker), CI simulation, (3) piano target with piano A3 masker, unprocessed, (4) piano target with piano A3 masker, CI simulation, (5) piano target with piano A5 masker, unprocessed, (6) piano target with piano A5 masker, CI simulation, (7) organ target (no masker), unprocessed, (8) organ target (no masker), CI simulation, (9) organ target with piano A3 masker, unprocessed, (10) organ target with piano A3 masker, CI simulation,

Table 4 | Experiment 2: Results of split-plot RM ANOVA for emotion identification.

		Observed power
BETWEEN-SUBJECT FACTOR		
Group	$F_{(1, 48)} = 4.66$; $p = 0.036$*	0.56
WITHIN-SUBJECT FACTORS		
Cue availability	$F_{(1, 48)} = 18.59$; $p < 0.001$*	0.99
Listening condition	$F_{(1, 48)} = 323.85$; $p < 0.001$*	1.00
Cue availability × group	$F_{(1, 48)} = 0.12$; $p = 0.733$	0.06
Listening condition × group	$F_{(1, 48)} = 0.21$; $p = 0.648$	0.07
Cue availability × listening condition	$F_{(1, 48)} = 1.19$; $p = 0.281$	0.19
Cue availability × listening condition × group	$F_{(1, 48)} = 0.03$; $p = 0.863$	0.05

**Significant (p < 0.05).*

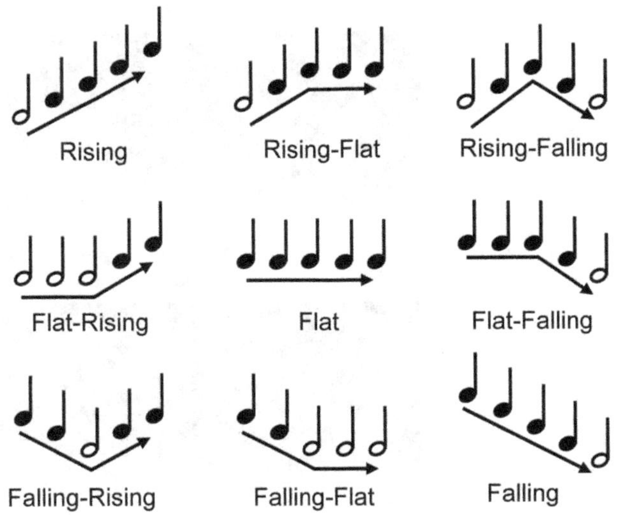

FIGURE 7 | The nine melodic contours used for MCI testing. The white note shows the lowest note of the contour (A3; 220 Hz).

(11) organ target with piano A5 masker, unprocessed, and (12) organ target with piano A5 masker, CI simulation. For conditions with a masker, participants were instructed that the masker would always be the "Flat" contour (i.e., the same note played five times in a row), and to ignore the masker and listen for the target, which would change in pitch. Responses were recorded using the test software, and the percent correct was calculated for each condition. The total testing time for all conditions was approximately 30 min.

RESULTS

Figure 9 shows box plots of MCI performance with unprocessed stimuli (left panel) or with the CI simulation (right panel), for musicians (white boxes) and non-musicians (red boxes), as a function of test condition. Note that in some cases, median and 25th/75th percentiles could not be displayed because performance was similarly good amongst participants; as such, only error bars and outliers are displayed. In general, musicians outperformed non-musicians; with unprocessed signals, musician performance was nearly perfect, even with the competing masker. Performance for both groups was much poorer with the CI simulation. The effects of the masker were unclear and somewhat counter-intuitive. In the CI simulation, performance was generally better with the A3 than with the A5 maskers, suggesting that listeners could not make use of the pitch difference between the target and the masker. Similarly, the effects of timbre were small in the CI simulation, as performance was generally similar between the piano and the organ. A split-plot RM ANOVA was performed on the data, with group as the between-subject factor, and target timbre (piano and organ) and masker pitch (no masker A3, A5) as within-subject factors. The complete analysis is presented in **Table 5**. There were significant main effects for group [$F_{(1, 48)} = 59.52$; $p < 0.001$], target timbre [$F_{(1, 48)} = 69.60$; $p < 0.001$], listening condition [$F_{(1, 48)} = 993.84$; $p < 0.001$], and masker pitch [$F_{(1.85, 88.71)} = 14.66$; $p < 0.001$]. *Post-hoc t-tests* showed a significant effect of group for all conditions for the unprocessed stimuli ($p < 0.001$). For the CI simulation, a significant musician effect was shown for the piano target with the piano A3 masker [$t_{(48)} = -5.10$, $p < 0.001$], the organ target with no masker [$t_{(48)} = -2.89$, $p = 0.006$], the organ target with the piano A3 masker [$t_{(48)} = -5.52$, $p < 0.001$] and the organ target with the piano A5 masker [$t_{(48)} = -4.22$, $p < 0.001$].

GENERAL DISCUSSION

The study showed an overall musician effect, however, the degree of the musician effect varied greatly across the three experiments. The musician effect was largest for the music test, even with melody contours degraded through a CI simulation, most likely as a direct consequence of music training. The musician effect was smaller for emotion identification, which relied strongly on perception of voice pitch contours, especially for the normalized stimuli where other potential cues, such as intensity and duration, were minimized; however, musicians still outperformed non-musicians even after the pitch cues were also degraded through the CI simulation. For speech perception, there was limited musician effect observed with only one of the speech tests used, word identification, and then only for one out of eight conditions tested, with the CI simulation and presented with background noise at +5 dB SNR.

THE MUSICIAN EFFECT

As outlined in the Introduction, there are two plausible explanations for why musicians may perceive speech better. First, musicians may be better able to detect pitch cues in stimuli, allowing for better segregation of acoustic cues that may improve speech intelligibility in challenging situations (Micheyl et al., 2006; Besson et al., 2007; Oxenham, 2008; Deguchi et al., 2012). Second, musicians may be better overall listeners due to better high-level auditory cognitive functioning, such as in working memory and auditory attention (Bialystok and DePape, 2009; Besson et al., 2011; Moreno et al., 2011; Barrett et al., 2013), which can also improve speech intelligibility, not only in noise (Parbery-Clark et al., 2009), but also in general. The present data

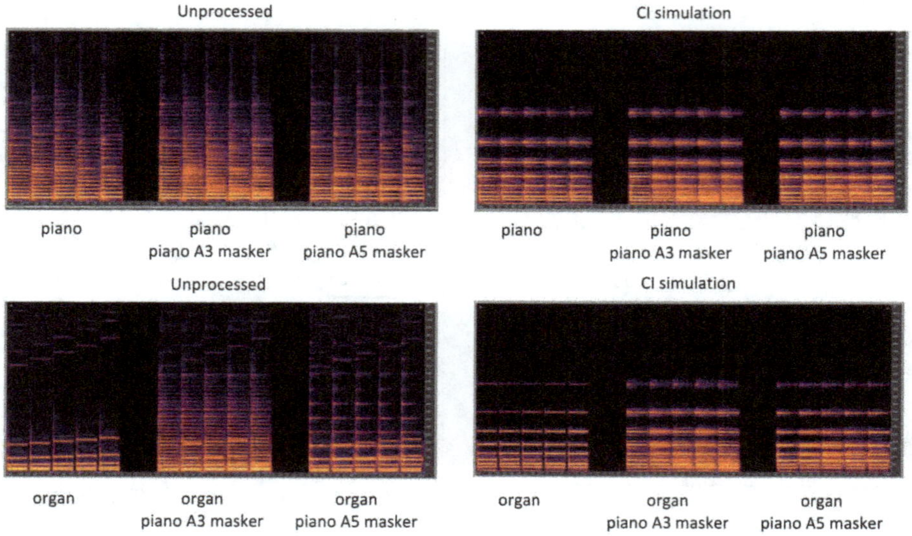

FIGURE 8 | Spectrograms for a Rising target melodic contour with 1-semitone spacing. The top panels show the piano target with the piano A3 and A5 maskers and the bottom panels show the organ target with the piano A3 and A5 maskers. The left panels show unprocessed signals and the right panels show signals processed by the CI simulation.

suggest that better pitch processing more strongly contributed to the musician effect, at least for the specific sets of experiments employed. This observation is in line with literature that has shown musicians to rely more heavily on pitch cues than non-musicians when stimuli are degraded (e.g., Fuller et al., 2014). Further, musicians seem to have a better pitch percept in pitch-related tasks in both speech and music, shown not only behaviorally, but also in imaging studies with an enhanced processing at different brain levels (Besson et al., 2011). Because it was not explicitly tested in this study, how higher-level cognitive processing may have contributed to the present pattern of results is difficult to judge. However, the observation that the musician effect increased as pitch cues became more meaningful across listening tasks suggests that pitch perception was a strong factor that differentiated musicians from non-musicians.

Prior evidence for transfer of music training to speech perception has been mixed. While Parbery-Clark et al. (2009) showed a small musician effect for identification of sentences presented in noise, but not processed otherwise, Ruggles et al. (2014) showed no musician effect for identification of sentences in noise, presented with or without voice pitch cues. In the present study, there was a significant musician effect for word identification (Experiment 1), yet, this was limited to one condition out of eight tested, only observed in noise and with CI simulation, and there was no musician effect for sentence recognition in noise, with or without CI simulation. The reason for not observing an effect in the latter may be that sentence recognition depends on also other factors besides pitch perception (e.g., segregating speech from noise, extracting meaning with help from semantics, context, prosody, and also using higher-level cognitive and linguistic processes). If the musician effect is largely based on pitch processing, it may be more difficult to observe with sentences; this effect may be stronger when perceiving subtle speech cues in phonetics-based tasks such as identification of syllables (Zuk et al., 2013) or words (in the present study), but this effect may diminish for linguistically rich materials, such as sentences, where listeners can compensate degradations using linguistic skills as well (Benard et al., 2014). Hence, overall, the present data combined with past studies imply that there could be some transfer of music training to better perception of speech, especially in degraded listening conditions, but this effect seems to be rather small. Further, this is perhaps a consequence of the musician advantage being mainly due to better processing of low-level acoustic cues, instead of a better overall cognitive processing.

The musician effect may be stronger in speech-related tasks in which pitch cues are more important. After all, perception of speech prosody is vital to real-life speech communication and depends strongly on perception of pitch cues (Wennerstrom, 2001; Besson et al., 2011). One novel aspect of the present study was to include the emotion identification task to explore this idea (Experiment 2). In this test, musicians were expected to have an advantage due to better utilization of pitch cues, as in comparison to neutral speech, angry and happy speech exhibit a wider pitch range as well as a higher mean pitch, while sad speech has a narrower range and lower mean pitch (Banse and Scherer, 1996; Luo et al., 2007). In line with this idea, Globerson et al. (2013) had observed that listeners with better F0 identification also exhibited better emotion identification in speech. However, other acoustic cues also contribute to vocal emotion identification, such as the level and the range of the duration and amplitude (controlled for in the present study), but also vocal energy, tempo, and pausing (not controlled; Hubbard and Assmann, 2013); hence, it was not known before the present study if musician advantage indeed would also present an advantage in perception of vocal emotion in speech. In the present study, we measured emotion identification in a nonsense word (thereby removing any semantic cues)

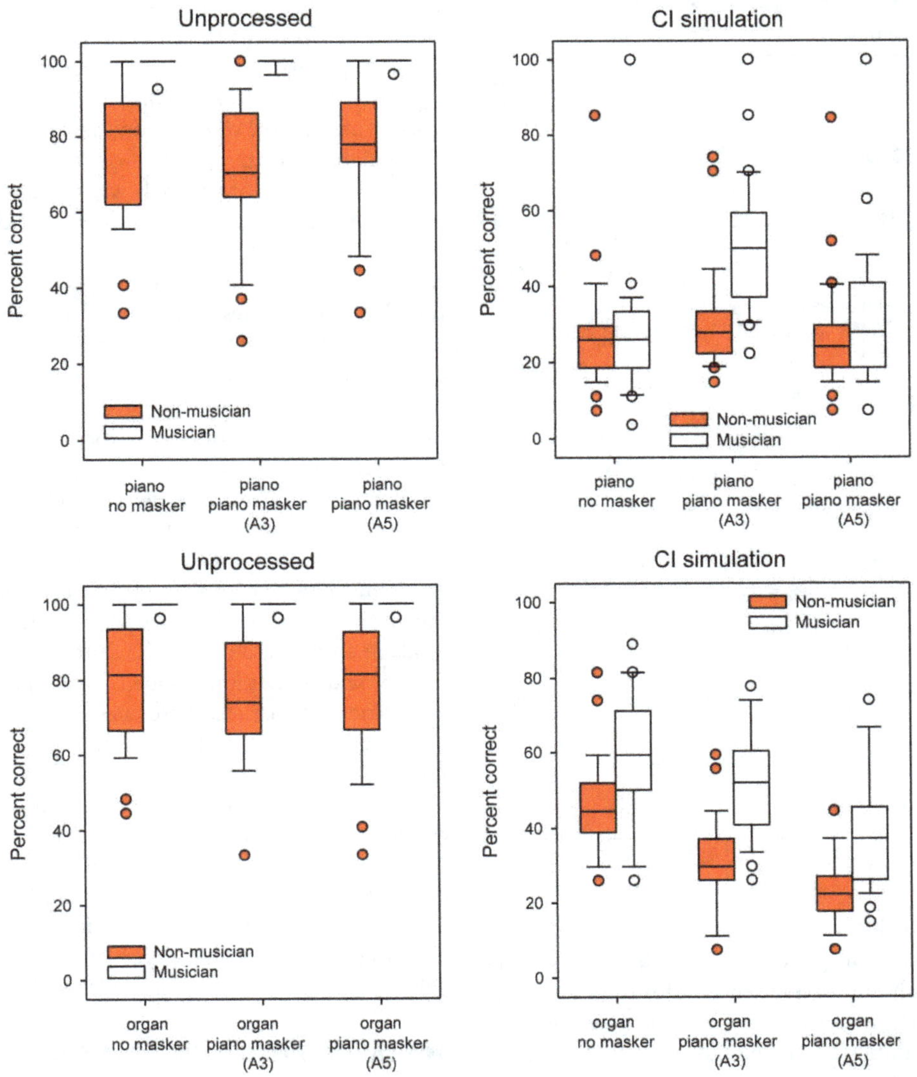

FIGURE 9 | Boxplots for MCI performance for each masker condition for musicians and non-musicians. The top and bottom panels show data for the piano and organ targets, respectively. The left and right panels show data with unprocessed stimuli or with the CI simulation, respectively. Within each panel, data is shown with no masker, with the A3 piano masker, and with the A5 piano masker. The error bars show the 10th and 90th percentiles and the circles show outliers.

in two versions; once with all cues intact, and once with normalized duration and amplitude cues, leaving mainly the pitch cues intact. There was a small but significant overall group effect, with no interactions with presence or absence of CI simulations or of normalization of other cues than pitch, confirming that generally musicians perceived vocal emotion in speech better than non-musicians. Consistent with previous literature (Thompson et al., 2004; Besson et al., 2007), the present data suggest that musicians may better utilize the pitch cues for vocal emotion identification, but interestingly, this is a persistent effect as they do so even when pitch cues are degraded through a CI simulation.

Note that, although twenty-five musicians and non-musicians were recruited based on a power-analysis prior to the study, the observed power for some analyses was low. This could either mean that there were not enough participants and/or that the musician effect was too small. For example, the observed power for the sentence test in stationary noise was 0.38 (**Table 3**). A power analysis based on the present results indicated that there would need to be a very large number of participants to achieve adequate power. Therefore, a musician effect for this specific test would not likely be found by increasing the number of participants in a realistic manner, and such a small effect might not be relevant in daily life. On the other hand, the observed power for the emotion test was 0.56 (**Table 4**), and while low, this was sufficient to produce statistically significant effects. For this test, to achieve power = 0.80, the number of participants would need to be increased to 46. As such, for this test, further research with more participants has the potential to produce more significant differences between musicians and non-musicians.

Table 5 | Experiment 3: Results from a split-plot RM ANOVA for melodic contour identification.

		Observed power
BETWEEN SUBJECT FACTOR		
Group	$F_{(1,\ 48)} = 59.52;\ p < 0.001$*	1.00
WITHIN SUBJECT FACTORS		
Target timbre	$F_{(1,\ 48)} = 69.60;\ p < 0.001$*	1.00
CI simulation	$F_{(1,\ 48)} = 993.84;\ p < 0.001$*	1.00
Masker pitch	$F_{(1.85,\ 88.71)} = 14.66;\ p < 0.001$*	1.00
Target timbre × masker pitch	$F_{(1.76,\ 84.69)} = 56.67;\ p < 0.001$*	1.00
Target timbre × CI simulation	$F_{(1,\ 48)} = 55.55;\ p < 0.001$*	1.00
Target timbre × group	$F_{(1,\ 48)} = 2.90;\ p = 0.095$	0.39
CI simulation × group	$F_{(1,\ 48)} = 11.19;\ p = 0.002$*	0.91
CI simulation × masker pitch	$F_{(1.96,\ 93.82)} = 27.51;\ p < 0.001$*	1.00
Masker pitch × group	$F_{(1.85,\ 88.71)} = 10.45;\ p < 0.001$*	0.98
Target timbre × CI simulation × Group	$F_{(1,\ 48)} = 19.86;\ p < 0.001$*	0.99
Target timbre × CI simulation × Masker	$F_{(1.95,\ 93.62)} = 46.22;\ p < 0.001$*	0.99
Target timbre × masker pitch × group	$F_{(1.76,\ 84.69)} = 3.21;\ p = 0.051$	0.56
Target timbre × CI simulation × masker pitch × group	$F_{(1.95,\ 93.62)} = 1.56;\ p = 0.217$	0.32

**Significant ($p < 0.05$).*

EFFECT OF THE CI SIMULATION

For all test conditions, mean performance was poorer with the CI simulation than with unprocessed speech, for both musicians and non-musicians. The effect of the CI simulation was more pronounced for more difficult listening tasks (e.g., speech recognition in noise, MCI). The musician effect persisted (or appeared, in the case of speech perception) with the application of the CI simulation, hinting that musicians were better able to extract acoustic cues in degraded conditions than non-musicians.

Interestingly, the effect of different types of noise also varied between unprocessed and CI-simulated conditions. In NH, a release of masking is observed when same listeners are tested with a steady noise vs. a fluctuating noise, usually resulting in better speech perception performance with the latter (Miller and Licklider, 1950; Başkent et al., 2014). This improvement is usually attributed to the glimpses of speech available through the valleys, i.e., low-level portions of the fluctuating noise, which provide samples of the speech that the listener can make use of to restore speech for enhanced intelligibility. In the present study, while there was such release from masking for unprocessed speech with fluctuating maskers, performance worsened with fluctuating maskers for the CI simulation. Such effects of dynamic maskers have been previously observed with real CI users and in CI simulations (Nelson et al., 2003; Fu and Nogaki, 2005). The limited spectral resolution, due to both the limited number of channels and the interactions between channels, is thought to increase susceptibility to fluctuating maskers in both CI users and CI simulations. Further, recent work by Bhargava et al. (2014) showed that perhaps the reduced quality of the speech glimpses due to signal degradations in CIs make them also more difficult to utilize the top-down reconstruction of speech in fluctuating noise. These factors can also limit melodic pitch perception in CI simulations. For example, Crew et al. (2012) showed that, even when the number of channels was increased, MCI performance was quite poor when there was substantial channel interaction in the CI simulations. Most likely, the current spread across electrodes in real CIs similarly causes spectral smearing, reducing the functional spectral resolution to be less than the number of nominal channels, thereby limiting the release from masking, as well as pitch perception.

Note that sinewave vocoding was used for the present CI simulation, rather than noise-band vocoding. The sinewave vocoder was used because of the greater specificity in terms of place of cochlear stimulation, as well as better representation of the temporal envelope, which may be "noisier" with noise-band carriers (e.g., Fu et al., 2004). One potential problem with sinewave vocoding, however, is the introduction of side-bands around the carrier frequency. Such side-band information would not be available in the case of real CIs. Although these side-bands may have provided additional (albeit weak) spectral cues beyond the eight sinewave carriers, these cues would have been available to both musicians and non-musicians in this study. It may be that musicians were better able to use this side-band information, or were better able to use pitch cues encoded in the temporal envelope. Either way, musicians in general performed better than non-musicians in the CI simulation. This observation gives support to previous literature (Gfeller et al., 2000; Galvin et al., 2007, 2012; Looi et al., 2012), and implies that musically trained CI users might be better able to perceive much-weakened pitch cues delivered by their devices (e.g., Fuller et al., 2014, under revision).

IMPLICATIONS FOR COCHLEAR IMPLANT USERS

The patterns of musician effect observed with unprocessed stimuli did not change largely with the CI simulations, except for generally poorer performance, and in case of speech intelligibility, the musician effect only appeared after the CI simulation was applied. This implies that the musician effect seems to persist despite the signal degradations associated with CI signal processing, or may become even more important in the presence of such degradations where listeners can benefit even more greatly if they can perceive any acoustic cues, albeit weak. While this sounds promising, one has to be cautious before drawing strong conclusions regarding actual CI users, whose demographics vary from that of young NH populations, and who also have to deal with additional factors related to the device front-end processing and nerve-electrode interface. One important consideration is that most post-lingually deafened CI users are typically older than the present study participants (Blamey et al., 2013), and have experienced a period of auditory deprivation (Lazard et al., 2012). Age alone can alter the cognitive and linguistic processes needed for speech perception in noise (e.g., Başkent et al., 2014), and auditory deprivation may lead to structural changes in the brain, affecting overall sound perception (e.g., Lazard et al., 2014). Thus, the sometimes small musician effects in this study, measured under ideal and well-controlled conditions, may be even smaller in actual CI users. Alternatively, to their benefit, real CI users will have had much greater experience with the CI signal processing than the NH participants of the present study had experience with the simulated CI. As the actual users of CIs have to rely on these degraded signals exclusively, and will have (had) more time to practice with them, the small effects observed in this study may have greater consequences for actual CI users' real-life performance.

Previous studies have shown significant benefits of musical training after implantation for post-lingually deafened CI users' music perception (Gfeller et al., 2000, 2002b; Galvin et al., 2007, 2012; Driscoll et al., 2009). In the present study, musical training, the main factor that differentiated the musician group from the non-musician group, was associated with better performance as pitch cues became more important in the listening task. Training melodic pitch perception in CI users may also benefit music perception and speech perception where pitch cues are relevant (emotion recognition, prosody perception, segregation of speech from background noise or distractor signals, etc.). However, such training will likely differ from the long-term music training experienced by the present group of NH musicians. Learning to play an instrument, with spectro-temporal fine-structure cues available and over a period of many years, may give rise to robust central pitch representations. Training melodic pitch perception after implantation may not provide such robust patterns. On the other hand, an earlier training provided to hearing-impaired children before they reach the level of profound hearing loss may provide positive results, due to yet strong plasticity experienced in childhood (Hyde et al., 2009; Moreno et al., 2009; Yucel et al., 2009; Torppa et al., 2014). Further research with pre- and post-lingually deafened CI musicians and non-musicians, with or without music training provided, may reveal whether patterns developed during previous acoustic hearing or during post-implantation electric hearing may benefit pitch, music, and speech perception after implantation.

CONCLUSIONS

In this study, performance of musicians and non-musicians was compared for a variety of speech and music listening tasks, with and without the spectro-temporal degradations associated with CI signal processing. Major findings include:

1. Cross-domain (music training to speech perception) effects were weak for speech intelligibility. The musician effect was minimal for word identification in noise, and non-existent for sentence identification in noise.
2. As pitch cues became more important for the listening task (i.e., vocal emotion identification, or MCI), the musician effect was more pronounced, suggesting that the musician effect may be rooted in better pitch perception.
3. Musicians tended to outperform non-musicians when listening to the CI simulation, especially for the MCI task. This suggests that musicians were better able to extract the relatively weak pitch and timbre information encoded in the CI simulations.

ACKNOWLEDGMENTS

We would like to thank Joeri Smit and Karin van der Velde for their help with collecting the data, Mirjam Broersma and Martijn Goudbeek for providing the emotion stimuli, Steven Gilbers for help with the emotion data and Qian Jie Fu and the Emily Shannon Fu Foundation for the help and support with the testing software. The second author is supported by NIH R01-DC004792. The fourth author is supported by an otological/neurotological stipendium from the Heinsius-Houbolt Foundation. The last author is supported by a Rosalind Franklin Fellowship from the University Medical Center Groningen, University of Groningen, and the VIDI grant 016.096.397 from the Netherlands Organization for Scientific Research (NWO) and the Netherlands Organization for Health Research and Development (ZonMw). The study is part of the research program of our department: Healthy Aging and Communication.

REFERENCES

Banse, R., and Scherer, K. R. (1996). Acoustic profiles in vocal emotion expression. *J. Pers. Soc. Psychol.* 70, 614–636. doi: 10.1037/0022-3514.70.3.614

Barrett, K. C., Ashley, R., Strait, D. L., and Kraus, N. (2013). Art and science: how musical training shapes the brain. *Front. Psychol.* 4:713. doi: 10.3389/fpsyg.2013.00713

Başkent, D., and Shannon, R. V. (2006). Frequency transposition around dead regions simulated with a noiseband vocoder. *J. Acoust. Soc. Am.* 119, 1156. doi: 10.1121/1.2151825

Başkent, D., and Shannon, R. V. (2007). Combined effects of frequency compression-expansion and shift on speech recognition. *Ear Hear.* 28, 277–289. doi: 10.1097/AUD.0b013e318050d398

Başkent, D., van Engelshoven, S., and Galvin, J. J. III. (2014). Susceptibility to interference by music and speech maskers in middle-aged adults. *J. Acoust. Soc. Am.* 135, EL147–EL153. doi: 10.1121/1.4865261

Benard, M. R., Mensink, J. S., and Başkent, D. (2014). Individual differences in top-down restoration of interrupted speech: links to linguistic and cognitive abilities. *J. Acoust. Soc. Am.* 135, EL88–EL94. doi: 10.1121/1.4862879

Besson, M., Chobert, J., and Marie, C. (2011). Transfer of training between music and speech: common processing, attention, and memory. *Front. Psychol.* 2:94. doi: 10.3389/fpsyg.2011.00094

Besson, M., Schon, D., Moreno, S., Santos, A., and Magne, C. (2007). Influence of musical expertise and musical training on pitch processing in music and language. *Restor. Neurol. Neurosci.* 25, 399–410.

Bhargava, P., Gaudrain, E., and Başkent, D. (2014). Top-down restoration of speech in cochlear-implant users. *Hear. Res.* 309, 113–123. doi: 10.1016/j.heares.2013.12.003

Bialystok, E., and DePape, A. M. (2009). Musical expertise, bilingualism, and executive functioning. *J. Exp. Psychol. Hum. Percept. Perform.* 35, 565–574. doi: 10.1037/a0012735

Bierer, J. A. (2010). Probing the electrode-neuron interface with focused cochlear implant stimulation. *Trends Amplif.* 14, 84–95. doi: 10.1177/1084713810375249

Blamey, P., Artieres, F., Başkent, D., Bergeron, F., Beynon, A., Burke, E., et al. (2013). Factors affecting auditory performance of post-linguistically deaf adults using cochlear implants: an update with 2251 patients. *Audiol Neurotol.* 18, 36–47. doi: 10.1159/000343189

Boersma, P., and Weenink, D. (2012). *PRAAT: Doing Phonetics by Computer (Version 5.3.16).* Institute of Phonetic Sciences, University of Amsterdam. Available online at: http://www.fon.hum.uva.nl/praat

Bosman, A. J., and Smoorenburg, G. F. (1995). Intelligibility of Dutch CVC syllables and sentences for listeners with normal hearing and with three types of hearing impairment. *Audiology* 34, 260–284. doi: 10.3109/00206099509071918

Chartrand, J. P., and Belin, P. (2006). Superior voice timbre processing in musicians. *Neurosci. Lett.* 405, 164–167. doi: 10.1016/j.neulet.2006.06.053

Crew, J. D., Galvin, J. J. 3rd., and Fu, Q. J. (2012). Channel interaction limits melodic pitch perception in simulated cochlear implants. *J. Acoust. Soc. Am.* 132, EL429–EL435. doi: 10.1121/1.4758770

Deguchi, C., Boureux, M., Sarlo, M., Besson, M., Grassi, M., Schon, D., et al. (2012). Sentence pitch change detection in the native and unfamiliar language in musicians and non-musicians: Behavioral, electrophysiological and psychoacoustic study. *Brain Res.* 1455, 75–89. doi: 10.1016/j.brainres.2012.03.034

Dreschler, W. A., Verschuure, H., Ludvigsen, C., and Westermann, S. (2001). ICRA noises: artificial noise signals with speech-like spectral and temporal properties for hearing instrument assessment. International collegium for rehabilitative audiology. *Audiology* 40, 148–157. doi: 10.3109/00206090109073110

Driscoll, V. D., Oleson, J., Jiang, D., and Gfeller, K. (2009). Effects of training on recognition of musical instruments presented through cochlear implant simulations. *J. Am. Acad. Audiol.* 20, 71–82. doi: 10.3766/jaaa.20.1.7

Friesen, L. M., Shannon, R. V., Başkent, D., and Wang, X. (2001). Speech recognition in noise as a function of the number of spectral channels: comparison of acoustic hearing and cochlear implants. *J. Acoust. Soc. Am.* 110, 1150–1163. doi: 10.1121/1.1381538

Fu, Q. J., Chinchilla, S., and Galvin, J. J. 3rd. (2004). The role of spectral and temporal cues in voice gender discrimination by normal-hearing listeners and cochlear implant users. *J. Assoc. Res. Otolaryngol.* 5, 253–260. doi: 10.1007/s10162-004-4046-1

Fu, Q. J., and Nogaki G. (2005). Noise susceptibility of cochlear implant users: the role of spectral resolution and smearing. *J. Assoc. Res. Otolaryngol.* 6, 19–27. doi: 10.1007/s10162-004-5024-3

Fuller, C., Free, R., Maat, B., and Başkent, D. (2012). Musical background not associated with self-perceived hearing performance or speech perception in postlingual cochlear-implant users. *J. Acoust. Soc. Am.* 132, 1009–1016. doi: 10.1121/1.4730910

Fuller, C., Galvin, J. J. III., Free, R., and Başkent, D. (2014). Musician effect in cochlear implant simulated gender categorization. *J. Acoust. Soc. Am.* 135, EL159–EL165. doi: 10.1121/1.4865263

Galvin, J. J. 3rd., Eskridge, E., Oba, S., and Fu, Q. J. (2012). Melodic contour identification training in cochlear implant users with and without a competing instrument. *Semin. Hear.* 33, 399–409. doi: 10.1055/s-0032-1329227

Galvin, J. J. 3rd., Fu, Q. J., and Nogaki, G. (2007). Melodic contour identification by cochlear implant listeners. *Ear Hear.* 28, 302–319. doi: 10.1097/01.aud.0000261689.35445.20

Galvin, J. J. 3rd., Fu, Q. J., and Oba, S. (2008). Effect of instrument timbre on melodic contour identification by cochlear implant users. *J. Acoust. Soc. Am.* 124, EL189–EL195. doi: 10.1121/1.2961171

Galvin, J. J. 3rd., Fu, Q. J., and Shannon, R. V. (2009). Melodic contour identification and music perception by cochlear implant users. *Ann. N.Y. Acad. Sci.* 1169, 518–533. doi: 10.1111/j.1749-6632.2009.04551.x

Gfeller, K., Turner, C., Mehr, M., Woodworth, G., Fearn, R., Knutson, J. F., et al. (2002a). Recognition of familiar melodies by adult cochlear implant recipients and normal-hearing adults. *Cochlear Implants Int.* 3, 29–53. doi: 10.1179/cim.2002.3.1.29

Gfeller, K., Turner, C., Oleson, J., Zhang, X., Gantz, B., Froman, R., et al. (2007). Accuracy of cochlear implant recipients on pitch perception, melody recognition, and speech reception in noise. *Ear Hear.* 28, 412–423. doi: 10.1097/AUD.0b013e3180479318

Gfeller, K., Witt, S., Adamek, M., Mehr, M., Rogers, J., Stordahl, J., et al. (2002b). Effects of training on timbre recognition and appraisal by postlingually deafened cochlear implant recipients. *J. Am. Acad. Audiol.* 13, 132–145.

Gfeller, K., Witt, S., Stordahl, J., Mehr, M., and Woodworth, G. (2000). The effects of training on melody recognition and appraisal by adult cochlear implant recipients. *J. Acad. Rehabil. Audiol.* 33, 115–138.

Globerson, E., Amir, N., Golan, O., Kishon-Rabin, L., and Lavidor, M. (2013). Psychoacoustic abilities as predictors of vocal emotion recognition. *Atten. Percept. Psychophys.* 78, 1799–1810. doi: 10.3758/s13414-013-0518-x

Goudbeek, M., and Broersma, M. (2010). "Language specific effects of emotion on phoneme duration," in *Proceedings of the 11th Annual Conference of the International Speech Communication Association (Interspeech 2010)* (Makuhari), 2026–2029.

Greenwood, D. D. (1990). A cochlear frequency–position function for several species—29 years later. *J. Acoust. Soc. Am.* 87, 2592–2605.

Heng, J., Cantarero, G., Elhilali, M., and Limb, C. J. (2011). Impaired perception of temporal fine structure and musical timbre in cochlear implant users. *Hear. Res.* 280, 192–200. doi: 10.1016/j.heares.2011.05.017

Holden, L. K., Finley, C. C., Firszt, J. B., Holden, T. A., Brenner, C., Potts, L. G., et al. (2013). Factors affecting open-set word recognition in adults with cochlear implants. *Ear Hear.* 34, 342–360. doi: 10.1097/AUD.0b013e3182741aa7

Hubbard, D. J., and Assmann, P. F. (2013). Perceptual adaptation to gender and expressive properties in speech: the role of fundamental frequency. *J. Acoust. Soc. Am.* 133, 2367–2376. doi: 10.1121/1.4792145

Hyde, K. L., Lerch, J., Norton, A., Forgeard, M., Winner, E., Evans, A. C., et al. (2009). The effects of musical training on structural brain development: a longitudinal study. *Ann. N.Y. Acad. Sci.* 1169, 182–186. doi: 10.1111/j.1749-6632.2009.04852.x

Kong, Y. Y., Cruz, R., Jones, J. A., and Zeng, F. G. (2004). Music perception with temporal cues in acoustic and electric hearing. *Ear Hear.* 25, 173–185. doi: 10.1097/01.AUD.0000120365.97792.2F

Kraus, N., and Chandrasekaran, B. (2010). Music training for the development of auditory skills. *Nat. Rev. Neurosci.* 11, 599–605. doi: 10.1038/nrn2882

Lazard, D. S., Innes-Brown, H., and Barone, P. (2014). Adaptation of the communicative brain to post-lingual deafness. Evidence from functional imaging. *Hear. Res.* 307, 136–143. doi: 10.1016/j.heares.2013.08.006

Lazard, D. S., Vincent, C., Venail, F., Van de Heyning, P., Truy, E., Sterkers, O., et al. (2012). Pre-, per- and postoperative factors affecting performance of postlinguistically deaf adults using cochlear implants: a new conceptual model over time. *PLoS ONE* 7:e48739. doi: 10.1371/journal.pone.0048739

Limb, C. J., and Roy, A. T. (2014). Technological, biological, and acoustical constraints to music perception in cochlear implant users. *Hear. Res.* 308, 13–26. doi: 10.1016/j.heares.2013.04.009

Looi, V., Gfeller, K., and Driscoll, V. (2012). Music appreciation and training for cochlear implant recipients: a review. *Semin. Hear.* 33, 307–334. doi: 10.1055/s-0032-1329222

Luo, X., Fu, Q. J., and Galvin, J. J. 3rd. (2007). Vocal emotion recognition by normal-hearing listeners and cochlear implant users. *Trends Amplif.* 11, 301–315. doi: 10.1177/1084713807305301

McDermott, H. J. (2004). Music perception with cochlear implants: a review. *Trends Amplif.* 8, 49–82. doi: 10.1177/108471380400800203

Micheyl, C., Delhommeau, K., Perrot, X., and Oxenham, A. J. (2006). Influence of musical and psychoacoustical training on pitch discrimination. *Hear. Res.* 219, 36–47. doi: 10.1016/j.heares.2006.05.004

Miller, G. A., and Licklider, J. C. R. (1950). The intelligibility of interrupted speech. *J. Acoust. Soc. Am.* 22, 167. doi: 10.1121/1.1906584

Moreno, S., Bialystok, E., Barac, R., Schellenberg, E. G., Cepeda, N. J., and Chau, T. (2011). Short-term music training enhances verbal intelligence and executive function. *Psychol. Sci.* 22, 1425–1433. doi: 10.1177/0956797611416999

Moreno, S., Marques, C., Santos, A., Santos, M., Castro, S. L., and Besson, M. (2009). Musical training influences linguistic abilities in 8-year-old children: more evidence for brain plasticity. *Cereb. Cortex* 19, 712–723. doi: 10.1093/cercor/bhn120

Musacchia, G., Strait, D., and Kraus, N. (2008). Relationships between behavior, brainstem and cortical encoding of seen and heard speech in musicians and non-musicians. *Hear. Res.* 241, 34–42. doi: 10.1016/j.heares.2008.04.013

Nelson, P. B., Jin, S. H., Carney, A. E., and Nelson, D. A. (2003). Understanding speech in modulated interference: cochlear implant users and normal-hearing listeners. *J. Acoust. Soc. Am.* 113, 961–968. doi: 10.1121/1.1531983

Oxenham, A. J. (2008). Pitch perception and auditory stream segregation: implications for hearing loss and cochlear implants. *Trends Amplif.* 12, 316–331. doi: 10.1177/1084713808325881

Parbery-Clark, A., Skoe, E., Lam, C., and Kraus, N. (2009). Musician enhancement for speech-in-noise. *Ear Hear.* 30, 653–661. doi: 10.1097/AUD.0b013e3181b412e9

Plomp, R., and Mimpen, A. M. (1979). Speech-reception threshold for sentences as a function of age and noise level. *J. Acoust. Soc. Am.* 66, 1333–1342. doi: 10.1121/1.383554

Ruggles, D. R., Freyman, R. L., and Oxenham, A. J. (2014). Influence of musical training on understanding voiced and whispered speech in noise. *PLoS ONE* 9:e86980. doi: 10.1371/journal.pone.0086980

Schon, D., Magne, C., and Besson, M. (2004). The music of speech: Music training facilitates pitch processing in both music and language. *Psychophysiology* 41, 341–349. doi: 10.1111/1469-8986.00172.x

Shannon, R. V., Zeng, F. G., Kamath, V., Wygonski, J., and Ekelid, M. (1995). Speech recognition with primarily temporal cues. *Science* 270, 303–304. doi: 10.1126/science.270.5234.303

Stickney, G. S., Zeng, F. G., Litovsky, R., and Assmann, P. (2004). Cochlear implant speech recognition with speech maskers. *J. Acoust. Soc. Am.* 116, 1081. doi: 10.1121/1.1772399

Strait, D. L., Kraus, N., Skoe, E., and Ashley, R. (2009). Musical experience and neural efficiency: effects of training on subcortical processing of vocal expressions of emotion. *Eur. J. Neurosci.* 29, 661–668. doi: 10.1111/j.1460-9568.2009.06617.x

Thompson, W. F., Schellenberg, E. G., and Husain, G. (2004). Decoding speech prosody: do music lessons help? *Emotion* 4, 46–64. doi: 10.1037/1528-3542.4.1.46

Torppa, R., Faulkner, A., Huotilainen, M., Järvikivi, J., Lipsanen, J., Laasonen, M., et al. (2014). The perception of prosody and associated auditory cues in early-implanted children: the role of auditory working memory and musical activities. *Int. J. Audiol.* 53, 182–191. doi: 10.3109/14992027.2013.872302

Versfeld, N. J., Daalder L., Festen, J. M., and Houtgast, T. (2000). Method for the selection of sentence materials for efficient measurement of the speech reception threshold. *J. Acoust. Soc. Am.* 107, 1671–1684. doi: 10.1121/1.428451

Wennerstrom, A. (2001). *The Music of Everyday Speech: Prosody and Discourse Analysis.* New York, NY: Oxford University Press.

Won, J. H., Drennan, W. R., Kang, R. S., and Rubinstein, J. T. (2010). Psychoacoustic abilities associated with music perception in cochlear implant users. *Ear Hear.* 31, 796–805. doi: 10.1097/AUD.0b013e3181e8b7bd

Wong, P. C., Skoe, E., Russo, N. M., Dees, T., and Kraus, N. (2007). Musical experience shapes human brainstem encoding of linguistic pitch patterns. *Nat. Neurosci.* 10, 420–422. doi: 10.1038/nn1872

Yucel, E., Sennaroglu, G., and Belgin, E. (2009). The family oriented musical training for children with cochlear implants: speech and musical perception results of two year follow-up. *Int. J. Pediatr. Otorhinolaryngol.* 73, 1043–1052. doi: 10.1016/j.ijporl.2009.04.009

Zuk, J., Ozernov-Palchik, O., Kim, H., Lakshminarayanan, K., Gabrieli, J. D. E., Tallal, P., et al. (2013). Enhanced syllable discrimination thresholds in musicians. *PLoS ONE* 8:e80546. doi: 10.1371/journal.pone.0080546

7

Neurobiological, cognitive and emotional mechanisms in Melodic Intonation Therapy

Dawn L. Merrett[1], Isabelle Peretz[2] and Sarah J. Wilson[1]*

[1] *Melbourne School of Psychological Sciences, The University of Melbourne, Melbourne, VIC, Australia*
[2] *Department of Psychology, Université de Montréal, Montréal, QC, Canada*

Correspondence:
Sarah J. Wilson, Melbourne School of Psychological Sciences, The University of Melbourne, 12th Floor, Redmond Barry Building, Melbourne, VIC 3010, Australia
e-mail: sarahw@unimelb.edu.au

Singing has been used in language rehabilitation for decades, yet controversy remains over its effectiveness and mechanisms of action. Melodic Intonation Therapy (MIT) is the most well-known singing-based therapy; however, speculation surrounds when and how it might improve outcomes in aphasia and other language disorders. While positive treatment effects have been variously attributed to different MIT components, including melody, rhythm, hand-tapping, and the choral nature of the singing, there is uncertainty about the components that are truly necessary and beneficial. Moreover, the mechanisms by which the components operate are not well understood. Within the literature to date, proposed mechanisms can be broadly grouped into four categories: (1) neuroplastic reorganization of language function, (2) activation of the mirror neuron system and multimodal integration, (3) utilization of shared or specific features of music and language, and (4) motivation and mood. In this paper, we review available evidence for each mechanism and propose that these mechanisms are not mutually exclusive, but rather represent different levels of explanation, reflecting the neurobiological, cognitive, and emotional effects of MIT. Thus, instead of competing, each of these mechanisms may contribute to language rehabilitation, with a better understanding of their relative roles and interactions allowing the design of protocols that maximize the effectiveness of singing therapy for aphasia.

Keywords: Melodic Intonation Therapy, singing, language rehabilitation, aphasia, mechanisms, neuroplasticity, cognitive, mood

The relationship between singing and language impairment has been discussed in case studies and in the research literature for hundreds of years. One such case from 1745 CE presented an individual who had a putative stroke in the left hemisphere and was unable to speak, but was able to sing hymns and say certain rhythmic prayers (Dalin, cited in Benton and Joynt, 1960). Reports of many other individuals who were able to sing accurately and fluently with lyrics despite expressive language impairments prompted a study by Yamadori et al. (1977) to investigate singing ability in those with non-fluent (Broca's) aphasia following stroke or head trauma in frontal regions of the left hemisphere. They found that most of their participants could sing the melody correctly, while about 50% of participants, including some with severe Broca's aphasia, could sing the lyrics fluently and without errors. This remarkable *dissociation* between singing and language ability was accompanied in the literature by reports of an observed *association* between singing and language recovery. Over the years, clinicians reported the successful use of singing to assist aphasia rehabilitation (for example, Mills, 1904; Backus, 1945; Gerstman, 1964), and this eventually led to the first formalized singing treatment for aphasia – Melodic Intonation Therapy (MIT).

Melodic Intonation Therapy was introduced for English speakers in 1973 by Albert, Sparks, and Helm. Key features of the method include the intoning (singing) of common phrases at a slow pace with left hand-tapping, following a hierarchy of steps that eventually moves from singing to speech (Sparks and Holland, 1976; Helm-Estabrooks and Albert, 2004; Sparks, 2008). MIT has become well-known throughout the world and has been modified extensively by clinicians and researchers, including adaption to many other languages, cultures, and even other disorders of speech and language (for example, Marshall and Holtzapple, 1976; Goldfarb and Bader, 1979; Miller and Toca, 1979; Van Eeckhout et al., 1982; Neumeister et al., 1983; Seki and Sugishita, 1983; van der Lugt-van Wiechen and Visch-Brink, 1989; Popovici and Mihilescu, 1992; Helfrich-Miller, 1994; Carroll, 1996; Carlomagno et al., 1997; Baker, 2000; Bonakdarpour et al., 2003; Hough, 2010; Vines et al., 2011; Conklyn et al., 2012). Yet despite its ubiquity, a number of key questions regarding MIT remain unanswered: How effective is the method? In what contexts does it work? Which components of the method are critical? What mechanisms are involved?

Previous MIT and singing therapy studies have attempted to answer these questions, but have been limited by a number of factors. Both the difficulty in obtaining homogeneous participant samples and the time and resultant cost to implement the MIT protocol have led to a proliferation of case studies or very small patient samples. The heterogeneity of approaches, all of which have been labeled MIT, often prevents direct comparison across these case studies and small samples. Although a significant number of publications now suggest that MIT and some modifications of MIT promote improved language function, the overall quality of this evidence remains poor (Hurkmans et al., 2012; van der Meulen et al., 2012). While the existing research appears to be sufficient to answer the basic question of whether MIT works, the questions of (i) how well it works, in terms of its effect size and in comparison to other treatment options, (ii) when it works, including for which patient groups and treatment protocols, and (iii) why it works, are all still open to debate. Carefully designed studies and randomized controlled trials will provide some of the answers being sought, and several research groups are currently working toward this end (Schlaug et al., 2008; van der Meulen et al., 2012).

In the midst of these unanswered questions, the existing literature provides a significant amount of speculation about which components of the MIT protocol might be essential and what mechanisms of action might be linked to those components. Unfortunately, few studies have attempted to systematically address these issues. Opinions about the utility of the various features of MIT and possible mechanisms of action have been articulated primarily in the discussion sections of relevant research articles. However, as new MIT studies including both behavioral and neuroimaging components have emerged along with relevant findings in both music neuroscience and neurorehabilitation, it would be useful to reassess the existing theories against the available evidence. Several recent reviews have focused primarily on the MIT method (Norton et al., 2009), protocol variations (Zumbansen et al., 2014), and efficacy (Hurkmans et al., 2012; van der Meulen et al., 2012), with somewhat limited discussion of the putative mechanisms of MIT. The aim of the current review is to examine these putative mechanisms in detail, synthesize the existing evidence, and suggest directions for future basic and clinical research.

CONTEXT FOR THIS REVIEW

As mentioned previously, the principal components of MIT are melodic intoning (on a minor third or a simple melody), the use of common, formulaic phrases and sentences, left hand-tapping, and slow rhythmic verbalization (usually one syllable per second, although slower durations or more varied rhythms have also been used; see Sparks et al., 1974; Laughlin et al., 1979). Early explanations for the effects of MIT centered around the notion that the musical components of MIT, particularly the intoning, might promote the use of the right hemisphere for language production (Albert et al., 1973) or allow the right hemisphere to better support residual left-hemisphere function (Sparks et al., 1974; Berlin, 1976). However, other possible explanations were put forward, such as the motivational impacts of MIT (Sparks et al., 1974). The originators of MIT were careful to point out that a psychological mechanism could play a role, but was "probably too simplistic an explanation" (Sparks et al., 1974). Their method papers also suggest that notwithstanding some degree of clinical flexibility, adherence to the general methodology, including each of the principal MIT components, is necessary for successful treatment (Sparks and Holland, 1976). Presumably, they felt that each of these components had an important role in the therapy's effects.

Despite these early views, many discussions of MIT over the past decades have taken a reductionist approach to the therapy, sometimes suggesting that careful research should determine *which* component is responsible for its therapeutic effects. For example, one of the significant debates in the MIT literature is whether rhythm *or* melody is the effective component (or more effective component). The most common finding in both cross-sectional speech facilitation studies and longitudinal treatment studies that attempt to parse melodic and/or rhythmic components is that rhythm, rather than melody, may account for most of MIT's effects (Boucher et al., 2001; Stahl et al., 2011, 2013). However, although rhythm clearly plays a fundamental role in MIT and the role of melody is still somewhat ambiguous, it may be an oversimplification, or at least premature given the available evidence, to assume that rhythm alone can account for observed treatment effects in their entirety. While the importance of fundamental research to better understand the contribution of individual MIT components should not be underestimated, we believe that a reductionist interpretation of fundamental research should be avoided. For example, given the inherent rhythmicity of singing and the pitch contours intrinsic to rhythmic speech, fully separating the rhythmic and melodic components of MIT may not be possible, thereby limiting the interpretation of studies that compare the effects of melody and rhythm. In addition, potential interaction effects between components, or indirect contributions of components to therapeutic efficacy, may not be accounted for when considering the role of each component separately, especially with a limited number of outcome measures.

In a similar manner, the search for specific mechanisms of action has often been simplified into a contest between two opposing views: right-hemisphere versus left-hemisphere facilitation. For instance, does MIT promote up-regulation of neural activity in the right-hemisphere language homologs or up-regulation of neural activity in perilesional left hemisphere? Since there is some evidence for each of these views, along with several other potential mechanisms, it seems that searching for a single explanatory mechanism that underpins the effects of this therapy is unlikely to be fruitful. It may be that different mechanisms are in operation across different individuals, based on pre-morbid factors (such as genetics and musicianship), lesion factors (such as location, size, time since onset), and syndrome factors (aphasia vs. aphasia with apraxia of speech, dysarthria, etc.). It may also be that various mechanisms are operating synergistically. Within the literature to date, proposed mechanisms can be broadly grouped into four categories: (1) neuroplastic reorganization of language function, (2) activation of the mirror neuron system and multimodal integration, (3) utilization of shared or specific features of music and language, and (4) motivation and mood. We propose that these mechanisms are not mutually exclusive, but rather represent different levels of explanation, reflecting the neurobiological, cognitive, and emotional effects of MIT. The evidence for our proposal and for the various individual mechanisms is reviewed below.

NEUROPLASTIC REORGANIZATION OF LANGUAGE FUNCTION

The use of MIT to facilitate language reorganization in the brain is by far the most discussed putative mechanism. The first attempt to provide a neurobiological explanation for MIT's effects was the early hypothesis, mentioned above, that the musical components promote right-hemisphere involvement in language processing. This hypothesis was based on behavioral data available at the time that indicated right-hemisphere lateralization for music processing (for example, Kimura, 1964; Bogen and Gordon, 1971). It was supported by the finding that individuals with intact right hemispheres had better outcomes after receiving MIT than those with bilateral lesions (Naeser and Helm-Estabrooks, 1985). Recent functional and structural neuroimaging cases from Schlaug and colleagues also provide some support for this hypothesis. They found an increase in right-hemisphere language activation and improved language production following MIT in two patients (Schlaug et al., 2008). They also reported increased volume of the right arcuate fasciculus, a white-matter tract connecting temporal and frontal language regions, after intensive MIT (Schlaug et al., 2009; Zipse et al., 2012). In addition, MIT combined with anodal transcranial direct current stimulation over the right inferior frontal region (to increase brain excitability) led to greater language improvements than MIT with sham stimulation (Vines et al., 2011). These studies, spanning a number of different modalities, suggest right-hemisphere involvement in MIT-mediated language recovery.

However, a number of other studies have reported contradictory results. A PET study in a group treated with Thérapie Mélodique et Rythmique (TMR), the French version of MIT, suggested that TMR phrases actually led to left-hemisphere language activation, while normal speech led to homologous right-hemisphere activation (Belin et al., 1996). In a magnetoencephalography study of two cases, MIT led to increased left-hemisphere activation in both cases and divergent changes in right-hemisphere activation (Breier et al., 2010). In the individual who showed improvement with MIT, right-hemisphere activation decreased, while in the individual who showed no improvement, right-hemisphere activation increased. This same pattern of divergent functional activation patterns (using pre- and post-fMRI) and language outcomes after MIT was seen in two recent cases reported by Al-Janabi et al. (2014). They found decreased right-hemisphere activation in the individual who showed language improvements, despite the use of excitatory repetitive transcranial magnetic stimulation (rTMS) in the right hemisphere. Furthermore, Laine et al. (1994) described a patient who showed increased left-hemisphere activation after MIT without a right-hemisphere decrease, and this patient did not respond to the treatment. This is consistent with Belin et al.'s (1996) interpretation in their imaging study that right activation reflects maladaptive language processing associated with persistent aphasia.

This debate mirrors a broader ongoing debate in the aphasia literature about the role of the right hemisphere in language recovery. A substantial body of research has shown that areas of the brain that are normally less involved in some language tasks, particularly in the right hemisphere, may be activated to a much greater extent following left-hemisphere insult (for example, Saur et al., 2006; Richter et al., 2008). However, the timing of this right-hemisphere involvement and the extent to which it reflects beneficial functional reorganization are still controversial. Currently, it is thought that right-hemisphere activation occurs commonly in the post-acute phase, with a return to perilesional left-hemisphere activation over the following months reflecting optimal language recovery or successful rehabilitation (Saur et al., 2006). Yet, some imaging studies have shown activation in right-hemisphere language homologs in chronic aphasia. This may be reflective of ongoing disfluency (Naeser et al., 2004), but in some cases, it appears to be predictive of future neuroplastic reorganization and rehabilitation gains (Richter et al., 2008) or even the result of successful rehabilitation (Crinion and Price, 2005).

Such reorganization and its relationship to functional language outcomes appear to be dependent on a number of factors, including the size and location of the lesion and the related severity of aphasia (Marchina et al., 2011; Wang et al., 2013). In the case of a small lesion in the language-dominant (typically left) hemisphere, areas surrounding the lesion may be more likely to take over the function of the affected language region. Alternatively, in the case of a large lesion, homologous regions in the opposite hemisphere may take on language functions (Crosson et al., 2007b). As Schlaug et al. (2009) have argued, using the right hemisphere for language processing might be the only option for individuals who have large left-hemisphere lesions. It seems that both hemispheres can contribute to functional language under some circumstances, whereas activation in either hemisphere can inhibit good recovery in others (Crosson et al., 2007b; Winhuisen et al., 2007; Turkeltaub et al., 2012). Within the right hemisphere of a single individual, some activation could be helpful and other activation detrimental. Evidence suggests that within the inferior frontal gyrus, inhibition of the right pars triangularis using rTMS contributes to language improvement, while inhibition of the right pars opercularis contributes to language disturbance (Naeser et al., 2005; Turkeltaub et al., 2012).

Given the large degree of variability in language reorganization both during spontaneous recovery and following various treatments, the existing contradictory findings in the MIT literature are not so surprising. The cases reported in the literature are far from homogeneous with regard to the time since the lesion, the size of the lesion, or the location of the lesion. In addition, both genetic and environmental factors, such as music training, can influence neuroplastic capacity (discussed in Merrett et al., 2013). If MIT is able to promote neuroplastic reorganization of the language network, it must do so within the context of these individual differences. The same therapy could lead to different patterns of structural and functional neuroplasticity across individuals who had different brain structure and function to start with. A highly relevant example is the way that the relationship between the singing and language networks in the brain is modulated by singing expertise (Wilson et al., 2011). Since MIT is a singing-based therapy, this variable relationship between the singing and language networks could potentially influence both the efficacy of MIT and the resulting language reorganization. Unfortunately, singing expertise has not typically been thoroughly evaluated in MIT studies to date.

It should also be noted that the results of neuroimaging studies of aphasic language function, both within and outside the MIT literature, should be interpreted in light of the type of language task used for functional imaging and the therapy protocol. A significant body of evidence (reviewed in Van Lancker Sidtis, 2012) indicates that formulaic language production depends on right-hemisphere and subcortical regions, in contrast to the generation of more spontaneous language, which typically depends on the left hemisphere. Formulaic language includes common, highly stereotyped expressions, which are generally used contextually and stored as a unit in memory (Van Lancker Sidtis, 2012). Differences in the degree of formulaicity in functional imaging tasks both between and within studies may significantly impact the lateralization of activation. The use of non-propositional language tasks during functional imaging, such as counting or repeating everyday phrases, may lead to greater right-hemisphere activation than tasks that are more generative in nature. Stahl et al. (2013) suggested that these task-based differences in language lateralization may account for the existing imaging findings. More generally, they also proposed that the use of right-hemisphere language regions could be a function of intensive training of formulaic phrases in MIT, providing an alternative hypothesis to that of music-based promotion of right-hemisphere activation. Formulaic phrases, such as "good morning," "cup of coffee," and "How are you?" are often used in the early stages of MIT, and these may be the only phrases that are trained in individuals with severe aphasia who are unable to progress to more complex material. Even if the MIT phrases in a given protocol include less formulaic material, such phrases may become like speech formulas over time with intense repetition. Although the MIT protocols discussed by Sparks (2008) and Helm-Estabrooks and Albert (2004) suggest using a broad range of material to ensure that there is little repetition, the phrases used in MIT are typically highly repetitive in practice. In conjunction with the individual differences mentioned above, the role of formulaicity may explain many of the disparities in previous neuroimaging studies.

It has often been assumed that MIT must have a common mechanism (across all treated individuals with aphasia) by which it promotes language reorganization, such as the exploitation of right-hemisphere music processing regions for language or the use of right corticostriatal formulaic language circuits. While it is likely correct that MIT is effective in activating any intact brain regions that are involved in music processing (both right *and* left) as well as those involved in formulaic language, the assumption that there is a common neuroplastic mechanism and/or that this mechanism is musical or linguistic in nature may be flawed. Rather than depending on the musical or linguistic components to promote a specific type of language reorganization, it may be that MIT can help to promote neuroplasticity of the language network more generically, simply because it allows individuals with aphasia to practice language production intensely. Evidence suggests that treatments that promote intense, complex practice can effectively induce neuroplasticity (Green and Bavelier, 2008; Kleim and Jones, 2008). Other aphasia rehabilitation strategies that have demonstrated some positive effects, such as intensive language–action therapy, are based on such principles (Difrancesco et al., 2012). Furthermore, a significant relationship between intensity and speech and language outcomes was found when existing treatment studies were reviewed (Bhogal et al., 2003). MIT may make language production easier (discussed further below) and thereby encourage intense practice, which could in turn lead to training-induced reorganization.

In sum, evidence from a variety of neuroimaging studies demonstrates that MIT can promote both functional and structural neuroplasticity. It remains unclear how induced neuroplastic change interacts with individual patient characteristics and whether this neuroplasticity is directly related to specific components of the therapy. It is worth noting that the recommended "ideal candidate" for MIT has a language profile that includes poor repetition, paucity of output, and stereotypic utterances (Sparks et al., 1974). Given this profile, the ideal candidate for MIT is likely to be an individual with severe aphasia and a large anterior left-hemisphere lesion. However, many MIT studies are carried out with participants who do not meet the criteria for ideal candidates and who have large variations in lesion size and location, including those with small lesions and only mild to moderate non-fluent aphasia. Different mechanisms may be involved across individuals who have excellent responses to MIT and/or meet the ideal candidate profile versus those who only show a partial response or have different language impairment profiles. The relationship between neuroplastic mechanisms, individual factors, and clinical outcomes needs further exploration. In addition to advancing our understanding of brain plasticity and individual differences, future work addressing these questions will be of great value clinically.

OBSERVATION, IMITATION, INTEGRATION, AND THE MIRROR NEURON SYSTEM

Melodic Intonation Therapy is a multimodal therapy, as the therapist provides both an auditory and visual model for the patient, and the protocol contains elements of observation, imitation, and synchronization. A number of different hypotheses have been raised as to how these aspects of the therapy might explain its effects, although these have not been subjected to direct empirical investigation. These hypotheses include: (1) a proposal by Schlaug et al. (2008) that the left hand-tapping used in MIT engages a right sensorimotor integration network in which hand and articulatory movements are closely linked and (2) a proposal by Racette et al. (2006) that the synchronized singing in MIT could promote activation of an "auditory–vocal interface" to improve articulatory motor function. What links these hypotheses together as a category of putative mechanisms is their connection to integration/association functions of the brain and possibly the human mirror neuron system.

Left hand-tapping has been considered a crucial component of the MIT protocol since its inception, although a number of cases have successfully used a modification of MIT without the tapping (for example, Hough, 2010). In their case study, Goldfarb and Bader (1979) demonstrated improvements in phrase repetition using intonation alone compared to normal speech, but hand-tapping appeared to further improve performance. A number of potential mechanisms have been proposed for this MIT component, including enhancement or reinforcement of the rhythmic aspects of MIT and pacing of speech (both discussed below), as well as the up-regulation of right-hemisphere activity related to articulation through sensorimotor coupling. From theoretical, neurophysiological, and behavioral perspectives, speech and language are strongly linked to hand motor control (Meister et al., 2003, 2006; Binkofski and Buccino, 2004; Gentilucci and Dalla Volta, 2008). Based on such findings, Schlaug et al. (2008) have hypothesized that left hand-tapping could activate a right-hemisphere sensorimotor network that is used for articulatory movement. Articulation is often impaired in individuals with non-fluent aphasia because of comorbid motor speech disorders such as apraxia of speech and dysarthria. Given the close proximity of oral and hand movement representations in the motor control system, Schlaug et al. proposed that hand-tapping could lead to a priming effect for orofacial and articulatory movements. Lending indirect support to the idea, an unrelated study has demonstrated that completing a complex, non-symbolic left hand movement in conjunction with naming led to improved performance and increased right-hemisphere activity in aphasic individuals (Crosson et al., 2007a, 2009). The reasoning behind this treatment was that it might activate intention mechanisms in the right frontal lobe and thereby prime right-hemisphere language activity. Another proposal regarding hand-tapping is that the sound of the tapping may promote sensorimotor integration, i.e., a neurobiological coupling between the sound and the co-occurring hand and articulatory actions (Lahav et al., 2007; Schlaug et al., 2008). Such sensorimotor integration has often been linked theoretically and neuroanatomically to the putative mirror neuron system (Lahav et al., 2007).

Mirror neurons are neurons that exhibit multimodal response properties – they are stimulated by certain actions whether those actions are being performed or being perceived (visually or aurally). Recent work, such as Mukamel et al. (2010), demonstrates that neurons with mirror properties occur widely throughout the brain; however, it is widely held that humans have a "mirror neuron system" which consists of specific neural regions including the premotor cortex, inferior frontal gyrus, and inferior parietal areas (Iacoboni and Mazziotta, 2007). While the functions (and even the existence) of a mirror neuron system in humans have been hotly debated, the evidence appears strong that inferior frontal and inferior parietal regions, among others, are activated both in the observation (seeing and/or hearing) and the execution of known actions (Buccino et al., 2001; Gazzola and Keysers, 2009). Such findings have been enthusiastically applied in clinical neuroscience rehabilitation paradigms (Ertelt et al., 2007; Celnik et al., 2008; Bang et al., 2013). For example, Ertelt et al. (2007) combined physical practice with action observation of purposeful hand and arm movements (using video) for upper arm rehabilitation after stroke. They found a significant improvement over controls who completed physical practice only. The results have been attributed to activation of the mirror neuron system, particularly after neuroimaging of object manipulation before and after action observation treatment showed increased activity in parieto-frontal areas considered core regions of the system.

Whether there is an actual mirror neuron system or a more general perception–action integration network in the brain, this mechanism has been proposed to explain the positive effects of MIT (Racette et al., 2006; Overy and Molnar-Szakacs, 2009). The MIT protocol provides the patient with a visual and auditory model to observe, to imitate, and to synchronize with. If observation, imitation, and synchronization of singing or intoned speech are interacting with a neural perception–action integration system, they might be expected to impact motor aspects of speech most strongly (Fadiga et al., 2002; Wilson et al., 2004). Indeed, some of the benefits of MIT are perhaps attributable to improvements in speech articulation (Sparks and Holland, 1976; Wilson et al., 2006) that subsequently lead to improvements in language output. Racette et al. (2006) compared word production and intelligibility in individuals with aphasia when singing and speaking both alone and with an auditory model. They found that choral singing (with a model) led to better word intelligibility than singing alone or choral speaking. Although the advantage of choral singing over choral speaking may be explained at least in part by the slower rate of production in singing than in natural speech, there is still a distinct advantage for singing along compared to singing alone that is unrelated to tempo. The authors suggest that this may be due to activation of a right-hemisphere "auditory–vocal interface" or mirror neuron system, as the improvements appear to depend on the opportunity to sing together and synchronize with an auditory model.

Such a mechanism would not be specific to MIT or singing, but rather, would apply more generally to any speech/language therapy that provides similar multimodal modeling or synchronization opportunities. Fridriksson et al. (2012) recently found that mimicking an auditory–visual speech model induced significantly greater speech output and fluency than an auditory-only model or spontaneous speech in a group of individuals with non-fluent aphasia and concomitant apraxia of speech. If this mechanism alone could account for MIT's effects, MIT may not offer benefit beyond other multimodal therapies. However, Racette et al. (2006) suggested that the left-hemisphere lesions that typically lead to aphasia may impair the left-hemisphere auditory–vocal interface involved in generative speech, while the intact right-hemisphere auditory–vocal interface may be more responsive to singing or formulaic speech. If so, this could explain why MIT, which includes singing common phrases, would be better placed than other therapies to take advantage of such a system. It is worthwhile noting that singing or intoning activates a bilateral fronto-temporal network that overlaps with the putative mirror neuron system to a certain degree (Ozdemir et al., 2006; Kleber et al., 2007; Wilson et al., 2011). Nonetheless, there is no direct evidence that MIT leverages this system through intonation or hand-tapping. Further investigation into the role of the mirror neuron system in singing, in articulatory motor function, and in language rehabilitation more generally is clearly warranted and may provide insight into the neurobiological mechanisms underlying MIT.

SHARED OR SPECIFIC FEATURES OF MUSIC AND LANGUAGE

One of the current debates in the literature is the extent to which music and language overlap in terms of their neural representation and processing. While differences between the two cannot be denied, there are features that are shared at least superficially by music and language, such as pitch, rhythm, timbre, and syntax (reviewed in Patel, 2008). These shared features have prompted proposals that there could be common processing pathways for music and language, such as Patel's shared syntactic integration resource hypothesis (Patel, 2003). The idea of common processing pathways for language and music provides a potential cognitive mechanism for MIT that is clearly linked to some of the neuroplasticity hypotheses discussed above. MIT could take advantage of the shared features of music and language, such as pitch and/or rhythm, to access language indirectly through music processing pathways. This is a somewhat controversial proposal. For example, there is significant neuropsychological evidence for modularity of the two systems, with evidence of clear dissociations between language impairment and music impairment (Peretz and Coltheart, 2003; Peretz, 2009). Logically, the more cognitive overlap between music and language, the more likely that dysfunction in the language system would be accompanied by dysfunction in music processing as well. To date, a fully coherent explanation is lacking for how intoning or singing could overlap cognitively with the language network in such a way that it would be independent enough to remain intact despite damage to the language network but interdependent enough to take on language function.

Two possible arguments for this mechanism come from the research literature comparing speaking and singing. First, both speaking and singing are known to be processed bilaterally in the brain, using proximal regions that appear to overlap to a large degree, but with speaking more left lateralized and singing more right lateralized (Jeffries et al., 2003; Brown et al., 2006; Callan et al., 2006; Ozdemir et al., 2006). It appears that sung word production may be less reliant on the left-hemisphere language network than spoken words, even when lyric type and tempo are taken into account. This difference in lateralization may provide the means whereby language functions could co-opt relevant right-hemisphere regions of the singing network in the presence of a left-hemisphere lesion. However, this is difficult to reconcile with the bulk of the neuroimaging findings after MIT treatment presented above. Another study that has investigated the neurocognitive relationship between singing and speaking provides an alternative argument by considering the role of expertise (Wilson et al., 2011). These researchers found that singing expertise is associated with a decoupling of the singing network from the language network, with more focal, left lateralized functional activation for singing that is proximal but posterior to language activation. When considered in conjunction with putative neuroplasticity mechanisms, this raises a number of hypotheses, including (1) that MIT would be more effective in individuals with previous singing experience who have already developed a specialized singing network or (2) that through regular singing practice, MIT could promote the development of a more "expert" singing network that would occupy left-hemisphere perilesional regions. The first hypothesis is indirectly supported in the existing literature, given that Wilson et al. (2006) found that MIT was more effective than rhythmic speech in their case study of a trained musician, while Stahl et al. (2013) did not find an advantage of singing over rhythmic speech in a group of non-musicians. Additional studies are needed to disentangle the relationship between music and language in aphasia and in MIT relative to expertise. Despite being poorly understood, it is possible that an intact singing network would best facilitate language production.

Another set of hypothesized mechanisms steers clear of this debate about shared cognitive processing and simply suggests that specific features of music and/or language can facilitate speech production. A range of possible beneficial effects of the melodic and rhythmic components of MIT has been suggested. For example, Racette et al. (2006) suggested that singing or intoning phrases may provide more time for motor planning and execution than normal spoken language. This could make production more fluent and allow less demanding rehearsal. Lending support to this idea, Laughlin et al. (1979) showed that longer syllable lengths in MIT increased the number of correct phrases produced by patients with non-fluent aphasia. Other studies in dysarthric speakers have indicated that pacing and intervention techniques that reduce speech rate can improve intelligibility, although the exact relationship between speech rate and intelligibility is uncertain (for example, Yorkston et al., 1990; Pilon et al., 1998; Hustad et al., 2003). It may be that the slower articulation of singing benefits some patients, while being less helpful for others (Racette et al., 2006). In another example of a possible effect of melody, Wilson et al. (2006) found a long-term benefit for the production of rehearsed phrases that had a melodic and rhythmic component over those with only a rhythmic component in a musically-trained individual with aphasia. They proposed that the melodic component may have promoted separate representation in memory, leading to superior phrase encoding and retrieval.

Other rhythmic aspects of MIT have also been implicated as facilitators. In the TMR protocol (French version of MIT), word accentuation is greatly emphasized, despite the fact that French does not have the language element of lexical stress, creating a strong sense of rhythm (Van Eeckhout et al., 1982). Singing may be more rhythmic than speech, at least in French. The hand-tapping and steady rhythm used in MIT could also act as a metronome, as pacing is known to be beneficial with articulatory impairments (Brendel and Ziegler, 2008). In their study of the facilitatory effects of singing on aphasic speech, Racette et al. (2006) suggest that increased temporal regularity may be an alternative or additional explanation as to why singing along with a model is more beneficial than speaking along in a syllable-timed language such as French. As a final point regarding rhythmic facilitation, Stahl et al. (2011) suggested that rhythm may be particularly useful in facilitating speech for aphasic individuals who have large basal ganglia lesions. The benefits of rhythm for speech production were evident in this group, whereas a group with no or small lesions in the basal ganglia did not show a rhythmic facilitation effect, suggesting once again a possible interaction between mechanisms and patient variables such as lesion size and location.

In addition to musical features such as melody and rhythm that might act as facilitators, the use of a specific type of language within the therapy may also play a significant role. In the early stages of MIT, most therapists use common, high-probability phrases (Helm-Estabrooks and Albert, 2004). Although the stated goal of the therapy is to improve generative language, the incorporation of formulaic phrases into a functional vocabulary for the patient may become a treatment objective in and of itself, particularly for individuals with severe aphasia. This has been described as palliative use of MIT by Zumbansen et al. (2014). Whether or not the restoration of generative language function is the goal, the use of formulaic phrases may facilitate language by tapping into corticostriatal regions implicated in formulaic, non-generative language (Van Lancker Sidtis, 2012). This language feature may also interact with a number of putative mechanisms of action, including promoting the use of right-hemisphere language regions (as discussed above, Stahl et al., 2013) and motivating patients (discussed below).

MOTIVATION, MOOD, AND AROUSAL

Although regarded as "probably too simplistic an explanation" (Sparks et al., 1974), a potential role for psychological or emotional mechanisms in the efficacy of MIT should not be discounted. These putative mechanisms have received far less attention in the MIT literature, but indirect evidence suggests that they may be highly significant. Singing is a pleasurable and non-threatening way for individuals with aphasia to express themselves vocally, which may help to enhance motivation to continue with an intensive therapy regimen (Racette et al., 2006). A substantial literature exists regarding the use of music as a motivator in sport and exercise, where it can lead to increased output and endurance (Karageorghis and Priest, 2011). This may also occur in the rehabilitation domain, as internal motivation has been shown to be a strong predictor of rehabilitation adherence (Chan et al., 2009). Music therapy has even been used successfully with mental health clients with low motivation for other therapies (Gold et al., 2013). Such studies imply that music might be intrinsically motivating. Neurobiological evidence for a relationship between music and motivation comes from studies showing that pleasurable experiences during music listening activate the brain's reward/motivation circuitry (Blood and Zatorre, 2001; Menon and Levitin, 2005) and are associated with striatal dopamine release, a neurotransmitter associated with pleasure, motivation, and reward (Salimpoor et al., 2011). Outside of the music domain, the use of formulaic phrases in the early stages of MIT might also enhance motivation, given that these are usually highly familiar and desirable phrases to rehearse, and may even be chosen in conjunction with the patient. Although motivation has not been studied directly in MIT, our own experience is that patients with aphasia report being highly motivated by MIT and have been able to successfully complete intense daily therapy sessions.

As a musical form of language rehabilitation, MIT could potentially harness not only music's capacity to engage and motivate, but also its ability to influence mood in a positive direction (Pelletier, 2004; Västfjäll et al., 2012). Simply listening to music has been shown to improve negative mood in both healthy adults (Boothby and Robbins, 2011) and in stroke patients (Särkämö et al., 2008; Kim et al., 2011). Active music making, such as singing, also increases positive mood, decreases negative mood, and positively influences biochemistry (Kuhn, 2002; Unwin et al., 2002; Grape et al., 2003; Kreutz et al., 2004). Although it has not been empirically assessed to date, the influence of MIT on mood and motivation may explain some of its efficacy. The use of rehabilitation therapies, such as singing, that can jointly influence both language function and mood might be of great import in the treatment of post-stroke aphasia, since low mood and clinical depression are common comorbidities of stroke (Robinson, 2003; Berthier, 2005).

CONCLUSION

The various mechanisms discussed above provide possible explanations of MIT's effects, spanning neurobiological, cognitive, and emotional domains. Previous discussions regarding MIT have often presented these mechanisms as competing hypotheses, requiring a definitive answer as to which (one) mechanism is causal. However, given the direct evidence for many of these hypotheses and the indirect evidence for others, we take the opinion that, broadly speaking, these are different levels of explanation rather than competing explanations, and they reflect the diverse ways that MIT and its various components can influence speech and language rehabilitation. In almost every case, these are not mutually exclusive hypotheses, and each could contribute to the overall effect of MIT.

This may explain why MIT has been considered an effective treatment option by many clinicians, despite the lack of carefully controlled evidence and the uncertainty as to the mechanisms involved. As mentioned previously, other speech and language therapies have been developed that are based on or explained by many of the mechanisms discussed here, including constraint-induced aphasia therapy, a form of intensive language–action therapy (Pulvermüller et al., 2001; Difrancesco et al., 2012), speech entrainment (Fridriksson et al., 2012), and intention treatment (Crosson et al., 2009). The reported success of these treatments lends credibility to the proposal that similar mechanisms underlie successful treatment with MIT. However, unlike therapies with a single target mechanism, MIT may be uniquely placed to take advantage of many of these mechanisms of action simultaneously. There are three potential implications of this that will be discussed here and that we believe should be the focus of future research.

First, the use of multiple mechanisms could have an additive effect, making MIT a more efficient and/or effective treatment than therapies that target one mechanism. Ideally, the overall effectiveness of MIT compared to other treatment options would be evaluated with large-scale randomized controlled trials, some of which are reportedly underway. Yet, given the difficulty in obtaining this kind of evidence in heterogeneous aphasia populations, other methodologically rigorous methods of comparing MIT efficacy to that of other therapies should be sought. Using research participants with aphasia as their own controls is one possible option. The major caveat to this approach is the potential for carry-over or delayed treatment effects, but careful designs should minimize the problem. Despite concerns regarding generalizability to the larger clinical population, even single cases can help to address this issue if the study designs and statistics used are appropriate (Howard, 1986; Beeson and Robey, 2006). Few studies to date have directly compared MIT with other treatments, and statistical analysis and effect sizes have typically not been included in MIT case studies or case series. These shortcomings in the existing literature should be rectified in future studies so that questions about whether MIT is a more effective treatment can be appropriately addressed.

Second, the use of a variety of mechanisms could make MIT a more flexible treatment for a larger variety of patients, with the use of different mechanisms dependent on individual patient variables. As noted above, MIT was initially designed to treat non-fluent aphasia patients with a specific language profile; however, MIT has now been used to treat a large number of different speech and language disorders, particularly apraxia of speech and disorders of articulation. Furthermore, MIT has shown benefits to patients with vastly differing lesion locations, lesion sizes, severities of aphasia, and language profiles (but see Zumbansen et al., 2014, for a dissenting view). It may be that the wide variety of mechanisms of action confers flexibility on the therapy, making it functional for a number of different disorders or language profiles that would benefit from different mechanisms. A "one-size fits all" approach to speech and language therapy is unlikely to be fruitful and thus is not particularly desirable, whereas clinical constraints and practical considerations would suggest that broadly applicable therapeutic techniques are of value.

Third, the various proposed mechanisms of action in MIT could have a synergistic effect. Evidence from the basic neuroscience literature suggests likely interactions between the various mechanisms implicated in MIT. For example, neuroplasticity is negatively influenced by stress and depression (reviewed in Pittenger and Duman, 2007). As mentioned previously, mood disorders are often comorbid with post-stroke aphasia. If MIT is able to positively influence mood, then treatment-induced neuroplasticity may also be enhanced. Koelsch (2009) has also suggested that emotional processes modulate mirror neuron system activity, potentially linking these two putative MIT mechanisms. Other examples, already discussed elsewhere in this review, include the relationship between cognitive and neurobiological mechanisms and the role of motivation in facilitating intense training that could mediate neuroplasticity. Both the specific musical features of MIT and the communicative content, such as formulaic phrases, may interact with motivation and mood mechanisms. In short, these neurobiological, cognitive, and emotional mechanisms could certainly influence each other, and may lead to different, and perhaps greater, treatment effects than if they were to act in isolation.

Consideration of the mechanisms involved in MIT leads to many questions that can and should be further investigated, including the nature of MIT-induced neuroplasticity, the role of the mirror neuron system, the interaction between underlying cognitive processes for music and language, the role of phrase formulaicity, the relative contribution of mood and motivation, and the facilitatory effects of various musical and non-musical MIT components. However, we suggest that regarding these as competing mechanisms may not be the most fruitful approach to understanding this multi-faceted therapy. Although prior research has aimed to clarify which MIT component and/or mechanism is responsible for its effects, this review advocates for multiple and perhaps synergistically acting mechanisms. Multivariate research methods that can take multiple mechanisms of action into account may be the catalyst for resolving both the ambiguity and some of the existing discrepancies that surround this therapy. A better understanding of not only the individual actions of each component but also the interaction of their related mechanisms would allow further refinements to the MIT protocol to maximize the effectiveness of singing therapy for aphasia.

REFERENCES

Albert, M. L., Sparks, R. W., and Helm, N. A. (1973). Melodic intonation therapy for aphasia. *Arch. Neurol.* 29, 130–131. doi:10.1001/archneur.1973.00490260074018

Al-Janabi, S., Nickels, L., Sowman, P. F., Burianova, H., Merrett, D. L., and Thompson, W. F. (2014). Augmenting melodic intonation therapy with non-invasive brain stimulation to treat impaired left-hemisphere function: two case studies. *Front. Psychol.* 5:37. doi:10.3389/fpsyg.2014.00037

Backus, O. L. (1945). The rehabilitation of aphasic veterans. *J. Speech Disord.* 10, 149–153.

Baker, F. A. (2000). Modifying the Melodic Intonation Therapy program for adults with severe non-fluent aphasia. *Music Ther. Perspect.* 18, 110–114. doi:10.1093/mtp/18.2.110

Bang, D.-H., Shin, W.-S., Kim, S.-Y., and Choi, J.-D. (2013). The effects of action observational training on walking ability in chronic stroke patients: a double-blind randomized controlled trial. *Clin. Rehabil.* 27, 1118–1125. doi:10.1177/0269215513501528

Beeson, P. M., and Robey, R. R. (2006). Evaluating single-subject treatment research: lessons learned from the aphasia literature. *Neuropsychol. Rev.* 16, 161–169. doi:10.1007/s11065-006-9013-7

Belin, P., Eeckhout, P. V., Zilbovicius, M., Remy, P., François, C., Guillaume, S., et al. (1996). Recovery from nonfluent aphasia after melodic intonation therapy: a PET study. *Neurology* 47, 1504–1511. doi:10.1212/WNL.47.6.1504

Benton, A. L., and Joynt, R. J. (1960). Early descriptions of aphasia. *Arch. Neurol.* 3, 205–222. doi:10.1001/archneur.1960.00450020085012

Berlin, C. I. (1976). On: melodic intonation therapy for aphasia by R. W. Sparks and A. L. Holland. *J. Speech Hear. Disord.* 41, 298–300.

Berthier, M. L. (2005). Poststroke aphasia – epidemiology, pathophysiology and treatment. *Drugs Aging* 22, 163–182. doi:10.2165/00002512-200522020-00006

Bhogal, S. K., Teasell, R., and Speechley, M. (2003). Intensity of aphasia therapy, impact on recovery. *Stroke* 34, 987–993. doi:10.1161/01.STR.0000062343.64383.D0

Binkofski, F., and Buccino, G. (2004). Motor functions of the Broca's region. *Brain Lang.* 89, 362–369. doi:10.1016/S0093-934X(03)00358-4

Blood, A. J., and Zatorre, R. J. (2001). Intensely pleasurable responses to music correlate with activity in brain regions implicated in reward and emotion. *Proc. Natl. Acad. Sci. U.S.A.* 98, 11818–11823. doi:10.1073/pnas.191355898

Bogen, J. E., and Gordon, H. W. (1971). Musical tests for functional lateralization with intracarotid amobarbital. *Nature* 230, 524–525. doi:10.1038/230524a0

Bonakdarpour, B., Eftekharzadeh, A., and Ashayeri, H. (2003). Melodic intonation therapy in Persian aphasic patients. *Aphasiology* 17, 75–95. doi:10.1080/729254891

Boothby, D. M., and Robbins, S. J. (2011). The effects of music listening and art production on negative mood: a randomized, controlled trial. *Arts Psychother.* 38, 204–208. doi:10.1016/j.aip.2011.06.002

Boucher, V., Garcia, L. J., Fleurant, J., and Paradis, J. (2001). Variable efficacy of rhythm and tone in melody-based interventions: implications for the assumption of a right-hemisphere facilitation in non-fluent aphasia. *Aphasiology* 15, 131–149. doi:10.1080/02687040042000098

Breier, J. I., Randle, S., Maher, L. M., and Papanicolaou, A. C. (2010). Changes in maps of language activity activation following melodic intonation therapy using magnetoencephalography: two case studies. *J. Clin. Exp. Neuropsychol.* 32, 309–314. doi:10.1080/13803390903029293

Brendel, B., and Ziegler, W. (2008). Effectiveness of metrical pacing in the treatment of apraxia of speech. *Aphasiology* 22, 77–102. doi:10.1080/02687030600965464

Brown, S., Martinez, M. J., and Parsons, L. M. (2006). Music and language side by side in the brain: a PET study of the generation of melodies and sentences. *Eur. J. Neurosci.* 23, 2791–2803. doi:10.1111/j.1460-9568.2006.04785.x

Buccino, G., Binkofski, F., Fink, G. R., Fadiga, L., Fogassi, L., Gallese, V., et al. (2001). Action observation activates premotor and parietal areas in a somatotopic manner: an fMRI study. *Eur. J. Neurosci.* 13, 400–404. doi:10.1111/j.1460-9568.2001.01385.x

Callan, D. E., Tsytsarev, V., Hanakawa, T., Callan, A. M., Katsuhara, M., Fukuyama, H., et al. (2006). Song and speech: brain regions involved with perception and covert production. *Neuroimage* 31, 1327–1342. doi:10.1016/j.neuroimage.2006.01.036

Carlomagno, S., Van Eeckhout, P., Blasi, V., Belin, P., Samson, Y., and Deloche, G. (1997). The impact of functional neuroimaging methods on the development of a theory for cognitive remediation. *Neuropsychol. Rehabil.* 7, 311–326. doi:10.1080/713755542

Carroll, D. (1996). *A Study of the Effectiveness of an Adaptation of Melodic Intonation Therapy in Increasing the Communicative Speech of Young Children with Down Syndrome.* M.A. in Music Education, McGill University, Montreal.

Celnik, P., Webster, B., Glasser, D. M., and Cohen, L. G. (2008). Effects of action observation on physical training after stroke. *Stroke* 39, 1814–1820. doi:10.1161/STROKEAHA.107.508184

Chan, D. K., Lonsdale, C., Ho, P. Y., Yung, P. S., and Chan, K. M. (2009). Patient motivation and adherence to postsurgery rehabilitation exercise recommendations: the influence of physiotherapists' autonomy-supportive behaviors. *Arch. Phys. Med. Rehabil.* 90, 1977–1982. doi:10.1016/j.apmr.2009.05.024

Conklyn, D., Novak, E., Boissy, A., Bethoux, F., Chemali, K., Smith, A., et al. (2012). The effects of modified melodic intonation therapy on nonfluent aphasia: a pilot study. *J. Speech Lang. Hear. Res.* 55, 1463–1471. doi:10.1044/1092-4388(2012/11-0105)

Crinion, J., and Price, C. J. (2005). Right anterior superior temporal activation predicts auditory sentence comprehension following aphasic stroke. *Brain* 128, 2858–2871. doi:10.1093/brain/awh659

Crosson, B., Fabrizio, K. S., Singletary, F., Cato, M. A., Wierenga, C. E., Parkinson, R. B., et al. (2007a). Treatment of naming in nonfluent aphasia through manipulation of intention and attention: a phase 1 comparison of two novel treatments. *J. Int. Neuropsychol. Soc.* 13, 582–594. doi:10.1017/S1355617707070737

Crosson, B., McGregor, K., Gopinath, K. S., Conway, T. W., Benjamin, M., Chang, Y. L., et al. (2007b). Functional MRI of language in aphasia: a review of the literature and the methodological challenges. *Neuropsychol. Rev.* 17, 157–177. doi:10.1007/s11065-007-9024-z

Crosson, B., Moore, A. B., McGregor, K. M., Chang, Y.-L., Benjamin, M., Gopinath, K., et al. (2009). Regional changes in word-production laterality after a naming treatment designed to produce a rightward shift in frontal activity. *Brain Lang.* 111, 73–85. doi:10.1016/j.bandl.2009.08.001

Difrancesco, S., Pulvermüller, F., and Mohr, B. (2012). Intensive language-action therapy (ILAT): the methods. *Aphasiology* 26, 1317–1351. doi:10.1080/02687038.2012.705815

Ertelt, D., Small, S., Solodkin, A., Dettmers, C., McNamara, A., Binkofski, F., et al. (2007). Action observation has a positive impact on rehabilitation of motor deficits after stroke. *Neuroimage* 36, T164–T173. doi:10.1016/j.neuroimage.2007.03.043

Fadiga, L., Craighero, L., Buccino, G., and Rizzolatti, G. (2002). Speech listening specifically modulates the excitability of tongue muscles: a TMS study. *Eur. J. Neurosci.* 15, 399–402. doi:10.1046/j.0953-816x.2001.01874.x

Fridriksson, J., Hubbard, H. I., Hudspeth, S. G., Holland, A. L., Bonilha, L., Fromm, D., et al. (2012). Speech entrainment enables patients with Broca's aphasia to produce fluent speech. *Brain* 135, 3815–3829. doi:10.1093/brain/aws301

Gazzola, V., and Keysers, C. (2009). The observation and execution of actions share motor and somatosensory voxels in all tested subjects: single-subject analyses of unsmoothed fMRI data. *Cereb. Cortex* 19, 1239–1255. doi:10.1093/cercor/bhn181

Gentilucci, M., and Dalla Volta, R. (2008). Spoken language and arm gestures are controlled by the same motor control system. *Q. J. Exp. Psychol.* 61, 944–957. doi:10.1080/17470210701625683

Gerstman, H. L. (1964). A case of aphasia. *J. Speech Hear. Disord.* 29, 89–91.

Gold, C., Mössler, K., Grocke, D., Heldal, T. O., Tjemsland, L., Aarre, T., et al. (2013). Individual music therapy for mental health care clients with low therapy motivation: multicentre randomised controlled trial. *Psychother. Psychosom.* 82, 319–331. doi:10.1159/000348452

Goldfarb, R., and Bader, E. (1979). Espousing melodic intonation therapy in aphasia rehabilitation: a case study. *Int. J. Rehabil. Res.* 2, 333–342. doi:10.1097/00004356-197909000-00002

Grape, C., Sandgren, M., Hansson, L. O., Ericson, M., and Theorell, T. (2003). Does singing promote well-being? An empirical study of professional and amateur singers during a singing lesson. *Integr. Physiol. Behav. Sci.* 38, 65–74. doi:10.1007/BF02734261

Green, C. S., and Bavelier, D. (2008). Exercising your brain: a review of human brain plasticity and training-induced learning. *Psychol. Aging* 23, 692–701. doi:10.1037/a0014345

Helfrich-Miller, K. R. (1994). A clinical perspective: melodic intonation therapy for developmental apraxia. *Clin. Commun. Disord.* 4, 175–182.

Helm-Estabrooks, N., and Albert, M. L. (2004). "Melodic Intonation Therapy," in *Manual of Aphasia and Aphasia Therapy*, (Austin, TX: Pro-Ed), 221–233.

Hough, M. S. (2010). Melodic Intonation Therapy and aphasia: another variation on a theme. *Aphasiology* 24, 775–786. doi:10.1080/02687030903501941

Howard, D. (1986). Forum: evaluating intervention beyond randomised controlled trials: the case for effective case studies of the effects of treatment in aphasia. *Int. J. Lang. Commun. Disord.* 21, 89–102. doi:10.3109/13682828609018546

Hurkmans, J., De Bruijn, M., Boonstra, A. M., Jonkers, R., Bastiaanse, R., Arendzen, H., et al. (2012). Music in the treatment of neurological language and speech disorders: a systematic review. *Aphasiology* 26, 1–19. doi:10.1080/02687038.2011.602514

Hustad, K. C., Jones, T., and Dailey, S. (2003). Implementing speech supplementation strategies: effects on intelligibility and speech rate of individuals with chronic severe dysarthria. *J. Speech Lang. Hear. Res.* 46, 462–474. doi:10.1044/1092-4388(2003/038)

Iacoboni, M., and Mazziotta, J. C. (2007). Mirror neuron system: basic findings and clinical applications. *Ann. Neurol.* 62, 213–218. doi:10.1002/ana.21198

Jeffries, K. J., Fritz, J. B., and Braun, A. R. (2003). Words in melody: an H(2)15O PET study of brain activation during singing and speaking. *Neuroreport* 14, 749–754. doi:10.1097/00001756-200304150-00018

Karageorghis, C. I., and Priest, D.-L. (2011). Music in the exercise domain: a review and synthesis (Part I). *Int. Rev. Sport Exerc. Psychol.* 5, 44–66. doi:10.1080/1750984X.2011.631026

Kim, D. S., Park, Y. G., Choi, J. H., Im, S.-H., Jung, K. J., Cha, Y. A., et al. (2011). Effects of music therapy on mood in stroke patients. *Yonsei Med. J.* 52, 977–981. doi:10.3349/ymj.2011.52.6.977

Kimura, D. (1964). Left-right differences in the perception of melodies. *Q. J. Exp. Psychol.* 16, 355–358. doi:10.1080/17470216408416391

Kleber, B., Birbaumer, N., Veit, R., Trevorrow, T., and Lotze, M. (2007). Overt and imagined singing of an Italian aria. *Neuroimage* 36, 889–900. doi:10.1016/j.neuroimage.2007.02.053

Kleim, J. A., and Jones, T. A. (2008). Principles of experience-dependent neural plasticity: implications for rehabilitation after brain damage. *J. Speech Lang. Hear. Res.* 51, S225–S239. doi:10.1044/1092-4388(2008/018)

Koelsch, S. (2009). A neuroscientific perspective on music therapy. *Ann. N. Y. Acad. Sci.* 1169, 374–384. doi:10.1111/j.1749-6632.2009.04592.x

Kreutz, G., Bongard, S., Rohrmann, S., Hodapp, V., and Grebe, D. (2004). Effects of choir singing or listening on secretory immunoglobulin A, cortisol, and emotional state. *J. Behav. Med.* 27, 623–635. doi:10.1007/s10865-004-0006-9

Kuhn, D. (2002). The effects of active and passive participation in musical activity on the immune system as measured by salivary immunoglobulin A (SIgA). *J. Music Ther.* 39, 30–39. doi:10.1093/jmt/39.1.30

Lahav, A., Saltzman, E., and Schlaug, G. (2007). Action representation of sound: audiomotor recognition network while listening to newly acquired actions. *J. Neurosci.* 27, 308–314. doi:10.1523/JNEUROSCI.4822-06.2007

Laine, M., Tuomainen, J., and Ahonen, A. (1994). Changes in hemispheric brain perfusion elicited by Melodic Intonation Therapy: a preliminary experiment with single photon emission computed tomography (SPECT). *Logoped. Phoniatr. Vocol.* 19, 19–24. doi:10.3109/14015439409101070

Laughlin, S. A., Naeser, M. A., and Gordon, W. P. (1979). Effects of three syllable durations using the Melodic Intonation Therapy technique. *J. Speech Hear. Res.* 22, 311–320.

Marchina, S., Zhu, L. L., Norton, A., Zipse, L., Wan, C. Y., and Schlaug, G. (2011). Impairment of speech production predicted by lesion load of the left arcuate fasciculus. *Stroke* 42, 2251–2256. doi:10.1161/STROKEAHA.110.606103

Marshall, N., and Holtzapple, P. (1976). "Melodic Intonation Therapy: variations on a theme," in *Clinical Aphasiology Conference*, ed. R. Brookshire (Wemme, OR: BRK), 115–141.

Meister, I. G., Boroojerdi, B., Foltys, H., Sparing, R., Huber, W., and Töpper, R. (2003). Motor cortex hand area and speech: implications for the development of language. *Neuropsychologia* 41, 401–406. doi:10.1016/S0028-3932(02)00179-3

Meister, I. G., Sparing, R., Foltys, H., Gebert, D., Huber, W., Töpper, R., et al. (2006). Functional connectivity between cortical hand motor and language areas during recovery from aphasia. *J. Neurol. Sci.* 247, 165–168. doi:10.1016/j.jns.2006.04.003

Menon, V., and Levitin, D. J. (2005). The rewards of music listening: response and physiological connectivity of the mesolimbic system. *Neuroimage* 28, 175–184. doi:10.1016/j.neuroimage.2005.05.053

Merrett, D. L., Peretz, I., and Wilson, S. J. (2013). Moderating variables of music training-induced neuroplasticity: a review and discussion. *Front. Psychol.* 4:606. doi:10.3389/fpsyg.2013.00606

Miller, S. B., and Toca, J. M. (1979). Adapted Melodic Intonation Therapy: a case study of an experimental language program for an autistic child. *J. Clin. Psychiatry* 40, 201–203.

Mills, C. K. (1904). Treatment of aphasia by training. *JAMA* 43, 1940–1949. doi:10.1001/jama.1904.92500260002d

Mukamel, R., Ekstrom, A. D., Kaplan, J., Iacoboni, M., and Fried, I. (2010). Single-neuron responses in humans during execution and observation of actions. *Curr. Biol.* 20, 750–756. doi:10.1016/j.cub.2010.02.045

Naeser, M. A., and Helm-Estabrooks, N. (1985). CT scan lesion localization and response to Melodic Intonation Therapy with nonfluent aphasia cases. *Cortex* 21, 203–223. doi:10.1016/S0010-9452(85)80027-7

Naeser, M. A., Martin, P. I., Baker, E. H., Hodge, S. M., Sczerzenie, S. E., Nicholas, M., et al. (2004). Overt propositional speech in chronic nonfluent aphasia studied with the dynamic susceptibility contrast fMRI method. *Neuroimage* 22, 29–41. doi:10.1016/j.neuroimage.2003.11.016

Naeser, M. A., Martin, P. I., Nicholas, M., Baker, E. H., Seekins, H., Kobayashi, M., et al. (2005). Improved picture naming in chronic aphasia after TMS to part of right Broca's area: an open-protocol study. *Brain Lang.* 93, 95–105. doi:10.1016/j.bandl.2004.08.004

Neumeister, C., Wioland, F., Metz-Lutz, M. N., Dziony, M. C., and North, P. (1983). Adaption de la Melodic Intonation Therapy au rythme du français parlé. *Rééduc. Orthophon.* 21, 149–161.

Norton, A., Zipse, L., Marchina, S., and Schlaug, G. (2009). Melodic Intonation Therapy: shared insights on how it is done and why it might help. *Ann. N. Y. Acad. Sci.* 1169, 431–436. doi:10.1111/j.1749-6632.2009.04859.x

Overy, K., and Molnar-Szakacs, I. (2009). Being together in time: musical experience and the mirror neuron system. *Music Percept.* 26, 489–504. doi:10.1371/journal.pone.0013812

Ozdemir, E., Norton, A., and Schlaug, G. (2006). Shared and distinct neural correlates of singing and speaking. *Neuroimage* 33, 628–635. doi:10.1016/j.neuroimage.2006.07.013

Patel, A. D. (2003). Language, music, syntax and the brain. *Nat. Neurosci.* 6, 674–681. doi:10.1038/nn1082

Patel, A. D. (2008). *Music, Language and the Brain.* New York, NY: Oxford University Press, Inc.

Pelletier, C. L. (2004). The effect of music on decreasing arousal due to stress: a meta-analysis. *J. Music Ther.* 41, 192–214. doi:10.1093/jmt/41.3.192

Peretz, I. (2009). Music, language and modularity framed in action. *Psychol. Belg.* 49, 157–175. doi:10.5334/pb-49-2-3-157

Peretz, I., and Coltheart, M. (2003). Modularity of music processing. *Nat. Neurosci.* 6, 688–691. doi:10.1038/nn1083

Pilon, M. A., Mcintosh, K. W., and Thaut, M. H. (1998). Auditory vs visual speech timing cues as external rate control to enhance verbal intelligibility in mixed spastic ataxic dysarthric speakers: a pilot study. *Brain Inj.* 12, 793–803. doi:10.1080/026990598122188

Pittenger, C., and Duman, R. S. (2007). Stress, depression, and neuroplasticity: a convergence of mechanisms. *Neuropsychopharmacology* 33, 88–109. doi:10.1038/sj.npp.1301574

Popovici, M., and Mihilescu, L. (1992). Melodic intonation in the rehabilitation of Romanian aphasics with bucco-lingual apraxia. *Rom. J. Neurol. Psychiatry* 30, 99–113.

Pulvermüller, F., Neininger, B., Elbert, T., Mohr, B., Rockstroh, B., Koebbel, P., et al. (2001). Constraint-induced therapy of chronic aphasia after stroke. *Stroke* 32, 1621–1626. doi:10.1161/01.STR.32.7.1621

Racette, A., Bard, C., and Peretz, I. (2006). Making non-fluent aphasics speak: sing along! *Brain* 129, 2571–2584. doi:10.1093/brain/awl250

Richter, M., Miltner, W. H. R., and Straube, T. (2008). Association between therapy outcome and right-hemispheric activation in chronic aphasia. *Brain* 131, 1391–1401. doi:10.1093/brain/awn043

Robinson, R. G. (2003). Poststroke depression: prevalence, diagnosis, treatment, and disease progression. *Biol. Psychiatry* 54, 376–387. doi:10.1016/S0006-3223(03)00423-2

Salimpoor, V. N., Benovoy, M., Larcher, K., Dagher, A., and Zatorre, R. J. (2011). Anatomically distinct dopamine release during anticipation and experience of peak emotion to music. *Nat. Neurosci.* 14, 257–262. doi:10.1038/nn.2726

Särkämö, T., Tervaniemi, M., Laitinen, S., Forsblom, A., Soinila, S., Mikkonen, M., et al. (2008). Music listening enhances cognitive recovery and mood after middle cerebral artery stroke. *Brain* 131, 866–876. doi:10.1093/brain/awn013

Saur, D., Lange, R., Baumgaertner, A., Schraknepper, V., Willmes, K., Rijntjes, M., et al. (2006). Dynamics of language reorganization after stroke. *Brain* 129, 1371–1384. doi:10.1093/brain/awl090

Schlaug, G., Marchina, S., and Norton, A. (2008). From singing to speaking: why singing may lead to recovery of expressive language function in patients with Broca's aphasia. *Music Percept.* 25, 315–323. doi:10.1525/mp.2008.25.4.315

Schlaug, G., Marchina, S., and Norton, A. (2009). Evidence for plasticity in white-matter tracts of patients with chronic Broca's aphasia undergoing intense intonation-based speech therapy. *Ann. N. Y. Acad. Sci.* 1169, 385–394. doi:10.1111/j.1749-6632.2009.04587.x

Seki, K., and Sugishita, M. (1983). Japanese-applied Melodic Intonation Therapy for Broca aphasia. *No To Shinkei* 35, 1031–1037.

Sparks, R. (2008). "Melodic intonation therapy," in *Language Intervention Strategies in Aphasia and Related Neurogenic Communication Disorders*, 5th Edn, ed. R. Chapey (Baltimore, MD: Lippincott Williams & Wilkins), 837–851.

Sparks, R., Helm, N., and Albert, M. (1974). Aphasia rehabilitation resulting from Melodic Intonation Therapy. *Cortex* 10, 303–316. doi:10.1016/S0010-9452(74)80024-9

Sparks, R., and Holland, A. L. (1976). Method: melodic intonation therapy for aphasia. *J. Speech Hear. Disord.* 41, 287–297.

Stahl, B., Henseler, I., Turner, R., Geyer, S., and Kotz, S. A. E. (2013). How to engage the right brain hemisphere in aphasics without even singing: evidence for two paths of speech recovery. *Front. Hum. Neurosci.* 7:35. doi:10.3389/fnhum.2013.00035

Stahl, B., Kotz, S. A., Henseler, I., Turner, R., and Geyer, S. (2011). Rhythm in disguise: why singing may not hold the key to recovery from aphasia. *Brain* 134, 3083–3093. doi:10.1093/brain/awr240

Turkeltaub, P. E., Coslett, H. B., Thomas, A. L., Faseyitan, O., Benson, J., Norise, C., et al. (2012). The right hemisphere is not unitary in its role in aphasia recovery. *Cortex* 48, 1179–1186. doi:10.1016/j.cortex.2011.06.010

Unwin, M. M., Kenny, D. T., and Davis, P. J. (2002). The effects of group singing on mood. *Psychol. Music* 30, 175–185. doi:10.1177/0305735602302004

van der Lugt-van Wiechen, K., and Visch-Brink, E. (1989). Die melodic intonation therapy bei patienten mit einer globalen aphasie; das hemmen von recurring utterances. *Sprache Stimme Gehör* 13, 142–145.

van der Meulen, I., Van De Sandt-Koenderman, M. E., and Ribbers, G. M. (2012). Melodic Intonation Therapy: present controversies and future opportunities. *Arch. Phys. Med. Rehabil.* 93, S46–S52. doi:10.1016/j.apmr.2011.05.029

Van Eeckhout, P., Pillon, B., Signoret, J.-L., Deloche, G., and Seron, X. (1982). "Rééducation des réductions sévères de l'expression orale: la thérapie mélodique et rythmée," in *Rééduquer le Cerveau*, ed. P. Mardaga (Bruxelles: Solédi), 109–121.

Van Lancker Sidtis, D. (2012). Formulaic language and language disorders. *Annu. Rev. Appl. Linguist.* 32, 62–80. doi:10.1017/S0267190512000104

Västfjäll, D., Juslin, P. N., and Hartig, T. (2012). "Music, subjective well-being, and health: the role of everyday emotions," in *Music, Health, and Well-Being*, eds R. Macdonald, G. Kreutz, and L. Mitchell (Oxford: Oxford University Press), 405–424.

Vines, B. W., Norton, A. C., and Schlaug, G. (2011). Non-invasive brain stimulation enhances the effects of melodic intonation therapy. *Front. Psychol.* 2:230. doi:10.3389/fpsyg.2011.00230

Wang, J., Marchina, S., Norton, A. C., Wan, C. Y., and Schlaug, G. (2013). Predicting speech fluency and naming abilities in chronic aphasic patients. *Front. Hum. Neurosci.* 7:831. doi:10.3389/fnhum.2013.00831

Wilson, S. J., Abbott, D. F., Lusher, D., Gentle, E. C., and Jackson, G. D. (2011). Finding your voice: a singing lesson from functional imaging. *Hum. Brain Mapp.* 32, 2115–2130. doi:10.1002/hbm.21173

Wilson, S. J., Parsons, K., and Reutens, D. C. (2006). Preserved singing in aphasia: a case study of the efficacy of Melodic Intonation Therapy. *Music Percept.* 24, 23–36. doi:10.1525/mp.2006.24.1.23

Wilson, S. M., Saygin, A. P., Sereno, M. I., and Iacoboni, M. (2004). Listening to speech activates motor areas involved in speech production. *Nat. Neurosci.* 7, 701–702. doi:10.1038/nn1263

Winhuisen, L., Thiel, A., Schumacher, B., Kessler, J., Rudolf, J., Haupt, W. F., et al. (2007). The right inferior frontal gyrus and poststroke aphasia: a follow-up investigation. *Stroke* 38, 1286–1292. doi:10.1161/01.STR.0000259632.04324.6c

Yamadori, A., Osumi, S., Masuhara, S., and Okubo, M. (1977). Preservation of singing in Broca's aphasia. *J. Neurol. Neurosurg. Psychiatr.* 40, 221–224. doi:10.1136/jnnp.40.3.221

Yorkston, K. M., Hammen, V. L., Beukelman, D. R., and Traynor, C. D. (1990). The effect of rate control on the intelligibility and naturalness of dysarthric speech. *J. Speech Hear. Disord.* 55, 550–560.

Zipse, L., Norton, A., Marchina, S., and Schlaug, G. (2012). When right is all that is left: plasticity of right-hemisphere tracts in a young aphasic patient. *Ann. N. Y. Acad. Sci.* 1252, 237–245. doi:10.1111/j.1749-6632.2012.06454.x

Zumbansen, A., Peretz, I., and Hébert, S. (2014). Melodic intonation therapy: back to basics for future research. *Front. Neurol.* 5:7. doi:10.3389/fneur.2014.00007

8

Moving to music: effects of heard and imagined musical cues on movement-related brain activity

Rebecca S. Schaefer[1]*, Alexa M. Morcom[2], Neil Roberts[3] and Katie Overy[4,5]

[1] *SAGE Center for the Study of the Mind, University of California, Santa Barbara, CA, USA*
[2] *School of Philosophy, Psychology and Language Sciences, University of Edinburgh, Edinburgh, UK*
[3] *Clinical Research Imaging Centre (CRIC), Queen's Medical Research Institute, University of Edinburgh, Edinburgh, UK*
[4] *Institute for Music in Human and Social Development, Reid School of Music, Edinburgh College of Art, University of Edinburgh, Edinburgh, UK*
[5] *Don Wright Faculty of Music, Department of Music Education, University of Western Ontario, London, ON, Canada*

Correspondence:
Rebecca S. Schaefer, SAGE Center for the Study of the Mind, Department of Psychological and Brain Sciences, University of California, Santa Barbara, CA 93106-9660, USA
e-mail: rebecca.schaefer@sagecenter.ucsb.edu

Music is commonly used to facilitate or support movement, and increasingly used in movement rehabilitation. Additionally, there is some evidence to suggest that music imagery, which is reported to lead to brain signatures similar to music perception, may also assist movement. However, it is not yet known whether either imagined or musical cueing changes the way in which the motor system of the human brain is activated during simple movements. Here, functional magnetic resonance imaging was used to compare neural activity during wrist flexions performed to either heard or imagined music with self-pacing of the same movement without any cueing. Focusing specifically on the motor network of the brain, analyses were performed within a mask of BA4, BA6, the basal ganglia (putamen, caudate, and pallidum), the motor nuclei of the thalamus, and the whole cerebellum. Results revealed that moving to music compared with self-paced movement resulted in significantly increased activation in left cerebellum VI. Moving to imagined music led to significantly more activation in pre-supplementary motor area (pre-SMA) and right globus pallidus, relative to self-paced movement. When the music and imagery cueing conditions were contrasted directly, movements in the music condition showed significantly more activity in left hemisphere cerebellum VII and right hemisphere and vermis of cerebellum IX, while the imagery condition revealed more significant activity in pre-SMA. These results suggest that cueing movement with actual or imagined music impacts upon engagement of motor network regions during the movement, and suggest that heard and imagined cues can modulate movement in subtly different ways. These results may have implications for the applicability of auditory cueing in movement rehabilitation for different patient populations.

Keywords: fMRI, music, music imagery, cued movement, neurorehabilitation

INTRODUCTION

The connection between musical rhythm and movement is an intuitive one, of which the most obvious manifestation is the widespread inclination to move to music. Coordinated movement necessarily depends on precise timing mechanisms and the inherent temporal structure of music can be used to make movements more regular (cf. Thaut et al., 2002; Bood et al., 2013). The connection between rhythm perception and movement has been demonstrated in cognitive neuroimaging studies: motor areas such as premotor cortex (PMC), basal ganglia, and cerebellum have been found to be activated when people listen to musical rhythms (Grahn and Brett, 2007; Chen et al., 2008). Motor network activation has also been found when people imagine music; additional to superior temporal and inferior frontal activation, the pre-supplementary motor area (pre-SMA), and PMC (both in BA6) have consistently been implicated in music imagery, and some studies have reported striatal and cerebellar activation (cf. Halpern and Zatorre, 1999; Leaver et al., 2009; Herholz et al., 2012). The neural activations of music imagination and music perception have also been found to show commonalities, both in terms of regional specificity measured using positron emission tomography (PET) or functional magnetic resonance imaging (fMRI) (cf. Halpern and Zatorre, 1999; Kraemer et al., 2005; Herholz et al., 2012) and in terms of temporal activation patterns measured using magneto-encephalography (MEG) or electro-encephalography (EEG) (Herholz et al., 2008; Schaefer et al., 2009, 2011a,b). Notably, the degree of such shared activation appears to vary with the complexity of the imagined musical stimulus, with more shared activation for simple stimuli than for complex stimuli such as ecologically valid music (Schaefer et al., 2013). The overlap between imagery and perception is not unique to the auditory modality; both visual and movement imagination have been found to activate modality-specific brain regions (Kosslyn et al., 2001; Pfurtscheller et al., 2006), and imagery content can even be decoded from the brain responses in visual and motor areas (Cichy et al., 2012; Oosterhof et al., 2012). The implication is that aspects of the imagined stimulus or action are being processed much in the way the actually perceived stimulus or performed action might be, usually with a weaker signature in modality-specific regions (Kosslyn et al., 2001) and together with additional, modality non-specific frontal and parietal activations that are related to imagery quality or vividness, likely involving memory and attentional processes related to the cognitive effort of imagining (Daselaar et al., 2010). Differences in activation patterns related to auditory imagery have also been reported between people with high- and low-imagery ability, showing differences in auditory and frontal regions (Herholz et al., 2012) although this vividness effect was not found in a previous study on non-musical auditory imagery (Olivetti Belardinelli et al., 2009).

Movement cueing refers to the use of an auditory stimulus to guide the temporal structure of a movement. The use of music as a cue for movement is common in recreational activities such as dancing or coordinated actions such as marching, and has been described as increasing athletic endurance (Karageorghis et al., 2010) and decreasing perceived exertion (Bood et al., 2013). However, aligning movement to a complex auditory stimulus such as music also involves cognitive operations such as periodicity detection and prediction (or beat induction, Honing, 2012) and tempo tracking. Auditory cueing is also used in rehabilitation of a range of movement disorders (Schaefer, in press), and several studies have indicated positive effects of music in movement rehabilitation. A meta-analysis of music-based gait interventions for Parkinson's disease (PD) showed small but significant effects on specific gait-related outcome measures (de Dreu et al., 2012), and significant effects have also been reported for rehabilitation of gait after stroke (Bradt et al., 2010). However, a worsening of gait has been reported in patients with Alzheimer's disease (AD) when walking to auditory cues (Wittwer et al., 2013), interpreted as related to impaired executive functioning, implying that attentional resources are necessary when aligning movements to music.

A small number of reports examine the use of imagined music as a cue for movement in rehabilitation settings. Schauer and Mauritz (2003) reported anecdotally that their music-based intervention was causing people to imagine the learned music while they walked, and more recently, imagined singing was successfully used to regularize gait in a small group of PD patients (Satoh and Kuzuhara, 2008). These reports suggest that a musical cue can potentially be endogenously generated through music imagery; however, there is currently no direct neural evidence to suggest that imagery might support movement in a similar way to perceived music.

When considering the possible mechanisms of movement cueing within the motor network of the brain, one possibility is that the motor network activations previously reported for musical rhythm perception (Grahn and Brett, 2007; Chen et al., 2008) may additively combine with the brain activation related to actual movements, leading to increased activation in basal ganglia, PMC, and (pre-)SMA. However, previous studies have found different rather than greater motor network activity when movement is cued by music compared to when it is carried out with no external cue, i.e., self-paced. Brown et al. (2006) used PET to directly compare music-cued dance-step foot movements in the supine position with the same movements in silence. This is to our knowledge the only brain imaging study, to date, to investigate movement cueing using naturalistic music stimuli, rather than a metronome, and compare it directly to self-paced movement. Results showed additional activation in lobule III of the cerebellar vermis during entrained relative to self-paced movement. This supports the longstanding notion that the cerebellum is involved in the timing of movement as well as in rhythm perception (Ivry and Keele, 1989; Schubotz et al., 2000). In a more recent fMRI study that directly compared cued and uncued conditions, using stepping movements and metronome stimuli, Toyomura et al. (2012) found greater left putamen activity for uncued movement relative to cued movement, which was attributed to self-pacing of the movement. The difference from Brown et al. (2006) findings may be due to the more recent study using either simpler movements (alternating foot raises as opposed to spatially organized dance steps), or may be due to simpler cueing stimuli (a metronome as opposed to tango music), or some interaction of these factors. Schaal et al. (2004), in a study focusing on rhythmic and discrete movements, reported that wrist flexions performed periodically to a metronome cue elicited similar, but weaker activation patterns in PMC to those elicited by self-paced movements. This suggests that the cue somehow facilitated the movement, leading to a reduced demand on the same neural resources. However, Schaal et al.'s study did neither focus on nor directly statistically compare, the cued and uncued movements, limiting possible interpretations. Collectively, brain imaging work has thus not yet provided clear indications of a neural basis for the potential clinical benefits of moving to music or imagined music.

In the current study, we used fMRI to evaluate the effects of musical cueing of a very simple movement on motor network activations, using an adaptation of the movement used by Schaal et al. (2004). We used two different cueing conditions: moving to music and moving to imagined music, with a control condition involving the same movement carried out without a cue, referred to as self-paced. We aimed to explore the activation of motor regions related to entraining movement to music, and the possible equivalence of using imagined and perceived music as cues. Possible differences between these conditions in terms of movement output were evaluated separately outside of the scanner in a behavioral study in a different group of participants. Based on the previous research findings reviewed above, a number of neural motor regions of interest are identified, namely, PMC (pre-)SMA, basal ganglia, and cerebellum. Considering the simple wrist flexion movement used here, reduced PMC activations were predicted to be found for cued (musical or imagined musical) compared to uncued movement (cf. Schaal et al., 2004). Based on previous results of musical cueing, cued movement was predicted to lead to activations in anterior cerebellum III (cf. Brown et al., 2006), and following the results of Toyomura et al. (2012), we expected that basal ganglia may be implicated in self-pacing movement. For music imagery without movement, the motor areas pre-SMA, PMC, and the cerebellum have been reported to be active (cf. Halpern and Zatorre, 1999; Leaver et al., 2009; Herholz et al., 2012). As the above-mentioned findings of reduced activation for imagery relative to perception only concerned modality-specific areas rather than activations found in the motor network, we hypothesized that, based on the reported shared activations between music perception and imagery, the activations in the pre-SMA, PMC, and the cerebellum when moving to music would be similar to those when moving to imagined music, contrasted with self-paced movement. Notably, Daselaar et al. (2010) reported bilateral striatum to be more active for (non-musical) auditory imagery than for perception, indicating that activation in this region may be increased for imagery-based cueing. The assessment of the movements with motion capture was predicted to show that for a simple movement such as wrist flexions, there would be no differences between conditions in terms of global movement parameters such as speed or range of movement.

MATERIALS AND METHODS

The fMRI and behavioral experiments were carried out in accordance with the code of ethical principles for medical research involving human subjects of the World Medical Association (Declaration of Helsinki), and was approved by the ethical committee of the University of Edinburgh and the West of Scotland Research Ethics Committee, UK, REC reference number 12/WS/0229.

PARTICIPANTS

Seventeen volunteers (8 female, mean age 27.3 years, range 20–46), recruited through University of Edinburgh networks, took part in the fMRI experiment after giving informed consent. All participants were self-reported right-handed [mean shortened Edinburgh handedness inventory (EHI; for details see Stimuli and Materials)] score 74.6, SD = 19.8, all classifying as right-handed (>40) except for one who scored ambidextrous at 25 points, but identified as right-handed. All had <5 years of formal music training (mean 2.2, SD = 2.2) but listened to music at least three times a week and reported being able to imagine music, and had no known neurological impairments. For the behavioral experiment, 10 additional right-handed volunteers were recruited with the same recruitment criteria, of which 1 had to be excluded due to data loss and 1 due to having more musical training than reported at the time of recruitment, resulting in 8 behavioral participants (5 female, mean age 23.6, range = 20–45), mean shortened EHI 89.6 (SD = 12.0, all classifying as right-handed), and a mean of 1.1 years (SD = 1.5) of formal music training.

STIMULI AND MATERIALS

Two experimental conditions and one control condition were presented in blocks: flexing the wrists either to music (music condition), or while imagining music (imagined music condition), or without a cue (self-paced condition), respectively. The tempo was indicated through a visual count-in cue, which was identical for all conditions. The wrist flexions were bilateral and identical for both hands, with one dorsiflexion and one plantar flexion per second, starting the movement block with a dorsiflexion each time after the count-in. The music fragment that was used consisted of bar 9–16 (15.8–31.6 s) of Stevie Wonder's "Another Star" (from "Songs in the Key of Life," 1976, Motown Records), available as Supplementary Material. This fragment was chosen for its tempo [120 bpm, which is in the range of preferred tempi for repeated movements, see Moelants (2003)], the fact that it is a natural performance with some rhythmic complexity that it has a vocal melody but no words, thus not including semantic content, and is sung by both men and women, which we hypothesized to facilitate the imagery for the music fragment.

To assess the recruitment criteria in terms of general auditory imagery ability and hand preference, the auditory part of the shortened Betts' questionnaire upon mental imagery (BQMI, Sheehan, 1967) and the EHI (Oldfield, 1971) were used. An exit questionnaire asked participants to rate the clarity and ease of the task on a five-point scale, give details of any prior musical training experience, and indicate when and how often they generally imagine music.

fMRI EXPERIMENT

Procedure

The procedure for the experiment is illustrated in **Figure 1**. Each block comprised a single sequence of wrist flexion movements, instructed to be performed with a maximal range within the limits of comfort, preceded by a cue indicating the movement condition. For each condition, the instructions were first presented for 1.5–2.5 s, randomly jittered so that the timing of the instruction was uncorrelated with the block onset. Then, the word "Ready?" appeared for 1 s, then a black screen for 1 s, followed by a visual count-in of four pairs of dots closing in to the center, presented at intervals of 500 ms, after which a "+" appeared on the screen for 16 s while the movements were performed. The change from a "+" to a "−" indicated that the block was finished, and the participant should rest until the next block started. The inter-block rest period lasted 13–14 s, and each participant performed 10 blocks of each condition in a randomized order. Prior to task performance, participants practiced the movement, then listened to the music fragment until they indicated that they were able to imagine it easily (with no one taking more than 10 min of listening), and finally practiced five trials with the experiment instruction screens presented on a laptop. In case of involuntary imagery of the music during the self-paced condition, participants were suggested the back-up strategy of imagining the sound of a metronome, however, none required this strategy during scanning – all reported having no involuntary music imagery during the self-paced condition. Once the participant had confirmed that they understood the experiment by performing each condition appropriately, they were positioned comfortably in the scanner. The stimuli were presented using Presentation® software[1] (Version 0.70). Visual stimuli were presented using Nordic NeuroLabs goggles, and standard Siemens headphones were used to present the music. The full session included a structural scan lasting 6 min followed by two 20-min functional scanning runs, of which this study was the second. The first is reported elsewhere, and involved the same movement, but cued with a metronome. In terms of possible sequential effects, this means the participants had some practice in performing the wrist flexions in the scanner, which, given the simplicity of the movement, would not be expected to result in differences in motor network activations, and in any case would be expected to affect each condition of the currently discussed experiment equally. After the scanning runs, participants filled in the BMQI, EHI, and exit questionnaire.

Imaging data acquisition and analysis

Anatomical and functional images were acquired at the Clinical Research Imaging Centre (CRIC) at the Queen's Medical

[1]http://www.neurobs.com

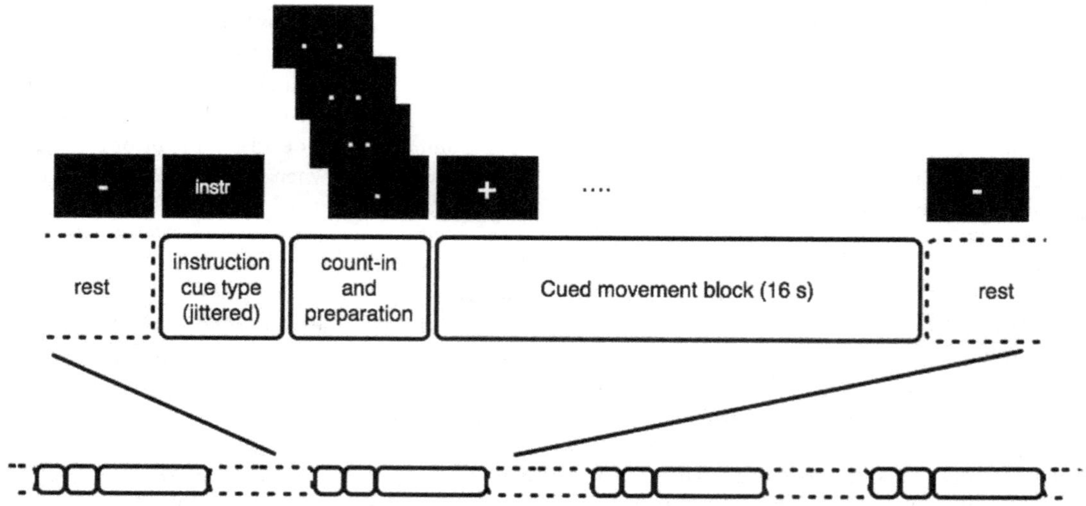

FIGURE 1 | Graphical representation of the stimulus structure.

Research Institute (QMRI) of the University of Edinburgh, UK, using a 3-T Siemens Magnetom Verio scanner with 12-channel matrix headcoil. For the anatomical images, an MPRAGE sequence was used (160 slices, TR = 2300 ms, TE = 2.98 ms, FOV = 240 mm × 256 mm × 160 mm, voxel size = 1 mm^3, TI = 900 ms, flip angle = 9°). Functional activations were assessed by acquiring T2*-weighted gradient-echo echo planar (EPI) images with blood oxygen level-dependent contrast (26 slices, TR = 1560 ms, TE = 26 ms, FOV = 192 mm × 192 mm × 130 mm, voxel size = 3 mm × 3 mm × 5 mm, flip angle = 90°, no gaps between the slices). The first six volumes were discarded to allow for T1 saturation effects.

Preprocessing

Data analyses were performed using Statistical Parametric Mapping software[2] (SPM8, version 4191) with MATLAB 7.10 (The MathWorks, Natick, MA, USA). The preprocessing steps were as follows: first, an outlier detection procedure was applied to ensure data quality; outlier slices with values >7 SD above the mean were identified and scans were replaced with the mean of the 2 neighboring scans to remove any faulty scans (replacing an average of 0.8 volumes, maximum 3 per participant, out of a total of 604 volumes). After realigning the functional data to one of the middle scans of the run with B-spline interpolation, and saving a mean image and the motion parameters, the structural image was coregistered to the mean functional image. Spatial normalization to MNI space then followed the optimized VBM5 procedure (Ashburner and Friston, 2005) with the "New Segment" option in SPM8: the structural image was segmented into six tissue types, and the resulting forward deformation field then applied to the functional images, reslicing to 3 mm × 3 mm × 3mm voxels. Finally, the functional data were spatially smoothed using a 6 mm × 6 mm × 6mm full-width at half maximum (FWHM) Gaussian kernel.

[2]www.fil.ion.ucl.ac.uk/spm/software/spm8/

Statistical analysis

Statistical inference employed a two-stage summary-statistic approach (Holmes and Friston, 1998; Penny and Holmes, 2006). First level general linear models (GLMs) for each subject were constructed with separate covariates for each of the three conditions (music, imagined music, and self-paced), modeled as sequences of 16 s blocks beginning at the onset times of each sequence of movement. Three additional covariates were included to account for the initial preparation and counting-in phase of each condition, modeled as sequences of 2 s blocks corresponding to the duration of the preparation time. This ensured that condition-specific movement effects of interest were not confounded with condition-specific movement preparation effects. Covariates were formed by convolution of block sequences with a canonical hemodynamic response function (HRF; Friston et al., 1998). Parameter estimates were then computed using the weighted least squares fit of the model to the data following pre-whitening with an AR(1) plus white noise model (Friston et al., 2002). Data for each session were high-pass filtered to 1/128 Hz and scaled to a grand mean of 100 across all voxels and scans within a session. Each GLM also included a session constant, and six movement regressors as covariates of no interest.

Second level analyses were conducted on first level contrast images, treating participants as a random effect. For each participant, three simple pairwise contrasts entered group-level one-sample t-tests, which compared parameter estimates between each movement condition (music and self-paced, imagined music and self-paced, music and imagined music). To focus on motor network effects, group analyses were conducted within a region of interest (ROI) mask created using the WFU Pickatlas toolbox (Maldjian et al., 2003). This mask comprised bilateral areas BA4, BA6, caudate, putamen, globus pallidus, motor thalamus (ventral anterior nucleus and ventrolateral nucleus; Mai and Forutan, 2012), and the entire cerebellum. Cluster significance was tested within the ROI mask using the AlphaSim tool included in the

AFNI toolbox[3] (Cox, 1996). This simulation indicated that with a cluster-forming threshold of 0.005, a family wise error (FWE) cluster correction at $P < 0.05$, required a minimum cluster size of 19 voxels. The locations of the clusters were determined using the probabilistic maps integrated in the SPM Anatomy Toolbox v1.8 (Eickhoff et al., 2005). The results of the ambidextrous participant were inspected in relation to the significant clusters, and were found not to show different results than the formally right-handed participants (as determined by the EHI).

BEHAVIORAL EXPERIMENT

Additional procedure and analysis

Except where noted, procedures for the behavioral experiment followed those described for the fMRI experiment, but the rest period between trials was now shortened to 5 s since a longer period of rest was not needed for behavioral data acquisition (see **Figure 1**). Participants assumed a supine position to mimic the fMRI set-up, with support pillows so that they could see a computer screen set-up in front of them and rest their arms while making the wrist flexion movements. An Ascension miniBIRD magnetic motion tracking system was used to capture the timing and extent of the wrist flexion, with a single 8 mm sensor attached to the middle finger of their right hand with medical tape (as a proxy for the movement of both hands) measuring with a sampling frequency of 100 samples per second. After 5 practice trials (during which the measurement was tested), 11 trials per condition were presented in a randomized order. This experiment included an additional condition in which movements were performed to a metronome, the results of which are discussed elsewhere. The experiment took approximately 20 min. Visual stimuli were presented using a 20″ computer screen, which was set-up in front of the participants who were in half supine position, and the sound was presented through stereo speakers (Genelec 1029A, 40 W, free field frequency response of 70 Hz – 18 kHz ± 2.5 dB) positioned to the sides of the screen and set at a comfortable listening level.

The data were analyzed in MATLAB 7.10 (The MathWorks, Natick, MA, USA). Using only the z-axis of the recording, movement blocks with obvious measurement artifacts (such as large spikes) were first removed by hand, leading to rejection of 5 blocks, leaving an average of 10.8 16-s movement blocks per condition (minimum = 8). The movement features analyzed were based on Schaal et al. (2004), and included the number of movements, range of the movements, mean period of a full flexion, and the mean and maximum velocity. Signals were first normalized to z-scores over all conditions, after which the number of movements, the (normalized) range, full back, and forth flexion period duration and velocity (displacement over time, mean, and maximum) were computed by extracting the dorsiflexions and plantar flexions for all individual trials and then averaging these over each condition and participant before averaging over the group. As there was unequal variance in all measures between conditions, the output measures are tested using the Friedman test (Friedman, 1937) as implemented in MATLAB, with *post hoc* comparisons tested separately.

RESULTS

QUESTIONNAIRE RESULTS

The results of the EHI and musical background questions are reported above in Section "Participants." All participants (fMRI and behavioral) indicated that they were not highly familiar with the music fragment and found the task easy, while most participants indicated that they found the experiment enjoyable (14/17 for the fMRI group and 7/8 for the behavioral group). On the BQMI measure of imagery ability, which uses a 5-point scale (where 1 is high-imagery ability), the fMRI group had an average score of 2.05 (SD = 0.8), and the behavioral group had an average score of 2.48 (SD = 1.17). These are not statistically different between groups using the Mann–Whitney test, and both are slightly below the normative average of 3.01 (SD = 1.53), reported originally by Sheehan (1967), indicating somewhat better imagery vividness in these participants than average, in accordance with the recruitment criteria.

BEHAVIORAL RESULTS

The mean number of movements, the mean amplitude of the wrist flexions, the mean period, and the mean and maximum velocity of the movements are shown for each condition in **Table 1**. Given that the tempo of the music (which was the same as the instructed tempo for the silent and imagery-cued conditions) was 120 bpm, the 16 s blocks should lead to 16 flexions and a mean period of 1 s. As the amplitudes (or extent of the movement) were normalized between participants they are reported in terms of the z-score, and both velocity measurements are thus in arbitrary units. The movements were found to be highly similar; the Friedman test revealed no statistically significant differences between the conditions for any of the outcome measures. These results indicate that large-scale differences in velocity or range were not found between the different movement conditions.

[3]http://afni.nimh.nih.gov/afni/

Table 1 | Behavioral results: wrist flexions for each cueing condition.

Condition	Wrist flexions	Amplitude (z-scores)	Period (s)	Velocity (arbitrary units)	Maximum velocity (arbitrary units)
Self-paced	15.56 (1.37)	2.84 (0.07)	1.07 (0.09)	0.05 (0.005)	0.16 (0.005)
Music	16.09 (0.94)	2.83 (0.07)	0.99 (0.04)	0.05 (0.003)	0.18 (0.003)
Imagined music	16.12 (1.29)	2.85 (0.08)	1.02 (0.07)	0.05 (0.005)	0.17 (0.005)

The number of movements, the mean amplitude, and mean period of each back and forth flexion, and mean and maximum velocity over the whole block of movement are shown with SD in brackets. Between-condition comparisons did not reveal any significant differences ($P > 0.05$, Friedman test).

fMRI RESULTS

Significant clusters of activity within the regions of interest are summarized in **Table 2** and illustrated in **Figures 2–4**. There was significantly increased activity for the music condition relative to the self-paced condition in a cluster in the left cerebellum, lobule VI (**Figure 2**), but no region showed significantly increased activity for the self-paced condition relative to the music condition.

The comparisons between the imagined music condition and the self-paced condition revealed significant activity increases for imagined music relative to self-paced in the right pre-SMA and in the right globus pallidus (see **Figure 3**). Again, no region showed significantly increased activity for self-paced relative to imagined music.

Finally, comparisons between the two cued conditions (music and imagined music), showed music-specific activations in left cerebellum lobule VIIa and the vermis of lobule IX, whereas for imagery, activation was seen in bilateral pre-SMA (see **Figure 4**). The cerebellar cluster did not overlap with the cerebellar activation identified in the contrast between music and self-paced, but the pre-SMA cluster did show five voxels overlap with that found in the contrast between imagined music and self-paced.

Table 2 | Regions showing significant between-condition differences in BOLD activation.

Contrast	Anatomical region	Cluster size	Peak voxel (*x, y, z*)	*z*-Value
Music > self-paced	Left cerebellum VI	28	−27, −58, −23	2.97
			−18, −64, −23	2.95
Imagined music > self-paced	Right globus pallidus	19	18, −4, 1	5.24
	Right pre-SMA	20	9, 11, 64	3.17
			12, 5, 73	3.40
Music > imagined music	Left cerebellum VIIa	218	−24, −76, −32	4.03
			−18, −70, −32	3.98
			−30, −76, −38	3.97
	Cerebellar vermis IX	37	3, −55, −47	3.28
			12, −43, −47	3.11
Imagined music > music	Bilateral Pre-SMA	117	−9, 8, 67	4.16
			12, 8, 67	3.20

See Section "Statistical Analysis" for details of analysis and thresholding.

DISCUSSION

In the current study, brain activity within motor regions during a simple wrist flexion movement task was found to vary according to how this movement was cued. We observed differential responses in cerebellum, globus pallidus, and pre-SMA according to whether wrist flexion movements were performed to music, to imagined music or were self-paced. Self-paced movement did not elicit significant additional activity relative to either of the cued conditions. A closely matched behavioral study showed that these neural differences were not related to gross differences in performance: the number, amplitude, and velocity of the movements showed no significant differences between conditions. Thus, in the cued conditions, increased activations in specific motor areas were associated with a similar behavioral output, suggesting differing neural processes to lead to the same movement.

Our data provide a direct comparison of musically cued and uncued movements while keeping movement complexity minimal, and both converge and diverge from previous findings. As predicted, we observed pre-SMA activation during movement cued by musical imagery relative to heard music as well as relative to self-paced movements. However, the hypothesized activity increase in anterior cerebellum III and activity reduction in PMC for musically cued compared with self-paced movement were not seen. The areas that were active in the cued conditions over the self-paced condition (left cerebellum VI for music, and right pallidum and right pre-SMA for music imagery) are all regions that have previously been implicated in finger tapping tasks cued by auditory pacing signals (Witt et al., 2008), but have not previously been found in direct comparisons of cued to uncued movement. We now consider these findings in turn.

MUSICAL CUEING

Performing wrist flexions to music, as compared to self-cued movement, yield activation in lobule VI of the left cerebellum. This area has previously emerged as involved in musical processing (cf. Peretz and Zatorre, 2005; Alluri et al., 2012), but is also involved in a variety of other cognitive and motor tasks (Stoodley and Schmahmann, 2009). Our finding differs from those of Brown et al. (2006) PET study, which examined activity for patterned dance steps performed to natural music contrasted to the same steps but self-paced, and reported cerebellar activation in lobule III of the vermis, which was interpreted as specific to entrainment to musical rhythm. Although this study is to our knowledge the only other study directly comparing musically cued movement to uncued movement, there are several basic differences in the study design that could cause divergence from these previous findings. It is possible that the very simple movement used in the current experiment, based on a previous research report (Schaal et al., 2004), may lead to different cueing effects from more complex movements. Recurring wrist flexions are easy to perform without too extensive effort or attention, fitting with the rationale for the current experiment, which had the aim of assessing the effect of auditory cues for simple movements, whereas it may be the case that for more complex movements, such as the tango dance steps used in Brown et al. (2006), the effects of auditory cues are different, involving the cerebellar vermis, or alternately that the musical style is relevant for the effect of a cue on motor network activation. The increased sample size used in the current study ($N = 17$) as compared to previous work on cued movement [studies by Brown et al. (2006), Schaal et al. (2004), and Toyomura et al. (2012) had Ns of 10, 11, and 12, respectively] lends some support to the current findings as a robust reflection of mechanisms of simple movements cued by a musical stimulus.

In previous studies, multiple motor areas including cerebellum VI have been reported as being activated during rhythm perception [such as cerebellum VIII (pre-)SMA, PMC, putamen, see Chen et al. (2008), Grahn and Brett (2007)]. Thus, one possibility is that the cerebellum VI activation found in the current study is purely due to music listening. In that case, it is of interest that this

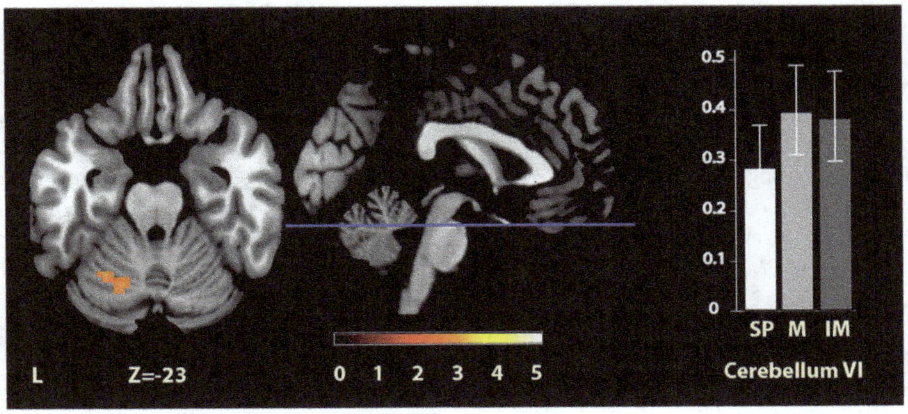

FIGURE 2 | Musically cued versus self-paced movement. The section shows the left cerebellum VI region activation cluster for music relative to self-paced conditions, displayed on the MRIcron reference T1 image in MNI space, FWE cluster corrected at $P < 0.05$. The parameter estimate plot shows mean percent signal change of the self-paced (white, SP), music (mid-gray, M), and imagined music (dark gray, IM) conditions relative to rest in cluster peak voxel $x = -27$, $y = -58$, $z = -23$.

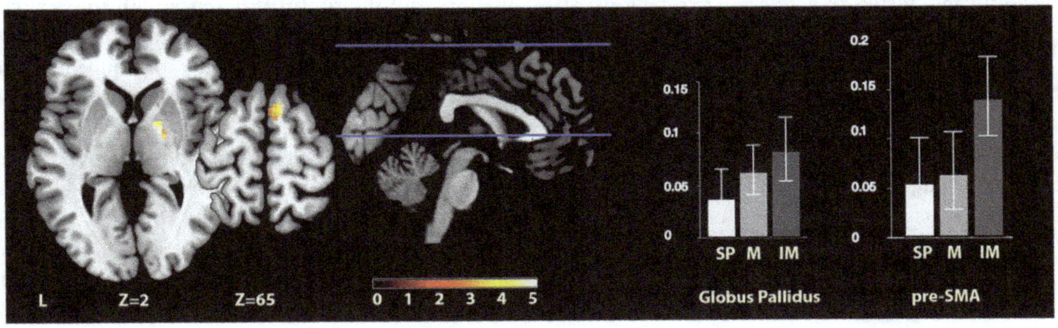

FIGURE 3 | Imagery-cued versus self-paced movement. The sections show activation clusters in the right globus pallidus and pre-SMA for imagined music relative to self-paced conditions, displayed on the MRIcron reference T1 image in MNI space, FWE cluster corrected at $P < 0.05$. The parameter estimate plots show percent signal change of self-paced (white, SP), music (mid-gray, M), and imagined music (dark gray, IM) conditions relative to rest in cluster peak voxels $x = 18$, $y = -4$, $z = 1$ (globus pallidus) and $x = 9$, $y = 11$, $z = 64$ (pre-SMA).

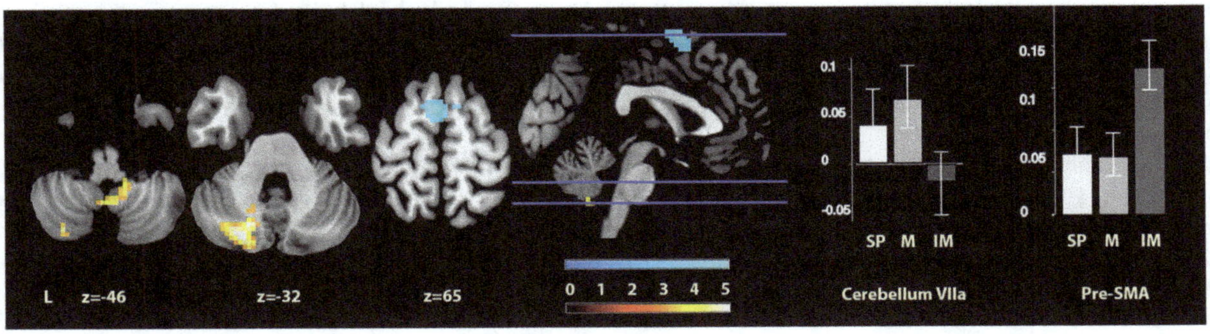

FIGURE 4 | Musically cued versus imagery-cued movement. The sections show the cerebellar activations for music relative to imagined music conditions in orange and the pre-SMA activations of imagined music relative to music conditions in blue, displayed on the MRIcron reference T1 image in MNI space, FWE cluster corrected at $P < 0.05$. The parameter estimate plots show percentage signal change of self-paced (white, SP), music (mid-gray, M), and imagined music (dark gray, IM) conditions relative to rest in cluster peak voxels $x = -24$, $y = -76$, $z = -32$ (cerebellum VIIa) and $x = -6$, $y = 1$, $z = 69$ (pre-SMA).

cerebellar area was the only motor region found to be significantly activated by music perception in the current context of continuous movement, suggesting that, whereas the perception-related activation in other motor regions does not persist while performing a movement, this is not the case for the cerebellum VI region. Alternatively, this region may respond specifically to musically cued movement, and be crucial for aligning movement to sound. Based on the data presented here, it is not possible to distinguish between these potential explanations. However, it appears likely that cerebellum VI, with its connections to PMd and M1, as well as frontal and parietal areas (Bernard et al., 2012), acts as a hub of connectivity linking perceptual and motor processes [much like the anterior cerebellar activation was interpreted in Brown et al. (2006)], and has a distinct role compared to other movement-related regions involved in music processing. Future studies may reveal further motor region effects for cued movements of varying complexity, as here we only examined the simplest case, a regularly recurring, easy movement.

IMAGERY-BASED CUEING

When comparing movement cued by imagery to self-paced movement, we found significant clusters of activity in two regions: one in the right pre-SMA and one in the right globus pallidus. The former was expected from previous literature on music imagination (cf. Halpern and Zatorre, 1999; Leaver et al., 2009; Herholz et al., 2012) and is found here to persist in the context of movement. In previous literature, this activation has been proposed to relate to sequential control through chunking and memory processes (Leaver et al., 2009), and has also been implicated in free musical improvisation of melodies and rhythms (de Manzano and Ullén, 2012), which in a different way also includes imagery, memory, and sequencing processes. More generally, pre-SMA is associated with self-initiation of actions and cognitive involvement in action (Nachev et al., 2008). Although not reported consistently, activation in the pallidum has also been noted previously in the context of music imagery, specifically vividness in anticipatory imagery (Leaver et al., 2009), while striatal activation has been reported for vividness of (non-musical) auditory imagery as compared to perception (Daselaar et al., 2010). The current finding of pallidum activation is specifically interesting in the context of movement cueing in clinical situations, as the globus pallidus is one of the main sites for which deep brain stimulation (DBS) has been found to be effective in reducing motor impairments [another site being the subthalamic nucleus, cf. Follett et al., 2010]. In PD, this stimulation has for example been reported not only to reduce tremor and improve gait (Follett et al., 2010) but also to reduce symptoms in various types of dystonia (Kupsch et al., 2006; Walsh et al., 2013), Huntington's disease (Edwards et al., 2012), and Tourette's syndrome (Priori et al., 2013). The finding that this area is especially active during imagery-cued movement needs further investigation and replication before a robust connection with these patient populations can be established; however, this first brain imaging result of moving to imagined music shows promise for further development of paradigms using music imagery in clinical situations. The beta and gamma frequency bands of electrical activity in the internal globus pallidus (as measured in cervical dystonia patients with implanted electrodes) are modulated by the preparation of self-initiated movements and the execution of both self-initiated and externally triggered movements (Tsang et al., 2012). For PD, bilateral thalamus and pallidum size are positively correlated with disease duration (Geevarghese et al., 2014), and altered pallidal–frontal processing is associated with executive dysfunction (Dirnberger et al., 2005). Moreover, patients with focal basal ganglia lesions are reported to be affected in the ability to execute a steady sequence of periodic actions (Schwartze et al., 2011). The finding that this area is more active for imagined music than during self-paced sustained movement, but not significantly different from musically cued movement may be related to the relative endogenous effort involved in pacing movement through imagery.

COMPARISON OF MUSICAL CUEING AND IMAGERY-BASED CUEING

Directly contrasting the two cued movement conditions showed significantly greater activity for musical cueing in two main clusters in the cerebellum (i.e., lobule VIIa of the left hemisphere and lobule IX of the vermis), and significantly greater activity for imagery-based cueing in bilateral pre-SMA. The latter result was predicted on the basis of previous literature on music imagination, and the robust difference with musical cueing indicates that the pre-SMA was uniquely significantly activated by imagined music. Regarding our hypothesis of equivalence between music and imagined music, when considered alongside the results discussed above (see Musical Cueing and Imagery-Based Cueing), the cerebellum VI and pallidum regions, which responded to musical and imagery-based cueing compared with self-paced movement, respectively, did not show reliably different activity when these two conditions were contrasted directly with one another. This is supported by inspection of the parameter estimates in both regions, suggesting intermediate responses for the contrasts with self-paced movement for imagined music for cerebellum VI and music for the pallidum. Thus, our data are consistent with the hypothesis that moving to music and to imagined music engages some of the same parts of the movement network, and also suggests that these regions are engaged to differing degrees.

In terms of the unpredicted activation differences that were found for music-based cueing as compared to imagery-based cueing; the cerebellar left lobule VII and vermis IX activations could be interpreted as relating to temporal prediction. A recent study by Pecenka et al. (2012) reported left cerebellum VIIa activation to correlate negatively with temporal prediction accuracy while timing movement to a metronome with a slightly varying tempo (although their other reported activations of SMA and precentral gyrus, which are also included in our search volume, were not found for our music condition). Additionally, cerebellum VIIa has been implicated in perceptual prediction without moving (O'Reilly et al., 2008). The activation in lobule IX of the vermis, reportedly connecting to superior temporal gyrus (Bernard et al., 2012), may also be related to perceptual processes during music listening. This finding offers some exploratory detail on the different role that cerebellar lobule VI may have as opposed to lobule VIIa and IX in aligning movement to auditory cues, in that cerebellum VI appears to be more involved in both external and internal rhythm processing, whereas lobule VIIa and IX may be specifically implicated in perceiving versus self-generating a rhythmic stimulus. Future studies will be necessary to verify and refine this interpretation.

LIMITATIONS

A number of study limitations need to be kept in mind when considering these interpretations. Firstly, the current design did not include trial-to-trial vividness measures, and we thus relied on self-report from the participants after scanning that they were successfully imagining the music. This is a potential limitation as previous results indicate that imagery ability and vividness may affect the brain signatures of imagery (cf. Olivetti Belardinelli et al., 2009; Herholz et al., 2012). However, the regions previously reported to be implicated in imagery vividness were not motor areas and thus outside our regions of interest for the current study. Moreover, all participants in our study were pre-selected for imagery skills, all participants reported imagining the music easily, and we found significant differences in brain activity between imagery and self-paced conditions, suggesting that the manipulation was successful. A second potential limitation of the study is that, although the movements were evaluated behaviorally outside the scanner that sample size was relatively small and the measures of amplitude, period, velocity, and number of completed flexions were somewhat crude, possibly missing more subtle aspects of movement, such as movement fluidity or jerk. Such differences have been previously reported for more complex cued movements that have longer trajectories (e.g., Thaut et al., 2002). Nevertheless, there is no reason to assume that differences in these subtle aspects of the currently used movement, if present, would explain the differences in the brain activity we observed. Finally, since our results were obtained from simple movements carried out by healthy volunteers, further research will be needed to assess how the differences in neural processing are affected by either more complex movements or by the specific neural deficits of particular patient groups. Future neuroscientific and behavioral investigations aimed at detecting subtle differences in movement due to heard and imagined musical cueing will be of substantial converging interest for interpreting the present findings and those of the clinical studies.

CONCLUSION AND FUTURE DIRECTIONS

The current work presents, a first step in researching the neural mechanisms of moving to heard and imagined music, using ecologically valid music and simple movements. A cognitive task – music imagination – is shown to impact upon the activation of the motor network of the brain, in line with anecdotal clinical reports of imagined music facilitating movement, implicating brain areas in the cerebellum and basal ganglia long known to be important for the timing of movement. Thus, cognitive aspects of music processing, likely involving some representation of the musical rhythm, are demonstrated to affect movement processing at the level of the motor network of the brain.

Future work may benefit from investigating different styles of music, taking into account personal music preference as well as specific rhythmic characteristics of the musical stimulus. Additionally, other movements may be examined, using different limbs, different degrees of complexity, or the extent to which the movements are rhythmic or discrete in nature. This study only employed one musical extract, while recent behavioral work has shown that style of music can modulate the effects of cueing in terms of movement vigor (Leman et al., 2013), suggesting that this difference in vigor may also lead to more extensive motor network activation. Furthermore, the ability to move to an auditory cue appears to differ across individuals (Tierney and Kraus, 2013), for which test batteries of synchronization skills have recently been developed (Farrugia et al., 2012; Fujii and Schlaug, 2013). Thus, also taking individual differences into account for paradigms using both heard and imagined cueing may inform the usefulness of auditory cues in movement rehabilitation for specific patient groups, ideally permitting selection of cues or cueing strategies that are optimally useful given a specific neurological problem. The usability of music imagination as a cue will depend fully on the imagery ability of a specific patient group or individual, which can currently be assessed through imagery ability measures such as the BQMI questionnaire used here, similar to those used for movement imagery in movement rehabilitation [for an example with stroke patients, see Malouin et al. (2007)]. Systematic clinical evaluation of the applicability of moving to heard and imagined music is necessary to evaluate whether the current fMRI findings have consequences for the specific patient groups that could benefit from musical or imagined musical cueing.

ACKNOWLEDGMENTS

We thank Rob McIntosh for use of the motion tracking equipment, Madhurima Chakraborty for running the behavioral experiment, and Caryn Cobb for help with coding the questionnaires. We acknowledge the support of the European Commission under the Marie Curie Intra-European Fellowship Program (grant FP7-2010-PEOPLE-IEF 276529), the SAGE Center for the Study of the Mind at the University of California at Santa Barbara, and the Clinical Research Imaging Centre (CRIC) at the University of Edinburgh. Neil Roberts and Alexa M. Morcom are members of the University of Edinburgh Centre for Cognitive Ageing and Cognitive Epidemiology, part of the cross-council Lifelong Health and Wellbeing Initiative (grant G0700704/84698).

REFERENCES

Alluri, V., Toiviainen, P., Jääskeläinen, I. P., Glerean, E., Sams, M., and Brattico, E. (2012). Large-scale brain networks emerge from dynamic processing of musical timbre, key and rhythm. *Neuroimage* 59, 3677–3689. doi:10.1016/j.neuroimage.2011.11.019

Ashburner, J., and Friston, K. J. (2005). Unified segmentation. *Neuroimage* 26, doi:10.1016/j.neuroimage.2005.02.018

Bernard, J. A., Seidler, R. D., Hassevoort, K. M., Benson, B. L., Welsh, R. C., Wiggins, J. L., et al. (2012). Resting state cortico-cerebellar functional connectivity networks: a comparison of anatomical and self-organizing map approaches. *Front. Neuroanat.* 6:31. doi:10.3389/fnana.2012.00031

Bood, R. J., Nijssen, M., van der Kamp, J., and Roerdink, M. (2013). The power of auditory-motor synchronization in sports: enhancing running performance by coupling cadence with the right beats. *PLoS ONE* 8:e70758. doi:10.1371/journal.pone.0070758

Bradt, J., Magee, W. L., Dileo, C., Wheeler, B. L., and McGilloway, E. (2010). Music therapy for acquired brain injury. *Cochrane Database Syst. Rev.* (7):CD006787. doi:10.1002/14651858.CD006787.pub2

Brown, S., Martinez, M. J., and Parsons, L. M. (2006). The neural basis of human dance. *Cereb. Cortex* 16, 1157–1167. doi:10.1093/cercor/bhj057

Chen, J. L., Penhune, V. B., and Zatorre, R. J. (2008). Listening to musical rhythms recruits motor regions of the brain. *Cereb. Cortex* 18, 2844–2854. doi:10.1093/cercor/bhn042

Cichy, R. M., Heinzle, J., and Haynes, J. (2012). Imagery and perception share cortical representations of content and location. *Cereb. Cortex* 22, 372–380. doi:10.1093/cercor/bhr106

Cox, R. W. (1996). AFNI: software for analysis and visualization of functional magnetic resonance neuroimages. *Comput. Biomed. Res.* 29, 162–173. doi:10.1006/cbmr.1996.0014

Daselaar, S. M., Porat, Y., Huijbers, W., and Pennartz, C. M. A. (2010). Modality-specific and modality-independent components of the human imagery system. *Neuroimage* 52, 677–685. doi:10.1016/j.neuroimage.2010.04.239

de Dreu, M. J., van der Wilk, S. D., Poppe, E., Kwakkel, G., and van Wegen, E. E. H. (2012). Rehabilitation, exercise therapy and music in patients with Parkinson's disease: a meta-analysis of the effects of music-based movement therapy on walking ability, balance and quality of life. *Parkinsonism Relat. Disord.* 18(Suppl. 1), S114–S119. doi:10.1016/S1353-8020(11)70036-0

de Manzano, Ö., and Ullén, F. (2012). Activation and connectivity patterns of the presupplementary and dorsal premotor areas during free improvisation of melodies and rhythms. *Neuroimage* 63, 272–280. doi:10.1016/j.neuroimage.2012.06.024

Dirnberger, G., Frith, C. D., and Jahanshahi, M. (2005). Executive dysfunction in Parkinson's disease is associated with altered pallidal-frontal processing. *Neuroimage* 25, 588–599. doi:10.1016/j.neuroimage.2004.11.023

Edwards, T. C., Zrinzo, L., Limousin, P., and Foltynie, T. (2012). Deep brain stimulation in the treatment of chorea. *Mov. Disord.* 27, 357–363. doi:10.1002/mds.23967

Eickhoff, S. B., Stephan, K. E., Mohlberg, H., Grefkes, C., Fink, G. R., Amunts, K., et al. (2005). A new SPM toolbox for combining probabilistic cytoarchitectonic maps and functional imaging data. *Neuroimage* 25, 1325–1335. doi:10.1016/j.neuroimage.2004.12.034

Farrugia, N., Benoit, C., Harding, E., Kotz, S. A., and Dalla Bella, S. (2012). "BAASTA: battery for the assessment of auditory sensorimotor and timing abilities," in *Proceedings of the 12th International Conference on Music Perception & Cognition*, eds E. Cambouropoulos, C. Tsougras, P. Mavromatis, and K. Pastiades (Thessaloniki: School of Music Studies, Aristotle University of Thessaloniki), 292.

Follett, K. A., Weaver, F. M., Stern, M., Hur, K., Harris, C. L., Luo, P., et al. (2010). Pallidal versus subthalamic deep-brain stimulation for Parkinson's disease. *N. Engl. J. Med.* 362, 2077–2091. doi:10.1056/NEJMoa0907083

Friedman, M. (1937). The use of ranks to avoid the assumption of normality implicit in the analysis of variance. *J. Am. Stat. Assoc.* 32, 675–701. doi:10.1080/01621459.1937.10503522

Friston, K. J., Fletcher, P., Josephs, O., Holmes, A., Rugg, M. D., and Turner, R. (1998). Event-related fMRI: characterizing differential responses. *Neuroimage* 7, 30–40. doi:10.1006/nimg.1997.0306

Friston, K. J., Glaser, D. E., Henson, R. N., Kiebel, S., Phillips, C., and Ashburner, J. (2002). Classical and Bayesian inference in neuroimaging: applications. *Neuroimage* 16, 484–512. doi:10.1006/nimg.2002.1091

Fujii, S., and Schlaug, G. (2013). The Harvard beat assessment test (H-BAT): a battery for assessing beat perception and production and their dissociation. *Front. Hum. Neurosci.* 7:771. doi:10.3389/fnhum.2013.00771

Geevarghese, R., Lumsden, D. E., Hulse, N., Samuel, M., and Ashkan, K. (2014). Subcortical structure volumes and correlation to clinical variables in Parkinson's disease. *J. Neuroimaging.* doi:10.1111/jon.12095

Grahn, J. A., and Brett, M. (2007). Rhythm and beat perception in motor areas of the brain. *J. Cogn. Neurosci.* 19, 893–906. doi:10.1162/jocn.2007.19.5.893

Halpern, A. R., and Zatorre, R. J. (1999). When that tune runs through your head: a PET investigation of auditory imagery for familiar melodies. *Cereb. Cortex* 9, 697–704. doi:10.1093/cercor/9.7.697

Herholz, S. C., Halpern, A. R., and Zatorre, R. J. (2012). Neuronal correlates of perception, imagery, and memory for familiar tunes. *J. Cogn. Neurosci.* 24, 1382–1397. doi:10.1162/jocn_a_00216

Herholz, S. C., Lappe, C., Knief, A., and Pantev, C. (2008). Neural basis of music imagery and the effect of musical expertise. *Eur. J. Neurosci.* 28, 2352–2360. doi:10.1111/j.1460-9568.2008.06515.x

Holmes, A. P., and Friston, K. J. (1998). Generalisability, random effects and population inference. *Neuroimage* 7, 754.

Honing, H. (2012). Without it no music: beat induction as a fundamental musical trait. *Ann. N. Y. Acad. Sci.* 1252, 85–91. doi:10.1111/j.1749-6632.2011.06402.x

Ivry, R. B., and Keele, S. W. (1989). Timing functions of the cerebellum. *J. Cogn. Neurosci.* 1, 136–152. doi:10.1162/jocn.1989.1.2.136

Karageorghis, C. I., Priest, D. L., Williams, L. S., Hirani, R. M., Lannon, K. M., and Bates, B. J. (2010). Ergogenic and psychological effects of synchronous music during circuit-type exercise. *Psychol. Sport Exerc.* 11, 551–559. doi:10.1016/j.psychsport.2010.06.004

Kosslyn, S. M., Ganis, G., and Thompson, W. L. (2001). Neural foundations of imagery. *Nat. Rev. Neurosci.* 2, 635–642. doi:10.1038/35090055

Kraemer, D. J. M., Macrae, C. N., Green, A. E., and Kelley, W. M. (2005). Sound of silence activates auditory cortex. *Nature* 434, 158. doi:10.1038/434158a

Kupsch, A., Benecke, R., Müller, J., Trottenberg, T., Schneider, G.-H., Poewe, W., et al. (2006). Pallidal deep-brain stimulation in primary generalized or segmental dystonia. *N. Engl. J. Med.* 355, 1978–1990. doi:10.1056/NEJMoa063618

Leaver, A. M., Van Lare, J., Zielinski, B., Halpern, A. R., and Rauschecker, J. P. (2009). Brain activation during anticipation of sound sequences. *J. Neurosci.* 29, 2477–2485. doi:10.1523/JNEUROSCI.4921-08.2009

Leman, M., Moelants, D., Varewyck, M., Styns, F., van Noorden, L., and Martens, J.-P. (2013). Activating and relaxing music entrains the speed of beat synchronized walking. *PLoS ONE* 8:e67932. doi:10.1371/journal.pone.0067932

Mai, J. K., and Forutan, F. (2012). "Thalamus," in *The Human Nervous System*, 3rd Edn, eds J. K. Mai and G. Paxinos (San Diego: Academic Press), 618–677. doi:10.1016/B978-0-12-374236-0.10019-7

Maldjian, J. A., Laurienti, P. J., Kraft, R. A., and Burdette, J. H. (2003). An automated method for neuroanatomic and cytoarchitectonic atlas-based interrogation of fMRI data sets. *Neuroimage* 19, 1233–1239. doi:10.1016/S1053-8119(03)00169-1

Malouin, F., Richards, C. L., Jackson, P. L., Lafleur, M. F., Durand, A., and Doyon, J. (2007). The kinesthetic and visual imagery questionnaire (KVIQ) for assessing motor imagery in persons with physical disabilities: a reliability and construct validity study. *J. Neurol. Phys. Ther.* 31, 20–29. doi:10.1097/01.NPT.0000260567.24122.64

Moelants, D. (2003). "Dance music: movement and tempo preferences," in *Proceedings of the 5th Triennial ESCOM Conference*, eds R. Kopiez, A. C. Lehmann, I. Wolther, and C. Wolf (Hanover: Hanover University of Music and Drama), 649–652.

Nachev, P., Kennard, C., and Husain, M. (2008). Functional role of the supplementary and pre-supplementary motor areas. *Nat. Rev. Neurosci.* 9, 856–869. doi:10.1038/nrn2478

Oldfield, R. C. (1971). The assessment and analysis of handedness: the Edinburgh inventory. *Neuropsychologia* 9, 97–113. doi:10.1016/0028-3932(71)90067-4

Olivetti Belardinelli, M., Palmiero, M., Sestieri, C., Nardo, D., Di Matteo, R., Londei, A., et al. (2009). An fMRI investigation on image generation in different sensory modalities: the influence of vividness. *Acta Psychol.* 132, 190–200. doi:10.1016/j.actpsy.2009.06.009

Oosterhof, N. N., Tipper, S. P., and Downing, P. E. (2012). Visuo-motor imagery of specific manual actions: a multi-variate pattern analysis fMRI study. *Neuroimage* 63, 262–271. doi:10.1016/j.neuroimage.2012.06.045

O'Reilly, J. X., Mesulam, M. M., and Nobre, A. C. (2008). The cerebellum predicts the timing of perceptual events. *J. Neurosci.* 28, 2252–2260. doi:10.1523/JNEUROSCI.2742-07.2008

Pecenka, N., Engel, A., and Keller, P. E. (2012). Neural correlates of auditory temporal predictions during sensorimotor synchronization. *Front. Hum. Neurosci.* 7:380. doi:10.3389/fnhum.2013.00380

Penny, W., and Holmes, A. (2006). "Random effects analysis," in *Statistical Parametric Mapping: The Analysis of Functional Brain Images*, eds K. Friston, J. Ashburner, S. Kiebel, T. Nichols, and W. Penny (London: Elsevier), 156–165.

Peretz, I., and Zatorre, R. J. (2005). Brain organization for music processing. *Annu. Rev. Psychol.* 56, 89–114. doi:10.1146/annurev.psych.56.091103.070225

Pfurtscheller, G., Brunner, C., Schlogl, A., and da Silva, F. H. L. (2006). Mu rhythm (de)synchronization and EEG single-trial classification of different motor imagery tasks. *Neuroimage* 31, 153–159. doi:10.1016/j.neuroimage.2005.12.003

Priori, A., Giannicola, G., Rosa, M., Marceglia, S., Servello, D., Sassi, M., et al. (2013). Deep brain electrophysiological recordings provide clues to the pathophysiology of Tourette syndrome. *Neurosci. Biobehav. Rev.* 37, 1063–1068. doi:10.1016/j.neubiorev.2013.01.011

Satoh, M., and Kuzuhara, S. (2008). Training in mental singing while walking improves gait disturbance in Parkinson's disease patients. *Eur. Neurol.* 60, 237–243. doi:10.1159/000151699

Schaal, S., Sternad, D., Osu, R., and Kawato, M. (2004). Rhythmic arm movement is not discrete. *Nat. Neurosci.* 7, 1137–1145. doi:10.1038/nn1322

Schaefer, R. S. (in press). Auditory rhythmic cueing in movement rehabilitation: findings and possible mechanisms. *Philos. Trans. R. Soc. Lond. B.*

Schaefer, R. S., Desain, P., and Farquhar, J. (2013). Shared processing of perception and imagery of music in decomposed EEG. *Neuroimage* 70, 317–326. doi:10.1016/j.neuroimage.2012.12.064

Schaefer, R. S., Desain, P., and Suppes, P. (2009). Structural decomposition of EEG signatures of melodic processing. *Biol. Psychol.* 82, 253–259. doi:10.1016/j.biopsycho.2009.08.004

Schaefer, R. S., Vlek, R. J., and Desain, P. (2011a). Decomposing rhythm processing: electroencephalography of perceived and self-imposed rhythmic patterns. *Psychol. Res.* 75, 95–106. doi:10.1007/s00426-010-0293-4

Schaefer, R. S., Vlek, R. J., and Desain, P. (2011b). Music perception and imagery in EEG: alpha band effects of task and stimulus. *Int. J. Psychophysiol.* 82, 254–259. doi:10.1016/j.ijpsycho.2011.09.007

Schauer, M., and Mauritz, K. (2003). Musical motor feedback (MMF) in walking hemiparetic stroke patients: randomized trials of gait improvement. *Clin. Rehabil.* 17, 713–722. doi:10.1191/0269215503cr668oa

Schubotz, R. I., Friederici, A. D., and von Cramon, D. Y. (2000). Time perception and motor timing: a common cortical and subcortical basis revealed by fMRI. *Neuroimage* 11, 1–12. doi:10.1006/nimg.1999.0514

Schwartze, M., Keller, P. E., Patel, A. D., and Kotz, S. A. (2011). The impact of basal ganglia lesions on sensorimotor synchronization, spontaneous motor tempo, and the detection of tempo changes. *Behav. Brain Res.* 216, 685–691. doi:10.1016/j.bbr.2010.09.015

Sheehan, P. W. (1967). A shortened form of Betts' questionnaire upon mental imagery. *J. Clin. Psychol.* 23, 386–389. doi:10.1002/1097-4679(196707)23:3<386::AID-JCLP2270230328>3.0.CO;2-S

Stoodley, C. J., and Schmahmann, J. D. (2009). Functional topography in the human cerebellum: a meta-analysis of neuroimaging studies. *Neuroimage* 44, 489–501. doi:10.1016/j.neuroimage.2008.08.039

Thaut, M. H., Kenyon, G. P., Hurt, C. P., McIntosh, G. C., and Hoemberg, V. (2002). Kinematic optimization of spatiotemporal patterns in paretic arm training with stroke patients. *Neuropsychologia* 40, 1073–1081. doi:10.1016/S0028-3932(01)00141-5

Tierney, A., and Kraus, N. (2013). The ability to move to a beat is linked to the consistency of neural responses to sound. *J. Neurosci.* 33, 14981–14988. doi:10.1523/JNEUROSCI.0612-13.2013

Toyomura, A., Shibata, M., and Kuriki, S. (2012). Self-paced and externally triggered rhythmical lower limb movements: a functional MRI study. *Neurosci. Lett.* 516, 39–44. doi:10.1016/j.neulet.2012.03.049

Tsang, E. W., Hamani, C., Moro, E., Mazzella, F., Lozano, A. M., Hodaie, M., et al. (2012). Movement related potentials and oscillatory activities in the human internal globus pallidus during voluntary movements. *J. Neurol. Neurosurg. Psychiatry* 83, 91–97. doi:10.1136/jnnp.2011.243857

Walsh, R. A., Sidiropoulos, C., Lozano, A. M., Hodaie, M., Poon, Y.-Y., Fallis, M., et al. (2013). Bilateral pallidal stimulation in cervical dystonia: blinded evidence of benefit beyond 5 years. *Brain* 136, 761–769. doi:10.1093/brain/awt009

Witt, S. T., Laird, A. R., and Meyerand, M. E. (2008). Functional neuroimaging correlates of finger-tapping task variations: an ALE meta-analysis. *Neuroimage* 42, 343–356. doi:10.1016/j.neuroimage.2008.04.025

Wittwer, J. E., Webster, K. E., and Hill, K. (2013). Effect of rhythmic auditory cueing on gait in people with Alzheimer disease. *Arch. Phys. Med. Rehabil.* 94, 718–724. doi:10.1016/j.apmr.2012.11.009

9

Individual differences in beat perception affect gait responses to low- and high-groove music

Li-Ann Leow*, Taylor Parrott and Jessica A. Grahn

The Brain and Mind Institute, University of Western Ontario, London, ON, Canada

****Correspondence:***
Li-Ann Leow, Department of Psychology, The Brain and Mind Institute, The Natural Sciences Centre, University of Western Ontario, London, ON N6A 5B7, Canada
e-mail: liann.leow@gmail.com

Slowed gait in patients with Parkinson's disease (PD) can be improved when patients synchronize footsteps to isochronous metronome cues, but limited retention of such improvements suggest that permanent cueing regimes are needed for long-term improvements. If so, music might make permanent cueing regimes more pleasant, improving adherence; however, music cueing requires patients to synchronize movements to the "beat," which might be difficult for patients with PD who tend to show weak beat perception. One solution may be to use high-groove music, which has high beat salience that may facilitate synchronization, and affective properties, which may improve motivation to move. As a first step to understanding how beat perception affects gait in complex neurological disorders, we examined how beat perception ability affected gait in neurotypical adults. Synchronization performance and gait parameters were assessed as healthy young adults with strong or weak beat perception synchronized to low-groove music, high-groove music, and metronome cues. High-groove music was predicted to elicit better synchronization than low-groove music, due to its higher beat salience. Two musical tempi, or rates, were used: (1) preferred tempo: beat rate matched to preferred step rate and (2) faster tempo: beat rate adjusted to 22.5% faster than preferred step rate. For both strong and weak beat-perceivers, synchronization performance was best with metronome cues, followed by high-groove music, and worst with low-groove music. In addition, high-groove music elicited longer and faster steps than low-groove music, both at preferred tempo and at faster tempo. Low-groove music was particularly detrimental to gait in weak beat-perceivers, who showed slower and shorter steps compared to uncued walking. The findings show that individual differences in beat perception affect gait when synchronizing footsteps to music, and have implications for using music in gait rehabilitation.

Keywords: gait rehabilitation, rhythmic auditory cueing, beat perception, basal ganglia, music rehabilitation, Parkinson's disease, rhythmic auditory stimulation

INTRODUCTION

Music and rhythm engage the motor system (Grahn and Brett, 2007; Chen et al., 2008a; Stupacher et al., 2013), ostensibly through extensive connections between the auditory and motor areas of the brain (Petrides and Pandya, 2006). The propensity of music to facilitate movement (Rossignol and Jones, 1976) has been exploited in gait rehabilitation, in which rhythmic auditory cues such as metronome tones are used to regulate movement (Rubinstein et al., 2002; Lim et al., 2005). In Parkinson's disease (PD), a disease characterized by death of basal ganglia dopaminergic neurons (Kish, 1988), rhythmic auditory cues show promise in improving gait impairments, which are not easily treated by pharmacological interventions (Rubinstein et al., 2002; Lim et al., 2005). Patients typically show slower gait than healthy controls, mainly because they have shorter stride lengths (Morris et al., 1994a), which result from deficient internal regulation of movement amplitude and movement timing (Morris et al., 1994a). Cueing-based interventions typically require patients to synchronize footsteps to metronome cues set at either their preferred step rate or slightly faster than preferred step rate (Spaulding et al., 2012). Cueing appears to ameliorate deficient internal regulation of movement timing, not movement amplitude, by regulating step rate (Morris et al., 1994b). However, as the primary reason for slowed gait in PD is from shortened step length (smaller movement amplitude), not from slower step rate (Morris et al., 1994b), step length does not consistently increase after auditory cueing (Lim et al., 2005). Furthermore, the effect sizes of auditory cueing are not large and benefits tend not to persist over time (Nieuwboer et al., 2007). Consequently, long-term functional improvements may require that cueing become a permanent part of patients' lives (Lim et al., 2005; Nieuwboer et al., 2007). If permanent auditory cues are required, then music, compared to metronome cues, might better motivate patients to adhere to rehabilitation regimes (de Bruin et al., 2010). Little, however, is known about exactly *what* auditory features of music, or even what task instructions, are most important to achieve the best functional outcomes in music-based therapies, limiting clinicians' ability to optimize music for gait interventions.

Most forms of music-based movement therapy instruct patients to synchronize movements in time with the "beat," or perceived pulse, in music. The beat is a regularly recurring perceived salience that arises in response to rhythm and music (Meyer and Cooper, 1960; London, 2012). The beat is not necessarily a strict property of a rhythmic stimulus, but rather is a psychological percept induced by the stimulus. This is why beats can be perceived through silent gaps in the music (Meyer and Cooper, 1960; London, 2012). The ability to perceive the beat differs widely across individuals (Grahn and McAuley, 2009; Grahn and Schuit, 2013; Sowinski and Dalla Bella, 2013; Launay et al., 2014). At the extreme end of the spectrum, case studies find some individuals so impaired at perceiving a beat that they are called "beat-deaf" (Phillips-Silver et al., 2011). However, less extreme impairments also exist (Grahn and McAuley, 2009). Poor beat perception is present in patients with PD as well as patients with focal basal ganglia lesions (Grahn and Brett, 2009; Schwartze et al., 2011). Not surprisingly, difficulty in perceiving the beat appears to result in difficulties in synchronizing movements to the beat in music (Phillips-Silver et al., 2011; Benoit et al., 2014). Hence, patients with PD and others with poor beat perception might benefit more from rehabilitation studies using auditory cues that have clear and unambiguous beats.

The clarity of the beat in music (i.e., beat salience) is associated with a musical characteristic called "groove" (Madison, 2006). Although groove is operationally defined as how much music evokes the desire to move (Madison, 2006), groove has also been consistently associated with greater beat salience, both when beat salience is assessed subjectively through participant ratings (Janata et al., 2012), as well as objectively through music analysis algorithms (Madison, 2006). Tapping to the beat of high-groove music is perceived to be easier than low-groove music (Madison, 2006; Janata et al., 2012). Therefore, synchronizing footsteps to the beat in high-groove music might help those with poor beat perception improve gait.

Apart from greater beat salience, high levels of groove might also improve gait by modulating an individual's affective state. In particular, high-groove music elicits higher arousal as well as a positive affective state (Janata et al., 2012). Even at rest, high-groove music modulates excitability of the motor system more than low-groove music (Stupacher et al., 2013). Gait is sensitive to changes in the state of affect and arousal (Naugle et al., 2011). Affective properties of music can evoke faster gait (Leman et al., 2013a). This might be because altering the affective state increases movement vigor, which is a greater willingness to expend more energy for movement, such as by moving more quickly or by increasing movement amplitude (Mazzoni et al., 2007). Therefore, in addition to increasing ease of synchronization to the beat, high-groove music might also increase arousal and positive affect, such that movements during synchronization are more vigorous (i.e., faster or larger).

Overall, then, beat perception ability, beat salience, and the affective properties of music may all affect gait parameters when synchronizing movements to music. These factors might, therefore, determine the extent to which patients benefit from music-cued rehabilitation. To gain a better understanding of how beat perception ability might affect gait in complex clinical populations who often show multiple cognitive and perceptual deficits, it is important to first understand how beat perception ability affects gait in neurologically intact healthy adults. Here, we examined how beat perception ability affected gait spatiotemporal parameters when healthy adults synchronized footsteps to the beat of low-groove music, high-groove music, and metronome cues. We predicted slower and more cautious gait (i.e., slower and wider strides) with low-groove music than with high-groove music, due to the low beat salience and low arousal properties of low-groove music. To evaluate whether gait changes in the high-groove condition were primarily due to high beat salience or physiological/arousal factors, we compared the high groove and metronome conditions. Metronomes have the highest beat salience, as only the beat is present. However, metronomes have not been shown to modulate physiological arousal or affective state. Thus, if high-groove music elicits similar gait changes as metronome cues, the changes are likely due to high beat salience. If high-groove music alters gait more than metronome cues, then the affective properties of high-groove music likely also contribute to gait changes.

Beat perception ability was assessed with a perceptual beat alignment test (BAT), which measures beat perception in music with no motor requirement, and is sensitive to individual differences in beat perception ability in the general population (Iversen, 2008; Müllensiefen et al., 2012). We hypothesized that beat perception ability would affect gait spatiotemporal parameters when synchronizing footsteps to the beat in music. We divided our group into "strong" and "weak" beat-perceivers based on their BAT performance. Strong beat-perceivers were predicted to successfully maintain gait velocity while synchronizing, as beat perception would not be difficult for them. Conversely, weak beat-perceivers were predicted to show slower and more cautious gait (i.e., slower strides) while synchronizing, as beat perception would be more difficult, and could create an attention-demanding "dual task." Finally, we predicted that the low-groove music condition would elicit slower and more cautious gait than the high-groove music condition, in both strong and weak beat-perceivers, due to its lower beat salience. We measured only the immediate effects of cueing on gait spatiotemporal parameters, not carryover effects [e.g., McIntosh et al. (1997)].

MATERIALS AND METHODS

PARTICIPANTS

Forty-three healthy undergraduate psychology students from the University of Western Ontario with self-reported normal hearing (age range 18–20, 24 females) participated in this study for course credit. One participant was excluded due to incomplete data. The study was approved by the Human Research Ethics Committee at the University of Western Ontario. All participants provided written informed consent.

PROCEDURE

Beat alignment test (BAT)

We used the BAT from the Goldsmiths Music Sophistication Index v1.0 (Müllensiefen et al., 2012), which is modeled after the original BAT (Iversen, 2008). We selected the BAT because it is brief and easy to implement, and is easily used in a clinical setting. In addition, the BAT assesses beat perception in the context of music, and is therefore more directly relevant to the current step synchronization task than other assessments of beat perception, which do not use music. In the test, participants decided whether metronome beeps superimposed over instrumental music clips were correctly aligned with the perceptual beat of that clip. Beeps were aligned to the beat in four trials. The remaining trials contained either (1) a tempo error (eight trials): beeps were 2% faster or slower than the true beat tempo, or (2) a phase error (five trials): beeps were ahead of the actual beat by 10 or 17.5% of the length of the beat interval. Participants completed 3 practice trials and 17 test trials. Stimulus order was randomized for each participant. After listening to the whole clip, participants were asked to judge whether the beeps were in time with the beat by pressing the "y" key to indicate yes and the "n" key to indicate no. Participants were also asked to rate their confidence in their answer (1 = not sure, 2 = somewhat sure, 3 = very sure). Participants completed three practice trials (1 aligned, 1 tempo error, 1 phase error) to familiarize themselves with the task.

Step synchronization task stimulus selection

The pool of step synchronization task stimuli were originally selected based on input from lab members. Ten lab members rated a range of unfamiliar musical clips on perceived groove, and a balanced set of high and low-groove clips was selected on the basis of these ratings. Relatively obscure music was selected because strong beat-perceivers may listen to music more often, and thus be more familiar with any well-known music clips than weak beat-perceivers. Obscure music would be equally unfamiliar to all participants. As the tempo of the beat in music can be subjective (McKinney and Moelants, 2006), three lab members with musical training tapped to the beat of each music clip to determine the tempo of each song. Music clips on which raters did not all tap the same tempo were removed from the set. This resulted in a set of 20 instrumental music clips, with 10 low-groove music clips and 10 high-groove music clips. From this set, six clips were selected for each participant in the experiment, using their individual ratings (see below). For a list of stimuli and details of the selection method, see the Supplementary Material. Clip loudness was normalized to the same relative volume using Audacity (Free Software Inc., Boston, USA). Metronome sequences were created using 50 ms 1 kHz sine tones. All auditory stimuli were trimmed to start on a beat.

Prior to starting the step synchronization task, each participant rated the 20 pre-selected music clips on groove, familiarity, and enjoyment on a 10-point Likert scale, so that the final selection of clips used in the step synchronization task was tailored to each participant's ratings. The rating scale items were as follows: (1) Groove: how much did the music make you want to move? 1 = did not want to move, 10 = very much wanted to move. (2) Familiarity: how familiar are you with the music clip? 1 = not at all familiar to me, 10 = very familiar to me. (3) How enjoyable is this piece of music? 1 = not at all enjoyable, 10 = very enjoyable. Based on individual ratings, the three music clips rated as lowest on groove and the three music clips rated as highest on groove were selected for each participant. To reduce the likelihood that familiarity with the music clip would confound the results, only low familiarity clips (ratings < 4 on familiarity) were used for the step synchronization task. Ratings data for the stimuli are listed in the Supplementary Material.

Step synchronization task procedure

First, each participant's preferred gait step rate (number of steps per minute) during uncued walking was determined by having the participant walk eight lengths of a 16 foot Zeno pressure sensor walkway (one "walk" was one length of the walkway) in silence. Previous studies using similar walkways have shown that six walks results in a sufficient number of steps for reliable estimation of gait parameters (Hollman et al., 2010).The sampling rate of the walkway was 120 Hz. The tempo of each auditory stimulus (low-groove music, high-groove music, and metronome cues) was adjusted in Audacity (Free Software Inc., Boston, USA) to two tempi: (1) the participant's preferred step rate and (2) 22.5% faster than the participant's preferred step rate. This faster rate was selected in accordance with previous step synchronization studies in older adults (Roerdink et al., 2011). Previous work with similarly large tempo manipulations (Fujii and Schlaug, 2013) has shown that Audacity successfully preserves pitch properties of the stimuli. Auditory inspection of the stimulus waveforms did not reveal any hisses or clicks as a result of the tempo change. Participants completed 18 walking trials under the following cue conditions: low-groove music (three trials), high-groove music (three trials), and metronome sequences (three trials). Due to a technical error, for 18 participants, only 1 metronome trial was collected. One stimulus was played during each trial, and trials were completed in random order. Participants were allowed as much time as needed to find the beat before starting to walk. To reduce the effects of acceleration and deceleration on steady-state gait, walks started and finished at a line marked 1 m beyond the end of the mat, and participants were instructed to continue stepping to the beat when turning at the marked line. To prevent fatigue, participants were allowed as much time as necessary to rest between trials. Each test session lasted approximately 1 h.

DATA ANALYSIS

Synchronization performance

Synchronization is typically measured by assessing both phase-matching performance (the extent to which the phase of the steps matches the phase of the beats) and period-matching performance (the extent to which the tempo of the steps matches the tempo of the beats). However, we were only able to evaluate period matching performance, not phase-matching performance for the following reasons. First, it is unknown whether subjects aim to synchronize the first contact time of their step (e.g., heel-strike), the last contact time of their step (e.g., toe-offset), or some time point between the heel-strike and the toe-offset, to the beat. Synchronizing the heel-strike or the toe-offset can result in significant differences in synchronization accuracy (Chen et al., 2006). Furthermore, we do not know whether the synchronization time point within each footfall is consistent between individuals, or even between walking trials from the same individual. An estimation method that assumes that all subjects consistently synchronize at the same time point could systematically bias the data if strong beat-perceivers and weak beat-perceivers differed in their point of synchronization. Second, we could not confidently estimate beat onsets for all the music clips. Beat onsets can be irregular due to common tempo changes in music. One option is to ask musically trained individuals to tap to the music, and use those times as beat times; however, this method assumes that musically trained individuals will tap on the beat with complete accuracy and consistency throughout the full set of music clips. We attempted to objectively estimate beat onsets with beat-tracking software (BeatRoot) (Dixon, 2007), but found that BeatRoot was inaccurate in estimating the beat locations of two low-groove songs and one high-groove song. These songs were used in at least 15% of all trials across participants. Similar occasional beat-tracking inaccuracies have been noted by BeatRoot's authors (Dixon, 2007). Finally, due to a technical problem, stimulus onset was accurately time-locked with step recordings of the pressure sensor mat for only a subset of participants: 18 weak beat-perceivers and 8 strong beat-perceivers. The small numbers of strong beat-perceivers made it unfeasible to statistically compare phase-matching performance between strong and weak beat-perceivers. We did explore phase synchronization performance using circular asynchronies across the remaining 26 datasets, assuming heel-strike as the first synchronization point, similar to previous work (McIntosh et al., 1997). These analyses yielded variable results (see Table S1 in Supplementary Material), perhaps unsurprisingly given the caveats above. We, therefore, limited our reported analyses to period-matching performance.

Period-matching performance

Ability to match step tempo to the stimulus tempo (i.e., period-matching accuracy) was assessed using the interbeat interval deviation (IBI deviation), which quantified how well step tempo was matched to the beat tempo on each trial (Chen et al., 2008b; Giovannelli et al., 2014). First, an automatic algorithm matched the first contact time of each step to the closest beat. Then, interstep intervals were calculated by subtracting the first contact times of consecutive steps. Interbeat intervals were calculated by subtracting beat onset times of consecutive beats. The IBI deviation was calculated by taking the absolute difference between each interstep interval and the corresponding interbeat interval. Then, to control for differences in interbeat intervals for different cue tempi, the IBI deviation was normalized to the mean interbeat interval for that trial – the absolute difference was divided by the mean interbeat interval (1).

$$\text{IBI deviation} = \frac{|\text{ mean interstep interval} - \text{interbeat interval }|}{\text{mean interbeat interval}} \tag{1}$$

Variability of period matching was assessed using the standard deviation of the IBI deviation.

Spatiotemporal gait parameters

Based on previous gait studies (Hollman et al., 2011), six gait parameters of interest were selected for analysis: stride velocity, step length, step time, double support time, stride width, and step length coefficient of variability. Gait speed was determined from stride velocity [the distance covered per unit time (cm/s) for every two consecutive steps]. Step length was the anterior–posterior distance from the first contact location of one step to the first contact location of the next step. Step time was the interval between the first contact time of one footprint to the first contact time of the next footprint. Thus, changes in velocity could result from changes in step length and/or changes in step time. In addition, to assess the attentional demands of gait synchronization, we also assessed double support time (% of time that both feet were simultaneously in contact with the ground), stride width distance between a line connecting two ipsilateral foot heel contacts (the stride) and the contralateral foot heel contact between those events, measured perpendicular to the stride, and step length coefficient of variation (standard deviation of step length normalized to the mean step length) (Hollman et al., 2011). Longer double support time, wider strides, and greater step length variability are associated with more cautious gait as a result of greater attentional demand during gait (Al-Yahya et al., 2011).

Statistical analyses

We were interested in how gait changed during the different music and metronome conditions compared to uncued walking. Hence, we obtained change scores of each gait parameter by subtracting the average gait parameters in each stimulus condition from the average gait parameters in uncued walking (Rochester et al., 2005). Then, to enable comparisons across individuals to be made on the same scale (e.g., a long-legged participant who takes long steps may have a greater absolute difference in step length than a short-legged participant who takes short steps), we normalized these change scores to gait parameters obtained from uncued walking.

$$\text{Normalized change score} = \frac{\text{Gait parameter} - \text{Uncued gait parameter}}{\text{Uncued gait parameter}} \tag{2}$$

To evaluate how beat perception ability affected gait synchronization to low-groove music, high-groove music, and metronome, Beat Perception (weak, strong beat-perceivers) by Cue (low groove, high groove, metronome) by Tempo (preferred step rate, faster step rate) mixed-measures ANOVAs were conducted for each gait parameter of interest. The Greenhouse-Geisser correction was applied when Mauchly's test of sphericity was significant. Pairwise comparisons using Dunn-Sidak corrections for multiple comparisons identified significant differences between conditions.

RESULTS

BEAT ALIGNMENT TEST SCORES

Beat alignment test scores were calculated as the proportion correct from all 17 trials. Scores ranged from 0.47 to 1, $M = 0.69$, $SD = 0.15$, consistent with previous findings (Iversen, 2008; Grahn and Schuit, 2013). A split of 0.65 was used to classify participants as strong beat-perceivers (scores above 0.65, $n = 19$) and weak beat-perceivers (scores equal to or below 0.65, $n = 23$). The use of the 0.65 split was justified by similar BAT median scores in other versions of the BAT (Iversen, 2008; Grahn and Schuit, 2013). Strong beat-perceivers had more years of musical training ($M = 5.11$, $SD = 4.45$, $SEM = 1.05$) than weak beat-perceivers ($M = 2.91$, $SD = 3.51$, $SEM = 0.74$), although this difference was not statistically significant [$t(39) = 1.77$, $p = 0.08$].

PERIOD-MATCHING PERFORMANCE

Figure 1, top panel, shows period-matching accuracy, or how well participants matched step tempo to cue tempo, as indicated by interbeat interval deviation. Smaller values indicate

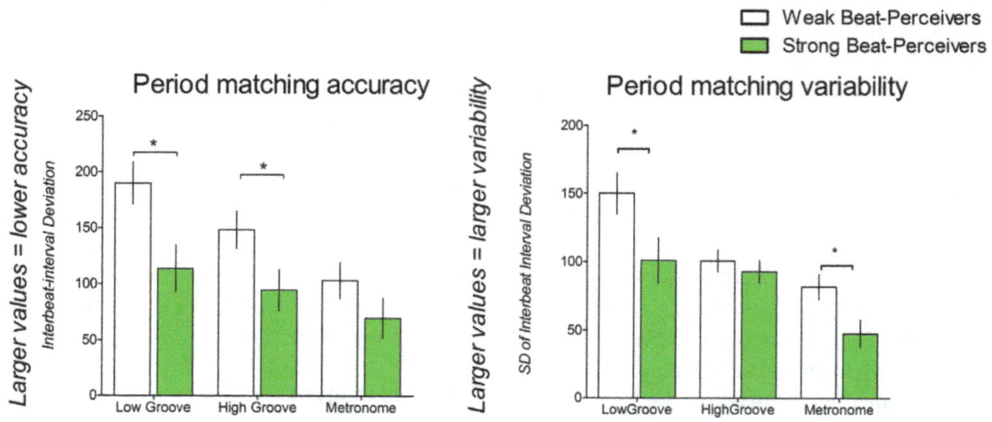

FIGURE 1 | Period-matching accuracy as estimated by IBI deviation, and period-matching variability as estimated by standard deviation of the IBI deviation. Weak beat-perceivers are shown in clear bars; strong beat-perceivers are shown in green bars.

more accurate period matching. Only the faster tempo condition was analyzed, as the cues at preferred tempo were specifically matched to each participant's preferred step tempo; therefore, the periods were expected to match regardless of synchronization ability. Weak beat-perceivers were worse at matching step tempo to the cue tempo than strong beat-perceivers (see **Figure 1**), as shown by a significant main effect of Beat Perception [$F(1,40) = 5.92$, $p = 0.02$, $\eta^2_p = 0.13$]. A significant main effect of Cue [$F(2,80) = 17.46$, $p < 0.001$, $\eta^2_p = 0.30$] indicates that period-matching accuracy differed between cue types. Period matching was best for metronome cues (86.53 ± 12.06), followed by high-groove music (121.44 ± 12.43), and was worst for low-groove music (151.79 ± 14.04). All conditions differed significantly from each other. Period matching was significantly less accurate for low-groove music compared to high-groove music ($p = 0.001$), and for low-groove music compared to metronome cues ($p < 0.001$). Period matching was also significantly less accurate for high-groove music compared to metronome cues ($p = 0.003$). The Cue × Beat Perception interaction was not significant: [$F(2,80) = 1.89$, $p = 0.16$, $\eta^2_p = 0.04$], indicating that period matching in strong and weak beat-perceivers was similarly affected by the different cue types.

The variability of period matching was indicated by the standard deviation of the IBI deviation (see **Figure 1**), with smaller values indicating less variable period matching. Weak beat-perceivers showed more variable period matching for all cues than strong beat-perceivers, as shown by a significant main effect of Beat Perception [$F(1,40) = 5.79$, $p = 0.02$, $\eta^2_p = 0.13$]. A significant main effect of Cue [$F(2,80) = 20.88$, $p < 0.001$, $\eta^2_p = 0.34$] indicated that variability differed between cue types. Period matching was least variable for metronome cues (64.73 ± 6.71), followed by high-groove music (96.68 ± 5.87), and was most variable for low-groove music (125.50 ± 11.33). All conditions differed significantly from each other. Period matching was more variable for low-groove music compared to high-groove music ($p = 0.036$), and more variable for low-groove music compared to metronome cues ($p < 0.001$). Period matching was more variable for high-groove music than for metronome cues ($p < 0.001$). The Cue × Beat Perception interaction was not significant [$F(2,80) = 2.45$, $p = 0.09$, $\eta^2_p = 0.058$].

GAIT PARAMETERS FOR DIFFERENT CUE CONDITIONS

Descriptive statistics for gait parameters measured in each cue condition are shown in **Table 1**.

Stride velocity, step length, and step time

Figure 2 shows the normalized change scores for stride velocity, step length, and step time. Left panels of **Figure 2** show that at preferred tempo, weak beat-perceivers showed slower stride velocity than strong beat-perceivers across all three cue types. This was large because weak beat-perceivers (clear bars) tended to reduce step length during cueing, unlike strong beat-perceivers (green bars), who successfully maintained step length. Right panels of **Figure 2** show that at the faster tempo, weak beat-perceivers (clear bars) sped up stride velocity while shortening step length and step time (right panel, middle graph), indicating that weak beat-perceivers sped up stride velocity by taking faster but shorter steps, whereas strong beat-perceivers sped up stride velocity by taking faster steps of similar length to those during uncued walking. The main effects of Beat Perception were significant for stride velocity [$F(1, 40) = 5.15$, $p = 0.029$, $\eta^2_p = 0.11$] and near significant for step length [$F(1, 40) = 3.21$, $p = 0.08$, $\eta^2_p = 0.07$]. The main effects of Beat Perception were not qualified by any significant interactions with Cue or Tempo.

There were significant Cue × Tempo interactions for stride velocity [$F(2, 80) = 11.027$, $p < 0.001$, $\eta^2_p = 0.22$] and step length [$F(2, 80) = 3.21$, $p = 0.04$, $\eta^2_p = 0.07$]. This interaction was because high-groove music elicited similar stride velocity and step length to metronome cues at preferred tempo [stride velocity: $t(41) = 0.5$, $p = 0.62$, step length: $t(41) = 0.53$, $p = 0.60$], but elicited slower and shorter steps than metronome cues at the faster tempo [stride velocity: $t(41) = 2.99$, $p = 0.005$, step length: [$t(41) = 2.96$, $p = 0.005$]. Low-groove music elicited significantly slower and shorter steps than high-groove music and metronome (see **Figure 2**), both at preferred tempo

Table 1 | Means and standard deviations of gait parameters for each cueing condition when cue tempo was set at preferred step tempo and at 22.50% faster than preferred tempo, averaged across all participants.

	Preferred tempo	Faster tempo (22.50% faster)
STRIDE VELOCITY (CM/S)		
Uncued	95.4 (14.4)	N/A
Low groove	88.4 (16.8)*	93.3 (22.0)
High groove	95.5 (18.6)	107.7 (20.9)*
Metronome	95.2 (17.3)	103.8 (19.2)*
STEP LENGTH (CM)		
Uncued	61.9 (6.5)	N/A
Low groove	61.0 (7.4)*	61.2 (8.2)*
High groove	59.8 (7.4)	58.8 (8.0)*
Metronome	60.8 (7.0)	59.9 (7.7)
STEP TIME (S)		
Uncued	0.37 (0.17)	N/A
Low groove	0.41 (0.18)*	0.29 (0.24)*
High groove	0.37 (0.17)	0.34 (0.16)*
Metronome	0.37 (0.17)	0.22 (0.25)*
STRIDE WIDTH (CM)		
Uncued	7.0 (2.5)	N/A
Low groove	8.6 (2.9)*	8.5 (2.7)*
High groove	7.8 (2.9)*	8.0 (2.9)*
Metronome	8.1 (2.7)*	7.2 (2.4)
DOUBLE SUPPORT (%)		
Uncued	25.62 (2.82)	N/A
Low groove	25.55 (3.04)	25.22 (3.18)
High groove	25.26 (3.23)	24.92 (3.49)
Metronome	24.97 (3.13)*	24.23 (3.33)*
STRIDE LENGTH VARIABILITY (CV)		
Uncued	0.051 (0.021)	N/A
Low groove	0.068 (0.022)*	0.070 (0.027)*
High groove	0.062 (0.018)*	0.072 (0.026)*
Metronome	0.055 (0.019)	0.057 (0.015)

Asterisks (*) indicate that the gait parameter for the cueing condition differed significantly ($p < 0.05$) from uncued gait.

[stride velocity: $t(41) = 4.62$, $p < 0.001$, step length $t(41) = 2.43$, $p = 0.019$] and at faster tempo [$t(41) = 5.60$, $p < 0.001$, step length $t(41) = 2.14$, $p = 0.039$].

For step time, there was a significant Beat Perception × Cue × Tempo interaction [$F(1,40) = 7.52$, $p < 0.001$, $\eta^2_p = 0.16$]. This three-way interaction was because, at preferred tempo, weak beat-perceivers slowed step times more than strong beat-perceivers with low-groove music [$t(25.29) = 1.99$, $p = 0.057$] but not with high-groove music [$t(40) = 0.97$, $p = 0.34$] and metronome cues [$t(40) = 0.77$, $p = 0.45$]. At the faster tempo, weak beat-perceivers sped up step times more than strong beat-perceivers with metronome cues [$t(40) = 2.47$, $p = 0.018$] but not with low-groove music [$t(40) = 1.07$, $p = 0.29$] or high-groove music [$t(40) = 0.82$, $p = 0.42$]. With faster tempo metronome cues, the markedly briefer step times in weak beat-perceivers were accompanied by reduced step length, and thus, the increase in stride velocity to fast metronome cues (**Figure 2**, top right panel, clear bars) was accomplished by taking shorter but faster steps.

Stride width, double support time, and stride length variability

Wider strides, longer double support time, and greater stride length variability indicate greater attentional demands and greater cautiousness during gait (Al-Yahya et al., 2011). **Figure 3** shows the normalized change scores for stride width, stride length variability, and double support time. For stride width, significant main effects of Beat Perception [$F(1,40) = 4.41$, $p = 0.04$, $\eta^2_p = 0.099$] and Cue [$F(2,80) = 9.64$, $p < 0.001$, $\eta^2_p = 0.19$] were qualified by a significant three-way Beat Perception × Cue × Tempo interaction [$F(1,40) = 3.27$, $p = 0.043$, $\eta^2_p = 0.076$]. At preferred tempo, weak beat-perceivers increased stride width more than strong beat-perceivers with low-groove music [$t(40) = 2.29$, $p = 0.027$], but not with high-groove music [$t(40) = 1.96$, $p = 0.056$], or with metronome cues [$t(40) = 1.45$, $p = 0.15$]. At the faster tempo, weak beat-perceivers increased stride width more than strong beat-perceivers with high-groove music [$t(40) = 2.71$, $p = 0.01$], but not with low-groove music [$t(40) = 1.61$, $p = 0.12$], or with metronome cues [$t(40) = 0.13$, $p = 0.9$].

For double support time, the main effect of Beat Perception was not significant [$F(1,40) = 2.05$, $p = 0.16$, $\eta^2_p = 0.05$], and there were no significant interactions between Beat Perception and other factors. There was a significant main effect of Cue [$F(2,40) = 7.85$, $p = 0.001$, $\eta^2_p = 0.16$], which was not qualified by any interactions, as both strong and weak beat-perceivers decreased double support time more with metronome cues than with low-groove music ($p = 0.001$) or high-groove music ($p = 0.049$).

For stride length variability, the marginally significant main effect of Beat Perception [$F(1,40) = 3.46$, $p = 0.07$, $\eta^2_p = 0.08$] was qualified by a significant Cue x Beat Perception interaction [$F(2,40) = 4.40$, $p = 0.015$, $\eta^2_p = 0.10$], as weak beat-perceivers showed greater increases in stride length variability than strong beat-perceivers with low-groove music [preferred: $t(40) = 1.84$, $p = 0.07$, faster: $t(40) = 2.22$, $p = 0.03$], and metronome cues [preferred: $t(40) = 2.79$, $p = 0.008$, faster: $t(40) = 1.96$, $p = 0.05$], but not with high-groove music [preferred: $t(40) = 0.71$, $p = 0.48$, faster: $t(40) = 0.11$, $p = 0.91$].

In summary, weak beat-perceivers showed larger increases in stride width and stride length variability than strong beat-perceivers, and this pattern of results was particularly evident with low-groove music.

DISCUSSION

The primary finding of this study is that individual differences in beat perception ability determined whether gait was maintained or impaired by synchronizing to music and metronome cues. Weak beat-perceivers showed slower gait than strong beat-perceivers, perhaps because weak beat-perceivers had more difficulty in synchronizing footsteps to the beat, as shown by poorer performance in period matching their step tempo to the cue tempo. Conversely, strong beat-perceivers showed faster gait than weak beat-perceivers, perhaps because strong beat-perceivers found it easier to synchronize footsteps to the beat, as shown

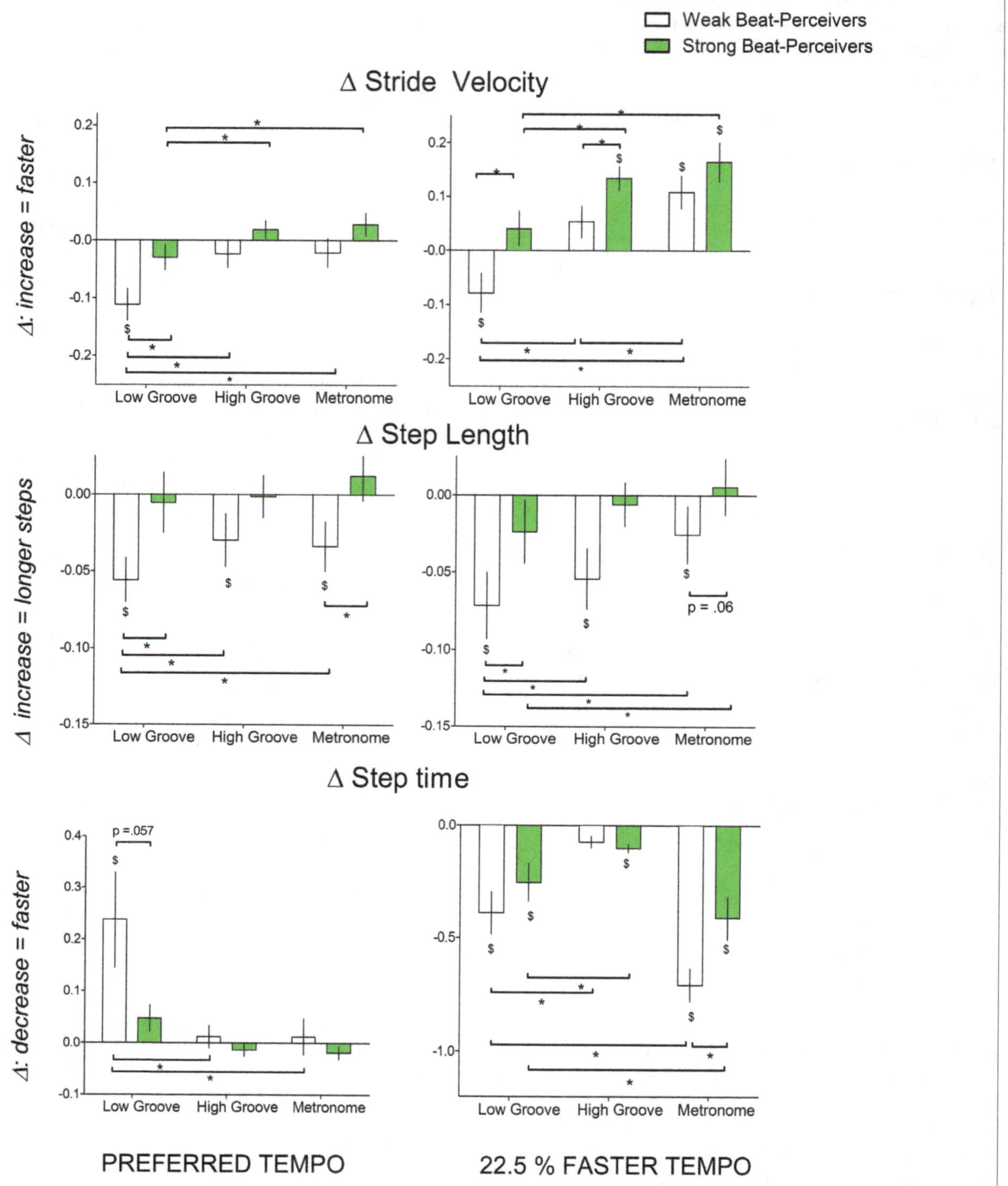

FIGURE 2 | Normalized change scores in gait parameters indicating gait speed (stride velocity (cm/s), step length (cm), step time (s)) with all three cue types (low-groove music, high-groove music, metronome cues) at different tempi: left panel, preferred tempo and right panel, faster tempo. All normalized change scores shown are a proportion of uncued gait. Weak beat-perceivers are shown in clear bars; strong beat-perceivers are shown in green bars. Values close to zero show that gait parameters showed little change compared to uncued walking. Dollar signs ($) indicate significant differences relative to uncued walking at $p < 0.05$. Asterisks (*) indicate significance differences at $p < 0.05$.

by better period-matching performance in strong beat-perceivers than weak beat-perceivers. Collectively, these findings suggest that beat perception ability may affect outcomes in music-based gait rehabilitation, particularly in patients with PD, who show beat perception deficits (Grahn and Brett, 2009), as well as cautious, less vigorous movement (Mazzoni et al., 2007).

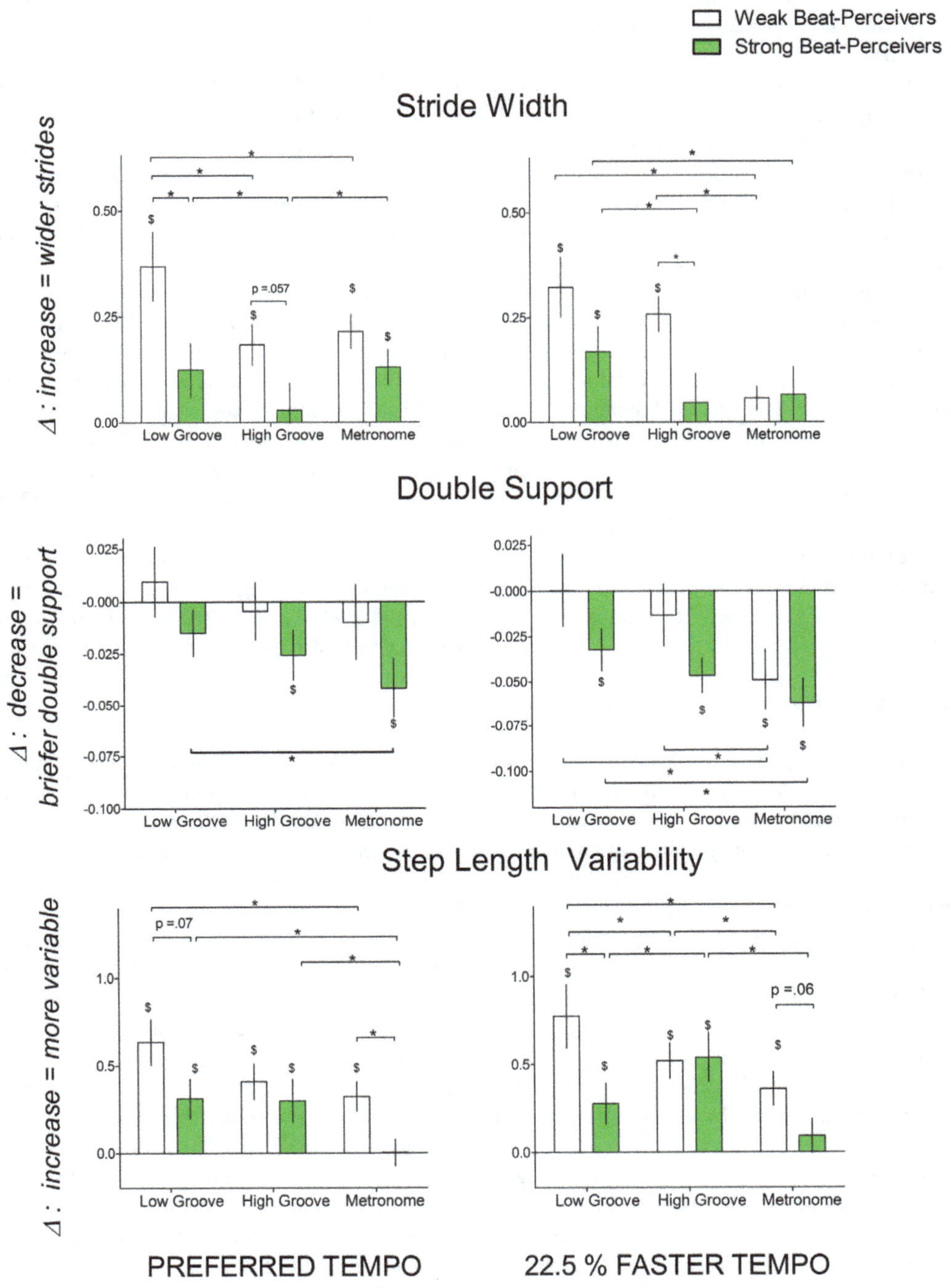

FIGURE 3 | Normalized change scores for gait parameters indicating the attentional demands of synchronization [stride width (cm), double support time (% of gait cycle), and step length variability] with each cue type (low-groove music, high-groove music, metronome cues) at different tempi: left panel, preferred tempo and right panel, faster tempo. All normalized change scores here are a proportion of uncued gait. Weak beat-perceivers are shown in clear bars; strong beat-perceivers are shown in green bars. Values close to zero show that gait parameters showed little change compared to uncued walking. Dollar signs ($) indicate significant differences relative to uncued walking at $p < 0.05$. Asterisks (*) indicate significance differences between conditions at $p < 0.05$.

GAIT RESPONSES TO AUDITORY CUES DEPEND ON BEAT PERCEPTION ABILITY

Weak beat-perceivers showed overall slower, shorter, and wider steps than strong beat-perceivers when synchronizing to auditory cues, regardless of cue tempo. These effects were particularly evident with low-groove music, which reduced step length at both preferred and faster tempos in weak beat-perceivers. Slower, shorter and wider strides are commonly evoked by greater attentional demands in dual task paradigms [for a review, see Al-Yahya et al. (2009)]. Therefore, the shorter, slower, and wider steps in weak beat-perceivers might be because synchronizing movements to auditory cues is more attention-demanding for weak beat-perceivers than strong beat-perceivers. Our findings suggest that for weak beat-perceivers, synchronizing footsteps to the beat might be an attention-demanding task that slows and shortens strides.

In weak beat-perceivers, negative effects of synchronization on gait parameters (e.g., step length and double support time) were evident even with metronome cues, when there was no need to extract the beat structure. Such findings appear at first glance to contradict previous studies that report that weak beat-perceivers show intact synchronization performance when tapping to metronome cues (Sowinski and Dalla Bella, 2013; Launay et al., 2014). However, as only the timing of finger tapping was assessed in these previous studies, it remains possible that weak beat-perceivers might alter spatial kinematics when tapping to metronome cues similarly to the gait alterations observed here. Walking might also be more sensitive than finger tapping to individual differences in beat perception ability – recent work has shown that reproducing a rhythm by walking is more difficult than by finger tapping or foot tapping (Iannarilli et al., 2013). Thus, gait synchronization may be more likely to be affected by poorer beat perception than finger tapping synchronization.

EFFECT OF CUE PROPERTIES ON SYNCHRONIZATION ACCURACY AND GAIT PARAMETERS

Low-groove music appears to be harder to synchronize to, and also to have a generally detrimental effect on gait. Tempo-matching was less accurate and more variable with low-groove music compared to high-groove music and compared to metronome, as low-groove music elicited larger and more variable deviations from interbeat intervals. This difficulty cannot be explained by differences in tempo, as the same tempo manipulations were done for low-groove music and high-groove music. Low-groove music was particularly detrimental to gait kinematics, as it elicited slower, shorter, and wider steps compared to uncued walking. High-groove music and metronome cues elicited similar effects on relevant gait parameters such as stride velocity and step length, suggesting that high-groove music might be a viable alternative to metronome cues.

Our finding that high-groove music did not elicit faster, longer steps than metronome cues appears inconsistent with previous findings of faster stride velocity with music than with metronome cues (Styns et al., 2007; Leman et al., 2013b). Several methodological differences might explain the difference in results. First, highly familiar music was used in these previous studies (Styns et al., 2007), unlike the current study, which used unfamiliar music. Familiarity with the beat structure of the music might increase the ease of extracting the beat and synchronization to the beat, therefore, reducing the attentional demands of synchronization that could counteract positive effects of groove on step length. Studies that directly compare the effects of low and high familiarity music would be needed to determine whether familiarity is important for high-groove music to elicit more beneficial effects than metronome cues. Another approach may be to accent the beat structure of low familiarity music with metronome cues. This would reduce the attentional demands of beat extraction, potentially improving gait outcomes, especially for weak beat-perceivers.

AUDITORY CUES INCREASED GAIT VELOCITY BY ALTERING STEP TIME, NOT STEP LENGTH

Under all cueing conditions, even when cue tempo was sped up, step length did not significantly increase compared to uncued walking. Stride velocity increased, but by decreasing step time, not by increasing step length. That is, participants moved faster, but by taking briefer and more frequent steps, not by taking longer steps. These findings are consistent with previous findings of shorter (Cubo et al., 2004; Dibble et al., 2004) or unaltered step lengths during synchronization to metronome cues, both for patients with PD (Morris et al., 1994a; Howe et al., 2003; Almeida et al., 2007) and healthy adults (Wittwer et al., 2013). These findings are important because the slowing of gait in PD results primarily from steps that are too short (Morris et al., 1994b, 1996), thus simply presenting faster cues may not help increase step length (Morris et al., 1994a). In fact, several studies suggest that metronome cueing only lengthens steps if patients with PD are also intentionally increasing step lengths while stepping in time to the cue (Nieuwboer et al., 2007; Baker et al., 2008; Rochester et al., 2011). Therefore, synchronizing footsteps to auditory cues might not be sufficient to elicit increased step length: intention to increase step length might also be necessary.

IMPLICATIONS FOR GAIT REHABILITATION IN PARKINSON'S DISEASE

In the current study, gait performance depended strongly on beat perception ability. The effects of beat perception ability might explain previous reports of variable outcomes of music-based rehabilitation in PD [for a review, see de Dreu et al. (2012)]. Functional neuroimaging studies demonstrate involvement of the basal ganglia in internally generating and maintaining the beat (Grahn and Rowe, 2013). Deficient basal ganglia function impairs beat perception in patients with PD (Grahn and Brett, 2009) and patients with focal basal ganglia lesions (Schwartze et al., 2011), suggesting that intact basal ganglia function might be necessary to perceive the beat. Difficulty generating and maintaining the beat could limit the ability of patients with PD to improve from rehabilitation paradigms when they are required to synchronize footsteps to the beat (Nombela et al., 2013). Weaker beat perception in patients with PD might further increase the attentional demand of synchronizing footsteps to the beat, thereby worsening gait in patients with PD, as they generally show weaker attentional control than healthy individuals when walking (Yogev et al., 2005).

For patients with PD with weak beat perception, synchronization to the beat in music might elicit weaker gait performance than synchronization to metronome cues. One way of reducing the difficulty of synchronization in weak beat-perceivers is to make the musical beat structure unambiguous by embedding metronome cues into music. This method of embedding music with metronome cues has previously elicited faster and longer strides in comparison to silence (Thaut et al., 1996; McIntosh et al., 1997) and in comparison to metronome cues alone (Wittwer et al., 2013). Music combined with metronome cues might therefore evoke additive effects that facilitate longer, faster strides. In addition, using familiar music might be beneficial, as familiarity with music and consequently familiarity with the beat structure might reduce the attentional demands of extracting the beat, such that gait might be less impaired in weak beat-perceivers. This is consistent with the finding that patients with PD increased stride velocity and stride length when they synchronized footsteps to the beat of highly familiar music for 30 min daily over 3 weeks (de Bruin et al., 2010).

LIMITATIONS

The BAT perception test is a brief measure of beat perception ability, but does not provide as much information as more extensive beat perception measures, such as the BAASTA (Benoit et al., 2014) or the Harvard BAT (Fujii and Schlaug, 2013). We also did not test for pitch perception deficits, which have previously been shown to result in difficulties with rhythm perception (Foxton et al., 2006). The BAT was selected because it uses ecologically valid music, similar to that used during walking, and it is brief, easily implemented, and also practical to administer in rehabilitation contexts. Even with these limitations, the categorization of strong and weak beat-perceivers revealed distinct gait responses when synchronizing to the beat: participants classified as weak beat-perceivers by this task showed overall worse gait performance when required to synchronize footsteps to the beat. The BAT perception test might, therefore, be useful in tailoring gait rehabilitation protocols for weak and strong beat-perceivers. While weak beat-perceivers might benefit from increasing the beat salience of music by embedding metronome cues into music, strong beat-perceivers might not require this, and embedding metronomes may even reduce their enjoyment of the rehabilitation. It remains to be seen if the BAT is sensitive enough to characterize beat perception ability in more variable populations such as older adults or neurologically impaired patients such as individuals with PD. In addition, the current study did not examine short-term carryover effects of cueing on gait, which have been reported for clinical populations such as PD (Thaut et al., 1996). Future examinations could determine which stimulus cue properties provide the longest persistence of carryover benefits in clinical populations.

Another limitation of this study, and our understanding of gait synchronization more generally, is that it is unclear which timepoint within each footfall is synchronized to the beat. In bipedal gait, each foot stays in contact with the ground for long periods of time (up to 800 ms in our data), and thus foot contact times can be longer than the interbeat interval. This contrasts with assessments of synchronization performance with finger tapping, in which the finger contact time is brief and discrete. In bipedal gait, participants could synchronize any timepoint between the first contact time (typically the heel-strike) and the last contact time of the step (the toe-off). Synchronizing using the heel-strike or the toe-off can result in significant differences in synchronization accuracy (Chen et al., 2006). Although previous work estimated synchronization performance using the first contact time (Thaut et al., 1996), there is no clear evidence that individuals intend for that to be the synchronized point. Furthermore, we do not know whether the synchronized time point is consistent between individuals, conditions, or even within each walking trial. To assess synchronization accuracy, future studies will need to determine what timepoint of the footfall is synchronized, and whether strong and weak beat-perceivers differ in their selection of the synchronization timepoint.

SUMMARY

The primary finding of this study is that beat perception ability affects whether gait performance is impaired or maintained when synchronizing footsteps to the beat in music. When synchronizing to auditory cues, strong beat-perceivers either maintained or improved gait performance, whereas weak beat-perceivers showed slower, more cautious gait, particularly with low-groove music, in which beat locations are less salient. High-groove music and metronome cues generally resulted in better gait performance than low-groove music in both weak and strong beat-perceivers. Taken together, these findings suggest that tailoring auditory cues according to patient beat perception ability in gait rehabilitation might elicit better outcomes.

REFERENCES

Almeida, Q. J., Frank, J. S., Roy, E. A., Patla, A. E., and Jog, M. S. (2007). Dopaminergic modulation of timing control and variability in the gait of Parkinson's disease. *Mov. Disord.* 22, 1735–1742. doi:10.1002/mds.21603

Al-Yahya, E., Dawes, H., Collett, J., Howells, K., Izadi, H., Wade, D. T., et al. (2009). Gait adaptations to simultaneous cognitive and mechanical constraints. *Exp. Brain Res.* 199, 39–48. doi:10.1007/s00221-009-1968-1

Al-Yahya, E., Dawes, H., Smith, L., Dennis, A., Howells, K., and Cockburn, J. (2011). Cognitive motor interference while walking: a systematic review and meta-analysis. *Neurosci. Biobehav. Rev.* 35, 715–728. doi:10.1016/j.neubiorev.2010.08.008

Baker, K., Rochester, L., and Nieuwboer, A. (2008). The effect of cues on gait variability – reducing the attentional cost of walking in people with Parkinson's disease. *Parkinsonism Relat. Disord.* 14, 314–320. doi:10.1016/j.parkreldis.2007.09.008

Benoit, C. E., Dalla Bella, S., Farrugia, N., Obrig, H., Mainka, S., and Kotz, S. A. (2014). Musically cued gait-training improves both perceptual and motor timing in Parkinson's disease. *Front. Hum. Neurosci.* 8, 494. doi:10.3389/fnhum.2014.00494

Chen, H. Y., Wing, A. M., and Pratt, D. (2006). The synchronisation of lower limb responses with a variable metronome: the effect of biomechanical constraints on timing. *Gait Posture* 23, 307–314. doi:10.1016/j.gaitpost.2005.04.001

Chen, J. L., Penhune, V. B., and Zatorre, R. J. (2008a). Listening to musical rhythms recruits motor regions of the brain. *Cereb. Cortex* 18, 2844–2854. doi:10.1093/cercor/bhn042

Chen, J. L., Penhune, V. B., and Zatorre, R. J. (2008b). Moving on time: brain network for auditory-motor synchronization is modulated by rhythm complexity and musical training. *J. Cogn. Neurosci.* 20, 226–239. doi:10.1162/jocn.2008.20018

Cubo, E., Leurgans, S., and Goetz, C. G. (2004). Short-term and practice effects of metronome pacing in Parkinson's disease patients with gait freezing while in the 'on' state: randomized single blind evaluation. *Parkinsonism Relat. Disord.* 10, 507–510. doi:10.1016/j.parkreldis.2004.05.001

de Bruin, N., Doan, J. B., Turnbull, G., Suchowersky, O., Bonfield, S., Hu, B., et al. (2010). Walking with music is a safe and viable tool for gait training in Parkinson's disease: the effect of a 13-week feasibility study on single and dual task walking. *Parkinsons Dis.* 2010, 483530. doi:10.4061/2010/483530

de Dreu, M. J., Van Der Wilk, A. S. D., Poppe, E., Kwakkel, G., and Van Wegen, E. E. H. (2012). Rehabilitation, exercise therapy and music in patients with Parkinson's disease: a meta-analysis of the effects of music-based movement therapy on walking ability, balance and quality of life. *Parkinsonism Relat. Disord.* 18(Suppl. 1), S114–S119. doi:10.1016/S1353-8020(11)70036-0

Dibble, L. E., Nicholson, D. E., Shultz, B., Macwilliams, B. A., Marcus, R. L., and Moncur, C. (2004). Sensory cueing effects on maximal speed gait initiation in persons with Parkinson's disease and healthy elders. *Gait Posture* 19, 215–225. doi:10.1016/S0966-6362(03)00065-1

Dixon, S. (2007). Evaluation of the audio beat tracking system beat root. *J. New Music Res.* 36, 39–50. doi:10.1080/09298210701653310

Foxton, J. M., Nandy, R. K., and Griffiths, T. D. (2006). Rhythm deficits in 'tone deafness'. *Brain Cogn.* 62, 24–29. doi:10.1016/j.bandc.2006.03.005

Fujii, S., and Schlaug, G. (2013). The Harvard Beat Assessment Test (H-BAT): a battery for assessing beat perception and production and their dissociation. *Front. Hum. Neurosci.* 7:771. doi:10.3389/fnhum.2013.00771

Giovannelli, F., Innocenti, I., Rossi, S., Borgheresi, A., Ragazzoni, A., Zaccara, G., et al. (2014). Role of the dorsal premotor cortex in rhythmic auditory-motor entrainment: a perturbational approach by rTMS. *Cereb. Cortex.* 24, 1009–1016. doi:10.1093/cercor/bhs386

Grahn, J. A., and Brett, M. (2007). Rhythm and beat perception in motor areas of the brain. *J. Cogn. Neurosci.* 19, 893–906. doi:10.1162/jocn.2007.19.5.893

Grahn, J. A., and Brett, M. (2009). Impairment of beat-based rhythm discrimination in Parkinson's disease. *Cortex* 45, 54–61. doi:10.1016/j.cortex.2008.01.005

Grahn, J. A., and McAuley, J. D. (2009). Neural bases of individual differences in beat perception. *Neuroimage* 47, 1894–1903. doi:10.1016/j.neuroimage.2009.04.039

Grahn, J. A., and Rowe, J. B. (2013). Finding and feeling the musical beat: striatal dissociations between detection and prediction of regularity. *Cereb. Cortex* 23, 913–921. doi:10.1093/cercor/bhs083

Grahn, J. A., and Schuit, D. (2013). Individual differences in rhythmic ability: Behavioral and neuroimaging investigations. *Psychomusicology* 22, 105–121. doi:10.1037/a0031188

Hollman, J. H., Childs, K. B., Mcneil, M. L., Mueller, A. C., Quilter, C. M., and Youdas, J. W. (2010). Number of strides required for reliable measurements of pace, rhythm and variability parameters of gait during normal and dual task walking in older individuals. *Gait Posture* 32, 23–28. doi:10.1016/j.gaitpost.2010.02.017

Hollman, J. H., Mcdade, E. M., and Petersen, R. C. (2011). Normative spatiotemporal gait parameters in older adults. *Gait Posture* 34, 111–118. doi:10.1016/j.gaitpost.2011.03.024

Howe, T., Lovgreen, B., Cody, F., Ashton, V., and Oldham, J. (2003). Auditory cues can modify the gait of persons with early-stage Parkinson's disease: a method for enhancing parkinsonian walking performance? *Clin. Rehabil.* 17, 363–367. doi:10.1191/0269215503cr621oa

Iannarilli, F., Vannozzi, G., Iosa, M., Pesce, C., and Capranica, L. (2013). Effects of task complexity on rhythmic reproduction performance in adults. *Hum. Mov. Sci.* 32, 203–213. doi:10.1016/j.humov.2012.12.004

Iversen, J. R., and Patel, A. D. (2008). "The beat alignment test (BAT): surveying beat processing abilities in the general population," in *Proceedings of the 10th International Conference on Music Perception and Cognition (ICMPC10).* eds K. Miyazaki, Y. Hiraga, M. Adachi, Y. Nakajima, and M. Tsuzaki. Sapporo. 465–468.

Janata, P., Tomic, S. T., and Haberman, J. M. (2012). Sensorimotor coupling in music and the psychology of the groove. *J Exp Psychol* 141, 54–75. doi:10.1037/a0024208

Kish, S. J. (1988). Uneven pattern of dopamine loss in the striatum of patients with idiopathic Parkinson's disease. *N. Engl. J. Med.* 318, 876–880. doi:10.1056/NEJM198804073181402

Launay, J., Grube, M., and Stewart, L. (2014). Dysrhythmia: a specific congenital rhythm perception deficit. *Front. Psychol.* 5:18. doi:10.3389/fpsyg.2014.00018

Leman, M., Moelants, D., Varewyck, M., Styns, F., Van Noorden, L., and Martens, J.-P. (2013a). Activating and relaxing music entrains the speed of beat synchronized walking. *PLoS ONE* 8:e67932–e67932. doi:10.1371/journal.pone.0067932

Leman, M., Moelants, D., Varewyck, M., Styns, F., Van Noorden, L., and Martens, J. P. (2013b). Activating and relaxing music entrains the speed of beat synchronized walking. *PLoS ONE* 8:e67932. doi:10.1371/journal.pone.0067932

Lim, I., Van Wegen, E., De Goede, C., Deutekom, M., Nieuwboer, A., Willems, A., et al. (2005). Effects of external rhythmical cueing on gait in patients with Parkinson's disease: a systematic review. *Clin. Rehabil.* 19, 695–713. doi:10.1191/0269215505cr906oa

London, J. (2012). *Hearing in Time.* Oxford University Press.

Madison, G. (2006). Experiencing groove induced by music: consistency and phenomenology. *Music Percept.* 24, 201–208. doi:10.1525/mp.2006.24.2.201

Mazzoni, P., Hristova, A., and Krakauer, J. W. (2007). Why don't we move faster? Parkinson's disease, movement vigor, and implicit motivation. *J. Neurosci.* 27, 7105–7116. doi:10.1523/JNEUROSCI.0264-07.2007

McIntosh, G. C., Brown, S. H., Rice, R. R., and Thaut, M. H. (1997). Rhythmic auditory-motor facilitation of gait patterns in patients with Parkinson's disease. *J. Neurol. Neurosurg. Psychiatry* 62, 22–26. doi:10.1136/jnnp.62.1.22

McKinney, M. F., and Moelants, D. (2006). Ambiguity in tempo perception: what draws listeners to different metrical levels? *Music Percep. Interdiscip. J.* 24, 155–166. doi:10.1525/mp.2006.24.2.155

Meyer, L., and Cooper, G. (1960). *The Rhythmic Structure of Music.* Chicago, IL: University of Chi-cago Press.

Morris, M. E., Iansek, R., Matyas, T. A., and Summers, J. J. (1994a). Ability to modulate walking cadence remains intact in Parkinson's disease. *J. Neurol. Neurosurg. Psychiatry* 57, 1532–1534. doi:10.1136/jnnp.57.12.1532

Morris, M. E., Iansek, R., Matyas, T. A., and Summers, J. J. (1994b). The pathogenesis of gait hypokinesia in Parkinson's disease. *Brain* 117, 1169–1181. doi:10.1093/brain/117.5.1169

Morris, M. E., Iansek, R., Matyas, T. A., and Summers, J. J. (1996). Stride length regulation in Parkinson's disease: normalization strategies and underlying mechanisms. *Brain* 119, 551–568. doi:10.1093/brain/119.2.551

Müllensiefen, D., Gingras, B., Stewart, L., and Musil, J. (2012). *The Goldsmiths Musical Sophistication Index (Gold-MSI): Technical Report and Documentation v1.0.* London: Goldsmiths, University of London.

Naugle, K. M., Hass, C. J., Joyner, J., Coombes, S. A., and Janelle, C. M. (2011). Emotional state affects the initiation of forward gait. *Emotion* 11, 267–277. doi:10.1037/a0022577

Nieuwboer, A., Kwakkel, G., Rochester, L., Jones, D., Van Wegen, E., Willems, A. M., et al. (2007). Cueing training in the home improves gait-related mobility in Parkinson's disease: the RESCUE trial. *J. Neurol. Neurosurg. Psychiatry* 78, 134–140. doi:10.1136/jnnp.200X.097923

Nombela, C., Hughes, L. E., Owen, A. M., and Grahn, J. A. (2013). Into the groove: can rhythm influence Parkinson's disease? *Neurosci. Biobehav. Rev.* 37, 2564–2570. doi:10.1016/j.neubiorev.2013.08.003

Petrides, M., and Pandya, D. N. (2006). Efferent association pathways originating in the caudal prefrontal cortex in the macaque monkey. *J. Comp. Neurol.* 498, 227–251. doi:10.1002/cne.21048

Phillips-Silver, J., Toiviainen, P., Gosselin, N., Piche, O., Nozaradan, S., Palmer, C., et al. (2011). Born to dance but beat deaf: a new form of congenital amusia. *Neuropsychologia* 49, 961–969. doi:10.1016/j.neuropsychologia.2011.02.002

Rochester, L., Baker, K., Nieuwboer, A., and Burn, D. (2011). Targeting dopa-sensitive and dopa-resistant gait dysfunction in Parkinson's disease: selective responses to internal and external cues. *Mov. Disord.* 26, 430–435. doi:10.1002/mds.23450

Rochester, L., Hetherington, V., Jones, D., Nieuwboer, A., Willems, A. M., Kwakkel, G., et al. (2005). The effect of external rhythmic cues (auditory and visual) on walking during a functional task in homes of people with Parkinson's disease. *Arch. Phys. Med. Rehabil.* 86, 999–1006. doi:10.1016/j.apmr.2004.10.040

Roerdink, M., Bank, P. J. M., Peper, C. L. E., and Beek, P. J. (2011). Walking to the beat of different drums: practical implications for the use of acoustic rhythms in gait rehabilitation. *Gait Posture* 33, 690–694. doi:10.1016/j.gaitpost.2011.03.001

Rossignol, S., and Jones, G. M. (1976). Audio-spinal influence in man studied by the H-reflex and its possible role on rhythmic movements synchronized to sound. *Electroencephalogr. Clin. Neurophysiol.* 41, 83–92. doi:10.1016/0013-4694(76)90217-0

Rubinstein, T. C., Giladi, N., and Hausdorff, J. M. (2002). The power of cueing to circumvent dopamine deficits: a review of physical therapy treatment of gait disturbances in Parkinson's disease. *Mov. Disord.* 17, 1148–1160. doi:10.1002/mds.10259

Schwartze, M., Keller, P. E., Patel, A. D., and Kotz, S. A. (2011). The impact of basal ganglia lesions on sensorimotor synchronization, spontaneous motor tempo, and the detection of tempo changes. *Behav. Brain Res.* 216, 685–691. doi:10.1016/j.bbr.2010.09.015

Sowinski, J., and Dalla Bella, S. (2013). Poor synchronization to the beat may result from deficient auditory-motor mapping. *Neuropsychologia* 51, 1952–1963. doi:10.1016/j.neuropsychologia.2013.06.027

Spaulding, S. J., Barber, B., Colby, M., Cormack, B., Mick, T., and Jenkins, M. E. (2012). Cueing and gait improvement among people with Parkinson's disease: a meta-analysis. *Arch. Phys. Med. Rehabil.* 94, 562–570. doi:10.1016/j.apmr.2012.10.026

Stupacher, J., Hove, M. J., Novembre, G., Schutz-Bosbach, S., and Keller, P. E. (2013). Musical groove modulates motor cortex excitability: a TMS investigation. *Brain Cogn.* 82, 127–136. doi:10.1016/j.bandc.2013.03.003

Styns, F., Van Noorden, L., Moelants, D., and Leman, M. (2007). Walking on music. *Hum. Mov. Sci.* 26, 769–785. doi:10.1016/j.humov.2007.07.007

Thaut, M. H., Mcintosh, G. C., Rice, R. R., Miller, R. A., Rathbun, J., and Brault, J. M. (1996). Rhythmic auditory stimulation in gait training for Parkinson's disease patients. *Mov. Disord.* 11, 193–200. doi:10.1002/mds.870110213

Wittwer, J. E., Webster, K. E., and Hill, K. (2013). Music and metronome cues produce different effects on gait spatiotemporal measures but not gait variability in healthy older adults. *Gait Posture.* 37, 219–222. doi:10.1016/j.gaitpost.2012.07.006

Yogev, G., Giladi, N., Peretz, C., Springer, S., Simon, E. S., and Hausdorff, J. M. (2005). Dual tasking, gait rhythmicity, and Parkinson's disease: which aspects of gait are attention demanding? *Eur. J. Neurosci.* 22, 1248–1256. doi:10.1111/j.1460-9568.2005.04298.x

10

Musically cued gait-training improves both perceptual and motor timing in Parkinson's disease

Charles-Etienne Benoit[1,2,3], Simone Dalla Bella[1,3,4]*, Nicolas Farrugia[2,5], Hellmuth Obrig[2,6], Stefan Mainka[7] and Sonja A. Kotz[2,8]*

[1] Department of Cognitive Psychology, University of Finance and Management in Warsaw, Warsaw, Poland
[2] Max Planck Institute for Human Cognitive and Brain Sciences, Leipzig, Germany
[3] Movement to Health Laboratory (M2H), EuroMov, Montpellier-1 University, Montpellier, France
[4] Institut Universitaire de France, Paris, France
[5] Goldsmiths, University of London, London, UK
[6] Clinic for Cognitive Neurology, University Hospital, University of Leipzig, Leipzig, Germany
[7] Neurologisches Fachkrankenhaus für Bewegungsstörungen/Parkinson, Beelitz-Heilstätten, Germany
[8] School of Psychological Sciences, The University of Manchester, Manchester, UK

Correspondence:
Simone Dalla Bella, Movement to Health (M2H) Laboratory, Institut Universitaire de France (IUF), University of Montpellier-1, EuroMov, 700 Avenue du Pic Saint Loup, Montpellier 34090, France
e-mail: simone.dalla-bella@univ-montp1.fr;
Sonja A. Kotz, Department of Neuropsychology, Max Planck Institute for Human Cognitive and Brain Sciences, Stephanstrasse 1a, Leipzig 04103, Germany
e-mail: kotz@cbs.mpg.de

It is well established that auditory cueing improves gait in patients with idiopathic Parkinson's disease (IPD). Disease-related reductions in speed and step length can be improved by providing rhythmical auditory cues via a metronome or music. However, effects on cognitive aspects of motor control have yet to be thoroughly investigated. If synchronization of movement to an auditory cue relies on a supramodal timing system involved in perceptual, motor, and sensorimotor integration, auditory cueing can be expected to affect both motor and perceptual timing. Here, we tested this hypothesis by assessing perceptual and motor timing in 15 IPD patients before and after a 4-week music training program with rhythmic auditory cueing. Long-term effects were assessed 1 month after the end of the training. Perceptual and motor timing was evaluated with a battery for the assessment of auditory sensorimotor and timing abilities and compared to that of age-, gender-, and education-matched healthy controls. Prior to training, IPD patients exhibited impaired perceptual and motor timing. Training improved patients' performance in tasks requiring synchronization with isochronous sequences, and enhanced their ability to adapt to durational changes in a sequence in hand tapping tasks. Benefits of cueing extended to time perception (duration discrimination and detection of misaligned beats in musical excerpts). The current results demonstrate that auditory cueing leads to benefits beyond gait and support the idea that coupling gait to rhythmic auditory cues in IPD patients relies on a neuronal network engaged in both perceptual and motor timing.

Keywords: Parkinson disease, auditory cueing, timing, motor behavior, perception

INTRODUCTION

Idiopathic Parkinson's disease (IPD) is one of the most common movement disorders. Although substantial progress has been made regarding the treatment of its cardinal motor symptoms, progressive brady- or akinesia, rigor, and tremor lead to disability and are a major challenge for the health care system (Elbaz et al., 2002). Clinically, gait disorder and postural instability leading to falls and fractures represent a major challenge for the patients as the disease progresses (Bloem, 1992; Koller and Montgomery, 1997; Grabli et al., 2012). However, even if motor deficits can be alleviated by a number of therapeutic regimes (Samii et al., 2004), cognitive and affective deficits emerge as additional challenges in the disease's progression. These may dramatically influence patients' quality of life and have been increasingly recognized to undermine independent living (e.g., Morris et al., 2001; Bloem et al., 2004).

While many motor symptoms in IPD can be alleviated by pharmacological treatment and deep-brain stimulation, effects on gait dysfunctions are rather meager, inconstant, and decrease over time (Blin et al., 1990; Grabli et al., 2012; Sharma et al., 2012). Therefore, physical therapy is an essential ingredient of IPD management. It is non-invasive, cost-efficient, and may slow the progress of the disease (Kwakkel et al., 2007). One way of compensating for gait disorders is the use of temporally predictable external cues (Lim et al., 2005; Spaulding et al., 2012). Rhythmic auditory cues have been shown to enhance gait spatio-temporal parameters such as speed and stride length (Lim et al., 2005). Typically patients are instructed to match their walking speed to a repeated isochronous sound (i.e., metronome) or to the beat of music (Thaut et al., 1996; McIntosh et al., 1997; Nieuwboer et al., 2007; de Bruin et al., 2010). Auditory cueing is efficient during stimulation (Howe et al., 2003; Willems et al., 2006; Arias and Cudeiro, 2008), but has also been shown to carry over to uncued gait after training (Nieuwboer et al., 2007). Some studies report a reduction of its benefit between 4 and 6 weeks after training (Thaut et al., 2001) with considerable deterioration almost to pre-test values after 12 weeks post-intervention (Nieuwboer et al., 2001). Other studies reported stable cueing benefits even after 4–6 weeks (Marchese et al., 2000; Lehman et al., 2005).

The neuronal mechanism underlying the sustained benefits of cueing-based training is largely elusive. It has been suggested that coupling movement to an external rhythmic stimulus reinforces compensatory neuronal networks enhancing motor behavior in IPD (Nombela et al., 2013; see also Kotz and Schwartze, 2011). One candidate is the sensorimotor network underlying temporal processing. Structuring actions in time is a key element to achieve precise and stable coordinated movement such as gait. As IPD patients also display timing deficits (Hallett, 2008; Allman and Meck, 2012; Wu et al., 2012), one cause of gait dysfunctions in self-initiated and self-paced movements may be reduced by enhancing general timing functions. Indeed, dopamine depletion, a characteristic of this disorder, leads to malfunctioning of the basal-ganglia–cortical circuitry crucially involved in timing (Wing, 2002; Coull et al., 2011; Merchant et al., 2013). An external rhythmic cue may modulate the activity within the impaired timing system. Presenting an external temporally predictable cue, to which patients can synchronize their steps, provides a regularizing temporal input to the timing system.

External cues generate temporal expectations (e.g., via a process called "entrainment"; Jones, 1976; Large and Jones, 1999; Large, 2008) allowing to predict when a next event (e.g., a step) should occur. This may facilitate movement optimization and execution. Rhythm-driven expectations can regularize and stabilize movement by synchronizing the timing of an action execution to the beat structure of an auditory stimulus (e.g., Nombela et al., 2013). Since this process is probably supported by a neural circuitry less affected by IPD, it may compensate progressive malfunctioning of the basal-ganglia–cortical circuitry (e.g., Lewis et al., 2007). The compensatory system is likely to involve cerebello-thalamo-cortical circuitry (see also Kotz et al., 2009; Kotz and Schwartze, 2011; Nombela et al., 2013), a hypothesis which has received some support from studies with IPD patients. Cerebellar connections to the SMA are hyperactivated when action is externally cued (Sen et al., 2010). Moreover, activity of the cerebellar anterior lobule is enhanced following 1-month of cueing-based training (del Olmo et al., 2006).

The aforementioned circuitry is likely to support auditory cueing and its effects on gait kinematics, and is part of a domain-general system affording both perceptual and motor timing (Coull et al., 2011; Merchant et al., 2013; Schwartze and Kotz, 2013). Therefore, it is expected that auditory cueing may not merely improve motor control during gait, but more generally to enhance performance in tasks involving perceptual and motor timing (e.g., hand tapping or duration discrimination). Effects of auditory cueing beyond gait kinematics have not been systematically investigated so far. The goal of the present study was therefore to test whether a 1-month training of gait via auditory cueing enhances perceptual and motor timing. This hypothesis was tested by submitting a group of IPD patients to the Battery for the Assessment of Auditory Sensorimotor and Timing Abilities (BAASTA), a comprehensive set of tasks for the assessment of perceptual and motor timing abilities. Patients were tested before, right after, and 1 month following the training. Impairment prior to training was assessed in comparison to a group of healthy age-matched participants (controls) considered as baseline. Improvement in perceptual and motor timing was expected in response to external cueing. Moreover, as long-term benefits of auditory cueing on gait have been observed several weeks after training (Nieuwboer et al., 2007), we addressed the question whether improvement in timing abilities would similarly persist 1 month after the training.

MATERIALS AND METHODS

PARTICIPANTS

Fifteen right-handed non-demented patients (10 males) with IPD, aged 49–80 years ($M = 67.2$, $SD = 7.5$) participated in the study (see **Table 1**). Scores of the Unified Parkinson's Disease Rating Scale (UPDRS) and staging according to Hoehn and Yahr (H&Y) were assessed by an experienced neurologist (H.O.). Patients did not discontinue medication, and the levodopa equivalent daily dose was on average 363 mg. They were clinically assessed at the Clinic for Cognitive Neurology at the University Hospital in Leipzig, Germany. Patients showed moderate symptoms of IPD, with an average H&Y stage of 2 ($SD = 0.7$) and a UPDRS of 37.7 ($SD = 18.8$). Inclusion criteria were low scores (<5; $M = 1.29$) on the Geriatric Depression Scale (Yesavage et al., 1982), absence of a hearing impairment, absence of musical training as assessed by a customized questionnaire for musical aptitudes. Additional neuropsychological testing included the Token-test (De Renzi and Vignolo, 1962), the consortium to establish a registry for Alzheimer's disease (CERAD) (Welsh et al., 1994) and the Parkinson neuropsychometric dementia assessment (PANDA) (Kalbe et al., 2008). No other severe neurological or psychiatric illness was reported. Twenty (10 males) right-handed healthy adults, who matched the patients in age ($M = 66.4$, $SD = 7.8$) and education ($M = 14.4$ years; $SD = 3.0$) formed the control group. Healthy controls had no history of neurological or psychiatric disorders, showed no hearing impairments and did not actively practice music. All participants, recruited via the database of the Max Planck Institute for Human Cognitive and Brain Sciences, Leipzig, Germany, gave informed consent and were remunerated for their participation. The study was approved by the Ethics Committee of the University of Leipzig, Germany.

PROCEDURE

IPD patients took part in an auditory cuing training program. A 2-day assessment of perceptual and movement kinematics was administered before, after, and 1 month following the intervention. Controls were assessed only once. IPD patients were tested while they were in an ON-state. Details about the training program and the evaluation of perceptual and motor timing are provided in detail below.

TRAINING

The training sessions took place at the Day Clinic for Cognitive Neurology at the University of Leipzig. Patients were asked to walk while following a familiar German folk song. No explicit instructions to synchronize their footsteps to the beat of music were provided. The song was played without lyrics and the beat of the song was emphasized with a superimposed salient high-pitch bell sound. The beat rate of the auditory stimulus was set to ±10% of

Table 1 | Demographic and clinical characteristics for IPD patients and healthy controls.

	Patients		Controls	
	Mean (SD)	*n*	Mean (SD)	*n*
Demographics				
Females	–	5	–	10
Males	–	10	–	10
Handedness				
Right	–	15	–	20
Age	67.2 (7.5)	15	66.4 (7.8)	20
Years of education	14.7 (2.7)	15	14.4 (3.0)	20
Age at onset	59.3 (7.4)	15	–	–
Disease duration	7.9 (2.7)	15	–	–
Clinical Characteristics				
UPDRS				
I (mentation, behavior, and mood)	2.47 (1.8)	15	–	–
II (activities of daily living)	12 (6.11)	15	–	–
III (motor examination)	23.3 (12.4)	15	–	–
Total score	37.7 (18.8)	15	–	–
Hoehn and Yahr	2.0 (0.7)	15	–	–
0.5	–	1	–	–
1	–	2	–	–
2	–	6	–	–
2.5	–	5	–	–
3	–	1	–	–
Schwab and England	87.9 (5.8)	15	–	–
Medication				
L-Dopa LED	136.0 (159.3)	14	–	–
Ago LED	253.0 (201.2)	14	–	–
Total LED	363.0 (260.5)	15	–	–

a patient's spontaneous walking cadence as assessed prior to the first training session. The chosen beat rate [i.e., +10% ($n = 8$) or −10% ($n = 7$)] was the one which led to the longest step length as assessed in prior testing (Willems et al., 2006). Patients underwent three training sessions per week for 1 month. Medication was kept constant over the whole course of the study. Stimuli were delivered via a portable MP3-player (Sansa-Clip) and headphones (Sansa-Clip earbuds). Each training session lasted 30 min and consisted of three phases. In the first phase (10 min) the patient walked to the auditory rhythmic stimulus for 8 min. The stimulus was then stopped while the patient continued walking for 2 min at the same speed. In the second phase (10 min), the patient performed stop-and-go trials, in which the auditory stimulus was played for 30 s. At the end of the stimulus presentation, the patient stopped walking and restarted at the onset of the next stimulus presentation. During the last 2 min, the patient repeated the stop-and-go trials without the stimulus. The third phase (10 min) was the same as phase 1.

BATTERY FOR THE ASSESSMENT OF AUDITORY SENSORIMOTOR AND TIMING ABILITIES (BAASTA)

Patients and controls were submitted to the BAASTA, which consists of a series of perceptual timing and motor timing tasks sketched out below. The test battery was administered over 2 days.

PERCEPTUAL TIMING TASKS

The first three tasks (duration discrimination, anisochrony detection with tones, and anisochrony detection with music) allow estimating thresholds of duration discrimination of two tones and to detect an interval embedded in an isochronous sequence of tones or in a musical excerpt. Thresholds are estimated using a maximum-likelihood adaptive procedure (MLP) (Green, 1993) implemented in the MLP toolbox (Grassi and Soranzo, 2009) in MATLAB. Participants performed 3 blocks of 16 trials each. In each trial, the stimulus difference was changed adaptively depending on the participants' response. Thresholds corresponded to the midpoint of the psychometric curve defined as a probability of 63.1% of correct detection (Grassi and Soranzo, 2009). Stimuli were delivered via headphones (Sennheiser HD201) at a comfortable sound pressure level. A response was provided verbally by participants and entered by the experimenter via a computer keyboard. The tasks were preceded by four practice trials with feedback.

DURATION DISCRIMINATION

The goal of this test is to measure the ability to discriminate two subsequent durations. The participants are presented with pairs of pure tones (frequency = 1 kHz; interval between tones = 600 ms). The first tone lasts 600 ms (standard duration) while the second tone (comparison) varies between 600 and 1000 ms. The duration of the second tone is controlled by the MLP algorithm. Participants' task is to note if the second tone lasts "longer" than the first or has the "same" duration.

ANISOCHRONY DETECTION WITH TONES

This test assesses the sensitivity to time shifts (i.e., anisochrony) in a sequence of isochronous stimuli (Hyde and Peretz, 2003; Sowinski and Dalla Bella, 2013). Participants listen to sequences of five tones (tone frequency = 1047 Hz, duration = 150 ms). Isochronous sequences have a constant inter-onset-interval (IOI) while in non-isochronous sequences the fourth tone occurs earlier than expected based on the IOI of the preceding tones. This displacement results in reciprocal time shifts between tones 3/4 (shortened) and 4/5 (lengthened). The standard IOI is 600 ms. The magnitude of the local shift, up to 30% of the IOI (180 ms), is controlled by the MLP algorithm. After each sequence, participants are asked to judge whether the sequence was "regular" or "irregular."

ANISOCHRONY DETECTION WITH MUSIC

The purpose of the third task is to assess participants' ability to detect a time shift (i.e., deviant beat) in a short musical excerpt (Sowinski and Dalla Bella, 2013). In each trial, a computer-generated musical excerpt is presented to participants. The excerpt is a two-bar fragment (i.e., eight quarter notes overall) taken from Bach's "Badinerie" orchestral suite for flute BWV 1067, played with a piano timbre at a tempo of 100 beats/min (IOI = 600 ms; beat = quarter note). The IOI between musical beats is not manipulated in a regular sequence, while a local time shift (as in the previous task) is introduced at the onset of the fifth beat in an irregular sequence. The standard IOI between musical beats is 600 ms. The magnitude of the time shift, up to 30% (180 ms) of the IOI between musical beats, is controlled by the MLP algorithm. Participants' task is to judge whether the sequence was "regular" or "irregular."

BEAT ALIGNMENT TEST

This task examines sensitivity to the beat conveyed by a musical stimulus. The task is an adapted version of the beat alignment task (Iversen and Patel, 2008; Fujii and Schlaug, 2013). Participants are presented with four musical excerpts including a salient beat structure. Two are fragments from Bach's "Badinerie" and two from Rossini's "William Tell Overture." Each excerpt includes 20 beats (beat = quarter note). An isochronous sequence with a triangle timbre is superimposed on the music starting on the seventh beat. The isochronous sequence is either aligned to the musical beat or unaligned. In the latter case either relative phase is changed (with the tones preceding or following the beats by 33% of the IOI between beats, while keeping the same tempo of the musical stimulus), or period (with the tones being presented at a slower or faster rate by 10% of the quarter note duration). The 4 musical excerpts are presented at 3 different tempi (IOIs of 450, 600, and 750 ms, respectively), for a total of 24 beat-aligned trials and 48 beat-unaligned trials (72 trials overall). After each excerpt, participants are asked whether the isochronous sounds are aligned to the musical beat (perception of a regular pulse evoked by music).

MOTOR TIMING TASKS

Motor timing is assessed by hand tapping (Aschersleben, 2002; Repp, 2005). Participants are instructed to tap as regularly as possible with their right hand either without stimulation (unpaced tapping) or in the presence of a rhythmic auditory stimulus (paced tapping). Tapping is recorded via a Roland SPD-6 MIDI percussion pad controlled by MAX-MSP software (version 5.1). Stimuli are delivered over headphones (Sennheiser HD201) at a comfortable sound pressure level. No auditory feedback is provided during tapping. The tasks are preceded by practice trials.

UNPACED TAPPING

The aim of this task is to assess the tapping rate and variability in the absence of a pacing stimulus. Participants are instructed to tap regularly at a comfortable rate for 60 s, while maintaining tapping rate as constant as possible. The same task is realized also with the left hand. Unpaced tapping tasks are repeated once more at the end of all the motor timing tasks of the BAASTA.

PACED TAPPING TO AN ISOCHRONOUS SEQUENCE

This task assesses sensorimotor synchronization with isochronous sequences of tones. Participants are instructed to synchronize their taps to an isochronous sequence of 60 piano tones (tone frequency = 1319 Hz). The sequence is presented at three IOIs: 600, 450, and 750 ms. Each tapping trial at a given tempo is repeated twice.

PACED TAPPING TO MUSIC

In this task, the ability to synchronize to the beat of a musical stimulus is tested. Participants synchronize their taps to the beat of a well-formed musical excerpt from Bach's "Badinerie" and from Rossini's "William Tell Overture" (quarter note IOI = 600 ms), each including 64 beats. The tapping trial for each musical excerpt is repeated twice.

SYNCHRONIZATION–CONTINUATION

The purpose of this test is to assess motor timing when participants continued tapping at a given rate after prior synchronization with an isochronous sequence (Wing and Kristofferson, 1973a,b; O'Boyle et al., 1996). Participants synchronize to a series of 10 piano tones presented isochronously at 3 tempi (600, 450, or 750 ms) and are instructed to continue tapping at the same rate (continuation phase) for a duration corresponding to 30 IOIs in the absence of a pacing stimulus. The end of the trial is indicated by a low-pitch tone. Each tapping trial at a given tempo is repeated twice.

ADAPTIVE TAPPING

This final test examines the ability to adapt to tempo change in a synchronization–continuation task, using an adaptive tapping task (Schwartze et al., 2011). Series of 10 tones are presented to participants. The first six tones of the sequences have an IOI of 600 ms, while the remaining four tones either maintain the same IOI or, in 67% of the trials, show a slower tempo (with a final IOI of 630 or 670 ms) or a faster tempo (with a final IOI of 570 or 525 ms). Participants are instructed to synchronize to the initial tempo, to adapt to the tempo change, and to continue tapping at the new tempo after the presentation of the last tone for a duration corresponding to 10 IOIs. At the end of each trial, participants are asked whether they perceived acceleration, deceleration, or no tempo change in the sequence. There are 10 blocks with 6 trials per block (4 with tempo change, 2 without), presented in random order.

GAIT ASSESSMENT

Gait kinematics in the absence of auditory cues was assessed with a Vicon MX Motion Capture System during the second day of testing. Sixteen passive reflective markers (14 mm) were attached to participants' lower body (four on the hip, three on each leg and foot, respectively) in accordance with the Conventional Gait Model (Baker, 2006). Participants were asked to walk for 1 min at their spontaneous walking speed. The trial was repeated twice. The performance was recorded using Vicon Nexus Software.

ANALYSIS

Perceptual timing tasks

In duration discrimination and anisochrony detection tasks, the smallest threshold value obtained across the three blocks (i.e., the best performance), expressed in percent of IOI (Weber Ratio) was retained as the final threshold. In the Beat Alignment Test (BAT), the number of Hits (i.e., when a misaligned metronome was correctly detected; maximum = 48 items) and of FAs (i.e., when a misalignment was erroneously reported; maximum = 24 items) was calculated. Trials with a FA rate higher than 30% were discarded. The percent of Hits minus FAs was computed to obtain an unbiased measure of detection performance.

Motor timing tasks

In the Unpaced tapping tasks, and in the continuation phase of the synchronization–continuation and adaptive tapping tasks accuracy of motor timing was obtained by computing the mean inter-tap interval (ITI). Tapping variability was calculated with the Coefficient of Variation (CV) of the ITI (i.e., the ratio of the SD of the ITIs over the mean ITI). In Paced tapping tasks, synchronization accuracy was obtained by calculating the mean absolute asynchrony (i.e., not signed) between the taps and pacing stimuli/beats. Small asynchrony indicates high accuracy. Synchronization variability is indicated by the standard error of asynchrony between taps and pacing stimuli. Both synchronization accuracy and precision are indicated in percent of the IOI. For both paced tapping and synchronization–continuation tasks, the results obtained in the trial showing the lowest variability were submitted to further analysis. Finally, in the adaptive tapping task, adaptation of tapping to the tempo change was measured with the adaptation index corresponding to the mean ITI of the continuation phase divided by the target ITI calculated for all tempi (see Schwartze et al., 2011). The adaptation indexes for faster (plus) and slower tempi (minus) were calculated separately. The sensitivity index (D-prime) for detecting tempo changes was also computed (Schwartze et al., 2011).

Statistical analysis

Since data were not normally distributed in both groups in more than 50% of the cases as assessed with Kolmogorov–Smirnov test, groups and condition were compared with non-parametric tests. To assess whether IPD patients were impaired prior to the training program, their performance was compared to that of controls with Mann–Whitney's tests. If patients' performance in the BAASTA was impaired at baseline, pre-/post-performance was compared with Wilcoxon matched-pairs tests. Patients' individual performance was compared to that of controls via corrected t-tests (Crawford and Garthwaite, 2002).

RESULTS

GAIT

When walking at comfortable speed in the absence of an external cue, patients showed lower stride length ($M = 980.4$ mm) as compared to controls ($M = 1152.3$ mm) ($U = 76, p < 0.01$). Cueing training increased stride length ($M = 1037.0$ mm at post-test; $W = -70, p < 0.05$) and this benefit was maintained 1 month after the training had ended ($M = 1028.9$ mm; $W = -78, p < 0.05$).

BAASTA

Before submitting data to the following analyses, trials were screened for outliers (e.g., for perceptual tasks, blocks with a higher false alarm rate higher than 30%; for motor tasks, taps with ITI deviating by more than three times the interquartile range from the median). A low number of outliers was found in both patients and controls. Overall in the perceptual tasks, 3.3% of the trials were rejected for patients and 3.8% for controls. In the motor tasks, <1% of taps were discarded for both patients and controls.

The effect of training on perceptual and motor timing abilities was examined for the tasks of the BAASTA where patients showed impaired performance relative to controls pre-training. The mean results obtained in these tasks are shown in **Figure 1** (perceptual tasks), and **Figure 2** (motor tasks). Patients showed higher thresholds than controls ($U = 75.5$, $p < 0.05$) in the duration discrimination task before the training. Patients improved following the training, an effect that was not confirmed post-training but in the follow-up evaluation ($W = 66.0$, $p < 0.05$). One month following the intervention, the difference between patients' and controls' discrimination thresholds was no longer significant. Patients displayed worse detection of anisochronies in musical stimuli than controls ($U = 87.5$, $p < 0.05$); yet, training did not improve patients' performance in this task. Finally, in the BAT, patients had more difficulties in detecting misaligned beats before intervention when compared to controls ($U = 74.5$, $p < 0.05$). This difference was present for tempi with inter-beat-intervals of 600 and 750 ms ($U = 84.5$, $p < 0.05$ and $U = 68.0$, $p < 0.05$, respectively). No difference between patients ($M = 11.8$, SEM = 0.8) and controls ($M = 12.9$, SEM = 0.9) was found at the fastest tempo (450 ms). The detection of misaligned beats generally improved when tested at follow-up. The difference pre-/post-training just failed to reach significance ($W = -49.0$, $p = 0.07$). This effect of training was mostly driven by patients' performance at the average tempo ($W = -37.0$, $p < 0.05$). Patients' performance at the follow-up testing did not significantly differ from that of controls.

In the unpaced tapping tasks patients did not differ from controls before the training, in terms of accuracy (IPD: $M = 580.4$, SEM = 78.5; controls: $M = 600.3$, SEM = 63.9) and variability

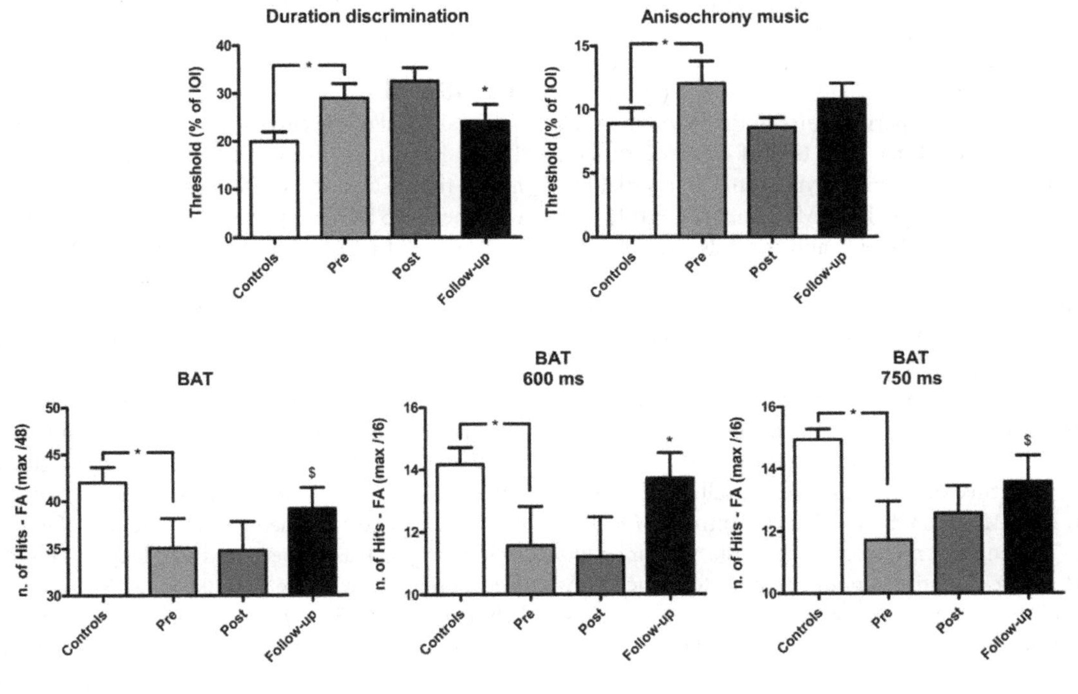

FIGURE 1 | Mean performance of IPD patients and controls in the perceptual tasks of the BAASTA. Tasks where patients differed from controls before the cueing training are selectively reported. Error bars indicate the standard error of the mean (SEM). Note: $*p < 0.05$; $marginally significant difference.

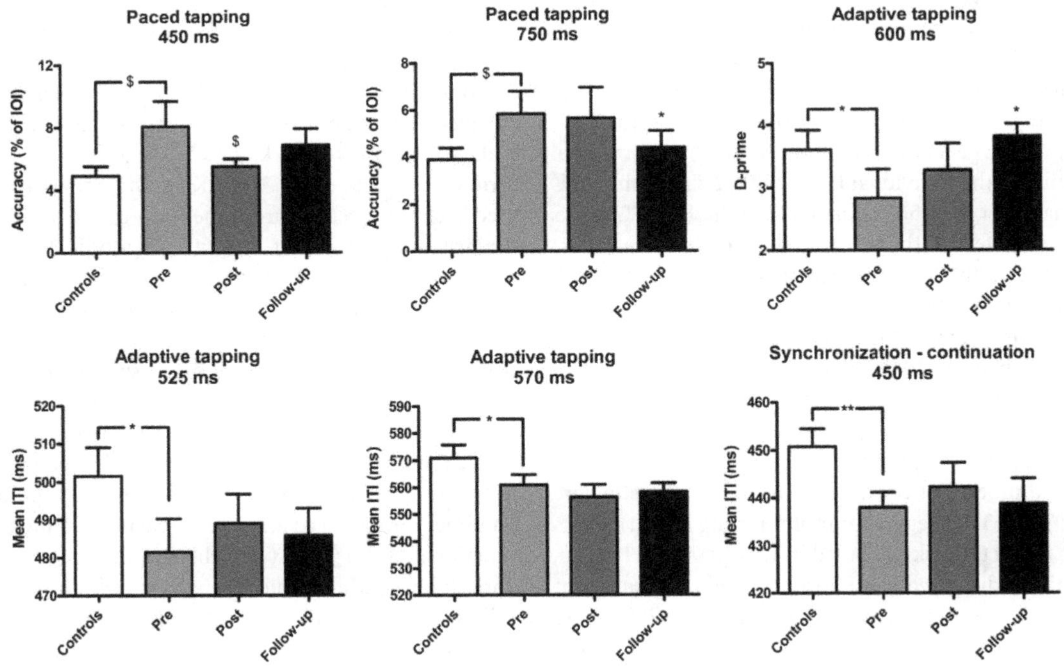

FIGURE 2 | Mean performance of IPD patients and controls in the motor tasks of the BAASTA. Tasks where patients differed from controls before the cueing training are selectively reported. Error bars indicate the standard error of the mean (SEM). $*p < 0.05$; $**p < 0.01$; $marginally significant difference.

(IPD: $M = 0.05$, SEM $= 0.08$; controls: $M = 0.05$, SEM $= 0.004$). In paced tapping tasks, patients tended to be less accurate than controls when synchronizing with an isochronous sequence, a difference showing a statistical trend (at 450 ms, $U = 102.0$, $p = 0.06$; at 750 ms, $U = 102.5$, $p = 0.06$). The effect of the training was mostly visible in the follow-up session. Training led to increased synchronization accuracy with the isochronous sequences at the fastest tempo (450 ms) as confirmed by a statistical trend ($W = 50$, $p = 0.08$). A significant increase of synchronization accuracy was found in the follow-up session (at 750 ms; $W = 72.0$, $p < 0.05$). Patients' performance in the follow-up evaluation did not statistically differ from that of controls. Patients and controls did not differ in terms of synchronization variability before the training (on average, IPD: $M = 0.6$, SEM = 0.1; controls: $M = 0.6$, SEM = 0.06). Patients and controls did not differ in terms of synchronization accuracy (on average, IPD: $M = 7.3$, SEM = 1.4; controls: $M = 6.9$, SEM = 0.8) and variability (on average, IPD: $M = 0.8$, SEM = 0.2; controls: $M = 0.7$, SEM = 0.08) when they synchronized with music.

In the synchronization–continuation task, patients tested prior to training were less accurate than controls only at the fastest tempo (450 ms, $U = 78.0$, $p < 0.01$). However, the two groups did not differ in terms of variability across all tempi (average variability, IPD: $M = 0.03$, SEM = 0.003; controls: $M = 0.03$, SEM = 0.002). Training had no effect on this task. Similar results were obtained in the adaptive tapping task. Before the training, patients exhibited lower accuracy than controls at the fastest tempi in the continuation phase (at 570 ms, $U = 100.0$, $p < 0.05$, and at 525 ms, $U = 94.0$, $p < 0.05$). Moreover, patients performed worse in detecting tempo changes at 600 ms ($U = 99.5$, $p < 0.05$). Both groups displayed similar tapping variability (on average, IPD: $M = 0.05$, SEM = 0.007; Controls: $M = 0.05$, SEM = 0.005), and comparable adaptation indexes (on average, IPD: $M = 1.5$, SEM = 0.2; Controls: $M = 1.4$, SEM = 0.1). Training was effective only in improving the detection of tempo changes, an effect visible when comparing pre-intervention to follow-up ($W = -43$, $p < 0.05$). Patients' perception in the follow-up session did not significantly differ from the performance of healthy controls.

Further analyses targeted the benefits of training on perceptual and motor timing at the individual level. **Table 2** shows the individual performance of the 15 IPD patients on the BAASTA tasks showing significant effects at the group level. z-Scores for each testing session relative to the performance of controls are reported. Significant results are highlighted by the gray shading. Notably there are important individual differences in patients. After the training, some of them performed comparably to age-matched controls ($n = 4$), others showed improvement in perceptual/motor timing ($n = 8$) while the remaining did not respond to the training ($n = 3$). The percent of patients showing perceptual, motor, or perceptual and motor deficits at the three times of testing are summarized in **Table 3**. Perceptual or motor timing impairment is defined here based on the tasks included in **Table 2**. As can be seen, 73% of the patients displayed some form of timing impairment before the training. Post-intervention, poor timing abilities were found in 67% of the patients, while in the follow-up evaluation, only 40% of the patients still showed impaired timing.

In summary, training successfully yielded improvements in gait kinematics, which were still present in follow-up tests 1 month after the training ended. Prior to training patients performed worse in several tests of the BAASTA. Training improved performance in three perceptual and two motor tasks at the group level. However, there were important individual differences: four patients were unimpaired at the training onset, eight patients improved their performance with training, while three did not respond to the intervention.

DISCUSSION

The main goal of the current study was to examine the effects of a 1-month auditory cueing gait-training program on perceptual and motor timing abilities in IPD patients. Performance was assessed with the BAASTA battery. Prior to the intervention, patients exhibited impaired perceptual timing across all BAASTA tasks except for anisochrony detection in isochronous sequences. On the contrary, motor timing was relatively spared, except lower accuracy in continuing tapping at a given rate, and in tapping along with an isochronous sequence. These findings are in line with previous evidence that IPD is associated with a malfunctioning timing system (Harrington et al., 1998, 2011; Spencer and Ivry, 2005; Smith et al., 2007; Koch et al., 2008; Merchant et al., 2008, 2013; Wearden et al., 2008; Jones and Jahanshahi, 2009). Moreover, we could confirm that auditory cueing has a beneficial effect on uncued gait by showing increased speed and step length. This effect outlasted the training (Marchese et al., 2000; Nieuwboer et al., 2001, 2007; Lehman et al., 2005). Our results show a stable effect of training on perceptual and motor timing tasks even after the training ended. In some tasks a delayed effect of cueing on perceptual and motor timing was observed (i.e., duration discrimination, BAT, paced tapping with a metronome, and adaptive tapping). The mechanisms leading to such delayed training effects require further study, for example, by controlling factors such as additional practice or placebo effects (for a discussion, see below).

Most notably, benefits of the training extended beyond gait, improving perceptual and motor timing abilities in a number of non-gait tasks assessed by the BAASTA. Benefits of auditory cueing on gait kinematics are likely to be mediated by a cerebello-thalamo-cortical network, which is also involved in timing (for reviews, see Kotz et al., 2009; Kotz and Schwartze, 2011). More specifically, projections from the SMA to the primary motor cortex may support motor output and modulate or stabilize gait kinematics over time. Compensation of a dysfunctional basal ganglia timing system via rhythmic auditory cues may be afforded by this compensatory cerebello-thalamo-cortical network (Sen et al., 2010). For example, evidence of hypermetabolism in the cerebellum of IPD patients, as a result of cueing training (del Olmo et al., 2006), provides preliminary support for this hypothesis. This circuitry plays a key role in domain-general timing (Kotz and Schwartze, 2011) and may underlie perceptual timing and coupling movement to an external pacing stimulus (Wing, 2002). Functional and/or structural changes in this compensatory network due to auditory cueing may affect both gait kinematics as well as perceptual and motor timing. Additional regions that may be associated with the observed timing benefits of cueing include temporal and parietal cortical areas (Nombela et al., 2013). For example, increased activation of the dentate nucleus near the midline and in the right temporo-parietal junction during a sensorimotor task was observed in IPD following auditory cueing training (del Olmo et al., 2006). The dentate nucleus has been linked to timekeeping (Malapani et al., 1998; Casini and Ivry, 1999) and the right inferior parietal and superior temporal cortex are involved in the coding of temporal intervals (Platel et al.,

Table 2 | Patients' individual perfomances (*z*-scores) on the tasks of the BAASTA showing an effect of the cueing training at a group level.

Patient	Duration discrimination *z*-Score			BAT *z*-Score			D-prime 600 ms *z*-Score			Paced tapping accuracy 450 ms *z*-Score			Paced tapping accuracy 750 ms *z*-Score		
	Pre	Post	Follow-up	Pre	Post	Follow-up	Pre	Post	Follow-up	Pre	Post	Follow-up	Pre	Post	Follow-up
1	2.27	2.04	−0.14	−2.16	−2.16	−0.58	−0.23	0.43	0.43	−0.28	−0.40	2.28	−0.23	−0.48	−0.69
2	0.51	2.43	−0.47	−2.30	−2.02	−1.15	−1.11	−1.11	0.43	−0.46	0.26	−0.04	0.11	0.04	−0.42
3	0.44	−0.14	−0.14	0.72	0.86	0.86	0.43	0.43	0.43	0.43	0.30	0.33	−0.77	−0.90	−0.18
4	0.93	0.57	0.89	0.72	0.86	0.43	−0.75	−0.23	−0.23	−1.00	−0.37	0.18	−0.43	−0.61	−0.30
5	1.47	2.23	0.68	−1.87	−1.73	−0.43	0.42	0.43	0.43	1.22	0.26	−0.85	−0.50	−0.69	−0.97
6	−1.07	0.47	−0.53	0.00	−0.86	−1.30	−1.39	−0.23	0.43	4.56	1.88	3.54	−0.34	−0.46	−0.64
7	0.20	1.18	−0.75	NaN	NaN	NaN	0.43	−2.05	0.43	1.14	−0.53	0.36	2.30	0.59	0.40
8	2.27	3.36	1.62	−2.74	−2.16	0.14	0.43	0.43	−0.75	6.89	0.79	−0.51	3.86	0.30	0.38
9	−1.16	0.51	−0.59	0.29	0.43	0.14	−0.23	0.43	0.43	−0.34	−0.24	−1.05	−0.59	−0.26	−1.02
10	3.32	2.66	3.52	0.58	0.86	0.43	−1.11	−0.23	−0.10	1.12	0.71	2.27	1.93	8.74	3.25
11	0.23	2.59	4.30	−4.61	−3.74	−2.16	−3.78	0.49	0.43	4.69	0.12	3.19	5.12	2.39	2.45
12	3.48	−0.17	−0.56	0.58	0.00	0.72	0.43	0.43	0.43	−0.09	−0.80	−0.57	0.21	0.21	−0.74
13	1.07	3.23	−0.24	−0.86	−1.30	0.29	0.43	0.43	0.43	1.10	0.79	2.13	1.78	1.98	1.82
14	0.64	0.44	0.47	−2.30	−3.89	−3.31	−2.79	−3.58	−1.39	−0.42	0.58	−0.46	1.17	1.25	0.46
15	0.93	0.20	−1.00	0.58	0.29	0.29	0.43	0.43	0.43	−1.04	−0.11	−0.09	0.04	0.24	−0.46

Values highlighted in gray indicate significant differences between the performances of patients and of healthy controls, as assessed with corrected t-tests (Crawford and Garthwaite, 2002). 'NaN' indicates missing values.

$p < 0.05$; $p < 0.01$; $p < 0.001$.

Table 3 | Percentage of IPD patients who exhibited impaired perceptual and/or motor timing relative to healthy controls pre-, post-training, and at the follow-up.

	Pre	Post	Follow-up
Perceptual only	5/15 (33%)	6/15 (40%)	1/15 (7%)
Motor only	3/15 (20%)	1/15 (7%)	3/15 (20%)
Perceptual and motor	3/15 (20%)	3/15 (20%)	2/15 (13%)
No impairment	4/15 (27%)	5/15 (33%)	9/15 (60%)

1997; Liegeois-Chauvel et al., 1998). Yet, the contribution of these regions to the benefits of auditory cueing is not clear to date and deserves further enquiry. In line with previous research, we find considerable variability between individual patients (Merchant et al., 2008). We observed a spectrum of individual profiles. Some patients were impaired in either or both perceptual and motor timing, while others performed comparable to healthy controls. For tasks positively affected by the training, eight patients showed an improvement after training, while six patients improved in perceptual timing, one in motor timing, and one in both timing functions. Four out of the six patients who improved in the BAT (beat-based timing) showed a comparable profile in the duration discrimination task (interval-based timing). Among the non-responders, 4 out of 15 showed no timing impairments prior to the training. Differences between patients may point to different loci of impairment within the neuronal network supporting perceptual and motor timing. The observed variability across tasks may be accounted for in the context of a hybrid model of timing, recently proposed by Merchant and collaborators (Merchant et al., 2008, 2013). The model postulates a partially distributed network, involving a core timing mechanism (e.g., cortico-thalamo-basal ganglia structures) and task-driven context-dependent mechanisms, engaged by specific behavioral contexts/tasks. A viable hypothesis is that performance variability between individuals and across tasks may therefore stem from the interaction between the core timing system and context- or task-dependent areas (for a discussion, see Merchant et al., 2013). A similar account may explain why in a functionally degenerated network, such as in IPD, training may show rather variable effects.

The study has some limitations that need to be addressed in further studies. One caveat is that the observed effects may be placebo effects in therapy. Indeed, placebo effects in PD can be very strong, and have been reported for dopamine release (e.g., de la Fuente-Fernandez et al., 2001). Moreover, there is a possibility that patients kept performing additional auditory cueing training at home after the end of the 1-month training session. We cannot exclude this possibility, even if patients were not encouraged to do so and even if the cueing device was not made available to the patients after the training. Finally, since BAASTA was administered three times for each patients, learning may act as a confound when considering the effects of training on perceptual and motor timing. Note, however, that the effects of the training on perceptual and motor timing abilities was selective, and confined to a subset of tasks of the BAASTA. Moreover, a thorough look at the individual performance of PD patients reveals different patterns of improvement due to training (e.g., delayed vs. immediate effects of training). These findings speak against a general explanation of improvements due to auditory cueing as a mere placebo, learning or practice effect. Indeed, these factors should indistinctly affect all tasks and patients in a similar fashion. Nevertheless, these factors should be carefully considered in further studies. A possibility which was not implemented in the present study is to include a control condition, where participants would perform a similar task in the absence of auditory cueing (e.g., music listening, or walking in the absence of a cue). This condition would allow pinpointing the contribution of coupling perception and action, which is characteristic of an auditory cueing training, compared to merely listening to music or uncued motor activity. In addition, submitting healthy participants to the BAASTA in a test–retest design will allow examining the contribution of practice and assessing which tasks of the battery are more susceptible to learning effects.

In summary, a training scheme relying on musically paced gait over 4 weeks in patients with mild to moderate IPD was shown to produce beneficial effects on perceptual and motor timing beyond gait. We suggest that such a generalization is mediated by a domain-general system, which governs perceptual and motor timing beyond gait. Such a network may be recruited when patients have to couple steps to auditory stimuli. These findings are relevant for theories about the functional and neuronal underpinnings of timing in performance and perception. However, they may also be considered as a first step toward the development of novel strategies for training cognitive aspects of IPD, extending beyond motor symptoms. Training targeted to cognitive functioning may be highly needed, since IPD has been increasingly recognized to not only affect movement but also cognition (Svenningsson et al., 2012). Training schemes bridging motor performance and cognition may be an important building block for devising efficient intervention strategies to delay cognitive decline in IPD.

ACKNOWLEDGMENTS

The authors would like to acknowledge the contributions of Jana Kynast, Julia Schuler, and Anja Hutschenreiter. This research was funded by the European Community's Seventh Framework Programme under the EBRAMUS project (FP7 Initial Training Network) – grant agreement no. 238157.

REFERENCES

Allman, M. J., and Meck, W. H. (2012). Pathophysiological distortions in time perception and timed performance. *Brain* 135, 656–677. doi:10.1093/brain/awr210

Arias, P., and Cudeiro, J. (2008). Effects of rhythmic sensory stimulation (auditory, visual) on gait in Parkinson's disease patients. *Exp. Brain Res.* 186, 589–601. doi:10.1007/s00221-007-1263-y

Aschersleben, G. (2002). Temporal control of movements in sensorimotor synchronization. *Brain Cogn.* 48, 66–79. doi:10.1006/brcg.2001.1304

Baker, R. (2006). Gait analysis methods in rehabilitation. *J. Neuroeng. Rehabil.* 3, 4. doi:10.1186/1743-0003-3-4

Blin, O., Ferrandez, A. M., and Serratrice, G. (1990). Quantitative analysis of gait in Parkinson patients: increased variability of stride length. *J. Neurol. Sci.* 98, 91–97. doi:10.1016/0022-510X(90)90184-O

Bloem, B. R. (1992). Postural instability in Parkinson's disease. *Clin. Neurol. Neurosurg.* 94(Suppl.), S41–S45. doi:10.1016/0303-8467(92)90018-X

Bloem, B. R., Hausdorff, J. M., Visser, J. E., and Giladi, N. (2004). Falls and freezing of gait in Parkinson's disease: a review of two interconnected, episodic phenomena. *Mov. Disord.* 19, 871–884. doi:10.1002/mds.20115

Casini, L., and Ivry, R. B. (1999). Effects of divided attention on temporal processing in patients with lesions of the cerebellum or frontal lobe. *Neuropsychology* 13, 10–21. doi:10.1037/0894-4105.13.1.10

Coull, J. T., Cheng, R. K., and Meck, W. H. (2011). Neuroanatomical and neurochemical substrates of timing. *Neuropsychopharmacology* 36, 3–25. doi:10.1038/npp.2010.113

Crawford, J. R., and Garthwaite, P. H. (2002). Investigation of the single case in neuropsychology: confidence limits on the abnormality of test scores and test score differences. *Neuropsychologia* 40, 1196–1208. doi:10.1016/S0028-3932(01)00224-X

de Bruin, N., Doan, J. B., Turnbull, G., Suchowersky, O., Bonfield, S., Hu, B., et al. (2010). Walking with music is a safe and viable tool for gait training in Parkinson's disease: the effect of a 13-week feasibility study on single and dual task walking. *Parkinsons Dis.* 2010, 483530. doi:10.4061/2010/483530

de la Fuente-Fernandez, R., Ruth, T. J., Sossi, V., Schulzer, M., Calne, D. B., and Stoessl, A. J. (2001). Expectation and dopamine release: mechanism of the placebo effect in Parkinson's disease. *Science* 293, 1164–1166. doi:10.1126/science.1060937

De Renzi, E., and Vignolo, L. A. (1962). The token test: a sensitive test to detect receptive disturbances in aphasics. *Brain* 85, 665–678. doi:10.1093/brain/85.4.665

del Olmo, M. F., Arias, P., Furio, M. C., Pozo, M. A., and Cudeiro, J. (2006). Evaluation of the effect of training using auditory stimulation on rhythmic movement in Parkinsonian patients – a combine motor and [18F]-FDG PET study. *Parkinsonism Relat. Disord.* 12, 155–164. doi:10.1016/j.parkreldis.2005.11.002

Elbaz, A., Bower, J. H., Maraganore, D. M., Mcdonnell, S. K., Peterson, B. J., Ahlskog, J. E., et al. (2002). Risk tables for parkinsonism and Parkinson's disease. *J. Clin. Epidemiol.* 55, 25–31. doi:10.1016/S0895-4356(01)00425-5

Fujii, S., and Schlaug, G. (2013). The Harvard Beat Assessment Test (H-BAT): a battery for assessing beat perception and production and their dissociation. *Front. Hum. Neurosci.* 7:771. doi:10.3389/fnhum.2013.00771

Grabli, D., Karachi, C., Welter, M. L., Lau, B., Hirsch, E. C., Vidailhet, M., et al. (2012). Normal and pathological gait: what we learn from Parkinson's disease. *J. Neurol. Neurosurg. Psychiatr.* 83, 979–985. doi:10.1136/jnnp-2012-302263

Grassi, M., and Soranzo, A. (2009). MLP: a MATLAB toolbox for rapid and reliable auditory threshold estimation. *Behav. Res. Methods* 41, 20–28. doi:10.3758/BRM.41.1.20

Green, D. M. (1993). A maximum-likelihood method for estimating thresholds in a yes-no task. *J. Acoust. Soc. Am.* 93, 2096–2105. doi:10.1121/1.406162

Hallett, M. (2008). The intrinsic and extrinsic aspects of freezing of gait. *Mov. Disord.* 23(Suppl. 2), S439–S443. doi:10.1002/mds.21836

Harrington, D. L., Castillo, G. N., Greenberg, P. A., Song, D. D., Lessig, S., Lee, R. R., et al. (2011). Neurobehavioral mechanisms of temporal processing deficits in Parkinson's disease. *PLoS ONE* 6:e17461. doi:10.1371/journal.pone.0017461

Harrington, D. L., Haaland, K. Y., and Hermanowicz, N. (1998). Temporal processing in the basal ganglia. *Neuropsychology* 12, 3–12. doi:10.1037/0894-4105.12.1.3

Howe, T. E., Lovgreen, B., Cody, F. W., Ashton, V. J., and Oldham, J. A. (2003). Auditory cues can modify the gait of persons with early-stage Parkinson's disease: a method for enhancing parkinsonian walking performance? *Clin. Rehabil.* 17, 363–367. doi:10.1191/0269215503cr621oa

Hyde, K. L., and Peretz, I. (2003). "Out-of-pitch" but still "in-time". An auditory psychophysical study in congenital amusic adults. *Ann. N. Y. Acad. Sci.* 999, 173–176. doi:10.1196/annals.1284.023

Iversen, J. R., and Patel, A. D. (2008). The Beat Alignment Test (BAT): surveying beat processing abilities in the general population. *Proceedings of the 10th International Conference on Music Perception and Cognition*; Sapporo, Japan. 465–468.

Jones, C. R., and Jahanshahi, M. (2009). The substantia nigra, the basal ganglia, dopamine and temporal processing. *J. Neural Transm. Suppl.* 73, 161–171. doi:10.1007/978-3-211-92660-4_13

Jones, M. R. (1976). Time, our lost dimension: toward a new theory of perception, attention, and memory. *Psychol. Rev.* 83, 323–355. doi:10.1037/0033-295X.83.5.323

Kalbe, E., Calabrese, P., Kohn, N., Hilker, R., Riedel, O., Wittchen, H. U., et al. (2008). Screening for cognitive deficits in Parkinson's disease with the Parkinson neuropsychometric dementia assessment (PANDA) instrument. *Parkinsonism Relat. Disord.* 14, 93–101. doi:10.1016/j.parkreldis.2007.06.008

Koch, G., Costa, A., Brusa, L., Peppe, A., Gatto, I., Torriero, S., et al. (2008). Impaired reproduction of second but not millisecond time intervals in Parkinson's disease. *Neuropsychologia* 46, 1305–1313. doi:10.1016/j.neuropsychologia.2007.12.005

Koller, W. C., and Montgomery, E. B. (1997). Issues in the early diagnosis of Parkinson's disease. *Neurology* 49, S10–S25. doi:10.1212/WNL.49.1_Suppl_1.S10

Kotz, S. A., and Schwartze, M. (2011). Differential input of the supplementary motor area to a dedicated temporal processing network: functional and clinical implications. *Front. Integr. Neurosci.* 5:86. doi:10.3389/fnint.2011.00086

Kotz, S. A., Schwartze, M., and Schmidt-Kassow, M. (2009). Non-motor basal ganglia functions: a review and proposal for a model of sensory predictability in auditory language perception. *Cortex* 45, 982–990. doi:10.1016/j.cortex.2009.02.010

Kwakkel, G., De Goede, C. J., and Van Wegen, E. E. (2007). Impact of physical therapy for Parkinson's disease: a critical review of the literature. *Parkinsonism Relat. Disord.* 13(Suppl. 3), S478–S487. doi:10.1016/S1353-8020(08)70053-1

Large, E. W. (2008). "Resonating to musical rhythm: theory and experiment," in *The Psychology of Time*, ed. S. Grondin (West Yorkshire: Emerald), 189–231.

Large, E. W., and Jones, M. R. (1999). The dynamics of attending: how we track time. *Psychol. Rev.* 106, 119–159. doi:10.1016/j.neuroimage.2011.11.065

Lehman, D. A., Toole, T., Lofald, D., and Hirsch, M. A. (2005). Training with verbal instructional cues results in near-term improvement of gait in people with Parkinson disease. *J. Neurol. Phys. Ther.* 29, 2–8. doi:10.1097/01.NPT.0000282256.36208.cf

Lewis, M. M., Slagle, C. G., Smith, A. B., Truong, Y., Bai, P., Mckeown, M. J., et al. (2007). Task specific influences of Parkinson's disease on the striato-thalamo-cortical and cerebello-thalamo-cortical motor circuitries. *Neuroscience* 147, 224–235. doi:10.1016/j.neuroscience.2007.04.006

Liegeois-Chauvel, C., Peretz, I., Babai, M., Laguitton, V., and Chauvel, P. (1998). Contribution of different cortical areas in the temporal lobes to music processing. *Brain* 121(Pt 10), 1853–1867. doi:10.1093/brain/121.10.1853

Lim, I., Van Wegen, E., De Goede, C., Deutekom, M., Nieuwboer, A., Willems, A., et al. (2005). Effects of external rhythmical cueing on gait in patients with Parkinson's disease: a systematic review. *Clin. Rehabil.* 19, 695–713. doi:10.1191/0269215505cr906oa

Malapani, C., Dubois, B., Rancurel, G., and Gibbon, J. (1998). Cerebellar dysfunctions of temporal processing in the seconds range in humans. *Neuroreport* 9, 3907–3912. doi:10.1097/00001756-199812010-00026

Marchese, R., Diverio, M., Zucchi, F., Lentino, C., and Abbruzzese, G. (2000). The role of sensory cues in the rehabilitation of parkinsonian patients: a comparison of two physical therapy protocols. *Mov. Disord.* 15, 879–883. doi:10.1002/1531-8257(200009)15:5<879::AID-MDS1018>3.0.CO;2-9

McIntosh, G. C., Brown, S. H., Rice, R. R., and Thaut, M. H. (1997). Rhythmic auditory-motor facilitation of gait patterns in patients with Parkinson's disease. *J. Neurol. Neurosurg. Psychiatr.* 62, 22–26. doi:10.1136/jnnp.62.1.22

Merchant, H., Harrington, D. L., and Meck, W. H. (2013). Neural basis of the perception and estimation of time. *Annu. Rev. Neurosci.* 36, 313–336. doi:10.1146/annurev-neuro-062012-170349

Merchant, H., Luciana, M., Hooper, C., Majestic, S., and Tuite, P. (2008). Interval timing and Parkinson's disease: heterogeneity in temporal performance. *Exp. Brain Res.* 184, 233–248. doi:10.1007/s00221-007-1097-7

Morris, M. E., Huxham, F. E., Mcginley, J., and Iansek, R. (2001). Gait disorders and gait rehabilitation in Parkinson's disease. *Adv. Neurol.* 87, 347–361.

Nieuwboer, A., De Weerdt, W., Dom, R., Truyen, M., Janssens, L., and Kamsma, Y. (2001). The effect of a home physiotherapy program for persons with Parkinson's disease. *J. Rehabil. Med.* 33, 266–272. doi:10.1080/165019701753236455

Nieuwboer, A., Kwakkel, G., Rochester, L., Jones, D., Van Wegen, E., Willems, A. M., et al. (2007). Cueing training in the home improves gait-related mobility in Parkinson's disease: the RESCUE trial. *J. Neurol. Neurosurg. Psychiatr.* 78, 134–140. doi:10.1136/jnnp.200X.097923

Nombela, C., Hughes, L. E., Owen, A. M., and Grahn, J. A. (2013). Into the groove: can rhythm influence Parkinson's disease? *Neurosci. Biobehav. Rev.* 37(10 Pt 2), 2564–2570. doi:10.1016/j.neubiorev.2013.08.003

O'Boyle, D. J., Freeman, J. S., and Cody, F. W. (1996). The accuracy and precision of timing of self-paced, repetitive movements in subjects with Parkinson's disease. *Brain* 119(Pt 1), 51–70. doi:10.1093/brain/119.1.51

Platel, H., Price, C., Baron, J. C., Wise, R., Lambert, J., Frackowiak, R. S., et al. (1997). The structural components of music perception. A functional anatomical study. *Brain* 120(Pt 2), 229–243.

Repp, B. H. (2005). Sensorimotor synchronization: a review of the tapping literature. *Psychon. Bull. Rev.* 12, 969–992. doi:10.3758/BF03206433

Samii, A., Nutt, J. G., and Ransom, B. R. (2004). Parkinson's disease. *Lancet* 363, 1783–1793. doi:10.1016/S0140-6736(04)16305-8

Schwartze, M., Keller, P. E., Patel, A. D., and Kotz, S. A. (2011). The impact of basal ganglia lesions on sensorimotor synchronization, spontaneous motor tempo, and the detection of tempo changes. *Behav. Brain Res.* 216, 685–691. doi:10.1016/j.bbr.2010.09.015

Schwartze, M., and Kotz, S. A. (2013). A dual-pathway neural architecture for specific temporal prediction. *Neurosci. Biobehav. Rev.* 37(10 Pt 2), 2587–2596. doi:10.1016/j.neubiorev.2013.08.005

Sen, S., Kawaguchi, A., Truong, Y., Lewis, M. M., and Huang, X. (2010). Dynamic changes in cerebello-thalamo-cortical motor circuitry during progression of Parkinson's disease. *Neuroscience* 166, 712–719. doi:10.1016/j.neuroscience.2009.12.036

Sharma, A., Szeto, K., and Desilets, A. R. (2012). Efficacy and safety of deep brain stimulation as an adjunct to pharmacotherapy for the treatment of Parkinson disease. *Ann. Pharmacother.* 46, 248–254. doi:10.1345/aph.1Q508

Smith, J. G., Harper, D. N., Gittings, D., and Abernethy, D. (2007). The effect of Parkinson's disease on time estimation as a function of stimulus duration range and modality. *Brain Cogn.* 64, 130–143. doi:10.1016/j.bandc.2007.01.005

Sowinski, J., and Dalla Bella, S. (2013). Poor synchronization to the beat may result from deficient auditory-motor mapping. *Neuropsychologia* 51, 1952–1963. doi:10.1016/j.neuropsychologia.2013.06.027

Spaulding, S. J., Barber, B., Colby, M., Cormack, B., Mick, T., and Jenkins, M. E. (2012). Cueing and gait improvement among people with Parkinson's disease: a meta-analysis. *Arch. Phys. Med. Rehabil.* 94, 562–570. doi:10.1016/j.apmr.2012.10.026

Spencer, R. M., and Ivry, R. B. (2005). Comparison of patients with Parkinson's disease or cerebellar lesions in the production of periodic movements involving event-based or emergent timing. *Brain Cogn.* 58, 84–93. doi:10.1016/j.bandc.2004.09.010

Svenningsson, P., Westman, E., Ballard, C., and Aarsland, D. (2012). Cognitive impairment in patients with Parkinson's disease: diagnosis, biomarkers, and treatment. *Lancet Neurol.* 11, 697–707. doi:10.1016/S1474-4422(12)70152-7

Thaut, M. H., McIntosh, G. C., Rice, R. R., Miller, R. A., Rathbun, J., and Brault, J. M. (1996). Rhythmic auditory stimulation in gait training for Parkinson's disease patients. *Mov. Disord.* 11, 193–200. doi:10.1002/mds.870110213

Thaut, M. H., McIntosh, K. W., McIntosh, G. C., and Hoemberg, V. (2001). Auditory rhythmicity enhances movement and speech motor control in patients with Parkinson's disease. *Funct. Neurol.* 16, 163–172.

Wearden, J. H., Smith-Spark, J. H., Cousins, R., Edelstyn, N. M., Cody, F. W., and O'Boyle, D. J. (2008). Stimulus timing by people with Parkinson's disease. *Brain Cogn.* 67, 264–279. doi:10.1016/j.bandc.2008.01.010

Welsh, K. A., Butters, N., Mohs, R. C., Beekly, D., Edland, S., Fillenbaum, G., et al. (1994). The consortium to establish a registry for Alzheimer's disease (CERAD). Part V. A normative study of the neuropsychological battery. *Neurology* 44, 609–614.

Willems, A. M., Nieuwboer, A., Chavret, F., Desloovere, K., Dom, R., Rochester, L., et al. (2006). The use of rhythmic auditory cues to influence gait in patients with Parkinson's disease, the differential effect for freezers and non-freezers, an explorative study. *Disabil. Rehabil.* 28, 721–728. doi:10.1080/09638280500386569

Wing, A. M. (2002). Voluntary timing and brain function: an information processing approach. *Brain Cogn.* 48, 7–30. doi:10.1006/brcg.2001.1301

Wing, A. M., and Kristofferson, A. B. (1973a). Response delays and the timing of discrete motor responses. *Percept. Psychophys.* 14, 5–12. doi:10.3758/BF03198607

Wing, A. M., and Kristofferson, A. B. (1973b). The timing of interresponse intervals. *Percept. Psychophys.* 13, 455–460. doi:10.3758/BF03205802

Wu, T., Wang, J., Wang, C., Hallett, M., Zang, Y., Wu, X., et al. (2012). Basal ganglia circuits changes in Parkinson's disease patients. *Neurosci. Lett.* 524, 55–59. doi:10.1016/j.neulet.2012.07.012

Yesavage, J. A., Brink, T. L., Rose, T. L., Lum, O., Huang, V., Adey, M., et al. (1982). Development and validation of a geriatric depression screening scale: a preliminary report. *J. Psychiatr. Res.* 17, 37–49. doi:10.1016/0022-3956(82)90033-4

11

Reducing chronic visuo-spatial neglect following right hemisphere stroke through instrument playing

Rebeka Bodak[1]*, Paresh Malhotra[2], Nicolò F. Bernardi[3], Gianna Cocchini[4] and Lauren Stewart[4]*

[1] *Department of Clinical Medicine, Aarhus University, Aarhus, Denmark*
[2] *Division of Brain Sciences, Imperial College London, London, UK*
[3] *Department of Psychology, McGill University, Montreal, QC, Canada*
[4] *Department of Psychology, Goldsmiths University of London, London, UK*

Correspondence:
Rebeka Bodak, Department of Clinical Medicine, Center of Functionally Integrative Neuroscience, Aarhus University Hospital, Building 10G, Nørrebrogade 44, 8000 Aarhus C, Denmark
e-mail: rebeka_bodak@hotmail.com;
Lauren Stewart, Department of Psychology, Goldsmiths, University of London, New Cross, London SE14 6NW, UK
e-mail: l.stewart@gold.ac.uk

Unilateral visuo-spatial neglect is a neuropsychological syndrome commonly resulting from right hemisphere stroke at the temporo-parietal junction of the infero-posterior parietal cortex. Neglect is characterized by reduced awareness of stimuli presented on patients' contralesional side of space. Inspired by evidence of increased spatial exploration of patients' left side achieved during keyboard scale-playing, the current study employed a music intervention that involved making sequential goal-directed actions in the neglected part of space, in order to determine whether this would bring about clinically significant improvement in chronic neglect. Two left neglect patients completed an intervention comprising four weekly 30-min music intervention sessions involving playing scales and familiar melodies on chime bars from right to left. Two cancellation tests [Mesulam shape, Behavioral Inattention Test (BIT) star], the neglect subtest from the computerized TAP (Test of Attentional Performance) battery, and the line bisection test were administered three times during a preliminary baseline phase, before and after the four intervention sessions during the intervention phase to investigate short-term effects, and 1 week after the last intervention session to investigate whether any changes in performance would persist. Both patients demonstrated significant short-term and longer-lasting improvements on the Mesulam shape cancellation test. One patient also showed longer-lasting effects on the BIT star cancellation test and scored in the normal range 1 week after the intervention. These findings provide preliminary evidence that active music-making with a horizontally aligned instrument may help neglect patients attend more to their affected side.

Keywords: neglect, stroke, rehabilitation, music therapy, motivation, auditory–motor, spatial attention

INTRODUCTION

Spatial neglect is a frequent consequence of right hemispheric stroke, ranging from 13 to 82%, with a number of studies suggesting that approximately half of these individuals manifest some degree of neglect (Stone et al., 1993; Bowen et al., 1999; Buxbaum et al., 2004; Ringman et al., 2004). It is a heterogeneous neuropsychological syndrome frequently associated with damage to the inferior parietal lobe (Vallar, 1993; Heilman, 2003; Mort et al., 2003), superior temporal gyrus (Karnath et al., 2001), and occasionally with lesions to the white matter tracts (Doricchi et al., 2008).

Demonstrated through a bias toward ipsilesional space, neglect patients present with impaired attention to stimuli located on the contralesional (usually the left) side of the patient's body and environment. This leads to difficulties engaging in everyday tasks (Luauté et al., 2006; Bowen and Lincoln, 2008), which in turn reduces functional independence. Importantly, the presence of neglect is associated with worse rehabilitation outcome (Jehkonen et al., 2006).

Several rehabilitation techniques have been implemented to reduce neglect. These include training in visual scanning (e.g., Pizzamiglio et al., 2004), prism adaptation (e.g., Rossetti et al., 1998; Humphreys et al., 2006), limb activation (Reinhart et al., 2012), transcutaneous electrical nervous stimulation (TENS) technique (Vallar et al., 1995; Beschin et al., 2012), and virtual reality treatments (Kim et al., 2011; Borghese et al., 2013; see also Rode et al., 2010, for a review). Despite the large body of research investigating treatment techniques for neglect, recent systematic reviews demonstrate a lack of efficacy of existing rehabilitation approaches, with no consensus regarding which technique is most effective (Luauté et al., 2006; Bowen and Lincoln, 2008) and no strong evidence that these approaches lead to improvements in activities of daily living (see for example, review by Barrett et al., 2012).

An intervention based around music-making may hold special promise as a potential new approach. Playing an instrument offers the opportunity to train cognitive and motor skills (Zatorre et al., 2007). For many people, active music-making can be intrinsically rewarding (Altenmüller and Schlaug, 2013), and patients anecdotally report high levels of engagement with rehabilitation exercises that are embedded within a musical context (Bodak, personal communication). The use of music-making as a rehabilitation approach falls under the broad domain of neurologic music therapy (NMT); a neuro-scientifically motivated model of practice, which consists of 20 standardized research-based music therapy techniques (Thaut, 2008). The techniques cover three overarching rehabilitation areas including sensorimotor, speech and language, and cognitive training. As noted in research by Hommel et al. (1990), one of the cognitive training techniques is musical neglect training, which Thaut (2008) defines as a technique that "includes active performance exercises on musical instruments that is structured in time, tempo, and rhythm, and is in appropriate spatial configurations, to focus attention to a neglected or inattended visual field" (p. 196). While evidence on this issue is scarce, one empirical study provides preliminary evidence that making music may ameliorate neglect. Cioffi et al. (2011, 2014) reported that when neglect patients were asked to play consecutive keys on a piano from right to left (into the neglected side), they proceeded further to the left when responses were systematically paired with descending tones, as opposed to random pairing or silence. This improvement may be explained by research findings showing that tasks comprising the active production of a predictable sequence yield better performance (Ishiai et al., 1990, 1997). This suggests that taking advantage of the sequence completion, which is a core component of musical scales and melodies, may facilitate spatial exploration in neglect patients. However, the extent to which this increased spatial exploration might persist and/or translate to improvement on clinical tests of neglect, is unknown.

With this in mind, the aim of the present study was to explore whether a period of active music-making with a horizontally aligned instrument (chime bars) leads to a reduction in attentional bias outside the music session as measured by performance on standard clinical tests for neglect.

MATERIALS AND METHODS

DESIGN

The study followed a within-subject case study design (**Figure 1**) with participants acting as their own controls. The experiment comprised three phases in the following order: (1) a no-intervention control phase of 6 weeks, during which baseline measures were obtained, followed by (2) an intervention phase of 4 weeks, ending with (3) a single follow-up testing session 1 week after the last intervention session. The dependent variable was performance on tests of visuo-spatial attention, measured within subjects in terms of (a) accuracy on two paper and pencil cancellation tests, (b) accuracy on a computerized target detection task (number of omitted targets in both cases), (c) reaction time on this computer task, and (d) accuracy on the line bisection test (percentage of rightward deviation).

MATERIALS

Two cancellation tests [Mesulam shape cancellation test, Mesulam, 1985; Star cancellation test as a part of the Behavioral Inattention Test (BIT), Wilson et al., 1987], the neglect subtest from the computerized Test of Attentional Performance (TAP, Zoccolotti et al., 2000) battery, and the line bisection test (Halligan et al., 1990) were administered three times during a 6-week baseline period (Phase 1), before and after each of the four sessions during the intervention phase investigating short-term effects (Phase 2), and at follow-up 1 week after the final intervention session investigating longer-lasting effects (Phase 3).

MESULAM SHAPE CANCELLATION TEST

This target detection task is presented to patients on an A4 sheet of paper. It is administered in landscape layout with its center presented to patients at their midline where the researcher sits directly opposite. The test comprises 300 filled and unfilled, familiar (i.e., stars, circles, squares, and triangles), and unfamiliar distractor shapes spatially positioned at random. The target shape is a non-darkened bisected circle with six spines on its outer circumference. Patients are instructed to draw a line through all targets, of which there are a total of 60 with 15 in each quadrant.

BIT STAR CANCELLATION TEST

Like the Mesulam shape cancellation test, this target detection task is also presented to patients on an A4 sheet of paper, in landscape orientation, with the researcher sitting directly opposite. The test comprises 52 darkened large stars, 10 short words, and 13 randomly laid out letters, which are all spread around 56 filled small stars. The targets comprise 54 of the 56 small stars where the two in the center are crossed out by the researcher and excluded from calculations. Patients are instructed to cross out all targets, which are subdivided into 6 sections with 27 on each side.

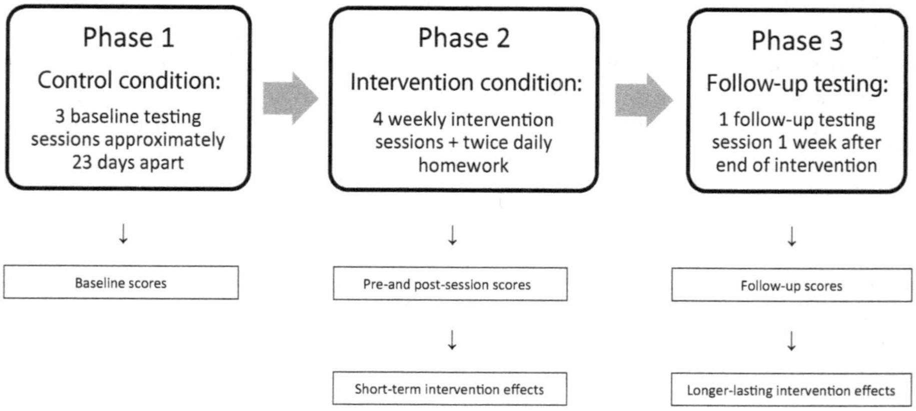

FIGURE 1 | Outline of experimental design.

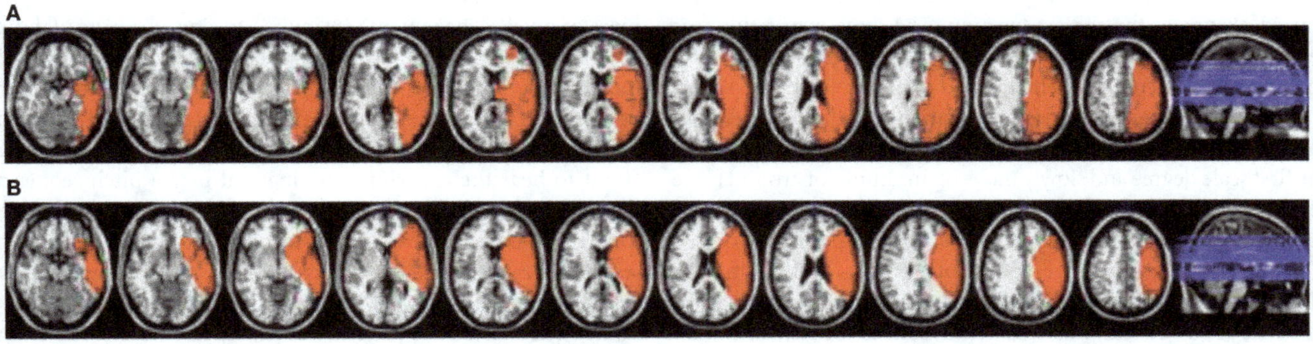

FIGURE 2 | (A) Patient 1's lesion reconstruction (in red) plotted from magnetic resonance imaging acquisitions onto a standard MRI-based template. **(B)** Patient 2's lesion reconstruction (in red) plotted from magnetic resonance imaging acquisitions onto a standard MRI-based template.

TEST OF ATTENTIONAL PERFORMANCE

In this computerized test, patients are instructed to look at and name letters in the center of the screen throughout the 5-min test. The aim of the task is to detect a total of 44 (11 in each quadrant) stimuli, consisting of successive rapidly changing numbers, by pressing a key. Accuracy and response speed for correctly detected targets is recorded.

LINE BISECTION

Patients are required to bisect three 180 mm centered horizontal lines on separate landscape A4 sheets of paper.

PATIENTS

Two outpatients diagnosed with chronic unilateral left-sided spatial neglect following a right hemisphere stroke were recruited to the study. Both patients were right-handed, medically stable, native English-speaking adults who had no known hearing impairment and no prior musical training. Patient 1 had reduced visual acuity in one eye (secondary to previous retinal vein occlusion). Other than this, there was no known prior neurological, cognitive, or psychiatric disease. The study was approved by the National Research Ethics Service and both patients gave full consent.

Patient 1 was a 46-year-old male who sustained an ischemic stroke 5 years and 11 months prior to commencement of baseline testing. His stroke resulted in a large right middle cerebral artery territory infarct involving the frontal, parietal, and temporal lobes (**Figure 2A**). Patient 2 was a 63-year-old male who sustained an ischemic stroke 4 years and 5 months prior to commencement of baseline testing. His stroke also resulted in a large right middle cerebral artery territory infarct involving the frontal, parietal, and temporal lobes (**Figure 2B**). Patient 2 required a hemicraniectomy involving temporary removal of part of the skull to help reduce brain swelling.

PROCEDURE

The four weekly 30-min intervention sessions involved playing scales and familiar melodies on 12 chime bars (C_4–G_5), which were arranged horizontally, increasing in pitch from right to left (**Figure 3**). A series of foam frames were used to enable flexibility in the spatial layout using three fixed frame sizes. Chime bars were placed adjacent to each other either (1) one chime bar width apart on the smallest frame (level one), (2) one and a half chime bar widths apart on the middle frame (level two), or (3) two chime bar widths apart on the largest frame (level three). This enabled the intervention sessions to be calibrated for each patient, according to the precise limits of spatial exploration seen. Patients started on level one, and progressed up a level when they played all 12 bars in a row from right to left three consecutive times in one session without errors. When starting at level one, the space between the sixth and the seventh chime bars was at the patient's midline, with half of the bars reaching to the patient's right, and the other half reaching to the patient's left. From this point on, the chime bar at the patient's far right became the anchor point for successive levels. Namely, it remained in the same place in relation to the patient's midline throughout the intervention phase, such that the increasing distance between bars stretched out into the left field only, encouraging leftward movement.

FIGURE 3 | During the intervention session, the patients observed and repeated the experimenter modeling simple scales and melodies. A series of three foam frames allowed the spacing between chime bars to be increased as performance improved (see text for more details).

Sessions followed an ABA format where part A comprised playing up to one and a half octaves of a C major scale, and part B comprised playing familiar melodies. During the scale-playing, the patient was instructed to "play all the bars, one after the other, right to left, starting here." At the end of the instruction, the researcher would point to the bar on the patient's far right to ensure that they started playing at the correct location. The same instruction was repeated three consecutive times both at the start and at the end of each session. Patients were encouraged to play at their own speed.

Both patients reported prior familiarity with the two melodies used in part B – *Frère Jacques* and *Do-Re-Mi.* Both songs start at the first scale degree and slowly move up in chunks of around three (*Frère Jacques* and the first half of *Do-Re-Mi*) to six (the second half of *Do-Re-Mi*) notes at a time.

Frère Jacques has a range of six notes (C4–A4) and each subphrase of the song repeats itself twice, allowing for repetition and encouraging memorization. The benefit of the range was that patients would not be required to cross their midline to complete the song before they had reached level two. Patients progressed to *Do-Re-Mi* after they had played *Frère Jacques* once all the way through from beginning to end with no instruction from the researcher. Self corrected errors were permitted.

Do-Re-Mi has a range of an octave; eight white notes (C4–C5). Therefore, unlike *Frère Jacques,* in order to play the whole song the patient had to cross their midline on all three levels. The subphrases of the second half of the song comprised around six consecutive notes, which encouraged patients to cover a larger spatial array and draw their attention further to their left.

The researcher sat directly opposite the patient throughout the intervention and modeled playing the melodies. This was achieved by initially singing and playing the song that was being worked on from beginning to end, and then breaking it down into small sections for the patient to play back. Each small section was repeated three times before progressing to the next section, to help the patient become familiar with the playing. Each section was then slowly put together, ultimately building it up into a complete piece of music. The patient was invited to sing along throughout.

The scales and familiar melodies that were the focus of each music session were consolidated through structured homework between each session, which was administered via a CD. The patient heard the experimenter verbally explain that they were about to hear the experimenter sing and play a pitch sequence, which they should listen to and repeat. Each exercise corresponded to one CD track. The patient was instructed to complete only the set of exercises (tracks) that were worked on during the intervention session that week, which was clearly written out on a homework sheet. Each patient was provided with a set of chime bars and the foam frame that was appropriate to their respective level at any given week. The patients were asked to work through three sets of the assigned homework exercises twice a day, and to log each completed session.

RESULTS

BASELINE PERIOD

The mean baseline responses from each test are summarized in **Table 1**. Responses confirmed that both patients scored within the pathological range for neglect across all tests prior to the intervention period with respect to responses made on the left side, as well as in total (left and right side combined). Further, Patient 1's right side target detection responses on the TAP fell within the pathological range.

SHORT-TERM AND LONGER-LASTING TREATMENT EFFECTS

To determine whether significant short-term changes in performance had occurred as a function of the intervention sessions,

Table 1 | Baseline descriptive statistics.

Test				Patient 1		Patient 2	
		Unit	Max. score	Mean	SD	Mean	SD
Mesulam shape	Left	Omissions	30	26	2.65	8[a]	1.00
	Right	Omissions	30	1.33	1.53	0.33	0.58
	Total	Omissions	60	27.33[a]	4.04	8.33[a]	1.53
BIT star	Left	Omissions	27	17.67[a]	2.52	3[a]	2.00
	Right	Omissions	27	1.67	1.53	2	2.65
	Total	Omissions	54	19.33[a]	4.04	5[a]	3.61
TAP	Left	Omissions	22	19[a]	N/A	21[a]	N/A
	Right	Omissions	22	10.67[a]	4.73	1.33	0.58
	Total	Omissions	44	29.67[a]	4.73	22.33[a]	0.58
TAP (mean reaction time)	Left	ms	∞	1276[a]	386.99	N/A	N/A
	Right	ms	∞	869	135.35	903.67	113.32
	Total	ms	∞	1073[a]	174.79	946.70[a]	66.32
Line bisection[b]		mm		10.22[a]	6.43	18.56[a]	9.14

[a]*Within pathological range as reported in previous studies: Mesulam shape (Mesulam, 1985; Machner et al., 2012), BIT Star (Wilson et al., 1987), TAP (Zimmermann and Fimm, 2007), line bisection (Halligan et al., 1990; Mort et al., 2003).*

[b]*Average rightward deviation from true center from nine separate 180 mm lines (three each testing session).*

N/A, not available; unable to compute as either no variation between baseline scores (left TAP omissions) or unavailable mean reaction times resulting from either zero or only one detected stimuli on the left side.

Table 2 | Summary of results.

Test		Unit	Patient 1				Patient 2			
			Average pre	Average post	Mean baseline	Follow-up	Average pre	Average post	Mean baseline	Follow-up
Mesulam shape	Left	Omissions	**24**	**13**	**26**	**11**	**5**	**2**	**8**	**1**
	Total	Omissions	**27**	**13**	**27**	**13**	**6**	**2**	**8**	**1**
BIT star	Left	Omissions	8	6	**18**	**8**	5	3	3	1
	Total	Omissions	10	7	**19**	**10**	6	3	5	1
TAP	Left	Omissions	21	20	19	19	21	21	21	20
	Total	Omissions	29	27	30	23	22	22	22	24
Line bisection[a]		mm	11	14	10	17	20	10	19	16

Bold typeface indicates a significant improvement.

[a]*Average rightward deviation from the true center from three separate 180 mm lines during each testing session.*

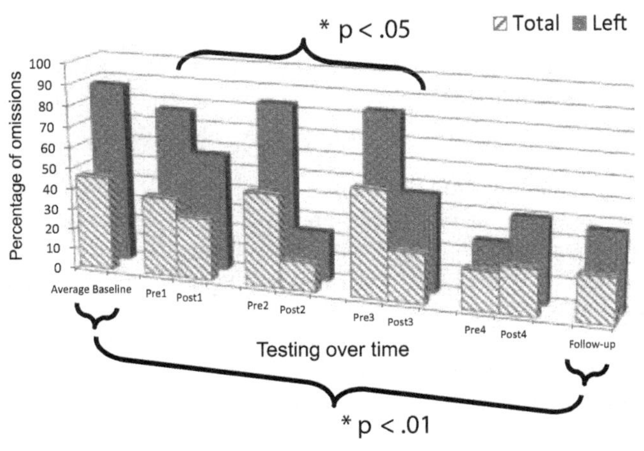

FIGURE 4 | Plot of Patient 1's average baseline, intervention period, and follow-up responses on the *Mesulam shape cancellation test*.

one sample t-tests were conducted using change scores (calculated by subtracting the pre-intervention scores from post-intervention scores) for each patient's left side and total (combined left and right) responses on each of the four tests. To test for longer-lasting treatment effects, z-scores were calculated, comparing scores on each test at follow-up for each patient against the corresponding mean baseline scores.

A summary of significant short-term (average pre and average post) and longer-lasting (mean baseline and follow-up) improvement can be seen for each patient in **Table 2**.

MESULAM SHAPE CANCELLATION TEST: PATIENT 1

Change scores for post versus pre-intervention sessions revealed a non-significant trend, both for responses on the left side, $t(3) = 1.675$, $p = 0.096$, and in total, $t(3) = 1.954$, $p = 0.073$ (**Figure 4**). An apparent lack of change post versus pre-intervention for session four appeared to be attributable to a ceiling effect resulting from a lasting improvement between the end of session three and the start of session four. When session four was omitted from the analysis, performance post versus pre-intervention for the remaining three sessions was significantly improved, both for responses on the left side, $t(2) = 3.352$, $p = 0.040$, and in total, $t(2) = 3.126$, $p = 0.045$.

Comparison of mean baseline performance with performance at follow-up showed significant improvement, both for responses on the left side, $z = 5.76$, $p < 0.001$, and in total, $z = 3.55$, $p < 0.001$ (**Figure 4**).

MESULAM SHAPE CANCELLATION TEST: PATIENT 2

Change scores for post versus pre-intervention sessions revealed significant improvement, both for responses on the left side, $t(3) = 2.777$, $p = 0.035$, and in total, $t(3) = 4.382$, $p = 0.011$ (**Figure 5**). Additionally, performance was in the normal range as evidenced by omitting a total of two or fewer targets after sessions one (Post1), three (Post3), and four (Post4).

Comparison of mean baseline performance with performance at follow-up showed significant improvement, both for responses on the left side, $z = 7.00$, $p < 0.001$, and in total, $z = 4.79$, $p < 0.001$ (**Figure 5**). Moreover, at the follow-up session, performance was in the normal range on the test as evidenced by omitting a total of only one target.

BIT STAR CANCELLATION TEST: PATIENT 1

Change scores for post versus pre-intervention sessions did not reveal significant improvement, neither for responses on the left side, $t(3) = 0.551$, $p = 0.310$, nor in total, $t(3) = 0.742$, $p = 0.256$ (**Figure 6**).

Comparison of mean baseline performance with performance at follow-up showed significant improvement, both for responses on the left side, $z = 3.84$, $p < 0.001$, and in total, $z = 2.31$, $p = 0.021$ (**Figure 6**).

BIT STAR CANCELLATION TEST: PATIENT 2

Change scores for post versus pre-intervention sessions did not reveal significant improvement, neither for responses on the left side, $t(3) = 0.651$, $p = 0.281$, nor in total, $t(3) = 0.762$, $p = 0.762$ (**Figure 7**).

Comparison of mean baseline performance with performance at follow-up did not show significant improvement, neither for responses on the left side, $z = 1.00$, $p = 0.317$, nor in total, $z = 1.12$,

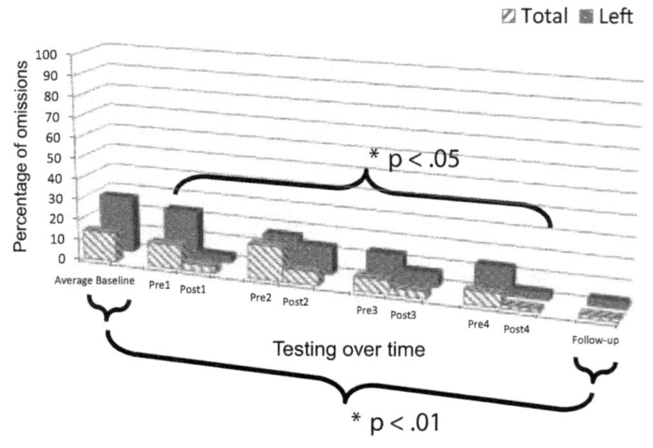

FIGURE 5 | Plot of Patient 2's average baseline, intervention period, and follow-up responses on the *Mesulam shape cancellation test*.

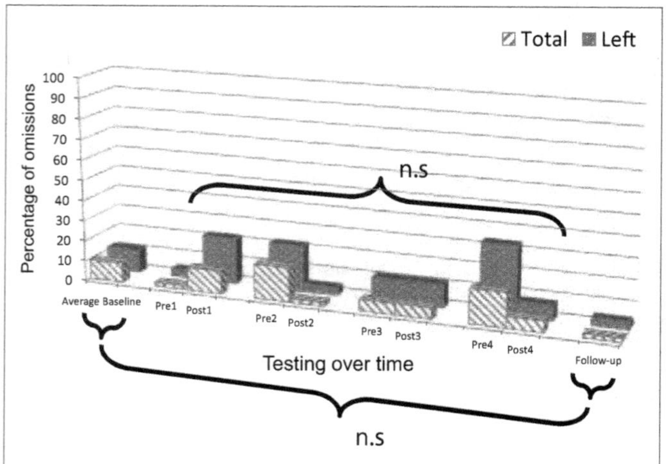

FIGURE 7 | Plot of Patient 2's average baseline, intervention period, and follow-up responses on the *BIT star cancellation test*.

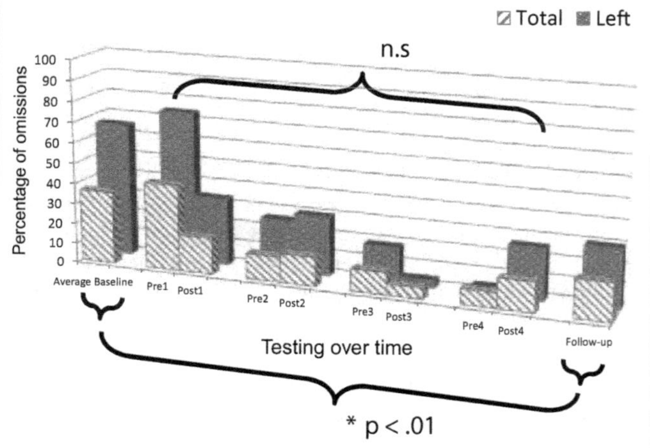

FIGURE 6 | Plot of Patient 1's average baseline, intervention period, and follow-up responses on the *BIT star cancellation test*.

$p = 0.263$ (**Figure 7**). Performance was in the normal range on the test as evidenced by omitting a total of only one target three times during the study including before session one (Pre1), after session two (Post2), and at follow-up.

TEST OF ATTENTIONAL PERFORMANCE (TAP)

Although response time data were collected, mean response times could not be computed owing to a paucity of correctly detected targets in both patients.

TAP (OMISSIONS): PATIENT 1

Change scores for post versus pre-intervention sessions did not reveal significant improvement, neither for responses on the left side, $t(3) = 0.577$ $p = 0.302$, nor in total, $t(3) = 0.739$, $p = 0.257$.

Analysis of longer-lasting effects could not be computed for responses on the left side because of insufficient variation in performance during the baseline period (omissions scores were identical for all three baseline testing sessions). Comparison of mean baseline performance with performance at follow-up did not show significant improvement on total test responses, $z = 1.41$, $p = 0.159$.

TAP (OMISSIONS): PATIENT 2

Change scores for post versus pre-intervention sessions did not reveal significant improvement, neither for responses on the left side, $t(3) = -1.000$, $p = 0.196$, nor in total, $t(3) = -0.293$, $p = 0.395$.

As for Patient 1, analysis of longer-lasting effects could not be computed for responses on the left side because of insufficient variation in performance during the baseline period (omissions scores were identical for all three baseline testing sessions). Comparison of mean baseline performance with performance at follow-up showed significant decline in performance on total test responses, $z = -2.88$, $p = 0.004$, attributable to a change in performance on the right side.

LINE BISECTION TEST: PATIENT 1

Change scores for post versus pre-intervention sessions did not reveal significant improvement on test responses, $t(3) = -2.189$, $p = 0.058$.

Comparison of mean baseline performance with performance at follow-up did not show significant improvement on test responses, $z = -1.11$, $p = 0.267$.

LINE BISECTION TEST: PATIENT 2

Change scores for post versus pre-intervention sessions did not reveal significant improvement on test responses, $t(3) = 1.242$, $p = 0.151$.

Comparison of mean baseline performance with performance at follow-up did not show significant improvement on test responses, $z = 0.028$, $p = 0.780$.

DISCUSSION

Operating within the broad framework of NMT (Thaut, 2008), the aim of the present study was to explore whether musical training on a horizontally aligned instrument (chime bars) would increase spatial awareness in patients with chronic unilateral neglect. It was hypothesized that patients would perform better on neglect tests after, compared to before, the music intervention sessions (demonstrating short-term treatment effects), and that patients would perform better on neglect tests at follow-up one week after the intervention compared to the baseline period (demonstrating a longer-lasting treatment effect).

As predicted, short-term treatment effects were found for both participants on the Mesulam shape cancellation test. For Patient 1, improvement was observed after sessions one, two, and three. At the beginning of sessions two and three, however, performance returned to a similar level seen at baseline. Interestingly, this fluctuation seemed to stabilize after session three, which may be explained by a consolidation of repeated effects of the intervention and weekly homework. While no significant short-term improvements were seen on the BIT star cancellation test for either patient, for Patient 1 at least, this may be explained due to a large and sustained treatment effect following session one, leaving little room for further short-term improvements.

Longer-lasting treatment effects were found for both participants on the Mesulam shape cancellation test. Patient 1 showed this longer-lasting treatment effect on the BIT star cancellation test, despite not showing significant short-term improvements (supporting the above suggestion that an early and sustained improvement occurred in session one). Furthermore, Patient 2 performed in the clinically normal range on both the Mesulam shape and BIT star cancellation tests at follow-up.

An important possibility to consider is whether or not the improvements seen during the intervention period may be at least in part owing to the repeated testing and hence increased familiarity with the clinical tests. We consider this unlikely for two reasons: first, neither patient showed systematic improvement during the baseline period on either of the cancellation tasks, which would be expected according to a "practice effect" explanation. Second, a recent study examining test–retest reliability of two cancellation tasks, including the Mesulam cancellation task, in 15 chronic neglect patients over five consecutive days, demonstrated stable performance that did not show a significant practice effect (Machner et al., 2012).

While significant improvements were observed on the Mesulam shape cancellation test, and to some extent on the BIT star cancellation test, similar improvements were not found on the TAP or the line bisection. One reason for the improved performance on the paper and pencil cancellation tasks may be that these tasks most closely mirror the nature of the intervention, whereby patients were required to constantly orient their attention and make movements toward their left side in order to find the next chime bar to play. Moreover, the cancellation tasks, like the music training, involved sequential processing of information, rather than repeated responses in the same location as was required for the line bisection and TAP. Thus, there might be a more effective transfer of "trained" behavior contributing to this finding.

Clearly, many aspects of the musical intervention used here may have contributed to the improvements seen in both patients and further studies may attempt to isolate some of the potential underlying mechanisms of the intervention. Music-making of the kind involved here is by nature visuomotor and goal-directed, both of which have been highlighted as important factors for rehabilitation of spatial attention (Harvey et al., 2003; Harvey and Rossit, 2012). In addition, the sequential aspect of the intervention, whereby patients played back simple and short scales and melodies with a predetermined sequence and clear end-point is likely to have played a role, echoing Ishiai and colleagues' findings, which showed that patients performed better on tasks of visuo-spatial attention when such tasks required them to sequentially number targets (1990) and complete sequences (1997). Further, the spatially systematic nature of the pitch-based feedback may have also played an important role: Cioffi et al. (2011, 2014), showed that patients with neglect proceeded further to the left while playing a keyboard when responses were systematically paired with tones, as opposed to random pairing of key/pitch or silence. Determining the relative contributions of the pitch feedback versus the role of making repeated physical movements in the neglected part of space could be tested by comparing (1) the current combined auditory–motor intervention against (2) a motor only intervention with silent chime bars or woodblocks that produce sound with no changing pitch against (3) an auditory only intervention comprising vertical or stationary playing at midline, with pitch feedback.

As with any intervention approach where lasting effects are desired, it will be important to determine the dose–response relationship: how many sessions are optimal to achieve lasting treatment effects, how long do such effects last, and do they translate into improvement in activities of daily living, as measured by more ecological tasks such as the Catherine Bergego Scale (Azouvi, 2003). While both patients in the study had chronic neglect, further work will be required to ascertain whether such an intervention can improve neglect in the acute stage. Similarly, while neglect is typically a heterogeneous syndrome (Hillis, 2006), our findings are most relevant to patients with peripersonal neglect and it remains an empirical question as to whether the benefits would extend, e.g., to presentations of auditory or personal neglect.

The current study has demonstrated that active music-making holds promise as an effective intervention for neglect patients. Further research in this as yet untapped area has key implications for the improvement of existing clinical interventions and development of future treatment protocols. A deeper understanding of the underlying mechanisms has the capacity to contribute to the expanding scientific knowledge base of music interventions relevant to improving quality of life in this clinical group.

ACKNOWLEDGMENTS

The authors would like to thank the patients for participating in the study. They would also like to acknowledge the support of Korina Li, Clinical Research Fellow at Imperial College London, and the Neuro-disability Research Trust. Rebeka Bodak was supported by a Ph.D. Mobility Fellowship from Aarhus University. Lauren Stewart was supported by a grant from the Leverhulme Trust RPG-297.

REFERENCES

Altenmüller, E., and Schlaug, G. (2013). Neurologic music therapy: the beneficial effects of music making on neurorehabilitation. *Acoust. Sci. Technol.* 34, 5–12. doi:10.1250/ast.34.5

Azouvi, P., Olivier, S., de Montety, G., Samuel, C., Louis-Dreyfus, A., and Tesio, L. (2003). Behavioral assessment of unilateral neglect: study of the psychometric properties of the Catherine Bergego Scale. *Arch. Phys. Med. Rehabil.* 84, 51–57. doi:10.1053/apmr.2003.50062

Barrett, A. M., Goedert, K. M., and Basso, J. C. (2012). Prism adaptation for spatial neglect after stroke: translational practice gaps. *Nat. Rev. Neurosci.* 8, 567–577. doi:10.1038/nrneurol.2012.170.Prism

Beschin, N., Cocchini, G., Allen, R., and Della Sala, S. (2012). Anosognosia and neglect respond differently to the same treatments. *Neuropsychol. Rehabil.* 22, 550–562. doi:10.1080/09602011.2012.669353

Borghese, N., Bottini, G., and Sedda, A. (2013). Videogame based neglect rehabilitation: a role for spatial remapping and multisensory integration? *Front. Hum. Neurosci.* 7:116. doi:10.3389/fnhum.2013.00116

Bowen, A., and Lincoln, N. (2008). Cognitive rehabilitation for spatial neglect following stroke. *Cochrane Database Syst. Rev.* 4, CD003586. doi:10.1002/14651858.CD003586

Bowen, A., McKenna, K., and Tallis, R. C. (1999). Reasons for variability in the reported rate of occurrence of unilateral spatial neglect after stroke. *Stroke* 30, 1196–1202. doi:10.1161/01.STR.30.6.1196

Buxbaum, L. J., Ferraro, M. K., Veramonti, T., Farne, A., Whyte, J., Ladavas, E., et al. (2004). Hemispatial neglect: subtypes, neuroanatomy, and disability. *Neurology* 62, 749–756. doi:10.1212/01.WNL.0000113730.73031.F4

Cioffi, M. C., Bernardi, N. F., Maravita, A., Ronchi, R., Fumagalli, F., Bricolo, E., et al. (2011). "Can active music-making facilitate spatial exploration?", in *Poster session presented at: The Neurosciences and Music IV: Learning and Memory*, Edinburgh, UK.

Cioffi, M. C., Bernardi, N. F., Ronchi, R., Maravita, A., Bricolo, E., Zigiotto, L., et al. (2014). "Improving left spatial neglect by scale-playing", in *Poster session presented at: The Neurosciences and Music V: Cognitive Stimulation and Rehabilitation*, Dijon, France.

Doricchi, F., Thiebaut de Schotten, M., Tomaiuolo, F., and Bartolomeo, P. (2008). White matter (dis)connections and gray matter (dys)functions in visual neglect: gaining insights into the brain networks of spatial awareness. *Cortex* 44, 983–995. doi:10.1016/j.cortex.2008.03.006

Halligan, P. W., Manning, L., and Marshall, J. C. (1990). Individual variation in line bisection: a study of four patients with right hemisphere damage and normal controls. *Neuropsychologia* 28, 1043–1051. doi:10.1016/0028-3932(90)90139-F

Harvey, M., Hood, B., North, A., and Robertson, I. H. (2003). The effects of visuomotor feedback training on the recovery of hemispatial neglect symptoms: assessment of a 2-week and follow-up intervention. *Neuropsychologia* 41, 886–893. doi:10.1016/S0028-3932(03)00003-4

Harvey, M., and Rossit, S. (2012). Visuospatial neglect in action. *Neuropsychologia* 50, 1018–1028. doi:10.1016/j.neuropsychologia.2011.09.030

Heilman, K. M., Watson, R. T., and Valenstein, E. (2003). "Neglect and related disorders", in *Clinical Neuropsychology*, eds K. M. Heilman, and E. Valenstein, (New York: OUP), 296–346. doi:10.1016/j.neuropsychologia.2011.09.030

Hillis, A. E. (2006). Neurobiology of unilateral spatial neglect. *Neuroscientist* 12, 153–163. doi:10.1177/1073858405284257

Hommel, M., Peres, B., Pollak, P., Memin, B., Besson, G., Gaio, J.-M., et al. (1990). Effects of passive tactile and auditory stimuli on left visual neglect. *Arch. Neurol.* 47, 573–576. doi:10.1001/archneur.1990.00530050097018

Humphreys, G., Watelet, A., and Riddoch, M. (2006). Long-term effects of prism adaptation in chronic visual neglect: a single case study. *Cogn. Neuropsychol.* 23, 463–478. doi:10.1080/02643290500202755

Ishiai, S., Seki, K., Koyama, Y., and Izumi, Y. (1997). Disappearance of unilateral spatial neglect following a simple instruction. *J. Neurol. Neurosurg. Psychiatr.* 63, 23–27. doi:10.1136/jnnp.63.1.23

Ishiai, S., Sugishita, M., Odajima, N., Yaginuma, M., Gono, S., and Kamaya, T. (1990). Improvement of unilateral spatial neglect with numbering. *Neurology* 40, 1395–1398. doi:10.1212/WNL.40.9.1395

Jehkonen, M., Laihosalo, M., and Kettunen, J. (2006). Anosognosia after stroke: assessment, occurrence, subtypes and impact on functional outcome reviewed. *Acta Neurol. Scand.* 114, 293–306. doi:10.1111/j.1600-0404.2006.00723.x

Karnath, H. O., Ferber, S., and Himmelbach, M. (2001). Spatial awareness is a function of the temporal not the posterior parietal lobe. *Nature* 411, 950–953. doi:10.1038/35082075

Kim, Y. M., Chun, M. H., Yun, G. J., Song, Y. J., and Young, H. E. (2011). The effect of virtual reality training on unilateral spatial neglect in stroke patients. *Ann. Rehabil. Med.* 35, 309–315. doi:10.5535/arm.2011.35.3.309

Luauté, J., Halligan, P., Rode, G., Rossetti, Y., and Boisson, D. (2006). Visuo-spatial neglect: a systematic review of current interventions and their effectiveness. *Neurosci. Biobehav. Rev.* 30, 961–982. doi:10.1016/j.neubiorev.2006.03.001

Machner, B., Mah, Y.-H., Gorgoraptis, N., and Husain, M. (2012). How reliable is repeated testing for hemispatial neglect? Implications for clinical follow-up and treatment trials. *J. Neurol. Neurosurg. Psychiatr.* 83, 1032–1034. doi:10.1136/jnnp-2012-303032

Mesulam, M. M. (1985). *Principles of Behavioural Neurology. Tests of Directed Attention and Memory.* Philadelphia: Davis.

Mort, D. J., Malhotra, P., Mannan, S. K., Rorden, C., Pambakian, A., Kennard, C., et al. (2003). The anatomy of visual neglect. *Brain* 126, 1986–1997. doi:10.1093/brain/awg200

Pizzamiglio, L., Fasotti, L., Jehkonen, M., Antonucci, G., Magnotti, L., and Boelen, D. (2004). The use of opto-kinetic stimulation in rehabilitation of the hemi-neglect disorder. *Cortex* 40, 441–450. doi:10.1016/S0010-9452(08)70138-2

Reinhart, S., Schmidt, L., Kuhn, C., Rosenthal, A., Schenk, T., Keller, I., et al. (2012). Limb activation ameliorates body-related deficits in spatial neglect. *Front. Hum. Neurosci.* 6:188. doi:10.3389/fnhum.2012.00188

Ringman, J. M., Saver, J. L., Woolson, R. F., Clarke, W. R., and Adams, H. P. (2004). Frequency, risk factors, anatomy, and course of unilateral neglect in an acute stroke cohort. *Neurology* 63, 468–474. doi:10.1212/01.WNL.0000133011.10689.CE

Rode, G., Vallar, G., and Jacquin-Courtois, S. (2010). Bodily representations disorders and sensory manipulations. *Rev Neuropsychol* 2, 235–243. doi:10.3917/rne.023.0235

Rossetti, Y., Rode, G., Pisella, L., Farne, A., Li, L., Boisson, D., et al. (1998). Prism adaptation to a rightward optical deviation rehabilitates left hemispatial neglect. *Nature* 395, 166–169. doi:10.1038/25988

Stone, S. P., Halligan, P. W., and Greenwood, R. J. (1993). The incidence of neglect phenomena and related disorders in patients with an acute right or left hemisphere stroke. *Age Ageing* 22, 46–52. doi:10.1093/ageing/22.1.46

Thaut, M. H. (2008). *Rhythm, Music and the Brain: Scientific Foundations and Clinical Applications.* London: Taylor & Francis.

Vallar, G. (1993). "The anatomical basis of spatial neglect in humans", in *Unilateral Neglect: Clinical and Experimental Studies*, eds I. H. Robertson, and J. Marshall (Hove, UK:Lawrence Erlbaum Associates), 27–53.

Vallar, G., Rusconi, M. L., Barozzi, S., Bernardini, B., Ovadia, D., Papagno, C., et al. (1995). Improvement of left visuo-spatial hemineglect by left-sided transcutaneous electrical stimulation. *Neuropsychologia* 33, 73–82. doi:10.1016/0028-3932(94)00088-7

Wilson, B., Cockburn, J., and Halligan, P. W. (1987). *Behavioural Inattention Test.* Bury St. Edmunds: Thames Valley Test Company.

Zatorre, R. J., Chen, J. L., and Penhune, V. B. (2007). When the brain plays music: auditory-motor interactions in music perception and production. *Nat. Rev. Neurosci.* 8, 547–558. doi:10.1038/nrn2152

Zimmermann, P., and Fimm, B. (2007). *Test of Attentional Performance.* Vera Fimm: Psychologishe Testsysteme.

Zoccolotti, P., Matano, A., Deloche, G., Cantagallo, A., Passadori, A., Leclercq, M., et al. (2000). Patterns of attentional impairment following closed brain injury: a collaborative European study. *Cortex* 36, 93–107. doi:10.1016/S0010-9452(08)70839-6

12

The combination of rhythm and pitch can account for the beneficial effect of melodic intonation therapy on connected speech improvements in Broca's aphasia

Anna Zumbansen*[1,2,3], *Isabelle Peretz*[2,3,4] and *Sylvie Hébert*[1,2,3]

[1] *Faculty of Medicine, School of Speech Pathology and Audiology, Université de Montréal, Montreal, QC, Canada*
[2] *CRBLM, Centre for Research on Brain, Language and Music, McGill University, Montreal, QC, Canada*
[3] *BRAMS, International Laboratory for Research on Brain, Music, and Sound, Université de Montréal, Montreal, QC, Canada*
[4] *Faculty of Arts and Science, Department of Psychology, Université de Montréal, Montreal, QC, Canada*

Correspondence:
Sylvie Hébert, École d'orthophonie et d'audiologie, Université de Montréal, C.P.6128, Succursale Centre-Ville, Montréal, QC H3C 3J7, Canada
e-mail: sylvie.hebert@umontreal.ca

Melodic intonation therapy (MIT) is a structured protocol for language rehabilitation in people with Broca's aphasia. The main particularity of MIT is the use of intoned speech, a technique in which the clinician stylizes the prosody of short sentences using simple pitch and rhythm patterns. In the original MIT protocol, patients must repeat diverse sentences in order to espouse this way of speaking, with the goal of improving their natural, connected speech. MIT has long been regarded as a promising treatment but its mechanisms are still debated. Recent work showed that rhythm plays a key role in variations of MIT, leading to consider the use of pitch as relatively unnecessary in MIT. Our study primarily aimed to assess the relative contribution of rhythm and pitch in MIT's generalization effect to non-trained stimuli and to connected speech. We compared a melodic therapy (with pitch and rhythm) to a rhythmic therapy (with rhythm only) and to a normally spoken therapy (without melodic elements). Three participants with chronic post-stroke Broca's aphasia underwent the treatments in hourly sessions, 3 days per week for 6 weeks, in a cross-over design. The informativeness of connected speech, speech accuracy of trained and non-trained sentences, motor-speech agility, and mood was assessed before and after the treatments. The results show that the three treatments improved speech accuracy in trained sentences, but that the combination of rhythm and pitch elicited the strongest generalization effect both to non-trained stimuli and connected speech. No significant change was measured in motor-speech agility or mood measures with either treatment. The results emphasize the beneficial effect of both rhythm and pitch in the efficacy of original MIT on connected speech, an outcome of primary clinical importance in aphasia therapy.

Keywords: aphasia, melodic intonation therapy, treatment, speech, pitch and rhythm

INTRODUCTION

Aphasia is an acquired loss or impairment of the ability to communicate by language following brain damage (usually in the left hemisphere) and is present in more than one-third of stroke survivors (Wade et al., 1986; Dickey et al., 2010). Aphasia takes multiple forms. People with Broca's aphasia, one of the aphasic syndromes, have preserved simple verbal comprehension ability but have difficulty understanding complex syntactic sentences and, on the expressive side of language, they experience word-retrieval difficulty (i.e., anomia), grammar and syntax deficit (i.e., agrammatism), and apraxia of speech, a motor-speech disorder affecting the planning or programing of speech movements (AAN, 1994; Basso, 2003).

In its original form, Melodic Intonation Therapy (MIT, Albert et al., 1973; Sparks et al., 1974) is a formalized impairment-based approach of language rehabilitation in people with Broca's aphasia (AAN, 1994) (see Zumbansen et al., 2014 for a synthesis of MIT variations). The particularity of MIT in comparison to other therapies for aphasia is that it trains patients to produce speech using a form of singing to facilitate their speech output. The so-called intoned-speech technique is a musical stylization of the normal speech prosody using a few pitches (usually only two, separated by a third or a fourth) and a simple rhythm (quarter and eighth notes) on a slow tempo (Sparks, 2008). The stressed syllables of words are produced with higher voice intensity on the high pitch and a quarter note, whereas the unstressed syllables are produced with lower voice intensity on the low pitch and the eighth note. Patients first learn to intone speech through a structured, intensive therapeutic protocol where they are asked to produce numerous and varied short sentences, with the help of additional facilitation techniques, such as unison production, lip-reading, hand-tapping of the rhythm, and use of formulaic phrases that are often better produced in Broca's aphasia. Each sentence is repeated several times, first in unison with the clinician and gradually more autonomously but always with the intoned-speech technique. After a series of sessions, the last level of the program guides patients to return to a normal speech output and patients are supposed to intone speech only internally. The goal of MIT is to improve propositional speech, that is, the generative and controlled language on which people rely most to express their ideas in everyday life (Jackson, 1878; Van Lancker-Sidtis and Rallon, 2004). MIT has been rated as promising for the treatment of Broca's aphasia (AAN, 1994). It has been studied in several efficacy studies that have reported improvements in participants' natural connected speech (Sparks et al., 1974; Bonakdarpour et al., 2003; Schlaug et al., 2008, 2009; van der Meulen et al., 2014).

The role of the melodic elements in MIT has intrigued scientists since the very early publications of MIT and a variety of mechanisms have been proposed to explain MIT's efficacy (reviewed in Merrett et al., 2014; Zumbansen et al., 2014). To date, however, few have been tested. The early idea in the 1970s was that musical components could engage music processing regions of the right cerebral hemisphere and that these regions could potentially take over the role of the damaged left hemisphere language regions (Berlin, 1976; Helm-Estabrooks, 1983). The right-hemisphere contribution has been the most studied aspect of MIT but has not been unanimously supported (e.g., Belin et al., 1996). In fact, language hemisphere lateralization after stroke primarily depends on individual factors, and it is still unclear if any speech and language therapy can force the lateralization of language in one hemisphere or the other during brain reorganization after stroke (Anglade et al., 2014).

The role of melodic components in MIT has otherwise been studied at the behavioral level mainly with attempts to understand how rhythm or pitch could account for the beneficial effect of MIT. In transversal studies, the rhythmic component of intoned-speech production appears to be responsible for on-line facilitation of patients' speech accuracy (Laughlin et al., 1979; Boucher et al., 2001; Stahl et al., 2011). Longitudinal studies have used variations of MIT where only a limited set of sentences (10 to 15) is repeatedly trained (i.e., palliative variations of MIT, see Zumbansen et al., 2014) and examined if participants improved their speech accuracy in normally spoken sentences trained either with intoned speech (i.e., with rhythm and pitch), with rhythmic speech (i.e., without musical pitch) or non-trained (Wilson et al., 2006; Stahl et al., 2013). Significant improvement was obtained for trained sentences compared to non-trained items and pitch did not add any beneficial effect over rhythm on speech accuracy immediately post-treatment. Therefore, the utility of pitch in MIT is currently questioned. In both studies, no transfer of improvements to the non-trained phrases was observed. One possible explanation is that these versions of MIT did not include a basic characteristic of the original MIT, namely the numerous sentences that have to be presented to avoid the use of rote memory (Sparks, 2008), a strategy that was pointed as a generalization factor by several authors (Thompson, 1989; Nadeau et al., 2008). Changes in natural connected speech, the ultimate goal of MIT, were not assessed in these studies.

For a long time, many studies have measured treatment efficacy on trained material only (e.g., number of correct syllables produced in sentences repeatedly trained). Others have used verbal tasks with non-trained items such as sentence repetition and picture naming to capture improvement in specific speech and language abilities (Brady et al., 2012). However, these tasks may not reveal how patients use language in natural speech. In reviewing efficacy studies in the aphasia literature, Beeson and Robey (2006) have distinguished direct effects on trained stimuli, generalization to non-trained stimuli, and generalization to connected speech. Here too we will refer to these effects as direct effect, indirect effect, and generalization, respectively. A common way to measure connected speech improvements in functional communication is to count the presence of Correct Information Units (CIU) in a speech sample. Nicholas and Brookshire (1993) define CIUs as words that are intelligible in context and accurately convey information relevant to the eliciting stimulus. Informativeness, the efficiency in conveying and transmitting correct information to the listener, can be calculated by dividing the number of CIUs in a speech sample by the number of words in the sample. This measure has been validated to assess language in the connected speech of people with aphasia and healthy individuals (Nicholas and Brookshire, 1993).

Little is known about the mechanisms that promote generalization to connected speech in aphasia therapy. A number of treatment components are thought to play a role in this effect (see Frey, 2013 for a recent literature and expert panel review), but to our knowledge, none has been explicitly tested as a generalization mechanism to natural discourse in impairment-based aphasia treatments. Studies on therapeutic protocols such as MIT that were designed to elicit improvements in connected speech can give insights in treatment factors promoting this type of generalization. Interestingly, the melodic characteristics of MIT, which set this treatment apart from other speech and language therapies, seem to play a role in MIT's generalization effect. In a study with two participants with Broca's aphasia, Schlaug et al. (2008) compared the original MIT with a control treatment differing from MIT only by the absence of the pitch and rhythmic components. MIT led to greater improvement than the non-musical treatment on measures including informativeness of connected speech. The melodic components were deemed key efficacy factors for MIT. A firmer conclusion is anticipated with the results of an ongoing randomized control trial comparing the two treatments on language outcome in connected speech (Schlaug and Norton, 2011).

Our study aims to assess the relative contribution of the rhythmic and pitch features of MIT's generalization effect to connected speech. Thus, we designed a variation of MIT (hereafter referred to as melodic therapy) that includes basic characteristics thought to promote generalization (large number of various sentences and intensive treatment delivery). We compared this melodic therapy (MT) with two control treatments: rhythmic therapy (RT), that is, MT without musical pitch, and spoken therapy (ST), without pitch or rhythmic aspects. Furthermore, in order to capture the degrees of direct and indirect effects elicited by the melodic components, we measured speech accuracy in a subset of 10 sentences that were repeatedly trained at each treatment session and in 10 non-trained sentences.

Other proposed mechanisms related to the melodic aspect of MIT have never been assessed. One of them is that singing could keep patients motivated to continue with an intensive therapy regimen because it is a pleasurable activity (Racette et al., 2006). Data demonstrating that music and singing can positively influence mood in healthy individuals and in various clinical populations has also led to the suggestion that the singing aspect of MIT could benefit patients' mood (Merrett et al., 2014). Finally, we have suggested that MIT could mostly benefit apraxia of speech, the motor-speech symptom of Broca's aphasia's syndrome (Zumbansen et al., 2014). Indeed, the best responders to MIT have this symptom in common. In a first attempt to evaluate these suggested mechanisms, we tested the mood and the motor-speech agility of the participants as additional, secondary outcomes.

MATERIALS AND METHODS

PARTICIPANTS

Three native French-speaking, right-handed men with aphasia (FL, FS, and JPL) participated in the study. They were recruited through an association of persons with aphasia located in the greater Montreal area. Each had experienced a single ischemic unilateral left hemisphere cerebrovascular accident more than 1 year prior to their involvement in the study and had been through the standard public rehabilitation services, which commonly discharge aphasic patients when their language improvements reach a plateau. They had not received any speech-language therapy since. None of the participants had experienced neurological or psychiatric problems before the stroke. An examination by a certified audiologist attested that they had no hearing deficit. **Table 1** summarizes patients' characteristics, and **Table 2** presents the scores of francophone language tests and non-verbal cognitive tests. Each subject had a clinical profile consistent with Broca's aphasia, that is, naming deficits, agramatism, apraxia of speech, and relatively preserved simple verbal comprehension compared to expressive difficulties. FL and JPL had a moderate degree of aphasia whereas FS had a more severe clinical profile, especially because he experienced more severe apraxia of speech than the other participants in connected speech. FL and FS had a right upper-limb hemiplegia while JPL had almost completely recovered from it. The three participants had been treated for focal epilepsy and JPL has also been treated for depression since his stroke. All three participants were good candidates for MIT according to the American Academy of Neurology (1994): they had Broca's aphasia and were willing to undergo intensive individual speech and language treatment. They gave their informed consent and the study was approved by the Ethical Committee of the Montreal University Geriatric Institute.

VERBAL MATERIAL

A total of 240 2- to 8-syllable-long phrases were created by two graduate students in speech and language pathology and the first author (an experienced speech and language therapist). Phrases were selected so as to fit participants' daily living, as would do a typical clinician in aphasia therapy. They were split into 180 New-phrases (2- to 8-syllable long) and 60 Test-phrases (4- to 5-syllable long). The 180 New-phrases were used for the purpose of the interventions. The same 180 sentences were used in the same order for the three consecutive treatments, so that one phrase was presented once for each treatment, leaving a minimal interval of

Table 1 | Participants' characteristics.

Participant	Sex	Age	Education (in years)	Years of formal musical training	Months post-stroke (at recruitment)	Aphasia diagnosis
FL	M	57	17	0	20	Moderate Broca's aphasia
FS	M	50	13	0	24	Severe Broca's aphasia
JPL	M	48	16	0	21	Moderate Broca's aphasia

Table 2 | Participants's language and non-verbal cognitive diagnostic assessments.

	FL	FS	JPL
MT-86 aphasia battery (Nespoulous et al., 1992)			
Expression			
Naming/31	**17** [28]	**8** [28]	**17** [23]
Narrative discourse/18	**9** [9]	**2** [9]	**7** [8]
Global reduction of fluency	**Moderate**	**Severe**	**Moderate**
Agrammatism	**Severe**	**Severe**	**Severe**
Syntactic deviations	**Moderate**	**Severe**	**Moderate**
Anomia	**Moderate**	**Severe**	**Moderate**
Phonetic deviations	**Moderate**	**Severe**	**Moderate**
Phonemic deviations (and/or jargon)	**Moderate**	**Severe**	**Moderate**
Semantic deviations	**Moderate**	**Mild**	**Mild**
Repetition/30	**16** [24]	**9** [24]	**12** [27]
Comprehension/47	**24** [40]	**33** [40]	**34** [39]
Words/9	9	8	9
Sentences/38	**15**	**25**	**25**
Verbal fluency test (Cardebat et al., 1990)			
Phonemic fluency	**2** (−2.6)	**8** (−2.2)	**8** (−2.2)
Semantic fluency	**6** (−3.9)	**7** (−3.7)	**23** (−2.3)
Abbreviated MBEMA (Peretz et al., 2013)			
Pitch/20	15	**9** (−4.1)	14
Rhythm/20	17	16	17
Memory/20	15	**13** (−3.6)	17
PEGV (Agniel et al., 1992)			
Visual agnosia/66	62	62	66
WAIS (Wechsler, 1997a)			
Matrix reasoning/26	22	11	23
WMS (Wechsler, 1997b)			
Spatial span/32	10	15	17
Tower of London – Drexel University (Culbertson and Zillmer, 2001)			
Total move score	7	32	20

When available, the maximum score is indicated next to the test name. Measures considered below the relevant norms for patient's demographics are printed in bold and number of standard deviations (SD) to the mean is indicated next to the scores in parentheses. Cut-off scores for patients' age and education are in square brackets. MBEMA, Montreal Battery of Evaluation of Musical Abilities; PEGV, Protocole d'évaluation des gnosies visuelles (Visual agnosia diagnostic battery); WAIS-III, Wechsler Adult Intelligence Scale – third edition; WMS, Wechsler Memory Scale – third edition.

6 weeks between two presentations. Test-phrases served to assess the direct and indirect effects of the treatments. These items were four- to five-syllable long, that is, of medium difficulty compared to the New-phrases.

All sentences were recorded in three modes: intoned, rhythmically spoken, and normally spoken, for a total of 720 recordings (see an example in **Figure 1**). The stimuli were produced by a natural voice in the way a speech and language therapist would do in a real clinical setting following the instructions of the different production modes and with the help of pitch and tempo cues given prior to the recordings. In the intoned mode, the stimuli had pitch variation on two notes separated by a fourth interval. We chose G# and C# according to an estimate of participants' vocal speech range to allow them to reproduce the pitches without vocal strain. Stimuli were presented by a female voice and were reproduced one octave lower by participants. Each syllable had to be produced on a single pitch. The high pitch was associated with syllables that are stressed in natural prosody of French (e.g., the last syllable of a clause) and with the syllables of function words (e.g., prepositions, pronouns, and articles), according to a French adaptation of MIT (Therapie Mélodique et Rythmée, Van Eeckhout and Bhatt, 1984), because they are often omitted in Broca's aphasic speech. In addition to musical pitch variation, the intoned sentences were produced with rhythm: syllables had to be temporally organized on a regular beat of 100 bpm with high pitch twice as long as low pitches. In the rhythmically spoken mode, phrases had to be produced only with the rhythmic element following the same tempo cue as in the intoned mode and otherwise with continuous voice frequency variation typical of speech. In the normally spoken mode, both above mentioned pitch and rhythm elements were absent. The sentences were produced with clear and slow articulation and with prosody consistent with the French morpho-syntactic rules, as would do clinicians in standard aphasia therapy. Mean syllable duration was computed by dividing each stimulus duration in milliseconds by its number of syllables. Significant differences were found across stimuli modes. In average, compared to melodic syllables ($M = 1130$, $SD = 146$), rhythmic syllables ($M = 1040$, $SD = 146$) were 90 ms shorter while spoken syllables ($M = 556$, $SD = 94$) were twice shorter.

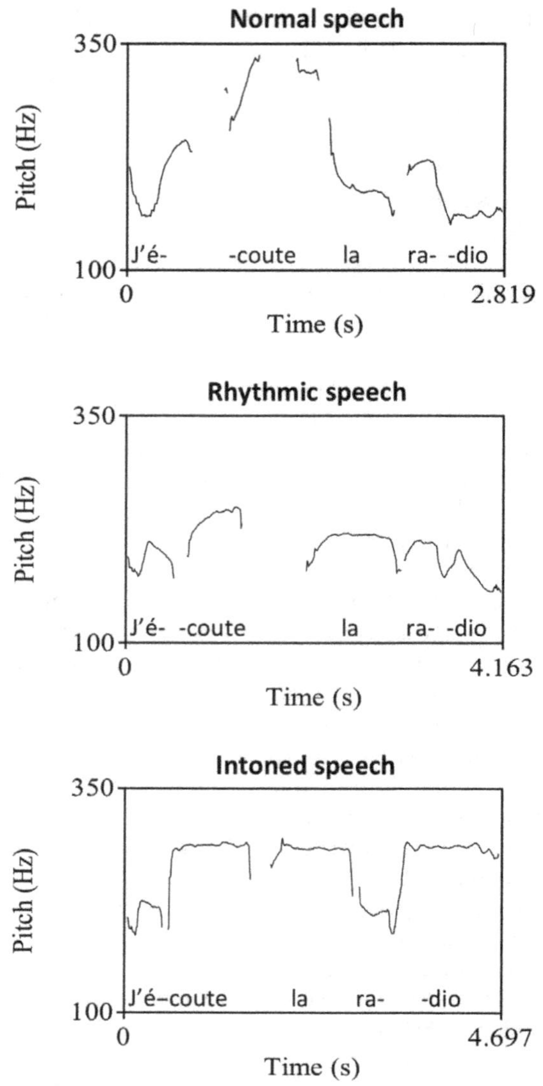

FIGURE 1 | Sentence example ("I listen to the radio") in normal, rhythmic, and intoned speech. Graphs represent the fundamental frequency of the voice in recordings as extracted by the software for speech analysis, Praat (Boersma and Weenick, 2013).

TREATMENTS

Each treatment (MT, RT, and ST) was administered by a trained graduate student in speech and language therapy, at a frequency of 3 one-hour sessions/week for 6 weeks (i.e., 18 sessions/treatment). They differed only with regard to the presence or absence of hand-tapping and musical elements in the stimuli. In the MT, patients had to repeat intoned sentences and were guided to tap the rhythm along with their left hand (hereafter simply referred to as hand-tapping). The RT consisted of rhythmically spoken stimuli and hand-tapping. In the ST, patients were presented with normally spoken stimuli and no hand-tapping was elicited.

During sessions, participant and therapist sat facing each other at a table in a quiet room. Participants had to listen and produce 20 phrases (see examples in **Table 3**), each following a progressive procedure in four steps: two times in unison, two times in unison with therapist fading-out at half-way, one time in repetition alone, and finally alone in response to a question. Half of the sentences were New-phrases ranging from two to eight syllables (one phrase of two, three, seven, and eight syllables and two of four, five, and six syllables), beginning with the shortest and progressing on to the longest sentences. The other half were Test-phrases repeatedly trained at each session to ultimately assess the direct effect of the treatment. The stimuli were first heard from an iPod connected to speakers and immediately reproduced by the therapist to allow lip-reading. Up to four attempts were allowed in the steps where unison was used. If the participant still failed to produce the phrase successfully, the item was discontinued and the next phrase was presented. When errors occurred at the two last steps, the preceding step was reintroduced before trying again and if this second attempt failed, the item was discontinued.

Table 3 | Characteristics and examples of sentences worked out during a treatment session.

Presentation order	Item status	Number of syllables	Sentences
1	New	2	Parfait (*All right*)
2	New	3	Il fait froid (*It's cold*)
3	New	4	Je te regarde (*I'm watching you*)
4	New	4	Prends le courrier (*Take the mail!*)
5	New	5	La porte est ouverte (*The door is open*)
6	New	5	Voici mon adresse (*Here is my address*)
7	New	6	Donne-moi de tes nouvelles (*Give me some news of you*)
8	New	6	J'écoute de la musique (*I listen to music*)
9	New	7	Dis bonjour à ta famille (*Say hi to your family*)
10	New	8	Je n'ai pas fini de manger (*I have not finished eating*)
11	Trained at each session	4	À la prochaine (*See you later*)
12	Trained at each session	4	Bon appétit (*Enjoy your meal*)
13	Trained at each session	4	Ça me fait mal (*It hurts*)
14	Trained at each session	4	Combien ça coûte (*How much is it*)
15	Trained at each session	4	Prends soin de toi (*Take care*)
16	Trained at each session	5	J'ai de la visite (*I have visitors*)
17	Trained at each session	5	J'ai un rendez-vous (*I have an appointment*)
18	Trained at each session	5	Je ne comprends pas (*I don't understand*)
19	Trained at each session	5	Je ne viendrai pas (*I won't come*)
20	Trained at each session	5	Pouvez-vous m'aider (*Could you help me*)

GENERAL PROCEDURE

The study took place at the aphasic association where participants were recruited. We followed a Latin cross-over design and used the random number generation function of Microsoft Excel to allocate participants to treatment sequences: FL underwent the treatment sequence MT–RT–ST, FS underwent RT–ST–MT and JPL followed the order ST–MT–RT. Evaluations were conducted before and after each treatment phase, for a total of four evaluation periods, hereafter referred to as T1, T2, T3, and T4. Moreover, performance was measured three times within each evaluation period (T1a, T1b, T1c; T2a, T2b, T2c; T3a, T3b, T3c; T4a, T4b, T4c), with a minimum of 2-day intervals between assessments, to ensure that results would not be biased by day-to-day variations in participants' general state. One list of 20 Test-phrases was used for each intervention phase. They were split into 10 stimuli to be repeatedly trained at each treatment session and 10 non-treated stimuli and were counterbalanced between participants.

ASSESSMENT OF TREATMENT OUTCOMES

Language outcomes were assessed through the repetition of trained and non-trained stimuli (direct and indirect treatment effects) and in connected speech (generalization effect) elicited in a picture description task. Motor-speech ability and mood were assessed with adapted standardized test (see below). All the assessments were videotaped and verbal performance was transcribed in order to be analyzed by a different person than the therapist.

The primary outcome was the change from pre- to post-treatment in discourse informativeness (in percent CIU in connected speech). Speech samples were elicited in a description task of 15 complex line drawing pictures of several characters acting in daily situations. This number is well above the recommended minimum number of stimuli (5) (Brookshire and Nicholas, 1994) to ensure adequate test–retest stability of informativeness in people with aphasia. Moreover, in order to control for day-to-day variations within each evaluation period, the pictures were split into three groups of five to collect speech samples on three different days. Informativeness was scored with the help of the software, Cordial Analyseur (Synapse-Développement, 2010), for words' counts.

Secondary outcomes were the changes from pre- to post-treatment in number of correct syllables in the trained and non-trained sentences. The productions were obtained in a repetition task of the audio-recorded Test-phrases in the normally spoken mode. No lip-reading was possible. Correct syllables were rated with 1 point and syllables with an error on a single phoneme were given 0.5 point, following the procedure of Racette et al. (2006).

In a first attempt to monitor changes in apraxia of speech with MIT and in absence of a validated test in French, we chose the Diadochokinetic rate subtest of the Apraxia battery for adults (ABA2, Dabul, 2000), the best validated diagnostic battery currently available. The task consists of rapid repetitions of syllables to assess motor-speech agility. We used the total score of this ABA2 subtest.

Finally, we assessed participants' mood with the visual analog mood scales (VAMS, Stern, 1997). On each scale, drawings of two faces are connected with a vertical 10-cm line. One face has a neutral expression while the other represents a mood state (afraid, confused, sad, angry, energetic, tired, happy, or tense). Participants have to mark on the line how they feel. This test is particularly well adapted to patients with aphasia since it requires minimal verbal abilities. T-scores on the eight mood subscales of the VAMS served for this secondary outcome.

RESULTS

PRIMARY OUTCOMES – GENERALIZATION EFFECTS TO LANGUAGE IN CONNECTED SPEECH

Participants were considered as single cases (**Figure 2**). We compared participants' mean informativeness score computed from the 15 picture descriptions before and after each treatment. In FL, the Wilcoxon signed-rank tests revealed a significant progression only from T1 to T2, that is, with MT ($Z = -2.101$, $p = 0.036$). In FS, there was a significant improvement only from T3 to T4, with MT ($Z = -2.017$, $p = 0.044$). In JPL, significant change was only found from T2 to T3, with MT again ($Z = -2.329$, $p = 0.024$). In sum, in all three participants, MT had a significant generalization effect in terms of informativeness in connected speech while RT and ST had not.

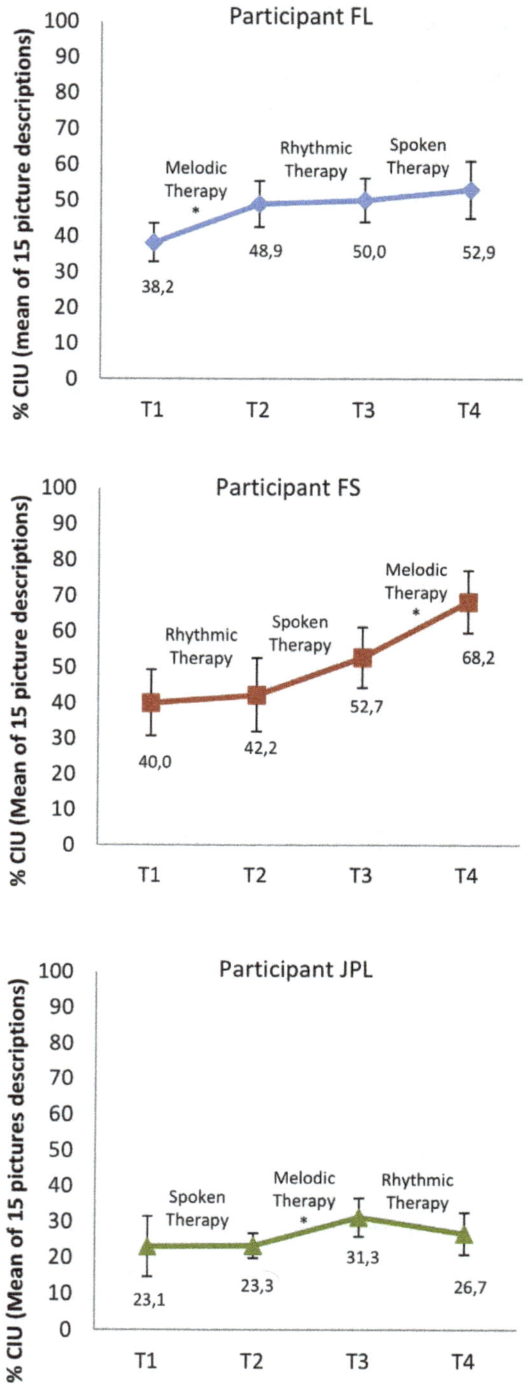

FIGURE 2 | Informativeness in connected speech at each assessment time (T1–T4), before and after treatments (i.e., generalization effects). Error bars represent 95% confidence intervals. The star indicate pre–post-treatment differences in non-parametric statistical tests when $p < 0.05$. CIU: Correct information units.

SECONDARY OUTCOMES

Direct and indirect treatment effects

Test-phrases were repeatedly assessed at three different days (a, b, and c) within each evaluation period before and after treatments (**Table 4** and **Figure 3**). A preliminary analysis with Friedman tests revealed no significant difference between the repeated assessments of each list of Test-phrases within the evaluation periods of each participant. Thus, the measures appeared to be stable before or after treatments and we compared pre- to post-treatment data with Wilcoxon tests based on the mean scores of the three repeated assessments of each treated (tr) and non-treated (ntr) Test-phrase.

In FL, the number of correct syllables in trained Test-phrases improved significantly with all treatments (MT[T1–T2]tr: $Z = -2.040$, $p = 0.041$; RT[T2–T3]tr: $Z = -2.431$, $p = 0.015$; ST[T3–T4]tr: $Z = -2.134$, $p = 0.033$). The production of non-trained Test-phrases also improved significantly with MT (MT[T1–T2]ntr: $Z = -2.383$, $p = 0.017$) but not with RT or ST (RT[T2–T3]ntr: $Z = -1.023$, $p = 0.306$; ST[T3–T4]: $Z = -0.178$, $p = 0.859$). Because there were improvements both in trained and non-trained phrases with MT, we seek to determine if speech accuracy better improved on trained versus non-trained items with this therapy. We computed for each phrase the gain in number of syllables from pre to post MT, and we compared the mean syllable gain on trained stimuli with the mean syllable gain on non-trained stimuli. We found no significant difference between the two progressions (MT[T1–T2]tr–ntr: $Z = -0.153$, $p = 0.878$).

In FS, the number of correct syllables improved significantly with all treatments in trained and non-trained Test-phrases (MT[T3–T4]tr: $Z = -2.666$, $p = 0.008$; RT[T1–T2]tr: $Z = -2.810$, $p = 0.005$; ST[T2–T3]tr: $Z = -2.668$, $p = 0.008$; MT[T3–T4]ntr: $Z = -2.245$, $p = 0.025$; RT[T1–T2]ntr: $Z = -2.809$, $p = 0.005$; ST[T2–T3]: $Z = -2.040$, $p = 0.041$). The progression was significantly greater on trained phrases than non-trained phrases following RT or ST (RT[T1–T2]tr–ntr: $Z = -2.398$, $p = 0.016$; ST[T2–T3]tr–ntr: $Z = -2.191$, $p = 0.028$) but not with MT (MT[T3–T4]tr–ntr: $Z = -0.833$, $p = 0.405$).

In JPL, there was also a significant improvement on trained Test-phrases with all treatments (MT[T2–T3]tr: $Z = -2.703$, $p = 0.007$; RT[T3–T4]tr: $Z = -2.807$, $p = 0.005$; ST[T1–T2]tr: $Z = -2.553$, $p = 0.011$). Furthermore, the production of non-trained Test-phrases also improved significantly with MT and RT (MT[T2–T3]ntr: $Z = -2.807$, $p = 0.005$; RT[T3–T4]ntr:

Table 4 | Mean number of correct syllables per test-phrases ($n = 10$) before and after each treatment.

Treatment	Participant	Trained				Non-trained				Comparison of increases
		Pre-	Post-	Pre-post comparison	Increase	Pre-	Post-	Pre-post comparison	Increase	
Melodic therapy	FL	2.50 (1.00)	3.58 (0.91)	*	1.09 (1.44)	2.12 (1.08)	3.10 (0.76)	*	0.98 (0.84)	NS
	FS	2.92 (0.88)	3.95 (0.75)	*	1.03 (0.68)	2.38 (0.81)	3.08 (0.84)	*	0.71 (0.78)	NS
	JPL	2.08 (0.85)	4.22 (0.69)	*	2.13 (1.05)	2.50 (0.73)	3.85 (0.64)	*	1.35 (0.54)	NS
Rhythmic therapy	FL	2.73 (0.79)	3.75 (0.55)	*	1.02 (0.97)	2.97 (1.01)	3.50 (0.81)	NS	0.53 (1.35)	Trained > non-trained
	FS	1.72 (0.75)	3.87 (0.85)	*	2.15 (0.72)	2.03 (0.61)	3.03 (0.68)	*	1.00 (0.66)	Trained > non-trained
	JPL	3.00 (0.92)	4.35 (0.69)	*	1.35 (0.66)	3.38 (0.61)	4.00 (0.36)	*	0.63 (0.70)	Trained > non-trained
Spoken therapy	FL	3.37 (0.54)	4.18 (0.56)	*	0.82 (0.82)	3.48 (1.02)	3.72 (0.71)	NS	0.24 (1.02)	Trained > non-trained
	FS	2.18 (1.03)	4.00 (0.67)	*	1.82 (0.96)	2.30 (0.81)	2.93 (0.77)	*	0.63 (0.78)	Trained > non-trained
	JPL	2.51 (0.54)	3.98 (1.07)	*	1.47 (1.05)	2.25 (0.88)	2.58 (1.02)	NS	0.33 (1.29)	Trained > non-trained

*Standard deviations (SD) are indicated in parentheses. *Significant differences in non-parametric statistical tests when $p < 0.05$.*

$Z = -2.383$, $p = 0.017$) but not with ST (ST[T1–T2]ntr: $Z = -0.866$, $p = 0.386$). The progression was significantly greater on trained phrases than non-trained phrases following RT (RT[T3–T4]tr–ntr: $Z = -2.091$, $p = 0.037$) but not with MT (MT[T2–T3]tr–ntr: $Z = -1.614$, $p = 0.107$).

In sum, all treatments had a significant direct effect in each participant. The indirect effect of MT was also significant and no weaker than its direct effect, while RT had a significant indirect effect in two of three participants and was weaker than its direct effect. In only one participant, ST had a significant indirect effect and it was weaker than the direct effect.

Measure of motor-speech agility

We used the published norms to determine if changes on the Diadochokinetic score were significant within and between evaluation periods (Dabul, 2000). No significant variation appeared in any participant, for any treatment according to the norms.

Mood

The participants scored within the norms at the eight-mood subscales of the VAMS (Stern, 1997), and there was no significant variation (i.e., more than 20 T-score points) during the study.

DISCUSSION

Our primary goal was to assess the relative contribution of rhythm and pitch in MIT's generalization effect by comparing three treatments (MT, RT, and ST) differing only by the presence or absence of these two melodic features. Only the MT, which had both pitch and rhythm, had a significant effect on the informativeness of connected speech in the participants regardless of the treatment order. Furthermore, all three forms of therapies led to improvements on trained sentences (direct effect) but their capacity to generalize these gains to non-trained sentences (indirect effect) varied. The MT showed an effect on non-trained material that was as large as the direct effect. In the other treatments, the indirect effect, when significant, was weaker than the direct effect. Finally, the presence of rhythm (in RT) had an indirect effect in two of the three participants, whereas the treatment with no melodic elements (ST) was associated with indirect effect in only one participant.

The findings show that MT was the most effective in terms of generalization effects. It replicates the results of Schlaug et al. (2008, 2009) who found better language improvements in the connected speech of one participant with MIT compared to a control therapy that did not use the musical components. With three additional participants with Broca's aphasia, our study further supports that the combination of rhythm and pitch is valuable to language recovery in MIT. Furthermore, we found that the addition of musical pitch to the rhythmic element was associated with generalization effect to connected speech, whereas the use of rhythm only did not.

The finding of indirect effects in all participants with MT and in two participants with RT is in apparent contradiction with the results of the two previous longitudinal studies investigating the differential role of rhythm and pitch in MIT. Stahl et al. (2013) showed improvements in trained phrases but not on non-trained stimuli in two groups of subjects who underwent a melodic or a rhythmic treatment. In a controlled single case study, Wilson et al. (2006) also found significant changes in phrases trained with intoned speech or with rhythmic speech, but not in non-trained verbal material. However, none of these participants was presented with diverse New-phrases during treatment sessions that are supposed to promote generalization in original MIT (Sparks, 2008;

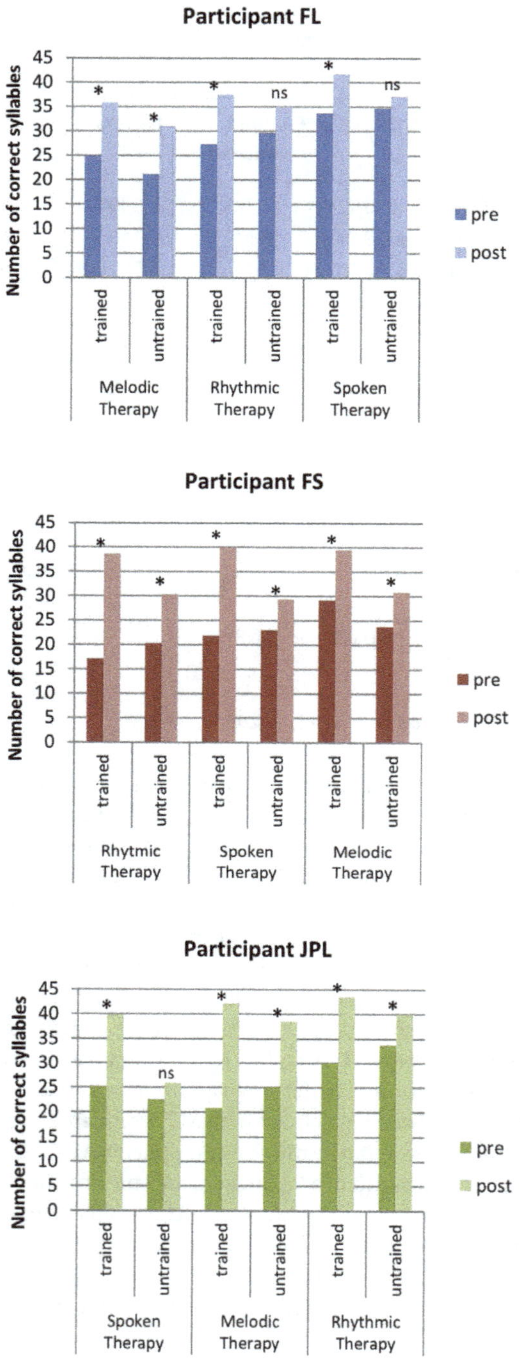

FIGURE 3 | Speech accuracy in trained and non-trained Test-phrases before and after each treatment (i.e., direct and indirect effects). Columns represent the total number of correct syllables in 10 phrases produced in a normally spoken repetition task. The star indicate pre–post-treatment differences in non-parametric statistical tests when $p < 0.05$.

Zumbansen et al., 2014). In fact, in the study of Stahl et al., the control group of participants who were allocated to standard therapy improved on non-trained phrases. The standard therapy consisted of a wide range of language tasks and verbal stimuli. As stressed by several authors and expert panels, the variety of verbal tasks, stimuli, and contexts may well be a key factor in the generalization effect of a speech and language therapy approach (Thompson, 1989; Nadeau et al., 2008; Frey, 2013).

One important question is to understand how pitch and rhythm, when combined, lead to some generalized language improvements. Pitch processing engages right-lateralized cerebral activity (Peretz and Zatorre, 2005), while rhythm and temporality in simple singing has been associated with left hemispheric areas that are close to language centers (Jungblut et al., 2012). So far, better language recovery has been reported with the recruitment of left perilesional cortex rather than interhemispheric compensation in post-stroke aphasia (Heiss et al., 1999; Rosen et al., 2000; Heiss and Thiel, 2006; Anglade et al., 2014). Because intoned speech engages left perilesional areas to a greater extent than normal speech in participants with aphasia after stroke (Laine et al., 1994; Belin et al., 1996), one could hypothesize that rhythm in intoned speech could be responsible for this left-hemispheric activation, leaving the pitch component as relatively unnecessary. However, in light of our behavioral results, we suggest that pitch could act as a facilitator to effectively get access to reactivation of perilesional areas for language production. Pitch information adds a redundant cue to rhythmicity in the intoned-speech technique; the high pitch is produced on the stressed syllables, which are also pronounced on the longer note, while the low pitch is on the unstressed syllables and shorter notes. We propose that pitch changes could help processing the rhythmic patterns and bootstrapping the reactivation of rhythm- and language-related left-hemispheric areas, possibly through transcallosal pathways following the classical Hebbian axiom "neurons that fire together wire together". More brain imaging studies are clearly needed to better understand the brain correlates associated with the beneficial effect of pitch and rhythm combination on generalized language recovery after stroke. It is most plausible that the brain mechanisms of MIT vary depending on individual factors, such as the lesion size and location. In this regard, longitudinal brain imaging data from two studies with original MIT have shown increased right-hemisphere activation and white matter plasticity in nine patients with large left hemisphere lesions (Schlaug et al., 2008, 2009) and Schlaug et al. (2009) have argued that using the right hemisphere for language processing might be the only option for language improvements in such patients. When reactivation of left language areas is not possible, the pitch element of MIT could be even more crucial.

Although the three participants of our study had quite similar clinical and demographic profiles, individual differences can not easily be ruled out in clinical studies. Among the participants, FS had the lowest level of education, the most severe aphasia, and he scored lower in reasoning, planning, and musical abilities, particularly pitch processing (see the subtest of the WAIS, the Tower of London, and the Abbreviated MBEMA in **Table 2**). FS had theoretically more room for improvement, whereas FL and JPL were probably closer to a plateau. This could explain why FS showed indirect effects with all treatments and benefited most from the MT. Interestingly, FS did improve with MT despite his low musical abilities, suggesting that severely affected patients without good musical abilities can still benefit from pitch and rhythm combination in MIT. Melodic aspects probably affect such patients differently than patients with preserved musical skills. Turning our attention on therapists, we speculate that the use of both melodic components in MIT (compared to rhythm only) could also better entrain the clinician in a favorable attitude toward the patient to facilitate speech production during sessions, by synchronizing all facilitation techniques (unison production, lip-reading, and hand-tapping) and by enhancing the common focus of both patient and therapist. Future studies could explore the impact of melody on the therapist engagement during therapy sessions, a point of view rarely addressed in speech and language therapy.

We did not find support here for the suggestion that the musical elements of MIT would improve patient's mood and motivation. We did not capture any mood changes that were significant according to the norms of the VAMS (Stern, 1997), whether participants were pharmacologically treated for depression (JPL) or not (FL and FS). The potential mood mechanism of MIT is based on the fact that music has been shown to have a strong effect on emotions and mood (reviewed in Juslin and Vastfjall, 2008; Koelsch, 2010). Post-stroke depression is associated with greater degree of cognitive impairment and with lower cognitive recovery when controlling for the size of the lesion (Robinson et al., 1986) and music listening leads to better cognitive recovery along with a decrease of depressed and confused mood when compared to stories listening in post-stroke rehabilitation (Särkämö et al., 2008). It was suggested that the power of music on mood could explain a part of the beneficial effects of singing therapies on language recovery. Yet, the effect of music on mood has been shown in rich musical contexts, where subjects listen to, play, or sing real music pieces. In contrast, the musical content of MIT is made of few (usually only two) pitches, its rhythmical structure is poor and there is neither musical syntax nor harmony. A controlled experiment with healthy participants showed that the use of monophonic tones and isochronous beat alone had no significant impact on mood when compared to real musical pieces (Koelsch et al., 2010). Thus, the musical context of MIT might not be sufficient to elicit significant mood changes.

According to the motor-speech hypothesis of MIT's effect (Zumbansen et al., 2014), the improvements in language production after MIT may be due to the reduction of apraxia of speech, one of the symptoms distinguishing Broca's aphasia from other aphasic syndromes. It would explain why this specific form of aphasia responds well and consistently to MIT while other forms rarely do (AAN, 1994). In the present study, we did not capture any significant changes in motor-speech agility as measured by one of the sub-tests of the ABA2 (Dabul, 2000). Testing the motor-speech hypothesis of MIT is a challenge due to the lack of quantitative and unanimously accepted assessment tools for apraxia of speech (Ballard et al., 2000). The ABA2 is the best-validated clinical tool currently available. We chose the motor-speech agility subtest because it could be administered to French-speaking participants and we planned to use the norms to decide if changes would be significant. However, ABA2 is a diagnostic tool and it was not validated to detect changes over time in apraxia of speech. Moreover, it is surprising that no significant change was detected on this score when speech accuracy improved on non-trained phrases. For these reasons, we believe that the Diadochokinetic rate subtest of the ABA2 with its current norms is probably not sensitive enough to detect the changes in apraxia of speech with therapy. There is a need to develop sensitive, quantitative assessment methods of apraxia of speech that could be used at the individual level to document intervention-related progress.

Ours is the first study assessing the differential contribution of rhythm and pitch in a version of MIT that preserves all the basic generalization characteristics of the original protocol. As already mentioned, the mood and motor-speech hypotheses had never been assessed. Few speech and language therapies have been tested in such depth with regard to the mechanisms at work in language recovery effects. Given the high inter-individual variability in patients with aphasia, we chose a Latin square cross-over design to be able to compare participants with themselves. Interventions with carry-over effects, as is the case in our study, are theoretically not suited to this design type since periods of wash-out are necessary for the dependent variable to return to baseline before starting the next intervention phase. However, despite the carry-over effects, we were able to capture treatment-related differential improvements. We readily acknowledge that the best experimental design would have been a randomized controlled group study. However, due to the difficulty in recruiting large number of patients with aphasia, especially with the strict selection criteria we applied, it is somewhat unrealistic to investigate the finer aspects of treatment mechanisms in this way.

Finally, the version of MIT that we designed for experimental purposes gave good results at three levels of therapeutic effects with significant improvements on trained, non-trained, and connected speech in the three participants. Combining various verbal materials with a set of repetitive stimuli may constitute an interesting therapeutic mixed principle because it would allow the clinician to evaluate the best language gains achievable by a patient. If only direct effects are obtained in patients with the most severe language impairments, the clinician could focus on real palliative versions of MIT (i.e., that are designed to train a few ready-made useful sentences for the patients' daily living), and this strategy could be used as a complement to communication-based approaches in speech and language therapy. However, before turning to a fully palliative approach, the mixed principle could allow some patients to show connected speech gains.

ACKNOWLEDGMENTS

This work was supported by the Centre for Research on Brain, Language and Music (CRBLM) and by scholarships to Anna Zumbansen from the Collaborative Research and Training Experience (CREATE) Program in Auditory Cognitive Neuroscience from the Natural Sciences and Engineering Research Council of Canada (NSERC), the Quebec Bio-Imaging Network (QBIN), and the Faculty of Graduate Studies of Université de Montréal. We thank Philippe Fournier for testing participants' hearing thresholds, and Bernard Bouchard for helping in audio stimuli analysis. We especially thank Alice Perdereau, Sarah André, and Isabelle Marcoux for their help in implementing the study protocol and data collection, and the association Aphasie Rive-Sud for its long-lasting collaboration in participant recruitment and for providing a testing space during the study.

REFERENCES

AAN. (1994). Assessment: melodic intonation therapy. *Neurology* 44, 566–568.

Agniel, A., Joanette, Y., Doyon, B., and Duchein, C. (1992). *Protocole Montréal – Toulouse. Evaluation des gnosies visuelles et auditives.* Isbergues: L'Ortho Edition.

Albert, M. L., Sparks, R. W., and Helm, N. A. (1973). Melodic intonation therapy for aphasia. *Arch. Neurol.* 29, 130–131. doi:10.1001/archneur.1973.00490260074018

Anglade, C., Thiel, A., and Ansaldo, A. I. (2014). The complementary role of the cerebral hemispheres in recovery from aphasia after stroke: a critical review of literature. *Brain Inj.* 28, 138–145. doi:10.3109/02699052.2013.859734

Ballard, K. J., Granier, J. P., and Robin, D. A. (2000). Understanding the nature of apraxia of speech: theory, analysis, and treatment. *Aphasiology* 14, 969–995. doi:10.1080/02687030050156575

Basso, A. (2003). *Aphasia and its Therapy.* New York: Oxford University Press.

Beeson, P. M., and Robey, R. R. (2006). Evaluating single-subject treatment research: lessons learned from the aphasia literature. *Neuropsychol. Rev.* 16, 161–169. doi:10.1007/s11065-006-9013-7

Belin, P., Van Eeckhout, P., Zilbovicius, M., Remy, P., François, C., Guillaume, S., et al. (1996). Recovery from nonfluent aphasia after melodic intonation therapy: a PET study. *Neurology* 47, 1504–1511. doi:10.1212/WNL.47.6.1504

Berlin, C. I. (1976). On: melodic intonation therapy for aphasia by R. W. Sparks and A. L. Holland. *J. Speech Hear. Disord.* 41, 298–300.

Boersma, P., and Weenick, D. (2013). *Praat Software.* Amsterdam: University of Amsterdam.

Bonakdarpour, B., Eftekharzadeh, A., and Ashayeri, H. (2003). Melodic intonation therapy in Persian aphasic patients. *Aphasiology* 17, 75–95. doi:10.1080/729254891

Boucher, V., Garcia, L. J., Fleurant, J., and Paradis, J. (2001). Variable efficacy of rhythm and tone in melody-based interventions: implications for the assumption of a right-hemisphere facilitation in non-fluent aphasia. *Aphasiology* 15, 131–149. doi:10.1080/02687040042000098

Brady, M. C., Kelly, H., Godwin, J., and Enderby, P. (2012). Speech and language therapy for aphasia following stroke. *Cochrane Database Syst. Rev.* 5:CD000425. doi:10.1002/14651858.CD000425.pub3

Brookshire, R. H., and Nicholas, L. E. (1994). Test-retest stability of measures of connected speech in aphasia. *Clin. Aphasiol.* 22, 119–133.

Cardebat, D., Doyon, B., Puel, M., Goulet, P., and Joanette, Y. (1990). Evocation lexicale formelle et sémantique chez des sujets normaux. Performances et dynamiques de production en fonction du sexe, de l'âge et du niveau d'étude. *Acta Neurol. Belg.* 90, 207–217.

Culbertson, C. W., and Zillmer, E. A. (2001). *Tower of London Drexel University (TOL DX): Technical Manual.* Toronto, ON: Multi-Health Systems Incorporated (MHS).

Dabul, B. L. (2000). *Apraxia Battery for Adults, Second Edition (ABA2).* Austin, TX: PRO-ED.

Dickey, L., Kagan, A., Lindsay, M. P., Fang, J., Rowland, A., and Black, S. (2010). Incidence and profile of inpatient stroke-induced aphasia in Ontario, Canada. *Arch. Phys. Med. Rehabil.* 91, 196–202. doi:10.1016/j.apmr.2009.09.020

Frey, K. L. (2013). *Patient Characteristics and Treatment Components that Mediate Improvements in Connected Speech in Persons with Chronic Post-Stroke Aphasia: A Delphi Study Involving a Communication Disorders Expert Panel.* Boulder, CO: University of Colorado Boulder.

Heiss, W.-D., Kessler, J., Thiel, A., Ghaemi, M., and Karbe, H. (1999). Differential capacity of left and right hemispheric areas for compensation of poststroke aphasia. *Ann. Neurol.* 45, 430–438. doi:10.1002/1531-8249(199904)45:4<430::AID-ANA3>3.0.CO;2-P

Heiss, W.-D., and Thiel, A. (2006). A proposed regional hierarchy in recovery of post-stroke aphasia. *Brain Lang.* 98, 118–123. doi:10.1016/j.bandl.2006.02.002

Helm-Estabrooks, N. A. (1983). "Exploiting the right hemisphere for language rehabilitation: melodic intonation therapy," in *Cognitive Processing in the Right Hemisphere,* ed. E. Perecman (New York: Academic Press), 229–240.

Jackson, J. H. (1878). On affections of speech from disease of the brain. *Brain* 1, 304–330. doi:10.1093/brain/1.3.304

Jungblut, M., Huber, W., Pustelniak, M., and Schnitker, R. (2012). The impact of rhythm complexity on brain activation during simple singing: an event-related fMRI study. *Restor. Neurol. Neurosci.* 30, 39–53. doi:10.3233/RNN-2011-0619

Juslin, P. N., and Vastfjall, D. (2008). Emotional responses to music: the need to consider underlying mechanisms. *Behav. Brain Sci.* 31, 559. doi:10.1017/S0140525X08005293

Koelsch, S. (2010). Towards a neural basis of music-evoked emotions. *Trends Cogn. Sci.* 14, 131–137. doi:10.1016/j.tics.2010.01.002

Koelsch, S., Offermanns, K., and Franzke, P. (2010). Music in the treatment of affective disorders: an exploratory investigation of a new method for music-therapeutic research. *Music Percept.* 27, 307–316. doi:10.1525/mp.2010.27.4.307

Laine, M., Tuomainen, J., and Ahonen, A. (1994). Changes in hemispheric brain perfusion elicited by Melodic Intonation Therapy: a preliminary experiment with single photon emission computed tomography (SPECT). *Logoped. Phoniatr. Vocol.* 19, 19–24. doi:10.3109/14015439409101070

Laughlin, S. A., Naeser, M. A., and Gordon, W. P. (1979). Effects of three syllable durations using the melodic intonation therapy technique. *J. Speech Hear. Res.* 22, 311–320.

Merrett, D. L., Peretz, I., and Wilson, S. J. (2014). Neurobiological, cognitive, and emotional mechanisms in melodic intonation therapy. *Front. Hum. Neurosci.* 8:401. doi:10.3389/fnhum.2014.00401

Nadeau, S. E., Rothi, L. J. G., and Rosenbek, J. (2008). "Language rehabilitation from a neural perspective," in *Language Intervention Strategies in Aphasia and Related Neurogenic Communication Disorders,* ed. R. Chapey (Baltimore, MD: Lippincott Williams & Wilkins), 689–734.

Nespoulous, J.-L., Lecours, A. R., Lafond, D., Lemay, A., Puel, M., Cot, F., et al. (1992). *Protocole Montréal-Toulouse d'examen Linguistique de l'aphasie MT-86 M1béta Module Standard Initial,* 2nd Edn. Isbergues: Ortho-Edition.

Nicholas, L. E., and Brookshire, R. H. (1993). A system for quantifying the informativeness and efficiency of the connected speech of adults with aphasia. *J. Speech Hear. Res.* 36, 338–350.

Peretz, I., Gosselin, N., Nan, Y., Caron-Caplette, E., Trehub, S. E., and Béland, R. (2013). A novel tool for evaluating children's musical abilities across age and culture. *Front. Syst. Neurosci.* 7, doi:10.3389/fnsys.2013.00030

Peretz, I., and Zatorre, R. J. (2005). Brain organization for music processing. *Annu. Rev. Psychol.* 56, 89–114. doi:10.1146/annurev.psych.56.091103.070225

Racette, A., Bard, C., and Peretz, I. (2006). Making non-fluent aphasics speak: sing along! *Brain* 129, 2571–2584. doi:10.1093/brain/awl250

Robinson, R. G., Bolla-Wilson, K., Kaplan, E., Lipsey, J. R., and Price, T. R. (1986). Depression influences intellectual impairment in stroke patients. *Br. J. Psychiatry* 148, 541–547. doi:10.1192/bjp.148.5.541

Rosen, H. J., Petersen, S. E., Linenweber, M. R., Snyder, A. Z., White, D. A., Chapman, L., et al. (2000). Neural correlates of recovery from aphasia after damage to left inferior frontal cortex. *Neurology* 55, 1883–1894. doi:10.1212/WNL.55.12.1883

Särkämö, T., Tervaniemi, M., Laitinen, S., Forsblom, A., Soinila, S., Mikkonen, M., et al. (2008). Music listening enhances cognitive recovery and mood after middle cerebral artery stroke. *Brain* 131, 866–876. doi:10.1093/brain/awn013

Schlaug, G., Marchina, S., and Norton, A. (2008). From singing to speaking: why singing may lead to recovery of expressive language function in patients with Broca's aphasia. *Music Percept.* 25, 315–323. doi:10.1525/mp.2008.25.4.315

Schlaug, G., Marchina, S., and Norton, A. (2009). Evidence for plasticity in white matter tracts of chronic aphasic patients undergoing intense intonation-based speech therapy. *Ann. N. Y. Acad. Sci.* 1169, 385–394. doi:10.1111/j.1749-6632.2009.04587.x

Schlaug, G., and Norton, A. (2011). *Melodic-Intonation-Therapy and Speech-Repetition-Therapy for Patients with Non-Fluent Aphasia.* Available at: http://clinicaltrials.gov/ct2/show/study/NCT00903266

Sparks, R. W. (2008). "Melodic intonation therapy," in *Language Intervention Strategies in Aphasia and Related Neurogenic Communication Disorders,* ed. R. Chapey (Baltimore: Lippincott Williams & Wilkins), 837–851.

Sparks, R. W., Helm, N. A., and Albert, M. L. (1974). Aphasia rehabilitation resulting from melodic intonation therapy. *Cortex* 10, 303–316. doi:10.1016/S0010-9452(74)80024-9

Stahl, B., Henseler, I., Turner, R., Geyer, S., and Kotz, S. A. (2013). How to engage the right brain hemisphere in aphasics without even singing: evidence for two paths of speech recovery. *Front. Hum. Neurosci.* 7:35. doi:10.3389/fnhum.2013.00035

Stahl, B., Kotz, S. A., Henseler, I., Turner, R., and Geyer, S. (2011). Rhythm in disguise: why singing may not hold the key to recovery from aphasia. *Brain* 134, 3083–3093. doi:10.1093/brain/awr240

Stern, R. A. (1997). *Visual Analog Mood Scales, VAMS.* Odessa, FL: Psychological Assessment Resources.

Synapse-Développement. (2010). *Cordial Analyseur.* Toulouse: Synapse Développement.

Thompson, C. K. (1989). "Generalization in the treatment of aphasia," in *Generalization Strategies in the Treatment of Communication Disorders*, eds L. V. McReynolds and J. Spradlin (Burlington, ON: B.C. Decker Inc), 82–115.

van der Meulen, I., van de Sandt-Koenderman, W. M. E., Heijenbrok-Kal, M. H., Visch-Brink, E. G., and Ribbers, G. M. (2014). The efficacy and timing of melodic intonation therapy in subacute aphasia. *Neurorehabil. Neural Repair.* 28, 536–544. doi:10.1177/1545968313517753

Van Eeckhout, P., and Bhatt, P. (1984). Rythme, intonation, accentuation: la rééducation des aphasies non-fluentes sévères. *Rééducation Orthophonique* 22, 311–327.

Van Lancker-Sidtis, D., and Rallon, G. (2004). Tracking the incidence of formulaic expressions in everyday speech: methods for classification and verification. *Lang. Commun.* 24, 207–240. doi:10.1016/j.langcom.2004.02.003

Wade, D. T., Hewer, R. L., David, R. M., and Enderby, P. M. (1986). Aphasia after stroke: natural history and associated deficits. *J. Neurol. Neurosurg. Psychiatr.* 49, 11–16. doi:10.1136/jnnp.49.1.11

Wechsler, D. (1997a). *Wechsler Adult Intelligence Scale – Third Edition.* San Antonio, TX: Harcourt Assessment.

Wechsler, D. (1997b). *Wechsler Memory Scale – Third Edition.* San Antonio, TX: Psychological Corporation.

Wilson, S. J., Pearsons, K., and Reutens, D. C. (2006). Preserved singing in aphasia: a case study of the efficacity of Melodic Intonation Therapy. *Music Percept.* 24, 23–36. doi:10.1525/mp.2006.24.1.23

Zumbansen, A., Peretz, I., and Hébert, S. (2014). Melodic intonation therapy: back to basics for future research. *Front. Neurol.* 5:7. doi:10.3389/fneur.2014.00007

13

Music-supported motor training after stroke reveals no superiority of synchronization in group therapy

Floris T. Van Vugt[1,2*†], Juliane Ritter[1†], Jens D. Rollnik[3] and Eckart Altenmüller[1]

[1] Institute of Music Physiology and Musicians' Medicine, University of Music, Drama, and Media Hanover, Hanover, Germany
[2] Lyon Neuroscience Research Center, CNRS-UMR 5292, INSERM U1028, University Claude Bernard Lyon-1, Lyon, France
[3] BDH-Klinik, Institute for Neurorehabilitational Research (InFo), Teaching Hospital of Hanover Medical School, Hessisch Oldendorf, Germany

***Correspondence:**
Floris T. Van Vugt, Institute of Music Physiology and Musicians' Medicine, University of Music, Drama and Media Hanover, Emmichplatz 1, 30175 Hanover, Germany
e-mail: f.t.vanvugt@gmail.com

†These authors have contributed equally to this work.

Background: Music-supported therapy has been shown to be an effective tool for rehabilitation of motor deficits after stroke. A unique feature of music performance is that it is inherently social: music can be played together in synchrony.

Aim: The present study explored the potential of synchronized music playing during therapy, asking whether synchronized playing could improve fine motor rehabilitation and mood.

Method: Twenty-eight patients in neurological early rehabilitation after stroke with no substantial previous musical training were included. Patients learned to play simple finger exercises and familiar children's songs on the piano for 10 sessions of half an hour. Patients first received three individual therapy sessions and then continued in pairs. The patient pairs were divided into two groups. Patients in one group played synchronously (together group) whereas the patients in the other group played one after the other (in-turn group). To assess fine motor skill recovery the patients performed standard clinical tests such as the nine-hole-pegboard test (9HPT) and index finger-tapping speed and regularity, and metronome-paced finger tapping. Patients' mood was established using the Profile of Mood States (POMS).

Results: Both groups showed improvements in fine motor control. In metronome-paced finger tapping, patients in both groups improved significantly. Mood tests revealed reductions in depression and fatigue in both groups. During therapy, patients in the in-turn group rated their partner as more sympathetic than the together-group in a visual-analog scale.

Conclusions: Our results suggest that music-supported stroke rehabilitation can improve fine motor control and mood not only individually but also in patient pairs. Patients who were playing in turn rather than simultaneously tended to reveal greater improvement in fine motor skill. We speculate that patients in the former group may benefit from the opportunity to learn from observation.

Keywords: stroke rehabilitation, music therapy, motor improvement, synchronization, social, shared experience, mood

INTRODUCTION

Motor impairments are among the most common and most disabling consequences of stroke (Ward and Cohen, 2004; Dimyan and Cohen, 2011). Since effective therapeutic interventions are scarce (Woldag and Hummelsheim, 2002), several novel interventions including musical activities were developed (Bunketorp Käll et al., 2012; Chong et al., 2014). For example, stroke patients showed significant improvements in fine motor control after music-supported therapy in which they learned to play the piano and drums during several weeks (Schneider et al., 2007; Altenmüller et al., 2009; Amengual et al., 2013; Grau-Sánchez et al., 2013). These beneficial changes persisted in a 3-week follow-up test (Villeneuve and Lamontagne, 2013). The researchers found that patients' musical training transferred to motor benefits in a variety of clinical tasks measuring activities of daily living, revealing gains in fine motor control in these patients. Neurophysiologically, these behavioral improvements were accompanied by auditory-sensory-motor coactivation in the level of the cortex (Rojo et al., 2011) and by a shift in motor excitability patterns of the contra-lesional motor cortex of the patients as assessed with transcranial motor stimulation (Amengual et al., 2013; Grau-Sánchez et al., 2013).

A variety of explanations has been advanced for the performance improvement and the neuroplastic changes due to music-supported therapy in these patients: the brain's use of auditory feedback, the novelty of the intervention, and increased motivation (Altenmüller et al., 2009). However, we wondered whether the fact that music is a social activity played a role in the benefit of music-supported therapy. In healthy populations, music turned out to be an effective tool for supporting pro-social commitment, increasing group cohesion and cooperation (Overy, 2012). The particular aspect of music that is shown to be involved in creating group cohesion is synchronization. Performing (musical) movements in synchrony has been shown to improve feelings of reciprocal likeability (Hove and Risen, 2009), trust (Wiltermuth and Heath, 2009; Launay et al., 2013), pseudo-altruism (Kokal et al., 2011; Valdesolo and Desteno, 2011), and even destructive obedience (Wiltermuth, 2012). As a result of these findings, we hypothesized that music may be a powerful tool for promoting pro-social engagement in a rehabilitation therapy session. In support of this, it has been shown that participants in music therapy rehabilitation are more actively involved and cooperative than in other forms of therapy (Narme et al., 2012).

Furthermore, we hypothesized that greater engagement of patients in their rehabilitation would lead to an improved clinical outcome. Stroke victims often suffer from disturbances in motivation and mood (Caeiro et al., 2013). Social support (Sandin et al., 1994), in turn, has been associated with improved functional outcome after stroke (Glass et al., 1993). Neuroplastic changes of rehabilitation have been proposed to depend on a patients' emotional connection with the activities in question (Sanes and Donoghue, 2000). However, to date, no studies connected these two causalities (synchronization leads to social engagement which leads to functional improvement in motor function). We set out to directly test whether musical synchronization could enhance functional motor outcome after stroke.

The present study aimed to test the potential for music as a tool to create pro-social engagement on the part of patients. In particular, we hypothesized that the aspect of music that might boost social participation is synchronized musical playing. That is, do patients benefit from producing sounds in synchrony? In order to specifically test for the effect of synchronization whilst keeping other factors constant, we divided our patient population into pairs. Some pairs played in synchrony during their therapy whilst others played in turn.

We asked the following questions. First, is playing together in synchrony associated with changes in functional motor outcome? Secondly, we asked whether playing in synchrony or in turn influenced patients' mood. Thirdly, we asked whether patients' basic auditory-motor functioning (such as synchronizing to a metronome) was influenced by playing in synchrony or in turn.

METHODS

We assigned patients to one of two groups in a randomized design. Both groups received music therapy in pairs and they played the same selection of finger exercises and children's songs. Patients received 10 therapy sessions of half an hour. The first three therapy sessions were individual and the remaining seven were in pairs. The patients were divided into two groups. Patients in one group played in synchrony (together group) whereas the patients in the other group played one after the other (in-turn group). All patients received therapy in groups of two. Prior to therapy (PRE) and after therapy (POST), all patients completed a battery of tests described below. In between the three individual sessions and the seven joint sessions, we included a short session of measurements (INTER).

PATIENT GROUP CHARACTERISTICS

We aimed at obtaining a representative sample of patients from the hospital population. Consequently, we were not able to maintain high homogeneity of patient selection. However, we feel that by making this choice, our results are maximally relevant to clinical practice. Inclusion criteria were:

- light to moderate motor impairment in the upper extremity due to stroke (ischemia or hemorrhage);
- having residual voluntary movement capacity (practically, the patient was required to be able to move the arm and the index finger of the affected hand independently);
- age between 30 and 75 years;
- Barthel Index at least 25;
- right-handedness;
- less than 5 months had passed since patients' stroke at the time of inclusion in the study;
- being able to understand and agree with informed consent to participate.

Exclusion criteria were:

- previous musical training for more than 4 years;
- psychiatric problems (as assessed by standard clinical investigation);
- cognitive impairment or aphasia.

Initially, 36 patients were identified that matched the inclusion criteria and provided informed consent to participate. However, six patients (17%) were released from the hospital prior to finishing our therapy program. Furthermore, two patients (6%) dropped out of therapy because they no longer felt therapy was effective. Our final sample consisted of 28 patients. Patients were assigned quasi-randomly to the groups. Patients were included two or three at a time, since insufficient patients were available to include all patients at the same time. A custom designed computer script was used to quasi-randomly assign patients to groups making sure that (1) the number of patients in the two groups were as close as possible, and (2) the two groups were as closely matched as possible for age, gender, Barthel index, and nine-hole pegboard test score. We report clinical data about these patients in **Table 1**.

MUSIC TRAINING

Patients received 10 sessions of half an hour of piano training over the course of three to four weeks. The day before the first session and a day after the last session were dedicated to individual measurement sessions (PRE and POST), which are described in more details below.

The training program followed the same structure every day. In the beginning of the session, patients played simple finger exercises such as a five-tone scale up and down and other patterns with their paretic hand. Then patients learned to play one from a set of simple children's songs. If patients reached a sufficient level on one of the songs, they would be invited to learn additional songs from the set prepared by the therapist. See

Table 1 | Clinical data of the two patient groups.

	Together	In-turn	Statistical comparison
Number of patients	14	14	
Sex (female/male)	6/8	10/4	Fisher exact test $p = 0.2519$
Age (years)	65.6 (10.5)	67.1 (11.8)	$W = 85.0$, $p = 0.56$
Handedness (R/L)	14/0	13/1	Fisher exact test $p = 1$
Stroke type (Number of patients ischemia/hemorrhage)	12/2	12/2	Fisher exact test $p = 1$
Affected hand (Number of patients R/L)	9/5	8/6	Fisher exact test $p = 1$
Days since stroke (at PRE, days)	40.6 (25.6)	45.6 (29.9)	$W = 89.5$, $p = 0.71$
Lesion site (Number of patients with lesion at that site/Number of patients without lesion at that site)			
Left frontal	2/12	3/11	Fisher exact test $p = 1$
Left temporal	3/11	2/12	Fisher exact test $p = 1$
Left parietal	1/13	0/14	Fisher exact test $p = 1$
Left occipital	0/14	0/14	Fisher exact test $p = 1$
Left subcortical	6/8	7/7	Fisher exact test $p = 1$
Right frontal	2/12	2/12	Fisher exact test $p = 1$
Right temporal	3/11	2/12	Fisher exact test $p = 1$
Right parietal	1/13	1/13	Fisher exact test $p = 1$
Right occipital	3/11	1/13	Fisher exact test $p = 0.60$
Right subcortical	2/12	1/13	Fisher exact test $p = 1$
Barthel index PRE	48.2 (15.0)	48.9 (11.5)	$W = 96.5$, $p = 0.95$
Barthel index POST	72.1 (14.4)	67.7 (14.8)	$W = 104.0$, $p = 0.54$
Faces scale mood rating PRE	2.42 (1.22)	1.85 (1.23)	$W = 123.5$, $p = 0.22$
Therapy duration (days)	18.2 (3.0)	18.4 (5.1)	$W = 96.0$, $p = 0.94$

Continuous data are reported as mean (standard deviation). We report statistical comparison using Fisher exact test whenever appropriate, and Mann–Whitney test otherwise.

Supplementary Materials for more details about the contents of the music-supported therapy.

Each member in the patient pair played on their individual M-Key V2 MIDI controller keyboard that was chosen for its light touch. The two keyboards were connected through the M-Audio Midisport Uno MIDI-to-USB converter to a Linux laptop. The laptop ran a custom made C program that recorded the MIDI events and forwarded them to the software synthesizer Fluidsynth, which generated the sounds using a Steinway sound font. The program additionally changed the MIDI velocity value (loudness) to its maximum value. As a result, all sounds were maximally loud, regardless of how strong patients' keystroke was. This was done to prevent patients' typically very soft keystrokes from being inaudible. The sounds were then played through Creative Inspire T10 speakers (Creative Labs, Inc.) at a comfortable loudness level. The five keyboard keys used in the therapy were numbered. Songs and exercises were then written in a simplified musical notation as numbers in tabular form and presented visually to the patients as a memory aid (see Supplementary Materials for more information).

Patients played the piano with the hand of their affected extremity only. The therapist stood next to the patient and supported the patient's arm when so required. The patients were always encouraged to make as many of the movements by themselves as possible. For those patients who were more severely affected, the therapist initially pointed to the fingers or moved them gently, encouraging the patient to make the movements unassisted on the next trial. Throughout therapy, the therapist's aim was always to allow the patient to function as independently as possible instead of becoming dependent on the therapist.

In the together-condition, the two patients played different voices of the same musical materials (finger exercises or songs) in synchrony. The therapist indicated the tempo and started the patients at the same time. By contrast, in the in-turn group, patients always played one after the other and never in synchrony. While one patient was playing, the other patient waited.

NINE-HOLE PEGBOARD TEST

The nine-hole pegboard test (9HPT) is a clinical test to assess fine motor control. The patients' task is to place nine small sticks one by one (pegs) in nine holes and take them out again (Mathiowetz et al., 1985; Parker et al., 1986; Heller et al., 1987). The patients were seated comfortably with their affected arm resting on the table. The 9HPT board is placed within easy reach of the patient, with the side with the peg container at the side of the tested arm. The experimenter held a stopwatch that was started once the patient touched the first peg, and stopped once the patient released the last peg. This test was performed during the PRE and POST measurement sessions.

FINGER TAPPING MEASUREMENTS

We investigated patient's finger tapping performance of the affected hand as a measure of fine motor control. Three different tapping conditions were measured: (1) paced thumb-to-index tapping, (2) index finger speed tapping, (3) middle finger speed tapping. The tests are described in detail in what follows. In all conditions, patients were seated comfortably at a table on which they rested their arm. In order to have a portable, flexible and yet maximally accurate measurement of finger tapping performance, we custom-designed a measurement device. Finger motion was recorded by a triaxial accelerometer (ADXL 335) attached gently to the patient's index or middle finger tip (depending on the task). Tap contact was measured by a force sensitive resistor (FSR SEN09375), which consisted of a small sheet whose electrical resistance changes upon contact in a way that depends on the contact force. Both sensors were read out by an Arduino Duemilanove experimentation board running a custom made C program to sample sensors at 3 kHz. The data was then transferred online over USB to a Linux laptop running a custom Python program allowing the therapist to preview the data. We made the blueprints of the device set up as well as the custom programs available online for free for future research groups to use (http://github.com/florisvanvugt/immmotion).

In paced thumb-to-index tapping, patients were instructed to tap as regularly as possible in time with a metronome at 69 BPM (i.e., 1.15 Hz) during 60 s from the first tap (Calautti et al., 2006). The metronome sound was generated using direct digital synthesis (DDS) by the Arduino experimental board as follows. Essentially, we created a wave table (440 Hz, 20 ms) which was written to a PWM pin connected to an audio jack plug. A set of Creative Inspire T10 loudspeakers (Creative Labs, Inc.) were plugged into this connector. The patient was instructed to tap as follows. The side of the hand (at the little finger) rested lightly on the table and the fingers were held in a relaxed posture (neither at maximum flexion nor maximal extension). The index finger and thumb moved to touch each other and then moved apart again to a distance of about 5 cm (but at least 2 cm). The thumb-to-index tapping movement was chosen because it was previously argued to be more natural and a more reliable reflection of activities of daily living (Okuno et al., 2006).

In index finger speed tapping, we measured the maximum tapping rate and variability during approximately 14 s (measured from the first finger tap). Patients rested their elbow on the table and the patients' hand was palm down on the table. The fingers were held in a relaxed posture close to maximal extension but slightly bent so that the position could be sustained without muscular effort. No metronome was used in these speed tapping trials. The patients were instructed to tap as fast and as regularly as possible, lifting their finger at least 2 cm above the table on each cycle. The force sensor surface was placed on the table and the patients were instructed to tap on the same spot every time. In middle finger speed tapping, the procedure was the same as with index finger speed tapping but switching to the middle finger.

The raw data files containing the force trace over time were preprocessed using a custom developed python script (we do not report the accelerometer data here). The script discarded the first and last 0.5 s of data from the recordings and then converted the force sensor trace into Newtons using a previously established calibration table. We then smoothed the signal using a 160-sample Bartlett window (which amounted to approximately 53 ms at our sample rate). The script detected the tap onset landmarks (a sudden impact) when the force exceeded 0.05 Newton. Tap offsets (a release of contact from the tapping measurement surface) were defined as the time point when the force trace dropped below 0.05 Newton again at least 40 ms after the last tap onset. Similarly, the next onset was restricted to occur at least 75 ms after the last tap offset. All data files with their landmarks were furthermore visually inspected to ensure our method of analysis did not introduce any artifacts. In a number of cases the 0.05 Newton onset/offset threshold was adjusted manually to compensate for the fact that some patients tapped too softly or off the sensor surface. We furthermore recorded the maximal tapping force between subsequent tap onset and tap offsets; the intervals between adjacent onsets, which will be referred to as the inter-tap-intervals (ITIs) in what follows; and the duration between the tap onset and tap offset (tap dwell phase duration). Next, we discarded the ITIs that were larger than 2000 ms since these reflected pauses or interruptions in the patient's tapping behavior (such as asking the experimenter whether to continue tapping) instead of the patient's motor capacity. We also discarded ITIs shorter than 120 ms since there were disproportionately many as a result of double-tap recordings.

MOOD TEST: PROFILE OF MOOD STATES

Patients' mood was established using the Profile of Mood States (POMS) (Lorr et al., 1971). The short form has 35 adjectives (items). For each adjective the patients rated to what extent they are applicable to their mood over the last week, on a scale from 1 (not at all) to 5 (very strongly). The items load onto four category sub-scores: depression/anxiety, fatigue, vigor, and hostility (Curran et al., 1995). We used a previously validated German translation (Bullinger et al., 1990). The questionnaire was administered at PRE and POST. The experimenter read each of the items to the patients who then responded verbally.

MOOD TEST: FACES SCALE

In order to obtain a quick estimate of the development of a patient's mood throughout the therapy, we used a mood scale of faces (Kunin, 1955; Andrews and Crandall, 1976; McDowell, 2006). Patients were presented a list of smiley faces ranging from very happy to very sad (see Supplementary Materials). Patients were asked at the PRE measurement session which face best represented how they were feeling by pointing to the corresponding face. At the beginning of each therapy session, patients were asked to point how they had felt since the previous session. At the end of each therapy session, too, patients were asked again how they had felt during the therapy session. At the end of each joint therapy session, the patients were asked individually how they felt about the partner patient with whom they received therapy. The patients pointed to one of the faces in such a way that this was not seen by their partner so as to avoid social pressure effects. Finally, during the POST measurement patients were again asked to select the face representing how they felt at present. The therapist wrote down the letter code corresponding to the chosen face without allowing either patient to see the letter in question.

ETHICS

This study was performed in accordance with ethical guidelines proposed by the Medical University Hanover (MHH). The protocol was approved by the ethics board on 20 April 2011 (nr. 1056-2011).

DATA ANALYSIS

We performed parametric ANOVA whenever the data quantity and distribution could reasonably be assumed to fulfill its assumptions. We detected deviations from sphericity using Mauchley's Test and whenever it was significant we applied the Greenhause-Geisser correction. In those cases, we indicated significance as p_{GG} and omitted the uncorrected p-value for the sake of brevity. We report generalized effect sizes η^2_G (Bakeman, 2005). Groups were then compared using Tukey HSD contrasts.

RESULTS

NINE-HOLE PEGBOARD TEST

We performed an ANOVA with time to complete the pegboard test as dependent variable and factors group (in-turn or together) and measurement (PRE or POST). There was a main effect of time point [$F_{(1,26)} = 21.35$, $p < 0.0001$, $\eta^2_G = 0.02$] which indicated that both groups performed the 9HPT faster after therapy than before. Furthermore, there was a trend for an interaction effect between group and time point indicating that in-turn group tended to improve more than the together group [$F_{(1,26)} = 0.70$, $p = 0.065$, $\eta^2_G = 0.004$] (**Figure 1**). There was no main effect of group [$F_{(1,26)} = 0.74$, $p = 0.40$]. We feel that some caution may be needed in interpreting the interaction trend, since the in-turn group performed the test slightly slower at the PRE measurement ($M = 72.4$ s, $SD = 32.8$ s) than the together group ($M = 42.5$ s, $SD = 36.8$ s). However, this difference was not significant [$t_{(26.7)} = 1.13$, $p = 0.27$]. Furthermore, the effect might reflect two patients with larger improvement scores. However, these patients were not more than 3 SD away from the overall mean improvement or the mean improvement per group and were therefore not discarded as outliers.

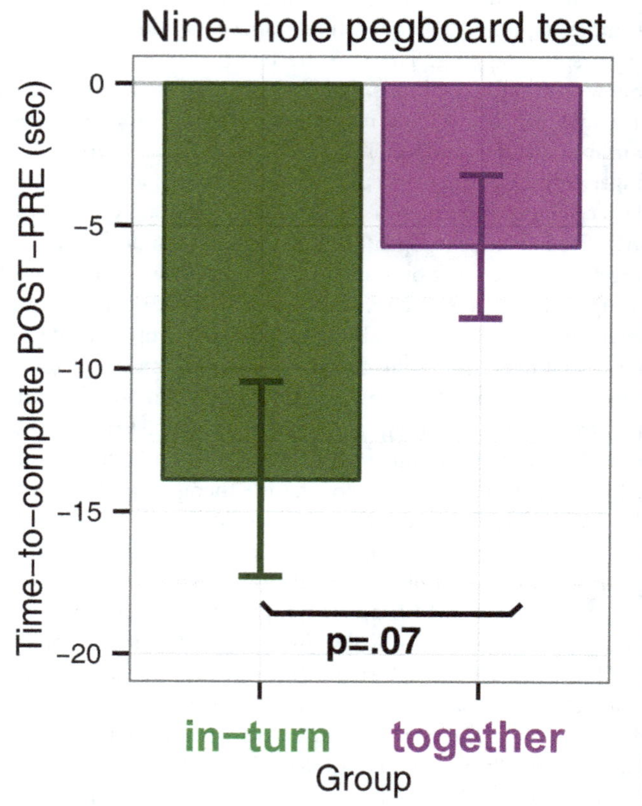

FIGURE 1 | Nine-hole pegboard test scores measured as the difference in time-to-complete POST minus time-to-complete at PRE (in seconds). A negative difference indicates that patients completed the Nine-hole pegboard test faster after therapy (POST) than before (PRE).

FINGER TAPPING TESTS

Index finger unpaced tapping

The PRE measurement of one patient (in the in-turn group) was invalid due to technical reasons and this patient was therefore removed from further analysis. We pooled the taps that were recorded before and after each therapy session and then computed the tapping speed and variability as follows. Speed was calculated as the median of the intervals (in ms). Variability was calculated by first discarding the taps that were 3 SD longer or shorter than the mean for that block, taking the standard deviation of the remaining intervals and then divided it by the mean for that block to obtain the coefficient-of-variation (CV in percent). We found no initial differences in tapping speed between the groups [$t_{(18.8)} = 1.09$, $p = 0.29$] or in tapping variability [$t_{(24.8)} = -1.2, p = 0.24$].

We performed an ANOVA on the log-transformed median tapping interval with factors session (PRE, POST, and the 10 therapy sessions) and group (in-turn, together). The main effect of group was not significant [$F_{(1,25)} = 0.15, p = 0.70$]. However, the main effect of measurement session was significant but became only a statistical trend after sphericity corrections [$F_{(11,275)} = 2.20, p = 0.01, p_{GG} = 0.10, \eta^2_G = 0.02$]. There was no interaction between group and session [$F_{(11,275)} = 0.72$, $p = 0.72$, $p_{GG} = 0.53$] (**Figure 2**).

We performed the same ANOVA with log-transformed coefficient-of-variability (CV) as dependent measure. We found no effect of group [$F_{(1,25)} = 0.09$, $p = 0.76$], measurement session [$F_{(11,275)} = 1.43, p = 0.16, p_{GG} = 0.20$] and no interaction [$F_{(11,275)} = 1.51, p = 0.12, p_{GG} = 0.17$] (**Figure 2**).

Middle finger unpaced tapping

Middle finger tapping was measured before (PRE) and after (POST) therapy. There were no differences in initial tapping speed [$t_{(13.0)} = 1.76, p = 0.11$]. There was a statistical trend for the in-turn group to tap more regularly ($M = 17.2$, $SD = 9.9$% CV) at the PRE measurement than the together group ($M = 30.2$, $SD = 19.0$% CV) [$t_{(24.0)} = -1.77, p = 0.09$].

An ANOVA with factors group (in-turn, together) and measurement session (PRE, POST) revealed no effect of group on middle finger tapping speed [$F_{(1,24)} = 1.89, p = 0.18$]. There was no effect of measurement session [$F_{(1,24)} = 1.86$, $p = 0.18$] and no interaction [$F_{(1,24)} = 0.20, p = 0.66$].

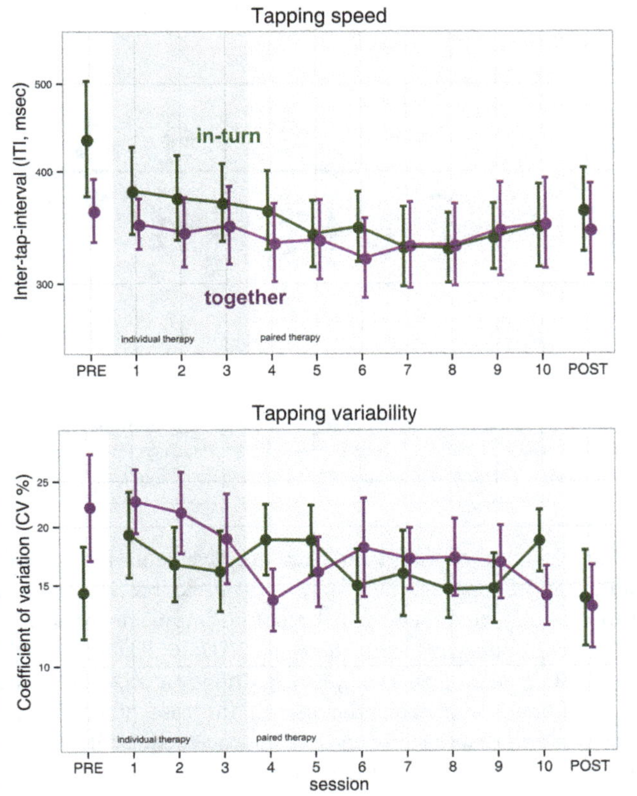

FIGURE 2 | Index finger tapping speed and regularity. Error bars indicate the standard error of the mean.

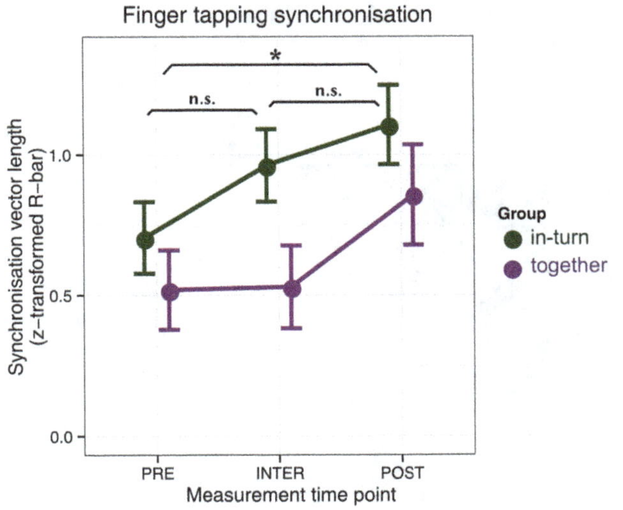

FIGURE 3 | Synchronization tapping performance before therapy (PRE), in between the individual and joint sessions (INTER), and after therapy (POST). Error bars indicate standard error of the mean. Significance of the main effect (across groups) is indicated: $^*p < 0.05$.

The same ANOVA was performed with tapping variability as dependent variable. We found no effect of group [$F_{(1,24)} = 0.88$, $p = 0.36$] or recording session (PRE,POST) [$F_{(1,24)} = 0.85$, $p = 0.36$]. There was a statistical trend for an interaction between group and session [$F_{(1,24)} = 3.29, p = 0.08, \eta^2_G = 0.04$]. However, in light of the subtle differences in middle finger tapping variability at the PRE measurement, we interpreted these findings as regression toward the mean.

Index-to-thumb paced tapping

Two patients were eliminated from further analysis because during one session their tapping was too soft to be reliably assessed (both from the *together* group). We used circular statistics to quantify the time-lock (synchronization) between patients' finger tap onsets and the metronome click onsets (Fisher, 1995). We then performed a repeated-measures ANOVA with factors group (together, in-turn) and measurement time point (PRE, INTER, and POST) (**Figure 3**). The main effect of group was not significant [$F_{(1,24)} = 2.54$, $p = 0.12$]. There was a main effect of recording time-point [$F_{(2,48)} = 10.98$, $p_{GG} = 0.0001$, $\eta^2_G = 0.09$]. This effect reflected the fact that patients' tapping was more synchronized after therapy relative to before ($p = 0.036$). There were no differences between the PRE and INTER measurements ($p = 0.60$) or the POST and INTER measurements ($p = 0.27$). There was no interaction between group and time-point [$F_{(2,48)} = 1.28, p_{GG} = 0.29$].

MOOD TESTS

For each factor of the POMS (depression/anxiety, fatigue, hostility, and vigor) we performed an ANOVA with factors group (together or in-turn) and time point (PRE, POST). We found a main effect of time point reflecting a reduction in depression [$F_{(1,26)} = 11.76$, $p = 0.002$, $\eta^2_G = 0.09$] and fatigue [$F_{(1,26)} = 6.56$, $p = 0.02$, $\eta^2_G = 0.07$]. No change was found in vigor [$F_{(1,26)} = 1.01$, $p = 0.32$] and a trend for improvement in hostility [$F_{(1,26)} = 3.95, p = 0.06$]. There were no main effects of group [all $F_{(1,26)} < 0.45$, $p > 0.51$] or interactions between group and time point [all $F_{(1,26)} < 0.19, p > 0.67$] (**Figure 4**).

FACES SCALE MOOD RATINGS

Patients were asked to rate their own mood on the faces scale, both during the PRE and POST measurement sessions and during the therapy sessions. There were no differences in rating between the groups at the PRE measurement [Mann-Whitney U, $Z = -1.22, p = 0.22$]. The in-turn group patients' self-mood ratings improved during therapy [Friedman test $\chi^2(11) = 27.36$, $p = 0.004$] as did those of the together group [Friedman test $\chi^2(11) = 36.08, p = 0.0001$]. There were no differences in rating during the POST measurement session [Mann-Whitney U, $Z = -0.62, p = 0.54$].

Patients were furthermore invited to rate how they experienced the therapy sessions. There was a tendency for the in-turn group to rate the first (individual) session more positive than the together group [Mann–Whitney U, $Z = -1.76$, $p = 0.08$], although first they still received therapy individually. This difference had disappeared by the third session [Mann–Whitney U, $Z = 0, p = 1.00$]. During the paired therapy (sessions 4–10), the in-turn group became more positive as therapy progressed [Friedman $\chi^2(6) = 13.87$, $p = 0.03$] but the together group stayed at the same level [Friedman $\chi^2(6) = 7.56$, $p = 0.27$]. There were nevertheless no differences in rating between the

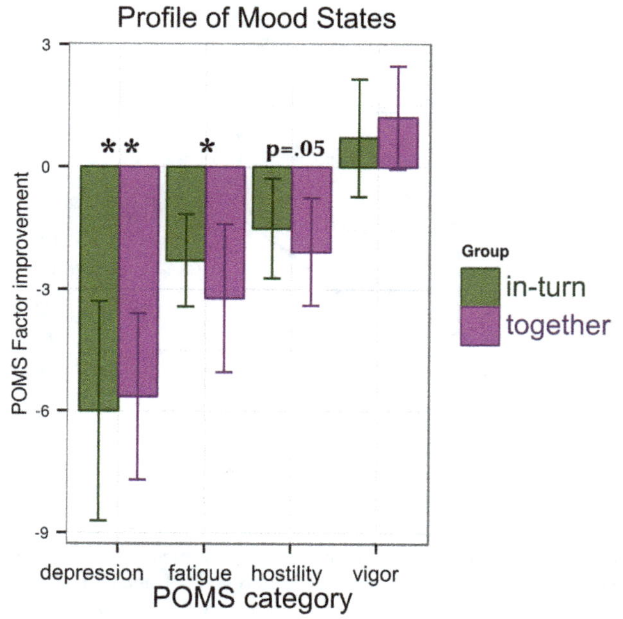

FIGURE 4 | Results of the mood tests: patients show reductions in depression/anxiety and fatigue that are similar between groups. A trend for improvement (decrease) in hostility is observed. Significance is indicated as follows: $^{*}p < 0.05$, $^{**}p < 0.01$.

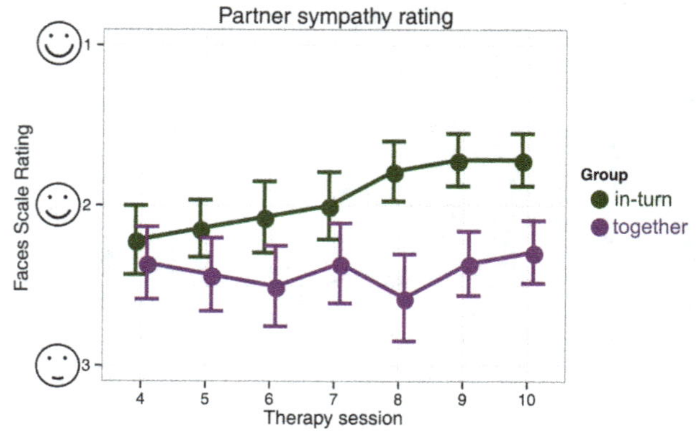

FIGURE 5 | Patient's likeability rating of their therapy partner. We indicate mean and standard errors of the ratings for each group for clarity of presentation, although our statistical analysis was non-parametric.

groups at the last (tenth) session [Mann–Whitney U, $Z = -0.25$, $p = 0.80$].

In the partner sympathy ratings, there were no differences in rating between the two groups in the first paired session (session 4) [Mann–Whitney U, $Z = -0.55$, $p = 0.58$]. The in-turn group showed a marked improvement in their rating of their therapy partner [Friedman $\chi^2(6) = 25.12$, $p = 0.0003$] whereas the together group showed no change in rating [Friedman $\chi^2(6) = 4.98$, $p = 0.55$] (**Figure 5**).

DISCUSSION

Our study was the first to implement music-supported therapy with pairs of patients instead of providing therapy to patients individually. We hypothesized that playing in synchrony would improve patient's social engagement and, through this greater engagement, improve their motor outcome. We controlled for potential benefits of patients sharing their musical rehabilitation experience (Overy, 2012) by having all patients receive therapy in pairs.

Firstly, our results reveal that music-supported stroke rehabilitation can be effective not only when patients are treated individually (as in previous studies) but also in pairs. We found improvements in patients' fine motor control in the 9HPT and synchronization tapping. The finding that music-supported rehabilitation is effective in pairs has practical implications. Paired therapy could considerably reduce the time investment on the part of the therapists. Furthermore, patients showed reductions in depression and fatigue. This indicates that music may have a beneficial effect on mood, in line with previous findings in healthy participants (Seinfeld et al., 2013).

Surprisingly, we found no clear improvements in index or middle finger tapping. This is in contrast to previous studies of music-supported therapy that reported improvements in finger tapping frequency (Schneider et al., 2007; Rodriguez-Fornells et al., 2012; Amengual et al., 2013; Chong et al., 2014) as a result of music-supported therapy. In the case of finger tapping speed, the absence of overall improvement could be due to the fact that finger tapping speed tended to show a u-shaped curve (**Figure 2**). Patients appeared to improve finger tapping speed in the first half of the therapy but then showed a tendency for a rebound in the second half of the therapy. Alternatively, there may be an effect of which therapist implements music-supported therapy on the rehabilitation outcome. On the other hand, we did find clear improvements in synchronization tapping.

The 9HPT showed a difference in rehabilitation outcome between patients playing in synchrony and patients playing in turn. Contrary to our hypothesis (that patients in the together group would show the greatest benefit), in this test we found a statistical trend for patients in the in-turn group to benefit more.

How could one explain that patients playing in-turn would show greater benefit than patients playing synchronously? We speculate that patients in the in-turn group may benefit from the opportunity to learn through observation. In healthy participants, seeing others perform a motor task leads to motor facilitation (Ménoret et al., 2013) and motor learning (McCullagh et al., 1989; Hodges et al., 2007; Wulf and Mornell, 2008) on the part of the observer. In particular, observers appear to benefit from observing both experts and novices perform a motor task, thus learning from errors as well as exemplary performance (Andrieux and Proteau, 2013). As a result, action observation has been proposed recently as a tool for motor-rehabilitation after stroke (Garrison et al., 2010, 2013; Sale and Franceschini, 2012). This finding suggests that stroke patients undergoing rehabilitation may benefit from first observing a therapist perform movements and then a patient peer perform those same movements, as they did in our in-turn group. In this way, observation during music-supported therapy might improve patients' rehabilitation outcome.

An alternative explanation for our findings is that the simultaneously occurring sounds in the together-condition confused patients, preventing them from dissociating sounds that they self-generated from those that were generated by their partner. This could have prevented the motor system from learning from auditory feedback (Altenmüller et al., 2009). A future study could remedy this problem by providing the two patients in each pair separate headphones in which their own sounds are louder than those of their partner. Another alternative explanation is that patients in the together-group were overwhelmed by the higher task demands. In this group, patients were required not only to produce the correct sequence of keystrokes, but also at the same time as their partner. This required them to observe the other person or listen to their keystrokes and predict when the next keystroke was going to occur (Keller and Repp, 2008; Sebanz and Knoblich, 2009; Pecenka and Keller, 2011). One can argue that coordinating one's actions with that of another person's actions is more challenging than performing the same actions alone. It is possible that the task demands in the together group were too high for the patients, causing the patients to be overtaxed and distracted or confused. This would provide an alternative explanation of the trend finding that the in-turn group shows greater rehabilitation benefit than the together group.

Furthermore, results indicate that patients in the in-turn group grew to like each other more over the course of therapy. This is contrary to previous findings where people moving in synchrony liked each other more than people who did not (Hove and Risen, 2009). Perhaps this difference between our study and previous ones is due to auditory-motor malfunctions in stroke patients, in line with previous suggestions (Rodriguez-Fornells et al., 2012). We found no differences in finger synchronization tapping performance between the groups, suggesting that the overall improvement in synchronization was due to a general improvement in motor capacity and not the fact that one group trained to synchronize during therapy. Similarly, the task of synchronization to another person may be so demanding for patients that the mechanisms that usually mediate synchrony-induced social effects (Wiltermuth and Heath, 2009; Wiltermuth, 2012) were unavailable.

At the outset of this study we had hypothesized two causalities. First, playing in synchrony would increase social engagement on the part of the patients. Second, this greater social engagement would then increase motor rehabilitation outcome. We found no evidence for the first causality. Instead, patients performing in turn rated their partner higher in sympathy ratings. As for the second causality, groups performed mostly similar with perhaps a small advantage for the group playing in turn. This suggests that greater social engagement might indeed improve motor outcome, in line with previous studies.

A limitation of this study is that we have not tested a control group who did not receive any musical intervention. As a result, effects found here that do not differ between groups cannot strictly be attributed to the musical intervention. However, the advantage of this approach is that any differences between the groups are likely due to the principal experimental manipulation (playing together vs. playing in turn). Our patient sample was relatively small and heterogeneous and the exact lesion sites of the stroke were unknown to us. Future studies could correlate lesion localization maps to performance and functional motor outcome of patients undergoing music-supported therapy in order to establish which patient groups might benefit maximally from music-supported therapy.

ACKNOWLEDGMENTS

This work was supported by the EBRAMUS, European Brain and Music Grant (ITN MC FP7, GA 238157). We are indebted to Britta Westner, M.A., for running a pilot study. We furthermore would like to thank Mr. Richter for valuable feedback about music-supported therapy. Also, Dr. Sabine Schneider kindly shared her knowledge of the previous implementation of the music-supported therapy that formed the basis for the current therapy program. We thank all the medical staff (doctors and nurses) in the Hessisch Oldendorf clinic for their cooperation and for indicating to us patients who might be suitable for inclusion in the study. Finally we wish to extend our gratitude to all the patients who devoted their time to participation in this study. We hope the therapy may benefit them in their daily lives.

REFERENCES

Altenmüller, E., Marco-Pallares, J., Münte, T. F., and Schneider, S. (2009). Neural reorganization underlies improvement in stroke-induced motor dysfunction by music-supported therapy. *Ann. N.Y. Acad. Sci.* 1169, 395–405. doi: 10.1111/j.1749-6632.2009.04580.x

Amengual, J. L., Rojo, N., Veciana de las Heras, M., Marco-Pallarés, J., Grau-Sánchez, J., Schneider, S., et al. (2013). Sensorimotor plasticity after music-supported therapy in chronic stroke patients revealed by transcranial magnetic stimulation. *PLoS ONE* 8:e61883. doi: 10.1371/journal.pone.0061883

Andrews, F. M., and Crandall, R. (1976). The validity of measures of self-reported well-being. *Soc. Indic. Res.* 3, 1–19. doi: 10.1007/BF00286161

Andrieux, M., and Proteau, L. (2013). Observation learning of a motor task: who and when? *Exp. Brain Res.* 229, 125–137. doi: 10.1007/s00221-013-3598-x

Bakeman, R. (2005). Recommended effect size statistics for repeated measures designs. *Behav. Res. Methods* 37, 379–384. doi: 10.3758/BF03192707

Bullinger, M., Heinisch, M., Ludwig, M., and Geier, S. (1990). Skalen zur Erfassung des Wohlbefindens: Psychosomatische Analysen zum "Profile of Mood States" (POMS) und zum "Psychological General Wellbeing Index" (PGWI). *Z. Differ. Diagn. Psychol.* 11, 53–61.

Bunketorp Käll, L., Lundgren-Nilsson, Å., Blomstrand, C., Pekna, M., Pekny, M., and Nilsson, M. (2012). The effects of a rhythm and music-based therapy program and therapeutic riding in late recovery phase following stroke: a study protocol for a three-armed randomized controlled trial. *BMC Neurol.* 12:141. doi: 10.1186/1471-2377-12-141

Caeiro, L., Ferro, J. M., and Costa, J. (2013). Apathy secondary to stroke: a systematic review and meta-analysis. *Cerebrovasc. Dis.* 35, 23–39. doi: 10.1159/000346076

Calautti, C., Jones, P. S., Persaud, N., Guincestre, J.-Y., Naccarato, M., Warburton, E. A., et al. (2006). Quantification of index tapping regularity after stroke with tri-axial accelerometry. *Brain Res. Bull.* 70, 1–7. doi: 10.1016/j.brainresbull.2005.11.001

Chong, H. J., Cho, S.-R., and Kim, S. J. (2014). Hand rehabilitation using MIDI keyboard playing in adolescents with brain damage: a preliminary study. *NeuroRehabilitation* 34, 147–155. doi: 10.3233/NRE-131026

Curran, S. L., Andrykowski, M. A., and Studts, J. L. (1995). Short form of the profile of mood states (POMS-SF): psychometric information. *Psychol. Assess.* 7, 80–83. doi: 10.1037/1040-3590.7.1.80

Dimyan, M. A., and Cohen, L. G. (2011). Neuroplasticity in the context of motor rehabilitation after stroke. *Nat. Rev. Neurol.* 7, 76–85. doi: 10.1038/nrneurol.2010.200

Fisher, N. I. (1995). *Statistical Analysis of Circular Data.* Cambridge, UK: Cambridge University Press.

Garrison, K. A., Aziz-Zadeh, L., Wong, S. W., Liew, S.-L., and Winstein, C. J. (2013). Modulating the motor system by action observation after. *Stroke* 44, 2247–2253. doi: 10.1161/STROKEAHA.113.001105

Garrison, K. A., Winstein, C. J., and Aziz-Zadeh, L. (2010). The mirror neuron system: a neural substrate for methods in stroke rehabilitation. *Neurorehabil. Neural Repair* 24, 404–412. doi: 10.1177/1545968309354536

Glass, T. A., Matchar, D. B., Belyea, M., and Feussner, J. R. (1993). Impact of social support on outcome in first stroke. *Stroke* 24, 64–70. doi: 10.1161/01.STR.24.1.64

Grau-Sánchez, J., Amengual, J. L., Rojo, N., de las Heras, M. V., Rubio, F., Altenmüller, E., et al. (2013). Plasticity in the sensorimotor cortex induced by Music-supported therapy in stroke patients: a TMS study. *Front. Hum. Neurosci.* 7:494. doi: 10.3389/fnhum.2013.00494

Heller, A., Wade, D. T., Wood, V. A., Sunderland, A., Hewer, R. L., and Ward, E. (1987). Arm function after stroke: measurement and recovery over the first three months. *J. Neurol. Neurosurg. Psychiatry* 50, 714–719. doi: 10.1136/jnnp.50.6.714

Hodges, N. J., Williams, A. M., Hayes, S. J., and Breslin, G. (2007). What is modelled during observational learning? *J. Sports Sci.* 25, 531–545. doi: 10.1080/02640410600946860

Hove, M. J., and Risen, J. L. (2009). It's all in the timing: interpersonal synchrony increases affiliation. *Soc. Cogn.* 27, 949–960. doi: 10.1521/soco.2009.27.6.949

Keller, P. E., and Repp, B. H. (2008). Multilevel coordination stability: integrated goal representations in simultaneous intra-personal and inter-agent coordination. *Acta Psychol. (Amst.)* 128, 378–386. doi: 10.1016/j.actpsy.2008.03.012

Kokal, I., Engel, A., Kirschner, S., and Keysers, C. (2011). Synchronized drumming enhances activity in the caudate and facilitates prosocial commitment - if the rhythm comes easily. *PLoS ONE* 6:e27272. doi: 10.1371/journal.pone.0027272

Kunin, T. (1955). The construction of a new type of attitude measure. *Pers. Psychol.* 8, 65–77. doi: 10.1111/j.1744-6570.1955.tb01189.x

Launay, J., Dean, R. T., and Bailes, F. (2013). Synchronization can influence trust following virtual interaction. *Exp. Psychol.* 60, 53–63. doi: 10.1027/1618-3169/a000173

Lorr, M., McNair, D., and Droppleman, L. (1971). *Manual: Profile of Mood States.* San Diego, CA: Educational and Industrial Testing Service.

Mathiowetz, V., Volland, G., Kashman, N., and Weber, K. (1985). Adult norms for the box and block test of manual dexterity. *Am. J. Occup. Ther.* 39, 386–391. doi: 10.5014/ajot.39.6.386

McCullagh, P., Weiss, M. R., and Ross, D. (1989). Modeling considerations in motor skill acquisition and performance: an integrated approach. *Exerc. Sport Sci. Rev.* 17, 475–513.

McDowell, I. (2006). *Measuring Health: a Guide to Rating Scales and Questionnaires.* Oxford: Oxford University Press. doi: 10.1093/acprof:oso/9780195165678.001.0001

Ménoret, M., Curie, A., des Portes, V., Nazir, T. A., and Paulignan, Y. (2013). Simultaneous action execution and observation optimise grasping actions. *Exp. Brain Res.* 227, 407–419. doi: 10.1007/s00221-013-3523-3

Narme, P., Tonini, A., Khatir, F., Schiaratura, L., Clément, S., and Samson, S. (2012). Non pharmacological treatment for Alzheimer's disease: comparison between musical and non-musical interventions. *Geriatr. Psychol. Neuropsychiatr. Vieil.* 10, 215–224. doi: 10.1684/pnv.2012.0343

Okuno, R., Yokoe, M., Akazawa, K., Abe, K., and Sakoda, S. (2006). Finger taps movement acceleration measurement system for quantitative diagnosis of Parkinson's disease. *Conf. Proc. IEEE Eng. Med. Biol. Soc.* 6623–6626. doi: 10.1109/IEMBS.2006.260904

Overy, K. (2012). Making music in a group: synchronization and shared experience. *Ann. N.Y. Acad. Sci.* 1252, 65–68. doi: 10.1111/j.1749-6632.2012.06530.x

Parker, V. M., Wade, D. T., and Langton Hewer, R. (1986). Loss of arm function after stroke: measurement, frequency, and recovery. *Int. Rehabil. Med.* 8, 69–73.

Pecenka, N., and Keller, P. E. (2011). The role of temporal prediction abilities in interpersonal sensorimotor synchronization. *Exp. Brain Res.* 211, 505–515. doi: 10.1007/s00221-011-2616-0

Rodriguez-Fornells, A., Rojo, N., Amengual, J. L., Ripollés, P., Altenmüller, E., and Münte, T. F. (2012). The involvement of audio-motor coupling in the music-supported therapy applied to stroke patients. *Ann. N.Y. Acad. Sci.* 1252, 282–293. doi: 10.1111/j.1749-6632.2011.06425.x

Rojo, N., Amengual, J., Juncadella, M., Rubio, F., Camara, E., Marco-Pallares, J., et al. (2011). Music-supported therapy induces plasticity in the sensorimotor cortex in chronic stroke: a single-case study using multimodal imaging (fMRI-TMS). *Brain Inj.* 25, 787–793. doi: 10.3109/02699052.2011.576305

Sale, P., and Franceschini, M. (2012). Action observation and mirror neuron network: a tool for motor stroke rehabilitation. *Eur. J. Phys. Rehabil. Med.* 48, 313–318.

Sandin, K. J., Cifu, D. X., and Noll, S. F. (1994). Stroke rehabilitation. 4. Psychologic and social implications. *Arch. Phys. Med. Rehabil.* 75, S52–S55.

Sanes, J. N., and Donoghue, J. P. (2000). Plasticity and primary motor cortex. *Annu. Rev. Neurosci.* 23, 393–415. doi: 10.1146/annurev.neuro.23.1.393

Schneider, S., Schönle, P. W., Altenmüller, E., and Münte, T. F. (2007). Using musical instruments to improve motor skill recovery following a stroke. *J. Neurol.* 254, 1339–1346. doi: 10.1007/s00415-006-0523-2

Sebanz, N., and Knoblich, G. (2009). Prediction in joint action: what, when, and where. *Top. Cogn. Sci.* 1, 353–367. doi: 10.1111/j.1756-8765.2009.01024.x

Seinfeld, S., Figueroa, H., Ortiz-Gil, J., and Sanchez-Vives, M. V. (2013). Effects of music learning and piano practice on cognitive function, mood and quality of life in older adults. *Front. Psychol.* 4:810. doi: 10.3389/fpsyg.2013.00810

Valdesolo, P., and Desteno, D. (2011). Synchrony and the social tuning of compassion. *Emotion* 11, 262–266. doi: 10.1037/a0021302

Villeneuve, M., and Lamontagne, A. (2013). Playing piano can improve upper extremity function after stroke: case studies. *Stroke Res. Treat.* 2013:159105. doi: 10.1155/2013/159105

Ward, N. S., and Cohen, L. G. (2004). Mechanisms underlying recovery of motor function after stroke. *Arch. Neurol.* 61, 1844–1848. doi: 10.1001/archneur.61.12.1844

Wiltermuth, S. S. (2012). Synchrony and destructive obedience. *Soc. Influ.* 7, 78–89. doi: 10.1080/15534510.2012.658653

Wiltermuth, S. S., and Heath, C. (2009). Synchrony and cooperation. *Psychol. Sci.* 20, 1–5. doi: 10.1111/j.1467-9280.2008.02253.x

Woldag, H., and Hummelsheim, H. (2002). Evidence-based physiotherapeutic concepts for improving arm and hand function in stroke patients. *J. Neurol.* 249, 518–528. doi: 10.1007/s004150200058

Wulf, G., and Mornell, A. (2008). Insights about practice from the perspective of motor learning: a review. *Music Perform. Res.* 2, 1–25. Available online at: http://mpr-online.net/Issues/Volume%202%20%5B2008%5D/Wulf%20and%20Mornell.pdf

14

Music mnemonics aid verbal memory and induce learning – related brain plasticity in multiple sclerosis

Michael H. Thaut[1]*, David A. Peterson[2,3], Gerald C. McIntosh[4] and Volker Hoemberg[5]

[1] *Center for Biomedical Research in Music, Colorado State University, Fort Collins, CO, USA*
[2] *Computational Neurobiology Laboratory, Salk Institute for Biological Studies, La Jolla, CA, USA*
[3] *Institute for Neural Computation, University of California San Diego, La Jolla, CA, USA*
[4] *Department of Neurology, University of Colorado Health, Fort Collins, CO, USA*
[5] *Department of Neurology, SRH Rehabilitation Hospital Bad Wimpfen, Bad Wimpfen, Germany*

***Correspondence:**
Michael H. Thaut, Center for Biomedical Research in Music, Colorado State University, Fort Collins, CO 80523, USA
e-mail: michael.thaut@colostate.edu

Recent research on music and brain function has suggested that the temporal pattern structure in music and rhythm can enhance cognitive functions. To further elucidate this question specifically for memory, we investigated if a musical template can enhance verbal learning in patients with multiple sclerosis (MS) and if music-assisted learning will also influence short-term, system-level brain plasticity. We measured systems-level brain activity with oscillatory network synchronization during music-assisted learning. Specifically, we measured the spectral power of 128-channel electroencephalogram (EEG) in alpha and beta frequency bands in 54 patients with MS. The study sample was randomly divided into two groups, either hearing a spoken or a musical (sung) presentation of Rey's auditory verbal learning test. We defined the "learning-related synchronization" (LRS) as the percent change in EEG spectral power from the first time the word was presented to the average of the subsequent word encoding trials. LRS differed significantly between the music and the spoken conditions in low alpha and upper beta bands. Patients in the music condition showed overall better word memory and better word order memory and stronger bilateral frontal alpha LRS than patients in the spoken condition. The evidence suggests that a musical mnemonic recruits stronger oscillatory network synchronization in prefrontal areas in MS patients during word learning. It is suggested that the temporal structure implicit in musical stimuli enhances "deep encoding" during verbal learning and sharpens the timing of neural dynamics in brain networks degraded by demyelination in MS.

Keywords: verbal memory, musical mnemonic, deep encoding, electroencephalogram, alpha/beta oscillations, learning-related neural synchrony

INTRODUCTION

The past two decades have seen an increasing awareness of cognitive deficits in multiple sclerosis (MS). Many MS patients have cognitive deficits (Borghi et al., 2013; Rahn et al., 2012; Rogers and Panegyres, 2007; Amato et al., 2001; Gaudino et al., 2001; Kujala et al., 1996; Rao, 1990; Peyser et al., 1980). It is estimated that up to 65% of persons with MS suffer from cognitive impairment affecting their quality of life, vocational ability, and social function. Although cognitive impairments in MS were described already in the nineteenth century, not until 2001 standard tests were codified to measure cognitive function in MS (Rahn et al., 2012).

Memory is one of the most prevalent types of cognitive deficit in MS and some memory deficits present in early phases of the disease (Gaudino et al., 2001; Landro et al., 2000; Thornton and Raez, 1997; Kujala et al., 1996; DeLuca et al., 1994; Peyser et al., 1980). However, no convincing evidence for effective pharmacological or other treatments for memory impairment in MS does exist (He et al., 2011). Furthermore, despite new memory test development (Camp et al., 2001) and several research studies aimed at isolating the memory problems in MS (Marie and Defer, 2001; Minden et al., 1990), the exact nature of memory deficits in MS remains unclear. One major theoretical approach attributes memory deficits in MS to inadequate learning processes (DeLuca et al., 1994) including reduced information processing speed which may prevent "deep encoding" of learning material (Rao et al., 1989; Litvan et al., 1988). More important clinically, however, as Rao (1995) has ardently noted for many years, is the lack of treatments for memory dysfunction in MS (Bennett et al., 1991).

In the past two decades, research has discovered the effectiveness of music as a temporal auditory language in neurorehabilitation (Thaut, 2005). The initial discoveries established the effect of music and rhythm in motor therapies, most comprehensively in stroke and Parkinson's disease (DeDreu et al., 2012; Thaut et al., 2007; Thaut et al., 1997; Thaut et al., 1996). Physiological priming (Rossignol and Melvill Jones, 1976), anticipatory perceptual cue timing, and neural auditory motor entrainment (Grahn and Watson, 2013; Thaut, 2013) have been proposed among the most prevalent underlying mechanisms. Music and rhythm intervention techniques (c.f., Rhythmic Auditory Stimulation RAS) are now considered evidence based and are widely used within neurologic rehabilitation (Hoemberg, 2013).

However, the recognition that timing and sequencing also have a critical function in cognitive abilities (Conway et al., 2009) has led to research investigating the potential role of music and rhythm as cognitive rehabilitation technique. Sound in music is inherently temporal and sequential and may serve as a "scaffold" to bootstrap the representation of temporal sequential patterns in cognitive functions such as memory (Conway et al., 2009). In support of this concept, many clinical reports have emphasized the relative "survival" of musical memories in neurologic memory disorders (Haslam and Cook, 2002; Baur et al., 2000), dementia, and Alzheimer's disease (Son et al., 2002; Foster and Valentine, 2001). Music processing may recruit not only declarative but also more automatic, procedural learning and memory systems that are spared in amnesia.

There is considerable evidence that music can also enhance memory for non-musical material (Thaut, 2005; Ho et al., 2003; Jakobson et al., 2003; Rainey and Larsen, 2002; Wallace, 1994). Previous evidence has shown that music memory provides access to verbal knowledge in patients with memory disorders (Cavaco et al., 2012; Moussard, 2012; Simmons-Stern et al., 2012; Sarkamo et al., 2008; Mammarella et al., 2007; Haslam and Cook, 2002; Foster and Valentine, 2001; Baur et al., 2000). Specific benefits of musical mnemonic rehearsal over verbal rehearsal when learning non-musical material have been shown with learning disabled and developmentally disabled students (Kern et al., 2007; Claussen and Thaut, 1997; Wolfe and Hom, 1993; Gfeller, 1983). In a study with autistic children – however without matched controls or a comparable control condition – a structured music listening protocol has shown to enhance a broad range of cognitive functions including memory (Bettison, 1996). However, Maeller (1996) demonstrated that music can improve memory in MS patients, with a trend toward greater improvement associated with severity of the disease.

The rhythmic-melodic pattern of a song as an auditory "scaffold" to bootstrap non-musical information may offer several advantages to facilitate "deep encoding" for the learning and retrieval process (Wallace, 1994). The rhythmic and melodic structure provides a temporal cue for the temporal order and sequencing of information. Additionally, the melody provides pitch contour cues to which information units can be mapped. The phrase structure of a melody segments information into chunks or single overarching units of information with distinct sound shapes, which is especially important when information units such as words in word lists are unrelated to each other (Snyder, 2000; Deutsch, 1982). In such process, several information units become segmented into one learning unit. Chunking is an important memory strategy because it reduces memory load (Gobet et al., 2001). Another critical element for learning via musical mnemonics is the fact that musical mnemonics, such as short songs, are composed of a relatively small "alphabet" of tones/pitches to which information units from a larger "alphabet" can be mapped (Dowling, 1973). Information such as a diatonic pitch scale (seven scale tones) is much easier to group and encode than data from large alphabets and we are much more likely to retain information from several small alphabets than the same total amount of information from a large alphabet. The English language uses 26 letters and up to 40 separate phonemes. Finally, in a well composed musical mnemonic the small tonal alphabet is organized into redundant repetitive and anticipatory units which are easy to remember (Snyder, 2000). By pairing verbal material with a simple melody (e.g., one word mapped to one note), a line of several unrelated words or numbers can now be bounded and encoded into a single "small alphabet" segment (Hitch et al., 1996; Deutsch, 1982).

Research on the neural basis of music and memory has mostly focused on musical memory formation. There are some studies that have investigated neural correlates of non-musical autobiographical recall elicited by music (Ford et al., 2011; Janata, 2009). However – despite the emerging behavioral evidence for musical mnemonics to assist in non-musical learning – no research has directly studied so far the neural correlates of non-musical memory training with musical mnemonics.

In other areas of brain and behavior function, there is emerging evidence that music modulates brain activity associated with non-musical functions of the nervous system. For example, we have evidence that rhythmic entrainment can be used for sensorimotor rehabilitation: the temporal structure of music can be harnessed to rehabilitate motor function and facilitate motor plasticity in brain damaged patient populations (Rojo et al., 2011; Luft et al., 2004; Hummelsheim, 1999). As another example, musical training evokes brain plasticity during speech perception (Kraus and Chandrasekaran, 2010). Therefore, in our study we included an investigation of neural correlates related to brain plasticity during verbal memory training using musical mnemonics. Plasticity in the functional organization of brain networks is important in recovering verbal learning and memory function after, for example, traumatic brain injury (Ricker et al., 2001). Music can play a role in brain plasticity, through both its pitch characteristics (Shahin et al., 2003) and temporal structure (Pantev et al., 1999; Merzenich et al., 1993). Music training (to discriminate pitch) produces enhanced plasticity of the N1 and P2 components of the auditory evoked potential (AEP) (Shahin et al., 2003). The temporal structure of music influences the brain oscillations associated with short-term memory for auditory patterns (Peterson and Thaut, 2002).

In this study, we investigated for the first time in persons with MS whether a musical template for verbal learning not only improves learning and memory but also involves a different pattern of short-term, system-level brain plasticity measured as changes in oscillatory network synchronization. Given the practical significance of sequencing in verbal information, we specifically investigated whether music would improve learning and memory for ordered word lists. We used the spectral power of the electroencephalogram (EEG) to measure oscillatory synchronization in patients with MS while they performed Rey's auditory verbal learning test (RAVLT).

MATERIALS AND METHODS

SUBJECTS

Subjects were 54 right-handed volunteers (38 female/16 male) with relapsing-remitting MS, with normal hearing, and no history of other neurological or psychiatric conditions. Subjects showed at least five brain lesions identified via MRI analysis. Subjects were stable on their immunomodulatory therapy and had <2 exacerbations within the 12-month prior to the study. Participants were not in an active exacerbation phase at the time of testing and were not treated with pulse-cortical steroids or cognition enhancing AChE inhibitors.

All subjects volunteered and provided written, informed consent approved by the institutional review board. Subjects were randomly assigned by computerized random number generator in concealed allocation to one of the two conditions: with and without a musical template, hereafter referred to as the "spoken" and "sung" conditions. Experimenters were blinded to assigned condition. There were no statistically significant differences between participant characteristics in the spoken and sung condition (**Table 1**).

Table 1 | Demographic data of MS participants: means (standard deviations).

	Spoken	Sung	$t(52)$	P
Age (years)	53.3 (9.3)	50.3 (10.1)	0.98	n.s.
Education (years)	15.3 (2.6)	14.7 (2.0)	1.15	n.s.
Private music training (years)	8.9 (13.9)	5.2 (4.5)	0.72	n.s.
EDSS	4.3 (0.9)	4.9 (1.3)	1.53	n.s.

EDSS, extended disability status scale (Kurtzke, 1983) (0 = no neurologic impairment, 10 = death due to MS).

TASK AND STIMULI

Unlike the more typical in-person administration of the RAVLT (Lezak, 1995), we used pre-recorded sound files and remotely recorded voice responses with the subjects isolated in a sound-proof booth to eliminate experimenter bias and to control for stimulus equality across subjects, to maximize consistency of the test procedures and to avoid the increased risk of artifacts in the simultaneously recorded EEG during interaction with another person. A single standard list of 15 words was repeated over 10 trials. Subjects were asked to recall as many words as possible after each list presentation (see **Figure 1**). The 15 words in the list were semantically unrelated. The listed words were presented at a rate of one per second and in the same order on every trial. On each trial, subjects were instructed to listen carefully as they would subsequently be asked to recall as many words as possible. Recall of the list (M1) was tested without further presentation of the original list after subjects heard and free-recalled a distractor list and again after a 20-min non-verbal distractor task (M2). Subjects were not given feedback on any trials.

In both conditions they were additionally instructed to recall items in the order they were presented on the word list.

Identical word lists were used in both experimental conditions. Overall durations for word list presentation in the spoken or sung conditions had the same length. List was presented via free field at 80 dB SPL. The same female voice was used to produce the sung and spoken word lists. In the musical mnemonic condition, the words were sung to the melody of an originally composed song. One-syllable words were assigned one-quarter note of 1 s duration, while two-syllable words were assigned one-eighth note of 0.5 s (500 ms) per syllable to generate melodic-rhythmic phrasing and to keep both conditions at 15 s durations (with 1 s rest at the end). We used an originally composed melody that was not familiar but was simple and repetitive in structure (AABA form).

The behavioral analysis measured results for overall recall of the words and for word chunks recalled in proper sequence, assessing chunk lengths of correct words' pairs across the list sequence.

ELECTROPHYSIOLOGICAL RECORDING AND ANALYSIS

We recorded from 128 scalp electrodes using Electrical Geodesic's Sensor Net. Continuous EEG was recorded using low- and high-cutoff frequencies of 1 and 100 Hz, respectively, with a 1-kHz sampling frequency. We used EGI's ocular artifact toolbox (precursor to the current Polygraphic Recording Analyzer, PRANA) to remove trials with ocular artifacts including eye movements and blinks. Spectral power was calculated over the 250–750 ms post-onset time window, common to most studies of verbal encoding (see, e.g., Staresina et al., 2005). Spectral power was computed for alpha and beta frequency bands, separately for each of the following subbands: alpha_1 (7–9 Hz), alpha_2 (9–11 Hz), alpha_3 (11–13 Hz), beta_1 (13–20 Hz), and beta_2 (20–34 Hz). Topographic EEG analysis was organized by quadrants defined by the following electrodes:

left anterior: F3, F7, FC3, FT7
right anterior: F4, F8, FC4, FT8
left posterior: CP3, TP7, P3, P7
right posterior: CP4, TP8, P4, P8.

We defined the "learning-related synchronization" (LRS) as the percent change in EEG spectral power averaged over the second through tenth encoding trials (collectively) relative to the power in the first encoding trial:

$$\text{LRS} = \frac{\text{power\_learned}}{\text{power\_notlearned}} \times 100 - 100.$$

Thus, LRS was defined in a fashion analogous to the more general event-related de-synchronization (ERD) or, more precisely, its inverted counterpart, the even-related synchronization (ERS) (Pfurtscheller, 1999). The primary difference is that the baseline for the LRS was not a period of time immediately preceding the trial of interest, but the first trial in which the same word was presented. By using the power ratio, we also mitigated absolute differences in subjects' baseline spectral EEG power. The LRS was calculated individually for every subject, frequency band, and electrode. We evaluated the average LRS from each of four quadrants: left anterior, right anterior, left posterior, and right posterior. For each frequency band the quadrant LRS averaged across subjects in each condition was compared between groups to test for change in short-term, systems-level plasticity associated with learning.

RESULTS

In overall recall, the music condition produced statistically significant results higher than in the spoken condition [two-way ANOVA: $F(1.52) = 4.12$; $p = 0.45$; mean squared error 0.057] (**Table 2**).

The analysis of pair-wise word order learning showed a statistically significant advantage for recall in music than spoken learning at the end of the last learning trial and the two subsequent memory trials [$F(1, 2) = 4.51$, $p = 0.038$, two-way ANOVA] (**Figure 2**).

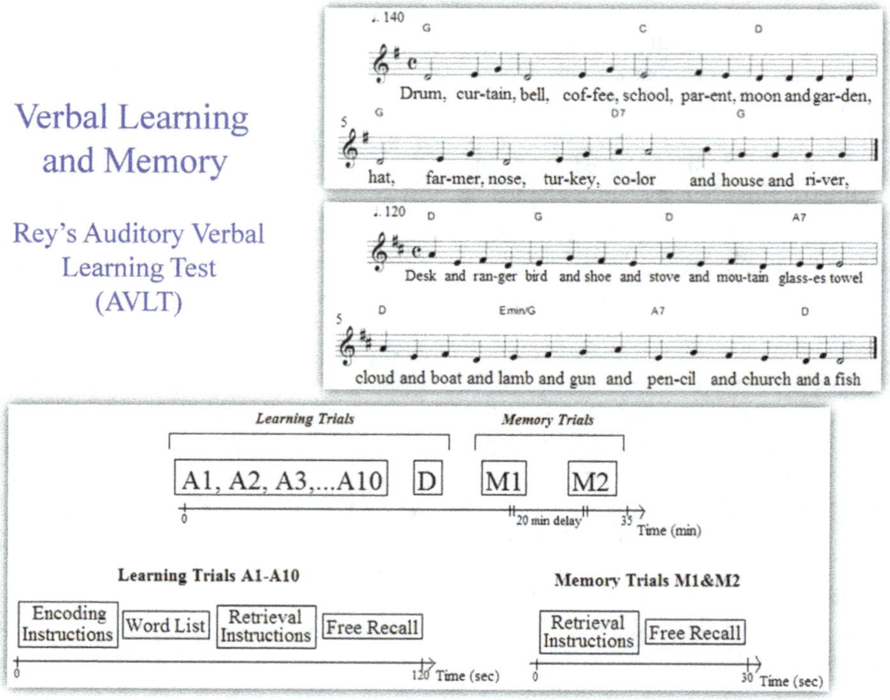

FIGURE 1 | Rey's auditory verbal learning test (RAVLT). There were 10 presentations of the same word list and one presentation of a new distractor word list. On each trial, subjects hear the full list of 15 words before being prompted to recall. Subjects are asked to perform free recall of the words again (without additional presentation) in two memory tests, M1 = immediate recall after the distractor list and M2 = recall after a 20 min delay and distractor task (D, distractor task).

Table 2 | Percentage means of recalled words at M1 and M2.

	M1	M2
Sung	77	76.6
Spoken	64.7	59.8

Musical verbal learning induced greater increase in word order recall in early and late phases of learning, whereas spoken verbal learning induced greatest increase in word order recall during the middle phase of learning. The spoken verbal learners' performance actually decreased slightly in the last two learning trials, and remained relatively lower than the musical verbal learners in the later recall trials.

When analyzed for a longer word order sequence (five words in correct order), the significant advantage for music disappeared during the acquisition trial. However, during M1 the significant difference between musical and spoken condition reemerged: the change between acquisition trials 6–10 and first recall was significantly higher for music than the spoken condition (**Figure 3**).

The stronger word order memory performance for the music condition was associated with low-alpha band ("alpha_1") LRS in bilateral frontal areas, whereas low-alpha power actually decreased in those same areas over the course of learning in the spoken condition (**Figure 4**). The difference between the groups' bilateral frontal alpha LRS was significant at the 0.05 level [$t(14) > 2.4$]. Both groups exhibited low-alpha LRS bilaterally in posterior regions, with no significant difference between the groups. In the upper beta band, both groups exhibited LRS (synchronization associated with verbal learning). In all but the left anterior quadrant, the spoken condition involved greater synchronization than the music condition, a difference that reached statistical significance in the left posterior area [$t(14) > 2.3, p < 0.05$].

Regression analysis between correct word order recall as a predictor of magnitude of overall word recall was highly significant in the sung condition for M1 ($p = 0.15$; $R^2 = 0.29$; beta = −0.54; Corr. = −0.54). Furthermore, higher EDSS scores were significant predictors for word order recall, only evident in the sung condition, however for both M1 and M2 (M1: $p = 0.001$; $R^2 = 0.57$; beta = 0.753; Corr. = 0.41) (M2: $p = 0.005$; $R^2 = 0.36$: beta + 0.60; Corr. = −0.42).

DISCUSSION

Subjects in the music condition showed significantly better total word memory, and more specifically, also paired word order memory than subjects in the spoken condition. Interestingly, general performance in word memory was significantly predicted in the music condition by correct word order recall, emphasizing the critical role of temporal structure in learning and retrieval of verbal information. Subjects who had better word order memory showed better overall word recall. This finding supports notions that music's facilitating mechanism is driven by its temporal structure

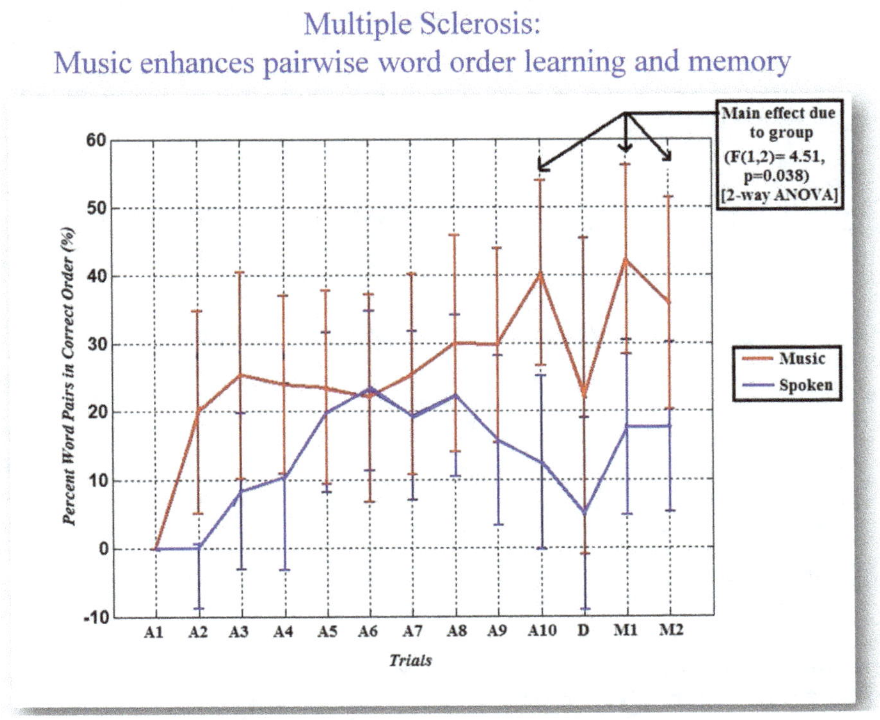

FIGURE 2 | Music enhances pair-wise word order learning and memory. *X*-axis: trial (learning trials 1–10, distractor trial "Dd," and memory trials 1 and 2). The % of recalled word pairs in correct order (*Y*-axis) is the change relative to trial 1. Bars are standard error.

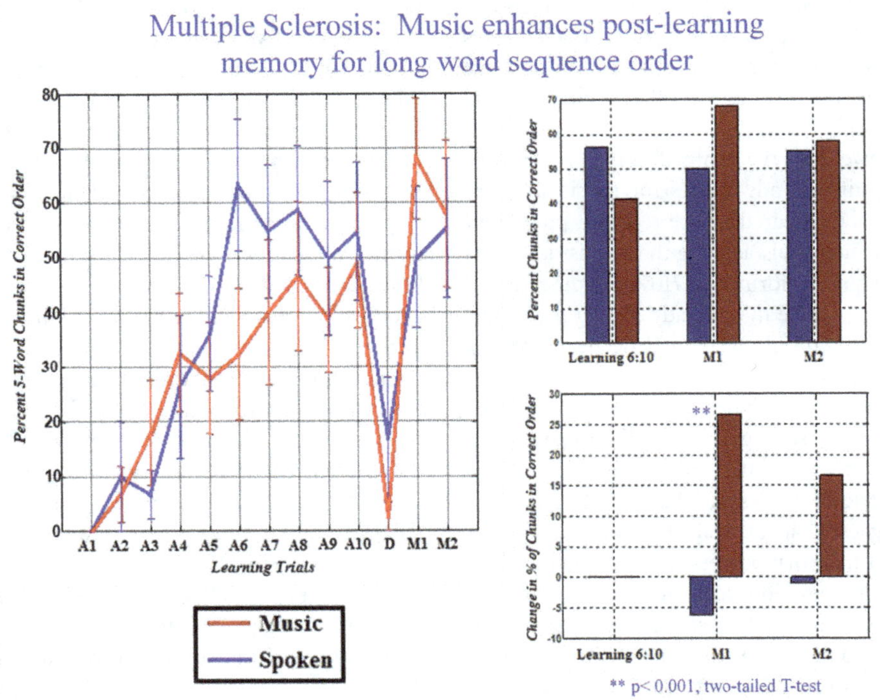

FIGURE 3 | Music enhances memory for correct five word order sequences only during recall but not during acquisition. *X*-axis: trial (learning trial 1–10, distractor trial "D," and memory trials 1 and 2). The % of recalled word sequences in correct order (*Y*-axis) is the change relative to trial 1. Bars are standard error. Bar graphs on right show % of correct word order for learning trials 6–10.

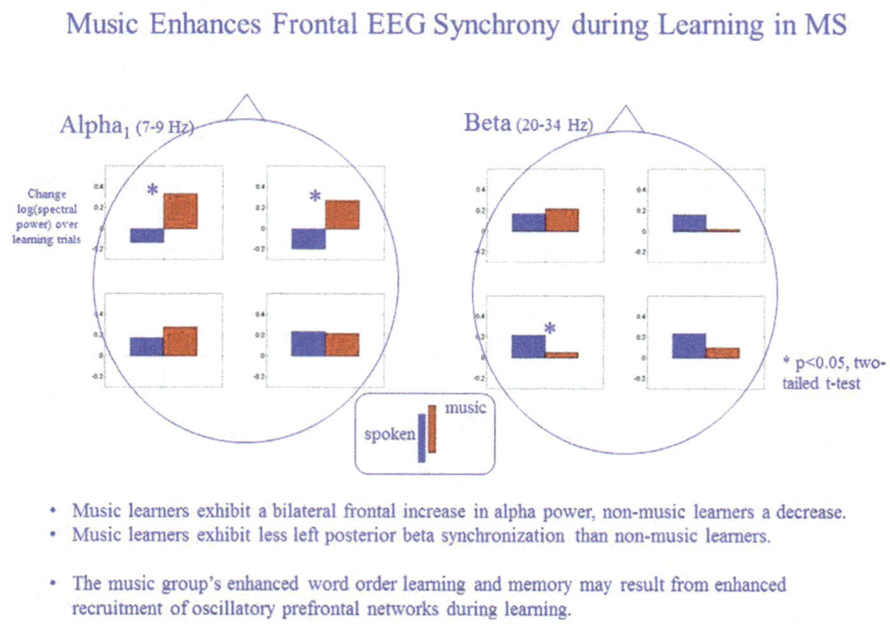

FIGURE 4 | Music induces a different form of learning-related synchronization (LRS) during verbal learning in MS than non-musical learning. Left: music enhances bilateral frontal alpha$_1$ LRS. Right: music is associated with significantly reduced left posterior beta LRS than conventional spoken verbal learning (*denotes statistically significant difference between the groups).

sequencing and chunking unrelated information units into single segments (Beatty and Monson, 1991). Temporal structure for sequencing and a small "alphabet" scaffold to reduce memory load are – based on the study data – suggested to facilitate "deep encoding" for patients with MS during the memory task. The advantages for the music assisted over the spoken memory condition were evident consistently during the learning as well as during the final retrieval stages of the RAVLT.

Important to note, however, is the contrast in the longer word order analysis where significant advantages for music in more complex task measure only appeared in the retrieval phase and not during the actual learning trials. During the acquisition trials both conditions showed equal performance. However, the retrieval advantage for music may indicate that already during the acquisition trials the musical mnemonic facilitated deeper encoding traces for word order memory.

Theoretical approaches have assigned memory impairments in MS to inadequate learning strategies rather than insufficient retrieval abilities. However, other suggestions have been made pointing at impaired retrieval processes (Rahn et al., 2012). In either case, our data suggest that musical mnemonics may successfully operate in both memory processes by enhancing deep encoding during initial information acquisition and providing critical cues for successful memory retrieval. Our results show that the advantage for deep encoding via music during more complex measures (repeating five words in correct order vs. word pairs) may not show immediately during acquisition trials. Evidence for enhanced deep encoding may not show until the retrieval phase indicating learning strategies based on "silent" processes whose success may not become evident until recall.

Several subjects in the sung condition sang the word lists back. The last point may be of clinical importance. In an earlier study (Peterson and Thaut, 2007), we found no differences when healthy subjects learned a version of the RAVLT in sung or spoken presentation. However, they were asked to speak the word lists back in both conditions during the two memory trials. We proposed as an explanation that the incongruence between learning and recall (speak back information presented in a song) created a transfer challenge that nullified a potential benefit for music. In the current study, we therefore did not require a change in recall modality (singing vs. speaking). This adjustment resulted in a significant advantage for music-assisted learning and may be an important clinical strategy for the use of musical mnemonics training as it is codified in the Neurologic Music Therapy Taxonomy (MMT) (Thaut and Hoemberg, 2014).

One important limitation in the current study is the absence of a healthy control group to confirm the differences found in the group with MS. However, memory is considered one of the core affected cognitive functions in MS and core functions are more affected than other more peripheral cognitive functions (Calabrese and Penner, 2007). Many assessment approaches to test for memory in MS use immediate and delayed recall of word lists (Wallin et al., 2006). As such we may consider the improvements during music in learning and recall using the tasks of the RAVLT a salient contribution to cognitive treatment for patients with MS.

Subjects in the music condition showed higher low-alpha power in bilateral frontal areas than subjects in the spoken condition. The increased power is usually attributed to an increase in oscillatory synchronization in recurrent cortical networks. However, it remains unknown whether it arises from a larger population of neurons recruited into the oscillatory assemblies, or greater phase synchrony in an assembly of a given size, or some combination of both.

The remarkable increase in neuronal synchronization in cortical networks in our cohort of people with MS after music-assisted training needs to be further investigated in light of the fact that the demyelination process of the disease will affect and interrupt network dynamics of neuronal cell assemblies. One might expect heterogeneous demyelination processes to variably increase propagation delays, thereby increasing noise in phase relationships among neurons in a given cell assembly and reducing synchrony (Calabrese et al., 2009). However, in light of research showing that increased frontal alpha power may represent less brain activity (Laufs et al., 2003) and increased power has been proposed as a sign for less mental effort (Jausovec, 1998), the results may indicate that music template assisted learning resulted in less mental effort by facilitating deep encoding.

This result is further underlined by the behavioral results that higher EDSS scores (higher disease states) were correlated with higher improvements in word order recall, suggesting that patients in more severe disease stages benefited particularly from music-facilitated "deep encoding" learning strategies. The results provide evidence that melodic-rhythmic templates, as commonly inherent in the temporal structure in music, may drive internal rhythm formation in recurrent cortical networks involved in learning and memory. It is particularly noteworthy that we found different short-term plasticity between the two conditions during encoding, a phase of memory processing associated with deficits in MS (Sweet et al., 2004; Marie and Defer, 2001). At a functional level, in light of past research implicating low-alpha band power in attentional processes (Klimesch, 1999; Fuster, 1997; Klimesch, 1997), the lower alpha band results in our study suggests that the influence of the musical condition may be at least partly mediated by an influence on attention. Relatedly, our low-alpha findings may also reflect some sort of adaptive processes, as seen in a conversion from relative de-synchronization (ERD) to synchronization (ERS) as subjects' transition from the first to subsequent minutes of listening to music (Krause et al., 1999). Future studies are needed to carefully control these various factors of modality, attention, and adaptation.

While the exact nature of the neurophysiologic mechanisms underlying the plasticity we measured with scalp EEG remains elusive, and the short-term nature of the learning task preclude changes in network structure, a few theories may be put forth. Musical mnemonics may activate or access alternative or compensatory pathway circuitry for memory functions to compensate for compromised prefrontal functions associated with learning and recall. The temporal pattern structure of a musical mnemonic may also facilitate deep encoding on a neurophysiological level through the stronger synchronization of the same neuronal cell assemblies underlying conventional verbal learning and memory. In either case, the temporal structure implicit in musical stimuli may sharpen the timing of neural dynamics in brain networks degraded by demyelination in MS.

Based on Gestalt perception and learning principles, it has also been proposed (Janata et al., 2002; Wallace, 1994; Deutsch, 1982) that musical patterns engage effective mechanisms by incorporating temporal structure and redundancy that chunks information into more manageable units (Deutsch, 1999; Gfeller, 1983). "Chunking" is known to be not only a critical mechanism in declarative memory learning and recall, but also in motor learning (Verwey, 2001). Chunking as a mechanism in grouping and structuring perceptual information may be an innate feature across a broad phylogenetic range of nervous systems to optimize sensory acquisition (Matzel et al., 1988). The intrinsic structure of sound patterns in music is a highly effective mechanism to facilitate perceptual grouping and chunking. The present study supports the notion that "musical chunking" can be exploited to rehabilitate verbal learning and memory. It extends previous research regarding the beneficial effect of musical template learning on verbal learning in healthy adult subjects (Peterson and Thaut, 2003). It also extends findings from a previous pilot study, which suggested that music can improve memory in MS patients (Maeller, 1996), by also showing that music-induced enhancements were significantly correlated with increases in severity of disease. The present study is to our knowledge the first research to investigate physiological correlates of enhanced memory capability in MS using musical mnemonics. A physiological correlate of enhanced memory indicates that it is possible to induce plasticity in the neuronal network activity of the dysfunctional brain.

There is a growing body of knowledge about the neurobiological correlates of verbal memory, music, chunking, and plasticity. Lesion (Peretz, 2002; Halpern, 2001), functional imaging (Parsons et al., 1998; Smith et al., 1998; Platel et al., 1997; Zatorre et al., 1996), EEG (Peterson and Thaut, 2002; Ruchkin et al., 1997) and MEG (Maess et al., 2001; Tecchio et al., 2000; Makeig and Jung, 1996) studies have illustrated that both music and verbal memory recruit widespread networks encompassing many brain regions. Theoretical work is beginning to link the behavioral level phenomenon of chunking to the dynamics of cell assemblies in cortex (Wickelgren, 1999). System-level research on brain plasticity has highlighted the importance of temporal structure in stimuli (Pantev et al., 1999; Merzenich et al., 1993) and associated cortical plasticity with verbal learning (Tallal, 2000). Collectively, the research suggests that physiological measures of brain network dynamics (Garrett et al., 2003; Fuster, 1997), such as spectral analysis of the scalp EEG (Basar et al., 1999; Niedermeyer and Lopes da Silva, 1999), can provide a window into how musical chunking may enhance verbal memory.

In conclusion, we evaluated the use of musical mnemonics as a specific strategy for enhancing verbal memory in MS patients and to identify neural "markers" for short-term plasticity in brain network activity that correspond to learning and improved memory. The combination of behavioral and physiological measures is suggestive of the therapeutic potential and underlying neurobiological mechanisms of musical mnemonics in verbal learning and memory, an area of dysfunction in MS that is underserved in basic research and therapeutic intervention. The finding that music can improve word order memory is significant given the increasingly recognized cognitive deficits in MS (Amato et al., 2001; Rao, 1990; Peyser et al., 1980). This is the first known study to extend earlier work on memory for temporal order in MS (Beatty and Monson, 1991) using an ecologically salient paradigm like the RAVLT.

ACKNOWLEDGMENTS

This research was funded by a Pilot Research Grant from the National Multiple Sclerosis Society (NMSS) to Michael H. Thaut and partial support to David A. Peterson from the National Science Foundation Grant "Mind, Machines, Motor Control" EFRI-1137279. The NMSS also assisted with advertising the study to local patients.

REFERENCES

Amato, M. P., Ponziani, G., Siracusa, G., and Sorbi, S. (2001). Cognitive dysfunction in early-onset multiple sclerosis – a reappraisal after 10 years. *Arch. Neurol.* 58, 1602–1606. doi:10.1001/archneur.58.10.1602

Basar, E., Basar-Eroglu, C., Karakas, S., and Schuermann, M. (1999). Oscillatory brain theory: a new trend in neuroscience. *IEEE Eng. Med. Biol. Mag.* 18, 56–66. doi:10.1109/51.765190

Baur, B., Uttner, I., Ilmberger, J., Fesl, G., and Mai, N. (2000). Music memory provides access to verbal knowledge in a patient with global amnesia. *Neurocase* 6, 415–421. doi:10.1080/13554790008402712

Beatty, W. W., and Monson, N. (1991). Memory for temporal-order in multiple-sclerosis. *Bull. Psychon. Soc.* 29, 10–12. doi:10.3758/BF03334753

Bennett, T., Dittmar, C., and Raubach, S. (1991). Multiple sclerosis: cognitive deficits and rehabilitation strategies. *Cogn. Rehabil.* 9, 18–23.

Bettison, S. (1996). The long-term effects of auditory training on children with autism. *J. Autism Dev. Disord.* 26, 361–374. doi:10.1007/BF02172480

Borghi, M., Cavallo, M., Carletto, S., Ostacoli, L., Zuffranieri, M., Picci, R. L., et al. (2013). Presence and significant determinants of cognitive impairment in a large sample of patients with multiple sclerosis. *PLoS ONE* 8, doi:10.1371/journal.pone0069820

Calabrese, M., Agosta, F., and Rinaldi, F. (2009). Cortical lesions and atrophy associated with cognitive impairment in relapsing-remitting multiple sclerosis. *Arch. Neurol.* 66, 1144–1150. doi:10.1001/archneurol.2009.174

Calabrese, P., and Penner, I. K. (2007). Cognitive dysfunctions in multiple sclerosis – a multiple disconnection syndrome. *J. Neurol.* 254, 18–21. doi:10.1007/s00415-007-2006-5

Camp, S. J., Thompson, A. J., and Langdon, D. W. (2001). A new test of memory for multiple sclerosis I: format development and stimuli design. *Mult. Scler.* 7, 255–262. doi:10.1177/135245850100700408

Cavaco, S., Feinstein, J. S., van Twillert, H., and Tranel, D. (2012). Musical memory in a patient with severe anterograde amnesia. *J. Clin. Exp. Neurospychol.* 34, 1089–1100. doi:10.1080/13803395.2012.728568

Claussen, D. W., and Thaut, M. H. (1997). Music as a mnemonic device for children with learning disabilities. *Can. J. Music Ther.* 5, 55–66.

Conway, C. M., Pisoni, D. B., and Kronenberger, W. G. (2009). The importance of sound for cognitive sequencing abilities. *Curr. Dir. Psychol. Sci.* 18, 275–279. doi:10.1111/j.1467-8721.2009.01651.x

DeDreu, M. J., van der Wilk, A. S., Poppe, E., Kwakkel, G., and van Wegen, E. E. (2012). Rehabilitation, exercise therapy and music in patients with Parkinson's disease: a meta-analysis of the effects of music-based movement therapy on walking ability, balance, and quality of life. *Parkinsonism Relat. Disord.* 18, 114–119. doi:10.1016/S1353-8020(11)70036-0

DeLuca, J., Barbieri-Berger, S., and Johnson, S. K. (1994). The nature of memory impairments in multiple sclerosis. *J. Clin. Exp. Neuropsychol.* 16, 183–189. doi:10.1080/01688639408402629

Deutsch, D. (1982). "Organizational processes in music," in *Music, Mind, and Brain*, ed. M. Clynes (New York: Plenum Press), 119–131.

Deutsch, D. (1999). *The Psychology of Music.* San Diego: Academic Press.

Dowling, W. J. (1973). Rhythmic groups and subjective chunks in memory for melodies. *Atten. Percept. Psychophys.* 14, 37–40. doi:10.3758/BF03198614

Ford, J. H., Addis, D. R., and Giovanello, K. S. (2011). Differential neural activity during search of specific and general autobiographical memories elicited by music cues. *Neuropsychologia* 49, 2514–2526. doi:10.1016/j.neuropsychologia.2011.04.032

Foster, N. A., and Valentine, E. R. (2001). The effect of auditory stimulation on autobiographical recall in dementia. *Exp. Aging Res.* 27, 215–228. doi:10.1080/036107301300208664

Fuster, J. M. (1997). Network memory. *Trends Neurosci.* 20, 451–459. doi:10.1016/S0166-2236(97)01128-4

Garrett, D., Peterson, D. A., Anderson, C. W., and Thaut, M. H. (2003). Comparison of linear, nonlinear, and feature selection methods for EEG signal classification. *IEEE Trans. Neural Syst. Rehabil. Eng.* 11, 141–144. doi:10.1109/TNSRE.2003.814441

Gaudino, E. A., Chiaravalloti, N. D., DeLuca, J., and Diamond, B. J. (2001). A comparison of memory performance in relapsing-remitting, primary progressive and secondary progressive multiple sclerosis. *Neuropsychiatry Neuropsychol. Behav. Neurol.* 14, 32–44.

Gfeller, K. E. (1983). Musical mnemonics as an aid to retention with normal and learning-disabled students. *J. Music Ther.* 20, 179–189. doi:10.1093/jmt/20.4.179

Gobet, F., Lane, P. C. R., Croker, S., Cheng, P. C., Jones, G., Oliver, I., et al. (2001). Chunking mechanisms in human learning. *Trends Cogn. Sci.* 5, 236–243. doi:10.1016/S1364-6613(00)01662-4

Grahn, J. A., and Watson, S. L. (2013). Perspectives on rhythm processing in motor regions of the brain. *Music Ther. Perspect.* 31, 15–24. doi:10.1111/j.1756-8765.2012.01213.x

Halpern, A. R. (2001). Cerebral substrates of musical imagery. *Ann. N. Y. Acad. Sci.* 930, 179–192.

Haslam, C., and Cook, M. (2002). Striking a chord with amnesic patients: evidence that song facilitates memory. *Neurocase* 8, 453–465. doi:10.1093/neucas/8.6.453

He, D., Zhou, H., Guo, D., Hao, Z., and Wu, B. (2011). Treatment of memory impairment in MS. *Cochrane Database Syst. Rev.* 10, CD008876.

Hitch, G. J., Burgess, N., Towse, J. N., and Culpin, V. (1996). Temporal grouping effects in immediate recall: a working memory analysis. *Q. J. Exp. Psychol.* 49, 116–139. doi:10.1080/027249896392829

Ho, Y. C., Cheung, M. C., and Chan, A. S. (2003). Music training improves verbal but not visual memory: cross-sectional and longitudinal explorations in children. *Neuropsychology* 17, 439–450. doi:10.1037/0894-4105.17.3.439

Hoemberg, V. (2013). "Neurorehabilitation approaches to facilitate motor recovery," in *Handbook of Clinical Neurology*, Vol. 110, eds M. P. Barnes and D. C. Good (New York: Elsevier), 161–174.

Hummelsheim, H. (1999). Rationales for improving motor function. *Curr. Opin. Neurol.* 12, 697–701. doi:10.1097/00019052-199912000-00007

Jakobson, L. S., Cuddy, L. L., and Kilgour, A. R. (2003). Time tagging: a key to musicians' superior memory. *Music Percept.* 20, 307–313. doi:10.1525/mp.2003.20.3.307

Janata, P. (2009). The neural architecture of music-evoked autobiographical memories. *Cereb. Cortex* 19, 2579–2595. doi:10.1093/cercor/bhp008

Janata, P., Tillmann, B., and Bharucha, J. J. (2002). Listening to polyphonic music recruits domain-general attention and working memory circuits. *Cogn. Affect. Behav. Neurosci.* 2, 121–140. doi:10.3758/CABN.2.2.121

Jausovec, N. (1998). Are gifted individuals less chaotic thinkers? *Pers. Indiv. Differ.* 25, 253–267. doi:10.1016/S0191-8869(98)00039-7

Kern, P., Wolery, M., and Aldridge, D. (2007). Use of songs to promote independence in morning greeting routines for young children with autism. *J. Autism Dev. Disord.* 37, 1264–1271. doi:10.1007/s10803-006-0272-1

Klimesch, W. (1997). EEG-alpha rhythms and memory processes. *Int. J. Psychophysiol.* 26, 319–340. doi:10.1016/S0167-8760(97)00773-3

Klimesch, W. (1999). EEG-alpha and theta oscialltions reflect cognitive and memory performance: a review and analysis. *Brain Res. Brain Res. Rev.* 29, 169–195. doi:10.1016/S0165-0173(98)00056-3

Kraus, N., and Chandrasekaran, B. (2010). Music training for the development of auditory skills. *Nat. Rev. Neurosci.* 11, 599–605. doi:10.1038/nrn2882

Krause, C. M., Porn, B., Lang, A. H., and Laine, M. (1999). Relative alpha desynchronization and synchronization during perception of music. *Scand. J. Psychol.* 40, 209–215. doi:10.1111/1467-9450.00118

Kujala, P., Portin, R., and Ruutiainen, J. (1996). Memory deficits and early cognitive deterioration in MS. *Acta Neurol. Scand.* 93, 329–335. doi:10.1111/j.1600-0404.1996.tb00005.x

Kurtzke, J. F. (1983). Some epidemiological trends in multiple sclerosis. *Trends Neurosci.* 6, 75–80. doi:10.1016/0166-2236(83)90042-5

Landro, N. I., Sletvold, H., and Celius, E. G. (2000). Memory functioning and emotional changes in early phase multiple sclerosis. *Arch. Clin. Neuropsychol.* 15, 37–46. doi:10.1016/S0887-6177(98)00151-6

Laufs, H., Kleinschmidt, A., Beyerle, A., Eger, E., Salek-Haddadi, A., Preibisch, C., et al. (2003). EEG-correlated fMRI of human alpha activity. *Neuroimage* 19, 1463–1476. doi:10.1016/S1053-8119(03)00286-6

Lezak, M. D. (1995). *Neuropsychological Assessment*, 3rd Edn. New York: Oxford University Press.

Litvan, I., Grafinan, J., Vendrell, P., and Martiney, J. M. (1988). Slowed information processing speed in multiple sclerosis. *Arch. Neurol.* 45, 281–285. doi:10.1001/archneur.1988.00520270059021

Luft, A. R., McCombe-Waller, S., Whitall, J., Forrester, L. W., Macko, R., Sorkin, J. D., et al. (2004). Repetitive bilateral arm training and motor cortex activation in chronic stroke. *JAMA* 292, 1853–1861. doi:10.1001/jama.292.15.1853

Maeller, D. H. (1996). *Rehearsal Strategies and Verbal Working Memory in Multiple Sclerosis.* Unpublished Master's thesis, Colorado State University, Fort Collins.

Maess, B., Koelsch, S., Gunter, T. C., and Friederici, A. D. (2001). Musical syntax is processed in Broca's area: an MEG study. *Nat. Neurosci.* 4, 540–545.

Makeig, S., and Jung, T. P. (1996). Tonic, phasic, and transient EEG correlates of auditory awareness in drowsiness. *Brain Res. Cogn. Brain Res.* 4, 15–25. doi:10.1016/0926-6410(95)00042-9

Mammarella, N., Fairfield, B., and Cornoldi, C. (2007). Does music enhance cognitive performance in healthy elderly adults? The Vivaldi effect. *Aging Clin. Exp. Res.* 19, 394–399. doi:10.1007/BF03324720

Marie, R. M., and Defer, G. L. (2001). Memory and executive functions in multiple sclerosis: preliminary findings with a cognitive battery. *Rev. Neurol.* 157, 402–408.

Matzel, L. D., Held, F. P., and Miller, R. R. (1988). Information and expression of simultaneous and backward associations: implications for contiguity theory. *Learn. Motiv.* 19, 317–344. doi:10.1016/0023-9690(88)90044-6

Merzenich, M. M., Schreiner, C., Jenkins, W., and Wang, X. (1993). Neural mechanisms underlying temporal integration, segmentation, and input sequence representation: some implications for the origin of learning disabilities. *Ann. N. Y. Acad. Sci.* 682, 1–22.

Minden, S. L., Moes, E. J., Ovav, J., Kaplan, E., and Reich, P. (1990). Memory impairment in multiple sclerosis. *J. Clin. Exp. Neuropsychol.* 12, 566–586. doi:10.1080/01688639008401002

Moussard, A. (2012). Music as an aid to learn new verbal information in Alzheimer's disease. *Music Percept.* 29, 521–531. doi:10.1525/mp.2012.29.5.521

Niedermeyer, E., and Lopes da Silva, F. (1999). *Electroencephalography: Basic Principles, Clinical Applications and Related Fields.* Baltimore, MD: Williams & Wilkins.

Pantev, C., Wollbrink, A., Roberts, L. E., Engelien, A., and Luetkenhoener, B. (1999). Short-term plasticity of the human auditory cortex. *Brain Res.* 842, 192–199. doi:10.1016/S0006-8993(99)01835-1

Parsons, L. M., Hodges, D. A., and Fox, P. T. (1998). Neural basis of the comprehension of musical harmony, melody, and rhythm. *J. Cogn. Neurosci.* 10, 96–96.

Peretz, I. (2002). Brain specialization for music. *Neuroscientist* 8, 372–380. doi:10.1177/107385840200800412

Peterson, D. A., and Thaut, M. H. (2002). Delay modulates spectral correlates in the human EEG of nonverbal auditory working memory. *Neurosci. Lett.* 328, 17–20. doi:10.1016/S0304-3940(02)00429-9

Peterson, D. A., and Thaut, M. H. (2003). Plasticity of Alpha and Theta synchronization during verbal learning with a musical template. *Proc. Soc. Neurosci.* 194.21.

Peterson, D. A., and Thaut, M. H. (2007). Music increases frontal EEG coherence during verbal learning. *Neurosci. Lett.* 41, 217–221. doi:10.1016/j.neulet.2006.10.057

Peyser, J. M., Edwards, K. R., Poser, C. M., and Filskov, S. B. (1980). Cognitive function in patients with multiple-sclerosis. *Arch. Neurol.* 37, 577–579. doi:10.1001/archneur.1980.00500580073013

Pfurtscheller, G. (1999). "EEG event-related desynchronization (ERD) and event-related synchronization (ERS)," in *Electroencephalography: Basic Principles, Clinical Applications, and Related Fields*, eds E. Niedermeyer and F. H. Lopes da Silva (Baltimore: Williams & Wilkins), 958–967.

Platel, H., Price, C., Baron, J. C., Wise, R., Lambert, J., Frackowiak, R. S., et al. (1997). The structural components of music perception: a functional anatomical study. *Brain* 120, 229–243. doi:10.1093/brain/120.2.229

Rahn, K., Slusher, B., and Kaplin, A. (2012). Cognitive impairment in multiple sclerosis: a forgotten disability remembered. *Cerebrum* 14,

Rainey, D. W., and Larsen, J. D. (2002). The effect of familiar melodies on initial learning and long-term memory for unconnected text. *Music Percept.* 20, 173–186. doi:10.1525/mp.2002.20.2.173

Rao, S. M. (1990). *Neurobehavioral Aspects of Multiple Sclerosis.* New York: Oxford University Press.

Rao, S. M. (1995). Neuropsychology of multiple-sclerosis. *Curr. Opin. Neurol.* 8, 216–220. doi:10.1097/00019052-199506000-00010

Rao, S. M., Staubinfaubert, P., and Leo, G. J. (1989). Information-processing speed in patients with multiple-sclerosis. *J. Clin. Exp. Neuropsychol.* 11, 471–477. doi:10.1080/01688638908400907

Ricker, J. H., Hillary, F. G., and DeLuca, J. (2001). Functionally activated brain imaging (O-15 PET and fMRI) in the study of learning and memory after traumatic brain injury. *J. Head Trauma Rehabil.* 16, 191–205. doi:10.1097/00001199-200104000-00007

Rogers, J. M., and Panegyres, P. K. (2007). Cognitive impairment in multiple sclerosis: evidence-based analysis and recommendations. *J. Clin. Neurosci.* 14, 919–927. doi:10.1016/j.jocn.2007.02.006

Rojo, N., Amenqual, J., Juncadella, M., Rubio, F., Camara, E., Marco-Pallares, J., et al. (2011). Music-supported arm training induces plasticity in the sensorimotor cortex in chronic stroke. *Brain Inj.* 25, 787–793. doi:10.3109/02699052.2011.576305

Rossignol, S., and Melvill Jones, G. (1976). Audiospinal influences in man studied by the H-reflex and its possible role in rhythmic movement synchronized to sound. *Electroencephalogr. Clin. Neurophysiol.* 41, 83–92. doi:10.1016/0013-4694(76)90217-0

Ruchkin, D. S., Berndt, R. S., Johnson, R., Ritter, W., Grafman, J., and Canoune, H. (1997). Modality-specific processing streams in verbal working memory: evidence from spatio-temporal patterns of brain activity. *Brain Res. Cogn. Brain Res.* 6, 95–113. doi:10.1016/S0926-6410(97)00021-9

Sarkamo, T., Tervaniemi, M., Latinen, S., Forsblom, A., Soinila, S., Mikkonen, M., et al. (2008). Music listening enhances cognitive recovery and mood after middle cerebral artery stroke. *Brain* 13, 866–876. doi:10.1093/brain/awn013

Shahin, A., Bosnyak, D. J., Trainor, L. J., and Roberts, L. E. (2003). Enhancement of neuroplastic P2 and N1c auditory evoked potentials in musicians. *J. Neurosci.* 23, 5545–5552.

Simmons-Stern, N. R., Deason, R. G., Brandler, B. J., Frustace, B. S., O'Connor, M. K., Ally, B. A., et al. (2012). Music based memory enhancement in Alzheimer's disease: promise and limitations. *Neuropsychologia* 50, 3295–3303. doi:10.1016/j.neuropsychologia.2012.09.019

Smith, E. E., Jonides, J., Marshuetz, C., and Koeppe, R. A. (1998). Components of verbal working memory: evidence from neuroimaging. *Proc. Natl. Acad. Sci. U.S.A.* 95, 876–882. doi:10.1073/pnas.95.3.876

Snyder, B. (2000). *Music and Memory.* Cambridge MA: MIT-Press.

Son, G. R., Therrien, B., and Whall, A. (2002). Implicit memory and familiarity among elders with dementia. *J. Nurs. Scholarsh.* 34, 263–267. doi:10.1111/j.1547-5069.2002.00263.x

Staresina, B. P., Bauer, H., Deecke, L., and Walla, P. (2005). Neurocognitive correlates of incidental verbal memory encoding: a magnetoencephalographic (MEG) study. *Neuroimage* 25, 430–443. doi:10.1016/j.neuroimage.2004.11.035

Sweet, L. H., Rao, S. M., Primeau, M., Mayer, A. R., and Cohen, R. A. (2004). Functional magnetic resonance imaging of working memory among MS patients. *J. Neuroimaging* 14, 150–158. doi:10.1111/j.1552-6569.2004.tb00232.x

Tallal, P. (2000). "Experimental studies of language learning impairments: From research to remediation," in *Speech and Language Impairments in Children: Causes, Characteristics, Intervention and Outcome*, ed. L. B. Leonard (Philadelphia, PA: Psychology Press/Taylor & Francis), 131–155.

Tecchio, F., Salustri, C., Thaut, M. H., Pasqualetti, P., and Rossini, P. M. (2000). Conscious and preconscious adaptation to rhythmic auditory stimuli: a magnetoencephalographic study of human brain responses. *Exp. Brain Res.* 135, 222–230. doi:10.1007/s002210000507

Thaut, M. H. (2005). *Rhythm, Music, and the Brain.* London: Taylor and Francis.

Thaut, M. H. (2013). Entrainment and the motor system. *Music Ther. Perspect.* 31, 25–30. doi:10.1093/mtp/31.1.31

Thaut, M. H., and Hoemberg, V. (2014). *Oxford Handbook of Neurologic Music Therapy.* Oxford: Oxford University Press.

Thaut, M. H., Leins, A. K., Rice, R. R., Argstatter, H., Kenyon, G. P., McIntosh, G. C., et al. (2007). Rhythmic auditory stimulation improves gait more than NDT/Bobath training in near-ambulatory patients early poststroke: a single blind randomized trial. *Neurorehabil. Neural Repair* 21, 455–459. doi:10.1177/1545968307300523

Thaut, M. H., McIntosh, G. C., and Rice, R. R. (1997). Rhythmic facilitation of gait training in hemiparetic stroke rehabilitation. *J. Neurol. Sci.* 151, 207–212. doi:10.1016/S0022-510X(97)00146-9

Thaut, M. H., McIntosh, G. C., Rice, R. R., Miller, R. A., Rathbun, J., and Brault, J. M. (1996). Rhythmic auditory stimulation in gait training with Parkinson's disease patients. *Mov. Disord.* 11, 193–200. doi:10.1002/mds.870110213

Thornton, A. E., and Raez, N. (1997). Memory impairment in multiple sclerosis: a quantitative review. *Neuropsychology* 11, 357–366. doi:10.1037/0894-4105.11.3.357

Verwey, W. B. (2001). Concatenating familiar movement sequences: the versatile cognitive processor. *Acta Psychol.* 106, 69–95. doi:10.1016/S0001-6918(00)00027-5

Wallace, W. T. (1994). Memory for music – effect of melody on recall of text. *J. Exp. Psychol. Learn. Mem. Cogn.* 20, 1471–1485. doi:10.1037/0278-7393.20.6.1471

Wallin, M. T., Wilken, J. A., and Kane, R. (2006). Cognitive dysfunction in multiple sclerosis: assessment, imaging, and risk factors. *J. Rehabil. Res. Dev.* 43, 63–72. doi:10.1682/JRRD.2004.09.0120

Wickelgren, W. A. (1999). Webs, cell assemblies, and chunking in neural nets: introduction. *Can. J. Exp. Psychol.* 53, 118–131. doi:10.1037/h0087304

Wolfe, D. E., and Hom, C. (1993). Use of melodies as structural prompts for learning and retention of sequential verbal information by preschool students. *J. Music Ther.* 30, 100–118. doi:10.1093/jmt/30.2.100

Zatorre, R. J., Halpern, A. R., Perry, D. W., Meyer, E., and Evans, A. C. (1996). Hearing in the mind's ear: a PET investigation of musical imagery and perception. *J. Cogn. Neurosci.* 8, 29–46. doi:10.1162/jocn.1996.8.1.29

15

Less effort, better results: how does music act on prefrontal cortex in older adults during verbal encoding? An fNIRS study

Laura Ferreri[1]*, Emmanuel Bigand[1], Stephane Perrey[2], Makii Muthalib[2], Patrick Bard[1] and Aurélia Bugaiska[1]

[1] *Laboratoire d'Etude de l'Apprentissage et du Développement (LEAD), CNRS UMR 5022, University of Burgundy, Dijon, France*
[2] *Movement to Health (M2H), EuroMov, Montpellier-1 University, Montpellier, France*

Correspondence:
Laura Ferreri, Laboratoire d'Etude de l'Apprentissage et du Développement (LEAD), Department of Psychology, CNRS UMR 5022, University of Burgundy, Pôle AAFE-Esplanade Erasme, BP 26513, Dijon F-21065, France
e-mail: lf.ferreri@gmail.com

Several neuroimaging studies of cognitive aging revealed deficits in episodic memory abilities as a result of prefrontal cortex (PFC) limitations. Improving episodic memory performance despite PFC deficits is thus a critical issue in aging research. Listening to music stimulates cognitive performance in several non-purely musical activities (e.g., language and memory). Thus, music could represent a rich and helpful source during verbal encoding and therefore help subsequent retrieval. Furthermore, such benefit could be reflected in less demand of PFC, which is known to be crucial for encoding processes. This study aimed to investigate whether music may improve episodic memory in older adults while decreasing the PFC activity. Sixteen healthy older adults ($\mu = 64.5$ years) encoded lists of words presented with or without a musical background while their dorsolateral prefrontal cortex (DLPFC) activity was monitored using a eight-channel continuous-wave near-infrared spectroscopy (NIRS) system (Oxymon Mk III, Artinis, The Netherlands). Behavioral results indicated a better source-memory performance for words encoded with music compared to words encoded with silence ($p < 0.05$). Functional NIRS data revealed bilateral decrease of oxyhemoglobin values in the music encoding condition compared to the silence condition ($p < 0.05$), suggesting that music modulates the activity of the DLPFC during encoding in a less-demanding direction. Taken together, our results indicate that music can help older adults in memory performances by decreasing their PFC activity. These findings open new perspectives about music as tool for episodic memory rehabilitation on special populations with memory deficits due to frontal lobe damage such as Alzheimer's patients.

Keywords: music, episodic encoding, fNIRS, prefrontal cortex, older adults

INTRODUCTION

Research in cognitive aging has reported that older adults often present declines in specific memory systems (Tulving, 1972). Working memory, episodic memory, and prospective memory have been shown to substantially decline in the course of normal aging, while procedural memory and some perceptual memory functions show few age-related changes (Mitchell, 1989; Luo and Craik, 2008).

Episodic memory can be defined as the type of awareness experienced when one thinks back to a specific moment in one's personal past and consciously recollects some prior episode or as it was previously experienced. This special kind of awareness is identifiable in all healthy and human adults (Wheeler et al., 1997). However, several studies have shown that healthy aging is often characterized by reduced access to contextually specific episodic memory details, resulting in larger deficits in source-memory performance than in item-memory performance (Craik et al., 1990; Glisky et al., 1995; Spencer and Raz, 1995; Dennis et al., 2008). Thus, older adults have difficulty remembering specific information about the circumstances under which an event was encountered, and they are less likely to remember the contextual features of events correctly (Johnson et al., 1993; Dodson et al., 2007), which can be considered to be a deficit in the ability to encode the spatio-temporal context of an event (Parkin and Walter, 1992; Bugaiska et al., 2007).

Several authors have observed that older adults produce lower scores than young adults on episodic memory tasks (mostly source-memory and recollection tasks) as a consequence of reduced executive function (Parkin and Walter, 1992; Bugaiska et al., 2007; see also Raz, 2000 and West, 1996). In particular, it has been claimed that impaired executive function reduces older adults' ability to initiate the memory encoding of target information appropriately for a durable explicit representation (Bunce, 2003; Bugaiska et al., 2007). Furthermore, it has been found that low memory performance in older adults is related to both an associative deficit and a lower level of strategic functioning (Naveh-Benjamin, 2000; Shing et al., 2008). Neuroimaging and behavioral studies investigating cognitive aging have revealed that these deficits in episodic memory are related to prefrontal cortex (PFC) limitations due to reductions in hemispheric specialization of cognitive functions in the frontal lobes (e.g., Souchay et al., 2000; Craik and Grady, 2002; Luo and Craik, 2008). This effect has been conceptualized in terms of a model called the hemispheric asymmetry reduction in older adults (HAROLD) (Cabeza, 2002), and may be due to dedifferentiation of function, deficits in function, or functional reorganization and compensation in frontal lobe regions (Rajah and D'Esposito, 2005). In line with the idea of an age-related memory encoding deficit, several neuroimaging findings confirm episodic memory impairments linked to reduced recruitment of mediotemporal and PFC regions, mainly during the encoding phase of memory tasks (Daselaar et al., 2004; Dennis et al., 2008), supporting the hypothesis that older adults fail to encode target items thoroughly (Craik and Lockhart, 1972; Burke and Light, 1981; Isingrini et al., 1995).

Improving episodic memory encoding in spite of PFC deficits is therefore a critical issue in aging research. It is well-known that enriching the encoding context of an event, for example, through enacted encoding or with emotional valence stimuli, can enhance memory performance at retrieval (Hamann, 2001; Lövdén et al., 2002). Music is a complex auditory stimulus, which evolves over time and has a strong emotional impact (Blood and Zatorre, 2001) and thus engages the whole brain through different cognitive activities and neural substrates (Altenmüller, 2003). Consequently, music is likely to enrich the encoding of memory items and can thus be used to improve memory performance.

Although the role of background music in learning and memory tasks is still an open and debated question in the literature (Schellenberg, 2003; Schellenberg, 2005; De Groot, 2006; Peterson and Thaut, 2007; Jäncke and Sandmann, 2010), the role that music plays in terms of emotions (Jäncke, 2008), reward (e.g., Salimpoor et al., 2013), and positive arousal (e.g., Judde and Rickard, 2010) has brought several authors to believe that music can be used to improve memory encoding in a variety of situations. In particular, research in music and neuroscience has shown how music could boost verbal memory performance not only in clinical populations (Brotons and Koger, 2000; Ho et al., 2003; Thaut et al., 2005; Thompson et al., 2005; Racette et al., 2006; Franklin et al., 2008; Särkämo et al., 2008; Simmons-Stern et al., 2010), but also in healthy young and older adults (Balch et al., 1992; Wallace, 1994; Balch and Lewis, 1996; Thompson et al., 2005; De Groot, 2006; Ferreri et al., 2013; Kang and Williamson, 2013). However, there has been little research investigating whether background music affects the memory performance of older adults.

In a previous study on healthy young subjects (Ferreri et al., 2013), we used functional near-infrared spectroscopy (fNIRS) to investigate the role of background music on memory performance and the dorsolateral prefrontal cortex (DLPFC), which has been shown to play a crucial role in organizational, associative (Murray and Ranganath, 2007; Ranganath, 2010), and semantic (Innocenti et al., 2010) memory encoding, and particularly for organizational processing, which helps build associations among items that are active in memory (Blumenfeld and Ranganath, 2007). fNIRS is a non-invasive optical neuroimaging technique that can be used to monitor cortical activation during cognitive tasks through the well-characterized neurovascular coupling mechanism related to neuronal activation, namely, an increase in oxygenated (O_2Hb) and a decrease in deoxygenated (HHb) hemoglobin concentrations (Jobsis, 1977; Ferrari and Quaresima, 2012). Moreover, fNIRS makes it possible to conduct more ecological cognitive experimental setups (subject sitting in a chair in a quiet room), which are not feasible in more traditional fMRI protocols, and it is thus suitable for investigating cortical activation in special populations such as older adults and neurological patients (Ferreri et al., in press). Recent fNIRS studies on verbal memory and learning have shown that facilitatory cues such as strategies (Matsuda and Hiraki, 2004, 2006; Matsui et al., 2007), pharmacological stimulants (Ramasubbu et al., 2012), or background music (Ferreri et al., 2013) during verbal encoding could result in deactivation, rather than greater activation, of PFC regions, suggesting less involvement/greater efficiency of high-cognitive functions mediated by PFC regions (such as the DLPFC) known to be crucial during memory encoding processes. In our previous experiment (Ferreri et al., 2013), we monitored bilateral DLPFC activation during verbal encoding with fNIRS and showed, for the first time, that background music during the encoding of verbal material can modulate DLPFC activity (i.e., decreased responses compared to a silent background) and, at the same time, facilitate the retrieval of the encoded material. We believe that these results open up interesting perspectives about how music could act on the DLPFC of people with memory disorders for whom the DLPFC is hypo-activated, impaired, or damaged, such as older adults or Alzheimer's patients. Indeed, because encoding information with music decreases activation of the DLPFC, and because age-related differences in episodic memory are mediated by the decline of executive functioning supported by the PFC (Parkin and Walter, 1992; Bugaiska et al., 2007; Clarys et al., 2009), one could assume that encoding with background music would also lead to an improvement of episodic memory in older adults and more generally in populations with impaired or damaged PFC. Therefore, in the present study we explored the role of background music in the memory performance and DLPFC activation of healthy older adults through an item/source-memory paradigm and using fNIRS to monitor DLPFC activation bilaterally during verbal encoding with or without music. We hypothesized that music would enhance the encoding of verbal material in older adults by enriching the context and supplying organizational, associative, and semantic processes. Considering previous fNIRS studies showing better behavioral performance and PFC deactivation in response to facilitatory cues (Matsuda and Hiraki, 2004, 2006; Matsui et al., 2007; Ramasubbu et al., 2012), we therefore expected to find improved episodic memory performance at a behavioral level together with minimal demand on PFC activity during music encoding condition as compared to silence encoding condition. In particular, a classical activation pattern should be observed for the silence encoding condition, namely an increase of O_2Hb and a decrease of HHb concentrations changes. On the other hand, we expected a DPLFC disengagement reflected in an inverse activation pattern, namely a decrease of O_2Hb and an increase of HHb concentrations.

MATERIALS AND METHODS

PARTICIPANTS

Sixteen healthy older adults, all right-handed, non-musicians, native French speakers (10 females, mean age 64.5 ± 2.5 years) volunteered to participate in the experiment. They scored above the 27-point cut-off on the mini-mental state examination (MMSE) to exclude dementia (Folstein et al., 1975). All the participants lived in their own homes, and reported themselves to be in good physical and mental health and to have normal or corrected-to-normal vision. All of them were recruited from the general "third age University" classes at the University of Burgundy and earn therefore a high-school degree. None were taking medication known to affect the central nervous system. Informed written consent was obtained from all participants prior to the experiment. The study conformed to the Helsinki Declaration, Convention of the Council of Europe on Human Rights and Biomedicine.

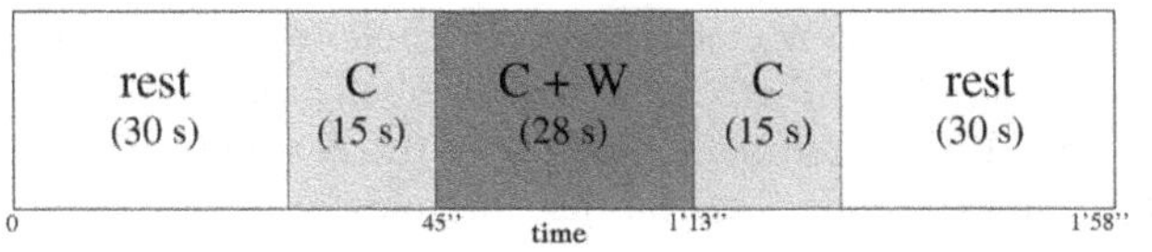

FIGURE 1 | Representation of one encoding block between two 30 s rest blocks. Each block consisted of 15 s of context (C) alone, either music or silence in the earphones, then 28 s of context and words (C + W) encoding (seven words for each block, 4 s per word), and then again 15 s of context (C) alone.

EXPERIMENTAL PROCEDURE

The procedure was the same as the one used in our previous study (Ferreri et al., 2013). All the participants were seated at a computer in a quiet, dim room and carried out a memory encoding task while their DLPFC activation was monitored using fNIRS neuroimaging. They then performed a retrieval task. After the eight fNIRS channels had been adjusted on the forehead scalp overlaying the DLPFC and the in-ear headphones inserted, participants were informed that they would be presented with different lists of words with two auditory contexts: music or silence. They were explicitly instructed to memorize both lists and the context in which the words were encoded. The background music used in all blocks was an upbeat, acoustic jazz piece ("If you see my mother" by Sidney Bechet), chosen for its positive valence and medium arousal quality. Verbal stimuli consisted of 42 taxonomically unrelated concrete nouns selected from the French "Lexique" database (New et al., 2004, http://www.lexique.org), randomly divided into six lists (7 words per list, 21 words for each encoding condition), equated for word length and occurrence frequency.

The encoding phase consisted of three blocks of "music encoding" and three blocks of "silence encoding," intermixed with 30-s rest periods. In each block, seven words were displayed successively with either a music or a silence background. The audio stimulation started 15 s before the first word was displayed, continued during the sequential display of words, and ended 15 s after the last word. Words in each block were presented at a rate of 4 s per word (28 s for the sequential presentation of seven words). Each block therefore lasted 58 s (15 s context, 28 s words, 15 s context) and was followed by a 30 s rest (silent) between each block (**Figure 1**). The order of music/silence blocks was counterbalanced, as were the order of the word lists and the order of words in the lists. During the rest periods, participants were instructed to try to relax and not think about the task; by contrast, during the context-only phases of the blocks (i.e., silence or music), they were instructed to concentrate on a fixation cross on the screen and to focus on the task. The entire encoding phase, together with fNIRS recording, took about 10 min.

Prior to the retrieval phase, participants performed two 5-min interference tasks: an "X–O" letter-comparison task (Salthouse et al., 1997) and a "plus–minus" task (Jersild, 1927; Spector and Bierdeman, 1976). They were then behaviorally tested for item and source-memory (Glisky et al., 1995). The retrieval test included the previously presented 42 words, together with 42 new words (lures) matched for word length and occurrence frequency. In a yes/no recognition task, participants were asked to say whether they had already seen each word before (yes/no button on the keyboard; item-memory task). If so, they were asked to indicate in which context they had seen it (music/silence/I do not know; source-memory task). In this way, we tested subjects' capacity to remember specific episodes. The presentation of task instructions and stimuli, as well as the recording of behavioral responses, were controlled by E-Prime software (Psychology Software Tools, Inc.) running on a laptop with a 15″ monitor.

fNIRS MEASUREMENTS

An eight-channel fNIRS system (Oxymon Mk III, Artinis Medical Systems B.V., The Netherlands) was used to measure the concentration changes of O_2Hb and HHb (expressed in micromolar) using an age-dependent constant differential path-length factor given by $4.99 + 0.0067 \times$ (age 0.814) (Duncan et al., 1996). Data were acquired at a sampling frequency of 10 Hz. The eight fNIRS optodes (four emitters and four detectors) were placed symmetrically over the dorsal part of the PFC (Brodmann areas 46 and 9, EEG electrodes AF7/8, F5/6, F3/4 and AF3/4 of the international 10/10 system) (Okamoto et al., 2004; Jurcak et al., 2007), and the distance between each emitter and detector was fixed at 3.5 cm (**Figure 3B**).

To optimize signal-to-noise ratio during the fNIRS recording, the eight optodes were masked from ambient light by a black plastic cap that was kept in contact with the scalp with elastic straps, and all cables were suspended from the ceiling to minimize movement artifacts (Cui et al., 2011). During data collection, O_2Hb and HHb concentration changes were displayed in real time, and signal quality and absence of movement artifacts were verified.

DATA ANALYSIS

BEHAVIORAL DATA

Each subject's item- and source-memory accuracy (hit) rates (number of hits for each condition during yes/no recognition) and false alarms were calculated for both the silence and music conditions. Source-memory was determined as the proportion of correct source judgments among item-memory hits.

fNIRS DATA

For each of the eight fNIRS measurement points, the O_2Hb and HHb signals were first low-pass filtered to eliminate task-irrelevant systemic physiological oscillations (fifth order digital Butterworth filter with cut-off frequency 0.1 Hz).

In order to determine the amount of activation during the encoding phase for the two conditions, data for each of the six experimental blocks were baseline-corrected using the mean of the O_2Hb and HHb signals during the last 5 s of "rest" block preceding each encoding block. We then sample-to-sample averaged (i.e., 10 samples/s) the baseline-corrected signals over the three blocks of each condition, yielding one average music and silence O_2Hb and HHb signal per participant. In order to determine the level of DLPFC activation during the encoding phase for the two verbal encoding context conditions, we computed the maximum O_2Hb and the minimum HHb values over the 28 s stimulus window (i.e., from $t = 15$ to 42 s), which indicated the maximum delta-to-baseline signal reached during the encoding phase.

Furthermore, in order to ascertain the DLPFC activation during the entire block of music/silence encoding conditions, we ran a complete time–series analysis in which we averaged O_2Hb and HHb concentrations over 5 s windows (so one average point for each 5 s) all over the block of the encoding, getting 13 successive measures of concentrations (from the first seconds of fixation point preceding the words to the end of the block, with the last 5 s of rest phase taken as baseline value). Considering O_2Hb increases and small HHb decreases as patterns of cortical activations (Jobsis, 1977), DLPFC activations were assessed by separately analyzing the baseline-corrected O_2Hb and HHb concentration changes, and also the total hemoglobin concentrations ($THb = O_2Hb + HHb$), for both the music and silence average block of each participant.

STATISTICAL ANALYSIS

For behavioral results, paired t-tests (one for each condition) were used to compare the item- and source-memory scores of the silence and music conditions. As well, paired t-tests were also used to test significant difference in false alarm rates for item and source-memory tasks, namely how many times they attributed a lure item (to have been) encoded with music or silence (music/silence item false alarms) and how many times subjects reported previously presented items (to have been) encoded in the wrong context (music/silence source false alarm). Furthermore, in order to account for bias with the source judgments, subjective source judgments were prorated according to prior item recognition. In this analysis, we took all the times where participants have said "music" (or "silence") for the source, and looked at the number of correct items for this set. Paired t-tests were applied to estimate significant means difference for these values. One-sample t-tests were used to ascertain that all the scores were significantly above chance level.

For fNIRS results, the O_2Hb, HHb, and THb concentrations were analyzed using a repeated-measures ANOVA with 2 (music/silence) × 2 (left/right hemisphere) × 4 (optodes) within subject factors, on which *post hoc* Bonferroni-corrected (confidence interval percentage = 99.3%) paired t-test comparisons determined which measurement points showed a significant difference between the two experimental conditions. Cohen's d and Eta-squared statistics were used to calculate the effect size of paired t-tests and repeated-measures ANOVA, respectively. Concerning the time–series analysis, we ran a 2 (conditions) × 2 (left/right hemisphere) × 4 (optodes) × 13 (time points, namely successive measures of concentrations) repeated-measure ANOVA for both O_2Hb and HHb values. Since SPSS software reports a partial Eta-squared value, which have been demonstrated to overestimate effect sizes (see Levine and Hullett, 2002), we calculated Eta-squared by dividing Type III Sum of squares of each condition and interaction by the corrected total (i.e., the sum of all Type III Sum of squares and error values computed in the statistics). The significance level was set at $p < 0.05$.

RESULTS

BEHAVIORAL RESULTS

Item-memory analysis revealed that subjects were significantly above chance level in yes–no recognition of items encoded with music and silence (one-sample t-test, $p < 0.001$). Whereas hits appeared constant across conditions for item-memory performance ($t = -0.674$, $p = 0.302$), there was a significant difference in false alarm rates ($t = 2.498$, $p = 0.02$, Cohen's d effect size $= -0.44$), suggesting that background music during encoding led to fewer errors in the recognition phase (**Figure 2A**). The one-sample t-tests on source-memory scores revealed that while performance in the music condition was significantly above chance level ($t = 3.537$, $p = 0.003$), source-memory performance in the silence condition was below chance level ($t = 0.418$, $p = 0.682$), suggesting that participants had difficulty remembering words in the silence condition, and that they remembered words better in the music condition. Results obtained by considering subjective source judgments according to prior item recognition showed that item recognition was better (i.e., proportion of hits from all responses) if subjects during the retrieval phase judged the item as being presented with music rather than silence context during the encoding phase ($t = 32.581$, $p = 0.021$). Furthermore, a paired t-test revealed that the participants tended to retrieve the musical context better than the silence context ($t = 31.57$, $p = 0.068$). Taken together, behavioral results show that a musical background source not only plays an interfering role, but rather

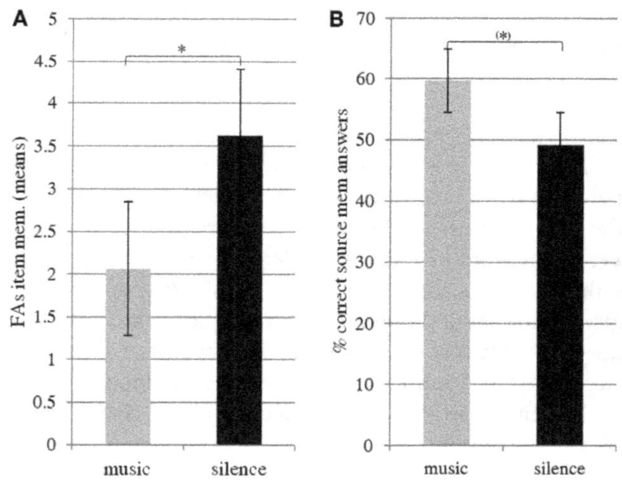

FIGURE 2 | Item-memory false alarm scores (A) and source memory correct answer scores (B). Paired t-tests showed fewer errors in item-memory performance and overall better source memory performance in the music condition than in the silence condition. One-sample t-tests revealed that music source memory scores were significantly above chance level, while silence source scores were not. * and (*) indicate, respectively, significant ($p < 0.05$) and marginally significant ($0.05 < p < 0.07$) difference in means.

helps subjects during verbal encoding thus improving subsequent retrieval performances (**Figure 2B**).

fNIRS RESULTS

The repeated-measures ANOVA on bilateral DLPFC O_2Hb values revealed a statistically significant main effect of condition [$F(1, 15) = 8.390$, $p = 0.011$], with greater bilateral O_2Hb increases in the silence than in the music encoding condition and a significant condition × laterality interaction [$F(1, 15) = 4.282$, $p = 0.056$], with music presenting higher O_2Hb values on the right hemisphere (although always lower than silence values). The strength of these effects computed by Eta-squared effect size revealed strong effect for the condition ($\eta^2 = 0.25$) and weak for the interaction ($\eta^2 = 0.01$). Furthermore, considering also HHb values, the repeated-measures ANOVA on THb values (**Figure 3A**) confirmed a main effect of condition [$F(1, 15) = 14.329$, $p = 0.009$, strong Eta-squared effect size $= 0.22$] in almost all channels, as shown by post hoc Bonferroni-corrected paired *t*-tests (**Figure 3A**). In line with several other fNIRS studies (e.g., Matsui et al., 2007; Okamoto et al., 2011), only HHb values did not show a significant effect.

Time–series analysis results are reported in **Figure 4**, which shows grand-average time-course of PFC O_2Hb and HHb concentration changes at each of the eight fNIRS channels in the music and silence encoding conditions. The repeated-measure ANOVA on the O_2Hb and HHb time-course series confirmed a main effect of condition [$F(1,15) = 7.893$, $p = 0.013$], corresponding to significantly greater O_2Hb increases bilaterally in silence than music condition, and a marginally significant condition × laterality interaction [$F(1,15) = 3.47$, $p = 0.082$]. Interestingly, while the increases in O_2Hb are visible bilaterally during the silence condition (and especially in left-hemisphere), time-course analysis revealed that the music condition was associated with a strong bilateral decrease of O_2Hb lasting all over the block of the encoding (and affecting also the 15-s post-words fixation point in some channels).

DISCUSSION

Based on previous results with young adults (Ferreri et al., 2013), the present study aimed to investigate the neural mechanisms involved in memory–music processes (and the role of background music in particular), using fNIRS to monitor cortical response during the encoding phase among older adults, who usually show impairment in PFC activity and episodic memory tasks.

Our fNIRS results showed that the bilateral DLPFC was activated (O_2Hb increase and HHb decrease) during the verbal

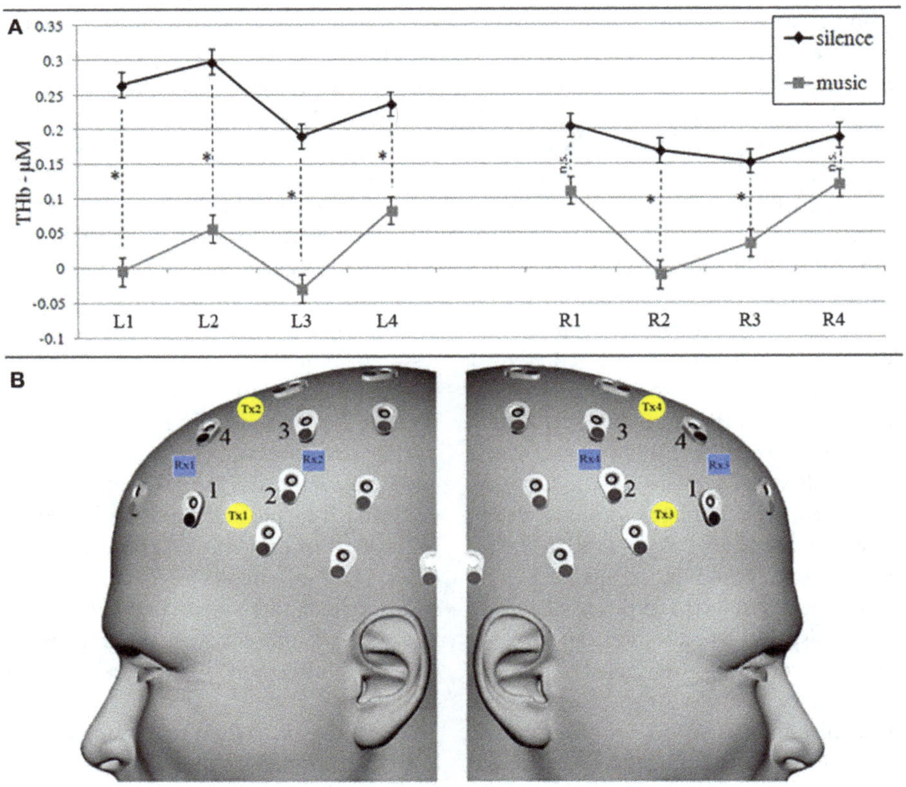

FIGURE 3 | Graphs of THb (A) concentration values (in micromoles) in silence and music conditions for each left and right fNIRS measurement channel (B). **(A)** Mean (±SEM) of THb ($O_2Hb + HHb$) concentration values for silence (black line) and music (gray lines) conditions. * Shows significant ($p < 0.05$) within-channel differences obtained by *post hoc* Bonferroni-corrected paired *t*-test comparisons. **(B)** fNIRS transmitters (left Tx1–Tx2, right Tx3–Tx4, yellow circles) and receivers (left Rx1–Rx2, right Rx3–Rx4, blue squares) were placed on the left and right forehead scalp region, corresponding to AF7/8, F5/6, F3/4, and AF3/4 EEG channels (international 10/10 system), respectively, renamed left/right channels 1, 2, 3, and 4.

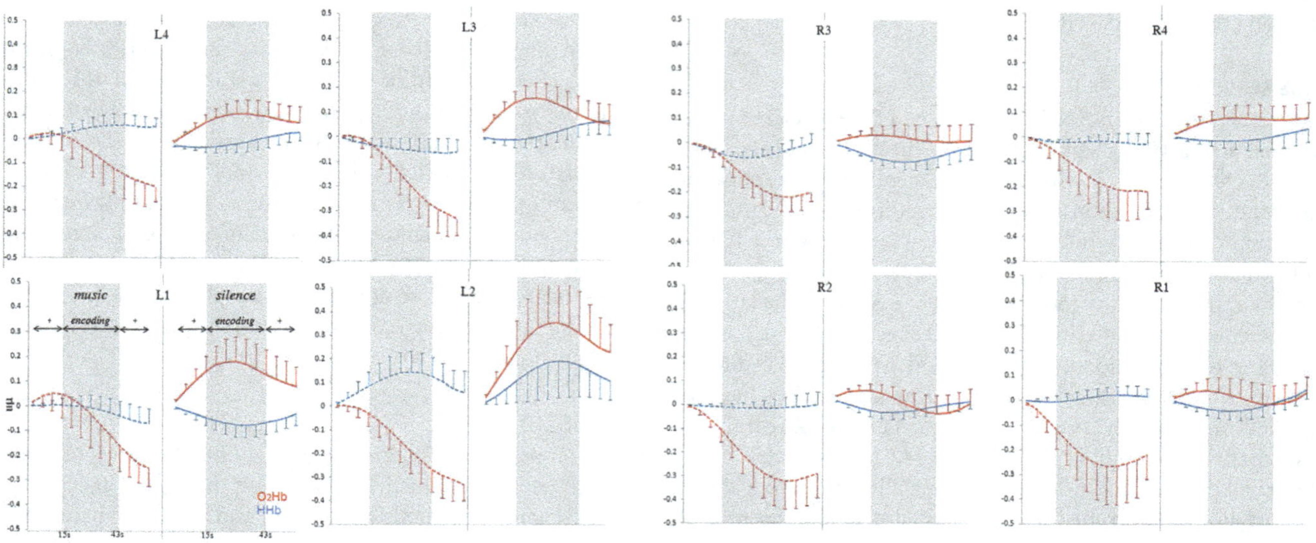

FIGURE 4 | Grand-average (±SEM) time-course of prefrontal cortex O_2Hb (red lines) and HHb (blue lines) concentration changes (vertical axis) over the left and right hemisphere during memory encoding (horizontal axis: time) for the silence (right side, solid lines) and music (left side, dashed lines) conditions.

encoding phase in the silence condition. Although recent studies suggest that caution should be exercised when applying fNIRS to infer PFC activation because of the task-evoked changes occurring in forehead skin perfusion (Kohno et al., 2007; Gagnon et al., 2011, 2012; Takahashi et al., 2011; Kirilina et al., 2012), these results confirm both the involvement of DLPFC during episodic memory encoding (Blumenfeld and Ranganath, 2007; Murray and Ranganath, 2007; Innocenti et al., 2010), and the suitability of fNIRS to investigate long-term memory processes (Kubota et al., 2006; Matsui et al., 2007; Okamoto et al., 2011; see also Cutini et al., 2012 for a review). The fNIRS results also showed a weak but significant interaction between memory encoding condition and hemispheric laterality, with greater left and right DLPFC activity (represented by O_2Hb increases) in the silence and music conditions, respectively. This condition by laterality interaction can be explained by the presence of music during the verbal encoding phase, which could have shifted the classic left-verbal lateralization to the right hemisphere, in support of evidence that left-lateralization is determined by the nature of the material (verbal or non-verbal) being encoded (e.g., Kelley et al., 1998). However, compared to our previous fNIRS results with young subjects (Ferreri et al., 2013) which found marked left-hemisphere lateralization during both the music and silence encoding conditions (discussed in relation to the HERA model, Tulving et al., 1994; Nyberg et al., 1996), we observed a reduction in hemispheric asymmetry in the present study involving older adults. Furthermore, the weak significance revealed by O_2Hb maximum values was not confirmed by time-course analysis, which revealed a marginal statistically significance, suggesting an absence of lateralization. This can be interpreted in relation to the HAROLD model (Cabeza, 2002), which predicts that DLPFC activity during cognitive performance tends to be less lateralized in older than in younger adults.

One of the main findings of the present study was that the eight measurement points surrounding the DLPFC made less demand on the DLPFC in the music than in the silence condition, resulting in decreased activity during the music verbal encoding phase (represented by an O_2Hb decrease, see **Figure 3**). In view of previous fNIRS studies which showed decreased PFC activity during cognitive tasks (Matsuda and Hiraki, 2004, 2006), and specifically those related to verbal learning in which subjects were helped to memorize words by a given strategy (Matsui et al., 2007) or by a pharmacological stimulant (Ramasubbu et al., 2012), we previously discussed PFC disengagement during memory encoding with background music as evidence that music plays a facilitating, less-demanding role for the PFC during word encoding (Ferreri et al., 2013). In particular, we focused our argument on the fact that the PFC, specifically the DLPFC, is known to be recruited during cognitive tasks demanding organizational (Blumenfeld and Ranganath, 2007) and relational inter-item processing during encoding (Murray and Ranganath, 2007). Therefore, one possible interpretation of the DLPFC deactivation is that music helped older adults to generate inter-item and item-source relationships, without demanding high-cognitive PFC processes, which usually intervene when highly structured items (e.g., those which can be organized into chunks) are presented (see for example, Bor et al., 2003).

In other words, the presence of a musical background could affect memory by modulating the neurocognitive state, which facilitates the encoding, thus increasing subjects' capacity to create associative bindings. Music could therefore modulate in a state-dependent manner the encoding mode, modifying the need of extra organizational and strategic encoding usually attributed to DPLFC, and facilitating the creation of richer associative links crucial for subsequent retrieval.

The behavioral results show that background music during the word encoding phase can assist memorization in older adults by reducing false alarm rates during recognition, confirming that item-memory performance can be improved by providing background music (Ferreri et al., 2013). Analysis of source-memory performance revealed that older adults could give details about the encoding context in the music condition more than in the silence condition, in which they were not able to retrieve the encoding context associated with the general information. These findings are in line with previous studies showing age-related impairments in remembering specific information about the circumstances under which a memory event was encountered (Johnson et al., 1993; Dodson et al., 2007). However, this difficulty was not encountered for the recollection of the musical context, suggesting that music could be a "good tool" to boost memory in older adults. Taken together, our results suggest that music can improve older adults' episodic memory performance and, at the same time, demand less DLPFC activation.

It is therefore crucial to discuss these findings in the framework of aging research, and their possible implications for research in music cognition. In particular, these results can be seen more broadly as part of the ongoing debate about whether music can boost non-musical abilities, and more specifically verbal memory. Several studies have shown that not only musical training (Chan et al., 1998; Ho et al., 2003; Franklin et al., 2008), but also simple exposure to background music or sung stimuli leads to short- and long-term verbal memory benefits in healthy young and older adults (Balch et al., 1992; Wallace, 1994; Balch and Lewis, 1996; Thompson et al., 2005) and clinical populations such as stroke patients (Särkämo et al., 2008), people with multiple sclerosis (Thaut et al., 2005), aphasics (Racette et al., 2006), and Alzheimer's patients (Thompson et al., 2005; Simmons-Stern et al., 2010). At the same time, it has also been claimed that music diverts participants' attention from the items to remember by generating a dual-task situation and thus causing a perturbing effect on the memorization of verbal material (Salame and Baddeley, 1989; Racette and Peretz, 2007; Jäncke and Sandmann, 2010; Moussard et al., 2012; Jäncke et al., 2014). Thus, as recently pointed out by Kang and Williamson (2013), a delicate balance exists between music that facilitates recall from memory and music, which acts as a drain on limited memory resources. Our results seem to support the idea that music can benefit verbal memory in aging rather than generate a dual-task situation, in which it is well-known that older adults are usually penalized (see for example, Verhaeghen et al., 2003).

It is well-known that normal aging presents episodic memory deficits (e.g., Craik et al., 1990; Light, 1991; Craik and Grady, 2002). These impairments have been shown to be related to PFC dysfunction or reduced activity (Souchay et al., 2000; Cabeza, 2002; Craik and Grady, 2002; Luo and Craik, 2008), especially during the encoding processes (Daselaar et al., 2004; Dennis et al., 2008). In particular, older adults' difficulty in episodic memory encoding has been shown to be related to an associative deficit, namely the difficulty in creating (and retrieving) cohesive episodes from unrelated attributes-units (Naveh-Benjamin, 2000), and also to a lower level of strategic functioning (Shing et al., 2008). The low episodic memory performance in our results could be related to associative deficits, which did not allow subjects to create appropriate strategies when encoding under the silence condition, obstructing the development of a durable memory trace. Interestingly, it has also been shown how this associative deficit in older participants can be circumvented by using appropriate associative strategies (e.g., creating a sentence linking pairs of words during encoding), which resulted in a significant improvement in episodic memory performance (Naveh-Benjamin et al., 2007). One possible explanation could therefore be that music helps older subjects to create strategies of associations during the encoding phase (between items and between the item and the source itself), which are not easily created under the silence condition, and in this way improves subsequent episodic memory performance. In line with this idea, it has been shown that certain situations can provide additional elaborative encoding, but it is only when using effortful processing, such as associative and integrative processing (Chalfonte and Johnson, 1996; Naveh-Benjamin, 2000), that older adults might find difficulty (Luo et al., 2007). A study by Luo et al. (2007) tested this hypothesis by devising a condition in which visually presented words were paired with an appropriate sound. Results showed that older adults benefited very little from associating sound to words, because of the additional demand this places on integrative processing. Thus, one possible reason for the enhancement of memory in a music condition is that it does not require effortful processing. This in turn would provide a mechanism to explain why less DLPFC activity was required for verbal encoding with background music, which, unlike the silence condition, does not require DLPFC involvement for the high-cognitive processing of verbal encoding, suggesting more automatic inter-item/item-source binding when there is background music. This explanation is supported by previous EEG findings that a few seconds of music can influence the semantic and conceptual processing of verbal material by priming the meaning of a word (Koelsch et al., 2004; Daltrozzo and Schön, 2009a,b). It is therefore possible that this semantic priming mechanism could also be reflected in easier associations and bindings between items when there is background music, thus requiring less demand on the DLPFC.

However, it is important to mention that a consistent part of the literature on episodic memory has shown how an item is better encoded when supported by semantically related contextual stimulation (see e.g., Engelkamp and Zimmer, 1984; Light, 1991; Lövdén et al., 2002). In our case, we have chosen a "Jazz" music piece, which could be a rich and pleasant encoding context for the subject, but that is not semantically related with the encoded items. Considering this, one could claim that the observed results are related to an increase of attention rather than due to associative and binding strategies linked to the background music. It has been discussed that, because of its intrinsic arousal potential, music might represent a powerful exogenous means of memory modulation, especially for long-term memory processes (Judde and Rickard, 2010). By comparing a musical versus non-musical context, it is therefore possible that music just improves subjects' attention thus increasing their performance. In this case, our findings would be line with previous behavioral studies, which attributed improved cognitive performance in the presence of a musical background to higher amounts of arousal and attention (Foster and Valentine, 2001; Thompson et al., 2005). In apparent conflict with this explanation there is the fact that, music being considered as an unrelated context, we should expect an attentional overload (with the attention divided between musical auditory stimulus and verbal encoding task) and observe music as an interference rather than an attention improving factor. This would be in line with the literature, which claims that music draws participants' attention away from the relevant information to remember thus creating a dual-task situation (e.g., Salame and Baddeley, 1989; Racette and Peretz, 2007; Jäncke and Sandmann, 2010; Moussard et al., 2012; Jäncke et al., 2014). In other words, we should have observed worse memory retrieval performance for the "unrelated" music condition when compared to silence condition which, even if semantically unrelated to the stimuli, allows the subjects to freely focus on the task without overloading their attentional field. This would be especially true for older adults, known to have impairments in inhibiting irrelevant information and therefore in dividing their attention during encoding (e.g., Park et al., 1989; Parks, 2007). However, in line with previous studies showing that background music (even when semantically unrelated) can help non-musical cognitive abilities (e.g., Balch et al., 1992; Wallace, 1994; Balch and Lewis, 1996; Thompson et al., 2005; De Groot, 2006; Ferreri et al., 2013; Kang and Williamson, 2013), our behavioral results show that music was not interfering with the memory encoding task, but rather helped subjects when presented as an encoding context. Furthermore, if an attentional explanation would be true, we should have expected our functional neuroimaging results to show greater PFC involvement in the music condition than in the silence condition. Several studies have indeed shown how alertness or attentional states significantly increase PFC activation (Ehlis et al., 2008; Herrmann et al., 2008), and these findings do not match with the decreased PFC activation found in our fNIRS data for the music encoding.

Another important point is that the PFC deactivation we found is in apparent conflict with previous fMRI study which showed that PFC, specifically the DLPFC, is recruited during cognitive tasks demanding inter-item organizational and strategic encoding (Blumenfeld and Ranganath, 2007; Murray and Ranganath, 2007) and that its activity usually increases when highly structured items are presented (e.g., Bor et al., 2003). As discussed by Ramasubbu et al. (2012), such PFC deactivation is in line with previous PET studies (e.g., Volkow et al., 2002) and the discrepancies between fMRI and near-infrared spectroscopy (NIRS) studies could be in part due to differences in methodologies and wide variation in correlation between O_2Hb–HHb and blood oxygen level-dependent (BOLD) responses (see e.g., Cui et al., 2011 for a combined fMRI–fNIRS study). However, it is reasonable to think that DLPFC deactivation goes with activation of other brain regions, and particularly subcortical regions. Starting from these considerations, although fNIRS spatial resolution limitations do not allow monitoring subcortical oxygenation changes, it is interesting to discuss another possible explanation for our findings, which relies on music-related emotional factors. It is well-known that a strong relationship exists between music and limbic-reward systems; music is indeed one of the most potent motivational rewards and several studies showed that pleasant music experiences are accompanied by activity in subcortical brain regions (e.g., ventral–tegmental area and nucleus accumbens) involved in motivation and reward processes (see e.g., Blood and Zatorre, 2001; Salimpoor et al., 2013). At the same time, it has also been demonstrated that mesolimbic reward circuit activations can precede memory formation during reward-motivated learning, suggesting the crucial role that the reward system plays in successful memory encoding processes (Adcock et al., 2006). It is therefore possible that the observed PFC disengagement is linked with implicit subcortical mesolimbic music-related activation, which most likely improved subjects' items learning and therefore the subsequent memory performance.

Further research on both behavioral (e.g., specific organizational and associative strategies, musical semantic related and unrelated material, pleasant and unpleasant music) and functional (e.g., with multi-channel fNIRS systems during both encoding and retrieval phases) levels may confirm these explanations and shed new light on which cognitive processes are involved during episodic encoding with music. However, in our opinion, these findings contribute to the ongoing debate about which neural mechanisms underlie the therapeutic effects of music. In particular, we believe that our results open up interesting perspectives about the use of music as a rehabilitation tool for people with memory deficits due to frontal lobe dysfunctions, such as Alzheimer's patients. The notion that memory for music can be preserved in patients with Alzheimer's disease has been raised by a number of case studies (Baird and Samson, 2009), and several studies have shown that the verbal memory of Alzheimer's patients can be improved by music (Thompson et al., 2005; Simmons-Stern et al., 2010). However, the processes underlying these improvements remain unclear. To investigate the effect of music on episodic performance in special populations such as Alzheimer's patients while non-invasively monitoring their PFC brain oxygenation through fNIRS could therefore offer a great opportunity to clarify how music could act on long-term memory processes and to understand better how and why music works in rehabilitation.

In conclusion, in line with the view that context is crucial during verbal episodic memory encoding, our findings suggest that music can create a rich and helpful context during the encoding of verbal material, improving the subsequent episodic memory performance of older adults, and that this improvement goes alongside less involvement of the PFC. Taken together, these results are in line with the idea that music is a good tool for memory rehabilitation and open up new perspectives about the cortical mechanisms involved in the therapeutic effects of music.

ACKNOWLEDGMENTS

This work was supported by the European Project EBRAMUS (European BRAin and MUSic) ITN – Grant Agreement Number 218357, the Conseil Régional de Bourgogne and the MAAMI ANR Project, TecSan Program, ANR-12-TECS-0014.

REFERENCES

Adcock, R. A., Thangavel, A., Whitfield-Gabrieli, S., Knutson, B., and Gabrieli, J. D. (2006). Reward-motivated learning: mesolimbic activation precedes memory formation. *Neuron* 50, 507–517. doi:10.1016/j.neuron.2006.03.036

Altenmüller, E. O. (2003). "How many music centers are in the brain?," in *The Cognitive Neuroscience of Music*, eds I. Peretz and R. J. Zatorre (Oxford, NY: Oxford University Press), 346–356.

Baird, A., and Samson, S. (2009). Memory for music in Alzheimer's disease: unforgettable? *Neuropsychol. Rev.* 19, 85–101. doi:10.1007/s11065-009-9085-2

Balch, W. R., Bowman, K., and Mohler, L. A. (1992). Music-dependent memory in immediate and delayed word recall. *Mem. Cognit.* 20, 21–28. doi:10.3758/BF03208250

Balch, W. R., and Lewis, B. S. (1996). Music-dependent memory: the roles of tempo change and mood mediation. *J. Exp. Psychol. Learn. Mem. Cogn.* 22, 1354–1363. doi:10.1037/0278-7393.22.6.1354

Blood, A. J., and Zatorre, R. J. (2001). Intensely pleasurable responses to music correlate with activity in brain regions implicated in reward and emotion. *Proc. Natl. Acad. Sci. U.S.A.* 98, 11818–11823. doi:10.1073/pnas.191355898

Blumenfeld, R. C., and Ranganath, C. (2007). Prefrontal cortex and long-term memory encoding: an integrative review of findings from neuropsychology and neuroimaging. *Neuroscientist.* 13, 280–291. doi:10.1177/1073858407299290

Bor, D., Duncan, J., Wiseman, R. J., and Owen, A. M. (2003). Encoding strategies dissociate prefrontal activity from working memory demand. *Neuron* 37, 361–367. doi:10.1016/S0896-6273(02)01171-6

Brotons, M., and Koger, S. M. (2000). The impact of music therapy on language functioning in dementia. *J. Music Ther.* 37, 183–195. doi:10.1093/jmt/37.3.183

Bugaiska, A., Clarys, D., Jarry, C., Taconnat, L., Tapia, G., Vanneste, S., et al. (2007). The effect of aging in recollective experience: the processing speed and executive functioning hypothesis. *Conscious. Cogn.* 16, 797–808. doi:10.1016/j.concog.2006.11.007

Bunce, D. (2003). Cognitive support at encoding attenuates age differences in recollective experience among adults of lower frontal lobe function. *Neuropsychology* 17, 353–361. doi:10.1037/0894-4105.17.3.353

Burke, D. M., and Light, L. L. (1981). Memory and aging: the role of retrieval processes. *Psychol. Bull.* 90, 513. doi:10.1037/0033-2909.90.3.513

Cabeza, R. (2002). Hemispheric asymmetry reduction in older adults: the HAROLD model. *Psychol. Aging* 17, 85. doi:10.1037/0882-7974.17.1.85

Chalfonte, B., and Johnson, M. K. (1996). Feature memory and binding in young and older adults. *Mem. Cognit.* 24, 403–416. doi:10.3758/BF03200930

Chan, A. S., Ho, Y., and Cheung, M. (1998). Music training improves verbal memory. *Nature* 396, 128. doi:10.1038/24075

Clarys, D., Bugaiska, A., Tapia, G., and Alexia Baudouin, A. (2009). Ageing, remembering, and executive function. *Memory* 17, 158–168. doi:10.1080/09658210802188301

Craik, F. I., and Grady, C. L. (2002). "Aging, memory, and frontal lobe functioning," in *Principles of Frontal Lobe Function*, eds D. T. Stuss and R. T. Knight (New York, NY: Oxford University Press), 528–540.

Craik, F. I., and Lockhart, R. S. (1972). Levels of processing: a framework for memory research. *J. Verbal Learn. Verbal Behav.* 11, 671–684. doi:10.1016/S0022-5371(72)80001-X

Craik, F. I., Morris, L. W., Morris, R. G., and Loewen, E. R. (1990). Relations between source amnesia and frontal lobe functioning in older adults. *Psychol. Aging* 5, 148. doi:10.1037/0882-7974.5.1.148

Cui, X., Bray, S., Bryant, D. M., Glover, G. H., and Reiss, A. L. (2011). A quantitative comparison of NIRS and fMRI across multiple cognitive tasks. *Neuroimage* 54, 2808–2821. doi:10.1016/j.neuroimage.2010.10.069

Cutini, S., Basso Moro, S., and Bisconti, S. (2012). Functional near infrared optical imaging in cognitive neuroscience: an introductory review. *J. Near Infrared Spectrosc.* 20, 75–92. doi:10.1255/jnirs.969

Daltrozzo, J., and Schön, D. (2009a). Conceptual processing in music as revealed by N400 effects on words and musical targets. *J. Cogn. Neurosci.* 21, 1882–1892. doi:10.1162/jocn.2009.21113

Daltrozzo, J., and Schön, D. (2009b). Is conceptual processing in music automatic? An electrophysiological approach. *Brain Res.* 1270, 88–94. doi:10.1016/j.brainres.2009.03.019

Daselaar, S. M., Prince, S. E., and Cabeza, R. (2004). When less means more: deactivations during encoding that predict subsequent memory. *Neuroimage* 23, 921–927. doi:10.1016/j.neuroimage.2004.07.031

De Groot, A. (2006). Effects of stimulus characteristics and background music on foreign language vocabulary learning and forgetting. *Lang. Learn.* 56, 463–506. doi:10.1111/j.1467-9922.2006.00374.x

Dennis, N. A., Hayes, S. M., Prince, S. E., Madden, D. J., Huettel, S. A., and Cabeza, R. (2008). Effects of aging on the neural correlates of successful item and source memory encoding. *J. Exp. Psychol. Learn. Mem. Cogn.* 34, 791. doi:10.1037/0278-7393.34.4.791

Dodson, C. S., Bawa, S., and Slotnick, S. D. (2007). Aging, source memory, and misrecollections. *J. Exp. Psychol. Learn. Mem. Cogn.* 33, 169. doi:10.1037/0278-7393.33.1.169

Duncan, A., Meek, J. H., Clemence, M., Elwell, C. E., Fallon, P., Tyszczuk, L., et al. (1996). Measurement of cranial optical path length as a function of age using phase resolved near infrared spectroscopy. *Pediatr. Res.* 39, 889–894. doi:10.1203/00006450-199605000-00025

Ehlis, A. C., Bähne, C. G., Jacob, C. P., Herrmann, M. J., and Fallgatter, A. J. (2008). Reduced lateral prefrontal activation in adult patients with attention-deficit/hyperactivity disorder (ADHD) during a working memory task: a functional near-infrared spectroscopy (fNIRS) study. *J. Psychiatr. Res.* 42, 1060–1067. doi:10.1016/j.jpsychires.2007.11.011

Engelkamp, J., and Zimmer, H. D. (1984). Motor programme information as a separable memory unit. *Psychol. Res.* 46, 283–299. doi:10.1007/BF00308889

Ferrari, M., and Quaresima, V. (2012). A brief review on the history of human functional near-infrared spectroscopy (fNIRS) development and fields of application. *Neuroimage* 63, 921–935. doi:10.1016/j.neuroimage.2012.03.049

Ferreri, L., Aucouturier, J. J., Muthalib, M., Bigand, E., and Bugaiska, A. (2013). Music improves verbal memory encoding while decreasing prefrontal cortex activity: an fNIRS study. *Front. Hum. Neurosci.* 7:779. doi:10.3389/fnhum.2013.00779

Ferreri, L., Bigand, E., Perrey, S., and Bugaiska, A. (in press). The promise of near-infrared spectroscopy (NIRS) for psychological research: a brief review. *Top. Cogn. Psychol.*

Folstein, M. F., Folstein, S. E., and McHugh, P. R. (1975). "Mini-mental state": a practical method for grading the cognitive state of patients for the clinician. *J. Psychiatr. Res.* 12, 189–198. doi:10.1016/0022-3956(75)90026-6

Foster, N. A., and Valentine, E. R. (2001). The effect of auditory stimulation on autobiographical recall in dementia. *Exp. Aging Res.* 27, 215–228.

Franklin, M. S., Moore, K. S., Yip, C. Y., Jonides, J., Rattray, K., and Moher, J. (2008). The effects of musical training on verbal memory. *Psychol. Music* 36, 353–365. doi:10.1177/0305735607086044

Gagnon, L., Perdue, K., Greve, D. N., Goldenholz, D., Kaskhedikar, G., and Boas, D. (2011). Improved recovery of the hemodynamic response in diffuse optical imaging using short optode separations and state-space modeling. *Neuroimage* 56, 1362–1371. doi:10.1016/j.neuroimage.2011.03.001

Gagnon, L., Yücel, M. A., Dehaes, M., Cooper, R. J., Perdue, K. L., Selb, J., et al. (2012). Quantification of the cortical contribution to the NIRS signal over the motor cortex using concurrent NIRS-fMRI measurements. *Neuroimage* 59, 3933–3940. doi:10.1016/j.neuroimage.2011.10.054

Glisky, E. L., Polster, M. R., and Routhieaux, B. C. (1995). Double dissociation between item and source memory. *Neuropsychology* 9, 229–235. doi:10.1037/0894-4105.9.2.229

Hamann, S. (2001). Cognitive and neural mechanisms of emotional memory. *Trends Cogn. Sci.* 5, 394–400. doi:10.1016/S1364-6613(00)01707-1

Herrmann, M. J., Woidich, E., Schreppel, T., Pauli, P., and Fallgatter, A. J. (2008). Brain activation for alertness measured with functional near infrared spectroscopy (fNIRS). *Psychophysiology* 45, 480–486. doi:10.1111/j.1469-8986.2007.00633.x

Ho, Y. C., Cheung, M. C., and Chan, A. A. (2003). Music training improves verbal but not visual memory: cross-sectional and longitudinal explorations in children. *Neuropsychology* 17, 439–450. doi:10.1037/0894-4105.17.3.439

Innocenti, I., Giovannelli, F., Cincotta, M., Feurra, M., Polizzotto, N. R., Bianco, G., et al. (2010). Event-related rTMS at encoding affects differently deep and shallow memory traces. *Neuroimage* 53, 325–330. doi:10.1016/j.neuroimage.2010.06.011

Isingrini, M., Fontaine, R., Taconnat, L., and Duportal, A. (1995). Aging and encoding in memory: false alarms and decision criteria in a word-pair recognition task. *Int. J. Aging Hum. Dev.* 41, 79–88. doi:10.2190/ERDG-LHA8-EBYN-L9LX

Jäncke, L. (2008). Music, memory and emotion Lutz Jäncke. *J. Biol.* 7, 21. doi:10.1186/jbiol82

Jäncke, L., Brügger, E., Brummer, M., Scherrer, S., and Alahmadi, N. (2014). Verbal learning in the context of background music: no influence of vocals and instrumentals on verbal learning. *Behav. Brain Funct.* 10, 10. doi:10.1186/1744-9081-10-10

Jäncke, L., and Sandmann, P. (2010). Music listening while you learn: no influence of background music on verbal learning. *Behav. Brain Funct.* 6, 1–14. doi:10.1186/1744-9081-6-3

Jersild, A. T. (1927). Mental set and shift. *Arch. Psychol.* 89, 5–82.

Jobsis, F. F. (1977). Noninvasive, infrared monitoring of cerebral and myocardial oxygen sufficiency and circulatory parameters. *Science* 198, 1264–1267. doi:10.1126/science.929199

Johnson, M. K., Hashtroudi, S., and Lindsay, D. S. (1993). Source monitoring. *Psychol. Bull.* 114, 3. doi:10.1037/0033-2909.114.1.3

Judde, S., and Rickard, N. (2010). The effect of post-learning presentation of music on long-term word-list retention. *Neurobiol. Learn. Mem.* 94, 13–20. doi:10.1016/j.nlm.2010.03.002

Jurcak, V., Tsuzuki, D., and Dan, I. (2007). 10/20, 10/10, and 10/5 systems revisited: their validity as relative head-surface-based positioning systems. *Neuroimage* 34, 1600–1611. doi:10.1016/j.neuroimage.2006.09.024

Kang, H. J., and Williamson, V. J. (2013). Background music can aid second language learning. *Psychol. Music.* doi:10.1177/0305735613485152

Kelley, W. M., Miezin, F. M., McDermott, K. B., Buckner, R. L., Raichle, M. E., Cohen, N. J., et al. (1998). Hemispheric specialization in human dorsal frontal cortex and medial temporal lobe for verbal and nonverbal memory encoding. *Neuron* 20, 927–936. doi:10.1016/S0896-6273(00)80474-2

Kirilina, E., Jelzow, A., Heine, A., Niessing, M., Wabnitz, H., Brühl, R., et al. (2012). The physiological origin of task-evoked systemic artefacts in functional near infrared spectroscopy. *Neuroimage* 61, 70–81. doi:10.1016/j.neuroimage.2012.02.074

Koelsch, S., Kasper, E., Sammler, D., Schulze, K., Gunter, T., and Friederici, A. D. (2004). Music, language and meaning: brain signatures of semantic processing. *Nat. Neurosci.* 7, 302–307. doi:10.1038/nn1197

Kohno, S., Miyai, I., Seiyama, A., Oda, I., Ishikawa, A., Tsuneishi, S., et al. (2007). Removal of the skin blood flow artifact in functional near-infrared spectroscopic imaging data through independent component analysis. *J. Biomed. Opt.* 12, 062111. doi:10.1117/1.2814249

Kubota, Y., Toichi, M., Shimizu, M., Mason, R. A., Findling, R. L., Yamamoto, K., et al. (2006). Prefrontal hemodynamic activity predicts false memory – a near-infrared spectroscopy study. *Neuroimage* 31, 1783–1789. doi:10.1016/j.neuroimage.2006.02.003

Levine, T. R., and Hullett, C. R. (2002). Eta squared, partial eta squared, and misreporting of effect size in communication research. *Hum. Commun. Res.* 28, 612–625. doi:10.1111/j.1468-2958.2002.tb00828.x

Light, L. L. (1991). Memory and aging: four hypotheses in search of data. *Annu. Rev. Psychol.* 42, 333–376. doi:10.1146/annurev.ps.42.020191.002001

Lövdén, M., Rönnlund, M., and Nilsson, L. G. (2002). Remembering and knowing in adulthood: effects of enacted encoding and relations to processing speed. *Aging Neuropsychol. Cogn.* 9, 184–200. doi:10.1076/anec.9.3.184.9612

Luo, L., and Craik, F. I. (2008). Aging and memory: a cognitive approach. *Can. J. Psychiatry* 53, 346–353.

Luo, L., Hendriks, T., and Craik, F. I. (2007). Age differences in recollection: three patterns of enhanced encoding. *Psychol. Aging* 22, 269. doi:10.1037/0882-7974.22.2.269

Matsuda, G., and Hiraki, K. (2004). "Prefrontal cortex deactivation during video game play," in *Gaming, Simulation and Society: Research Scope and Perspective*, eds R. Shiratori, K. Arai, and F. Kato (Tokyo: Springer-Verlag), 101–109.

Matsuda, G., and Hiraki, K. (2006). Sustained decrease in oxygenated hemoglobin during video games in the dorsal prefrontal cortex: a NIRS study of children. *Neuroimage* 29, 706–711. doi:10.1016/j.neuroimage.2005.08.019

Matsui, M., Tanaka, K., Yonezawa, M., and Kurachi, M. (2007). Activation of the prefrontal cortex during memory learning: near-infrared spectroscopy study. *Psychiatry Clin. Neurosci.* 61, 31–38. doi:10.1111/j.1440-1819.2007.01607.x

Mitchell, D. B. (1989). How many memory systems? Evidence from aging. *J. Exp. Psychol. Learn. Mem. Cogn.* 15, 31–49.

Moussard, A., Bigand, E., Belleville, S., and Peretz, I. (2012). Music as an aid to learn new verbal information in Alzheimer's disease. *Music Percept.* 29, 521–531. doi:10.1525/mp.2012.29.5.521

Murray, L. J., and Ranganath, C. (2007). The dorsolateral prefrontal cortex contributes to successful relational memory encoding. *J. Neurosci.* 27, 5515–5522. doi:10.1523/JNEUROSCI.0406-07.2007

Naveh-Benjamin, M. (2000). Adult age differences in memory performance: tests of an associative deficit hypothesis. *J. Exp. Psychol. Learn. Mem. Cogn.* 26, 1170. doi:10.1037/0278-7393.26.5.1170

Naveh-Benjamin, M., Brav, T. K., and Levy, O. (2007). The associative memory deficit of older adults: the role of strategy utilization. *Psychol. Aging* 22, 202. doi:10.1037/0882-7974.22.1.202

New, B., Pallier, C., Brysbaert, M., and Ferrand, L. (2004). Lexique 2: a new French lexical database. *Behav. Res. Methods Instrum. Comput.* 36, 516–524. doi:10.3758/BF03195598

Nyberg, L., Cabeza, R., and Tulving, E. (1996). PET studies of encoding and retrieval: the HERA model. *Psychon. Bull. Rev.* 3, 135–148. doi:10.3758/BF03212412

Okamoto, M., Dan, H., Sakamoto, K., Takeo, K., Shimizu, K., Kohno, S., et al. (2004). Three-dimensional probabilistic anatomical cranio-cerebral correlation via the international 10-20 system oriented for transcranial functional brain mapping. *Neuroimage* 21, 99–111. doi:10.1016/j.neuroimage.2003.08.026

Okamoto, M., Wada, Y., Yamaguchi, Y., Kyutoku, Y., Clowney, L., Singh, A. K., et al. (2011). Process-specific prefrontal contributions to episodic encoding and retrieval of tastes: a functional NIRS study. *Neuroimage* 54, 1578–1588. doi:10.1016/j.neuroimage.2010.08.016

Park, D. C., Smith, A. D., Dudley, W. N., and Lafronza, V. N. (1989). Effect of age and divided attention task presented during encoding and retrieval on memory. *J. Exp. Psychol. Learn. Mem. Cogn.* 15, 1185–1191. doi:10.1037/0278-7393.15.6.1185

Parkin, A. J., and Walter, B. M. (1992). Recollective experience, normal aging, and frontal dysfunction. *Psychol. Aging* 7, 290. doi:10.1037/0882-7974.7.2.290

Parks, C. M. (2007). The role of noncriterial recollection in estimating recollection and familiarity. *J. Mem. Lang.* 57, 81–100. doi:10.1016/j.jml.2007.03.003

Peterson, D. A., and Thaut, M. H. (2007). Music increases frontal EEG coherence during verbal learning. *Neurosci. Lett.* 412, 217–221. doi:10.1016/j.neulet.2006.10.057

Racette, A., Bard, C., and Peretz, I. (2006). Making non-fluent aphasics speak: sing along! *Brain* 129, 2571–2584. doi:10.1093/brain/awl250

Racette, A., and Peretz, I. (2007). Learning lyrics: to sing or not to sing? *Mem. Cognit.* 35, 242–253. doi:10.3758/BF03193445

Rajah, M. N., and D'Esposito, M. (2005). Region-specific changes in prefrontal function with age: a review of PET and fMRI studies on working and episodic memory. *Brain* 128, 1964–1983. doi:10.1093/brain/awh608

Ramasubbu, R., Sing, H., Zhu, H., and Dunn, J. F. (2012). Methylphenidate-mediated reduction in prefrontal hemodynamic responses to working memory task: a functional near-infrared spectroscopy study. *Hum. Psychopharmacol.* 27, 615–621. doi:10.1002/hup.2258

Ranganath, C. (2010). Binding items and contexts the cognitive neuroscience of episodic memory. *Curr. Dir. Psychol. Sci.* 19, 131–137. doi:10.1177/0963721410368805

Raz, N. (2000). "Aging of the brain and its impact on cognitive performance: integration of structural and functional findings," in *The Handbook of Aging and Cognition*, 2nd Edn, eds F. I. M. Craik and T. A. Salthouse (London: Lawrence Erlbaum Associates), 1–90.

Salame, P., and Baddeley, A. D. (1989). Effects of background music on phonological short-term memory. *Q. J. Exp. Psychol. A* 41, 107–122. doi:10.1080/14640748908402355

Salimpoor, V. N., van den Bosch, I., Kovacevic, N., McIntosh, A. R., Dagher, A., and Zatorre, R. J. (2013). Interactions between the nucleus accumbens and auditory cortices predict music reward value. *Science* 340, 216–219. doi:10.1126/science.1231059

Salthouse, T. A., Toth, J. P., Hancock, H. E., and Woodard, J. L. (1997). Controlled and automatic forms of memory and attention: process purity and the uniqueness of age-related influences. *J. Gerontol. B Psychol. Sci. Soc. Sci.* 52, 216–228. doi:10.1093/geronb/52B.5.P216

Särkämo, T., Tervaniemi, M., Latinen, S., Forsblom, A., Soinila, S., Mikkonen, M., et al. (2008). Music listening enhances cognitive recovery and mood after middle cerebral artery stroke. *Brain* 131, 866–876. doi:10.1093/brain/awn013

Schellenberg, E. G. (2003). "Does exposure to music have beneficial side effects?" in *The Cognitive Neuroscience of Music*, eds I. Peretz and R. J. Zatorre (Oxford, NY: Oxford University Press), 430–444.

Schellenberg, E. G. (2005). Music and cognitive abilities. *Curr. Dir. Psychol. Sci.* 14, 317–320. doi:10.1111/j.0963-7214.2005.00389.x

Shing, Y. L., Werkle-Bergner, M., Li, S. C., and Lindenberger, U. (2008). Associative and strategic components of episodic memory: a life-span dissociation. *J. Exp. Psychol. Gen.* 137, 495. doi:10.1037/0096-3445.137.3.495

Simmons-Stern, N. R., Budson, A. E., and Ally, B. A. (2010). Music as a memory enhancer in patients with Alzheimer's disease. *Neuropsychologia* 48, 3164–3167. doi:10.1016/j.neuropsychologia.2010.04.033

Souchay, C., Isingrini, M., and Espagnet, L. (2000). Aging, episodic memory feeling-of-knowing, and frontal functioning. *Neuropsychology* 14, 299. doi:10.1037/0894-4105.14.2.299

Spector, A., and Bierdeman, I. (1976). Mental set and mental shif revisited. *Am. J. Psychol.* 89, 669–679. doi:10.2307/1421465

Spencer, W. D., and Raz, N. (1995). Differential effects of aging on memory for content and context: a meta-analysis. *Psychol. Aging* 10, 527. doi:10.1037/0882-7974.10.4.527

Takahashi, T., Takikawa, Y., Kawagoe, R., Shibuya, S., Iwano, T., and Kitazawa, S. (2011). Influence of skin blood flow on near-infrared spectroscopy signals measured on the forehead during a verbal fluency task. *Neuroimage* 57, 991–1002. doi:10.1016/j.neuroimage.2011.05.012

Thaut, M. H., Peterson, D. A., and McIntosh, G. C. (2005). Temporal entrainment of cognitive functions musical mnemonics induce brain plasticity and oscillatory synchrony in neural networks underlying memory. *Ann. N. Y. Acad. Sci.* 1060, 243–254. doi:10.1196/annals.1360.017

Thompson, R. G., Moulin, C. J. A., Hayre, S., and Jones, R. W. (2005). Music enhances category fluency in healthy older adults and Alzheimer's disease patients. *Exp. Aging Res.* 31, 91–99. doi:10.1080/03610730590882819

Tulving, E. (1972). "Episodic and semantic memory," in *Organization of Memory*, eds E. Tulving and W. Donaldson (New York, NY: Academic Press), 381–403.

Tulving, E., Kapur, S., Craik, F. I. M., Moscovitch, M., and Houle, S. (1994). Hemispheric encoding/retrieval asymmetry in episodic memory: positron emission tomography findings. *Proc. Natl. Acad. Sci. U.S.A.* 91, 2016–2020. doi:10.1073/pnas.91.6.2016

Verhaeghen, P., Steitz, D. W., Sliwinski, M. J., and Cerella, J. (2003). Aging and dual-task performance: a meta-analysis. *Psychol. Aging* 18, 443. doi:10.1037/0882-7974.18.3.443

Volkow, N. D., Fowler, J. S., Wang, G. J., Ding, Y. S., and Gatley, S. J. (2002). Role of dopamine in the therapeutic and reinforcing effects of methylphenidate in humans: results from imaging studies. *Eur. Neuropsychopharmacol.* 12, 557–566. doi:10.1016/S0924-977X(02)00104-9

Wallace, W. T. (1994). Memory for music: effect of melody on recall of text. *J. Exp. Psychol. Learn. Mem. Cogn.* 20, 1471–1485. doi:10.1037/0278-7393.20.6.1471

West, R. L. (1996). An application of prefrontal cortex function theory to cognitive aging. *Psychol. Bull.* 120, 272–292. doi:10.1037/0033-2909.120.2.272

Wheeler, M. A., Stuss, D. T., and Tulving, E. (1997). Toward a theory of episodic memory: the frontal lobes and autonoetic consciousness. *Psychol. Bull.* 121, 331.

16

New learning of music after bilateral medial temporal lobe damage: evidence from an amnesic patient

Jussi Valtonen[1]*, Emma Gregory[2], Barbara Landau[2] and Michael McCloskey[2]

[1] *Institute of Behavioural Sciences, University of Helsinki, Helsinki, Finland*
[2] *Department of Cognitive Science, Johns Hopkins University, Baltimore, MD, USA*

***Correspondence:**
Jussi Valtonen, Institute of Behavioural Sciences, University of Helsinki, P.O. Box 9, Helsinki FI-00014, Finland
e-mail: jussi.valtonen@helsinki.fi

Damage to the hippocampus impairs the ability to acquire new declarative memories, but not the ability to learn simple motor tasks. An unresolved question is whether hippocampal damage affects learning for music performance, which requires motor processes, but in a cognitively complex context. We studied learning of novel musical pieces by sight-reading in a newly identified amnesic, LSJ, who was a skilled amateur violist prior to contracting herpes simplex encephalitis. LSJ has suffered virtually complete destruction of the hippocampus bilaterally, as well as extensive damage to other medial temporal lobe structures and the left anterior temporal lobe. Because of LSJ's rare combination of musical training and near-complete hippocampal destruction, her case provides a unique opportunity to investigate the role of the hippocampus for complex motor learning processes specifically related to music performance. Three novel pieces of viola music were composed and closely matched for factors contributing to a piece's musical complexity. LSJ practiced playing two of the pieces, one in each of the two sessions during the same day. Relative to a third unpracticed control piece, LSJ showed significant pre- to post-training improvement for the two practiced pieces. Learning effects were observed both with detailed analyses of correctly played notes, and with subjective whole-piece performance evaluations by string instrument players. The learning effects were evident immediately after practice and 14 days later. The observed learning stands in sharp contrast to LSJ's complete lack of awareness that the same pieces were being presented repeatedly, and to the profound impairments she exhibits in other learning tasks. Although learning in simple motor tasks has been previously observed in amnesic patients, our results demonstrate that non-hippocampal structures can support complex learning of novel musical sequences for music performance.

Keywords: music performance, learning, memory, hippocampus, brain damage, anterograde amnesia, single-patient study

INTRODUCTION

Performing music has been described as one of the most demanding forms of skilled serial action human beings are capable of (e.g., Palmer, 1997; Altenmüller and Schneider, 2009). The musician must execute intricate musical sequences expressively under precise timing constraints, following a hierarchically organized rhythmic structure while simultaneously preparing for subsequent notes. Behavioral studies have revealed many important aspects of the cognitive mechanisms that support music performance (Sloboda, 1984, 1985; Palmer and van de Sande, 1993, 1995; Chaffin and Imreh, 1997, 2002; Engel et al., 1997; Palmer, 1997, 2005, 2006; Drake and Palmer, 2000; Finney and Palmer, 2003; Palmer and Pfordresher, 2003; Stewart, 2005; Brodsky et al., 2008; Chaffin et al., 2009; Lehmann and Kopiez, 2009; Snyder, 2009; Simmons, 2012; van Vugt et al., 2012; Verrel et al., 2013). However, relatively few studies have shed light on the neural substrates. Among the reasons for the relative dearth of cognitive neuroscience research on music performance are technical difficulties in neuroimaging complex motor behavior, a lack of animal models, and the scarcity of musically proficient neuropsychological research patients [see Peretz and Zatorre (2005), Zatorre et al. (2007), and Levitin and Tirovolas (2009), for reviews on the cognitive neuroscience of music].

In this article, we address a central question concerning the neural bases for music performance, asking whether the hippocampus is necessary for learning to perform new musical pieces by sight-reading. We studied the learning of novel musical pieces by a newly identified amnesic patient, LSJ, who was a skilled amateur violist prior to suffering virtually complete bilateral destruction of her hippocampus due to herpes encephalitis.

The hippocampus, located within the brain's medial temporal lobes (MTL), is crucial for the acquisition of new declarative memories – memories that can be voluntarily retrieved (Scoville and Milner, 1957; Eichenbaum, 2000, 2013; Squire and Knowlton, 2000; Corkin, 2002; Insausti et al., 2013). In contrast, it has been argued that "procedural" or "motor" learning relies on structures other than the hippocampus and surrounding MTL areas (Squire et al., 2004; Eichenbaum, 2013; Reber, 2013). Consistent with this contention, a number of studies have reported that amnesic patients, including those with severe hippocampal damage, may show preserved capacities for certain forms of non-declarative learning (Milner, 1962; Corkin, 1968, 2002; Stefanacci et al., 2000; Eichenbaum, 2013). These results raise the possibility that learning to perform new pieces of music may be achievable in the absence of the hippocampus. However, it is not entirely clear that the forms of learning demonstrated by amnesic patients in prior studies are comparable in complexity to learning musical pieces for performance.

Learning to perform a piece of music has at times been equated with "procedural," "non-declarative," or "motor" learning (e.g., Crystal et al., 1989; Cowles et al., 2003; Cavaco et al., 2012; Simmons, 2012), implying that music performance recruits only learning processes for which the hippocampus is not critical. However, applying this terminology to music performance may be misleading. Stanley and Krakauer (2013) have recently argued that many motor skills such as music performance involve considerable cognitive complexity not required by the simple motor tasks that define procedural learning. As they point out, the distinction between declarative and procedural (or non-declarative) learning was originally based on studies with amnesic patient HM, who had portions of his hippocampus and surrounding MTL structures surgically removed. HM exhibited wide-ranging and profound impairments in various learning tasks requiring explicit retrieval, but showed improvement through repetition in simple motor tasks such as mirror drawing (Milner, 1962; Corkin, 1968, 2002; Eichenbaum, 2013). In contrast to how these results have often been interpreted, Stanley and Krakauer (2013) contend that what HM acquired in mirror drawing was not a motor skill but improved motor acuity, one component of motor skill. HM gained fine-tuned precision through repetition of explicitly indicated, identical motor movements. Complex motor skills such as music performance require not only motor acuity but also the ability to select the correct actions on the basis of factual knowledge (Stanley and Krakauer, 2013). Consistent with the distinction between gaining motor acuity and improvement in music performance skills, intact learning in simple motor acuity tasks (e.g., ones in which patient HM showed learning) does not guarantee the ability to learn to play a new piece of music (Beatty et al., 1999).

Sight-reading music requires being able to execute novel combinations of musical sequences that the performer has never encountered before. These demands distinguish sight-reading of music from the production of well-rehearsed motions (e.g., Lehmann and Kopiez, 2009). Unlike simple motor tasks such as mirror drawing, sight-reading of new music poses large cognitive demands (Kinsler and Carpenter, 1995; Furneaux and Land, 1999; Palmer, 2006). The separate dimensions of pitch, rhythm, and meter must be extracted from the notation, combined into a single representation for each event and prepared for execution in ordered sequences at a pre-specified rate. In addition, the processed elements must be held in a memory buffer while the rest of the sequence is being prepared (Kinsler and Carpenter, 1995; Palmer, 1997; Lehmann and Kopiez, 2009). Therefore, an essential aspect of what the sight-reader learns through practice with a new piece of music is more efficient mental planning of the ordered events (Palmer and van de Sande, 1993, 1995; Drake and Palmer, 2000; Palmer and Pfordresher, 2003; Palmer, 2006). In skilled musicians, these mental plans include representations both specific for and independent of the motor programs used to execute them (Sloboda, 1984; Palmer and Meyer, 2000; Meyer and Palmer, 2003; Palmer, 2005, 2006; Brodsky et al., 2008).

In all likelihood, both hippocampal and non-hippocampal structures normally support the complex processes involved in learning to perform a novel piece. Several lines of indirect evidence suggest that the hippocampus is especially important. First, outside the domain of music, the hippocampus has been shown to be important both for the learning of single items and for the ability to form associations between previously unrelated items (Henke et al., 1999; Eichenbaum, 2000; Stark et al., 2002; O'Kane et al., 2004; Squire et al., 2004; Schapiro et al., 2014). As musical pieces are composed from a limited number of basic elements, the ability to form associations between items should be of central importance in learning any new piece of music. Second, some have suggested that the hippocampus plays a special role in memory under conditions that require combining information from multiple sources (Squire and Knowlton, 2000; Nadel and Peterson, 2013); music performance requires integrating separate aspects of musical information related to pitch, rhythm, and meter from visual, auditory, and tactile sensory modalities. Third, music perception studies have shown that damage to the MTL region impairs the ability to learn new melodies in recognition tasks (Wilson and Saling, 2008), and fMRI studies indicate that the hippocampus is recruited in memory tasks involving recognition of novel melodies (Watanabe et al., 2008).

Additional evidence that the hippocampus is important for learning music comes from neuroimaging studies demonstrating that the hippocampus is engaged when complex temporal sequences are learned during motor performance. Specifically, evidence comes from the serial reaction time task (SRT task; Nissen and Bullemer, 1987; Janata and Grafton, 2003; Schendan et al., 2003), a temporal sequence learning paradigm thought to model some of the cognitive and motor aspects related to learning through music performance, albeit in a highly simplified form. In the SRT task, a visual cue appears in one of several spatial locations, and participants are instructed to press the corresponding button as quickly as possible. With practice, participants become faster in responding to repeated sequences than to random ones, even when they are unaware of any repeating patterns. Neuroimaging studies with neurologically intact subjects indicate that the MTL and hippocampus are engaged when complex SRT sequences are learned (Schendan et al., 2003; Robertson, 2007), indirectly suggesting that the hippocampus may also be recruited when new music is learned through performance. Hippocampal activation has also been observed during implicit sequence learning in studies of serial color matching (Gheysen et al., 2010) and oculomotor sequence learning (Albouy et al., 2008). One suggestion is that the hippocampus supports the learning of higher-order temporal associations in practiced sequences (Schendan et al., 2003; Albouy et al., 2008), a function that could be crucial for learning to perform a new piece of music.

Therefore, a relevant similarity between the SRT task and music performance could be that learning complex sequences requires forming higher-order associations among individual elements in both contexts. In terms of neural mechanisms, the MTL has been shown to be involved in learning when information about higher- but not lower-order patterns is acquired (Schendan et al., 2003; Robertson, 2007). In addition, studies with amnesic patients have shown preserved learning in simple forms of the SRT task (Reber and Squire, 1994, 1998), but other studies show impaired performance when the learning of higher-order associations is required (Curran, 1997). These group studies have included some patients with MTL damage, but as the extent of hippocampal damage is unreported and the results are considered at a group level only, the implications are not clear for the role of the hippocampus in learning. Together, however, the findings raise the possibility that learning of new music in the absence of the hippocampus may be unattainable. On the other hand, music performance by sight-reading differs from motor sequence learning tasks in various ways. For example, unlike the SRT task, music performance relies on a large body of previously acquired factual knowledge about musical rules, following a hierarchically organized rhythmic structure and making complex choices about fingerings and hand positions. Conceivably, such a wide range of previously obtained complex abilities could support learning in music performance in a way that is not possible in an SRT-type task. In addition, and perhaps not trivially, the music itself could matter for learning; in music performance, one produces esthetically and emotionally meaningful sounds absent from the SRT task.

Whether non-hippocampal structures alone can support any aspects of new music learning in a performance context is currently not known. Just two studies of brain-damaged individuals have examined whether the hippocampus is necessary for learning in music performance. Cowles et al. (2003) described SL, a patient presumed to have Alzheimer's disease, whose brain damage included bilateral atrophy in the MTL. SL was taught to play a new song on the violin from sheet music, which he was able to accomplish in two training sessions. Cowles et al. (2003) concluded that the learning of new music does not depend on an intact hippocampus. However, the extent of the patient's hippocampal damage is unreported, leaving unclear whether the observed learning was (at least partly) supported by remaining hippocampal tissue. In another study, Cavaco et al. (2012) studied a more severely amnesic patient, SZ. This amateur saxophonist had sustained MTL damage, including bilateral damage to the hippocampus, but was able to sight-read music and play in an orchestra. Cavaco et al. (2012) tested SZ's music performance on 11 target songs before and after biweekly practice with the orchestra over a period of 100 days. They found modest improvement for two of the five dimensions on which SZ's playing was rated: overall sight-reading accuracy and notes awareness (i.e., the correct identification of written notes and ability to correct one's errors). The magnetic resonance imaging (MRI) images for SZ indicate that at least some hippocampal tissue remained (see Cavaco et al., 2012). Hence, as in the Cowles et al. (2003) study, SZ's learning may have been supported by remaining hippocampal tissue. Further, no objective evaluations of the patient's performances before and after learning were reported by Cavaco et al. [or by Cowles et al. (2003)]. This makes it difficult to estimate the initial difficulty of the material for the patients, or to evaluate the learning trajectory by objective criteria. In addition, although the Cavaco et al. (2012) study is noteworthy for its ecologically valid setting and materials, neither the target nor control songs were pre-designed to control for any of the various factors possibly affecting performance, such as piece length, note type, key signature, or hand position changes[1].

In sum, it remains an open question whether the hippocampus is necessary for learning to perform a new piece of music, or whether at least some music performance learning can be supported by non-hippocampal structures alone. To investigate this issue, we studied the learning of novel musical pieces through sight-reading in a newly identified amnesic patient, LSJ. LSJ suffered near-complete destruction of her hippocampus bilaterally as a result of herpes encephalitis, and consequently exhibits extremely severe anterograde and retrograde amnesia. Prior to her illness, LSJ was a skilled amateur violist, and informal observations revealed that she could still play the viola by sight-reading at an advanced level. However, her anterograde amnesia is so severe that merely moments after performing a piece from sheet music, she shows no recollection of having encountered the piece before. We investigated whether LSJ could nevertheless show learning for new pieces of music, as revealed by improved performance resulting from practice.

Our study offers new evidence for three important reasons. First, unlike the patients in previous studies, LSJ has virtually no intact hippocampal tissue. Hence, any learning observed in her performance could not be attributed to hippocampal structures. Second, we used novel pieces of music that were specially designed to control for various factors affecting musical complexity, allowing for careful comparisons across pieces. Third, we carried out several analyses that provide a clearer basis for conclusions than in previous studies: LSJ's performance was evaluated before and after practice with a detailed note-by-note analyses and subjective whole-piece performance judgments made by a group of musicians.

Because some authors have argued that the hippocampus plays a critical role in memory consolidation for temporal sequence learning (Albouy et al., 2008, 2013a,b), we also wanted to investigate whether the learning could be retained in the absence of the hippocampus. Therefore, we tested LSJ's performance not only on the day of practice but also 14 days after practice.

MATERIALS AND METHODS

CASE DESCRIPTION

LSJ was 62 years old at the time of the study. Prior to contracting herpes simplex encephalitis (HSE) at age 57, she was a successful professional illustrator. Her illustrations appeared in books, magazines, and newspapers, including many New York Times articles and several covers for The New Yorker magazine. She has a Bachelor of Fine Arts degree.

Prior to her illness, LSJ was a skilled amateur violist and played in several chamber groups and orchestras. She received piano lessons from 6 to 11 years of age, violin lessons from ages 10 to 12, and viola lessons from age 12 until a few years after college. She played the viola in her school orchestra in junior high school,

[1] For two other related neuropsychological studies of music learning in which the role of the hippocampus was not investigated, see Fornazzari et al. (2006) and Baur et al. (2000).

in her high school orchestra for 4 years, in chamber music quartets with friends, and in a university orchestra for 2 years. During college, she played the viola in a theater orchestra and completed several college music courses in viola, violin, ensemble, and symphony orchestra. In the early 2000s, only a few years before her illness, she played viola and sang in the chorus of a community orchestra.

Structural MRI revealed severe bilateral damage to the MTL and anterior temporal damage in the left hemisphere (**Figure 1**). A volumetric analysis of LSJ's MTL region (**Table 1**; Schapiro et al., 2014) showed extensive bilateral damage to the hippocampus, parahippocampal cortex, entorhinal cortex, and perirhinal cortex, as compared to age-matched controls. Most importantly, the analysis demonstrated the near-complete elimination of the hippocampus bilaterally.

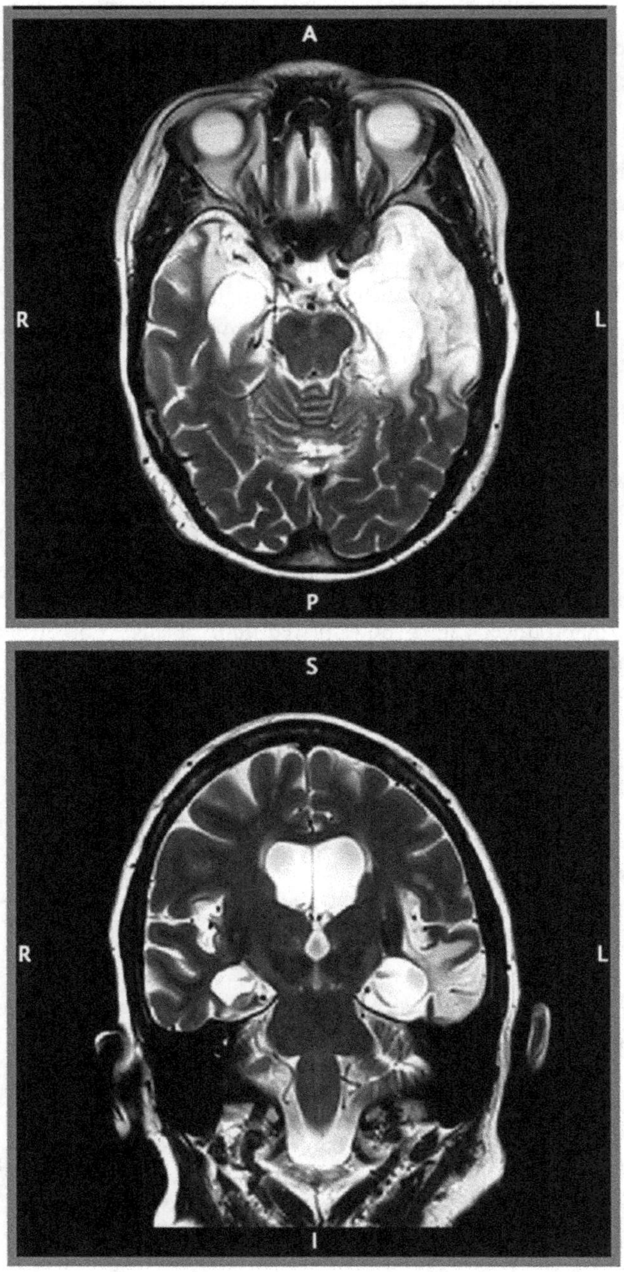

FIGURE 1 | Magnetic resonance images of patient LSJ's brain: axial (Top) and coronal (Bottom) view.

LSJ's general intellectual capabilities are largely spared, and her speech production, comprehension, reading, and visuo-spatial skills are intact or nearly so [see **Table 2**; for full neuropsychological profile see Gregory et al. (2014)]. On the Wechsler Adult Intelligence Scale IV (Wechsler, 2008), she scored at the 30th percentile. Her single-word reading and spelling were in the normal range, 58th percentile and 55th percentile, respectively, on the Wide Range Achievement Test III (Wilkinson, 1993), and her vocabulary score was at the 63rd percentile on the Peabody Picture

Table 1 | Remaining brain volume in patient LSJ by MTL region (Schapiro et al., 2014).

MTL region	Remaining volume relative to age-matched controls ($N = 4$)	
	Left (%)	**Right (%)**
Hippocampus	4	0
Parahippocampal cortex	12	62
Entorhinal cortex	0	43
Perirhinal cortex	2	50

Table 2 | LSJ's performance on the WAIS-IV, WMS-III, and MBEA [for full neuropsychological test profile see Gregory et al. (2014)].

Test	Score	
Wechsler Adult Intelligence Scale IV (WAIS-IV)		
Full scale	92 (30th percentile)	
Verbal comprehension	96 (39th percentile)	
Perceptual reasoning	104 (55th percentile)	
Working memory	83 (13th percentile)	
Processing speed	86 (18th percentile)	
Wechsler Memory Scale III (WMS-III)		
Auditory immediate	56 (0.2 percentile)	Impaired
Visual immediate	57 (0.2 percentile)	Impaired
Immediate memory	47 (<0.1 percentile)	Impaired
Auditory delayed	58 (0.3 percentile)	Impaired
Visual delayed	56 (0.2 percentile)	Impaired
Auditory recognition delayed	55 (0.1 percentile)	Impaired
General memory	47 (<0.1 percentile)	Impaired
Working memory	76 (5 percentile)	Impaired
Montreal Battery of Evaluation of Amusia (MBEA)		
Scale	25	Pass
Contour	25	Pass
Interval	27	Pass
Rhythm	26	Pass
Meter	28	Pass
Incidental	16	Fail

Vocabulary Test-Revised (Dunn and Dunn, 1981). On the Boston Naming Test (Kaplan et al., 1983), she scored 49/60, at the low end of the normal range (49–59). In tests of visuo-spatial abilities, her performance was in the normal range on the Visual and Object Space Perception Battery (Warrington and James, 1991), and on the Block Design and Matrix Reasoning subtests on the WAIS-IV.

In sharp contrast to her largely preserved general intellectual functions, LSJ presents with extremely profound retrograde and anterograde amnesia (Gregory et al., 2014; Schapiro et al., 2014). Anecdotally, she does not seem to recognize any of our research team, despite having seen us many times; she shows no recollection of tasks she has completed only moments before; and she seems to lose awareness for everyday events very shortly after they have occurred. On the Wechsler Memory Scale III (Wechsler, 1997), she scored below the 0.1 percentile on the General Memory index, with performance severely impaired on all subscales except for working memory, which showed milder impairment (see **Table 2**). On the Warrington Recognition Memory Test (Warrington, 1984), she performed at chance for both words (26/50) and faces (28/50). Her direct copy of the Rey–Osterrieth figure was normal (34/36), but she scored 0/36 on a recall test after a 10-min delay. Her performance was impaired in tasks requiring statistical learning, the ability to extract regularities in the co-occurrence of items in sequences of shapes, syllables, scenes, or tones (Schapiro et al., 2014).

Thorough interviews with LSJ failed to show memory for even a single specific episode from her life before her illness. For example, she was unable to remember anything from her 10-year marriage including the day she married or was divorced, and even seemed uncertain as to whether she had ever been married. Gregory et al. (2014) found that her retrograde memory impairment extends across not only autobiographical and episodic memory, but also everyday general world knowledge and pre-morbid areas of expertise. Gregory et al. (2014) examined LSJ's memory for a range of everyday general world knowledge domains, including company names for commercial logos, events associated with everyday songs (e.g., New Year's with *Auld Lang Syne*), and commonly known facts about sports. LSJ performed far below the level of age- and education-matched controls in both cued recall and forced choice tests. She was also severely impaired relative to controls in tests of visual art and music knowledge, despite her extensive pre-morbid knowledge in those areas. She performed poorly in recalling or selecting the artists of famous paintings (e.g., Monet for *Waterlilies*), and she was unable to name the composer for any of the 61 clips from famous classical pieces (e.g., *Eine Kleine Nachtmusik*). When asked to choose the composer from three alternatives, she performed at chance.

Despite these broad and extensive memory impairments, many of LSJ's musical abilities appear to be preserved. On the Montreal Battery of Evaluation of Amusia (Peretz et al., 2003), she scored in the normal range on all subtests except the memory test (see **Table 2**). In a task constructed to assess her knowledge of musical symbols, she exhibited difficulties in verbally naming key signatures (4/26 trials correct) and notes and rests according to their duration (e.g., "a quarter-note," "a whole rest"; 12/24 and 5/16 trials correct, respectively), but was quite accurate at naming note pitches (88/96 trials correct), clefs (4/4 trials correct), the number of beats designated by note and rest durations (10/12 and 6/8 trials correct, respectively), and the pitches designated as sharps or flats by different key signatures (11/14). We are not able to determine whether her sight-reading or music performance skills are at her pre-morbid level, but when presented with sight-reading material on the viola at an easy to medium-level, she performs fluently and with expression. In performance, she exhibits no difficulty in understanding musical notation, either in the treble or the alto clef.

STIMULI, DESIGN, PROCEDURE, AND ANALYSES

Stimuli

To investigate LSJ's ability to learn through performance, three novel pieces of viola music were composed (A, B, and C) in a semiclassical style. To make the three pieces as comparable as possible, care was taken to control for various factors that contribute to a piece's complexity. For example, on a string instrument, a piece that requires frequent changes in hand position is considerably more difficult to sight-read than a piece that can be played throughout in first position. Similarly, it is important to control for the occurrences of specific musical events such as accidentals (sharps or flats outside the piece's key signature) or double-stops (two notes played simultaneously on two strings), because such events add to the cognitive processing load during sight-reading and often are, as in the case of double-stops, technically more difficult to play than single notes.

Therefore, across the three composed pieces, the following factors were closely matched (see **Tables 3** and **4**): piece length (both in measures and individual notes), key signature, time signature, note durations, double-stops and their durations, accidentals, clef changes, notes played in each of two clefs (alto and treble), harmonics (notes played by barely touching the string with the left-hand finger), slurs (notes played under a single bow stroke) and type of notes within slurs, notes played using the fourth finger, anticipated string crossings, anticipated hand position changes,

Table 3 | Number of notes by duration and clef in the pieces used in the experiment.

Note type	Piece		
	A	B	C
Dotted quarter notes	1	1	1
Eighth notes	145	145	145
Half notes	15	15	15
Quarter notes	80	78	80
Quarter triplets	6	6	6
Whole notes	1	1	1
Total	248	247	248
Quarter notes in treble clef	8	8	8
Half notes in treble clef	4	4	4
Eighth notes in treble clef	16	16	16
Total number of notes in treble clef	28	28	28
Total number of notes in alto clef	220	219	220
Total	248	247	248

Table 4 | Type and number of other musical events matched across pieces in the pieces used in the experiment.

Musical event	Piece		
	A	B	C
Quarter-note double-stops	4	4	4
Half-note double-stops	6	6	6
Eighth-note double-stops	2	2	2
A# accidentals	1	1	1
D# accidentals	3	3	3
Bb accidentals	2	2	2
Quarter-note slurs	6	6	6
Eighth-note slurs	52	52	52
Harmonics	2	1	1
Notes played with 4th finger	6	6	5
String crossings	119	119	119
Hand position shifts	4	4	4
Notes played in third position	24	24	21

and the number of notes played in each of the two anticipated hand positions.

All three pieces were composed so that they could be played on the viola in their entirety in the first and third positions. The number of anticipated position changes was matched by assuming that a violist will play in first position unless forced to move, and by introducing across the three pieces the same number of high notes that cannot be played in first position on the highest string (thereby forcing the performer to move up to third position for these notes). As shown in **Table 4**, hand position changes were anticipated to occur four times in each piece, with the largest part of the composition assumed to be played in first position.

The number of string crossings and use of the fourth finger were matched by assuming that a violist will only cross strings when necessary and, in a passage of running eighth notes, will use the fourth finger instead of playing an open string. It was also assumed that the violist will use each finger to play only a certain note in a given position, and elect to use the fourth finger only for the notes assigned to it in that position.

Although homogenous in all these respects, the three pieces sounded distinct. Within the same key signature, Piece A focused harmonically on the D major pentatonic, Piece B on D major, and Piece C on B minor (the relative minor of D major, sharing the same key signature). The pieces were all composed to conform to general conventions of Western classical tonal music. That is, they contained no deliberate violations of typical expectations an experienced performer would have of tonal or harmonic structure, meter, phrasing, or fingerings (for the sheet music and computer software performances of all three pieces, see Supplementary Material).

Design and procedure

LSJ practiced playing two of the pieces on the viola in two different sessions during the same day: Piece A was practiced in Session 1, and Piece B in Session 2 (see **Figure 2**). Piece C was not practiced and therefore served as a control for the other two.

During each practice session, LSJ completed 32 practice trials in which she played the material on the viola from the sheet music. The practice sessions were designed to model how a musician might rehearse a novel piece of music: the material was played at increasing tempos across a practice session, and included short segments as well as the whole piece.

In nine of the practice trials in each session, LSJ played the piece in its entirety at varying tempos controlled with a metronome: once at 96 bpm, once at 108 bpm, four times at 120 bpm, and three times at 144 bpm. Interspersed with the full-piece practice trials were 23 practice trials in which LSJ played short (4–9 bar) pre-specified segments of the piece at the different tempos. Each practice session lasted approximately an hour (62 and 69 min for sessions 1 and 2, respectively).

Test trials, in which LSJ played all three pieces in their entirety at 144 bpm, were administered immediately before and after each practice session and once again after a 14-day delay.

In all practice and test trials, LSJ was presented with sheet music and instructed to play it to the best of her ability, without interruption, and in time with the metronome. Before beginning, she was asked to play an unrelated piece from sheet music to warm-up. A professionally trained musician tuned LSJ's viola before each practice session.

On each of her many encounters with a piece, LSJ showed no awareness of having seen the piece before. In fact, she made the same humorous remark related to the pieces' title nearly every time she was presented with the sheet music, suggesting that she had no recollection either of having seen the sheet music before or of having made the same comment about it. Although LSJ generally performed the music willingly and seemed to enjoy playing, occasionally she expressed her discontent with being asked to play such difficult new material at a tempo she felt was too fast. She repeatedly indicated that she was playing the material for the very first time, even on the last test trials after repeated performances of all pieces. On these occasions, she was encouraged to do the best she could.

Since the time of her illness, LSJ has played the viola only occasionally. In the months prior to our study, she played for short periods several times per week, in the company of a family member.

Analyses

LSJ's test trial performance was evaluated via two methods: note-by-note analyses and subjective performance ratings by experienced string players.

Note-by-note analyses. Two independent coders counted the number of individual notes LSJ played correctly with respect to pitch, relative rhythm, note duration, and metronome-dictated tempo. One point was awarded for every correctly played note, and zero points were given for notes in which any of the above aspects were incorrect. In pitch, notes were allowed to deviate from the written notation by one half of a semitone or less to be considered correct. In rhythm and tempo, notes played slightly ahead or behind the beat were scored as correct, but those more than a half-beat off or in a clearly wrong rhythmic pattern or duration were scored as incorrect.

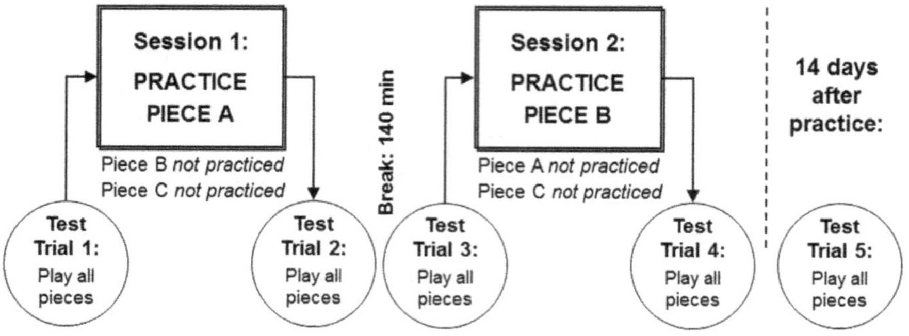

FIGURE 2 | Two practice sessions were conducted during the same day, in which LSJ practiced two pieces on the viola. Piece A was practiced in Session 1, and Piece B in Session 2. LSJ's performance on all pieces was evaluated at a tempo of 144 bpm in test trials before and after each practice session, and 14 days after practice.

One exception was made to the general scoring rule. As meter is temporally and hierarchically organized, a single rhythmic error can cause all subsequent notes to align incorrectly to the originally established meter, yielding a score of zero for all notes afterward. This occurs, for example, every time the performer misses or skips a beat, or plays an extraneous note. To avoid penalizing all consecutive notes because of a single error, coders identified the first run of four consecutive correctly played notes after such errors. This four-note run was used to establish a new meter with respect to the metronome, and coding was resumed from (and including) this four-note string. These four notes had to be correct in both pitch and rhythm and in synchrony with the metronome.

The coders were both skilled amateur musicians. The first coder was one of the authors (Jussi Valtonen), who was blind to test trial, but not to which pieces had been practiced. The second scorer was blind to both test trial and practiced pieces, and was otherwise not involved with the study. For all test trial performances, the two coders scored all notes in order from audio recordings of intact whole performances. The performances were scored in three blocks, with all test trials for one piece in one block. The order of the blocks and the order of test trial performances within each block were randomized for each of the two coders. Mean inter-rater reliability was 0.88 (0.87, 0.86, and 0.90 for Pieces A, B, and C, respectively). All discrepancies in coding were discussed and resolved between the two coders, and the resolved scorings were used for final analyses.

Subjective performance ratings. Subjective performance ratings were collected from six string instrumentalists, all blind to both test trial and to which pieces had been practiced. All raters were professional musicians or music students who had either the viola ($n = 4$) or the violin ($n = 2$) as their main instrument (mean number of years played 13.7; range 9–22). The raters were recruited from the Johns Hopkins Peabody Conservatory, where they pursued or had completed an undergraduate or graduate degree in viola or violin performance or had music as a minor subject. All raters reported prior experience in evaluating musical performances, either through formal music training, through teaching, or both.

The raters evaluated all LSJ's test trial performances on a 1–5 scale according to four qualitative dimensions of musical performance. Based on previous research (Zdzinski and Barnes, 2002), we chose three dimensions that form separate factors in string performance ratings: (1) *intonation*, reflecting pitch accuracy and the degree to which the pitches sound correct in context (1 = most pitches are out of tune, 5 = virtually all pitches are accurate, with virtually no adjustments needed to fix them), (2) *rhythm*, reflecting the rhythmic accuracy of executed patterns and how accurately they match the sheet music (1 = most rhythmic patterns are incorrect, 5 = virtually all rhythmic patterns are accurate), and (3) *tone*, reflecting the quality of sound in the played notes (1 = sound is unfocused, making it difficult to discern many notes, 5 = sound is clear, focused, and warm virtually throughout). In addition, the musicians were instructed to evaluate the performance (4) *overall*, taking into account all relevant aspects of skilled musical performance (values 1–5 were left for the rater to specify).

Before evaluating LSJ's performances, the raters were given the sheet music and familiarized themselves with the pieces by playing them on their own instrument. They also heard computer performances of each piece. Because the exact criteria and degree of precision required for an accurate performance are a matter of subjective opinion, and the relative weight given to expressive nuances will vary among raters, we attempted to calibrate different rating expectations before evaluations of test trials. To this end, the raters heard a recording of an error-free performance by LSJ of an unrelated song that she knows well. The raters were instructed to consider this performance as qualifying for a rating of 5 on the five-point scale.

Audio recordings of LSJ's test trial performances were presented to each rater in three blocks, with all test trials of one piece in one block. The order of blocks and the order of trials within each block were randomized across raters.

All raters provided written informed consent. LSJ provided oral assent, and her legal guardian provided written consent for her. The study protocol was approved by the Homewood Institutional Review Board at Johns Hopkins University.

RESULTS

NOTE-BY-NOTE SCORES

Note-by-note scorings of LSJ's viola performances showed that as expected, all three pieces were initially challenging for her to sight-read at the designated tempo. In her first test trial performances, before any pieces had been practiced, the mean percentage of correctly played notes across the three pieces was 29%, showing that the complexity of the sight-reading material clearly exceeded her capabilities at the requested tempo. Qualitatively, her performances in all trials included several temporal breakdowns and violations of the underlying beat, demonstrating that she was unable to maintain the expected temporal continuity in performance.

As all pieces were performed in five test trials, some improvement could potentially be expected to occur overall, merely as a function of repeated test trial performances and regardless of piece type. Learning effects resulting from training on Pieces A and B should be revealed by greater improvement for those pieces than for the unpracticed Piece C. In particular, we expected learning effects to be revealed by a positive linear trend that is larger for practiced than unpracticed pieces. In addition, we might also expect to see a quadratic trend, reflecting a plateauing of scores from Test Trial 4 to Test Trial 5, as no additional training took place over the delay.

To investigate potential learning in LSJ's performance, we compared three critical trials: Test Trial 1, administered before any pieces had been practiced, Test Trial 4, administered on the same day after both target pieces had been practiced, and Test Trial 5, administered 14 days after practice (see **Figure 2**). Because potential learning effects were expected to be similar for both practiced pieces, the data were collapsed across Pieces A and B and compared to the unpracticed Piece C.

As shown in **Figure 3**, the targeted learning effects can be seen very clearly in these trials. Overall, the mean percentages of correct notes increased across pieces from 29% in Test Trial 1 to 61% in Test Trial 5. A repeated-measures ANOVA (2 piece types × 3 test trials) showed a significant main effect of piece type [practiced versus unpracticed; $F(1,246) = 71.23$, $p < 0.001$], a significant main effect of test trial [$F(2,492) = 111.95$, $p < 0.001$], and a significant interaction [$F(2,492) = 19.58$, $p < 0.001$]. For the main effect of test trial, there was a significant linear trend across trials [$F(1,246) = 161.38$, $p < 0.001$], reflecting an overall improvement in note scores from Test Trial 1 to 5. The quadratic trend was also significant [$F(1,246) = 44.06$, $p < 0.001$], reflecting the increase in note scores immediately after practice (between Test Trials 1 and 4) followed by plateauing across the 14-day delay (from Test Trial 4 to 5).

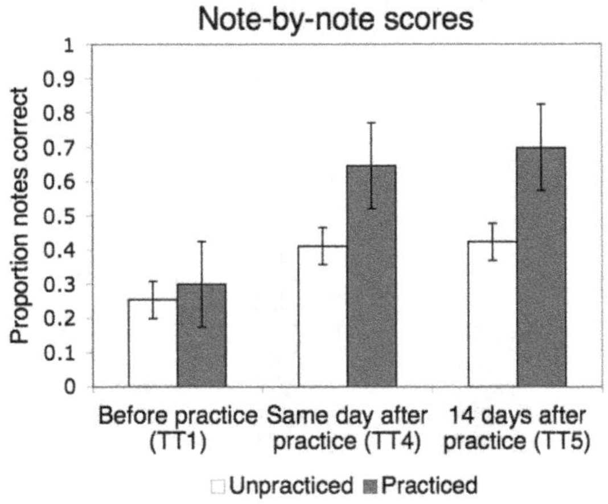

FIGURE 3 | Mean proportion of correctly played notes in LSJ's sight-reading performances on the viola before practice, after practice on the same day, and after a 14-day delay (Test Trials 1, 4, and 5, respectively). Results have been collapsed across the two practiced pieces, Piece A and Piece B. Error bars represent standard error of the mean.

Critically, the improvement in LSJ's performance was more pronounced in the practiced pieces relative to the unpracticed piece in both the linear and the quadratic trends, $F(1,246) = 43.66$, $p < 0.001$ and $F(1,246) = 3.95$, $p < 0.05$, respectively. As can be seen in **Figure 3**, note scores improved after practice both for unpracticed and practiced pieces, but this improvement was larger for the practiced pieces. The learning was also retained during the 14-day delay: as shown in the figure, the note scores for Test Trial 5 stayed almost exactly at the level of Test Trial 4 for both practiced and unpracticed pieces, but were higher for practiced pieces (mean scores 70 and 43% for practiced and unpracticed pieces, respectively, in Test Trial 5). The scores for practiced and unpracticed pieces improved by 40 versus 17 percentage points from Test Trial 1 to 5, respectively.

The learning effects observed in the analyses are also apparent when we examine the results for the individual pieces on each test trial (see **Table 5**). After each practice session, the piece practiced in that session showed the largest performance improvement. After Session 1, in which Piece A was practiced, the note-by-note score improved by 27 percentage points for piece A, versus 18 and 19 percentage points for pieces B and C, respectively. After Session 2, in which Piece B was practiced, Piece B showed a 36 percentage-point improvement, versus a 24 percentage-point improvement for Piece A and a 6 percentage-point decline for Piece C. After a piece was practiced, performance on that piece remained relatively stable. For example, the note score for Piece A immediately after practice was 66%, and remained high (76%) 2 weeks later. Similarly, the score for Piece B was 70% immediately after practice, and 64% after 2 weeks. The sole exception to this pattern was LSJ's poor score (35%) for Piece A on Test Trial 3 (the Session 2 pre-test immediately prior to practice on Piece B). On this particular trial, LSJ decided, either deliberately or by accident, to play most of the piece in half tempo, yielding a score of zero for all the corresponding notes. On the remaining test trials (Trials 4 and 5), her performance on Piece A was again much better (for a

Table 5 | Mean percentages of notes according to piece and test trial.

Test trial	Piece A correct (%)	Piece B correct (%)	Piece C correct (%)
1. Before practice	39	21	26
2. After practicing A	66	39	45
3. Before practicing B	35	34	47
4. After practicing B	59	70	41
5. After 14-day delay	76	64	43

Piece A was practiced between trials 1 and 2, and Piece B between trials 3 and 4. Piece C was not practiced.

figure showing note scores on all three pieces in all test trials, see Supplementary Material).

SUBJECTIVE PERFORMANCE RATINGS

Learning of the practiced pieces was also evident in the subjective performance ratings by string players (**Figure 4**). Mean ratings of overall musical performance increased across all pieces from 2.72 before practice to 3.39 immediately after practice, and ratings of intonation, rhythm, and tone from 3.11 to 3.44, from 2.56 to 3.50, and from 3.17 to 3.44, respectively. As illustrated in **Figure 4**, effects of learning for the practiced pieces can be seen in the ratings in all four dimensions.

As with note-by-note scores, the results were analyzed for the critical three test trials most comparable to each other, Test Trials 1, 4, and 5, with the data collapsed across the two practiced pieces. Separate repeated-measures ANOVAs (2 piece types × 3 test trials) revealed a significant main effect of test trial in all rating dimensions: intonation [$F(2,10) = 9.07$, $p < 0.01$], rhythm [$F(2,10) = 6.52$, $p < 0.05$], tone [$F(2,10) = 6.49$, $p < 0.05$], and overall ratings [$F(2,10) = 8.72$, $p < 0.01$], showing that performance ratings improved across test trials. The main effect of piece type (practiced versus unpracticed) was also significant for intonation [$F(1,5) = 17.1$, $p < 0.01$], tone [$F(1,5) = 7.66$, $p < 0.05$] and overall ratings [$F(1,5) = 13.35$, $p < 0.05$].

Most importantly, the interaction between piece type and test trial was significant in ratings of intonation [$F(2,10) = 6.150$, $p < 0.05$] and tone [$F(2,10) = 10.181$, $p < 0.01$], showing that practice had affected the ratings differently in the practiced pieces relative to the unpracticed piece in these dimensions. The interaction also approached significance in overall ratings [$F(2,10) = 3.545$, $p = 0.069$], but was not significant in rhythm ratings [$F(2,10) = 1.746$, $p = 0.224$]. For intonation and tone, ratings for the practiced pieces improved after practice and stayed the same or slightly declined over the 14-day delay, whereas ratings for the unpracticed piece showed less or no improvement and a marked decline over the delay [$F(1,5) = 9.494$, $p < 0.05$ and $F(1,5) = 16.304$, $p < 0.01$ for linear trend in practiced versus unpracticed pieces in intonation and tone ratings, respectively].

The pattern revealed by these analyses can also be seen in the ratings for the individual pieces on each test trial (see **Table 6**). After each practice session, the practiced piece showed the greatest improvement in ratings on each dimension, and thereafter showed better performance than the unpracticed piece.

DISCUSSION

We examined the learning of novel pieces of viola music by a newly identified amnesic patient who has bilateral MTL damage involving near-complete destruction of the hippocampus. Despite

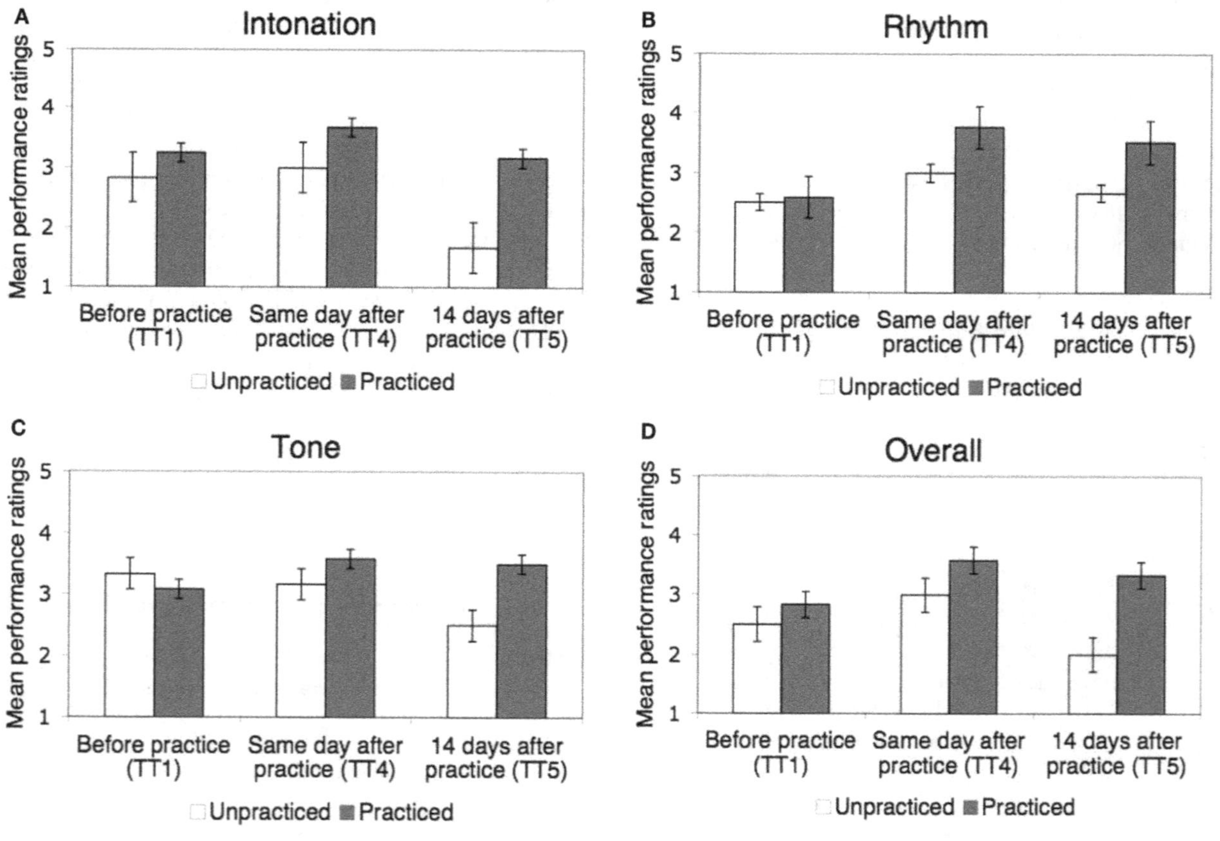

FIGURE 4 | LSJ's music performance on practiced and unpracticed pieces before and after practice on the same day and after a 14-day delay (Test Trials 1, 4, and 5, respectively) as evaluated by experienced string players. Performance was evaluated on a 1–5 scale separately for intonation **(A)**, rhythm **(B)**, tone **(C)**, and overall **(D)**. Results were collapsed across the two practiced pieces, Piece A and Piece B. Error bars represent standard errors of the mean.

Table 6 | Mean performance ratings for all evaluated performance dimensions according to piece and test trial.

Performance dimension	Test trial	Piece A	Piece B	Piece C
Intonation	1	2.83	3.67	2.83
	2	3.33	3.00	2.50
	3	3.33	2.67	2.67
	4	3.17	4.17	3.00
	5	3.33	3.00	1.67
Rhythm	1	2.83	2.33	2.50
	2	4.00	2.83	2.33
	3	2.83	2.17	2.67
	4	3.67	3.83	3.00
	5	4.33	2.67	2.67
Tone	1	3.17	3.00	3.33
	2	3.67	2.83	2.50
	3	3.50	2.83	2.67
	4	3.17	4.00	3.17
	5	3.83	3.17	2.50
Overall	1	2.83	2.83	2.50
	2	3.83	3.00	2.67
	3	3.17	2.17	2.67
	4	3.17	4.00	3.00
	5	3.67	3.00	2.00

Piece A was practiced between trials 1 and 2, and Piece B between trials 3 and 4. Piece C was not practiced.

her extreme anterograde amnesia and lack of recollection of having played the pieces, LSJ's performance improved for two pieces after practice relative to an unpracticed control piece[2]. These performance improvements were evident both in detailed note-by-note analyses, and in string instrumentalists' subjective ratings of whole-piece performances. Moreover, learning was apparent not only on the day of practice but also 14 days later. As LSJ has virtually no remaining hippocampal tissue, these results show that learning to perform new music can occur in the absence of the hippocampus. Although two previous studies have investigated music learning in patients with MTL damage, the underspecification of the patients' hippocampal damage makes the implications unclear, as it is impossible to rule out the contribution of remaining hippocampal tissue to learning. To our knowledge, our study is the first demonstration that non-hippocampal structures alone can support learning for music performance through sight-reading.

That such a complex learning process is possible without the hippocampus is somewhat surprising, given that the hippocampus is essential for memory functions that likely contribute to the learning process in neurologically intact musicians. For example, prior research has shown that the hippocampus is critical for both single item and associative declarative memory (Squire et al., 2004), and is engaged during the implicit learning of temporal-motor sequences (Schendan et al., 2003; Robertson, 2007; Gheysen et al., 2010). While the hippocampus is important in the normal process through which music is learned, our results suggest that non-hippocampal structures also can play a critical role.

The contrast between the learning observed in this study and LSJ's learning impairments in other tasks is remarkable: for example, LSJ fails to show statistical learning (Schapiro et al., 2014), which occurs largely automatically and implicitly in healthy adults (Kim et al., 2009). In the three experiments conducted by Schapiro et al. (2014), LSJ was passively exposed to visual shapes, spoken syllables, visual scenes, or auditory tones in sequences that contained temporal regularities. In contrast to control participants, she showed no ability to detect the regularities in any of the sequences. In addition, with regard to declarative memory, LSJ's ability to acquire new information is minimal and requires massive training. When trained on six commercial logos and their corresponding company names and product categories, LSJ showed very little learning after 114 practice sessions, totaling nearly 30 h of training (Gregory et al., 2013). In comparison, the learning effects observed in the current study were achieved rapidly, with only an hour of practice for each of the two pieces. On the other hand, however, LSJ's implicit learning abilities are not generally preserved for all music-related tasks: LSJ is also impaired at the MBEA incidental memory test (Peretz et al., 2003), a yes/no recognition task that probes familiarity for melodies presented in earlier tasks of the assessment battery. This finding, from a task that is arguably much simpler than the one used in the current study, suggests that LSJ's profound learning deficits extend also to measures of implicit learning in music perception, and stands in contrast to the learning seen in the current music performance experiment.

LSJ's learning of new musical pieces may be possible in part because musical performance is likely to draw on many different cognitive functions that may be supported by non-hippocampal structures, including those that were left intact after her illness. For example, learning new musical pieces might engage implicit learning mechanisms, which have been argued to be distributed across different brain regions (Reber, 2013)[3]. Playing an instrument requires processing information simultaneously from the visual, auditory, and tactile modalities and from sensory organs in muscles, tendons, joints, and skin (Sloboda, 1984; Palmer, 1997, 2006;

[2]It should be noted that note scores also improved for the unpracticed piece, albeit less markedly than for the pieces targeted for practice. As LSJ was exposed to the unpracticed control piece five times in the course of the experiment, the results may reflect improvement through the same learning mechanism as with the practiced pieces, merely to a lesser extent.

[3]It is important to note that the broad term implicit learning can refer to many distinct processes. While many amnesic patients with hippocampal damage have shown normal or near-normal learning in several implicit learning and implicit memory tasks (Corkin, 1968; Reber and Squire, 1994; Stefanacci et al., 2000; Verfaelllie et al., 2012; Eichenbaum, 2013; Reber, 2013), the evidence is mixed. Implicit learning is not always intact in amnesic patients (Cohen et al., 1997; Curran, 1997; Channon et al., 2002), and at least some forms of implicit learning do seem to depend on the hippocampus (Chun and Phelps, 1999; Squire and Knowlton, 2000). Determining the precise contribution of the hippocampus for implicit learning processes is difficult because measures of implicit learning often also recruit explicit memory processes (Gabrieli, 1998). An exhaustive review of these findings is beyond the scope of this paper, as our goal was to investigate whether the hippocampus is necessary for the learning of new music.

Altenmüller and Schneider, 2009; Chaffin et al., 2009). The correct note sequences have to be executed in concert with emotional processing and considerations for esthetic and musical expression. Neurally, areas that could support these functions are likely to encompass much of the brain, ranging from regions related to basic visual object recognition and sensorimotor functions to several separate pathways projecting from the primary auditory cortices to various targets (Peretz and Zatorre, 2005; Zatorre et al., 2007; Altenmüller and Schneider, 2009). With regard to specific aspects of music performance, several cortical and sub-cortical regions have been implicated in prior research. For example, controlling timing has been linked to the cerebellum, basal ganglia, and the supplementary motor area, while controlling aspects of rhythm has been connected to the dorsal premotor cortex, lateral cerebellar hemispheres, and prefrontal cortex. The inferior frontal regions have been implicated with retrieval processes from long-term representations [for reviews, see Janata and Grafton (2003), Peretz and Zatorre (2005), Zatorre et al. (2007), and Levitin and Tirovolas (2009)]. Conceivably, the recruitment of such a wide range of interconnected cortical and sub-cortical neural functions could support LSJ's new learning of musical pieces. Moreover, while virtually all of LSJ's hippocampal tissue has been destroyed, some tissue remains in her MTL (i.e., 40–60% of tissue in parahippocampal, entorhinal, and perirhinal cortices), and it is possible that this remaining tissue is contributing to learning.

LSJ not only learned new musical pieces within the practice sessions but also showed retention of the learning over a 14-day period. This result raises the question of how long-term memories can be preserved in the absence of the hippocampus. Some types of implicit learning can be retained for remarkably long time periods even in amnesic patients, including those with hippocampal damage (Gabrieli et al., 1993; Hayman et al., 1993; Hamann and Squire, 1995; Corkin, 2002). However, previous work has also indicated that the hippocampus is important for how declarative memories are stabilized or otherwise remain accessible over time (Nadel and Moscovitch, 1997; Squire et al., 2004; Bontempi and Frankland, 2005; Nadel and Peterson, 2013), and that the hippocampus is involved in memory consolidation for implicitly learned temporal-motor sequences (Albouy et al., 2008, 2013a,b). Our results suggest that structures outside of the hippocampus can support at least some of the processes by which memory representations for music performance are retained over time. Future research will be needed to shed light on how this occurs.

While music performance has at times been described as a case of "procedural," "non-declarative," or "motor" learning, we argued earlier that the learning of new musical pieces for performance is likely to go beyond what Stanley and Krakauer (2013) refer to as improved motor acuity. The current study and its results would also seem to support this suggestion. For one, the pieces did not pose novel motor acuity challenges for LSJ – for example, through exceptionally inconvenient fingerings or atypical position shifts – but rather asked her to carry out well-learned movements associated with familiar notes (although in novel sequences). In contrast, the pieces did pose cognitive challenges: even after practice, there were frequent occurrences of temporal discontinuities such as interruptions, temporal breakdowns, pauses, hesitations, and violations of the underlying beat. As Drake and Palmer (2000) point out, pauses and other forms of temporal disruption are considered a measure of cognitive load, both in music production and in other complex sequence planning tasks such as speech. Thus, there was considerable room for improvement in LSJ's ability to cope with the excessive cognitive load, and this – and not motor acuity – is likely where her learning occurred.

It is, of course, possible that LSJ also improved in motor acuity (for example, in the sequence-specific transitions between adjacent notes in these unique compositions), but this was not measured by our methods. Our methods focused on her acquisition of note accuracy, intonation, rhythm, and tone, and measured her ability to process written notation in order to execute the corresponding motor responses. In the note scores, notes counted as correct were as far as halfway between the correct and the adjacent pitch and therefore, notes counted as incorrect were very clearly off target or parts of long sequences she was not able to attempt to play at all. Her scores for correct notes increased from 30 to 70% on the practiced pieces, an improvement of more than 130%. Improved motor acuity may perhaps have helped move some very incorrectly executed notes to the zone of roughly correct, but it seems highly unlikely that such a large learning effect could be completely accounted for this way.

Many questions remain for future research concerning the specific cognitive and neural mechanisms underlying learning for music performance in LSJ and neurologically intact individuals. First, the current experiment did not assess one, specific cognitive ability, or even a collection of them that could be precisely specified. While many of the cognitive processes that underlie music performance have been identified in behavioral studies (e.g., Sloboda, 1985; Palmer, 2006), more theoretical and empirical work is needed to fully decompose the cognitive processes involved and their neural substrates. Second, we can ask whether neurologically intact violists with similar expertize would have shown more learning with the same amount of (non-standard) structured practice. Such research would speak regarding which aspects of learning can be supported by non-hippocampal structures and provide further ways to delineate the links between the cognitive and neural aspects of music performance. Third, a direct comparison of a hippocampal amnesic's performances in non-musical motor learning (e.g., the SRT task) and in music performance would shed more light both on the role of the hippocampus in different contexts of complex motor learning and on the different cognitive-motor processes involved in these tasks. In addition, some authors have argued that while acquiring conscious memories of the learning episode depends on the hippocampus, the subjective feeling of familiarity is supported by perirhinal cortex (Corkin, 2002). LSJ's apparent lack of awareness that the same musical material was being presented repeatedly in the practice and test trials suggests that she did not acquire a feeling of familiarity for the pieces, but it would have been interesting to collect familiarity judgments from her over the course of the study.

ACKNOWLEDGMENTS

We thank LSJ and her family for their cooperation and patience that made this study possible. We thank Joel Ramirez for composing the viola pieces used in the study and for help with data preparation for analyses, Erin Mahoney for assistance in note scoring, and James Caracoglia for help in recruiting and testing raters. This research was supported by a grant from the Brain Science Institute of the Johns Hopkins University to Barbara Landau and Michael McCloskey, and by grants from the Emil Aaltonen Foundation and The Finnish Cultural Foundation to Jussi Valtonen.

REFERENCES

Albouy, G., King, B. R., Maquet, P., and Doyon, J. (2013a). Hippocampus and striatum: dynamics and interaction during acquisition and sleep-related motor sequence memory consolidation. *Hippocampus* 23, 985–1004. doi:10.1002/hipo.22183

Albouy, G., Sterpenich, V., Vandewalle, G., Darsaud, A., Gais, S., Rauchs, G., et al. (2013b). Interaction between hippocampal and striatal systems predicts subsequent consolidation of motor sequence memory. *PLoS ONE* **8**:e59490. doi:10.1371/journal.pone.0059490

Albouy, G., Sterpenich, V., Balteau, E., Vandewalle, G., Desseilles, M., Dang-Vu, T., et al. (2008). Both the hippocampus and striatum are involved in consolidation of motor sequence memory. *Neuron* 58, 261–272. doi:10.1016/j.neuron.2008.02.008

Altenmüller, E., and Schneider, S. (2009). "Planning and performance", in *The Oxford Handbook of Music Psychology*, eds S. Hallam, I. Cross, and M. Thaut (Oxford, UK: Oxford University Press), 332–343.

Baur, B., Uttner, I., Ilmberger, J., Fesl, G., and Mai, N. (2000). Music memory provides access to verbal knowledge in a patient with global amnesia. *Neurocase* 6, 415–421. doi:10.1080/13554790008402712

Beatty, W. W., Rogers, C. L., Rogers, R. L., English, S., Testa, J. A., Orbelo, D. M., et al. (1999). Piano playing in Alzheimer's disease: longitudinal study of a single case. *Neurocase* 5, 459–469. doi:10.1080/13554799908402740

Bontempi, B., and Frankland, P. W. (2005). The organization of recent and remote memories. *Nat. Rev. Neurosci.* 6, 119–130. doi:10.1038/nrn1607

Brodsky, W., Kessler, Y., Rubinstein, B., Ginsborg, J., and Henik, A. (2008). The mental representation of music notation: notational audiation. *J. Exp. Psychol. Hum. Percept. Perform.* 34, 427–445. doi:10.1037/0096-1523.34.2.427

Cavaco, S., Feinstein, J. S., van Twillert, H., and Tranel, D. (2012). Musical memory in a patient with severe anterograde amnesia. *J. Clin. Exp. Neuropsychol.* 34, 1089–1100. doi:10.1080/13803395.2012.728568

Chaffin, R., and Imreh, G. (1997). Pulling teeth and torture: musical memory and problem solving. *Thinking Reasoning* 3, 315–336. doi:10.1080/135467897394310

Chaffin, R., and Imreh, G. (2002). Practicing perfection: piano performance as expert memory. *Psychol. Sci.* 13, 342–349. doi:10.1111/j.0956-7976.2002.00462.x

Chaffin, R., Logan, T. R., Begosh, K. T., Cross, I., and Thaut, M. (2009). "Performing from memory," in *The Oxford Handbook of Music Psychology*, ed. S. Hallam (Oxford: Oxford University Press), 352–363.

Channon, S., Shanks, D., Johnstone, T., Vakili, K., Chin, J., and Sinclair, E. (2002). Is implicit learning spared in amnesia? Rule abstraction and item familiarity in artificial grammar learning. *Neuropsychologia* 40, 2185–2197. doi:10.1016/S0028-3932(02)00037-4

Chun, M. M., and Phelps, E. A. (1999). Memory deficits for implicit contextual information in amnesic subjects with hippocampal damage. *Nat. Neurosci.* 2, 844–847. doi:10.1038/12222

Cohen, N. J., Poldrack, R. A., and Eichenbaum, H. (1997). Memory for items and memory for relations in the procedural/declarative memory framework. *Memory* 5, 131–178. doi:10.1080/741941149

Corkin, S. (1968). Acquisition of motor skill after bilateral medial temporal-lobe excision. *Neuropsychologia* 6, 255–265. doi:10.1016/0028-3932(68)90024-9

Corkin, S. (2002). What's new with the amnesic patient H.M.? *Nat. Rev. Neurosci.* 3, 153–160. doi:10.1038/nrn726

Cowles, A., Beatty, W. W., Nixon, S. J., Lutz, L. J., Paulk, J., Paulk, K., et al. (2003). Musical skill in dementia: a violinist presumed to have Alzheimer's disease learns to play a new song. *Neurocase* 9, 493–503. doi:10.1076/neur.9.6.493.29378

Crystal, H. A., Grober, E., and Masur, D. (1989). Preservation of musical memory in Alzheimer's disease. *J. Neurol. Neurosurg. Psychiatr.* 52, 1415–1416. doi:10.1136/jnnp.52.12.1415

Curran, T. (1997). Higher-order associative learning in amnesia: evidence from the serial reaction time task. *J. Cogn. Neurosci.* 9, 522–533. doi:10.1162/jocn.1997.9.4.522

Drake, C., and Palmer, C. (2000). Skill acquisition in music performance: relations between planning and temporal control. *Cognition* 74, 1–32. doi:10.1016/S0010-0277(99)00061-X

Dunn, L. M., and Dunn, L. M. (1981). *Peabody Picture Vocabulary Test-Revised.* Circle Pines, MN: American Guidance Service.

Eichenbaum, H. (2000). A cortical-hippocampal system for declarative memory. *Nat. Rev. Neurosci.* 1, 41–50. doi:10.1038/35036213

Eichenbaum, H. (2013). What H.M. taught us. *J. Cogn. Neurosci.* 25, 14–21. doi:10.1162/jocn_a_00285

Engel, K. C., Flanders, M., and Soechting, J. F. (1997). Anticipatory and sequential motor control in piano playing. *Exp. Brain Res.* 113, 189–199. doi:10.1007/BF02450317

Finney, S. A., and Palmer, C. (2003). Auditory feedback and memory for music performance: sound evidence for an encoding effect. *Mem. Cognit.* 31, 51–64. doi:10.3758/BF03196082

Fornazzari, L., Castle, T., Nadkarni, S., Ambrose, M., Miranda, D., Apanasiewicz, N., et al. (2006). Preservation of episodic musical memory in a pianist with Alzheimer disease. *Neurology* 66, 610–611. doi:10.1212/01.WNL.0000198242.13411.FB

Furneaux, S., and Land, M. F. (1999). The effects of skill on the eye-hand span during musical sight-reading. *Proc. Biol. Sci.* 266, 2435–2440. doi:10.1098/rspb.1999.0943

Gabrieli, J. D. E. (1998). Cognitive neuroscience of human memory. *Annu. Rev. Psychol.* 49, 87–115. doi:10.1146/annurev.psych.49.1.87

Gabrieli, J. D. E., Corkin, S., Mickel, S. F., and Growdon, J. H. (1993). Intact acquisition and long-term retention of mirror-tracing skill in Alzheimer's disease and in global amnesia. *Behav. Neurosci.* 107, 899–910. doi:10.1037/0735-7044.107.6.899

Gheysen, F., Van Opstal, F., Roggeman, C., Van Waelvelde, H., and Fias, W. (2010). Hippocampal contribution to early and later stages of implicit motor sequence learning. *Exp. Brain Res.* 202, 795–807. doi:10.1007/s00221-010-2186-6

Gregory, E., Landau, B., and McCloskey, M. (2013). "Non-hippocampal learning of novel associations and re-learning of previously known associations: evidence from a training study with an amnesic," in *Poster presented at the Psychonomic Society Annual Meeting, Nov. 14–17*, Toronto, CA.

Gregory, E., McCloskey, M., and Landau, B. (2014). Profound loss of general knowledge in retrograde amnesia: evidence from an amnesic artist. *Front. Hum. Neurosci.* **8**:287. doi:10.3389/fnhum.2014.00287

Hamann, S. B., and Squire, L. R. (1995). On the acquisition of new declarative knowledge in amnesia. *Behav. Neurosci.* 109, 1027–1044. doi:10.1037/0735-7044.109.6.1027

Hayman, C. A., Macdonald, C. A., and Tulving, E. (1993). The role of repetition and associative interference in new semantic learning in amnesia: a case experiment. *J. Cogn. Neurosci.* 5, 375–389. doi:10.1162/jocn.1993.5.4.375

Henke, K., Weber, B., Kneifel, S., Wieser, H. G., and Buck, A. (1999). Human hippocampus associates information in memory. *Proc. Natl. Acad. Sci. U.S.A.* 96, 5884–5889. doi:10.1073/pnas.96.10.5884

Insausti, R., Annese, J., Amaral, D. G., and Squire, L. R. (2013). Human amnesia and the medial temporal lobe illuminated by neuropsychological and neurohistological findings for patient E.P. *Proc. Natl. Acad. Sci. U.S.A.* 110, E1953–E1962. doi:10.1073/pnas.1306244110

Janata, P., and Grafton, S. T. (2003). Swinging in the brain: shared neural substrates for behaviors related to sequencing and music. *Nat. Neurosci.* 6, 682–687. doi:10.1038/nn1081

Kaplan, E., Goodglass, H., and Weintraub, S. (1983). *The Boston Naming Test.* Philadelphia: Lea & Febiger.

Kim, R., Seitz, A., Feenstra, H., and Shams, L. (2009). Testing assumptions of statistical learning: is it long-term and implicit? *Neurosci. Lett.* 461, 145–149. doi:10.1016/j.neulet.2009.06.030

Kinsler, V., and Carpenter, R. H. S. (1995). Saccadic eye movements while reading music. *Vision Res.* 35, 1447–1458. doi:10.1016/0042-6989(95)98724-N

Lehmann, A. C., and Kopiez, R. (2009). "Sight-reading," in *The Oxford Handbook of Music Psychology*, eds S. Hallam, I. Cross, and M. Thaut (Oxford, UK: Oxford University Press), 344–351.

Levitin, D. J., and Tirovolas, A. K. (2009). Current advances in the cognitive neuroscience of music. *Ann. N. Y. Acad. Sci.* 1156, 211–231. doi:10.1111/j.1749-6632.2009.04417.x

Meyer, R. K., and Palmer, C. (2003). Temporal and motor transfer in music performance. *Music Percept.* 21, 81–104. doi:10.1525/mp.2003.21.1.81

Milner, B. (1962). "Les troubles de la mémoire accompagnant des lésions hippocampiques bilatérales," in *Physiologie de l'Hippocampe*, ed. P. Passouant (Paris: Centre National de la Recherche Scientifique), 257–272.

Nadel, L., and Moscovitch, M. (1997). Memory consolidation, retrograde amnesia and the hippocampal complex. *Curr. Opin. Neurobiol.* 7, 217–227. doi:10.1016/S0959-4388(97)80010-4

Nadel, L., and Peterson, M. A. (2013). The hippocampus: part of an interactive posterior representational system spanning perceptual and memorial systems. *J. Exp. Psychol. Gen.* 142, 1242–1254. doi:10.1037/a0033690

Nissen, M. J., and Bullemer, P. (1987). Attentional requirements of learning: evidence from performance measures. *Cogn. Psychol.* 19, 1–32. doi:10.1016/0010-0285(87)90002-8

O'Kane, G., Kensinger, E. A., and Corkin, S. (2004). Evidence for semantic learning in profound amnesia: an investigation with patient H.M. *Hippocampus* 14, 417–425. doi:10.1002/hipo.20005

Palmer, C. (1997). Music performance. *Annu. Rev. Psychol.* 48, 115–138. doi:10.1146/annurev.psych.48.1.115

Palmer, C. (2005). Sequence memory in music performance. *Curr. Dir. Psychol. Sci.* 14, 247–250. doi:10.1111/j.0963-7214.2005.00374.x

Palmer, C. (2006). "The nature of memory for music performance skills," in *Music, Motor Control and the Brain*, eds E. Altenmüller, M. Wiesendanger, and J. Kesselring (Oxford: Oxford University Press), 39–53.

Palmer, C., and Meyer, R. K. (2000). Conceptual and motor learning in music performance. *Psychol. Sci.* 11, 63–68. doi:10.1111/1467-9280.00216

Palmer, C., and Pfordresher, P. Q. (2003). Incremental planning in sequence production. *Psychol. Rev.* 110, 683–712. doi:10.1037/0033-295X.110.4.683

Palmer, C., and van de Sande, C. (1993). Units of knowledge in music performance. *J. Exp. Psychol. Learn. Mem. Cogn.* 19, 457–470.

Palmer, C., and van de Sande, C. (1995). Range of planning in music performance. *J. Exp. Psychol. Hum. Percept. Perform.* 21, 947–962. doi:10.1037/0096-1523.21.5.947

Peretz, I., Champod, A. S., and Hyde, K. (2003). Varieties of musical disorders. *Ann. N. Y. Acad. Sci.* 999, 58–75. doi:10.1196/annals.1284.006

Peretz, I., and Zatorre, R. J. (2005). Brain organization for music processing. *Annu. Rev. Psychol.* 56, 89–114. doi:10.1146/annurev.psych.56.091103.070225

Reber, P. J. (2013). The neural basis of implicit learning and memory: a review of neuropsychological and neuroimaging research. *Neuropsychologia* 51, 2026–2042. doi:10.1016/j.neuropsychologia.2013.06.019

Reber, P. J., and Squire, L. R. (1994). Parallel brain systems for learning with and without awareness. *Learn. Mem.* 1, 217–229. doi:10.1101/lm.1.4.217

Reber, P. J., and Squire, L. R. (1998). Encapsulation of implicit and explicit memory in sequence learning. *J. Cogn. Neurosci.* 10, 248–263. doi:10.1162/089892998562681

Robertson, E. M. (2007). The serial reaction time task: implicit motor skill learning? *J. Neurosci.* 27, 10073–10075. doi:10.1523/JNEUROSCI.2747-07.2007

Schapiro, A. C., Gregory, E., Landau, B., McCloskey, M., and Turk-Browne, N. B. (2014). The necessity of the medial temporal lobe for statistical learning. *J. Cogn. Neurosci.* 26, 1736–1747. doi:10.1162/jocn_a_00578

Schendan, H., Searl, M. M., Melrose, R. J., and Stern, C. (2003). An fMRI study of the role of the medial temporal lobe in implicit and explicit sequence learning. *Neuron* 37, 1013–1025. doi:10.1016/S0896-6273(03)00123-5

Scoville, W. B., and Milner, B. (1957). Loss of recent memory after bilateral hippocampal lesions. *J. Neurol. Neurosurg. Psychiatr.* 20, 11–21. doi:10.1136/jnnp.20.1.11

Simmons, A. L. (2012). Distributed practice and procedural memory consolidation in musicians' skill learning. *J. Res. Music Educ.* 59, 357–368. doi:10.1177/0022429411424798

Sloboda, J. A. (1984). Experimental studies of music reading: a review. *Music Percept.* 2, 222–236. doi:10.2307/40285292

Sloboda, J. A. (1985). *The Musical Mind. The Cognitive Psychology of Music.* Oxford: Oxford University Press.

Snyder, B. (2009). "Memory for music," in *The Oxford Handbook of Music Psychology*, eds. S. Hallam, I. Cross and M. Thaut (Oxford: Oxford University Press), 107–118.

Squire, L. R., and Knowlton, B. (2000). "The medial temporal lobe, the hippocampus, and the memory systems of the brain," in *The New Cognitive Neurosciences, Second Edition*, ed. M. S. Gazzaniga (Cambridge, MA: MIT Press), 765–780.

Squire, L. R., Stark, C. E. L., and Clark, R. E. (2004). The medial temporal lobe. *Annu. Rev. Neurosci.* 27, 279–306. doi:10.1146/annurev.neuro.27.070203.144130

Stanley, J., and Krakauer, J. W. (2013). Motor skill depends on knowledge of facts. *Front. Hum. Neurosci.* **7**:503. doi:10.3389/fnhum.2013.00503

Stark, C., Bayley, P. J., and Squire, L. R. (2002). Recognition memory for single items and for associations is similarly impaired following damage to the hippocampal region. *Learn. Mem.* 9, 238–242. doi:10.1101/lm.51802

Stefanacci, L., Buffalo, E. A., Schmolck, H., and Squire, L. R. (2000). Profound amnesia after damage to the medial temporal lobe: a neuroanatomical and neuropsychological profile of patient E.P. *J. Neurosci.* 20, 7024–7036.

Stewart, L. (2005). A neurocognitive approach to music reading. *Ann. N. Y. Acad. Sci.* 1060, 377–386. doi:10.1196/annals.1360.032

van Vugt, F. T., Jabusch, H., and Altenmüller, E. (2012). Fingers phrase music differently: trial-to-trial variability in piano scale playing and auditory perception reveal motor chunking. *Front. Psychol.* **3**:495. doi:10.3389/fpsyg.2012.00495

Verfaelllie, M., LaRocque, K. F., and Keane, M. M. (2012). Intact implicit verbal relational memory in medial temporal lobe amnesia. *Neuropsychologia* 50, 2100–2106. doi:10.1016/j.neuropsychologia.2012.05.011

Verrel, J., Pologe, S., Manselle, W., Lindenberger, U., and Woollacott, M. (2013). Coordination of degrees of freedom and stabilization of task variables in a complex motor skill: expertise-related differences in cello bowing. *Exp. Brain Res.* 224, 323–334. doi:10.1007/s00221-012-3314-2

Warrington, E. K. (1984). *Recognition Memory Test.* Windsor: NFER-Nelson Publishing Company.

Warrington, E. K., and James, M. (1991). *The Visual Object and Space Perception Battery.* Bury St. Edmunds: Thames Valley Test Company.

Watanabe, T., Yagishita, S., and Kikyo, H. (2008). Memory of music: roles of right hippocampus and left inferior frontal gyrus. *Neuroimage* 39, 483–491. doi:10.1016/j.neuroimage.2007.08.024

Wechsler, D. (1997). *Wechsler Memory Scale*, 3rd Edn. San Antonio, TX: Psychological Corporation.

Wechsler, D. (2008). *Wechsler Adult Intelligence Scale*, 4th Edn. San Antonio, TX: Pearson Assessment.

Wilkinson, G. S. (1993). *WRAT3 Wide Range Achievement Test: Administration Manual.* Wilmington, DE: Wide Range, Inc.

Wilson, S. J., and Saling, M. M. (2008). Contributions of the right and left mesial temporal lobes to music memory: evidence from melodic learning difficulties. *Music Percept.* 25, 303–314. doi:10.1525/mp.2008.25.4.303

Zatorre, R. J., Chen, J. L., and Penhune, V. B. (2007). When the brain plays music: auditory-motor interactions in music perception and production. *Nat. Rev. Neurosci.* 8, 547–558. doi:10.1038/nrn2152

Zdzinski, S., and Barnes, G. (2002). Development and validation of a string performance rating scale. *J. Res. Music Educ.* 50, 245–255. doi:10.2307/3345801

17

Structural changes induced by daily music listening in the recovering brain after middle cerebral artery stroke: a voxel-based morphometry study

Teppo Särkämö[1,2]*, Pablo Ripollés[3,4], Henna Vepsäläinen[1], Taina Autti[5], Heli M. Silvennoinen[5], Eero Salli[5], Sari Laitinen[6], Anita Forsblom[7], Seppo Soinila[8] and Antoni Rodríguez-Fornells[3,4,9]

[1] Cognitive Brain Research Unit, Cognitive Science, Institute of Behavioural Sciences, University of Helsinki, Helsinki, Finland
[2] Finnish Centre of Interdisciplinary Music Research, University of Helsinki, Helsinki, Finland
[3] Cognition and Brain Plasticity Group, Bellvitge Biomedical Research Institute (IDIBELL), L'Hospitalet de Llobregat, Barcelona, Spain
[4] Department of Basic Psychology, University of Barcelona, Barcelona, Spain
[5] Department of Radiology, HUS Medical Imaging Center, Helsinki University Central Hospital, University of Helsinki, Helsinki, Finland
[6] Miina Sillanpää Foundation, Helsinki, Finland
[7] Department of Music, University of Jyväskylä, Jyväskylä, Finland
[8] Department of Neurology, Turku University Hospital, Turku, Finland
[9] Institució Catalana de Recerca i Estudis Avançats (ICREA), Barcelona, Spain

Correspondence:
Teppo Särkämö, Cognitive Brain Research Unit, Cognitive Science, Institute of Behavioural Sciences, University of Helsinki, Siltavuorenpenger 1B, P.O. Box 9, Helsinki FI-00014, Finland
e-mail: teppo.sarkamo@helsinki.fi

Music is a highly complex and versatile stimulus for the brain that engages many temporal, frontal, parietal, cerebellar, and subcortical areas involved in auditory, cognitive, emotional, and motor processing. Regular musical activities have been shown to effectively enhance the structure and function of many brain areas, making music a potential tool also in neurological rehabilitation. In our previous randomized controlled study, we found that listening to music on a daily basis can improve cognitive recovery and improve mood after an acute middle cerebral artery stroke. Extending this study, a voxel-based morphometry (VBM) analysis utilizing cost function masking was performed on the acute and 6-month post-stroke stage structural magnetic resonance imaging data of the patients ($n = 49$) who either listened to their favorite music [music group (MG), $n = 16$] or verbal material [audio book group (ABG), $n = 18$] or did not receive any listening material [control group (CG), $n = 15$] during the 6-month recovery period. Although all groups showed significant gray matter volume (GMV) increases from the acute to the 6-month stage, there was a specific network of frontal areas [left and right superior frontal gyrus (SFG), right medial SFG] and limbic areas [left ventral/subgenual anterior cingulate cortex (SACC) and right ventral striatum (VS)] in patients with left hemisphere damage in which the GMV increases were larger in the MG than in the ABG and in the CG. Moreover, the GM reorganization in the frontal areas correlated with enhanced recovery of verbal memory, focused attention, and language skills, whereas the GM reorganization in the SACC correlated with reduced negative mood. This study adds on previous results, showing that music listening after stroke not only enhances behavioral recovery, but also induces fine-grained neuroanatomical changes in the recovering brain.

Keywords: music, speech, stroke, magnetic resonance imaging, voxel-based morphometry, environmental enrichment, neuroplasticity, rehabilitation

INTRODUCTION

During the past 10 years, advanced magnetic resonance imaging (MRI) analysis methods, such as voxel-based morphometry (VBM) and diffusion tensor imaging (DTI), have provided novel information about the dynamics of the structural neuroplastic changes underlying spontaneous recovery and rehabilitation after stroke. Based on longitudinal VBM and DTI studies of stroke patients, the recovery of cognitive and motor deficits is associated with gray matter volume (GMV) changes in many frontal, temporal, cerebellar, and subcortical (e.g., hippocampus) areas (Grau-Olivares et al., 2010; Dang et al., 2013; Fan et al., 2013) as well as changes in the integrity of the white matter (WM) tracts connecting and projecting from these areas (Liang et al., 2008; van Meer et al., 2012; Thiebaut de Schotten et al., 2014). In longitudinal intervention studies, intensive motor rehabilitation using constraint-induced movement therapy (CIMT) has been shown to increase GMV in frontal and parietal sensory–motor areas and in the hippocampus (Gauthier et al., 2008) and intensive aphasia rehabilitation using constraint-induced language therapy (CILT) or melodic intonation therapy (MIT) has been observed to enhance the integrity of the WM tracks connecting frontal and temporal regions (arcuate fasciculus) in the left (Breier et al., 2011) and right (Schlaug et al., 2009) hemispheres, respectively. All in all, these findings suggest that both behavioral recovery and active rehabilitation after stroke are closely linked to fine-grained neuroanatomical changes in the recovering brain. However, very little is known about the wider potential effects of the *recovery environment* on structural brain plasticity after stroke in humans.

Converging evidence from both animal (Johansson, 2004; Nithianantharajah and Hannan, 2006) and human studies (Johansson, 2012; Janssen et al., 2014) indicates that an environmental enrichment (EE), which provides additional sensory, cognitive, motor, and/or social stimulation compared to a standard environment, plays an important role in enhancing behavioral recovery after an acute stroke. In addition, evidence from animal studies suggests that the post-stroke EE can induce a number of cellular and molecular neuroplastic effects in the brain, including increase in dendritic complexity (Biernaskie and Corbett, 2001; Johansson and Belichenko, 2002), neural stem and progenitor cells (Komitova et al., 2005; Matsumori et al., 2006), and neurotrophic and neural growth factor levels (Gobbo and O'Mara, 2004; Söderström et al., 2009), and that these changes are associated with better cognitive or motor recovery. Interestingly, especially a multisensory EE, which includes auditory, visual, and olfactory stimuli, has been found to be effective in improving cognitive and motor recovery and reducing lesion volume (Maegele et al., 2005a,b). Also evidence from developmental animal studies shows that a purely auditory EE, which contains complex sounds or music, can enhance the structure and function of the auditory cortex (Engineer et al., 2004; Bose et al., 2010) as well as improve learning and memory and upregulate various neurotransmitters (e.g., dopamine, glutamate) and neurotrophins associated with them (Sutoo and Akiyama, 2004; Angelucci et al., 2007; Nichols et al., 2007). Overall, these findings indicate that auditory enrichment can be beneficial for the brain and suggest that it could potentially contribute to better cognitive and neural recovery also after stroke.

In the human brain, music and speech constitute the two most complex and versatile auditory stimuli in terms of their acoustic richness and the breadth of the neural networks involved in their perception and learning (Zatorre, 2013). Neuroimaging studies of healthy subjects have demonstrated that music processing engages a vast bilateral network of temporal, frontal, parietal, cerebellar, and limbic/paralimbic areas associated with the perception of complex acoustic features (e.g., melody, rhythm), syntactic and semantic processing, attention and working memory, episodic and semantic memory, motor and rhythm processing, and experiencing emotions and reward (Blood and Zatorre, 2001; Janata et al., 2002a,b; Platel et al., 2003; Koelsch et al., 2004, 2005, 2006; Menon and Levitin, 2005; Bengtsson et al., 2009; Salimpoor et al., 2011, 2013; Alluri et al., 2012; Herdener et al., 2014; for recent reviews see, Koelsch, 2010, 2011; Zatorre, 2013). Evidence from VBM and DTI studies also indicates that frequent musical activities, such as playing an instrument or singing, can lead to long-term structural changes in the brain, especially in frontal, temporal, and parietal areas and in the WM pathways (e.g., corpus callosum, arcuate fasciculus) connecting them (Gaser and Schlaug, 2003; Hyde et al., 2009; Halwani et al., 2011; James et al., 2014). Improvements in attention and executive functioning have also been reported in healthy older adults after regular music playing activities, such as piano playing (Bugos et al., 2007), and one longitudinal study also highlighted the role of playing musical instruments and dancing as leisure activities associated with a reduced risk of developing dementia (Verghese et al., 2003). Regarding the potential rehabilitative use of music after stroke, results from recent clinical studies suggest that active music-based interventions that utilize singing (MIT) or instrument playing (music-supported therapy, MST), can be effective in improving speech and motor recovery through enhancing the functioning and connectivity of temporal auditory and frontal motor areas (Schlaug et al., 2008, 2009; Altenmüller et al., 2009; Rojo et al., 2011; Rodríguez-Fornells et al., 2012; Grau-Sánchez et al., 2013). Very little, however, is known about the potential neuroplastic changes induced by everyday musical activities, such as music listening, after stroke.

Previously, we performed a randomized controlled trial (RCT) concerning the potential rehabilitative effects of an enriched sound environment on stroke recovery. Sixty patients with an acute left ($n = 29$) or right ($n = 31$) hemisphere middle cerebral artery (MCA) brain infarction were randomized to a music group (MG) (daily listening to self-selected music), an audio book group (ABG) (daily listening to self-selected audio books), and a control group (CG) (standard care only) and their recovery was followed for 6 months using behavioral measures (neuropsychological tests and questionnaires on mood), an auditory magnetoencephalography (MEG) measurement, and structural MRI. Fifty-four patients completed the whole 6-month follow-up. Behavioral results showed that verbal memory and focused attention improved more in the MG than in the ABG or CG after the intervention period at the 3-month follow-up and also remained better at the longitudinal 6-month follow-up (Särkämö et al., 2008), suggesting that regular music listening enhanced cognitive recovery. Compared to the CG, the MG also experienced less depressed and confused mood at the 3-month follow-up (Särkämö et al., 2008). MEG results showed that the mismatch negativity (MMN) response to frequency changes strengthened more in the MG and ABG compared to the CG at the 6-month follow-up, indicating that regular exposure to both music and speech enhanced early auditory encoding in the recovering brain (Särkämö et al., 2010a).

In the present study, our aim was to determine with a VBM analysis of the longitudinal structural MRI data (baseline acute stage and 6-month stage) from the same patient sample whether daily music listening could also lead to structural GM and WM reorganization in the brain and if this change would also be related to the previously found positive effects of music on cognitive and emotional recovery after stroke.

MATERIALS AND METHODS

SUBJECTS AND STUDY DESIGN

Sixty stroke patients were recruited during 2004–2006 from the Department of Neurology of the Helsinki University Central Hospital (HUCH). All patients had an acute ischemic MCA stroke in the left ($n = 29$) or right ($n = 31$) temporal, frontal, parietal, or subcortical brain regions. Additional inclusion criteria were: no prior neurological/psychiatric disease, drug/alcohol abuse, or hearing deficit; right-handed; $\leq$75 years old; Finnish-speaking; and able to co-operate. Recruited patients were randomly assigned to one of three groups ($n = 20$ in each): an MG, an ABG, or a CG. Randomization was performed with a random number generator by a researcher not involved in the patient enrollment. The study was approved by the HUCH Ethics Committee, and all patients signed an informed consent. All patients received standard treatment for stroke in terms of medical care and rehabilitation.

During the follow-up, the patients underwent a neuropsychological assessment (including cognitive tests and questionnaires) and an auditory MEG measurement 1 week (baseline), 3 months, and 6 months post-stroke, and a structural MRI within 2 weeks of the stroke onset and 6 months post-stroke. Details regarding the methodology and results of the neuropsychological assessments and the MEG experiment are available in the previous published articles (Särkämö et al., 2008, 2010a).

Of the 60 patients originally recruited into the study, 55 completed the study up to the 3-month stage and 54 up to the 6-month stage. For the purpose of the longitudinal VBM analyses, appropriate MRI data were unavailable in three patients and the image quality was insufficient in two further patients. Thus, data from 49 patients were used in the present study. Demographic and clinical characteristics as well as the musical and linguistic activities of the patients are shown in **Tables 1** and **2**, presented separately for the patients with left hemisphere damage (LHD, $n = 23$) and right hemisphere damage (RHD, $n = 26$). There were no significant differences between the MG, ACG, and CG on any demographic or clinical variables, prior musical or linguistic activities, or in other rehabilitation received during the 6-month follow-up whereas the frequency of listening to music and audio books differed highly significantly between the groups both at the 3-month and the 6-month stage. However, there were no statistically significant differences between the MG and ABG on how many hours per day the patients listened to the provided material (music in the MG, audio books in the ABG) on average, although within the RHD patients the daily listening amounts were slightly higher in the MG than in the ABG. Overall, these results indicate that the groups were comparable and that the intervention protocol worked well.

INTERVENTION

As soon as possible after their enrollment to the study (mean 8.8 days post-stroke, range 3–21 days), the MG and ABG patients were individually contacted by a music therapist. In the MG, the therapist provided the patients with portable CD players and CDs of their own favorite music in any musical genre (mostly popular music with lyrics but also jazz, folk, or classical music). Similarly, the therapist provided the ABG with portable players and self-selected narrated audio books. The patients were trained in using the players and were instructed to listen to the material by themselves daily (for a minimum of 1 h per day) for the following 2 months in addition to standard care and rehabilitation. After this intervention period (3-month stage), they were encouraged to continue listening to the material on their own. In order to ensure that the patients were able to engage in the listening protocol, the therapist kept close weekly contact with the patients and the nurses and/or relatives of the patients were asked to help. Frequency of listening was verified from the listening diaries, which the patients kept during the intervention period and from questionnaires at the 3- and 6-month stages. The CG was not given any listening material and received only the standard care and rehabilitation during the follow-up.

MRI DATA ACQUISITION

Structural MRI was performed within 2 weeks of stroke onset and 6 months post-stroke using the 1.5 T Siemens Vision scanner of

Table 1 | Demographic and clinical characteristics of the patients ($n = 49$).

	Left hemisphere damage ($n = 23$)				Right hemisphere damage ($n = 26$)			
	MG ($n = 7$)	ABG ($n = 8$)	CG ($n = 8$)	*p*-value	MG ($n = 9$)	ABG ($n = 10$)	CG ($n = 7$)	*p*-value
DEMOGRAPHICAL CHARACTERISTICS								
Age (years)	55.3 (11.0)	57.9 (7.4)	60.0 (8.9)	0.615 (F)	59.6 (7.9)	59.4 (9.0)	63.4 (4.7)	0.519 (F)
Gender (male/female)	3/4	6/2	5/3	0.439 (χ^2)	6/3	2/8	3/4	0.111 (χ^2)
Education (years)	10.9 (4.4)	12.9 (3.1)	9.9 (3.4)	0.262 (F)	11.1 (4.5)	11.3 (2.9)	9.3 (3.9)	0.518 (F)
CLINICAL CHARACTERISTICS								
Time from stroke onset to acute MRI (days)	7.0 (3.2)	7.6 (3.7)	7.6 (2.8)	0.922 (F)	6.9 (1.6)	9.1 (3.4)	8.2 (4.3)	0.366 (F)
Time from stroke onset to 6-month MRI (days)	184.4 (6.2)	184.6 (15.9)	192.4 (16.2)	0.449 (F)	189.0 (5.9)	182.7 (8.8)	193.9 (22.0)	0.228 (F)
Hemiparesis (yes/no)	5/2	4/4	3/5	0.409 (χ^2)	9/0	10/0	7/0	–
Aphasia (yes/no)	4/3	6/2	6/2	0.701 (χ^2)				
Lesion size (max. diameter in cm)	47.0 (17.8)	39.7 (18.8)	52.5 (17.6)	0.384 (F)	57.3 (28.9)	58.5 (20.5)	62.1 (25.3)	0.924 (F)
OTHER REHABILITATION DURING THE 6-MONTH FOLLOW-UP[a]								
Physical therapy	19.7 (30.5)	11.3 (30.0)	4.0 (9.4)	0.732 (K)	26.9 (41.6)	30.2 (37.7)	20.1 (26.5)	0.991 (K)
Occupational therapy	14.3 (22.7)	0.4 (0.8)	8.0 (20.3)	0.627 (K)	9.8 (12.9)	10.0 (14.7)	5.9 (6.4)	0.886 (K)
Speech therapy	15.3 (20.5)	3.7 (9.4)	10.9 (11.5)	0.340 (K)	15.3 (20.5)	3.7 (9.4)	10.9 (11.5)	0.340 (K)
Neuropsychological rehabilitation	4.0 (10.9)	2.3 (4.3)	1.0 (1.9)	0.851 (K)	2.9 (5.1)	2.5 (4.9)	0.7 (1.0)	0.976 (K)

Data are mean (SD) unless otherwise stated. MG, music group; ABG, audio book group; CG, control group; F, one-way ANOVA; χ^2, chi-square test (likelihood ratio); K, Kruskal–Wallis test.

[a] Number of therapy sessions.

Table 2 | Musical and linguistic activities of the patients ($n = 49$).

	Left hemisphere damage ($n = 23$)				Right hemisphere damage ($n = 26$)			
	MG ($n = 7$)	**ABG ($n = 8$)**	**CG ($n = 8$)**	***p*-value**	**MG ($n = 9$)**	**ABG ($n = 10$)**	**CG ($n = 7$)**	***p*-value**
BEFORE STROKE								
Listening to music				0.592 (K)				0.617 (K)
Never	0 (0)	0 (0)	0 (0)		0 (0)	0 (0)	1 (14.3)	
Rarely	1 (14.3)	1 (12.5)	2 (25)		2 (22.2)	2 (20)	0 (0)	
Once a month	0 (0)	0 (0)	1 (12.5)		0 (0)	1 (10)	0 (0)	
Once a week	1 (14.3)	3 (37.5)	1 (12.5)		0 (0)	1 (10)	2 (28.6)	
2–3 Times a week	3 (42.9)	4 (50)	2 (25)		2 (22.2)	3 (30)	0 (0)	
Daily	2 (28.6)	0 (0)	2 (25)		5 (55.6)	3 (30)	4 (57.1)	
Listening to radio				0.991 (K)				0.163 (K)
Never	0 (0)	0 (0)	0 (0)		0 (0)	0 (0)	0 (0)	
Rarely	1 (14.3)	0 (0)	1 (12.5)		0 (0)	1 (10)	0 (0)	
Once a month	0 (0)	0 (0)	1 (12.5)		0 (0)	1 (10)	0 (0)	
Once a week	1 (14.3)	2 (25)	0 (0)		0 (0)	1 (10)	1 (14.3)	
2–3 Times a week	0 (0)	1 (12.5)	0 (0)		1 (11.1)	1 (10)	3 (42.9)	
Daily	5 (71.4)	5 (62.5)	6 (75)		8 (88.9)	6 (60)	3 (42.9)	
Reading				0.686 (K)				0.220 (K)
Never	0 (0)	0 (0)	0 (0)		0 (0)	0 (0)	0 (0)	
Rarely	0 (0)	0 (0)	0 (0)		0 (0)	0 (0)	0 (0)	
Once a month	0 (0)	0 (0)	1 (12.5)		1 (11.1)	0 (0)	0 (0)	
Once a week	0 (0)	1 (12.5)	1 (12.5)		4 (44.4)	4 (40)	0 (0)	
2–3 Times a week	3 (42.9)	1 (12.5)	1 (12.5)		2 (22.2)	2 (20)	3 (42.9)	
Daily	4 (57.1)	4 (50)	5 (62.5)		2 (22.2)	4 (40)	4 (57.1)	
DURING THE FIRST 3 MONTHS POST-STROKE								
Listening to music				0.003 (K)				0.001 (K)
Data missing	1 (14.3)	0 (0)	0 (0)		1 (11.1)	0 (0)	0 (0)	
Never	0 (0)	6 (75)	5 (62.5)		0 (0)	2 (20)	3 (42.9)	
Rarely	0 (0)	1 (12.5)	1 (12.5)		0 (0)	3 (30)	1 (14.3)	
Once a month	0 (0)	0 (0)	0 (0)		0 (0)	1 (10)	0 (0)	
Once a week	0 (0)	0 (0)	0 (0)		0 (0)	1 (10)	0 (0)	
2–3 Times a week	0 (0)	0 (0)	1 (12.5)		0 (0)	2 (20)	2 (28.6)	
Daily	6 (85.7)	1 (12.5)	1 (12.5)		8 (88.9)	1 (10)	1 (14.3)	
Listening to audio books				<0.001 (K)				<0.001 (K)
Data missing	1 (14.3)	0 (0)	0 (0)		0 (0)	0 (0)	0 (0)	
Never	5 (71.4)	0 (0)	6 (75)		9 (100)	1 (10)	6 (85.7)	
Rarely	1 (14.3)	0 (0)	2 (25)		0 (0)	0 (0)	0 (0)	
Once a month	0 (0)	0 (0)	0 (0)		0 (0)	0 (0)	0 (0)	
Once a week	0 (0)	1 (12.5)	0 (0)		0 (0)	0 (0)	0 (0)	
2–3 Times a week	0 (0)	2 (25)	0 (0)		0 (0)	0 (0)	0 (0)	
Daily	0 (0)	5 (62.5)	0 (0)		0 (0)	9 (90)	1 (14.3)	
Hours per day listening to group material[a]	1.6 (0.7)	1.3 (0.5)	–	0.484 (T)	2.1 (0.6)	1.4 (0.7)	–	0.076 (T)
DURING 3–6 MONTHS POST-STROKE								
Listening to music				0.010 (K)				0.018 (K)
Data missing	0 (0)	0 (0)	1 (12.5)		1 (11.1)	0 (0)	0 (0)	
Never	0 (0)	0 (0)	2 (25)		0 (0)	2 (20)	2 (28.6)	
Rarely	0 (0)	1 (12.5)	2 (25)		0 (0)	1 (10)	1 (14.3)	
Once a month	0 (0)	2 (25)	0 (0)		0 (0)	3 (30)	1 (14.3)	
Once a week	0 (0)	1 (12.5)	2 (25)		1 (11.1)	2 (20)	0 (0)	
2–3 Times a week	3 (42.9)	0 (0)	1 (12.5)		3 (33.3)	1 (10)	2 (28.6)	
Daily	4 (57.1)	4 (50)	0 (0)		4 (44.4)	1 (10)	1 (14.3)	

(Continued)

Table 2 | Continued

	Left hemisphere damage ($n = 23$)				Right hemisphere damage ($n = 26$)			
	MG ($n = 7$)	ABG ($n = 8$)	CG ($n = 8$)	p-value	MG ($n = 9$)	ABG ($n = 10$)	CG ($n = 7$)	p-value
Listening to audio books				<0.001 (K)				0.004 (K)
Data missing	0 (0)	0 (0)	1 (12.5)		0 (0)	0 (0)	0 (0)	
Never	6 (85.7)	0 (0)	5 (62.5)		8 (88.9)	2 (20)	6 (85.7)	
Rarely	1 (14.3)	0 (0)	2 (25)		0 (0)	1 (10)	0 (0)	
Once a month	0 (0)	2 (25)	0 (0)		0 (0)	0 (0)	0 (0)	
Once a week	0 (0)	0 (0)	0 (0)		0 (0)	2 (20)	0 (0)	
2–3 Times a week	0 (0)	3 (37.5)	0 (0)		1 (11.1)	1 (10)	1 (14.3)	
Daily	0 (0)	3 (37.5)	0 (0)		0 (0)	4 (40)	0 (0)	

Data shown as frequency (percentage) unless otherwise stated. MG, music group; ABG, audio book group; CG, control group; K, Kruskal–Wallis test; T, t-test.
[a]Music listening in the MG and audio book listening in the ABG [data are mean (SD)].

the HUCH Department of Radiology. Clinically, the MRI was used by two experienced neuroradiologists (authors Taina Autti and Heli M. Silvennoinen) to verify the stroke diagnosis and to evaluate the size and location of the lesion. The MRI sequence included a 3D set of high-resolution T1 images ($T_E = 3.68$ ms, $T_R = 1900$ ms, $T_I = 1100$ ms, flip angle 15°, isotropic voxel size of 1 mm^3), which were used in the present VBM analysis. In addition, also a smaller set of fluid-attenuated inversion recovery (2D FLAIR) images, which are sensitive to acute infarcts, were acquired and used in accurately locating the lesion area, especially in the acute stage.

VOXEL-BASED MORPHOMETRY ANALYSIS

Morphometric analysis was carried out using VBM (Ashburner and Friston, 2000) and Statistical Parametric Mapping software (SPM8; The Welcome Department of Imaging Neuroscience, London) under MATLAB 7.8.0 (The MathWorks Inc., Natick, MA, USA). The normalization of brain images is a prerequisite in any multi-subject voxel-wise MRI data analysis and especially important when dealing with abnormal brains. In order to achieve an accurate segmentation and normalization of lesioned GM and WM tissue, Unified Segmentation (Ashburner and Friston, 2005) with medium regularization and cost function masking (CFM) was applied to the structural T1-weighted images of each subject (Brett et al., 2001). The cost function masks were defined by manually depicting for each patient at each time (acute and 6-month stage) binary lesion masks of the lesioned tissue using the MRIcron software package[1] (Rorden and Brett, 2000). This technique has been widely used with patients suffering from stroke (Crinion et al., 2007; Andersen et al., 2010; Ripollés et al., 2012), achieving optimal normalization with no post-registration lesion shrinkage or out-of-brain distortion (Ripollés et al., 2012). During normalization, the GM and WM images were modulated in order to preserve the total amount of the signal. The resulting normalized GM and WM tissue probability maps were smoothed by using an isotropic spatial filter (FWHM = 6 mm) to reduce residual inter-individual variability.

All normalized and smoothed GM and WM images were further analyzed in order to compare the differences in the GMV or white matter volume (WMV). Because the processing of music and speech are generally known to involve the left and right hemispheres to a different degree (e.g., Zatorre et al., 2002; Tervaniemi and Hugdahl, 2003) and they are therefore differentially affected by lesion laterality, we performed separate analyses for the LHD patients (MG: $n = 7$, ABG: $n = 8$, CG: $n = 8$) and the RHD patients (MG: $n = 9$, ABG: $n = 10$, CG: $n = 7$). Thus, four separate mixed-design analysis of variance (ANOVA) models (GMV–LHD, GMV–RHD, WMV–LHD, WMV–RHD) were built with Group (MG/ABG/CG) as a between-subjects variable and Time (acute stage/6-month stage) as a within-subjects variable (thereby ensuring that each subject acted as its own control). Total intracranial volume (TIV) was included as a nuisance variable in order to correct for global differences for head size. Three different Group × Time interactions were calculated: MG > CG and ABG, ABG > CG and MG, CG > MG and ABG. In other words, we tested if the increments in post–pre GMV in one group (e.g., MG) were greater than in the other two groups (e.g., CG and ABG). In addition, *post hoc* paired t-tests were planned to check the direction of the effect of Time within each Group (6 months > acute). It has been suggested that combined intensity and cluster size thresholds such as $p < 0.005$ with a 10 voxel extent produce a desirable balance between Type I and Type II errors (Lieberman and Cunningham, 2009). Taking a slightly more stringent approach, the results are reported in tables at $p < 0.001$ (uncorrected threshold) with a cluster size of ≥50 voxels of spatial extent. For the sake of visual clarity, results are shown in figures at $p < 0.01$ (uncorrected threshold), although only clusters reported in the tables are labeled and commented throughout the text. Anatomical and cytoarchitectonical areas were identified using the Automated Anatomical Labeling (Tzourio-Mazoyer et al., 2002) and the Talairach Daemon database atlases (Lancaster et al., 2000) included in the xjView toolbox[2].

Finally, for any cluster of voxels where a significant Group × Time interaction was found, mean GMV or WMV increase (6 months − acute stage) was calculated for each patient and correlated with behavioral changes (also 6 months − acute

[1]http://www.mccauslandcenter.sc.edu/mricro/mricron/index.html

[2]http://www.alivelearn.net/xjview8/

stage) in cognitive tests and mood scales. For the cognitive measures, changes in the summary scores of the tests measuring the following cognitive domains were included: verbal memory, short-term and working memory, language skills, visuospatial cognition, executive functions, focused attention (correct responses and reactions times), and sustained attention (correct responses and reactions times; for details, see Särkämö et al., 2008). Similarly, for the mood measures, changes in the eight Profile of Mood States (POMS) scales (tension, depression, irritability, vigor, fatigue, inertia, confusion, and forgetfulness) were included (for details, see Särkämö et al., 2008).

RESULTS

GRAY AND WHITE MATTER VOLUME CHANGES DURING RECOVERY

Significant GMV increases were found post-intervention (6 months – acute) for all three groups of LHD patients (see **Table 3**; **Figure 1**) and RHD patients (see **Table 4**; **Figure 2**). Areas identified were mostly located in the temporal, frontal, motor, limbic, and cerebellar brain regions, especially in the contralesional hemisphere, with the largest and most extensive volume increases occurring in the MG.

In LHD patients, significant Group × Time interactions in GMV were found for the MG > ABG and CG contrast (see **Table 5**; **Figure 3**) in five different clusters: three in frontal areas [left and right superior frontal gyrus (SFG) and right medial SFG] and two in limbic areas [left ventral/subgenual anterior cingulate cortex (SACC) and right ventral striatum (VS) / globus pallidum). The reversed contrasts (ABG > CG and MG, CG > MG and ABG) did not yield any significant regions.

In RHD patients, there were no significant Group × Time interactions in GMV in any area at the selected threshold ($p < 0.001$ uncorrected). However, when using a slightly more lenient threshold ($p < 0.005$ uncorrected), a single cluster emerged in the left insula (MNI −33 −6 −8; 73 voxels of extent; $t(22) = 3.36$) for the MG > ABG and CG contrast (see **Figure 4**). Again, no other clusters were found using the reversed contrasts (ABG > CG and MG, CG > MG and ABG) at this same threshold.

There were no significant Time effects or Group × Time interactions in the WMV in LHD or RHD patients.

CORRELATION BETWEEN GRAY MATTER CHANGES AND BEHAVIORAL RECOVERY

In order to determine the functional relevance of the observed GMV increases induced by the music listening intervention, we performed correlation analyses with the longitudinal behavioral data (also 6 months – acute). In LHD patients, the increase in GMV in the identified frontal areas correlated significantly with improvement in verbal memory, language skills, and focused attention (see **Table 6** for individual cluster correlations; in **Figure 5** the frontal clusters are pooled together for illustrative

Table 3 | GMV increases (6-month – acute) in LHD patients ($n = 23$).

	Anatomical area	MNI coordinates	Cluster size	*t*-value
CG	Left cerebellum	−14 −59 −40	189	4.75
	Right temporal pole (BA 38)	34 5 −20	111	4.46
	Right cerebellum	14 −59 −42	59	4.27
	Left pons	−7 −29 −35	203	4.08
	Right posterior cingulate gyrus	12 −40 24	83	3.96
ABG	Right calcarine/cuneus (BA 17, 18)	17 −77 12	1084	5.14
	Left cerebellum	−7 −53 −17	166	4.75
	Right pons	−18 −35 −42	85	4.71
	Right calcarine (BA 17)	9 −82 4	239	4.66
	Right precentral gyrus (BA 6)	47 0 31	110	4.18
MG	Left ventral/subgenual anterior cingulate cortex (BA 10)	−10 34 −3	185	5.75
	Right superior frontal gyrus (BA 32, 6)	19 4 51	588	5.54
	Right middle frontal gyrus (BA 32, 9)	21 24 39	1367	5.39
	Right inferior frontal gyrus	31 13 21	153	5.35
	Right ventral striatum	12 15 −11	484	4.85
	Right fusiform gyrus (BA 19)	32 −45 −9	130	4.82
	Right orbitofrontal cortex (BA 11)	28 44 −6	264	4.80
	Right superior frontal gyrus (BA 10)	22 51 2	490	4.74
	Right superior medial frontal gyrus (BA 8)	8 32 51	76	4.67
	Right precuneus (BA 7)	19 −53 46	166	4.60
	Right posterior cingulate gyrus	14 −40 25	471	4.46
	Right ventral striatum/globus pallidum	14 6 −2	252	4.43
	Left supplementary motor area	−11 10 50	54	4.07

Results are reported at a $p < 0.001$ (uncorrected threshold) with 50 voxels of spatial extent. CG, control group; ABG, audio book group; MG, music group; BA, Brodmann area.

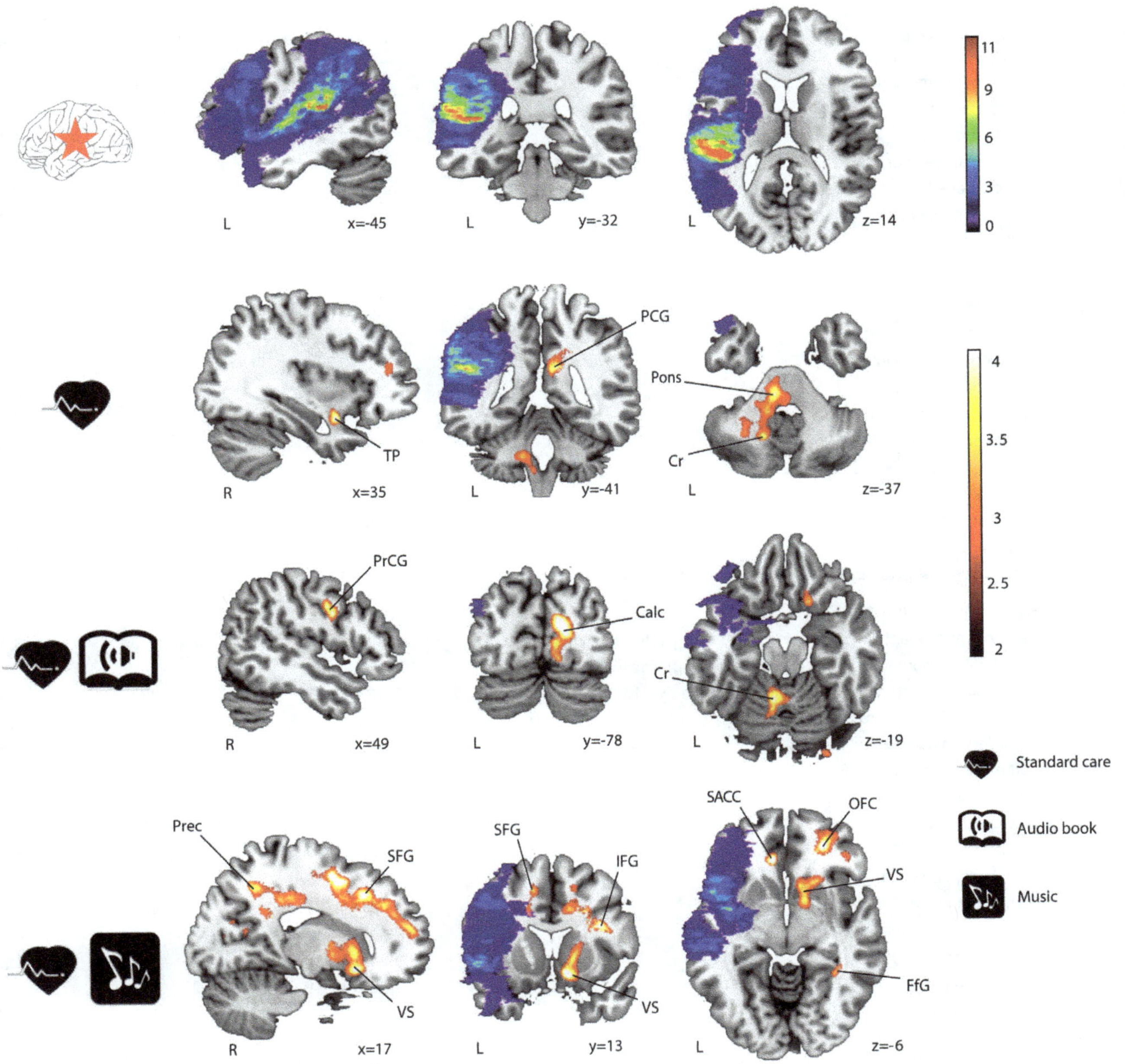

FIGURE 1 | GMV increases (6-month – acute) in LHD patients ($n=23$). Lesion overlap indicating the number of patients with damage at a particular voxel and GMV increases within the three groups are shown in blue–green–red and red–yellow, respectively. Neurological convention is used. Results are shown at $p < 0.01$ (uncorrected) with ≥ 50 voxels of spatial extent and overlaid over a canonical template with MNI coordinates at the bottom right of each slice. Only clusters surviving a $p < 0.001$ threshold are labeled (see also **Table 3**). TP, temporal pole; PCG, posterior cingulate gyrus; Cr, cerebellum; PrCG, precentral gyrus; Calc, calcarine; Prec, precuneus; SFG, superior frontal gyrus; VS, ventral striatum; IFG, inferior frontal gyrus; SACC, ventral/subgenual anterior cingulate cortex; OFC, orbitofrontal cortex; FfG, fusiform gyrus; L, left hemisphere; R, right hemisphere.

purposes). Similarly, increase in GMV in the limbic regions (left SACC) was significantly correlated with a decrease in self-reported depression, tension, fatigue, forgetfulness, and irritability and marginally correlated also with a decrease in self-reported confusion. In RHD patients, the GMV increases in the left insula cluster were also found to correlate with the improvement of language skills ($r = 0.63$, $p < 0.002$; **Figure 4**). There were no other significant correlations.

DISCUSSION

The novel key finding of the present VBM study was that regular music listening during the 6-month post-stroke stage can lead to structural reorganization in the recovering brain. Specifically, compared with patients who listened daily to audio books (ABG) or who did not receive any additional listening material (CG), the patients who listened daily to their own favorite music (MG) showed more increase in GMV from the acute to

Table 4 | GMV increases (6-month – acute) in RHD patients ($n = 26$).

	Anatomical area	MNI coordinates	Cluster size	*t*-value
CG	Left supramarginal gyrus (BA 40)	−44 −28 28	1597	6.13
	Left thalamus	−15 −6 6	946	5.97
	Left brainstem	−4 −20 −10	695	5.27
	Left inferior temporal lobe (BA 20, 21)	−44 −5 −35	208	4.42
	Right cerebellum	14 −42 −25	93	4.19
	Left sup./mid. occipital gyrus	−21 −86 12	405	4.18
	Left cuneus (BA 18)	−5 −85 22	340	4.18
	Left orbitofrontal cortex (BA 47)	−16 25 −21	85	3.97
ABG	Left cerebellum	−9 −52 −40	874	6.42
	Left posterior cingulum	−12 −43 21	322	5.85
	Right posterior cingulum	20 −43 26	79	4.83
	Left middle cingulum	−12 −11 35	546	4.78
	Right orbitofrontal cortex (BA 10)	15 53 1	185	4.66
	Right cerebellum	16 −71 −51	268	4.64
	Left thalamus	−15 −6 11	105	4.40
	Left insula	−33 −14 10	61	4.21
	Left precuneus	−20 −50 14	59	4.19
	Left precentral gyrus (BA 6)	−29 −11 45	102	4.18
	Left postcentral gyrus (BA 4)	−43 −17 51	169	4.13
MG	Right precuneus (BA 31)	16 −45 21	1544	6.35
	Left post/middle/ant cingulate gyrus; left sup./mid. frontal gyrus; left supp. motor area; left inferior frontal gyrus; *pars triangularis* (BA 32, 31, 24, 9)	−10 −12 34	11173	6.16
	Left supramarginal gyrus; left postcentral gyrus (BA 40)	−48 −23 27	1472	6.09
	Left inferior frontal gyrus; left precentral gyrus (BA 6)	−42 9 17	799	5.92
	Right middle cingulate gyrus (BA 24)	18 30 26	970	4.90
	Left orbitofrontal cortex (BA 47, 11)	−25 23 −16	1661	4.85
	Left inf./mid. temporal gyrus (BA 20)	−46 −5 −31	717	4.56
	Left fusiform gyrus	−34 −17 −27	266	4.42
	Left insula	−34 −12 −7	387	4.39
	Left parahippocampal gyrus	26 −65 −38	191	4.21
	Right cerebellum	11 31 −11	280	4.18
	Right anterior cingulate (BA 32)	19 43 4	72	4.14
	Left precentral gyrus	−34 5 35	188	4.12
	Left middle temporal gyrus	−56 −46 −8	372	4.06
	Right fusiform gyrus	36 −42 −16	246	4.05

Results are reported at a $p < 0.001$ (uncorrected threshold) with 50 voxels of spatial extent. CG, control group; ABG, audio book group; MG, music group; BA, Brodmann area.

the 6-month stage in a network of frontolimbic areas, primarily in the healthy contralesional side but also perilesionally. Importantly, the observed GMV increases in this network were directly associated with the behavioral improvement in cognitive functioning and reduction in negative mood shown previously for music listening (Särkämö et al., 2008; Forsblom et al., 2012). The area-specific correlations obtained (attention, memory, and language for frontal areas; mood for limbic regions), the lack of differences in the reversed contrasts (ABG > CG and MG, CG > MG and ABG), and the fact that effects emerge in areas that have previously been found to be closely associated with music processing and cognitive/emotional processing (see below), argue against our results being false positives. Moreover, given that the patient groups were comparable at baseline and the potential effects of other types of rehabilitation (standard stroke rehabilitation) and activities (audio book listening) were controlled for, these findings suggest that a musically enriched environment can be beneficial for acute stroke recovery and that neuroplastic changes in the frontolimbic network may underlie its efficacy.

In the present study, the frontal GMV increases associated with music listening in LHD patients were located in the left and right SFG and the right medial SFG and correlated with the improvement of verbal memory, language skills, and focused attention over the 6-month follow-up. These correlations are well in line with the previous findings of the study showing that music listening enhanced the recovery of verbal memory and focused attention

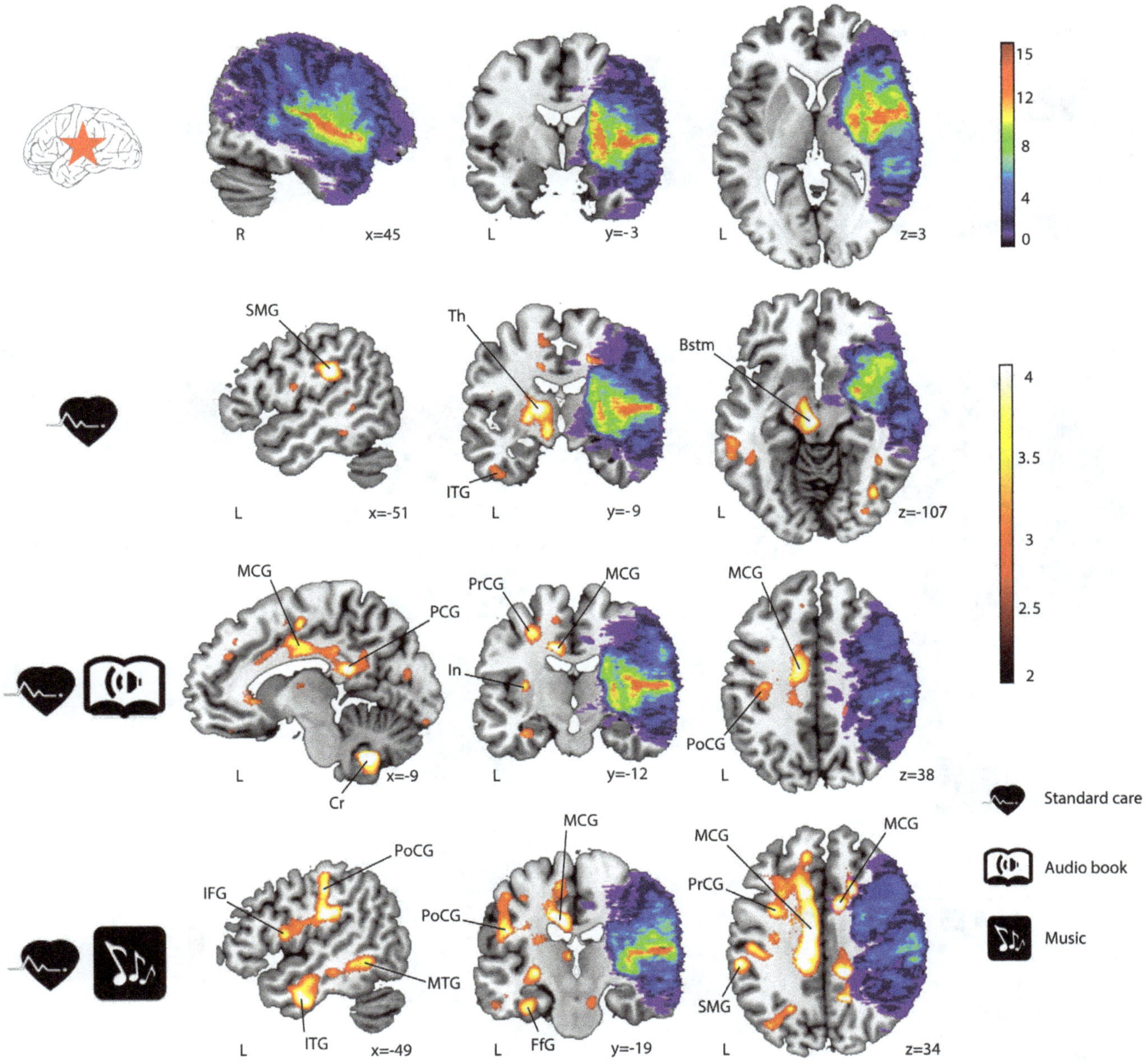

FIGURE 2 | GMV increases (6-month – acute) in RHD patients ($n = 26$). Lesion overlap indicating the number of patients with damage at a particular voxel and GMV increases within the three groups are shown in blue–green–red and red–yellow, respectively. Neurological convention is used. Results are shown at $p < 0.01$ (uncorrected) with ≥50 voxels of spatial extent and overlaid over a canonical template with MNI coordinates at the bottom right of each slice. Only clusters surviving a $p < 0.001$ threshold are labeled (see also **Table 4**). SMG, supramarginal gyrus; Th, thalamus; ITG, inferior temporal gyrus; Bstm, brainstem; MCG, middle cingulate gyrus; PCG, posterior cingulate gyrus; Cr, cerebellum; PrCG, precentral gyrus; In, insula; PoCG, postcentral gyrus; IFG, inferior frontal gyrus; MTG, middle temporal gyrus; FfG, fusiform gyrus; L, left hemisphere; R, right hemisphere.

Table 5 | GMV increases (6-month – acute) in the MG compared to the ABG and CG (LHD patients).

Anatomical area	MNI coordinates	Cluster size	*t*-value
Right superior frontal gyrus (BA 32)	22 25 38	347	4.88
Left ventral/subgenual anterior cingulate cortex (BA 10)	−10 37 −4	53	4.51
Right medial superior frontal gyrus (BA 8)	7 32 51	57	4.31
Right ventral striatum/globus pallidum	14 5 −3	57	4.03
Left superior frontal gyrus (BA 32)	−13 21 38	51	4.01

Time × Group interaction (MG > ABG and CG) at a $p < 0.001$ (uncorrected threshold) with 50 voxels of spatial extent. BA, Brodmann area.

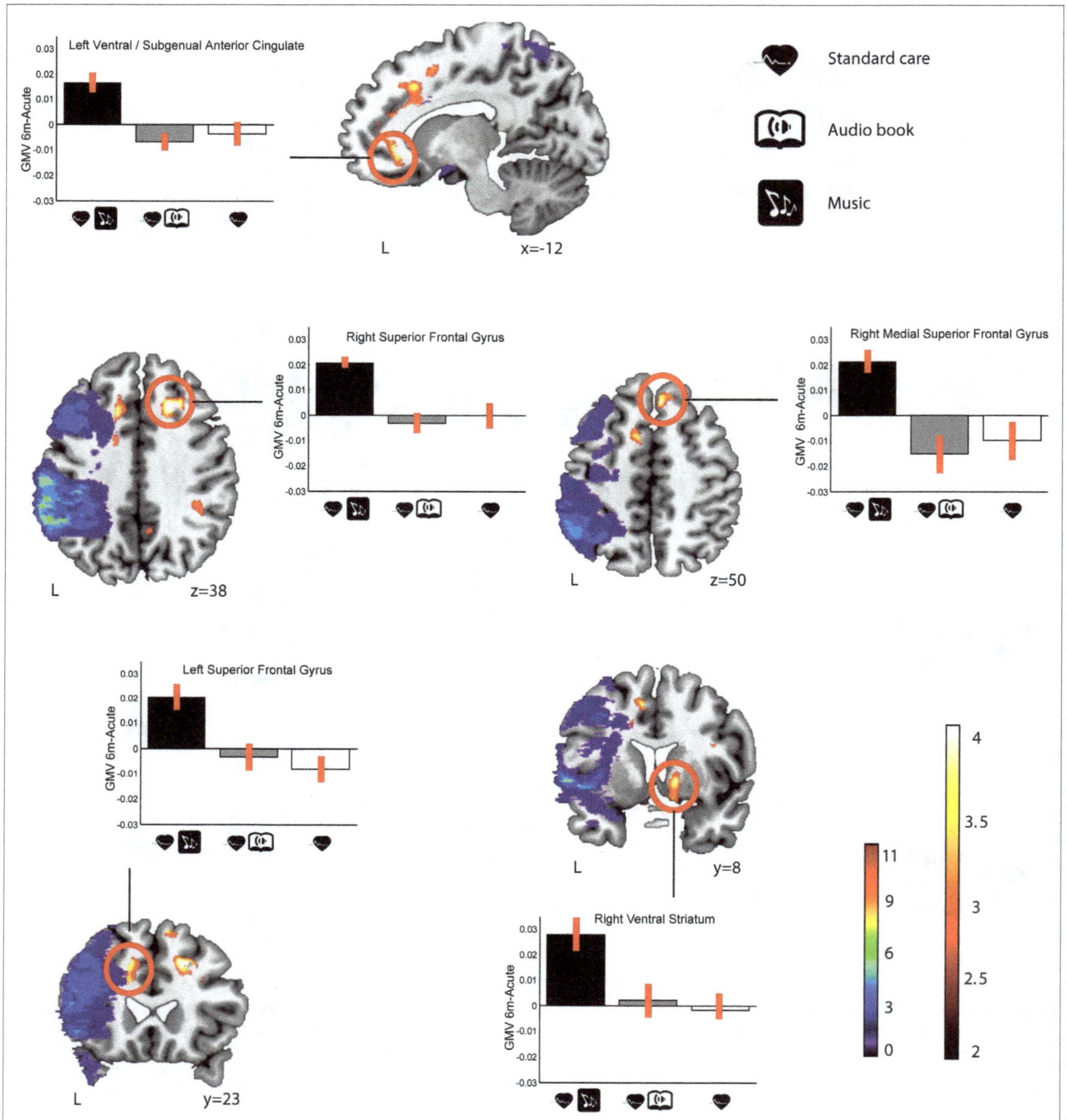

FIGURE 3 | GMV increases (6-month – acute) in the MG compared to the ABG and CG (LHD patients). Blue–green–red: lesion overlap indicating the number of patients showing damage at a particular voxel. Red–yellow: GMV increases for the MG compared to the ABG and CG (Group × Time interaction, MG > ABG and CG contrast). Bar graphs indicate GMV increases (mean ± SEM) for each of the clusters showing an interaction effect (white: CG, gray: ABG, black: MG). Neurological convention is used. Results are shown at $p < 0.01$ (uncorrected) with ≥50 voxels of spatial extent and overlaid over a canonical template with MNI coordinates at the bottom right of each slice (see also **Table 5**). L, left hemisphere.

more than audio book listening or standard care both 3 and 6 months post-stroke (Särkämö et al., 2008). In addition, in the original data ($n = 54$), there was also a slight trend toward a group difference in the domain of language [mixed-model ANOVA, Group × Time interaction, $F(2.4, 51.9) = 2.2, p = 0.108$)] over the 6-month follow-up, with more improvement in the MG than in

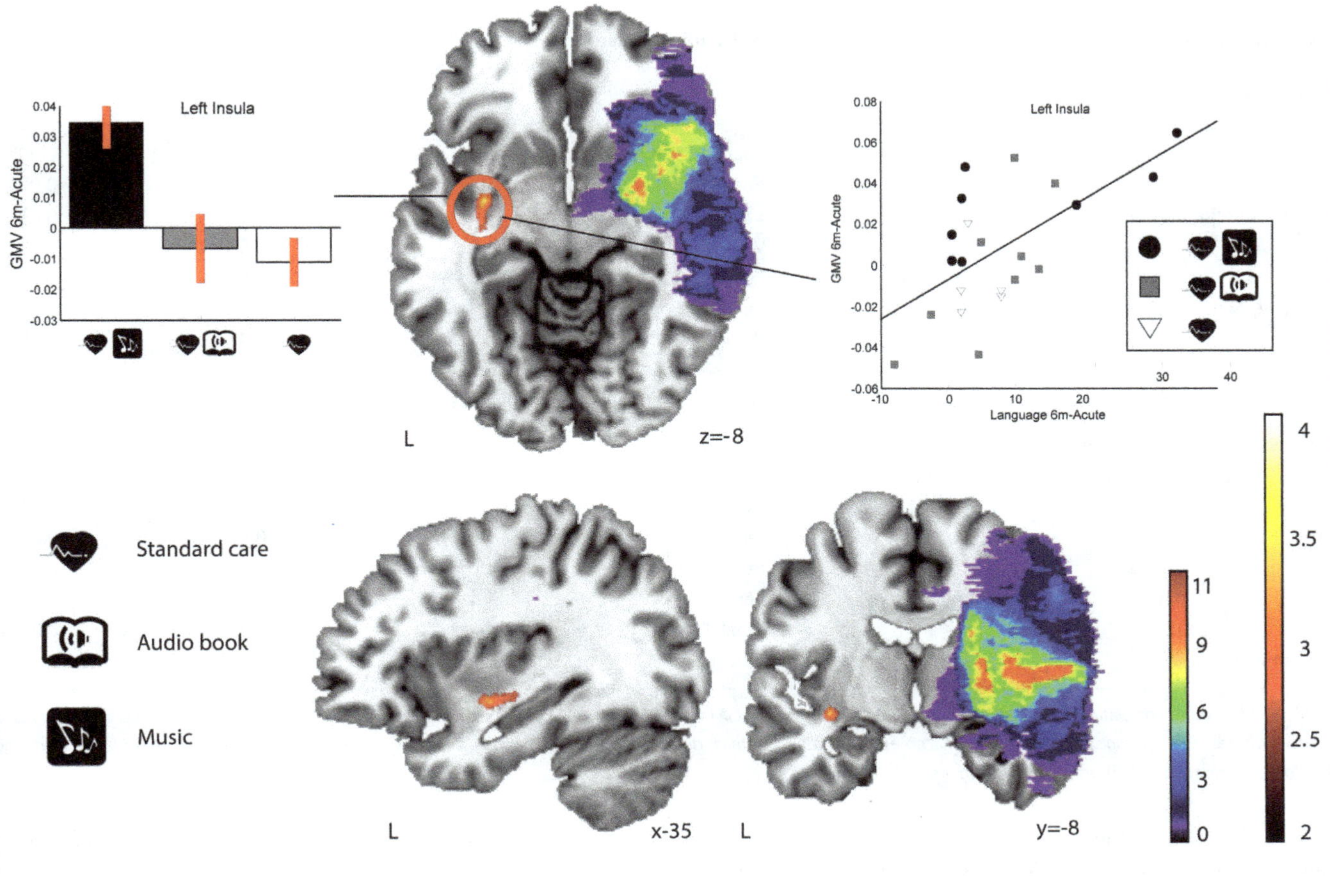

FIGURE 4 | GMV increases (6-month – acute) in the MG compared to the ABG and CG (RHD patients). Blue–green–red: lesion overlap indicating the number of patients showing damage at a particular voxel. Red–yellow: GMV increases for the MG compared to the ABG and CG (Group × Time interaction, MG > ABG, and CG contrast). Bar graphs (left) indicate GMV increases (mean ± SEM) for the only cluster (left insula) showing an interaction effect (white: CG, gray: ABG, black: MG). The scatter plot (right) shows the relationship between GMV increase in the insula cluster and improvement in language skills. Neurological convention is used. Results are shown at $p < 0.01$ (uncorrected) with ≥50 voxels of spatial extent and overlaid over a canonical template with MNI coordinates at the bottom right of each slice. L, left hemisphere.

the ABG ($p = 0.096$), suggesting that the correlation between GMV and language skills is also meaningful. In previous MEG and fMRI studies on music, the activity of the SFG has been linked to melody discrimination and production (Brown et al., 2006; Lappe et al., 2013), processing the emotional valence of music (Escoffier et al., 2013), and musical episodic memory (Platel et al., 2003). Cognitively, evidence from neuroimaging and lesion studies suggests that the SFG is involved in many domain-general cognitive functions, such as attention and working memory (du Boisgueheneuc et al., 2006; Huang et al., 2013), and together with the dorsal anterior cingulate cortex (DACC) it forms one key component of the *salience/central executive network* (Dosenbach et al., 2008). Interestingly, the DACC/SFG area seems to have a role also in language processing, including internally generated speech (Blank et al., 2003), and its activity has recently been linked also to aphasia recovery (Brownsett et al., 2014). Structural and functional changes in the SFG have also been reported following meditation practice (Kang et al., 2013) and cognitive training (Hoekzema et al., 2010), suggesting that changes in SFG are associated with improved cognition.

In addition to the frontal areas, we also found GMV increases induced by the music listening in LHD patients in two limbic areas: the left SACC and the right VS. Moreover, the GMV increase in the left SACC correlated with the reduction of negative mood (depression, confusion, tension, fatigue, forgetfulness, and irritability) in the POMS questionnaire. Again, this finding is well in line with our previous behavioral results showing that the music listening reduced depression and confusion more than standard care (Särkämö et al., 2008) and was also subjectively associated with better relaxation and positive mood than the audio book listening (Forsblom et al., 2012). Generally, the VS is considered to be a key part of the neural circuitry for reward and pleasure, and its dysfunction is associated with anhedonia, a hallmark symptom of depression (Der-Avakian and Markou, 2012; Eslinger et al., 2012). The nucleus accumbens (NAc) and parts of the caudate nucleus and putamen, the dopaminergic VS, have been strongly implicated in neuroimaging studies as underlying the emotional experience of music (Blood and Zatorre, 2001; Brown et al., 2004; Menon and Levitin, 2005; Koelsch et al., 2006; Mitterschiffthaler et al., 2007; Montag et al., 2011; Salimpoor et al., 2011, 2013). fMRI studies

Table 6 | Correlation between GMV increase and behavioral change (6-month – acute) in LHD patients.

Anatomical area	Behavioral measure	*r*-value	*p*-value
Frontal clusters pooled together	Language	0.51	0.012
	Verbal memory	0.56	0.009
	Focused attention (correct responses)	0.63	0.005
	Focused attention (reaction times)	−0.45	0.063
Right superior frontal gyrus	Language	0.52	0.011
	Verbal memory	0.59	0.004
	Focused attention (correct responses)	0.60	0.009
Left superior frontal gyrus	Language	0.42	0.044
	Verbal memory	0.41	0.050
	Focused attention (reaction times)	−0.61	0.008
Right medial superior frontal gyrus	Focused attention (correct responses)	0.62	0.006
Limbic cluster spooled together	–	–	–
Left ventral/subgenual anterior cingulate gyrus	Depression	−0.61	0.003
	Confusion	−0.41	0.061
	Tension	−0.48	0.029
	Fatigue	−0.65	0.001
	Forgetfulness	−0.55	0.008
	Irritability	−0.45	0.038
Right ventral striatum	–	–	–

Significant ($p < 0.05$) correlations and linear trends ($p < 0.1$) between the GM volume increases and changes in the summary scores of cognitive tests and the Profile of Mood States (POMS) mood scores [see Särkämö et al. (2008) for details] during follow-up (6 months – acute). Correlations are shown for individual clusters and for groups of clusters within frontal and limbic areas.

have implicated also the anterior cingulate in processing musical emotions (Brown et al., 2004; Mitterschiffthaler et al., 2007; Green et al., 2008; Janata, 2009; Escoffier et al., 2013), musical preferences (Berns et al., 2010; Kitayama et al., 2013), rhythm and melody perception (Jerde et al., 2011; Lee et al., 2011) and production (Brown et al., 2006; Berkowitz and Ansari, 2008), and singing (Kleber et al., 2007; Zarate and Zatorre, 2008). Generally, the ventral-rostral part of the ACC has a regulatory role in generating emotional responses, and its abnormal functioning has been linked to many psychiatric conditions (Etkin et al., 2011). In depressed patients, the activity of both the ACC and the VS to pleasant music has been found to be reduced compared to healthy controls (Osuch et al., 2009; Aust et al., 2013). In VBM studies, GM loss in the ACC has been linked to impaired recognition of musical emotions in frontotemporal dementia (Omar et al., 2011) and has also been documented as a key neuroanatomical component in the etiology of major depression (Grieve et al., 2013; Lai, 2013).

One possible interpretation for the increase in GMV in the subgenual part of the ACC could be related to the role of this subregion in affective appraisal, integration of emotional and motivational states, self-referential mental processing, and introspective thought (Northoff and Bermpohl, 2004; Vago and Silbersweig, 2012). Interestingly, Greicius et al. (2007) found using PET that the resting-state SACC activity was linked to the *default-mode network* in depressed patients and also correlated with the length of the depressive episode. In a recent fMRI study (Yoshimura et al., in press), the activity of medial prefrontal cortex and ventral ACC during a task of self-referential processing of positive emotional trait words was also observed to increase in depressed patients following cognitive behavioral therapy (CBT), suggesting that these areas are also linked to the amelioration of depression. Thus, given that pleasant and autobiographically salient music can activate the ventral ACC (Janata, 2009) and that music listening was also observed to evoke thoughts and memories about the past and improve mood in our stroke patients (Forsblom et al., 2012), it is possible that positive self-referential emotional processing associated with music listening could be driving the observed structural enhancement of the SACC and the concurrent reduction in depressed mood.

Within the RHD subgroup of patients, we observed more GMV increase in the MG compared to the other groups in a single contralesional (left) cluster in the insula, which also correlated with the recovery of language skills. Since this was seen only using a slightly less stringent statistical threshold ($p < 0.005$ uncorrected) and the RHD–MG listened to the intervention material slightly more often than the RHD–ABG ($p = 0.076$), this result should thus be interpreted with some caution. Although less is known about the specific role of the insula in music or language, current evidence from neuroimaging links it to the affective processing of music (Brown et al., 2004; Menon and Levitin, 2005; Koelsch et al., 2006; Montag et al., 2011; Omar et al., 2011; Trost et al., 2012) and voice (Blasi et al., 2011), musical creativity and improvisation (Brown et al., 2006; Engel and Keller, 2011; Villarreal et al., 2013), and perception of melody (Wehrum et al., 2011) and chords (Koelsch et al., 2005) as well as to verbal functions, especially speech articulation (Ackermann and Riecker, 2010; Price, 2010; Baldo et al., 2011). Overall, there was clearly less music-induced GM reorganization in RHD patients than in LHD patients. One

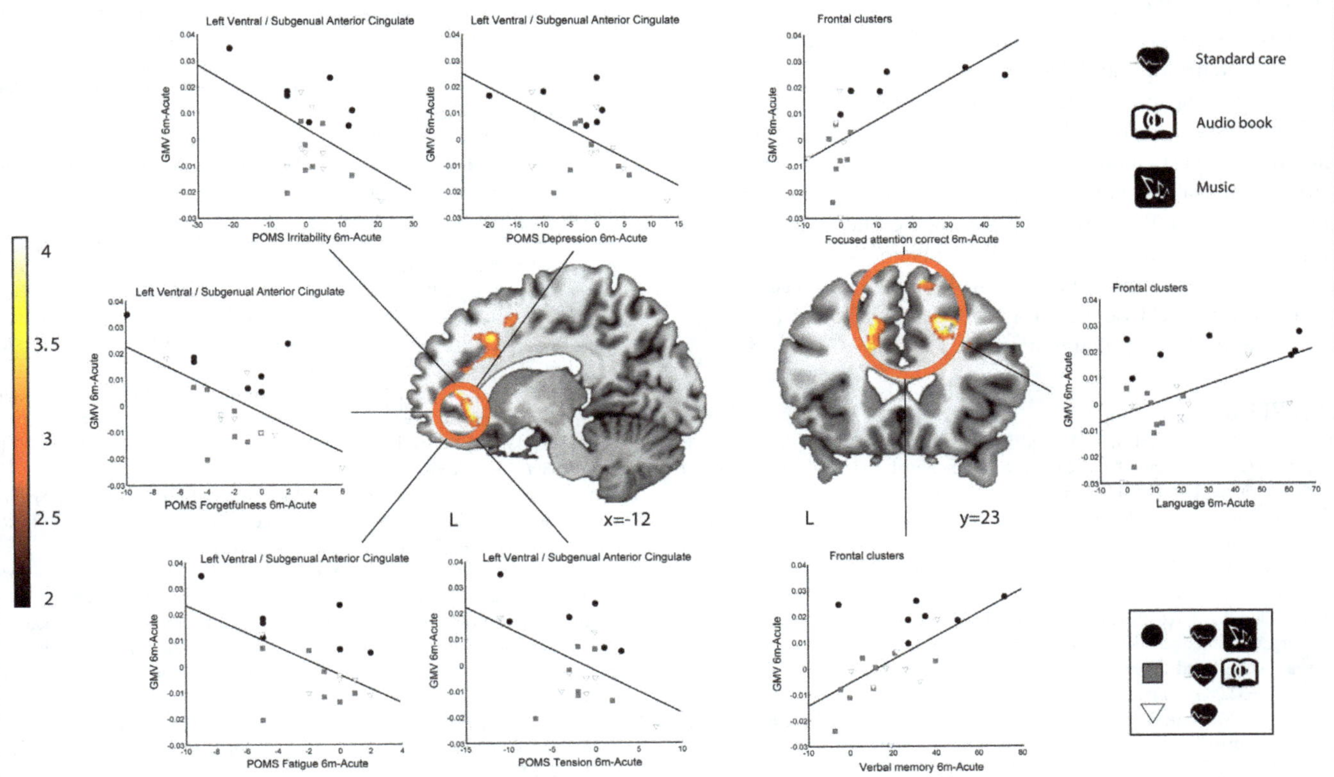

FIGURE 5 | Correlation between GMV increase and behavioral change (6-month – acute) in LHD patients. Red–yellow: GMV increases for the MG compared to the ABG and CG (Group × Time interaction). Scatter plots show the relationship between GMV increases and improvements in mood (left ventral/subgenual anterior cingulate cluster) and cognitive variables (three frontal clusters pooled together). Neurological convention is used. Results are shown at $p < 0.01$ (uncorrected) with ≥50 voxels of spatial extent and overlaid over a canonical template with MNI coordinates at the bottom right of each slice (see also **Table 6**). L, left hemisphere.

reason for this could be that the lesions in the right hemisphere were, on the average, larger and more extensive than in the left hemisphere ($p = 0.044$). Coupled with the fact that there is a level of right hemisphere dominance for music processing (Zatorre et al., 2002; Tervaniemi and Hugdahl, 2003) and, consequently, the majority of the RHD patients had some degree of amusia (see Särkämö et al., 2009, 2010b), it is possible that the music was not to able to engage the musical brain network in RHD patients to the same degree as in LHD patients. In addition, our sample size was relatively small (26 RHD patients and 23 LHD patients) and there was also considerable variability in the location and size of the lesions (see **Figures 1** and **2**, top row), which together can affect the sensitivity of the VBM analysis to detect potential volumetric changes over time, especially in the lesioned hemisphere. Thus, larger studies with more homogenous lesion characteristics are called for in the future to verify and extend the current findings.

In general, the exact anatomical nature of the GM and WM changes observed with the VBM method is still not understood very well - in VBM, a change in "volume" essentially refers to a change in GM intensity in the images (not the real volume of neurons, for instance) and is therefore non-specific with respect to the underlying tissue characteristics. According to the current view, the potential mechanisms for GM reorganization include axon sprouting, dendritic branching and synaptogenesis, neurogenesis, changes in glial number and morphology, and angiogenesis (Zatorre et al., 2012). These cellular changes as well as changes in neurotrophic and neural growth factor levels have been documented also in animal studies of post-stroke EE (Biernaskie and Corbett, 2001; Johansson and Belichenko, 2002; Gobbo and O'Mara, 2004; Komitova et al., 2005; Matsumori et al., 2006; Söderström et al., 2009) and auditory EE in healthy developing animals (Engineer et al., 2004; Angelucci et al., 2007; Nichols et al., 2007; Bose et al., 2010), providing experimental support for the enhanced cerebral reorganization induced by the musically enriched recovery environment in the present study.

In conclusion, the present study shows that daily music listening during the first month post-stroke stage can lead to fine-grained structural reorganization (as indicated by increased GMV) in a network of frontolimbic brain areas. Importantly, given that the frontolimbic plastic changes were also directly related to the cognitive and emotional recovery previously shown to be enhanced by music (Särkämö et al., 2008; Forsblom et al., 2012), these findings provide a plausible neuroanatomical correlate for the efficacy of music after stroke. At a more general level, they also provide the first evidence in humans that not only active therapist-led rehabilitation but also environmental enrichment has the potential to shape the structure of the recovering brain.

ACKNOWLEDGMENTS

We wish to express our gratitude to the staff of the HUCH Department of Neurology and Department of Radiology and other rehabilitation hospitals in the Helsinki metropolitan area for their collaboration, and especially to the patient subjects and their families for their participation and effort. We also wish to thank Mari Tervaniemi, Isabelle Peretz, Matti Laine, and Marja Hietanen for their assistance and expertise in planning the study. This work was funded by the Academy of Finland (grants no 77322, 141106, and 257077), the Jenny and Antti Wihuri Foundation (Helsinki, Finland), the National Doctoral Programme on Psychology (Finland), and the Finnish Brain Foundation.

REFERENCES

Ackermann, H., and Riecker, A. (2010). The contribution(s) of the insula to speech production: a review of the clinical and functional imaging literature. *Brain Struct. Funct.* 214, 419–433. doi:10.1007/s00429-010-0257-x

Alluri, V., Toiviainen, P., Jääskeläinen, I. P., Glerean, E., Sams, M., and Brattico, E. (2012). Large-scale brain networks emerge from dynamic processing of musical timbre, key and rhythm. *Neuroimage* 59, 3677–3689. doi:10.1016/j.neuroimage.2011.11.019

Altenmüller, E., Marco-Pallarés, J., Münte, T. F., and Schneider, S. (2009). Neural reorganization underlies improvement in stroke-induced motor dysfunction by music-supported therapy. *Ann. N. Y. Acad. Sci.* 1169, 395–405. doi:10.1111/j.1749-6632.2009.04580.x

Andersen, S. M., Rapcsak, S. Z., and Beeson, P. M. (2010). Cost function masking during normalization of brains with focal lesions: still a necessity? *Neuroimage* 53, 78–84. doi:10.1016/j.neuroimage.2010.06.003

Angelucci, F., Fiore, M., Ricci, E., Padua, L., Sabino, A., and Tonali, P. A. (2007). Investigating the neurobiology of music: brain-derived neurotrophic factor modulation in the hippocampus of young adult mice. *Behav. Pharmacol.* 18, 491–496. doi:10.1097/fbp.0b013e3282d28f50

Ashburner, J., and Friston, K. J. (2000). Voxel-based morphometry – the methods. *Neuroimage* 11, 805–821. doi:10.1006/nimg.2000.0582

Ashburner, J., and Friston, K. J. (2005). Unified segmentation. *Neuroimage* 26, 839–851. doi:10.1016/j.neuroimage.2005.02.018

Aust, S., Filip, K., Koelsch, S., Grimm, S., and Bajbouj, M. (2013). Music in depression: neural correlates of emotional experience in remitted depression. *World J. Psychiatry* 3, 8–17. doi:10.5498/wjp.v3.i2.8

Baldo, J. V., Wilkins, D. P., Ogar, J., Willock, S., and Dronkers, N. F. (2011). Role of the precentralgyrus of the insula in complex articulation. *Cortex* 47, 800–807. doi:10.1016/j.cortex.2010.07.001

Bengtsson, S. L., Ullén, F., Ehrsson, H. H., Hashimoto, T., Kito, T., Naito, E., et al. (2009). Listening to rhythms activates motor and premotor cortices. *Cortex* 45, 62–71. doi:10.1016/j.cortex.2008.07.002

Berkowitz, A. L., and Ansari, D. (2008). Generation of novel motor sequences: the neural correlates of musical improvisation. *Neuroimage* 41, 535–543. doi:10.1016/j.neuroimage.2008.02.028

Berns, G. S., Capra, C. M., Moore, S., and Noussair, C. (2010). Neural mechanisms of the influence of popularity on adolescent ratings of music. *Neuroimage* 49, 2687–2896. doi:10.1016/j.neuroimage.2009.10.070

Biernaskie, J., and Corbett, D. (2001). Enriched rehabilitative training promotes improved forelimb motor function and enhanced dendritic growth after focal ischemic injury. *J. Neurosci.* 21, 5272–5280.

Blank, S. C., Scott, S. K., Murphy, K., Warburton, E., and Wise, R. J. (2003). Speech production: Wernicke, Broca and beyond. *Brain* 125, 1829–1838. doi:10.1093/brain/awf191

Blasi, A., Mercure, E., Lloyd-Fox, S., Thomson, A., Brammer, M., Sauter, D., et al. (2011). Early specialization for voice and emotion processing in the infant brain. *Curr. Biol.* 21, 1220–1224. doi:10.1016/j.cub.2011.06.009

Blood, A. J., and Zatorre, R. J. (2001). Intensely pleasurable responses to music correlate with activity in brain regions implicated in reward and emotion. *Proc. Natl. Acad. Sci. U.S.A.* 98, 11818–11823. doi:10.1073/pnas.191355898

Bose, M., Muñoz-Llancao, P., Roychowdhury, S., Nichols, J. A., Jakkamsetti, V., Porter, B., et al. (2010). Effect of the environment on the dendritic morphology of the rat auditory cortex. *Synapse* 64, 97–110. doi:10.1002/syn.20710

Breier, J. I., Juranek, J., and Papanicolaou, A. C. (2011). Changes in maps of language function and the integrity of the arcuate fasciculus after therapy for chronic aphasia. *Neurocase* 17, 506–517. doi:10.1080/13554794.2010.547505

Brett, M., Leff, A. P., Rorden, C., and Ashburner, J. (2001). Spatial normalization of brain images with focal lesions using cost function masking. *Neuroimage* 14, 486–500. doi:10.1006/nimg.2001.0845

Brown, S., Martinez, M. J., and Parsons, L. M. (2004). Passive music listening spontaneously engages limbic and paralimbic systems. *Neuroreport* 15, 2033–2037. doi:10.1097/wnr.0b013e3282fd0dd8

Brown, S., Martinez, M. J., and Parsons, L. M. (2006). Music and language side by side in the brain: a PET study of the generation of melodies and sentences. *Eur. J. Neurosci.* 23, 2791–2803. doi:10.1111/j.1460-9568.2006.04785.x

Brownsett, S. L., Warren, J. E., Geranmayeh, F., Woodhead, Z., Leech, R., and Wise, R. J. (2014). Cognitive control and its impact on recovery from aphasic stroke. *Brain* 137, 242–254. doi:10.1093/brain/awt289

Bugos, J. A., Perlstein, W. M., McCrae, C. S., Brophy, T. S., and Bedenbaugh, P. H. (2007). Individualized piano instruction enhances executive functioning and working memory in older adults. *Aging Ment. Health* 11, 464–471. doi:10.1080/13607860601086504

Crinion, J., Ashburner, J., Leff, A., Brett, M., Price, C., and Friston, K. (2007). Spatial normalization of lesioned brains: performance evaluation and impact on fMRI analyses. *Neuroimage* 37, 866–875. doi:10.1016/j.neuroimage.2007.04.065

Dang, C., Liu, G., Xing, S., Xie, C., Peng, K., Li, C., et al. (2013). Longitudinal cortical volume changes correlate with motor recovery in patients after acute local subcortical infarction. *Stroke* 44, 2795–2801. doi:10.1161/strokeaha.113.000971

Der-Avakian, A., and Markou, A. (2012). The neurobiology of anhedonia and other reward-related deficits. *Trends Neurosci.* 35, 68–77. doi:10.1016/j.tins.2011.11.005

Dosenbach, N. U., Fair, D. A., Cohen, A. L., Schlaggar, B. L., and Petersen, S. E. (2008). A dual-networks architecture of top-down control. *Trends Cogn. Sci.* 12, 99–105. doi:10.1016/j.tics.2008.01.001

du Boisgueheneuc, F., Levy, R., Volle, E., Seassau, M., Duffau, H., Kinkingnehun, S., et al. (2006). Functions of the left superior frontal gyrus in humans: a lesion study. *Brain* 129, 3315–3328. doi:10.1093/brain/awl244

Engel, A., and Keller, P. E. (2011). The perception of musical spontaneity in improvised and imitated jazz performances. *Front. Psychol.* 2:83. doi:10.3389/fpsyg.2011.00083

Engineer, N. D., Percaccio, C. R., Pandya, P. K., Moucha, R., Rathbun, D. L., and Kilgard, M. P. (2004). Environmental enrichment improves response strength, threshold, selectivity, and latency of auditory cortex neurons. *J. Neurophysiol.* 92, 73–82. doi:10.1152/jn.00059.2004

Escoffier, N., Zhong, J., Schirmer, A., and Qiu, A. (2013). Emotional expressions in voice and music: same code, same effect? *Hum. Brain Mapp.* 34, 1796–1810. doi:10.1002/hbm.22029

Eslinger, P. J., Moore, P., Antani, S., Anderson, C., and Grossman, M. (2012). Apathy in frontotemporal dementia: behavioral and neuroimaging correlates. *Behav. Neurol.* 25, 127–136. doi:10.3233/ben-2011-0351

Etkin, A., Egner, T., and Kalisch, R. (2011). Emotional processing in anterior cingulate and medial prefrontal cortex. *Trends Cogn. Sci.* 15, 85–93. doi:10.1016/j.tics.2010.11.004

Fan, F., Zhu, C., Chen, H., Qin, W., Ji, X., Wang, L., et al. (2013). Dynamic brain structural changes after left hemisphere subcortical stroke. *Hum. Brain Mapp.* 34, 1872–1881. doi:10.1002/hbm.22034

Forsblom, A., Särkämö, T., Laitinen, S., and Tervaniemi, M. (2012). The effect of music and audio book listening on people recovering from stroke: the patient's point of view. *Music Med.* 2, 229–234. doi:10.1177/1943862110378110

Gaser, C., and Schlaug, G. (2003). Brain structures differ between musicians and non-musicians. *J. Neurosci.* 23, 9240–9245. doi:10.1016/S1053-8119(01)92488-7

Gauthier, L. V., Taub, E., Perkins, C., Ortmann, M., Mark, V. W., and Uswatte, G. (2008). Remodeling the brain: plastic structural brain changes produced by different motor therapies after stroke. *Stroke* 39, 1520–1525. doi:10.1161/strokeaha.107.502229

Gobbo, O. L., and O'Mara, S. M. (2004). Impact of enriched-environment housing on brain-derived neurotrophic factor and on cognitive performance after a transient global ischemia. *Behav. Brain Res.* 152, 231–241. doi:10.1016/j.bbr.2003.10.017

Grau-Olivares, M., Arboix, A., Junqué, C., Arenaza-Urquijo, E. M., Rovira, M., and Bartrés-Faz, D. (2010). Progressive gray matter atrophy in lacunar patients with vascular mild cognitive impairment. *Cerebrovasc. Dis.* 30, 157–166. doi:10.1159/000316059

Grau-Sánchez, J., Amengual, J. L., Rojo, N., Veciana de Las Heras, M., Montero, J., Rubio, F., et al. (2013). Plasticity in the sensorimotor cortex induced by music-supported therapy in stroke patients: a TMS study. *Front. Hum. Neurosci.* 7:494. doi:10.3389/fnhum.2013.00494

Green, A. C., Baerentsen, K. B., Stødkilde-Jørgensen, H., Wallentin, M., Roepstorff, A., and Vuust, P. (2008). Music in minor activates limbic structures: a relationship with dissonance? *Neuroreport* 19, 711–775. doi:10.1097/WNR.0b013e3282fd0dd8

Greicius, M. D., Flores, B. H., Menon, V., Glover, G. H., Solvason, H. B., Kenna, H., et al. (2007). Resting-state functional connectivity in major depression: abnormally increased contributions from subgenual cingulate cortex and thalamus. *Biol. Psychiatry* 62, 429–437. doi:10.1016/j.biopsych.2006.09.020

Grieve, S. M., Korgaonkar, M. S., Koslow, S. H., Gordon, E., and Williams, L. M. (2013). Widespread reductions in gray matter volume in depression. *Neuroimage Clin.* 3, 332–339. doi:10.1016/j.nicl.2013.08.016

Halwani, G. F., Loui, P., Rüber, T., and Schlaug, G. (2011). Effects of practice and experience on the arcuate fasciculus: comparing singers, instrumentalists, and non-musicians. *Front. Psychol.* 2:156. doi:10.3389/fpsyg.2011.00156

Herdener, M., Humbel, T., Esposito, F., Habermeyer, B., Cattapan-Ludewig, K., and Seifritz, E. (2014). Jazz drummers recruit language-specific areas for the processing of rhythmic structure. *Cereb. Cortex* 24, 836–843. doi:10.1093/cercor/bhs367

Hoekzema, E., Carmona, S., Tremols, V., Gispert, J. D., Guitart, M., Fauquet, J., et al. (2010). Enhanced neural activity in frontal and cerebellar circuits after cognitive training in children with attention-deficit/hyperactivity disorder. *Hum. Brain Mapp.* 31, 1942–1950. doi:10.1002/hbm.20988

Huang, S., Seidman, L. J., Rossi, S., and Ahveninen, J. (2013). Distinct cortical networks activated by auditory attention and working memory load. *Neuroimage* 83, 1098–1108. doi:10.1016/j.neuroimage.2013.07.074

Hyde, K. L., Lerch, J., Norton, A., Forgeard, M., Winner, E., Evans, A. C., et al. (2009). Musical training shapes structural brain development. *J. Neurosci.* 29, 3019–3025. doi:10.1523/jneurosci.5118-08.2009

James, C. E., Oechslin, M. S., Van De Ville, D., Hauert, C. A., Descloux, C., and Lazyras, F. (2014). Musical training yields opposite effects on grey matter density in cognitive versus sensorimotor networks. *Brain Struct. Funct.* 219, 353–366. doi:10.1007/s00429-013-0504-z

Janata, P. (2009). The neural architecture of music-evoked autobiographical memories. *Cereb. Cortex* 19, 2579–2594. doi:10.1093/cercor/bhp008

Janata, P., Birk, J. L., Van Horn, J. D., Leman, M., Tillmann, B., and Bharucha, J. J. (2002a). The cortical topography of tonal structures underlying Western music. *Science* 298, 2167–2170. doi:10.1126/science.1076262

Janata, P., Tillmann, B., and Bharucha, J. J. (2002b). Listening to polyphonic music recruits domain-general attention and working memory circuits. *Cogn. Aff. Behav. Neurosci.* 2, 121–140. doi:10.3758/CABN.2.2.121

Janssen, H., Ada, L., Bernhardt, J., McElduff, P., Pollack, M., Nilsson, M., et al. (2014). An enriched environment increases activity in stroke patients undergoing rehabilitation in a mixed rehabilitation unit: a pilot non-randomized controlled trial. *Disabil. Rehabil.* 36, 255–262. doi:10.3109/09638288.2013.788218

Jerde, T. A., Childs, S. K., Handy, S. T., Nagode, J. C., and Pardo, J. V. (2011). Dissociable systems of working memory for rhythm and melody. *Neuroimage* 57, 1572–1579. doi:10.1016/j.neuroimage.2011.05.061

Johansson, B. B. (2004). Functional and cellular effects of environmental enrichment after experimental brain infarcts. *Restor. Neurol. Neurosci.* 22, 163–174.

Johansson, B. B. (2012). Multisensory stimulation in stroke rehabilitation. *Front. Hum. Neurosci.* 6:60. doi:10.3389/fnhum.2012.00060

Johansson, B. B., and Belichenko, P. V. (2002). Neuronal plasticity and dendritic spines: effect of environmental enrichment on intact and postischemic rat brain. *J. Cereb. Blood Flow. Metab.* 22, 89–96. doi:10.1097/00004647-200201000-00011

Kang, D. H., Jo, H. J., Jung, W. H., Kim, S. H., Jung, Y. H., Choi, C. H., et al. (2013). The effect of meditation on brain structure: cortical thickness mapping and diffusion tensor imaging. *Soc. Cogn. Affect. Neurosci.* 8, 27–33. doi:10.1093/scan/nss056

Kitayama, S., Chua, H. F., Tompson, S., and Han, S. (2013). Neural mechanisms of dissonance: an fMRI investigation of choice justification. *Neuroimage* 69, 206–212. doi:10.1016/j.neuroimage.2012.11.034

Kleber, B., Birbaumer, N., Veit, R., Trevorrow, T., and Lotze, M. (2007). Overt and imagined singing of an Italian aria. *Neuroimage* 36, 889–900. doi:10.1016/j.neuroimage.2007.02.053

Koelsch, S. (2010). Towards a neural basis of music-evoked emotions. *Trends Cogn. Sci.* 14, 131–137. doi:10.1016/j.tics.2010.01.002

Koelsch, S. (2011). Toward a neural basis of music perception – a review and updated model. *Front. Psychol.* 2:110. doi:10.3389/fpsyg.2011.00110

Koelsch, S., Fritz, T., Schulze, K., Alsop, D., and Schlaug, G. (2005). Adults and children processing music: an fMRI study. *Neuroimage* 25, 1068–1076. doi:10.1016/j.neuroimage.2004.12.050

Koelsch, S., Fritz, T., V Cramon, D. Y., Müller, K., and Friederici, A. D. (2006). Investigating emotion with music: an fMRI study. *Hum. Brain Mapp.* 27, 239–250. doi:10.1002/hbm.20180

Koelsch, S., Kasper, E., Sammler, D., Schulze, K., Gunter, T., and Friederici, A. D. (2004). Music, language and meaning: brain signatures of semantic processing. *Nat. Neurosci.* 7, 302–307. doi:10.1038/nn1197

Komitova, M., Mattsson, B., Johansson, B. B., and Eriksson, P. S. (2005). Enriched environment increases neural stem/progenitor cell proliferation and neurogenesis in the subventricular zone of stroke-lesioned adult rats. *Stroke* 36, 1278–1282. doi:10.1161/01.str.0000166197.94147.59

Lai, C. H. (2013). Gray matter volume in major depressive disorder: a meta-analysis of voxel-based morphometry studies. *Psychiatry Res.* 211, 37–46. doi:10.1016/j.pscychresns.2012.06.006

Lancaster, J. L., Woldorff, M. G., Parsons, L. M., Liotti, M., Freitas, C. S., Rainey, L., et al. (2000). Automated Talairach atlas labels for functional brain mapping. *Hum. Brain Mapp.* 10, 120–131. doi:10.1002/1097-0193(200007)

Lappe, C., Steinsträter, O., and Pantev, C. (2013). Rhythmic and melodic deviations in musical sequences recruit different cortical areas for mismatch detection. *Front. Hum. Neurosci.* 7:260. doi:10.3389/fnhum.2013.00260

Lee, Y. S., Janata, P., Frost, C., Hanke, M., and Granger, R. (2011). Investigation of melodic contour processing in the brain using multivariate pattern-based fMRI. *Neuroimage* 57, 293–300. doi:10.1016/j.neuroimage.2011.02.006

Liang, Z., Zeng, J., Zhang, C., Liu, S., Ling, X., Xu, A., et al. (2008). Longitudinal investigations on the anterograde and retrograde degeneration in the pyramidal tract following pontine infarction with diffusion tensor imaging. *Cerebrovasc. Dis.* 25, 209–216. doi:10.1159/000113858

Lieberman, M. D., and Cunningham, W. A. (2009). Type I and Type II error concerns in fMRI research: re-balancing the scale. *Soc. Cogn. Affect. Neurosci.* 4, 423–428. doi:10.1093/scan/nsp052

Maegele, M., Lippert-Gruener, M., Ester-Bode, T., Garbe, J., Bouillon, B., Neugebauer, E., et al. (2005a). Multimodal early onset stimulation combined with enriched environment is associated with reduced CNS lesion volume and enhanced reversal of neuromotor dysfunction after traumatic brain injury in rats. *Eur. J. Neurosci.* 21, 2406–2418. doi:10.1111/j.1460-9568.2005.04070.x

Maegele, M., Lippert-Gruener, M., Ester-Bode, T., Sauerland, S., Schäfer, U., Molcanyi, M., et al. (2005b). Reversal of neuromotor and cognitive dysfunction in an enriched environment combined with multimodal early onset stimulation after traumatic brain injury in rats. *J. Neurotrauma* 22, 772–782. doi:10.1089/neu.2005.22.772

Matsumori, Y., Hong, S. M., Fan, Y., Kayama, T., Hsu, C. Y., Weinstein, P. R., et al. (2006). Enriched environment and spatial learning enhance hippocampal neurogenesis and salvages ischemic penumbra after focal cerebral ischemia. *Neurobiol. Dis.* 22, 187–198. doi:10.1016/j.nbd.2005.10.015

Menon, V., and Levitin, D. J. (2005). The rewards of music listening: response and physiological connectivity of the mesolimbic system. *Neuroimage* 28, 175–184. doi:10.1016/j.neuroimage.2005.05.053

Mitterschiffthaler, M. T., Fu, C. H., Dalton, J. A., Andrew, C. M., and Williams, S. C. (2007). A functional MRI study of happy and sad affective states induced by classical music. *Hum. Brain Mapp.* 28, 1150–1162. doi:10.1002/hbm.20337

Montag, C., Reuter, M., and Axmacher, N. (2011). How one's favorite song activates the reward circuitry of the brain: personality matters! Behav. *Brain Res.* 225, 511–514. doi:10.1016/j.bbr.2011.08.012

Nichols, J. A., Jakkamsetti, V. P., Salgado, H., Dinh, L., Kilgard, M. P., and Atzori, M. (2007). Environmental enrichment selectively increases glutamatergic responses in layer II/III of the auditory cortex of the rat. *Neuroscience* 145, 832–840. doi:10.1016/j.neuroscience.2006.12.061

Nithianantharajah, J., and Hannan, A. J. (2006). Enriched environments, experience-dependent plasticity and disorders of the nervous system. *Nat. Rev. Neurosci.* 7, 697–709. doi:10.1038/nrn1970

Northoff, G., and Bermpohl, F. (2004). Cortical midline structures and the self. *Trends Cogn. Sci.* 8, 102–107. doi:10.1016/j.tics.2004.01.004

Omar, R., Henley, S. M., Bartlett, J. W., Hailstone, J. C., Gordon, E., Sauter, D. A., et al. (2011). The structural neuroanatomy of music emotion recognition: evidence from frontotemporal lobar degeneration. *Neuroimage* 56, 1814–1821. doi:10.1016/j.neuroimage.2011.03.002

Osuch, E. A., Bluhm, R. L., Williamson, P. C., Théberge, J., Densmore, M., and Neufeld, R. W. (2009). Brain activation to favorite music in healthy controls and depressed patients. *Neuroreport* 20, 1204–1208. doi:10.1097/wnr.0b013e32832f4da3

Platel, H., Baron, J. C., Desgranges, B., Bernard, F., and Eustache, F. (2003). Semantic and episodic memory of music are subserved by distinct neural networks. *Neuroimage* 20, 244–256. doi:10.1016/S1053-8119(03)00287-8

Price, C. J. (2010). The anatomy of language: a review of 100 fMRI studies published in 2009. *Ann. N. Y. Acad. Sci.* 1191, 62–88. doi:10.1111/j.1749-6632.2010.05444.x

Ripollés, P., Marco-Pallarés, J., de Diego-Balaguer, R., Miró, J., Falip, M., Juncadella, M., et al. (2012). Analysis of automated methods for spatial normalization of lesioned brains. *Neuroimage* 60, 1296–1306. doi:10.1016/j.neuroimage.2012.01.094

Rodríguez-Fornells, A., Rojo, N., Amengual, J. L., Ripollés, P., Altenmüller, E., and Münte, T. F. (2012). The involvement of audio-motor coupling in the music-supported therapy applied to stroke patients. *Ann. N. Y. Acad. Sci.* 1252, 282–293. doi:10.1111/j.1749-6632.2011.06425.x

Rojo, N., Amengual, J. L., Juncadella, M., Rubio, F., Camara, E., Marco-Pallarés, J., et al. (2011). Music-supported therapy induces plasticity in the sensorimotor cortex in chronic stroke: a single-case study using multimodal imaging (fMRI-TMS). *Brain Inj.* 25, 787–793. doi:10.3109/02699052.2011.576305

Rorden, C., and Brett, M. (2000). Stereotaxic display of brain lesions. *Behav. Neurol.* 12, 191–200. doi:10.1155/2000/421719

Salimpoor, V. N., Benovoy, M., Larcher, K., Dagher, A., and Zatorre, R. J. (2011). Anatomically distinct dopamine release during anticipation and experience of peak emotion to music. *Nat. Neurosci.* 14, 257–262. doi:10.1038/nn.2726

Salimpoor, V. N., van den Bosch, I., Kovacevic, N., McIntosh, A. R., Dagher, A., and Zatorre, R. J. (2013). Interactions between the nucleus accumbens and auditory cortices predict music reward value. *Science* 340, 216–219. doi:10.1126/science.1231059

Särkämö, T., Pihko, E., Laitinen, S., Forsblom, A., Soinila, S., Mikkonen, M., et al. (2010a). Music and speech listening enhance the recovery of early sensory processing after stroke. *J. Cogn. Neurosci.* 22, 2716–2727. doi:10.1162/jocn.2009.21376

Särkämö, T., Tervaniemi, M., Soinila, S., Autti, T., Silvennoinen, H. M., Laine, M., et al. (2010b). Auditory and cognitive deficits associated with acquired amusia after stroke: a magnetoencephalography and neuropsychological follow-up study. *PLoS ONE* 5:e15157. doi:10.1371/journal.pone.0015157

Särkämö, T., Tervaniemi, M., Laitinen, S., Forsblom, A., Soinila, S., Mikkonen, M., et al. (2008). Music listening enhances cognitive recovery and mood after middle cerebral artery stroke. *Brain* 131, 866–876. doi:10.1093/brain/awn013

Särkämö, T., Tervaniemi, M., Soinila, S., Autti, T., Silvennoinen, H. M., Laine, M., et al. (2009). Cognitive deficits associated with acquired amusia after stroke: a neuropsychological follow-up study. *Neuropsychologia* 47, 2642–2651. doi:10.1016/j.neuropsychologia.2009.05.015

Schlaug, G., Marchina, S., and Norton, A. (2008). From singing to speaking: why singing may lead to recovery of expressive language function in patients with Broca's aphasia. *Music Percept.* 25, 315–323. doi:10.1525/mp.2008.25.4.315

Schlaug, G., Marchina, S., and Norton, A. (2009). Evidence for plasticity in white-matter tracts of patients with chronic Broca's aphasia undergoing intense intonation-based speech therapy. *Ann. N. Y. Acad. Sci.* 2009, 385–394. doi:10.1111/j.1749-6632.2009.04587.x

Söderström, I., Strand, M., Ingridsson, A. C., Nasic, S., and Olsson, T. (2009). 17beta-estradiol and enriched environment accelerate cognitive recovery after focal brain ischemia. *Eur. J. Neurosci.* 29, 1215–1224. doi:10.1111/j.1460-9568.2009.06662.x

Sutoo, D., and Akiyama, K. (2004). Music improves dopaminergic neurotransmission: demonstration based on the effect of music on blood pressure regulation. *Brain Res.* 1016, 255–262. doi:10.1016/j.brainres.2004.05.018

Tervaniemi, M., and Hugdahl, K. (2003). Lateralization of auditory-cortex functions. *Brain Res. Rev.* 43, 231–246. doi:10.1016/j.brainresrev.2003.08.004

Thiebaut de Schotten, M., Tomaiuolo, F., Aiello, M., Merola, S., Silvetti, M., Lecce, F., et al. (2014). Damage to white matter pathways in subacute and chronic spatial neglect: a group study and 2 single-case studies with complete virtual "in vivo" tractography dissection. *Cereb. Cortex* 24, 691–706. doi:10.1093/cercor/bhs351

Trost, W., Ethofer, T., Zentner, M., and Vuilleumier, P. (2012). Mapping aesthetic musical emotions in the brain. *Cereb. Cortex* 22, 2769–2783. doi:10.1093/cercor/bhr353

Tzourio-Mazoyer, N., Landeau, B., Papathanassiou, D., Crivello, F., Etard, O., Delcroix, N., et al. (2002). Automated anatomical labeling of activations in SPM using a macroscopic anatomical parcellation of the MNI MRI single-subject brain. *Neuroimage* 15, 273–289. doi:10.1006/nimg.2001.0978

Vago, D. R., and Silbersweig, D. A. (2012). Self-awareness, self-regulation, and self-transcendence (S-ART): a framework for understanding the neurobiological mechanisms of mindfulness. *Front. Hum. Neurosci.* 6:296. doi:10.3389/fnhum.2012.00296

van Meer, M. P., Otte, W. M., van derMarel, K., Nijboer, C. H., Kavelaars, A., van der-Sprenkel, J. W., et al. (2012). Extent of bilateral neuronal network reorganization and functional recovery in relation to stroke severity. *J. Neurosci.* 32, 4495–4507. doi:10.1523/jneurosci.3662-11.2012

Verghese, J., Lipton, R. B., Katz, M. J., Hall, C. B., Derby, C. A., Kuslansky, G., et al. (2003). Leisure activities and the risk of dementia in the elderly. *N. Engl. J. Med.* 348, 2508–2516. doi:10.1056/NEJMoa022252

Villarreal, M. F., Cerquetti, D., Caruso, S., SchwarczLópezAranguren, V., Gerschcovich, E. R., Frega, A. L., et al. (2013). Neural correlates of musical creativity: differences between high and low creative subjects. *PLoS ONE* 8:e75427. doi:10.1371/journal.pone.0075427

Wehrum, S., Degé, F., Ott, U., Walter, B., Stippekohl, B., Kagerer, S., et al. (2011). Can you hear a difference? Neuronal correlates of melodic deviance processing in children. *Brain Res.* 1402, 80–92. doi:10.1016/j.brainres.2011.05.057

Yoshimura, S., Okamoto, Y., Onoda, K., Matsunaga, M., Okada, G., Kunisato, Y., et al. (in press). Cognitive behavioral therapy for depression changes medial prefrontal and ventral anterior cingulate cortex activity associated with self-referential processing. *Soc. Cogn. Affect. Neurosci.* doi:10.1093/scan/nst009

Zarate, J. M., and Zatorre, R. J. (2008). Experience-dependent neural substrates involved in vocal pitch regulation during singing. *Neuroimage* 40, 1871–1887. doi:10.1016/j.neuroimage.2008.01.026

Zatorre, R. J. (2013). Predispositions and plasticity in music and speech learning: neural correlates and implications. *Science* 342, 585–589. doi:10.1126/science.1238414

Zatorre, R. J., Belin, P., and Penhune, V. B. (2002). Structure and function of auditory cortex: music and speech. *Trends Cogn. Sci.* 6, 37–46. doi:10.1016/S1364-6613(00)01816-7

Zatorre, R. J., Fields, R. D., and Johansen-Berg, H. (2012). Plasticity in gray and white: neuroimaging changes in brain structure during learning. *Nat. Neurosci.* 15, 528–536. doi:10.1038/nn.3045

18

Music as a mnemonic to learn gesture sequences in normal aging and Alzheimer's disease

Aline Moussard[1]*, Emmanuel Bigand[2], Sylvie Belleville[3] and Isabelle Peretz[4,5]

[1] Rotman Research Institute, Baycrest, University of Toronto, Toronto, ON, Canada
[2] Laboratoire d'Etude de l'Apprentissage et du Développement (LEAD – CNRS 5022), Université de Bourgogne, Dijon, France
[3] Centre de Recherche de l'Institut Universitaire de Gériatrie de Montréal (CRIUGM), Université de Montréal, Montréal, QC, Canada
[4] International Laboratory for Brain, Music and Sound Research (BRAMS), Université de Montréal, Montréal, QC, Canada
[5] Centre for Research on Brain, Language and Music (CRBLM), McGill University, Montréal, QC, Canada

Correspondence:
Aline Moussard, Rotman Research Institute, Baycrest, 3560 Bathurst Street, 724, Toronto, ON M6A 2E1, Canada
e-mail: amoussard@research.baycrest.org; alinemoussard@gmail.com

Strong links between music and motor functions suggest that music could represent an interesting aid for motor learning. The present study aims for the first time to test the potential of music to assist in the learning of sequences of gestures in normal and pathological aging. Participants with mild Alzheimer's disease (AD) and healthy older adults (controls) learned sequences of meaningless gestures that were either accompanied by music or a metronome. We also manipulated the learning procedure such that participants had to imitate the gestures to-be-memorized in synchrony with the experimenter or after the experimenter during encoding. Results show different patterns of performance for the two groups. Overall, musical accompaniment had no impact on the controls' performance but improved those of AD participants. Conversely, synchronization of gestures during learning helped controls but seemed to interfere with retention in AD. We discuss these findings regarding their relevance for a better understanding of auditory–motor memory, and we propose recommendations to maximize the mnemonic effect of music for motor sequence learning for dementia care.

Keywords: music, mnemonic, motor abilities, Alzheimer's disease, aging, imitation, movement

INTRODUCTION

Music has been shown to enhance the retention of newly acquired verbal information in normal aging and Alzheimer's disease (AD). Simmons-Stern et al. (2010) showed that after two exposures, patients with mild AD (mean MMSE = 24/30) were better at recognizing sung than spoken lyrics. Better retention of sung lyrics rather than spoken lyrics was found in a delayed free recall (10 min after learning) in mild AD patients and healthy controls (Moussard et al., 2014). We proposed that dual coding of lyrics and melody lead to a stronger memory trace, which enhances long-term retention. The strong links between music and language suggest a basis for the positive effect of music on verbal memory. According to numerous studies, the shared resources between these domains (Patel, 2008) could explain why adding musical information favors linguistic encoding and memorization. On the other hand, music has been shown to facilitate performance during various kinds of cognitive (including non-linguistic) tasks (Schellenberg, 2005). Accordingly, music may be viewed as having a large positive impact on cognition in general through broad effects on such aspects as attention, emotion, and motivation (arousal effect). The present study further investigates the positive impact of music on memory for non-linguistic material in healthy and AD older adults.

To our knowledge, no study has investigated the effect of a musical accompaniment for motor sequence learning. Yet strong links between music and motor functions suggest that music could represent an interesting aid for motor learning. Long- and short-term musical practice lead to strong plasticity effects in motor brain areas (Wan and Schlaug, 2010; Pantev and Herholz, 2011). Interestingly, listening to music activates motor regions (Brown and Martinez, 2007; Zatorre et al., 2007) and arousing musical pieces can enhance tonus and body posture (Forti et al., 2010). In dementia care, music is used to stimulate movement and alertness in patients with apathy (Cevasco and Grant, 2003; Holmes et al., 2006). A clinical case study showed that two out of three patients tested in the final stage of dementia showed greater reactions to musical than visual or tactile stimulations (Norberg et al., 2003). More generally, many reports from music therapy suggest a strong effect of music on tonus in dementia patients, though further scientific validation of these effects is needed (Aldridge, 1994).

Rhythm seems to be a key component in the relationship between music and motor functions. Motor synchronization is more strongly related to the auditory modality than the visual modality (Repp and Penel, 2004; Patel et al., 2005). In clinical care, auditory–motor synchronization enhances gait and movement production in Parkinson disease (Lim et al., 2005, for a review) and facilitates speech production in aphasia (Racette et al., 2006; Stahl et al., 2011; see Zumbansen et al., 2014, for review). By reinforcing auditory–motor coupling, synchronization during learning could reinforce encoding and facilitate memory retrieval. Moreover, synchronization and auditory–motor coupling could be enhanced by the presence of music accompaniment. In Racette and colleagues' study, singing (but not speaking) in unison with a demonstrator improves production and retention of sentences in aphasic patients (Racette et al., 2006). Several interpretations can account for a stronger effect of synchronization in musical than non-musical situations. Firstly, music provides cues for rhythmic synchronization and many studies showed strong sensory–motor integration effects, possibly mediated by the mirror neuron system (Chen et al., 2009; D'Ausilio, 2009; Overy and Molnar-Szakacs, 2009). Secondly, the affective component of music and its ability to communicate social and emotional meaning might play a role for synchronization between individuals (Molnar-Szakacs and Overy, 2006; Overy and Molnar-Szakacs, 2009). In the shared affective motion experience (SAME) model, Overy and Molnar-Szakacs (2009) propose that a large network involving the mirror neuron system and the emotional network (anterior insula and limbic system) is involved while experiencing a musical activity, which may explain why music is such a relevant stimulus in all human societies. According to the authors, imitation, synchronization, and shared experience may be key elements for successful therapeutic programs.

In the present pilot study, we investigate the learning and retention of sequences of gestures. We test the influence of two factors, musical accompaniment and synchronization of performance with a demonstrator during encoding, and the interaction between these. Musical accompaniment is expected to enhance recall performance because of links between music processing and motor functions and the general arousing effect of music. However, it could also be that music might distract participants, especially those with AD who may have more attentional deficits (e.g., Gorus et al., 2006). Dual coding resulting from music-based gesture-sequence learning might also lead to a detrimental effect for individuals with fewer cognitive resources. For these reasons, investigating the effects of musical accompaniment on motor memorization will provide both theoretical and clinical insights. Synchronization during the learning of gestures is expected to improve recall performance based on the effect of action on memory, which is well-documented in the literature. For example, learning a list of words describing actions is easier when these actions are mimed during encoding (e.g., Feyereisen, 2009). Additionally, we expected an interaction between synchronization and musical accompaniment, based on the specific links between music and sensory-motor integration described above.

MATERIALS AND METHODS

PARTICIPANTS

Eight AD participants (mean MMSE = 25.2/30; range 23–27) and seven healthy controls participated in the study. Healthy controls were recruited from the participant database of the Research Center of the Geriatric Institute of the University of Montreal (CRIUGM). We recruited AD participants from the Alzheimer Society of Montreal ($N = 6$) and from a cohort of patients followed at the CRIUGM ($N = 2$). AD participants met the NINCDS-ADRDA research criteria for probable AD (McKhann et al., 1984) and the DSM-IV clinical criteria for dementia of the Alzheimer's type (APA, 1994). Mixed dementias were excluded. Cognitively healthy individuals were used as controls. They were screened for cognitive impairment and selected to match AD patients for age and education. In all participants, exclusion criteria included history of psychiatric or neurological disorders, cerebrovascular diseases, hearing impairment, alcoholism, and dyslexia. All gave informed consent approved by the ethics board of IUGM for their participation in a larger study about music and memory. One control participant was excluded from the analyses because she was unable to complete all conditions, leaving a final pool of eight AD and six controls.

Neuropsychological assessment of participants is presented in **Table 1**. As expected, AD participants showed lower scores than controls for MMSE (Folstein et al., 1975) and verbal memory for words (Rey's 15 words; Rey, 1970) and stories (Gély-Nargeot et al., 1997). They also showed slightly inferior scores for verbal comprehension (Token test; De Renzi and Vignolo, 1962). They did not show significant differences from controls for verbal working memory (forward and backward digit spans), auditory attention (TEA, elevator task; Robertson et al., 1994), or praxis (imitation of meaningless gestures). There were no significant differences in the questionnaires of depression (Geriatric Depression Scale; Yesavage et al., 1983) and well-being (Bravo et al., 1996).

Assessment of auditory and musical abilities (**Table 2**) showed no difference between AD and control participants for musical experience; all were considered non-musicians according to the questionnaire of Ehrlé (1998). There were no differences for auditory perception (repetition of sentences; Moussard et al., 2012), nor musical perception abilities (Scale, Contour/Interval, and Rhythm subtests of the MBEMA; Peretz et al., 2013): all participants showed normal abilities to discriminate changes in melodies, which could either violate the key, the interval size, the contour, or the rhythm. Both groups of participants showed equivalent scores for the recognition of emotions – happiness, sadness, and fear – from short instrumental excerpts (from Vieillard et al., 2008). We also tested participants on their recognition of short instrumental familiar songs (e.g., *Brother John* versus non-familiar lures that were matched in terms of musical characteristics; task from Samson et al., 2012; see also Moussard et al., 2012). Participants showed preserved recognition in their ability to decide whether these songs were familiar or not to them.

DESIGN

Participants had to learn four different sets of 10 gestures. We first compared two conditions of accompaniment during gesture learning: (1) musical accompaniment, using familiar and danceable folkloric music from Quebec or (2) metronomic accompaniment set to the same tempo as the music of the first condition. Secondly, for each of these, the participant is asked to either (1) observe the gestures to-be-memorized once and then to reproduce them in synchrony with the experimenter before reproducing them alone or (2) observe the gestures twice before reproducing them alone (i.e., experiencing the same amount of exposure to the gestures but without any synchronized production). Thus, each participant learned four sets of gesture sequences: music accompaniment with synchronized production during learning (Music_Sync), music accompaniment without synchrony (Music_NoSync), metronome accompaniment with synchrony (Metronome_Sync), and metronome accompaniment without synchrony (Metronome_NoSync).

Table 1 | Neuropsychological assessment.

	Sex F/M	Age	Education (years)	Cognitive level	Verbal memory (Rev's 15 words)		Working memory		Attention	Language	Praxis	Mood and well-being	
				MMSE 30	Sum of 5 recalls/75	Recogn. 0.15	Digit span (forward)	Digit span (backward)	TEA (elevator task)/7	Token test/44	Praxis/12	Geriatric depression scale (GDS)/30	Well-being scale 100
AD													
HD	F	79	9	23	25	9	5	3	7	40	12	2	80
JO	M	77	17	23	12	2	5	3	6	29	11	0	84
JL	F	67	7	25	32	12	5	5	7	39	12	1	84
AM	F	84	12	25	22	8	7	4	6	32	12	7	54
JE	M	77	7	26	22	9	5	3	7	36	10	17	39
JR	M	79	16	26	17	7	6	4	7	42	12	5	69
RL	M	76	9	27	32	13	5	4	7	37	11	9	64
HU	F	83	16	27	19	4	6	5	7	35	11	6	94
Average		**77.8**	**11.6**	**25.2*** **	**22.6*** **	**8** **	**5.5**	**3.9**	**6.8**	**36.3** **	**11.4**	**5.9**	**71**
SD		**5.2**	**4.2**	**1.6**	**7**	**3.7**	**0.8**	**0.8**	**0.5**	**4.3**	**0.8**	**5.5**	**18.2**
CONTROLS													
RJ	F	77	15	28	63	15	5	4	7	44	11	1	85
RD	M	65	11	29	51	15	6	5	7	44	11	3	92
AL	F	70	15	29	62	15	5	4	7	43	12	1	68
LA	M	84	9	29	43	8	7	5	7	42	12	1	87
CB	F	70	8	30	45	12	5	4	7	36	11	4	79
AD	F	82	14	30	61	15	6	4	7	44	12	2	87
Average		**74.7**	**12**	**29.2**	**54.2**	**13.3**	**5.7**	**4.3**	**7**	**42.2**	**11.5**	**2**	**83**
SD		**7.5**	**3.1**	**0.8**	**9**	**2.9**	**0.8**	**0.5**	**0**	**3.1**	**0.5**	**1.3**	**8.5**

*Asterisks represent differences between AD and controls (**$p < 0.05$; ***$p < 0.01$).*

Table 2 | Auditory and musical assessment.

	Auditory test	Musical background	Musical abilities (adapted from MBMEA)			Memory for familiar music	Recognition of musical emotions (% correct)		
	Repetition of sentences/24	Questionnaire/27	Scale/20	Interval/ contour/20	Rhythm/20	Recognition/8	Joy	Sadness	Fear
AD									
HD	23	4	16	15	14	7	–	–	–
JO	21	7	18	17	18	7	81.3	18.8	25
JL	23	4	18	14	16	8	81.3	62.5	56.3
AM	22	6	19	20	18	8	93.8	56.3	43.8
JE	24	3	19	19	19	7	31.3	6.3	31.3
JR	23	9	18	19	19	8	93.8	37.5	43.8
RL	23	3	17	18	17	6	93.8	43.8	25
HU	24	10	19	20	19	8	100	43.8	18.8
Average	**22.9**	**5.8**	**18**	**17.8**	**17.5**	**7.4**	**82.1**	**38.4**	**34.8**
SD	**1**	**2.7**	**1.1**	**2.3**	**1.8**	**0.7**	**23.5**	**20**	**13.4**
CONTROLS									
RJ	24	5	18	16	18	8	100	56.3	25
RD	23	4	20	20	20	8	56.3	31.3	62.5
AL	23	3	18	19	18	5	87.5	50	50
LA	22	3	18	17	18	6	93.8	43.8	68.8
CB	23	4	17	14	15	4	81.3	25	43.8
AD	24	7	17	14	20	8	–	–	–
Average	**23.2**	**4.3**	**18**	**16.7**	**18.2**	**6.5**	**83.8**	**41.3**	**50**
SD	**0.8**	**1.5**	**1.1**	**2.5**	**1.8**	**1.8**	**16.9**	**13**	**17.1**

MATERIAL

Gestures

Twelve gestures involving simple and meaningless movements of arms, legs, head, and trunk were selected following the recommendations of a geriatric physiotherapist. They were performed in a secure sitting position (see **Figure 1A** for an illustration). Four sequences were created with a combination of 10 of the 12 gestures, to-be-learned sequentially. All 12 gestures were performed during a pre-experimental session to ensure that they could easily be done by participants. In case of discomfort with a gesture, it was replaced by one of the two supplementary gestures.

Accompaniment

Two musical excerpts were chosen among the repertoire of folkloric music from Quebec (Rigaudon), a style very similar to Irish jigs and reels. They had the same instrumentation, a very similar rhythm and the same tempo (116 bpm, which corresponds to a typical tempo in folkloric Rigaudon music). The excerpts were randomly assigned across the two synchrony conditions ("with" and "without") for each participant. An audible marker (a "beep" sound) was added to the recording to mark the beginning of each gesture (at the first beat of every measure), making for one gesture approximately every 2 s. To create the metronomic accompaniment, these beep tracks were isolated from the musical tracks, thus keeping the same tempo for the gesture sequences in both musical and metronome conditions. Both metronome tracks were also randomly assigned to the synchrony conditions across participants.

PROCEDURE

The learning procedure for each gesture-sequence occurred as follows. The participant and experimenter sat face to face. The participant was first familiarized with the complete sequence to-be-memorized by observing the experimenter performing it once, while the corresponding accompaniment played. Then, the first two gestures were taught to the participant following three steps. In the first step, the participant observed the first two gestures performed by the experimenter. The second step varied according to the learning condition, those being either (1) synchrony, where the experimenter's second performance of each gesture is shadowed by the participant, or (2) without synchrony, where the experimenter's second performance of gestures is simply observed again by the participant (as in step 1). Finally, in the third step (irrespective of condition), the participant was asked to reproduce the gestures by himself. All learning of subsequent gestures followed the same procedure. After each addition of a pair of gestures, the entire series of learned gestures up until that point was recapitulated. In other words, after adding gestures 3 and 4, gestures 1–4 were performed, and after adding gestures 5 and 6, gestures 1–6 were performed, and so on (always following the steps described above; see **Figure 1B** for an illustration of the learning procedure). Starting from the recall of the first six gestures, an additional two gestures were only added if participants reached a level of at least 65% during their previous recall (i.e., when they performed the gestures by themselves). This adaptive procedure ensured that the task was suited to each participant's capabilities and thus was adapted to both groups of participants.

A Example of gestures.

Gesture 1 Gesture 2 Gesture 3 Gesture 4 Gesture 5 Gesture 6

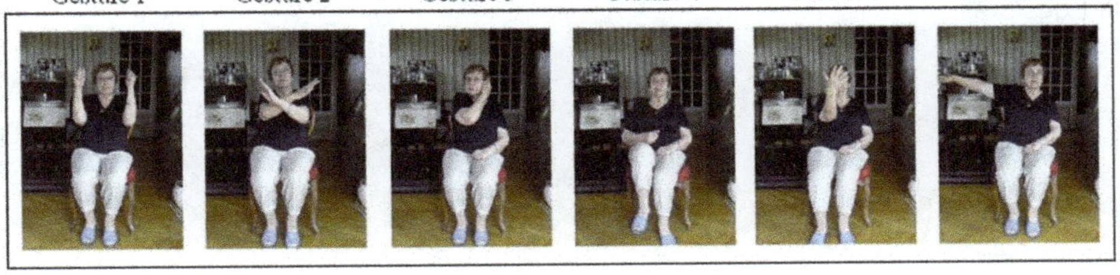

B Illustration of the learning procedure.

Learning trials for a full sequence	STEP 1: Observe		STEP 2: Observe (no synchrony condition) *OR* Reproduce together (synchrony condition)		STEP 3: Reproduce alone
1	Gestures 1 and 2	→	Gestures 1 and 2	→	Gestures 1 and 2
2	Gestures 3 and 4	→	Gestures 3 and 4	→	Gestures 3 and 4
3	Gestures 1 to 4	→	Gestures 1 to 4	→	**Gestures 1 to 4**
4	Gestures 5 and 6	→	Gestures 5 and 6	→	Gestures 5 and 6
5	Gestures 1 to 6	→	Gestures 1 to 6	→	**Gestures 1 to 6** ---------- Stop if score < 65 %
6	Gestures 7 and 8	→	Gestures 7 and 8	→	Gestures 7 and 8
7	Gestures 1 to 8	→	Gestures 1 to 8	→	**Gestures 1 to 8** ---------- Stop if score < 65 %
8	Gestures 9 and 10	→	Gestures 9 and 10	→	Gestures 9 and 10
9	Gestures 1 to 10	→	Gestures 1 to 10	→	**Gestures 1 to 10**

FIGURE 1 | (A) Examples of gestures; **(B)** illustration of learning procedure for a full sequence of 10 gestures. Bold font indicates recall trials that are considered in the statistical analysis.

The recapitulation of an entire series of learned gestures up until the last pair learned (i.e., gestures 1–4, 1–6, and if performance allowed, 1–8 and 1–10; see in bold in **Figure 1B**) served as our measure of immediate recall. Immediate recall scores were obtained by adding the scores of these recalls. Participants were tested again 10 min after the end of the learning session for a delayed recall trial: without being exposed to the sequence again, they were asked what they remembered from the sequence of gestures that they have been learned at the beginning of the session.

Music or metronome accompaniment was played for each of the three steps described above during learning and recall. Musical excerpt (see Accompaniment) was always associated to the same sequence of gestures and a given measure or musical phrase was always associated to a specific gesture, whether during observation or reproduction.

The four sequences (the product of the two learning conditions multiplied by the two accompaniment conditions; see Design above) were learned over four different sessions, each a week apart and presented in a randomized order for each subject. Each learning session lasted for an estimated 15 min. All sessions took place in the participant's home, always at the same hour of the day. Auditory stimuli were presented through a loudspeaker and the entire session was filmed.

DATA ANALYSIS

Two judges scored the produced gestures from videos; one of them was not involved in the study (intern students). Judges quantified recall according to four criteria: (1) gestures are present/absent (recalled gestures), (2) gestures are in the right/wrong order in the sequence (order), (3) gestures are well/poorly produced (quality of production), (4) wrong gestures are present (intrusions). When the two judges disagreed (in less than 10% of cases), a third judge (also not involved in the study) scored and arbitrated. Data were then analyzed using non-parametric statistics (Wilcoxon test). There was no clear influence of different conditions on measures of quality of production or intrusions, thus results will focus on the measures of recalled gestures and on gesture order in the sequence.

RESULTS

Immediate and delayed recall scores highlighted an outlier in the AD group (participant JL), with performance largely higher than the ones from the other seven AD participants. Scores of JL were

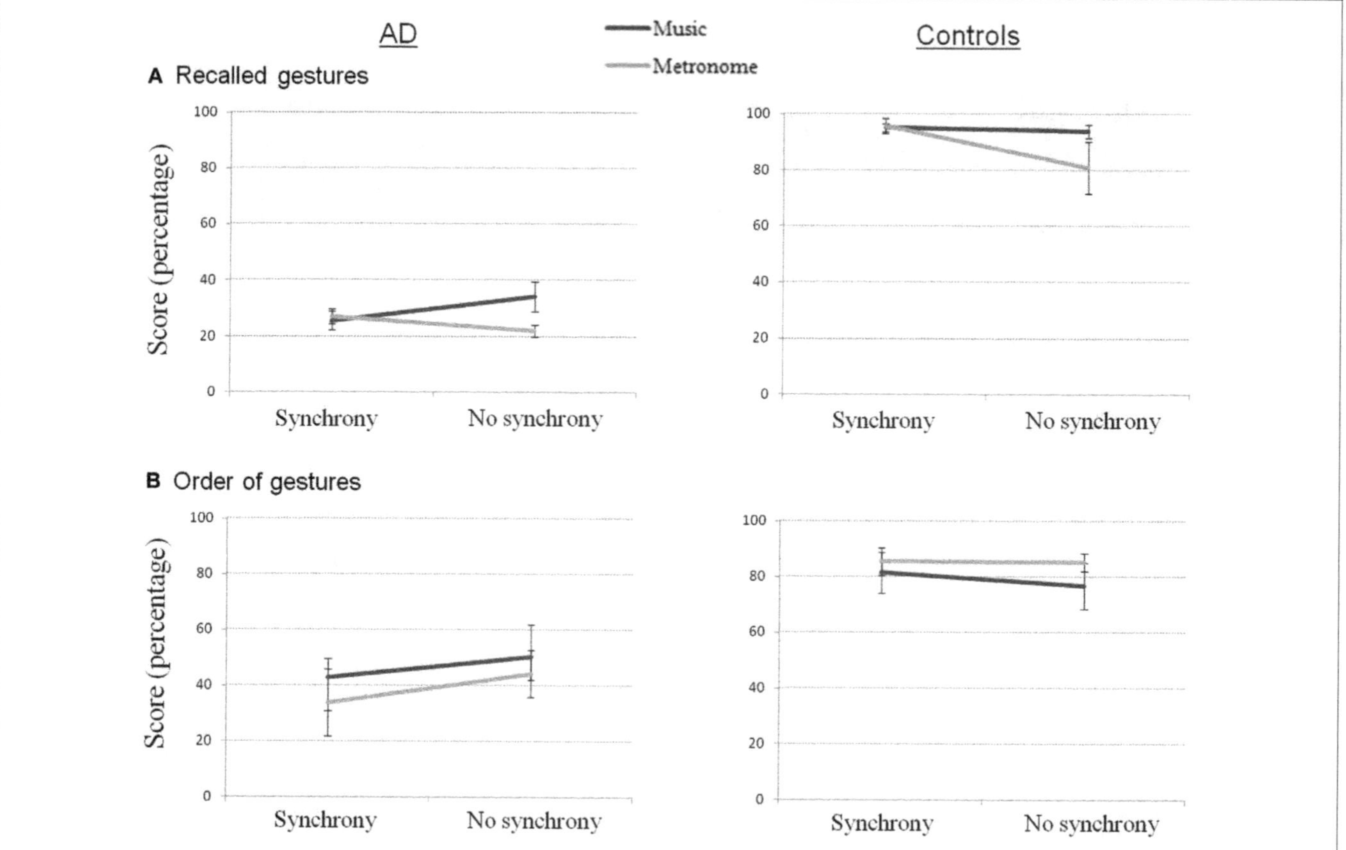

FIGURE 2 | Recalled gestures (A) and order of gestures (B) in immediate recall for AD and control participants.

thus analyzed separately and her data are presented after those of the groups.

IMMEDIATE RECALL

Immediate recall scores for our four measures are presented in **Figure 2**. Percentage of recalled gestures (out of 10 gestures expected for the complete sequence) showed strong differences between groups for all conditions (all contrasts $= p < 0.01$). Consistent with our hypothesis, performance was worst for both groups in the Metronome_NoSync condition. Statistically though, the only significant contrast was between Metronome_NoSync and Music_NoSync in the AD group ($Z = 2.11, p < 0.05$), showing an advantage in the music condition compared to the metronome condition when the gestures were learned without synchrony.

A ratio of well-ordered gestures to total number of gestures produced was derived from the second of our scoring criteria above. This score in AD participants was inferior to that of controls for all conditions (all contrasts $= p < 0.01$) except for the Music_NoSync condition, where the difference between groups did not reach significance. Within each group, no effect of condition reached significance (the only significant difference was the contrast between Music_NoSync and Metronome_Sync in controls).

DELAYED RECALL

Delayed recall scores (**Figure 3**) correspond to a ratio of recalled gestures out of the number of gestures that were learned (up to the point of failure). Performance showed again a strong effect of group for all conditions ($p < 0.05$). More correct gestures were recalled with the synchrony conditions for controls ($Z = 2.03$, $p < 0.05$), while more correct gestures were recalled when gestures were learned without synchrony in AD ($Z = 2.55$, $p < 0.05$). When considering the conditions separately, marginal effects confirmed this result. In AD, the Music_NoSync and Metronome_NoSync conditions were better than Music_Sync ($Z = 1.78$, $p = 0.075$ and $Z = 1.68$, $p = 0.093$, respectively) and Metronome_Sync ($Z = 1.86$, $p = 0.063$ and $Z = 1.83$, $p = 0.068$, respectively). In controls, the reverse pattern was shown, with Music_Sync better than Music_NoSync ($Z = 1.83, p = 0.068$).

Regarding order of gestures, better scores were observed for controls compared to AD for all conditions ($p < 0.05$) but Music_Sync. The Music_Sync condition was marginally better performed in AD compared to the Metronome_Sync ($Z = 1.83$, $p = 0.068$) and Metronome_NoSync ($Z = 1.68$, $p = 0.093$) conditions.

PARTICIPANT JL

Participant JL (MMSE = 25/30), from the AD group, showed relatively well-preserved abilities for the task, especially her score for the number of recalled gestures (similar to controls). Her score did not differ depending on experimental conditions for most of the measures. The only difference was found in immediate recall for gesture order, with worse performance for the music conditions

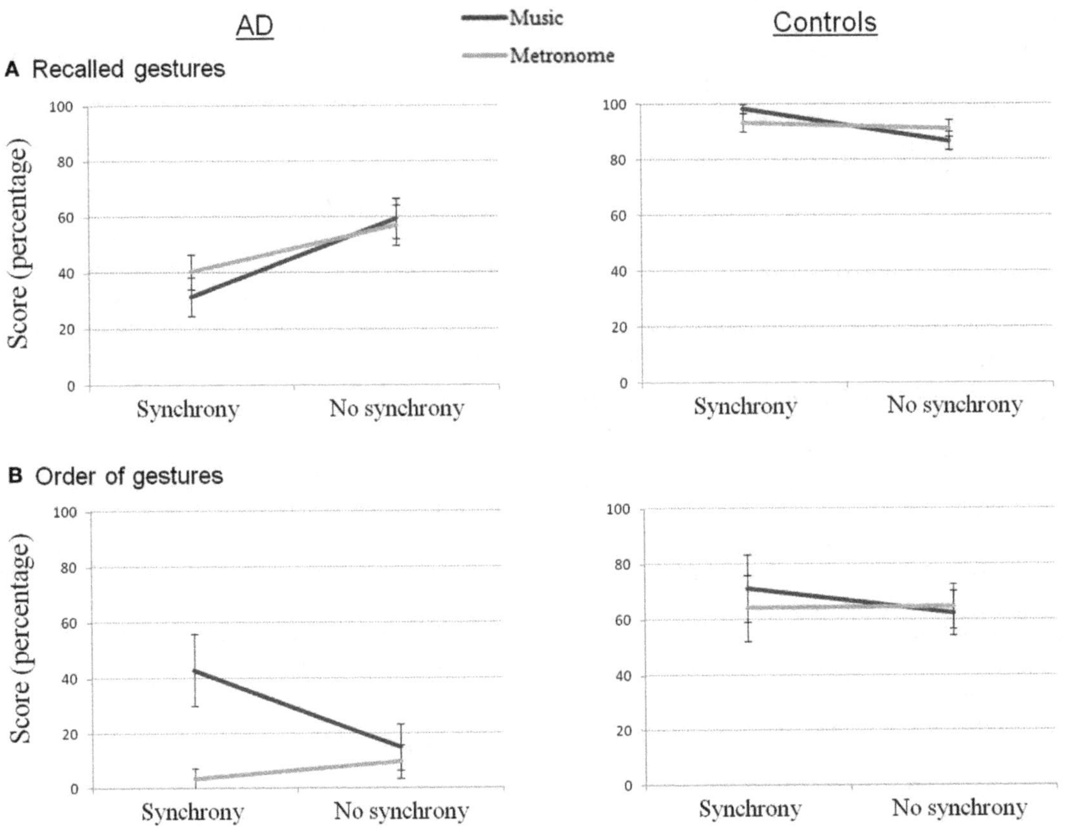

FIGURE 3 | Recalled gestures (A) and order of gestures (B) in delayed recall for AD and control participants.

(Music_Sync inferior to Metronome_Sync and Mus_NoSync inferior to Metronome_NoSync, Fisher test, $p < 0.05$).

DISCUSSION

Music has recently been shown to act as a mnemonic aid for recognition of lyrics in patients with AD (Simmons-Stern et al., 2010, 2012) as well as moderately increasing the retention of lyrics (Moussard et al., 2012, 2014). Music has also been shown to be strongly linked to motor functions (e.g., Zatorre et al., 2007). The present pilot study is the first study to investigate the potential of music as an aid for learning and retention of non-verbal information such as a sequence of gestures in both healthy old adults and AD individuals. The performance of participants was measured in terms of the number of gestures recalled and their order in the sequence of gestures, in both immediate and 10-min delayed recalls. Results showed different patterns for each group. AD participants showed a modest advantage for the music condition, as seen in the significantly greater percentage of gestures recalled in immediate recall and the marginal effect regarding the order of gestures in the sequence in delayed recall. AD participants also showed better performance for the sequences that were learned without synchrony (compared to with synchrony) in delayed recall. Control participants did not show any clear influences of accompaniment (music or metronome) but did show better scores in delayed recall when gestures were learned in synchrony.

Effects of synchronized production of gestures during learning were shown in delayed recall, with synchrony being helpful for controls but detrimental to AD participants. For controls, being more physically active during learning may help with maintaining motivation and attention. Dual or embodied coding of gestures might also have reinforced the memory trace, benefiting from tight auditory–motor coupling in the brain (Zatorre et al., 2007). This multimodal coding leads to multiple pathways involving a more complex brain network and deeper encoding (Craik and Tulving, 1975; Brown and Palmer, 2012). Moreover, the superiority of synchrony learning in the controls seems to be mainly driven by the fact that the Music_Sync condition led to the best performance out of all conditions. This finding supports our hypothesis that there is a positive interaction between music and motor synchrony during learning (Racette et al., 2006). The rhythmical and/or the emotional and affective richness of musical stimuli (see SAME model, Overy and Molnar-Szakacs, 2009) may have facilitated synchronization during learning and in turn strengthened the learning process. In AD participants, it may have been that imitating the gestures in synchrony was more demanding due to a limited ability to maintain attention or the fact that participants did not put as much effort into encoding when additional cues were provided (compared to the condition without this support). It is also possible that AD participants were not able to benefit from the synchrony learning to the same extent as the controls because of potential difficulties in motor functions due to the disease (e.g., Kurlan et al., 2000).

The fact that AD participants showed a modest increase in performance in the music condition for some of the measures while controls (and JL, the best performer of AD group) did not seem to be influenced by the accompaniment (either music or metronome) suggests that music is of greater benefit to those with more pronounced cognitive impairment. This might be due to several factors. Firstly, the dual coding between motor and auditory information may have reinforced the memory trace, ensuring higher quality of encoding and recall. It is important to note that adding musical information does not overload participant's attention as we might have expected considering limited cognitive resources. Secondly, the arousing characteristic of music is known to enhance short-term cognitive efficiency (e.g., Schellenberg et al., 2007). In a case study by Johnson et al. (1998), an AD patient showed improved performance at a spatial–temporal task after listening to an arousing musical excerpt. Enjoyable and energetic music could put participants into a more alert state, as well as decrease any stress related to the test situation and, in turn, help compensate for the cognitive impairment.

The positive effect of music compared to metronome for AD participants was smaller than anticipated. It is possible that the metronome condition played a mnemonic role itself and helped the learning, more so than learning in silence. Research in Parkinson's disease has shown that a regular beat was most often as helpful as music to support motor functions such as gait (Thaut et al., 2001). The imposed tempo for learning and retrieval may have helped structure the sequence during encoding and/or assist in planning the motor actions, making recall more automatic. This would have to be confirmed in a further study with a silent control condition.

It may also be the case that the associations between gestures and music were not optimal. Rigaudon is a style of music similar to Irish jigs, where the same musical phrase is repeated and only slightly modified throughout the excerpt. While this music is appropriate because it is familiar to older adults and stimulates movement, it may be better to use music with more variety. This could assist in the memorization of gestures as it would provide more distinctive cues and anchor points to associate with them. Similarly, using musical rhythm and its variability instead of having gestures on regular beats only could also provide more cues and help structure the sequence into smaller units (chunks; see Purnell-Webb and Speelman, 2008).

To conclude, music might be used as a mnemonic for gesture-sequence learning in AD patients, although synchronization of gesture production during encoding does not help performance. In healthy matched controls, synchronization during learning enhanced retention and interacted positively with music, thus supporting models of auditory–motor integration in healthy individuals. The main limitation of the study concerns the small sample size. With larger groups of participants, further studies will allow generalization of results to the AD population. Moreover, larger samples would allow correlational analyses aiming to determine profiles of individuals who would most benefit from music and/or synchronization for gesture-sequence learning. Further studies are also necessary to try to maximize the effect provided by the musical accompaniment and to assess how the to-be-learned gestures can be linked to the everyday needs of patients. For example, our procedure could be used to teach patients the series of gestures needed to use their new coffee machine or DVD player, to warm frozen food in the microwave, or to start load of laundry.

ACKNOWLEDGMENTS

We wish to thank Emilie Lepage (Geriatric Institute of the University of Montreal; IUGM) and the Montreal Alzheimer Society for recruitment of AD participants, Nadia Jaffer (IUGM) for the recruitment of control participants, and above all, all participants in the study. We are grateful to Amélie Racette for experimental materials and Patrick Bermudez for his insightful comments on the manuscript. Aline Moussard received a fellowship from the NSERC-CREATE program in Auditory Cognitive Neuroscience and a research award from the French Mederic-Alzheimer foundation. Preparation of this paper was supported by grants from the Natural Sciences and Engineering Research Council of Canada and the Canadian Institutes of Health Research to Isabelle Peretz and to Sylvie Belleville, a Canada Research Chair to Isabelle Peretz, and European EBRAMUS funding to Emmanuel Bigand. The research was conducted under the auspices of the Laboratory for Brain, Music, and Sound Research (BRAMS).

REFERENCES

Aldridge, D. (1994). Alzheimer's disease: rhythm, timing and music as therapy. *Biomed. Pharmacother.* 48, 275–281. doi:10.1016/0753-3322(94)90172-4

APA. (1994). *Diagnostic and Statistical Manual of Mental Disorders*, 4th Edn. Washington, DC: American Psychiatric Association.

Bravo, G., Gaulin, P., and Dubois, M.-F. (1996). Validation d'une échelle de bien-être général auprès d'une population francophone âgée de 50 à 75 ans. *Can. J. Aging* 15, 112–128. doi:10.1017/S0714980800013325

Brown, R. M., and Palmer, C. (2012). Auditory-motor learning influences auditory memory for music. *Mem. Cognit.* 40, 567–578. doi:10.3758/s13421-011-0177-x

Brown, S., and Martinez, M. J. (2007). Activation of premotor vocal areas during musical discrimination. *Brain Cogn.* 63, 59–69. doi:10.1016/j.bandc.2006.08.006

Cevasco, A. M., and Grant, R. E. (2003). Comparison of different methods for eliciting exercise-to-music for clients with Alzheimer's disease. *J. Music Ther.* 40, 41–56. doi:10.1093/jmt/40.1.41

Chen, J. L., Penhune, V. B., and Zatorre, R. J. (2009). The role of auditory and premotor cortex in sensorimotor transformations. *Ann. N. Y. Acad. Sci.* 1169, 15–34. doi:10.1111/j.1749-6632.2009.04556.x

Craik, F. I. M., and Tulving, E. (1975). Depth of processing and the retention of words in episodic memory. *J. Exp. Psychol. Gen.* 104, 268–294. doi:10.1037/0096-3445.104.3.268

D'Ausilio, A. (2009). Mirror-like mechanisms and music. *ScientificWorldJournal* 16, 1415–1422. doi:10.1100/tsw.2009.160

De Renzi, E., and Vignolo, L. A. (1962). The token test: a sensitive test to detect receptive disturbances in aphasics. *Brain* 85, 665–678. doi:10.1093/brain/85.4.665

Ehrlé, N. (1998). *Traitement Temporel de L'information Auditive et Lobe Temporal.* Unpublished Doctoral Dissertation, Université de Reims, Reims.

Feyereisen, P. (2009). Enactment effects and integration processes in younger and older adults' memory for actions. *Memory* 17, 374–385. doi:10.1080/09658210902731851

Folstein, M. F., Folstein, S. E., and McHugh, P. R. (1975). Mini mental state: a practical method for grading the cognitive state of patients for the clinician. *J. Psychiatr. Res.* 12, 189–198. doi:10.1016/0022-3956(75)90026-6

Forti, S., Filipponi, E., Di Berardino, F., Barozzi, S., and Cesarani, A. (2010). The influence of music on static posturography. *J. Vestib. Res.* 20, 351–356. doi:10.3233/VES-2010-0361

Gély-Nargeot, M. C., Cadilhac, C., Touchon, J., and Nespoulous, J. L. (1997). "La mémoire de textes chez les sujets sains et déments: application d'un nouvel outil d'évaluation pour neuropsychologues: mémo-textes," in *Perception Auditive et*

Compréhension du Langage, eds J. Lambert and J. L. Nespoulous (Marseille: Solal), 273–293.

Gorus, E., De Raedt, R., Lambert, M., Lemper, J. C., and Mets, T. (2006). Attentional processes discriminate between patients with mild Alzheimer's disease and cognitively healthy elderly. *Int. Psychogeriatr.* 18, 539–549. doi:10.1017/s1041610205002723

Holmes, C., Knights, A., Dean, C., Hodkinson, S., and Hopkins, V. (2006). Keep music live: music and the alleviation of apathy in dementia subjects. *Int. Psychogeriatr.* 18, 623–630. doi:10.1017/S1041610206003887

Johnson, J. K., Cotman, C. W., Tasaki, C. S., and Shaw, G. L. (1998). Enhancement of spatial-temporal reasoning after a Mozart listening condition in Alzheimer's disease: a case study. *Neurol. Res.* 20, 666–672.

Kurlan, R., Richard, I. H., Papka, M., and Marshall, F. (2000). Movement disorders in Alzheimer's disease: more rigidity of definitions is needed. *Mov. Disord.* 15, 24–29. doi:10.1002/1531-8257(200001)15:1<24::AID-MDS1006>3.0.CO;2-X

Lim, I., Van Wegen, E., De Goede, C., Deutekom, M., Nieuwboer, A., Willems, S., et al. (2005). Effects of external rhythmical cueing on gait in patients with Parkinson's disease: a systematic review. *Clin. Rehabil.* 19, 695–713. doi:10.1191/0269215505cr906oa

McKhann, G., Drachman, D., Folstein, M., Katzman, R., Proce, D., and Stadlan, E. M. (1984). Clinical diagnosis of Alzheimer disease: report of the NINCDS-ADRDA work group under the auspices of Health and human services task force on Alzheimer's disease. *Neurology* 34, 939–944. doi:10.1212/WNL.34.7.939

Molnar-Szakacs, I., and Overy, K. (2006). Music and mirror neurons: from motion to 'e'motion. *Soc. Cogn. Affect. Neurosci.* 1, 235–241. doi:10.1093/scan/nsl029

Moussard, A., Bigand, E., Belleville, S., and Peretz, I. (2014). Learning sung lyrics aids retention in normal aging and Alzheimer's disease. *Neuropsychol. Rehabil.* (in press).

Moussard, A., Bigand, E., Belleville, S., and Peretz, I. (2012). Music as an aid to learn new verbal information in Alzheimer's disease. *Music Percept.* 29, 521–531. doi:10.1525/mp.2012.29.5.521

Norberg, A., Melin, E., and Asplund, K. (2003). Reactions to music, touch and object presentation in the final stage of dementia: an exploratory study. *Int. J. Nurs. Stud.* 40, 473–479. doi:10.1016/S0020-7489(03)00062-2

Overy, K., and Molnar-Szakacs, I. (2009). Being together in time: musical experience and the mirror neuron system. *Music Percept.* 26, 486–504. doi:10.1525/MP.2009.26.5.489

Pantev, C., and Herholz, S. C. (2011). Plasticity of the human auditory cortex related to musical training. *Neurosci. Biobehav. Rev.* 35, 2140–2154. doi:10.1016/j.neubiorev.2011.06.010

Patel, A. D. (2008). *Music, Language, and the Brain.* New York: Oxford University Press.

Patel, A. D., Iversen, J. R., Chen, Y., and Repp, B. H. (2005). The influence of metricality and modality on synchronization with a beat. *Exp. Brain Res.* 163, 226–238. doi:10.1007/s00221-004-2159-8

Peretz, I., Gosselin, N., Nan, Y., Caron-Caplette, E., Trehub, S., and Béland, R. (2013). A novel tool for evaluating children's musical abilities across age and culture. *Front. Syst. Neurosci.* 7:30. doi:10.3389/fnsys.2013.00030

Purnell-Webb, P., and Speelman, C. P. (2008). Effects of music on memory for text. *Percept. Mot. Skills* 106, 927–957. doi:10.2466/pms.106.3.927-957

Racette, A., Bard, C., and Peretz, I. (2006). Making non-fluent aphasics speak: sing along! *Brain* 129, 2571–2584. doi:10.1093/brain/awl250

Repp, B. H., and Penel, A. (2004). Rhythmic movement is attracted more strongly to auditory than to visual rhythms. *Psychol. Res.* 68, 252–270. doi:10.1007/s00426-003-0143-8

Rey, A. (1970). *L'examen Clinique en Psychologie.* Paris: PUF.

Robertson, I. H., Ward, A., Ridgeway, V., and Nimmo-Smith, I. N. (1994). *Test of Everyday Attention.* Bury St Edmunds: Thames Valley Test.

Samson, S., Baird, A., Moussard, A., and Clément, S. (2012). Does pathological aging affect musical learning and memory? *Music Percept.* 29, 493–500. doi:10.1525/mp.2012.29.5.493

Schellenberg, E. G. (2005). Music and cognitive abilities. *Curr. Dir. Psychol. Sci.* 14, 317–320. doi:10.1111/j.0963-7214.2005.00389.x

Schellenberg, E. G., Nakata, T., Hunter, P. G., and Tamoto, S. (2007). Exposure to music and cognitive performance: tests of children and adults. *Psychol. Music* 35, 5–19. doi:10.1177/0305735607068885

Simmons-Stern, N. R., Budson, A. E., and Ally, B. A. (2010). Music as a memory enhancer in patients with Alzheimer's disease. *Neuropsychologia* 48, 3164–3167. doi:10.1016/j.neuropsychologia.2010.04.033

Simmons-Stern, N. R., Deason, R. G., Brandler, B. J., Frustace, B. S., O'Connor, M. K., Ally, B. A., et al. (2012). Music-based memory enhancement in Alzheimer's disease: promise and limitations. *Neuropsychologia* 50, 3295–3303. doi:10.1016/j.neuropsychologia.2012.09.019

Stahl, B., Kotz, S. A., Henseler, I., Turner, R., and Geyer, S. (2011). Rhythm in disguise: why singing may not hold the key to recovery from aphasia. *Brain* 134(Pt 10), 3083–3093. doi:10.1093/brain/awr240

Thaut, M. H., McIntosh, K. W., McIntosh, G. C., and Hoemberg, V. (2001). Auditory rhythmicity enhances movement and speech motor control in patients with Parkinson's disease. *Funct. Neurol.* 16, 163–172.

Vieillard, S., Peretz, I., Gosselin, N., Khalfa, S., Gagnon, L., and Bouchard, B. (2008). Happy, sad, scary and peaceful musical excerpts for research on emotions. *Cogn. Emot.* 22, 720–752. doi:10.1080/02699930701503567

Wan, C. Y., and Schlaug, G. (2010). Music making as a tool for promoting brain plasticity across the life span. *Neuroscientist* 16, 566–577. doi:10.1177/1073858410377805

Yesavage, J. A., Brink, T. L., Rose, T. L., Lum, O., Huang, V., Adey, M. B., et al. (1983). Development and validation of a geriatric depression screening scale: a preliminary report. *J. Psychiatr. Res.* 17, 37–49. doi:10.1016/0022-3956(82)90033-4

Zatorre, R. J., Chen, J. L., and Penhune, V. B. (2007). When the brain plays music: auditory-motor interactions in music perception and production. *Nat. Rev. Neurosci.* 8, 547–558. doi:10.1038/nrn2152

Zumbansen, A., Peretz, I., and Hébert, S. (2014). Melodic intonation therapy: back to basics for future research. *Front. Neurol.* 5:7 doi:10.3389/fneur.2014.00007

19

Intact brain processing of musical emotions in autism spectrum disorder, but more cognitive load and arousal in happy vs. sad music

Line Gebauer[1,2]*, Joshua Skewes[1], Gitte Westphael[1], Pamela Heaton[3] and Peter Vuust[1,4]

[1] *Music in the Brain, Department of Clinical Medicine, Center of Functionally Integrative Neuroscience, Aarhus University, Aarhus, Denmark*
[2] *Interacting Minds Centre, Aarhus University, Aarhus, Denmark*
[3] *Department of Psychology, Goldsmiths, University of London, London, UK*
[4] *The Royal Academy of Music, Aarhus, Denmark*

Correspondence:
Line Gebauer, Department of Clinical Medicine, Center of Functionally Integrative Neuroscience, Aarhus University, Noerrebrogade 44, Build. 10 G, 5th floor, Aarhus 8000, Denmark
e-mail: gebauer@pet.auh.dk; linegebauer@gmail.com

Music is a potent source for eliciting emotions, but not everybody experience emotions in the same way. Individuals with autism spectrum disorder (ASD) show difficulties with social and emotional cognition. Impairments in emotion recognition are widely studied in ASD, and have been associated with atypical brain activation in response to emotional expressions in faces and speech. Whether these impairments and atypical brain responses generalize to other domains, such as emotional processing of music, is less clear. Using functional magnetic resonance imaging, we investigated neural correlates of emotion recognition in music in high-functioning adults with ASD and neurotypical adults. Both groups engaged similar neural networks during processing of emotional music, and individuals with ASD rated emotional music comparable to the group of neurotypical individuals. However, in the ASD group, increased activity in response to happy compared to sad music was observed in dorsolateral prefrontal regions and in the rolandic operculum/insula, and we propose that this reflects increased cognitive processing and physiological arousal in response to emotional musical stimuli in this group.

Keywords: autism spectrum disorder, music, emotion, fMRI

INTRODUCTION

Music is highly emotional; it communicates emotions and synchronizes emotions between people (Huron, 2006; Overy, 2012). The social-emotional nature of music is often proposed as an argument for why music has sustained such prominence in human culture (Huron, 2001; Fitch, 2005). Indeed, people spend quite a large amount of their time listening to music. A recent Danish survey found that 79% of people between 12 and 76 years listened to music more than 1 h daily (Moesgaard, 2010), and when people are asked why they listen to music they consistently say that it is because music induces and regulates emotions (Dubé and Le Bel, 2003; Rentfrow and Gosling, 2003). Processing of emotional music is found to engage limbic and paralimbic brain areas, including regions related to reward processing (for reviews see Koelsch, 2010; Peretz, 2010; Zald and Zatorre, 2011). However, not everybody experience and process emotions in the same way. For instance, people with autism spectrum disorder (ASD) are often found to be impaired in recognizing, understanding and expressing emotions (Hobson, 2005).

ASD is a complex neurodevelopmental disorder characterized by difficulties in social and interpersonal communication, combined with stereotyped and repetitive behaviors and interests (APA, 2013). Despite somewhat conflicting findings, studies indicate that people with ASD have difficulties identifying emotions from facial expressions (Boucher and Lewis, 1992; Celani et al., 1999; Baron-Cohen et al., 2000; Philip et al., 2010; see however Jemel et al., 2006), affective speech (Lindner and Rosén, 2006; Golan et al., 2007; Mazefsky and Oswald, 2007; Philip et al., 2010; see however Jones et al., 2011), non-verbal vocal expressions (Hobson, 1986; Heaton et al., 2012) and body movements (Hubert et al., 2007; Hadjikhani et al., 2009; Philip et al., 2010). These difficulties in emotion recognition are associated with altered brain activations in people with ASD compared to neurotypical (NT) controls, i.e., with less activation in the fusiform gyrus and amygdala when viewing emotional faces (Critchley et al., 2000; Schultz et al., 2000; Ashwin et al., 2007; Corbett et al., 2009), and abnormal activation of superior temporal gyrus (STG)/sulcus and inferior frontal gyrus when listening to speech (Gervais et al., 2004; Wang et al., 2006; Eigsti et al., 2012; Eyler et al., 2012). Accordingly, it has been suggested that people with ASD do not automatically direct their attention to emotional cues in their surroundings, but instead tend to perceive emotions more analytically (Jemel et al., 2006; Nuske et al., 2013).

It has previously been advocated that general social-emotional difficulties could make people with ASD less emotionally affected by music and less able to recognize emotions expressed in music (Huron, 2001; Levitin, 2006). Nonetheless, anecdotal reports dating all the way back to Kanner's (1943) first descriptions of autism seems to suggest quite the opposite, namely, that people with autism enjoy listening to music, become emotionally affected by music, and often are musically talented. Behavioral studies have shown that people with ASD process musical contour and intervals just as well as NT individuals (Heaton, 2005), and that they display superior pitch processing (Bonnel et al., 1999; Heaton et al., 1999; Heaton, 2003) and pitch memory (Heaton, 2003; Stanutz et al., 2014). Interestingly, behavioral studies have shown that children and adults with ASD correctly identify a wide range of emotions in music just as well as NT individuals (Heaton et al., 2008; Allen et al., 2009a,b; Caria et al., 2011; Quintin et al., 2011). A qualitative study by Allen et al. (2009b) found that adults with ASD listened to music as often as people without ASD, and when asked why they listened to music, they reported being emotionally affected by the music and feeling a sense of belonging to a particular musical culture. Moreover, Allen et al. (2013) recently showed that physiological responses to music are intact in people with ASD, despite a lower verbal responsiveness to music in this group.

Only one brain imaging study of processing of musical emotions in ASD has been published to this date. Caria et al. (2011) scanned 8 adults with Asperger's syndrome (AS) while listening to excerpts of classical and self-chosen musical pieces. Emotion ratings of valence and arousal showed no difference between the two groups. Their main neurobiological finding was significant activations of a variety of cortical and subcortical brain regions, including bilateral STG, cerebellum, inferior frontal cortex, insula, putamen and caudate nucleus, in response to emotional music, which were common for the ASD and NT group. Yet, between-group comparisons revealed less brain activation in individuals with AS relative to NT individuals in response to both happy and sad music. For happy music, AS individuals showed decreased brain activation relative to NT individuals in the right precentral gyrus, supplementary motor area and cerebellum. When comparing self-chosen favorite happy music with standard happy music the ASD group showed decreased brain responses in supplementary motor area, insula and inferior frontal gyrus compared to the NT group. For sad music, individuals with AS showed decreased brain activation in precentral gyrus, insula and inferior frontal gyrus. Taken together, Caria et al. (2011) concludes that the most prominent difference between the two groups is the decreased activation of left insula in individuals with AS relative to NT individuals during processing of emotional music. This difference might be explained by higher levels of alexithymia (Fitzgerald and Bellgrove, 2006; Bird et al., 2010), an inability to identify and describe feelings, in the AS group compared to the NT group. This study is important in that it is the first to directly investigate the neural processing of emotional music in individuals with ASD. However, the study is limited by a fairly small sample size and it is not apparent if the ASD and the NT group were matched on IQ and/or verbal IQ. Previous studies have shown that differences in emotion processing might depend on verbal IQ rather than having ASD as such (Lindner and Rosén, 2006; Golan et al., 2007; Heaton et al., 2008; Anderson et al., 2010). Besides, the stimuli used by Caria et al. (2011) included a mix of familiar and unfamiliar music (5 familiar/self-chosen and 5 unfamiliar excerpts of happy and sad music respectively). More studies are needed to generalize these findings to larger groups of people with ASD. Empirical investigations of similarities and differences in the neurocognitive processing of music are relevant for understanding the nature of emotional impairments in individuals with ASD. In the literature on music emotions, the distinction between emotion perception and emotion induction is central (Gabrielsson, 2002; Juslin and Laukka, 2004; Konečni, 2008). The present study focused on emotion perception from music in individuals with ASD, because this study was designed to act as a parallel to ASD studies on emotion recognition in other domains (facial expressions, affective prosody, body movements etc.). Thus, the aim of the present study was to investigate emotion recognition and neural processing of happy, sad and neutral music in high-functioning adults with ASD compared to a group of NT individuals matched on age, gender, full-scale IQ and verbal IQ.

MATERIALS AND METHODS

PARTICIPANTS

A total of 43 participants were included in the study, 23 of these had a formal diagnosis of ASD. Participants with ASD were recruited through the national autism and Asperger's association, assisted living services for young people with ASD, and specialized educational facilities. The structural MRI of three participants with ASD showed abnormal ventricular enlargement (this is not an uncommon finding see Gillberg and Coleman, 1996) and were excluded before data analysis was begun. One ASD participant was unable to relax in the scanner and thus did not complete the testing. Consequently, a total of 19 high-functioning adults with ASD (2 females, 17 males) and 20 NT adults (2 females, 18 males) were included in the data analysis.

All participants were right-handed and native speakers of Danish, with normal hearing. Groups were matched on gender, age, IQ, and verbal IQ (**Table 1**). All participants were IQ-tested using Wechsler's Adult Intelligence Scale (WAIS-III, Wechsler, 1997). None of the NT participants had any history of neurological or psychiatric illness. All participants with ASD carried a previous formal diagnosis of ASD. Diagnoses were supported by the autism diagnostic observation schedule (ADOS-G, Lord et al., 2000) at the time of the study. All participants with ASD

Table 1 | Participant characteristics.

	ASD	NT	*t*-value *p*-value
Age (*SD*/range)	26.16 (5.63/20–36)	24.45 (4.57/19–41)	1.04 *ns*
Gender	2 F/17 M	2 F/18 M	−0.05 *ns*
Full-scale IQ[a] (*SD*/range)	108.32 (14.56/78–135)	114.50 (12.37/92–137)	−1.43 *ns*
Verbal IQ[b] (*SD*/range)	112.68 (23.7/74–186)	118.30 (13.8/90–143)	−1.05 *ns*
MET[c] melodic (*SD*/range)	35.47 (6.22/24–49)	37.10 (5.05/28–50)	−0.90 *ns*
MET[c] rhythmic (*SD*/range)	36.79 (5.67/24–45)	37.35 (4.43/28–48)	−0.32 *ns*

[a] *WAIS-III full-scale IQ (Wechsler, 1997).*

[b] *Verbal subscale of WAIS-III.*

[c] *The Musical Ear Test (Wallentin et al., 2010). ns, not significant at $p < 0.05$.*

were invited back in for the ADOS testing after the brain scanning session, but unfortunately five participants were unable to come back for testing due to long transportation, or because they needed special assistance. Thus, 14 out of the 19 ASD participants completed ADOS testing (**Table 2**). Nonetheless specialized psychiatrists had previously diagnosed all participants with ASD, and we were given access to their medical records to further confirm diagnoses. All ASD participants were medication naïve at the time of the study, and did not have any comorbid psychiatric disorders. All participants gave written informed consent and were compensated for their time and transportation expenses. The study was approved by the local ethics committee and was in accordance with the Helsinki declaration.

MEASURES OF MUSICAL EXPERIENCE

All participants completed a musical background questionnaire asking about their musical preferences, musical training, listening habits, and general physiological and emotional responses to music. For questions about physiological and emotional responses to music, participants rated how much they agreed (from 1 to 5, where 1 is least, 5 is most) with statements like "I find it easy to recognize whether a melody is happy or sad" or "I can feel my body responding physically when I listen to music." To compare musical abilities between the two groups, participants completed the Musical Ear Test (Wallentin et al., 2010), which measures melodic and rhythmic competence on a same/different listening task.

STIMULI

Emotional stimuli (happy/sad) were instrumental excerpts of 12 s duration, taken from the beginning of real music pieces of different genres (see Appendix A for a complete list of musical excerpts). Emotional stimuli were selected from a corpus of 120 musical excerpts based on pilot-data from a separate group of 12 neurotypical adults. The 120 musical excerpts were rated for emotionality by the pilot-group on a 5-point Likert-scale ranging from very sad to very happy. A total of 40 music excerpts (20 happy/20 sad) were selected for the fMRI experiment. The 20 happy excerpts, selected for the study, were all rated as happy or very happy by all participants in the pilot group. Similarly, the 20 sad excerpts were rated sad or very sad. During the piloting of the stimuli, people were asked whether they were familiar with the music, and if they could name the artist or part of the title of the piece. If any of the pilot-participants could name artist of part of the title of the musical piece from which the excerpt was taken, the excerpt was not included in the final stimulus sample for the fMRI-experiment. Besides the 20 happy and the 20 sad music excerpts, a 12 s chromatic scale was used as a neutral control condition. The neutral control condition acted as an "auditory baseline" for the two emotion conditions. This was done to have some degree of auditory stimulation across all conditions, while only the emotional intensity varies. Stimuli were all matched on duration and volume.

Table 2 | ADOS scores for ASD participants (N = 14).

ADOS total	11.2
(*SD*/range)	(4.5/3–18)
Communication	3.5
(*SD*/range)	(1.7/1–6)
Social interaction	7.2
(*SD*/range)	(3.9/1–12)
Imagination and creativity	0.33
(*SD*/range)	(0.5/0–1)
Stereotyped and repetitive behaviors	1.6
(*SD*/range)	(1.8/0–6)

Scores from the Autism Diagnostic Observation Schedule (ADOS, module 4, Lord et al., 2000) for 14 out of the 19 ASD participants. The remaining 5 ASD participants did not complete ADOS testing, see participant information for further information on this.

DESIGN

Participants listened to the music excerpts and rated the perceived emotion inside the fMRI-scanner. The study used a block-design, where 20 trials of happy instrumental music, 20 trials of sad and 20 trials of neutral music were presented in pseudo-random order. After hearing each excerpt (12 s), participants had 6 s to rate the perceived emotional intensity of the music on a visual analog scale from very sad over neutral to very happy (**Figure 1**). The visual analog scale was displayed on an MR compatible screen in the center of the participant's visual field and ratings were given with an MR compatible scroll ball. Participants were instructed that neutral was right in the middle, and the cursor always started out in the neutral position. No visual feedback was displayed during the music listening, but participants were instructed to lie with their eyes open during the entire scan. All participants

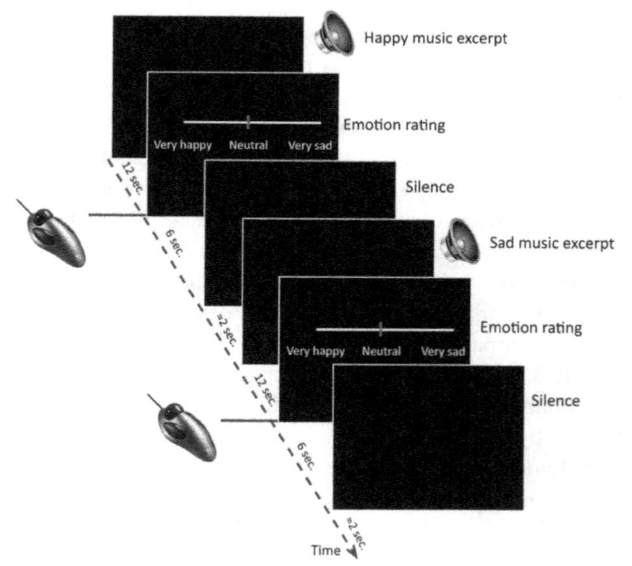

FIGURE 1 | Study design. The study consisted of 60 trials (20 happy, 20 sad, 20 neutral) inside the MR scanner. Each trial consisted of a musical excerpt of 12 s duration, followed a visual analog scale depicted on the screen in front of the participant for 6 s while participants indicated their emotion intensity ratings by using an MR-compatible scroll-ball mouse. After the rating there were approximately 2 s silence before the next trial began.

completed 5 trials outside the scanner, to make sure that they were familiar with the task and understood the instructions. It was emphasized that it was the emotion expressed in the music, and not the emotion or pleasantness experienced by the participant in response to the music, that should be rated. Participants also completed a similar task while listening to emotional linguistic stimuli. The data from this task will be analyzed and published separately of the present study.

MRI ACQUISITION

Brain imaging was obtained using a Siemens, 3T Trim Trio, whole-body magnetic resonance scanner located at the Centre of Functionally Integrative Neuroscience at Aarhus University Hospital, Denmark. Two 10,5 min experimental EPI-sequences were acquired with 200 volumes per session and the parameters; $TR = 3000$ ms, $TE = 27$ ms, flip angle $= 90°$, voxel size $= 2.00 \times 2.00 \times 2.00$ mm, #voxels $= 96 \times 96 \times 55$, slice thickness 2 mm, no gaps. Participants wore MR-compatible headphones inside a 12-channel head coil, and had a trackball in their right hand for the valence ratings. After the functional scans a sagittal T1-weighted anatomical scan with the parameters; $TR = 1900$ ms, $TE = 2.52$, flip angle $= 9°$, voxel size $= 0.98 \times 0.98 \times 1$ mm, # voxels $= 256 \times 256 \times 176$, slice thickness 1 mm, no gaps, 176 slices, was acquired for later co-registration with the functional data. Participants were instructed to lie still and avoid movement during the scan.

BEHAVIORAL DATA ANALYSIS

Age, gender, IQ, musicianship and answers on the background questionnaire were compared between groups using independent samples *t*-test. Emotion ratings were analyzed using a 2 (groups) $\times$ 3 (emotion condition: happy, neutral, or sad) mixed model analysis of variance (ANOVA).

fMRI ANALYSIS

fMRI data analysis was performed using Statistical Parametric Mapping (SPM8 version 4667; http://www.fil.ion.ucl.ac.uk/spm) (Penny et al., 2011). Preprocessing was done using default settings in SPM8. The functional images of each participant were motion corrected and realigned, spatially normalized to MNI space using the SPM EPI template and trilinear interpolation (Ashburner and Friston, 1999), and smoothed using an 8 mm full-width at half-maximum smoothing kernel.

For each participant, condition effects were estimated according to the general linear model (Friston et al., 1994). To identify clusters of significant activity across the two groups, one-sample t-contrasts for the main effect of emotional vs. neutral prosody were performed across all participants. For between group differences, random-effects analyses were performed using independent-samples *t*-tests. All results are thresholded at $p < 0.01$ after family wise error correction (FWE, Friston et al., 1996) with an extent threshold at 10 voxels. $p < 0.01$ after FWE correction is a relatively conservative significance threshold, thus to avoid type-2 errors all between-group analyses were also done with a threshold of $p < 0.05$ after FWE correction. Figures are t-statistics displayed on top of standard MNI T1-images. Labeling of brain regions is done according the Wake Forest University (WFU) PickAtlas (Lancaster et al., 2000; Tzourio-Mazoyer et al., 2002; Maldjian et al., 2003). However, the WFU PickAtlas does not label midbrain structures very precisely, so for identifying activity in ventral striatum and nucleus accumbens we used a midbrain atlas specialized for the basal ganglia (Ahsan et al., 2007). Tables indicate coordinates for peak-voxels significant at both peak and cluster-level.

RESULTS

BEHAVIORAL RESULTS

No statistically significant group differences were found with regard to gender, age, full-scale IQ or verbal IQ (**Table 1**). We found no group difference with regard to musicianship $t_{(37)} = -0.85$, $p = 0.403$, or musical abilities as measured with the Musical Ear Test (**Table 1**). On the 'musical background' questionnaire, 11 out of the 19 ASD participants, compared to 5 out of the 20 NT participants, reported that they experienced that specific tones had a great influence or special significance to them (i.e., were perceived as especially annoying or particularly pleasant) $t_{(37)} = 2.157, p = 0.038$. There were no statistically significant group differences to the questions regarding emotional impact and recognition ("I get emotionally affected by music"; "I find it easy to recognize whether a melody is happy or sad"; "when I am feeling down I often like to listen to sad music"; "It makes me happy to listen to happy music"; "If I am sad, it cheers me up to listen to happy music"). Nor did we see any differences on questions relating to physical arousal associated with music ("It energizes me to listen to music"; "I can feel my body responding physically when I listen to music"; "I often get chills when I listen to music").

EMOTION RATINGS

Mixed model ANOVA revealed a significant main effect of emotion condition $F_{(2,\ 37)} = 120.19$, $p < 0.000$. The ANOVA revealed no main effect of group $F_{(1,\ 37)} = 0.365$, $p = 0.550$ (**Figure 2**) and no significant group $\times$ emotion condition interaction $F_{(2,\ 37)} = 2.5, p = 0.091$. Additional independent samples *t*-test revealed no difference in the number of missing responses between the two groups $t_{(37)} = -0.928, p = 0.359$.

fMRI RESULTS

Between-group comparisons showed no differences on the contrasts; emotional (happy and sad) music vs. neutral music, happy vs. neutral music or sad vs. neutral music at $p < 0.01$ after FWE-correction, nor at a less conservative significance threshold of $p < 0.05$ FWE-corrected. However, the ASD group showed significantly greater activation in response to happy compared to sad music in left dorsolateral prefrontal regions i.e., middle frontal gyrus [$x = -24$, $y = 34$, $z = 42$; $T_{(1,\ 38)} = 7.75$; BA: 9], left rolandic operculum/insula [$x = -50, y = 2, z = 8$; $T_{(1,\ 38)} = 7.41$; BA: 6] and in superior frontal gyrus [$x = -26$, $y = 52$, $z = 32$; $T_{(38)} = 7.23$; BA: 9] (**Table 3** and **Figure 3**), than did the NT group.

Looking at both groups together, we found significant brain activation in response to emotional (happy and sad) music compared to neutral music in; bilateral STG [BA: 22], precentral gyrus [BA: 6, 4], parahippocampal gyrus [BA: 34, 28], left medial

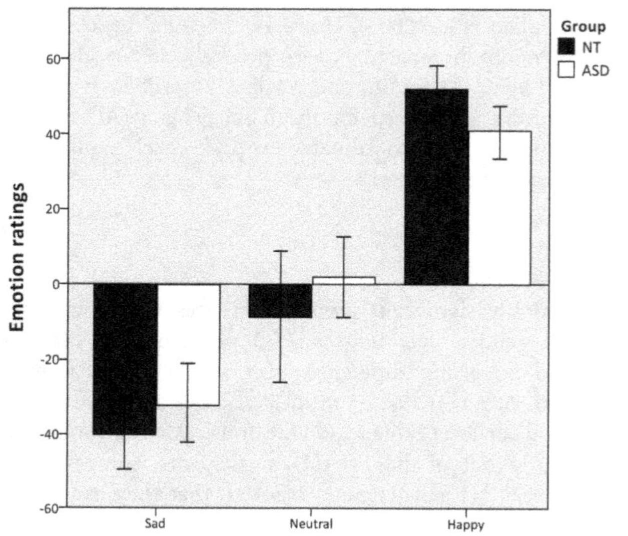

FIGURE 2 | Emotion ratings. Mean emotion ratings (on a visual analog scale from −100 to 100) of sad, neutral and happy musical excerpts. Error bars indicate 95% confidence intervals.

Table 3 | ASD > NT: group difference for happy vs. sad music (FWE $p < 0.01$).

		BA	x	y	z	k	T
Middle frontal gyrus	L	9	−24	34	42	27	7.75
Rorlandic operculum/insula	L	44	−50	−2	8	27	7.41
Superior frontal gyrus	L	9	−26	52	32	58	7.23

Peak coordinates from significant clusters after FWE correction at the peak level, $p < 0.01$, extent threshold = 10 voxels (Friston et al., 1996).

orbitofrontal gyrus [BA: 11], left midbrain, bilateral inferior frontal gyrus [BA: 47], right medial frontal gyrus [BA: 6], right ventral striatum/nucleus accumbens, and in orbitofrontal cortex [BA: 11] (**Table 4, Figure 4**).

Comparing processing of happy and sad music across groups showed increased activation bilaterally in STG [BA: 22, 38], anterior cingulate and cingulate cortex [BA: 32, 31], subcallosal gyrus, midbrain, medial frontal gyrus [BA: 9], and postcentral gyrus [BA: 3] (**Table 5**). No brain regions showed more activity in response to sad than happy music across groups.

DISCUSSION

Our results demonstrate intact emotion recognition, and mostly intact neural processing of emotional music in high-functioning adults with ASD compared to NT adults. Across both ASD and NT individuals we found increased activation in limbic and paralimbic brain areas, such as parahippocampal gyrus extending into amygdala, and midbrain structures, also including reward regions, such as medial orbitofrontal cortex and ventral striatum. These regions are highly interconnected and have previously been identified as core regions for emotional processing of music (Koelsch, 2010, see **Figure 4**), and for other emotional stimuli (Adolphs, 2002). Meanwhile, individuals with ASD displayed significantly greater activation in left dorsolateral prefrontal cortex (i.e., middle and superior frontal gyrus), and left rolandic operculum/insula, in response to happy contrasted with sad music, compared to NT individuals (**Figure 3**).

The difference in brain activation in response to happy compared to sad music between the two groups could be interpreted as heightened arousal and increased reliance on cognitive processing for emotion recognition of happy music in individuals with ASD. The dorsolateral prefrontal region is associated with higher cognitive functions, such as working memory and executive functions (Boisgueheneuc et al., 2006). With regard to emotion processing the medial parts of the pre-frontal cortex has been found to be involved in emotion appraisal (Etkin et al., 2011). Hence, the increased activation of the dorsolateral prefrontal cortex found in this study, is likely related to a more cognitively demanding emotion recognition strategy for happy music in the ASD group. This would be consistent with the findings of more analytical and cognitive strategies which have been suggested to govern face perception in individuals with ASD (Jemel et al., 2006), and with findings of atypicalities in verbal reporting of emotions (Heaton et al., 2012; Bird and Cook, 2013), including musical emotions in people with ASD (Allen et al., 2009a, 2013).

Meanwhile the insula is critically involved in mediating cognitive and emotional processing, for instance in emotion monitoring and regulation (Menon and Uddin, 2010; Gasquoine, 2014). The insula is highly connected with limbic, sensory and motor regions of the brain, and is considered a central in sensorimotor, visceral, interoceptive processing, homeostatic/allostatic functions, and emotional awareness of self and others (Craig, 2002; Critchley, 2005). Furthermore, the insula is posited to be involved in monitoring emotional salience (Craig, 2009). Consistent with this the insula is previously found to be involved in emotional responses to music (Blood and Zatorre, 2001; Brown et al., 2004; Griffiths et al., 2004; Trost et al., 2012). Hence activation of insula associated with emotional music found in these studies might be due to increased physiological arousal. Indeed, happy music is often found to be more arousing than sad music (see for instance, Trost et al., 2012). Thus the stronger insula activation found in the ASD group in this study might be linked to enhanced bodily arousal in response to happy music compared to NT individuals. This corresponds well with self-reports of individuals with ASD describing stronger physiological responses to music (Allen et al., 2009a).

Interestingly, in our study, we only found evidence for this differential brain processing between individuals with ASD and NT individuals in response to happy compared to sad music. Future studies are needed to clarify whether recruitment of extra cognitive resources is unique to the happy-sad differentiation or is related to other music emotions too.

While subtle brain processing differences were found between the two groups in recognizing happy music, we found no evidence of differences in emotion ratings between the ASD and NT group (**Figure 2**). The successful emotion recognition seen from our behavioral ratings was further substantiated by the data from the "music background"-questionnaire, where the ASD group reported that they got emotionally affected by listening

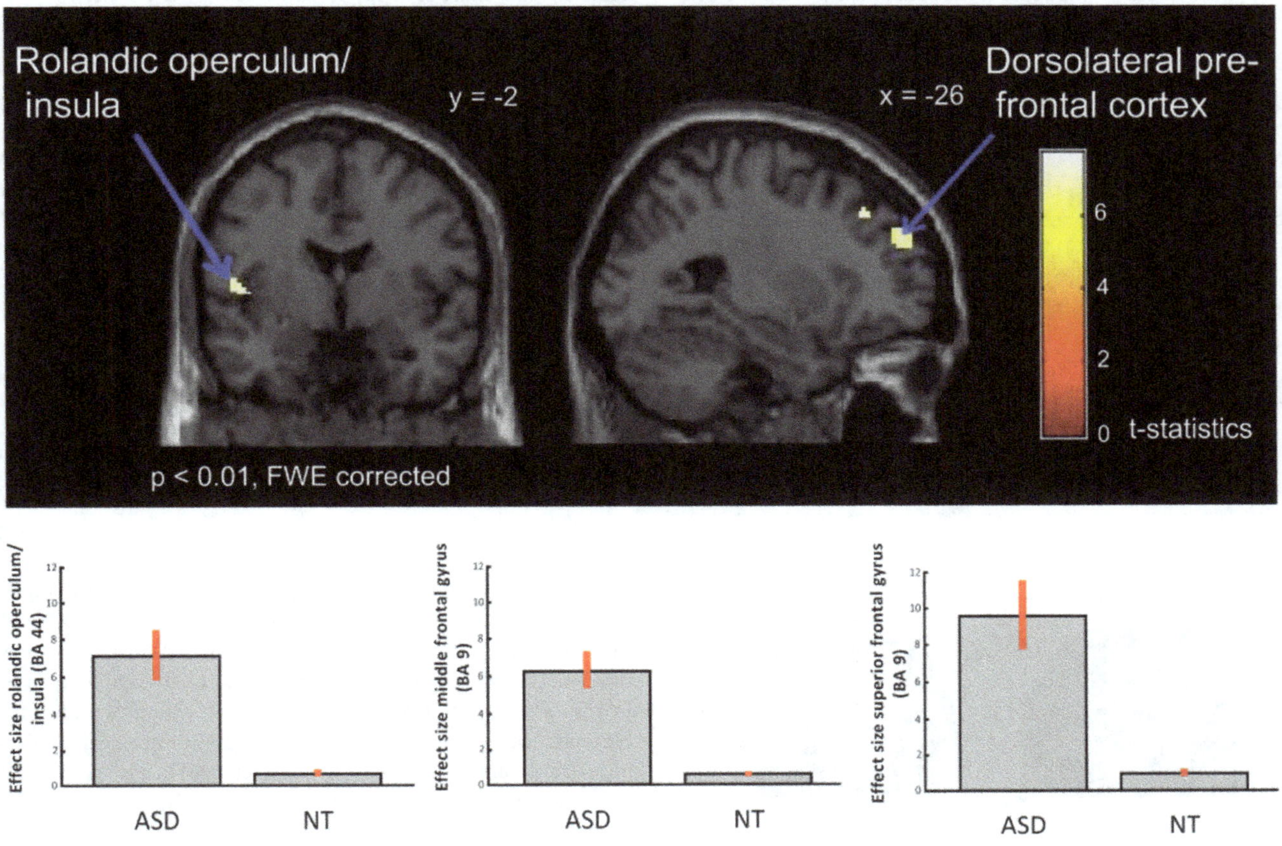

FIGURE 3 | ASD > NT: group difference for happy vs. sad music (FWE $p < 0.01$). Individuals with ASD showed increased activation in dorsolateral prefrontal cortex, i.e., middle and superior frontal gyrus, and in insula/rolandic operculum. Box plots show mean effect size for each group in the peak voxel for each region, with 95% confidence intervals.

to music, found it easy to recognize emotions from music, and experienced physiological arousal comparable to that of NT individuals when listening to music in everyday settings. This is consistent with previous findings of intact emotion recognition (Heaton et al., 2008; Quintin et al., 2011), and intact physiological responses to music in high-functioning individuals with ASD (Caria et al., 2011; Allen et al., 2013). Physiological arousal during music listening is associated with emotional and pleasurable responses (Grewe et al., 2005; Salimpoor et al., 2009). Thus, the presence of typical physiological responses to music indicates that people with ASD are not only capable of correctly recognizing emotions in music, but that they also experience full-fledged emotions from listening to music—though they might use an extra effort to report them. In summary our study shows that individuals with ASD do not have deficits in emotion recognition from music in general, but in certain instances rely on partially different strategies for decoding emotions from music, which may result in subtle differences in brain processing.

Looking at brain responses to emotional compared with neutral music we did not find any differences between the two groups. Across all participants we found increased activation in bilateral STG, parahippocampal gyrus extending into amygdala, inferior frontal gyrus, precentral gyrus, left midbrain, and right ventral striatum. This is consistent with what is generally found in studies of music emotion processing (Koelsch et al., 2006; Peretz, 2010; Brattico et al., 2011; Trost et al., 2012; Park et al., 2013). Indeed, music with a high impact on arousal, such as joyful music is associated with increased activation of the STG (Koelsch et al., 2006, 2013; Mitterschiffthaler et al., 2007; Brattico et al., 2011; Mueller et al., 2011; Trost et al., 2012), which also corresponds to our finding of increased STG activation in response to happy compared to sad music. Besides, being engaged in auditory processing, the STG is also central for social and emotional processing (Zilbovicius et al., 2006), and is proposed to code communicative and emotional significance from all social stimuli (Redcay, 2008). Music is a rich tool for communicating emotions (Huron, 2006; Juslin and Västfjäll, 2008), and accordingly emotional music will elicit more activation of the STG compared to neutral music, as was the case in our study. Also, the precentral and inferior frontal gyrus, were more active during emotional music than neutral. Precentral activity is found to correlate with the arousal dimension of music (Trost et al., 2012), and arousal levels are generally found to correlate with emotional responses to music (Grewe et al., 2005; Salimpoor et al., 2009). Increased activation of the inferior frontal gyrus

Table 4 | Main effect of emotional vs. neutral music (FWE $p < 0.01$).

		BA	*x*	*y*	*z*	*k*	*T*
Superior temporal gyrus	R	22	54	−14	6	3864	22.24
Superior temporal gyrus	L	22	−48	−16	4	2795	18.97
Precentral gyrus	R	6	54	−4	46	285	10.78
Medial frontal gyrus	L	11	−6	42	−14	314	9.50
Midbrain	L		−6	−24	−6	298	8.46
Inferior frontal gyrus	L	47	−26	28	−14	59	8.36
Precentral gyrus	L	4	−42	−18	54	400	8.22
Medial frontal gyrus	R	6	10	0	58	344	8.14
Parahippocampal gyrus	L	28	−18	−10	−16	57	7.49
Ventral striatum	R	25	2	6	−6	17	6.93
Inferior frontal gyrus	R	47	46	28	−4	92	6.88
Inferior frontal gyrus	L	47	−36	26	2	10	6.57
Inferior orbitofrontal gyrus	R	11	38	34	−16	11	6.44

Peak coordinates from significant clusters after FWE correction at the peak level, $p < 0.01$, extent threshold = 10 voxels (Friston et al., 1996).

Table 5 | Main effect of happy vs. sad music (FWE $p < 0.01$).

		BA	*x*	*y*	*z*	*k*	*T*
Superior temporal gyrus	L	22	−56	−10	2	2566	16.03
Superior temporal gyrus	R	22	56	−12	4	3275	14.54
Middle frontal gyrus	L	9	−24	34	42	256	9.11
Anterior cingulate cortex	L	32	−8	46	0	398	8.15
Subcallosal gyrus	L	11	−14	24	−10	24	7.96
Extra nuclear	R	-	24	2	−10	97	7.90
Superior temporal gyrus	R	38	36	10	−22	43	6.96
Medial frontal gyrus	L	9	−4	50	26	25	6.63
Postcentral gyrus	L	3	−52	−10	52	15	6.55
Superior temporal gyrus	L	22	−58	−60	16	10	6.51
Cingulate	-	31	0	−22	42	11	6.32

Peak coordinates from significant clusters after FWE correction at the peak level, $p < 0.01$, extent threshold = 10 voxels (Friston et al., 1996).

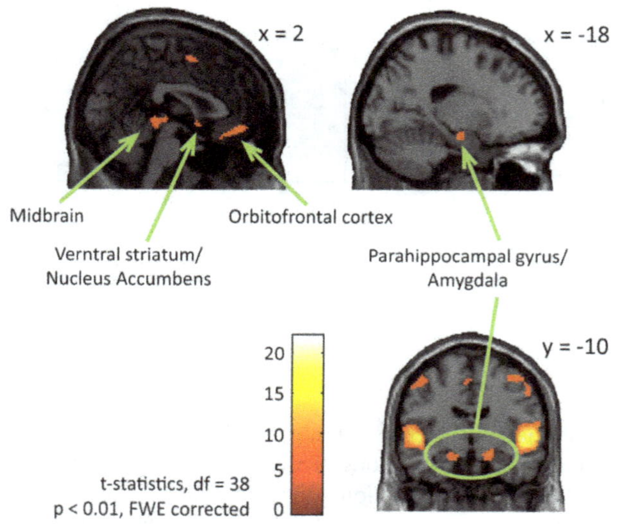

FIGURE 4 | ASD and NT—main effect of emotional vs. neutral music. The figure shows brain activations in response to emotional compared to neutral music across all participants, including activations in midbrain, parahippocampal gyrus extending into amygdala, ventral striatum/nucleus accumbens, and orbitofrontal cortex.

has also ben found in response to pleasant compared to scambled music, and is suggested to reflext music syntactic analysis (Koelsch et al., 2006).

We found increased activation of the parahippocampal gyrus extending into amygdala in response to emotional music across all individuals. Engagement of the parahippocampal gyrus and amygdala are primarily found to respond to negative affective states, including varying degrees of musical dissonance (Blood et al., 1999; Koelsch et al., 2006, 2008), but also to positive affective states and happy music (Mitterschiffthaler et al., 2007). In our study activation of the parahippocampal gyrus and amygdala was not significantly greater in response to sad compared to happy music, suggesting that these structures are implicated in processing of both happy and sad music. We found increased brain activation in midbrain structures, overlapping thalamus, in response to emotional music. Thalamus activity is found to correlate with music-induced psychophysiological arousal and pleasurable chills (Blood and Zatorre, 2001), and is central in processing temporal and ordinal complexity (Janata and Grafton, 2003). Indeed, emotional and pleasurable responses to music seem to be associated with optimal levels of complexity (Berlyne, 1971; North and Hargreaves, 1995; Witek et al., 2014), accordingly it makes sense that we find greater activity in these regions during emotional than neutral music.

Emotional music also engaged parts of the right ventral striatum, including nucleus accumbens, and medial orbitofrontal cortex, these regions are central parts of the brain's dopaminergic reward system (Gebauer et al., 2012), and have previously been associated with strong emotional and pleasurable responses to music (Blood and Zatorre, 2001; Brown et al., 2004; Menon and Levitin, 2005; Salimpoor et al., 2011, 2013). ASD is previously suggested to be associated with deficient reward processing (Kohls et al., 2013), however, the finding of intact activation of the reward system in response to emotional music suggests that music listening has the same pleasurable and motivational impact on people with ASD as it has on NT individuals.

Despite general agreement between the findings of this study and those of the previous neuroimaging study of emotional music perception in high-functioning adults with AS from Caria et al. (2011), there are some deviations. We found increased activation in the ASD group compared to the NT group in response to happy compared to sad music, and no group differences in processing of emotional compared to neutral music overall. Meanwhile, Caria et al. (2011) found less brain activation in various brain regions including precentral gyrus, cerebellum, supplementary motor area, insula and inferior frontal gyrus response to both happy and sad music in individuals with AS relative to NT individuals. However, the study designs are quite different: First, Caria et al. (2011) employed a relatively small study sample, and only had 5 trials in each condition for some of their comparisons. Second, our study required people to decode the emotional intensity of experimenter-selected music directly inside the scanner, while Caria et al. (2011) had their subjects bring half of the music themselves and had them rate the emotion and arousal of all music before the actual scanning. Consequently, our finding of intact emotion recognition and brain responses to music in individuals with ASD might be facilitated by the explicit nature of our task, where participants were directly instructed to evaluate the perceived emotion from the musical excerpts. Other studies have found that individuals with ASD in general perform better on emotion recognition tasks when given more explicit instructions (for review see Nuske et al., 2013) and show more "normalized" brain activity (Wang et al., 2007). Consequently, the difference in brain activation between this study and that of Caria et al. (2011) might relate to differences between active decoding of emotions from music and passive music listening. Also, the participants in Caria et al.'s (2011) study knew the music in advance, and it is well-established that familiarity influences the way we perceive music (Pereira et al., 2011; Van den Bosch et al., 2013), and may change the emotional experience inside the scanner.

Future studies should investigate differences in implicit and explicit emotion perception in music in ASD individuals, and preferably include more emotions than just happiness and sadness. It would also be interesting to conduct similar experiments using alternative scanning protocols such as sparse temporal sampling or interleaved steady state imaging, which might optimize signal intensity from auditory and subcortical regions compared to continuous scanning (Mueller et al., 2011; Perrachione and Ghosh, 2013). Finally, future studies should aim to investigate emotional responses to music in low-functioning and non-verbal individuals with ASD, since these might be the ones who could benefit the most from using music to communicate and share emotions.

CONCLUSION

Individuals with ASD showed intact emotion recognition from music, as expressed in their behavioral ratings, and in typical brain processing of emotional music overall, with activation of limbic and paralimbic areas, including reward regions. However, in response to happy compared to sad music individuals with ASD had increased activation of left dorsolateral prefrontal regions and rolandic operculum/insula, suggesting a more cognitively demanding strategy for decoding happy music, and potentially higher levels of physiological arousal in individuals with ASD.

ACKNOWLEDGMENT

This work was supported by the Lundbeck Foundation (R32-A2846 to Line Gebauer).

REFERENCES

Adolphs, R. (2002). Neural systems for recognizing emotion. *Curr. Opin. Neurobiol.* 12, 169–177. doi: 10.1016/S0959-4388(02)00301-X

Ahsan, R. L., Allom, R., Gousias, I. S., Habib, H., Turkheimer, F. E., Free, S., et al. (2007). Volumes, spatial extents and a probabilistic atlas of the human basal ganglia and thalamus. *Neuroimage* 38, 261–270. doi: 10.1016/j.neuroimage.2007.06.004

Allen, R., Davis, R., and Hill, E. (2013). The effects of autism and alexithymia on physiological and verbal responsiveness to music. *J. Autism Dev. Disord.* 43, 432–444. doi: 10.1007/s10803-012-1587-8

Allen, R., Hill, E., and Heaton, P. (2009a). The subjective experience of music in autism spectrum disorder. *Ann. N.Y. Acad. Sci.* 1169, 326–331. doi: 10.1111/j.1749-6632.2009.04772.x

Allen, R., Hill, E., and Heaton, P. (2009b). 'Hath Charms to Soothe...': an exploratory study of how high-functioning adults with asd experience music. *Autism* 13, 21–41. doi: 10.1177/1362361307098511

Anderson, J. S., Lange, N., Froehlich, A., DuBray, M. B., Druzgal, T. J., Froimowitz, M. P., et al. (2010). Decreased left posterior insular activity during auditory language in autism. *AJNR Am. J. Neuroradiol.* 31, 131–139. doi: 10.3174/ajnr.A1789

APA. (2013). *Diagnostic and Statistical Manual of Mental Disorders. 5th Edn.* Arlington, VA: American Psychiatric Publishing.

Ashburner, J., and Friston, K. J. (1999). Nonlinear spatial normalization using basis functions. *Hum. Brain Mapp.* 7, 254–266. doi: 10.1002/(SICI)1097-0193(1999)7:4<254::AID-HBM4>3.0.CO;2-G

Ashwin, C., Baron-Cohen, S., Wheelwright, S., O'Riordan, M., and Bullmore, E. T. (2007). Differential activation of the amygdala and the 'social brain' during fearful face-processing in asperger syndrome. *Neuropsychologia* 45, 2–14. doi: 10.1016/j.neuropsychologia.2006.04.014

Baron-Cohen, S., Ring, H. A., Bullmore, E. T., Wheelwright, S., Ashwin, C., and Williams, S. C. (2000). The amygdala theory of autism. *Neurosci. Biobehav. Rev.* 24, 355–364. doi: 10.1016/S0149-7634(00)00011-7

Berlyne, D. E. (1971). *Aesthetics and Psychobiology.* New York, NY: Appleton-Century-Crofts.

Bird, G., and Cook, R. (2013). Mixed emotions: the contribution of alexithymia to the emotional symptoms of autism. *Transl. Psychiatry* 3, e285. doi: 10.1038/tp.2013.61

Bird, G., Silani, G., Brindley, R., White, S., Frith, U., and Singer, T. (2010). Empathic brain responses in insula are modulated by levels of alexithymia but not autism. *Brain* 133(Pt 5), 1515–1525. doi: 10.1093/brain/awq060

Blood, A. J., and Zatorre, R. J. (2001). Intensely pleasurable responses to music correlate with activity in brain regions implicated in reward and emotion. *Proc. Natl. Acad. Sci. U.S.A.* 98, 11818–11823. doi: 10.1073/pnas.191355898

Blood, A. J., Zatorre, R. J., Bermudez, P., and Evans, A. C. (1999). Emotional responses to pleasant and unpleasant music correlate with activity in paralimbic brain regions. *Nat. Neurosci.* 2, 382–387. doi: 10.1038/7299

Boisgueheneuc, F. D., Levy, R., Volle, E., Seassau, M., Duffau, H., Kinkingnehun, S., et al. (2006). Functions of the left superior frontal gyrus in humans: a lesion study. *Brain* 129, 3315–3328. doi: 10.1093/brain/awl244

Bonnel, A., Mottron, L., Peretz, I., Trudel, M., Gallun, E., and Bonnel, A.-M. (1999). Enhanced pitch sensitivity in individuals with autism: a signal detection analysis. *J. Cogn. Neurosci.* 15, 226–235.

Boucher, J., and Lewis, V. (1992). Unfamiliar face recognition in relatively able autistic children. *J. Child Psychol. Psychiatry* 33, 843–850. doi: 10.1111/j.1469-7610.1992.tb01960.x

Brattico, E., Alluri, V., Bogert, B., Jacobsen, T., Vartiainen, N., Nieminen, S., et al. (2011). A functional MRI study of happy and sad emotions in music with and without lyrics. *Front. Psychol.* 2:308. doi: 10.3389/fpsyg.2011.00308

Brown, S., Martinez, M. J., and Parsons, L. M. (2004). Passive music listening spontaneously engages limbic and paralimbic systems. *Neuroreport* 15, 2033–2037. doi: 10.1097/00001756-200409150-00008

Caria, A., Venuti, P., and de Falco, S. (2011). Functional and dysfunctional brain circuits underlying emotional processing of music in autism spectrum disorders. *Cereb. Cortex* 21, 2838–2849. doi: 10.1093/cercor/bhr084

Celani, G., Battacchi, M. W., and Arcidiacono, L. (1999). The understanding of the emotional meaning of facial expressions in people with autism. *J. Autism Dev. Disord.* 29, 57–66. doi: 10.1023/A:1025970600181

Corbett, B. A., Carmean, V., Ravizza, S., Wendelken, C., Henry, M. L., Carter, C., et al. (2009). A functional and structural study of emotion and face processing in children with autism. [Research Support, N.I.H., Extramural]. *Psychiatry Res.* 173, 196–205. doi: 10.1016/j.pscychresns.2008.08.005

Craig, A. (2009). How do you feel—now? the anterior insula and human awareness. *Nat. Rev. Neurosci.* 10, 655–666. doi: 10.1038/nrn2555

Craig, A. D. (2002). How do you feel? Interoception: the sense of the physiological condition of the body. *Nat. Rev. Neurosci.* 3, 655–666. doi: 10.1038/nrn894

Critchley, H. D. (2005). Neural mechanisms of autonomic, affective, and cognitive integration. *J. Comp. Neurol.* 493, 154–166. doi: 10.1002/cne.20749

Critchley, H. D., Daly, E. M., Bullmore, E. T., Williams, S. C., Van Amelsvoort, T., Robertson, D. M., (2000). The functional neuroanatomy of social behaviour: changes in cerebral blood flow when people with autistic disorder process facial expressions. *Brain* 123(Pt 11), 2203–2212. doi: 10.1093/brain/123.11.2203

Dubé, L., and Le Bel, J. (2003). The content and structure of Laypeople's concept of pleasure. *Cogn. Emot.* 17, 263–295. doi: 10.1080/02699930302295

Eigsti, I.-M., Schuh, J., and Paul, R. (2012). The neural underpinnings of prosody in autism. *Child Neuropsychol.* 18, 600–617. doi: 10.1080/09297049.2011.639757

Etkin, A., Egner, T., and Kalisch, R. (2011). Emotional processing in anterior cingulate and medial prefrontal cortex. *Trends Cogn. Sci.* 15, 85–93. doi: 10.1016/j.tics.2010.11.004

Eyler, L. T., Pierce, K., and Courchesne, E. (2012). A failure of left temporal cortex to specialize for language is an early emerging and fundamental property of autism. *Brain* 135(Pt 3), 949–960. doi: 10.1093/brain/awr364

Fitch, W. T. (2005). The evolution of music in comparative perspective. *Ann. N. Y. Acad. Sci.* 1060, 29–49. doi: 10.1196/annals.1360.004

Fitzgerald, M., and Bellgrove, M. A. (2006). The overlap between alexithymia and Asperger's syndrome. *J. Autism Dev. Disord.* 36, 573–576. doi: 10.1176/appi.ajp.161.11.2134

Friston, K. J., Holmes, A., Poline, J.-B., Price, C. J., and Frith, C. (1996). Detecting activations in PET and fMRI: levels of inference and power. *Neuroimage* 4, 223–235. doi: 10.1006/nimg.1996.0074

Friston, K. J., Holmes, A. P., Worsley, K. J., Poline, J.-P., Frith, C. D., and Frackowiak, R. S. J. (1994). Statistical parametric maps in functional imaging: a general linear approach. *Hum. Brain Mapp.* 2, 189–210. doi: 10.1002/hbm.460020402

Gabrielsson, A. (2002). Emotion perceived and emotion felt: same or different? *Music. Sci.* 5(suppl. 1), 123–147. doi: 10.1177/10298649020050S105

Gasquoine, P. G. (2014). Contributions of the insula to cognition and emotion. *Neuropsychol. Rev.* 24, 77–87. doi: 10.1007/s11065-014-9246-9

Gebauer, L., Kringelbach, M. L., and Vuust, P. (2012). Ever-changing cycles of musical pleasure: the role of dopamine and anticipation. *Psychomusicology* 22, 152–167. doi: 10.1037/a0031126

Gervais, H., Belin, P., Boddaert, N., Leboyer, M., Coez, A., Sfaello, I., et al. (2004). Abnormal cortical voice processing in autism. *Nat. Neurosci.* 7, 801–802. doi: 10.1038/nn1291

Gillberg, C., and Coleman, M. (1996). Autism and medical disorders: a review of the literature. *Dev. Med. Child Neurol.* 38, 191–202. doi: 10.1111/j.1469-8749.1996.tb15081.x

Golan, O., Baron-Cohen, S., Hill, J. J., and Rutherford, M. D. (2007). The 'reading the mind in the voice' test-revised: a study of complex emotion recognition in adults with and without autism spectrum conditions. *J. Autism Dev. Disord.* 37, 1096–106. doi: 10.1007/s10803-006-0252-5

Grewe, O., Nagel, F., Kopiez, R., and Altenmüller, E. (2005). How does music arouse "Chills"? investigating strong emotions, combining psychological, physiological, and psychoacoustical methods. *Ann. N. Y. Acad. Sci.* 1060, 446–449. doi: 10.1196/annals.1360.041

Griffiths, T., Warren, J., Dean, J., and Howard, D. (2004). "When the feeling" S Gone": a selective loss of musical emotion. *J. Neurol. Neurosurg. Psychiatry* 75, 344–345. doi: 10.1136/jnnp.2003.015586

Hadjikhani, N., Joseph, R. M., Manoach, D. S., Naik, P., Snyder, J., Dominick, K., et al. (2009). Body expressions of emotion do not trigger fear contagion in autism spectrum disorder. *Soc. Cogn. Affect. Neurosci.* 4, 70–78. doi: 10.1093/scan/nsn038

Heaton, P. (2003). Pitch memory, labelling and disembedding in autism. *J. Child Psychol. Psychiatry* 44, 543–551. doi: 10.1111/1469-7610.00143

Heaton, P. (2005). Interval and contour processing in autism. *J. Autism Dev. Disord.* 35, 787–793. doi: 10.1007/s10803-005-0024-7

Heaton, P., Allen, R., Williams, K., Cummins, O., and Happe, F. (2008). Do social and cognitive deficits curtail musical understanding? Evidence from Autism and Down Syndrome. *Br. J. Dev. Psychol.* 26, 171–182. doi: 10.1348/026151007X206776

Heaton, P., Pring, L., and Hermelin, B. (1999). A pseudo-savant: a case of exceptional musical splinter skills. *Neurocase* 5, 503–509. doi: 10.1080/13554799908402745

Heaton, P., Reichenbacher, L., Sauter, D., Allen, R., Scott, S., and Hill, E. (2012). Measuring the effects of alexithymia on perception of emotional vocalizations in autistic spectrum disorder and typical development. *Psychol. Med.* 42, 2453–2459. doi: 10.1017/S0033291712000621

Hobson, P. (2005). "Autism and emotion," in *Handbook of Autism and Pervasive Developmental Disorders, Vol. 1: Diagnosis, Development, Neurobiology, and Behavior, 3rd Edn.*, eds F. R. Volkmar, R. Paul, A. Klin, and D. Cohen (Hoboken, NJ: John Wiley and Sons Inc), 406–422.

Hobson, R. P. (1986). The autistic child's appraisal of expressions of emotion. *J. Child Psychol. Psychiatry* 27, 321–342.

Hubert, B., Wicker, B., Moore, D. G., Monfardini, E., Duverger, H., Fonseca, D. D., et al. (2007). Brief report: recognition of emotional and non-emotional biological motion in individuals with autistic spectrum disorders. *J. Autism Dev. Disord.* 37, 1386–1392. doi: 10.1007/s10803-006-0275-y

Huron, D. (2001). Is music an evolutionary adaptation? *Ann. N. Y. Acad. Sci.* 930, 43–61. doi: 10.1111/j.1749-6632.2001.tb05724.x

Huron, D. (2006). *Sweet Anticipation: Music and the Psychology of Expectation.* Cambridge, MA: MIT Press.

Janata, P., and Grafton, S. T. (2003). Swinging in the brain: shared neural substrates for behaviors related to sequencing and music. *Nat. Neurosci.* 6, 682–687. doi: 10.1038/nn1081

Jemel, B., Mottron, L., and Dawson, M. (2006). Impaired face processing in autism: fact or artifact? *J. Autism Dev. Disord.* 36, 91–106. doi: 10.1007/s10803-005-0050-5

Jones, C. R. G., Pickles, A., Falcaro, M., Marsden, A. J. S., Happé, F., Scott, S. K., et al. (2011). A multimodal approach to emotion recognition ability in autism spectrum disorders. *J. Child Psychol. Psychiatry* 52, 275–285. doi: 10.1111/j.1469-7610.2010.02328.x

Juslin, P. N., and Laukka, P. (2004). Expression, perception, and induction of musical emotions: a review and a questionnaire study of everyday listening. *J. New Music Res.* 33, 217–238. doi: 10.1080/0929821042000317813

Juslin, P. N., and Västfjäll, D. (2008). Emotional responses to music: the need to consider underlying mechanisms. *Behav. Brain Sci.* 31, 559–575. discussion 575–621. doi: 10.1017/S0140525X08005293

Kanner, L. (1943). Autistic disturbances of affective contact. *Nervous Child* 2, 217–250.

Koelsch, S. (2010). Towards a neural basis of music-evoked emotions. *Trends Cogn. Sci.* 14, 131–137. doi: 10.1016/j.tics.2010.01.002

Koelsch, S., Fritz, T., Cramon, D. Y. V., Müller, K., and Friederici, A. D. (2006). Investigating emotion with music: an fMRI study. *Hum. Brain Mapp.* 27, 239–250. doi: 10.1002/hbm.20180

Koelsch, S., Fritz, T., and Schlaug, G. (2008). Amygdala activity can be modulated by unexpected chord functions during music listening. *Neuroreport* 19, 1815–1819. doi: 10.1097/WNR.0b013e32831a8722

Koelsch, S., Skouras, S., Fritz, T., Herrera, P., Bonhage, C., Küssner, M. B., et al. (2013). The roles of superficial amygdala and auditory cortex in music-evoked fear and joy. *Neuroimage* 81, 49–60. doi: 10.1016/j.neuroimage.2013.05.008

Kohls, G., Schulte-Rüther, M., Nehrkorn, B., Müller, K., Fink, G. R., Kamp-Becker, I., et al. (2013). Reward system dysfunction in autism spectrum disorders. *Soc. Cogn. Affect. Neurosci.* 8, 565–572. doi: 10.1093/scan/nss033

Konečni, V. J. (2008). Does music induce emotion? A theoretical and methodological analysis. *Psychol. Aesth. Creat. Arts* 2, 115–129. doi: 10.1037/1931-3896.2.2.115

Lancaster, J. L., Woldorff, M. G., Parsons, L. M., Liotti, M., Freitas, C. S., Rainey, L., et al. (2000). Automated talairach atlas labels for functional brain mapping. *Hum. Brain Mapp.* 10: 120–131. doi: 10.1002/1097-0193(200007)10:3<120::AID-HBM30>3.0.CO;2-8

Levitin, D. J. (2006). *This is Your Brain on Music: The Science of a Human Obsession.* New York, NY: Dutton.

Lindner, J. L., and Rosén, L. A. (2006). Decoding of emotion through facial expression, prosody and verbal content in children and adolescents with asperger's syndrome. *J. Autism Dev. Disord.* 36, 769–777. doi: 10.1007/s10803-006-0105-2

Lord, C., Risi, S., Lambrecht, L., Cook, E. H. Jr., Leventhal, B. L., DiLavore, P. C., et al. (2000). The autism diagnostic observation schedule-generic: a standard measure of social and communication deficits associated with the spectrum of autism. *J. Autism Dev. Disord.* 30, 205–223. doi: 10.1023/A:1005592401947

Maldjian, J. A., Laurienti, P. J., Burdette, J. B., and Kraft, R. A. (2003). An Automated method for neuroanatomic and cytoarchitectonic atlas- based interrogation of fMRI data sets. *Neuroimage* 19, 1233–1239. doi: 10.1016/S1053-8119(03)00169-1

Mazefsky, C. A., and Oswald, D. P. (2007). Emotion perception in asperger's syndrome and high-functioning autism: the importance of diagnostic criteria and cue intensity. *J. Autism Dev. Disord.* 37, 1086–1095. doi: 10.1007/s10803-006-0251-6

Menon, V., and Levitin, D. J. (2005). The rewards of music listening: response and physiological connectivity of the mesolimbic system. *Neuroimage* 28, 175–184. doi: 10.1016/j.neuroimage.2005.05.053

Menon, V., and Uddin, L. Q. (2010). Saliency, switching, attention and control: a network model of insula function. *Brain Struct. Funct.* 214, 655–667. doi: 10.1007/s00429-010-0262-0

Mitterschiffthaler, M. T., Fu, C. H. Y., Dalton, J. A., Andrew, C. M., and Williams, S. C. R. (2007). A functional MRI Study of happy and sad affective states induced by classical music. *Hum. Brain Mapp.* 28, 1150–1162. doi: 10.1002/hbm.20337

Moesgaard, K. (2010). *Musik Som Brandingplatform (Eng. Title. Music as Branding Plat Form).* Available online at: http://www.promus.dk/files/rapporter/mec_20musikundersoegelse_20september_202010.pdf

Mueller, K., Mildner, T., Fritz, T., Lepsien, J., Schwarzbauer, C., Schroeter, M. L., et al. (2011). Investigating brain response to music: a comparison of different fMRI acquisition schemes. *Neuroimage* 54, 337–343. doi: 10.1016/j.neuroimage.2010.08.029

North, A. C., and Hargreaves, D. J. (1995). Subjective complexity, familiarity and liking of popular music. *Psychomusicology* 14, 77–793. doi: 10.1037/h0094090

Nuske, H. J., Vivanti, G., and Dissanayake, C. (2013). Are emotion impairments unique to, universal, or specific in autism spectrum disorder? A comprehensive review. *Cogn. Emot.* 27, 1042–1061. doi: 10.1080/02699931.2012.762900

Overy, K. (2012). Making music in a group: synchronization and shared experience. *Ann. N.Y. Acad. Sci.* 1252, 65–68. doi: 10.1111/j.1749-6632.2012.06530.x

Park, M., Hennig-Fast, K., Bao, Y., Carl, P., Pöppel, E., Welker, L., et al. (2013). Personality traits modulate neural responses to emotions expressed in music. *Brain Res.* 1523, 68–76. doi: 10.1016/j.brainres.2013.05.042

Penny, W. D., Friston, K. J., Ashburner, J. T., Kiebel, S. J., and Nichols, T. E. (Eds.). (2011). *Statistical Parametric Mapping: The Analysis of Functional Brain Images.* London: Academic Press.

Pereira, C. S., Teixeira, J., Figueiredo, P., Xavier, J., Castro, S. L., and Brattico, E. (2011). Music and emotions in the brain: familiarity matters. *PLoS ONE* 6:e27241. doi: 10.1371/journal.pone.0027241

Peretz, I. (2010). "Towards a neurobiology of musical emotions," in *Handbook of Music and Emotion: Theory, Research, Applications*, ed P. J. J. Sloboda (Oxford: Oxford University Press), 99–126.

Perrachione, T. K., and Ghosh, S. S. (2013). Optimized design and analysis of sparse-sampling FMRI experiments. *Front. Neurosci.* 7:55. doi: 10.3389/fnins.2013.00055

Philip, R. C. M., Whalley, H. C., Stanfield, A. C., Sprengelmeyer, R., Santos, I. M., Young, A. W., et al. (2010). Deficits in facial, body movement and vocal emotional processing in autism spectrum disorders. *Psychol. Med.* 40, 1919–1929. doi: 10.1017/S0033291709992364

Quintin, E.-M., Bhatara, A., Poissant, H., Fombonne, E., and Levitin, D. J. (2011). Emotion perception in music in high-functioning adolescents with autism spectrum disorders. *J. Autism Dev. Disord.* 41, 1240–1255. doi: 10.1007/s10803-010-1146-0

Redcay, E. (2008). The superior temporal sulcus performs a common function for social and speech perception: implications for the emergence of autism. *Neurosci. Biobehav. Rev.* 32, 123–142. doi: 10.1016/j.neubiorev.2007.06.004

Rentfrow, P. J., and Gosling, S. D. (2003). The do re mi's of everyday life: the structure and personality correlates of music preferences. *J. Pers. Soc. Psychol.* 84, 1236–1256. doi: 10.1037/0022-3514.84.6.1236

Salimpoor, V. N., Benovoy, M., Larcher, K., Dagher, A., and Zatorre, R. J. (2011). Anatomically distinct dopamine release during anticipation and experience of peak emotion to music. *Nat. Neurosci.* 14, 257–262. doi: 10.1038/nn.2726

Salimpoor, V. N., Benovoy, M., Longo, G., Cooperstock, J., and Zatorre, R. (2009). The rewarding aspects of music listening are related to degree of emotional arousal. *PLoS ONE* 4:e7487. doi: 10.1371/journal.pone.0007487

Salimpoor, V. N., van den Bosch, I., Kovacevic, N., McIntosh, A. R., Dagher, A., and Zatorre, R. J. (2013). Interactions between the nucleus accumbens and auditory cortices predict music reward value. *Science* 340, 216–219. doi: 10.1126/science.1231059

Schultz, R. T., Gauthier, I., Klin, A., Fulbright, R. K., Anderson, A. W., Volkmar, F., et al. (2000). Abnormal ventral temporal cortical activity during face discrimination among individuals with autism and asperger syndrome. *Arch. Gen. Psychiatry* 57, 331–340. doi: 10.1001/archpsyc.57.4.331

Stanutz, S., Wapnick, J., and Burack, J. (2014). Pitch discrimination and melodic memory in children with autism spectrum disorder. *Autism* 18, 137–147. doi: 10.1177/1362361312462905

Trost, W., Ethofer, T., Zentner, M., and Vuilleumier, P. (2012). Mapping aesthetic musical emotions in the brain. *Cereb. Cortex* 22, 2769–2783. doi: 10.1093/cercor/bhr353

Tzourio-Mazoyer, N., Landeau, B., Papathanassiou, D., Crivello, F., Etard, O., Delcroix, N., et al. (2002). Automated anatomical labeling of activations in spm using a macroscopic anatomical parcellation of the mni mri single-subject brain. *Neuroimage* 15, 273–289. doi: 10.1006/nimg.2001.0978

Van den Bosch, I., Salimpoor, V. N., and Zatorre, R. J. (2013). Familiarity mediates the relationship between emotional arousal and pleasure during music listening. *Front. Hum. Neurosci.* 7:534. doi: 10.3389/fnhum.2013.00534

Wallentin, M., Nielsen, A. H., Friis-Olivarius, M., Vuust, C., and Vuust, P. (2010). The musical ear test, a new reliable test for measuring musical competence. *Learn. Individ. Differ.* 20, 188–196. doi: 10.1016/j.lindif.2010.02.004

Wang, A. T., Lee, S. S., Sigman, M., and Dapretto, M. (2006). Neural basis of irony comprehension in children with autism: the role of prosody and context. *Brain* 129(Pt 4), 932–943. doi: 10.1093/brain/awl032

Wang, A. T., Lee, S. S., Sigman, M., and Dapretto, M. (2007). Reading affect in the face and voice. *ArchGen Psychiatry* 64, 698–708. doi: 10.1001/archpsyc.64.6.698

Wechsler, D. (1997). *WAIS-III/WMS-III Technical Manual.* San Antonio, TX: The Psychological Corporation.

Witek, M., Clarke, E., Wallentin, M., Kringelbach, M. L., and Vuust, P. (2014). Rhythmic complexity, body-movement and pleasure in groove music. *PLoS ONE* 9:e94446. doi: 10.1371/journal.pone.0094446

Zald, D. H., and Zatorre, R. J. (2011). "Music," in *Neurobiology of Sensation and Reward*, Frontiers in Neuroscience, Chapter 19, ed J. A. Gottfried (Boca Raton, FL: CRC Press), 405–429.

Zilbovicius, M., Meresse, I., Chabane, N., Brunelle, F., Samson, Y., and Boddaert, N. (2006). Autism, the superior temporal sulcus and social perception. *Trends Neurosci.* 29, 359–366. doi: 10.1016/j.tins.2006.06.004

Permissions

All chapters in this book were first published by Frontiers; hereby published with permission under the Creative Commons Attribution License or equivalent. Every chapter published in this book has been scrutinized by our experts. Their significance has been extensively debated. The topics covered herein carry significant findings which will fuel the growth of the discipline. They may even be implemented as practical applications or may be referred to as a beginning point for another development.

The contributors of this book come from diverse backgrounds, making this book a truly international effort. This book will bring forth new frontiers with its revolutionizing research information and detailed analysis of the nascent developments around the world.

We would like to thank all the contributing authors for lending their expertise to make the book truly unique. They have played a crucial role in the development of this book. Without their invaluable contributions this book wouldn't have been possible. They have made vital efforts to compile up to date information on the varied aspects of this subject to make this book a valuable addition to the collection of many professionals and students.

This book was conceptualized with the vision of imparting up-to-date information and advanced data in this field. To ensure the same, a matchless editorial board was set up. Every individual on the board went through rigorous rounds of assessment to prove their worth. After which they invested a large part of their time researching and compiling the most relevant data for our readers.

The editorial board has been involved in producing this book since its inception. They have spent rigorous hours researching and exploring the diverse topics which have resulted in the successful publishing of this book. They have passed on their knowledge of decades through this book. To expedite this challenging task, the publisher supported the team at every step. A small team of assistant editors was also appointed to further simplify the editing procedure and attain best results for the readers.

Apart from the editorial board, the designing team has also invested a significant amount of their time in understanding the subject and creating the most relevant covers. They scrutinized every image to scout for the most suitable representation of the subject and create an appropriate cover for the book.

The publishing team has been an ardent support to the editorial, designing and production team. Their endless efforts to recruit the best for this project, has resulted in the accomplishment of this book. They are a veteran in the field of academics and their pool of knowledge is as vast as their experience in printing. Their expertise and guidance has proved useful at every step. Their uncompromising quality standards have made this book an exceptional effort. Their encouragement from time to time has been an inspiration for everyone.

The publisher and the editorial board hope that this book will prove to be a valuable piece of knowledge for researchers, students, practitioners and scholars across the globe.

List of Contributors

Shinya Fujii
Heart and Stroke Foundation Canadian Partnership for Stroke Recovery, Sunnybrook Research Institute, Toronto, ON, Canada

Catherine Y. Wan
Department of Radiology, Boston Children's Hospital, Harvard Medical School, Boston, MA, USA

Bjørn Petersen and Peter Vuust
Center for Functionally Integrative Neuroscience, Aarhus University Hospital, Aarhus, Denmark
Royal Academy of Music, Aarhus, Denmark

Ethan Weed
Center for Functionally Integrative Neuroscience, Aarhus University Hospital, Aarhus, Denmark
Department of Aesthetics and Communication-Linguistics, Aarhus University, Aarhus, Denmark

Pascale Sandmann
Central Auditory Diagnostics Lab, Department of Neurology, Cluster of Excellence "Hearing4all", Hannover Medical School, Hannover, Germany

Elvira Brattico
Brain and Mind Laboratory, Department of Biomedical Engineering and Computational Science, Aalto University, Aalto, Finland
Cognitive Brain Research Unit, Institute of Behavioral Sciences, University of Helsinki, Helsinki, Finland

Mads Hansen
Center for Functionally Integrative Neuroscience, Aarhus University Hospital, Aarhus, Denmark
Department of Psychology and Behavioural Sciences, Aarhus University, Aarhus, Denmark

Stine Derdau Sørensen
Department of Aesthetics and Communication-Linguistics, Aarhus University, Aarhus, Denmark

Luisa Lopez, Chiara Terribili, Sonia Buda and Sara Tilli
Developmental Neuropsychiatry Ward, Villaggio Eugenio Litta, Rome, Italy

Aline Moussard
Rotman Research Institute, Baycrest, University of Toronto, Toronto, ON, Canada

Lydia Timm and Deepashri Agrawal
Department of Neurology, Hannover Medical School, Hannover, Germany

Stefan Debener
Neuropsychology Laboratory, Department of Psychology, Carl von Ossietzky University of Oldenburg, Oldenburg, Germany
Cluster of Excellence Hearing4All, Oldenburg/Hannover, Germany

Andreas Büchner
Cluster of Excellence Hearing4All, Oldenburg/Hannover, Germany
Department of Otolaryngology, Hannover Medical School, Hannover, Germany

Reinhard Dengler
Department of Neurology, Hannover Medical School, Hannover, Germany
Cluster of Excellence Hearing4All, Oldenburg/Hannover, Germany

Matthias Wittfoth
Department of Clinical Psychology and Sexual Medicine, Hannover Medical School, Hannover, Germany

Elena Flaugnacco
Child Neurology and Psychiatry Ward, Institute for Maternal and Child Health-IRCCS Burlo Garofolo Pediatric Institute, Trieste, Italy
Center for the Child Health-Onlus, Trieste, Italy

Françoise Rochette and Emmanuel Bigand
Laboratoire d'Etude de l'Apprentissage et du Développement (LEAD - CNRS 5022), Université de Bourgogne, Dijon, France

Lorenzo Monasta, Marcella Montico and Luca Ronfani
Epidemiology and Biostatistics Unit, Institute for Maternal and Child Health-IRCCS Burlo Garofolo Pediatric Institute, Trieste, Italy

Stefania Zoia
Child Neurology and Psychiatry Ward, Institute for Maternal and Child Health-IRCCS Burlo Garofolo Pediatric Institute, Trieste, Italy

Alessandra Sila
Center for the Child Health-Onlus, Trieste, Italy

Daniele Schön
Institutde Neurosciences des Systémes, Aix-Marseille Université, Marseille, France
INSERM, U1106, Marseille, France

Christina D. Fuller, Bert Maat, Rolien H. Free and Deniz Başkent
Department of Otorhinolaryngology/Head and Neck Surgery, University Medical Center Groningen, University of Groningen, Groningen, Netherlands
Research School of Behavioral and Cognitive Neurosciences, Graduate School of Medical Sciences, University of Groningen, Groningen, Netherlands

John J. Galvin III
Department of Otorhinolaryngology/Head and Neck Surgery, University Medical Center Groningen, University of Groningen, Groningen, Netherlands
Research School of Behavioral and Cognitive Neurosciences, Graduate School of Medical Sciences, University of Groningen, Groningen, Netherlands
Division of Communication and Auditory Neuroscience, House Research Institute, Los Angeles, CA, USA
Department of Head and Neck Surgery, David Geffen School of Medicine, UCLA, Los Angeles, CA, USA

Dawn L. Merrett and Sarah J. Wilson
Melbourne School of Psychological Sciences, The University of Melbourne, Melbourne, VIC, Australia

Isabelle Peretz
Department of Psychology, Université de Montréal, Montréal, QC, Canada

Rebecca S. Schaefer
SAGE Center for the Study of the Mind, University of California, Santa Barbara, CA, USA

Alexa M. Morcom
School of Philosophy, Psychology and Language Sciences, University of Edinburgh, Edinburgh, UK

Katie Overy
Institute for Music in Human and Social Development, Reid School of Music, Edinburgh College of Art, University of Edinburgh, Edinburgh, UK
Don Wright Faculty of Music, Department of Music Education, University of Western Ontario, London, ON, Canada

Neil Roberts
Clinical Research Imaging Centre (CRIC), Queen's Medical Research Institute, University of Edinburgh, Edinburgh, UK

Li-Ann Leow, Taylor Parrott and Jessica A. Grahn
The Brain and Mind Institute, University of Western Ontario, London, ON, Canada

Charles-Etienne Benoit
Department of Cognitive Psychology, University of Finance and Management in Warsaw, Warsaw, Poland
Max Planck Institute for Human Cognitive and Brain Sciences, Leipzig, Germany
Movement to Health Laboratory (M2H), Euro Mov, Montpellier-1 University, Montpellier, France

Simone Dalla Bella
Department of Cognitive Psychology, University of Finance and Management in Warsaw, Warsaw, Poland
Movement to Health Laboratory (M2H), Euro Mov, Montpellier-1 University, Montpellier, France
Institut Universitaire de France, Paris, France

Nicolas Farrugia
Max Planck Institute for Human Cognitive and Brain Sciences, Leipzig, Germany
Goldsmiths, University of London, London, UK

Hellmuth Obrig
Max Planck Institute for Human Cognitive and Brain Sciences, Leipzig, Germany
Clinic for Cognitive Neurology, University Hospital, University of Leipzig, Leipzig, Germany

Stefan Mainka
Neurologisches Fachkrankenhaus für Bewegungss törungen/Parkinson, Beelitz- Heilstätten, Germany

Sonja A. Kotz
Max Planck Institute for Human Cognitive and Brain Sciences, Leipzig, Germany
School of Psychological Sciences, The University of Manchester, Manchester, UK

Rebeka Bodak
Department of Clinical Medicine, Aarhus University, Aarhus, Denmark

Paresh Malhotra
Division of Brain Sciences, Imperial College London, London, UK

Nicolò F. Bernardi
Department of Psychology, McGill University, Montreal, QC, Canada

Gianna Cocchini and Lauren Stewart
Department of Psychology, Goldsmiths University of London, London, UK

Juliane Ritter and Eckart Altenmüller
Institute of Music Physiology and Musicians' Medicine, University of Music, Drama, and Media Hanover, Hanover, Germany

Anna Zumbansen and Sylvie Hébert
Faculty of Medicine, School of Speech Pathology and Audiology, Université de Montréal, Montreal, QC, Canada
CRBLM, Centre for Research on Brain, Language and Music, McGill University, Montreal, QC, Canada
BRAMS, International Laboratory for Research on Brain, Music, and Sound, Université de Montréal, Montreal, QC, Canada

Isabelle Peretz
CRBLM, Centre for Research on Brain, Language and Music, McGill University, Montreal, QC, Canada
BRAMS, International Laboratory for Research on Brain, Music, and Sound, Université de Montréal, Montreal, QC, Canada
Faculty of Artsand Science, Department of Psychology, Université de Montréal, Montreal, QC, Canada

Floris T. Van Vugt
Institute of Music Physiology and Musicians' Medicine, University of Music, Drama, and Media Hanover, Hanover, Germany
Lyon Neuroscience Research Center, CNRS-UMR 5292, INSERM U1028, University Claude Bernard Lyon-1, Lyon, France

Jens D. Rollnik
BDH-Klinik, Institute for Neurorehabilitational Research (InFo), Teaching Hospital of Hanover Medical School, Hessisch Oldendorf, Germany

Michael H. Thaut
Center for Biomedical Research in Music, Colorado State University, Fort Collins, CO, USA

David A. Peterson
Computational Neurobiology Laboratory, Salk Institute for Biological Studies, La Jolla, CA, USA
Institute for Neural Computation, University of California San Diego, LaJolla, CA, USA

Gerald C. McIntosh
Department of Neurology, University of Colorado Health, Fort Collins, CO, USA

Volker Hoemberg
Department of Neurology, SRH Rehabilitation Hospital Bad Wimpfen, Bad Wimpfen, Germany

Laura Ferreri, Emmanuel Bigand, Patrick Bard and Aurélia Bugaiska
Laboratoire d'Etude de l'Apprentissage et du Développement (LEAD), CNRS UMR 5022, University of Burgundy, Dijon, France

Stephane Perrey and Makii Muthalib
Movement to Health (M2H), Euro Mov, Montpellier-1 University, Montpellier, France

Jussi Valtonen
Institute of Behavioural Sciences, University of Helsinki, Helsinki, Finland

Emma Gregory, Barbara Landau and Michael McCloskey
Department of Cognitive Science, Johns Hopkins University, Baltimore, MD, USA

Teppo Särkämö
Cognitive Brain Research Unit, Cognitive Science, Institute of Behavioural Sciences, University of Helsinki, Helsinki, Finland
Finnish Centre of Interdisciplinary Music Research, University of Helsinki, Helsinki, Finland

Pablo Ripollés
Cognition and Brain Plasticity Group, Bellvitge Biomedical Research Institute (IDIBELL), L'Hospitalet de Llobregat, Barcelona, Spain
Department of Basic Psychology, University of Barcelona, Barcelona, Spain

Henna Vepsäläinen
Cognitive Brain Research Unit, Cognitive Science, Institute of Behavioural Sciences, University of Helsinki, Helsinki, Finland

Taina Autti, Heli M. Silvennoinen and Eero Salli
Department of Radiology, HUS Medical Imaging Center, Helsinki University Central Hospital, University of Helsinki, Helsinki, Finland

Sari Laitinen
Miina Sillanpää Foundation, Helsinki, Finland

Seppo Soinila
Department of Neurology, Turku University Hospital, Turku, Finland

Antoni Rodríguez-Fornells
Cognition and Brain Plasticity Group, Bellvitge Biomedical Research Institute (IDIBELL), L'Hospitalet de Llobregat, Barcelona, Spain
Department of Basic Psychology, University of Barcelona, Barcelona, Spain
Institució Catalana de Recerca I Estudis Avançats (ICREA), Barcelona, Spain

Anita Forsblom
Department of Music, University of Jyväskylä, Jyväskylä, Finland

Aline Moussard
Rotman Research Institute, Baycrest, University of Toronto, Toronto, ON, Canada

Emmanuel Bigand
Laboratoire d'Etude de l'Apprentissage et du Développement (LEAD-CNRS5022), Université de Bourgogne, Dijon, France

Sylvie Belleville
Centre de Recherche de l'Institut Universitaire de Gériatrie de Montréal (CRIUGM), Université de Montréal, Montréal, QC, Canada

Isabelle Peretz
International Laboratory for Brain, Music and Sound Research (BRAMS), Université de Montréal, Montréal, QC, Canada
Centre for Research on Brain, Language and Music (CRBLM), McGill University, Montréal, QC, Canada

Line Gebauer
Music in the Brain, Department of Clinical Medicine, Center of Functionally Integrative Neuroscience, Aarhus University, Aarhus, Denmark
Interacting Minds Centre, Aarhus University, Aarhus, Denmark

Joshua Skewes and Gitte Westphael
Music in the Brain, Department of Clinical Medicine, Center of Functionally Integrative Neuroscience, Aarhus University, Aarhus, Denmark

Pamela Heaton
Department of Psychology, Goldsmiths, University of London, London, UK

Peter Vuust
Music in the Brain, Department of Clinical Medicine, Center of Functionally Integrative Neuroscience, Aarhus University, Aarhus, Denmark
The Royal Academy of Music, Aarhus, Denmark

Index

A

Alzheimer's Disease, 92, 115, 124, 152, 154, 170-173, 176, 185, 203, 210-211

Amygdala, 6, 212, 216-220

Anisochrony Detection, 116-118, 120

Aphasia, 9-10, 12-15, 80-90, 133-137, 139-143, 145, 187, 189, 200, 202-203, 211

Auditory Afferent Circuit, 6

Auditory Attention, 15, 30-31, 52-54, 56, 58, 61, 73, 201, 204

Auditory Evoked Potential, 29, 41

Auditory Perception, 3, 14, 30-31, 33-34, 36, 51, 66, 204

Auditory Working Memory, 30-31, 33-35, 37, 64, 161

Autism Spectrum Disorder, 10, 212, 219-221

B

Basal Ganglia, 3-4, 8, 10-15, 85, 91-92, 98-99, 101-102, 110, 112, 123-124, 184, 215, 219

Beat Alignment Test, 103, 105, 112, 117-118, 123

Beat Perception, 6, 12, 100, 102-103, 105-112, 123

C

Cerebellar Vermis, 92, 96

Cochlear Implants, 16, 28-32, 36-38, 48, 64, 77-79

Cochlear Nuclei, 3, 6

Coefficient Of Variation, 53, 56, 118

Cortical Motor Efferent Circuit, 6

D

Deep Brain Stimulation, 7-8, 98

Deep Encoding, 153-154, 158-159

Dyslexia, 12, 25, 28-29, 37, 50-53, 56, 59-63, 66, 204

Dystonia, 98, 101

E

Electroencephalography, 3, 16, 19-20, 40, 42, 45, 101, 161

F

Family Wise Error, 95, 215

Functional Magnetic Resonance Imaging, 2, 13, 91, 212

G

Gait Rehabilitation, 102, 110-112, 123

Globus Pallidus, 7-8, 91, 94, 96-98, 101

H

Hemodynamic Response Function, 94

I

Imagery-based Cueing, 93, 98

Independent Component Analysis, 20, 28, 42, 47, 172

Inferior Frontal Gyrus, 10, 82, 84, 90, 186, 192-195, 212-213, 217-218

Interbeat Interval Deviation, 105

L

Logistic Regression, 53, 56, 59

M

Magnetoencephalography, 13, 87, 188, 202

Melodic Contour Identification, 28, 48, 64-65, 71, 76, 78

Melodic Intonation Therapy, 9, 15, 80, 83, 87-90, 133, 142-143, 187, 211

Melodic Therapy, 133-134

Mesulam Shape Cancellation Test, 125-126, 129-131

Meter Perception Task, 54, 56, 59

Mismatch Negativity, 16-17, 29, 39-40, 48-49, 188

Motor Impairments, 10, 98, 144

Motor System, 10, 13, 91, 102-103, 151-152, 161

Multiple Sclerosis, 153, 160-162

Musical Cueing, 91-92, 96, 98-99

Musical Meter, 28, 37, 53, 56, 62

Musical Mnemonic, 153-155, 158-159

Musician Effect, 64-66, 69, 73-78

N

Neuroimaging, 6-7, 10-11, 13, 59, 81-85, 87, 91, 100-101, 110, 112, 161, 163-164, 170, 174-175, 186, 188, 197-198, 200, 202, 218

Neurological Disorders, 1, 66, 102

Neuroplasticity, 28, 37, 80, 82-83, 85, 87-89, 151, 187

Nine-hole Pegboard Test, 146, 148

Nucleus Accumbens, 6, 14, 170, 172, 197, 202, 215-216, 218, 221

O

Orbitofrontal Cortex, 6, 192-194, 216, 218

P

Parkinson's Disease, 1, 7-8, 11-15, 92, 100-102, 110-115, 122-124, 152-153, 162, 211

Periaqueductal Gray, 6-7

Period-matching Performance, 104-105, 108

Phonemic Blending, 52-53, 56, 58

Phonemic Segmentation, 52, 56, 58

Phonetic Discrimination, 30-31, 34-35, 61
Pitch Processing, 26, 46, 62, 64, 74, 77-78, 140, 213
Profile Of Mood States, 144, 147, 151-152, 192, 198
Psychiatric Disorders, 115, 214

R

Rhythm Reproduction, 53-54, 56, 58-60
Rhythm Training, 19, 28
Rhythmic Auditory Cueing, 8, 101-102, 114
Rhythmic Auditory Stimulation, 14, 102, 112, 124, 153, 161-162
Rhythmic Therapy, 10, 133-134
Rhythmic Vocalizations, 1, 6, 10

S

Sensorimotor Coupling, 1, 5, 83, 112
Sentence Identification, 66-68, 70, 77
Spatial Neglect, 125, 132
Speech Intelligibility, 1, 3, 7, 12, 39-41, 64-67, 73, 77
Speech Reception Threshold, 20, 68
Speech Sound Map, 5
Spoken Therapy, 133-134
Star Cancellation Test, 125-126, 129-131
Stroke Rehabilitation, 141, 144, 152, 161, 194, 201
Stuttering, 1, 3, 9, 11-15
Substantia Nigra, 7-8, 123
Subthalamic Nucleus, 8, 14, 98
Superior Temporal Gyrus, 3, 5, 11, 98, 125, 212, 218, 223
Superior Temporal Sulcus, 3, 221, 224, 231
Supplementary Motor Area, 3, 8, 13, 15, 91, 184, 192, 213
Synchronization, 1, 4-7, 9-14, 56, 61-62, 84, 99-106, 109-112, 114, 117-118, 120, 123-124, 144-145, 149-156, 158-161, 203-204, 210-211, 221

T

Temporal Processing, 12-13, 50-53, 55-56, 58-61, 65, 123
Test Of Attentional Performance, 125-127, 130, 132
Thalamus, 3-6, 8, 11, 91, 94, 98, 100, 194-195, 201, 218-219

U

Unpaced Tapping, 117-118, 148

V

Verbal Memory, 153-154, 159, 161, 164, 169-171, 187-188, 192, 194, 198, 204-205

W

Word Identification, 31, 64, 66-69, 74, 77

www.ingramcontent.com/pod-product-compliance
Lightning Source LLC
LaVergne TN
LVHW082215200926
848484LV00008B/2260